v

SECTION 8: CHILDBIRTH AND LACTATION 279

SECTION 9: GENDER-BASED VIOLENCE 321

Women, Health, & HEALTHCARE
Readings on Social, Structural, & Systemic Issues

Edited by
E. CABELL HANKINSON GATHMAN
University of Wisconsin-Madison

Kendall Hunt
publishing company

CONTENTS

PREFACE
&
ACKNOWLEDGEMENTS

By E. Cabell Hankinson Gathman

As a doctoral student in sociology at the University of Wisconsin-Madison, I was delighted when I was selected from several applicants outside the Department of Gender and Women's Studies to serve as a teaching assistant with Professor Jenny Higgins for Women and Their Bodies in Health and Disease (GWS 103) in the fall 2012 semester. It was a highlight in my graduate career both for the course content and the supportive community of its teaching team. At the time, that team comprised Jenny, myself, and five GWS masters students, amazing people doing interesting and creative scholarly work of their own, but who were also incredibly dedicated to making GWS 103 not only highly educational, but truly transformative for our students. I have always enjoyed teaching, particularly in areas of social inequality, but as part of the teaching team for GWS 103 I had a unique sense that our students were gaining not only important information and a critical lens, but the ability to advocate for themselves and others throughout their lives in an area that no one can avoid: health and healthcare. For many of them, the course literally forever changed the way that they saw the world, and gave them new confidence in their own ability to change it. I am extremely grateful to Jenny and Araceli Alonso, who also teaches the course, for the opportunity to curate some of the material that will help future GWS 103 students undergo similar intellectual and personal transformations.

This book is a new version of a venerable course reader that is beloved by decades' worth of GWS 103 students and teaching team members, many of whom have kept it in pride of place in their personal libraries for years after their immediate involvement with the course was past. This is not a new edition of that reader, but a new version that owes a great debt to the original created and revised multiple times by Nancy Worcester and Mariamne H. Whatley. I thank them for the generosity and insight that they offered me as I embarked on this project. Without Nancy and Mariamne, GWS 103 would not exist as the incredible community of activists and leaders that has been growing and evolving since 1978, and that gave me such warm welcome in 2012.

While unfortunately we had to reduce the total number of readings in this new version while also making room for new material, we tried to retain as many of the contributions of former GWS 103 teaching team members as possible. The authors you'll find in our table of contents still include former TAs and lecturers like Sue Pastor, Ronna Popkin, and Stephanie Rytilahti. Other seminal pieces from Mariamne and Nancy's original text, including but certainly not limited to Vanessa Northington Gamble's "Under the Shadow of Tuskegee," Megan Seely's "Take a Good Look," Loretta J. Ross's "The Color of Choice," Mariamne H. Whatley's "Male and Female Hormones Revisited," and Becky W. Thompson's "Making 'A Way Outa No Way" are included in this new reader as well. These consistent student favorites will continue to provide GWS 103 students with "mirrors, windows, and sliding glass doors"[1] into experiences that they may know well, but which are deeply underrepresented, a loss for those who are familiar and unfamiliar alike. Thanks to Nancy and Mariamne's longstanding involvement with the National Women's Health Network, that organization was particularly generous in granting permissions for use of their publications in this volume. We strongly encourage students to explore their website and follow their social media accounts for current news and information about women's health.[2]

We are also excited about the inclusion of new pieces from both academic and popular sources, such as public sociological work on trans and intersex issues reprinted with permission from the blog maintained by Cary Gabriel Costello of UW-Milwaukee, Lindsay King-Miller's first-person account of seeking fertility treatment as part of a queer couple in a system built upon the premise that everyone involved is cisgender and heterosexual, Johanna

Hedva's powerful message to "those who were never meant to survive but did" in her essay "Sick Woman Theory" (adapted from her original lecture "My Body Is a Prison of Pain so I Want to Leave It Like a Mystic But I Also Love It & Want It to Matter Politically"), and s.e. smith's disability activist critique of healthcare system claims to acting only in the best interest of disabled people, especially women, whose bodies are targeted for major surgical intervention without their individual informed consent. While all of the new content is exciting, I am perhaps most pleased to share the eleven new pieces written specifically for this book. Of these eleven, seven were written by eight former or incoming GWS 103 TAs. These new selections highlight the breadth and intellectual imagination of the UW-Madison Gender and Women Studies community and give our undergraduate students a focal point to imagine possible futures as scholars and researchers themselves.

Jasmia Hamilton and Brooke Barnhart collaborate to give us a comprehensive review of specific areas of disparity in women's health based on recent research. Jasmia also granted us permission to reprint two sections from her self-published *Black Teen Mom Manifesto*, which I hope will encourage all GWS 103 students to tell their stories for their own benefit and the benefit of others who need to hear them. Kadin Henningsen draws on his experience as a community educator with an approachable, but still complex, introduction to terminology, concepts, and health issues relevant to transgender people. Lacey Alexander makes use of both her GWS and healthcare training in a piece clearly demonstrating the existence and consequences of weight bias in healthcare. Kristin Ryder shares her expertise in contraception with an invaluable overview of currently available methods and discussion of factors influencing contraceptive choice. Miranda Welch, now a practicing doula, connects her GWS training to her practice with the LGBTQ+ community. Erica Koepsel also connects the literature with her current work in a piece that shows students what sexual health education, so often limited and disappointing, has the potential to be and do. Elise Nagy shares her original research on selfies and self-care in a piece that I think will particularly resonate with GWS 103 students.

I am also thankful to others outside the department who provided original content highlighting issues of particular complexity and importance to our students, both now and likely in their futures. Tanya Cook, who received her PhD from UW-Madison Sociology, provides an updated overview of pregnancy and birth outcomes with a focus on her special area of autonomy and choice, or the lack thereof, for birthing people. Michaela Null, an assistant professor of Sociology at UW-Fond du Lac who also teaches in Women's Studies, provides a staunch activist perspective with her piece on the right of fat people to dignity and respect, regardless of health metrics. Kristin Puhl draws on her training in both social psychology and medicine to report the results of her original research on the primary healthcare experiences of LGBTQ+ people. Finally, the book closes with a new piece on race and fat activism by Shannon Barber that also serves as a needed warning: We must center women of color and other marginalized voices in spaces where they are too often seen as source material to be consumed or repackaged by White women, rather than individuals to be uplifted and listened to.

Our students are ready to make the world a better place; this reader is just a beginning in their journey to imagine what that looks like and how to get there. Like everyone who has been part of the GWS 103 teaching team, I've lost track of the number of students whose informed and insightful contributions to discussion section were but a preamble to their ongoing contributions to the field of women's health. I'm excited to see what our students will achieve in the next 5, 10, and 15 years, and look forward to new editions of this reader that will include some of them!

REFERENCES

1. For an elaboration on this metaphor in regard to children's literature and the importance of representation in fiction, see Rudine Sims Bishop's "Mirrors, Windows, and Sliding Glass Doors," to which I was recently introduced by Angela Sparks, a continuing student in one of my courses and a working youth librarian. *Ed*

2. https://www.nwhn.org/; also see their Facebook page (https://www.facebook.com/TheNWHN) and Twitter account (@TheNWHN) *Ed*.

SECTION 1

WOMEN AND THE HEALTHCARE SYSTEM

"Diagnosing Gender Disparities in Health Care"

By Andrea Irwin

Taken from September/October 2007 Newsletter

Until I became a women's health advocate immersed in the nuances of Medicaid, health insurance, and other complicated policy issues, I never truly appreciated the numerous disparities that exist between the ways men and women access the healthcare system. Most of my female friends are now in their mid-to-late twenties and I am constantly amazed at the myriad medical concerns that are unique to the female anatomy. For starters, research shows that women's reproductive systems are just so much more complex than men's and women are more likely than men to need healthcare throughout their lifetimes. Our ovaries, uteruses, breasts, cervixes, and fallopian tubes are all subject to various cancers, infections and other complications making routine monitoring a necessity, in addition to women's overarching need for safe, effective and affordable birth control. Among my circle of friends we have experienced breast biopsies, vaginal ultrasounds, and colposcopies galore.

At a minimum, a young woman is advised to visit her gynecologist once a year to have a pelvic exam and Pap test, but she may require further and additional visits to receive contraception and STI/HIV testing, or to follow-up on any abnormalities discovered through these preventive screenings. For women with comprehensive health insurance, most of these preventive services are covered benefits—but, unfortunately, not all. Moreover, some of these services are not covered in a way that makes sense. For instance, I just learned that many insurance plans will not cover STI/HIV tests at a woman's annual physical visit, which forces a woman to make an additional appointment for these tests and adds an extra layer of stress and burden to an already anxiety-producing procedure. Luckily, my provider pointed this out to me, but most women are not likely to be aware of such hidden costs. Instead of creating disincentives for women to be smart, efficient consumers of healthcare, insurers should end this policy that may increase a woman's health expenses or lead her to avoid care altogether.

Even worse, some insurance plans do not cover contraceptives despite the fact that the plans usually cover other prescription drugs. And, even when plans do cover contraceptives, they may not cover Emergency Contraception (EC) now that it's sold over-the-counter. EC costs around $45, which impedes access for many young women. Some insurance plans (notably the federal government employees' plan) also refuse to pay for abortion services, despite the fact that abortion is a safe and legal procedure, and that plans cover all prenatal care and pregnancy-related services.[1] The typical first trimester abortion costs, on average, around $468, which is extremely expensive for many women, particularly young and low-income women.[1]

Beyond the reproductive health disparities between men and women in terms of needed services and covered benefits, young women are more likely than men to suffer from chronic conditions like rheumatoid arthritis, lupus, or asthma.[2] Over one-third (38%) of women suffer from chronic conditions that require ongoing treatment, compared with 30% of men.[2] I've seen my peers struggle with all of these illnesses first-hand, as well as with the on-going treatment and medications they necessitate.

Young women are also more prone to be diagnosed with anxiety, depression, eating disorders, and other mental health conditions that may require extensive therapy and/or medications, and which may also result in increased physical health problems if left untreated.[2] Twice as many women as men are diagnosed with certain mental health problems such as anxiety and depression.[2] Even for women who have health insurance, the costs of these services can add up and co-pays and deductibles can become very expensive.

Moreover, because most health insurance plans are not required to cover mental health services, many insurers refuse to cover treatment for some or all mental health conditions, or may set very low limits on the number of mental health visits an individual can receive. These practices leave many young women with no ability to seek needed treatment. The high prevalence of violence against women—and the media's negative influences on women's body image that have largely shaped our generation's tormented relationships with our bodies (and driven us to seek out carcinogenic cigarettes to stay thin, and cancer-causing tanning beds to improve our appearance)—also exacerbate women's need for comprehensive healthcare.[3] We need to advocate for policies that reduce the powerful, negative, influence of these harmful external forces on our health and promote universal healthcare for all.

While these insurance practices are bad for women, more than one-third of all young women between the ages of 19 and 24 aren't insured at all.[4] For these women, the situation is far more dire because, without health insurance, women are more likely to avoid needed healthcare. Women in this age group are also more likely than men to have high medical debts or to experience bankruptcy because of medical expenses.[2] This is due to both women's lower incomes on average (thanks to the gender gap in pay) and their greater healthcare needs.[4] Proposals that expand healthcare coverage to more people—including individuals who work part-time, run their own businesses, or stay at home to raise families—are essential to ensuring women's autonomy and full equality with men.

One major lesson I've learned is that young women tend to underestimate the value of healthcare to our lives and well-being. We constantly sacrifice our mental and physical health so that we can nurture our careers, and build financial nest eggs for our futures. Like the importance of setting up a 401(k) at work or pursuing higher education to ensure access to better employment opportunities, accessing quality healthcare when we are young is an investment women must learn to make in order to ensure our health throughout our lives. Young women need to share our stories and encourage our peers to empower and educate themselves about the importance of preventive care. Most importantly, we must demand that lawmakers develop and implement healthcare reform proposals that meet young women's unique healthcare needs.

I am fortunate to have comprehensive health insurance through my employer. I was also raised by a strong feminist mother with more than 30 years of nursing experience who helps me to navigate the increasingly convoluted healthcare system. My hope is that my generation will continue to advocate for improved healthcare services and access for all so that everyone can enjoy a brighter, healthier future and better quality of life than our grandmothers experienced.

REFERENCES

1. National Network of Abortion Funds. *Policy Report—Abortion Funding: A Matter of Justice.* Amherst, MA: NNAF. 2005, 2, 6.

2. The Commonwealth Fund and The National Women's Law Center. *Issue Brief—Women and Health Coverage: The Affordability Gap.* Washington, DC: CF. April, 2007, p. 4.

3. Charlie Guild Melanoma Foundation (CGMF) Website. "10 Facts About Melanoma." Richmond, CA: CGMF. No date. Accessed June 6, 2007 from http://www.charlie.org/melanoma_facts.html.

4. The National Women's Law Center (NWLC). *issue Brief—Women and Health Coverage: A Framework for Moving Forward.* Washington, DC: NWLC. April, 2007, p. 2.

"What's in the Health Care Law for Women? A Lot!"

By Keely Monroe

For the *National Women's Health Network*

Article taken from September/October 2012 Newsletter

Despite the huge and positive changes the health care law has made in the way health insurance works for people, the majority of Americans still don't support the law or have mixed views about it. Why is that? When polls break the law down into its component parts (like giving tax credits to small businesses or allowing young people to stay on their parents' plans), its specific sections are often very popular. The bottom line is that many people either know very little about what the law actually does, or believe the negative messages spread by anti-health care law activists in order to foster mistrust and opposition to the law. As an example of the sort of misinformation out there, my 82-year-old grandmother recently sent me a frantic email complaining that the health care law will eliminate care for people over age 75.[1] I know that's not true; you know that's not true; but my grandmother honestly believes that this is what is going to happen.

There is some good news, however; as people find out more about the law and as its provisions go into effect, overall support for health care reform is slowly increasing. As of July 2012, 48 percent of those surveyed said they supported the law, up from 43 percent the month before.[2] The National Women Health Network has been working to help increase support for the law—and awareness of how it's helping people—with our campaign, *Countdown to Coverage*. The campaign, launched in March of this year, is designed to raise women's awareness about the many benefits they stand to gain from the new law. The campaign draws on research released last year that shows that people don't know the concrete details about how the law will make health services more affordable and protect people from insurance company abuses. When people learned about the law's specific benefits, their views changed dramatically, in many cases flipping from opposition to support: for example, young women's support increased seven-fold and older women went from opposing the law to firmly supporting it.[3]

The health care law has already helped millions of people get the care they need by letting young adults stay on their parents' insurance plans until age 26; eliminating lifetime limits that used to let insurance companies end coverage when people reached a financial cap; and ensuring that children are not discriminated against for pre-existing conditions. On August 1st, women got a long list of *new* reasons to feel good about the health care law.

Enormous Coverage Benefits for Women Started August 1st

On August 1st, another historic and important change to the U.S. health care system went into effect. On that date, most health insurance plans were required to start covering important preventive health care services for women without charging anything extra, like co-pays or deductibles. These services include:

- Comprehensive contraceptive care;
- Counseling and testing for sexually transmitted infections, including Human papillomavirus (HPV) and HIV;
- Well-woman preventive care visits, so women can get the services they need at each specific age;
- Screening and counseling for intimate partner violence;
- Screening for gestational diabetes; and
- Breastfeeding counseling and equipment.

Preventive services are incredibly important in protecting the health of women and our families, but expensive co-pays have long been a serious barrier to access for many women, particularly young and low-income women. "Often because of cost, Americans used preventive services at about half the recommended rate... A report by the Commonwealth Fund found that in 2009 more than half of women delayed or avoided necessary care because of cost."[4] So, expanding access to these critical health services is an extraordinary accomplishment.

This is illustrated by looking at just one of the preventive care services, contraceptive care. Contraceptive care is a vital aspect of preventive health care because it helps women avoid unintended pregnancies and facilitates birth spacing, which are both important and necessary to ensure healthy mothers and healthy babies. Thanks to the Affordable Care Act (ACA), insurers will now have to provide coverage without co-pays for all contraceptive methods that have been approved by the Food and Drug Administration (FDA) including oral contraception, shots, the ring, intrauterine devices (IUDs), diaphragms, cervical caps, and tubal ligation. This means that all women who have health insurance—regardless of their age, contraceptive choices, or health status—can get affordable contraceptive care that's right for them. Thanks, Affordable Care Act!

Although the requirement that insurance companies start providing these preventive health services without co-pays went into effect on August 1, 2012, the changes in women's policies didn't all happen on that date. Every new insurance plan that a woman purchases after August 1 must include the new coverage, and all old plans that make a significant change in coverage must too. The U.S. Department of Health & Human Services estimates that approximately 47 million women will have access to the additional services without cost-sharing on or after August 1. Most plans run on a calendar year, and most make some changes each year so many women will first see the effect when their plan year starts on January 1, 2013. Women enrolled in student health plans are likely to see the benefit immediately, since these health plans are usually aligned with the start of the school year. So, if you go to your doctor for preventive health care in the next few months, you may still get charged a co-pay, but that experience will become more and more uncommon. To find out when your plan year starts, check your plan documents or ask your employer.

Countdown to Coverage

The *Countdown to Coverage* campaign strives to help women understand the law's concrete benefits and the many benefits they stand to gain. In addition, the campaign also collects and shares women's stories about how the law is making real changes to our lives. Its tagline is "the incredible true story of the Affordable Care Act (ACA)," because we all have our own story about how the law helps us stay healthy. Like Robyn, who tells her family's story:

> Last year, my son, Jax, was born with a genetic disorder and a serious heart condition. It's too early for me to know the actual cost of the medical services Jax needed and will continue to need, but I do know that the health care law has already helped to keep my family's health coverage secure by eliminating lifetime limits for health care costs. Before the health care law, my insurance company could have dropped my family's coverage once we met our plan's lifetime limit, but now we feel safer because the law guarantees that cannot happen. I also know that Jax can never be denied coverage due to his condition, because insurers can no longer refuse to cover children up to age 19 on the basis of pre-existing conditions. As of 2014, adults can't be denied coverage because of a pre-existing condition, either. The health care law helps protect my family and keep us healthy.

Earlier this year, we waited with anticipation for the U.S. Supreme Court to rule on the health care law's constitutionality. For those of us, like Robyn and Jax, who have already benefitted so much from the ACA, it was unfathomable that its benefits might be taken away if the Court ruled against the law. When the Court upheld the vast majority of the health care law, we all celebrated because it meant the law would continue to help women and families get the care we need to stay healthy.

Advocates were disappointed, however, that the Court decision may have jeopardized the part of the law that offered improved access to the poorest women and families. The health care law expanded eligibility for the Medicaid program to include people making less than 138 percent of the Federal Poverty Level annually (about $29,000 for a family of four). This expansion would help an estimated 17 million people get the health care services they need. To encourage states to implement the expansion, the health care law included both a carrot and a stick. The carrot: the Federal government provided a significant amount of financial support, so the states would not have to bear these costs. The stick: the Federal government could withhold all Medicaid funding (funds for the expansion as well as other Medicaid funding) from states that did not implement the expansion. But the Court ruled that withholding those funds is unconstitutional, so the stick has been taken away.

Unfortunately, some conservative governors are using that part of the decision to make political statements about their opposition to the health care law, declaring that they will not expand Medicaid in their states. If these governors follow through on their declarations, it will deprive some of the nation's poorest communities of the benefits of the law and access to care. It will also leave those states with some very burdensome health care costs that could have been paid for with Federal support, if they had implemented the Medicaid expansion. The Network and our allies will be advocating for full implementation of the health care law—including the Medicaid expansion—in all 50 states. And, as the furor of the election year dies down, we hope that more and more states will see the practical advantage of taking the carrot, rather than making a political stand that doesn't serve the interests of the states' residents and taxpayers.

What's Next?

In 2014, the health care law will make additional, significant changes to the health insurance system. As more and more aspects of the health care law go into effect, women will continue to gain more affordable coverage for the health care we need.

First, insurance companies will no longer be able to charge women more than men for the same insurance plan and they won't be able to place arbitrary annual limits on the amount of medical care they will cover per year; so, if you or a member of your family get sick, you'll remain covered no matter what type or amount of care you need. And, they won't be allowed to discriminate against people for having pre-existing conditions—a change that will impact pregnant women, cancer patients, survivors of abusive relationships, and many others. In addition, insurance companies will also be required to cover maternity care. This; is a huge advance for women, since many plans have historically excluded coverage for the care and

services that women need when we are pregnant and giving birth.

And, in the same year, families will start getting help paying for health insurance. Families that earn up to 400 percent of the FPL (about $88,400 for a family of four) will be eligible for Federal subsidies to buy health insurance. Families earning up to 138 percent of the FPL will be eligible for Medicaid, which will be available to them if they live in a state that implements the program expansion.

THIS is what the *Countdown to Coverage* campaign is all about: telling the Incredible True Story of the Affordable Care Act. From protecting women and their families from long-standing discriminatory practices by the insurance industry, to securing consistent and affordable health insurance, women stand to gain so much from the health care law. To find out more about what the health care law can do for you, and how you can help spread the word, please visit the *Countdown to Coverage* website: http://www. CountdowntoCoverage.org.

Keely Monroe was a Law Students for Reproductive Justice (LSRJ) fellow and NWHN Program Coordinator during 2011–2012.

REFERENCES

1. To read more on Medicare Facts and Fiction please see: http://www.medicareadvocacy.org/medicare-facts-fiction-quick-lessons-to-combat-medicare-spin/.

2. Ipsos and Reuters, "Healthcare Law Poll June 28–30, 2012," Ipsos Public Affairs, July 2012. Accessed on August 13 2012. Available online at: http://www.ipsos-na.com/download/pr.aspx?id=11782.

3. Lake C, Snell A, Glasscock C et al., "Finding s from a Survey of Likely Voters Nationwide." Lake Research Partners Powerpoint, August 2, 2011. Available online at: http://healthcareforamericanow.org/organizing-tools/.

4. US Department of Health and Human Services, *Affordable Care Act Rules on Expanding Access to Preventive Services for Women,* August 2, 2012. Available online at www.Healthcare.gov.

"State Of Women's Coverage: Health Plan Violations of the Affordable Care Act"

From The *National Women's Law Center*

Introduction

The Affordable Care Act (ACT) makes dramatic improvements for women's health coverage and women's health care by ending discriminatory health insurance practices, making health coverage more affordable and easier to obtain, and improving coverage for the essential health services women need.[1] Among other reforms, the law creates new Health Insurance Marketplaces, which operate in every state, where women can compare Qualified Health Plans (QHPs) and shop for affordable, comprehensive health coverage for themselves and their families. During the 2015 open enrollment period, nearly 6.3 million women purchased coverage from QHPs.[2]

As a result of this important law, pregnant women have coverage for prenatal care, labor and delivery, and postpartum care; women with chronic illnesses are able to manage their condition with coverage for prescription drugs, ambulatory care, and chronic disease management; women of reproductive age have comprehensive access to birth control that enables them to determine when and whether they become pregnant; and all women have access to a range of preventive services without the financial burden of cost-sharing to ensure they live longer, healthier lives.

This report examines how health plans have responded to these historic changes. More specifically, the analysis focuses on coverage options available to women on Marketplaces by studying issuers' coverage documents to determine whether or not Marketplace plans are covering women's preventive services, maternity care, and other services critical to women's health as required by the ACA.

This analysis shows that the vast majority of health insurance issuers considered in this report offer coverage that violates specific requirements of the law (see Appendix A for number of violations in each state). In addition, this analysis finds ACA violations with at least one issuer in every state included in this report, across a wide range of women's health concerns. Specifically, this analysis finds ACA violations related to maternity care, birth control, breastfeeding supports and supplies, genetic testing, well-woman visits, prescription drug coverage, care related to gender transition for transgender individuals, chronic pain treatment, and certain pre-existing conditions.

STATES INCLUDED IN THIS REPORT:

Alabama, California, Colorado, Connecticut, Florida, Maine, Maryland, Minnesota, Nevada, Ohio, Rhode Island, South Dakota, Tennessee, Washington, and Wisconsin

Although this report examines issuers offering plans on a subsection of Marketplaces, the extent of these violations suggests that similar violations also pervade QHP documents in other states.

These violations leave women without the coverage they need and that is required by law. This means women could be forced to pay for care that their plan should cover, or go without needed health care altogether.

To realize the full promise the ACA offers for women's health, state regulators and issuers must identify and correct violations before plans are sold on the Marketplaces, or whenever problems are identified.

Full report with end notes is available online from their website: http://nwlc.org/wp-content/uploads/2015/04/stateofwomenscoverage2015final.pdf.

Consumers should know their rights, and advocate for themselves. And advocates must work directly with consumers, issuers, and regulators to educate, identify problems, and correct violations. To that end, this report includes recommendations for issuers, consumers, advocates, and state and federal regulators, all of whom must ensure that the promise of the ACA becomes a reality for women across the country. The report also provides examples of how the National Women's Law Center (the Center) and its partners have worked directly with issuers and key regulators to correct many of these violations.

Methodology

This report analyzes the certificates of coverage for health plans offered in 15 states in 2014 and 2015. In six states, the report considers issuers for both plan years, while in other states the report examines issuers for one plan year. In some cases plan documents—sometimes called the "certificate of coverage" or "evidence of coverage"—were not available for all issuers in a state. However, two years of analysis provides a broad range of issuers and plans for this analysis.

The analysis encompasses more than 100 publicly available certificates of coverage from Alabama, California, Colorado, Connecticut, Florida, Maine, Maryland, Minnesota, Nevada, Ohio, Rhode Island, South Dakota, Tennessee, Washington, and Wisconsin (see Appendix B for a list of issuers by state and year).[3] The Center secured certificates of coverage through online searches and by working with state advocates across the country to access the documents. The states reflect a diverse sample in terms of geography, political environment, and use of a federal or state Marketplace.

> ### HOW ARE ISSUERS COUNTED IN THIS REPORT?
>
> Issuers are counted separately for each year that a violation occurs. For example, the finding that eight issuers in Connecticut impermissibly restrict coverage for infertility services counts one issuer twice when an issuer included this violation in both 2014 and 2015 plan documents.

This report highlights the violations that issuers included in their plans for both years. For the sake of readability, all findings are reported in present tense, although issuers may no longer offer some of the 2014 plans or may have corrected some of the 2014 violations. In cases where it is known an issuer or issuers have corrected these problems, there is a notation in the endnote. In each section, the report notes the number of issuers with violations. Issuers are counted separately for each year that a violation occurs. The endnotes include issuers' names, plan years, and states for each violation.

This analysis focuses on coverage areas of particular importance to women, including preventive services such as birth control, well-woman visits, and lactation supports; prenatal and maternity care; abortion services; and exclusion policies. It therefore does not address all possible ACA violations, or even all coverage limitations that women may face. Women experience a wide range of acute and chronic health issues, and issuers may limit coverage for these conditions in ways that this analysis does not capture.

In addition, this report relies on plan documents, not on medical management policies, formularies, benefit determinations, or other cost-containment strategies that also determine which services a plan covers. Moreover, as issuers, regulators, and advocates scrutinize plan documents, other violations may also become apparent. Additional problems with issuers' coverage policies are also likely to come to light as women use their coverage.

The ACA's Key Reforms for Women

Prior to the ACA, insurance coverage on the individual market often failed women. First, insurance companies could deny women coverage altogether, charge higher premiums or impose waiting periods based on their health history, and many plans charged women higher premiums simply for being women.[4] Second, issuers frequently did not cover important women's health services, such as maternity care, prescription drugs, and lactation counseling. In fact, before the ACA, the vast majority of individual market plans did not cover maternity care at all, while a limited number of insurers sold separate maternity riders for an additional premium.[5] Similarly, before the ACA took effect, 1.3 million Americans were enrolled in individual market plans that did not have prescription drug coverage.[6]

The ACA reformed the individual insurance market to ensure that plans sold on this market meet women's needs. Health insurance issuers must offer coverage to all applicants, regardless of whether they have a pre-existing condition, and can only vary premium prices based on geography, age, family size and, at state discretion, smoking status—not gender or health condition. The law also prohibits issuers from imposing a waiting period before covering a pre-existing condition.

The ACA requires all individual and small group market plans to cover Essential Health Benefits (EHB) such as maternity and newborn care, preventive and wellness services and chronic disease management, behavioral health services, and prescription drugs. By requiring plans in these markets to cover all of these benefits, the ACA corrects notable benefit gaps and significantly advances women's access to critical health services.

The ACA also created a historic opportunity to focus on disease prevention and early detection by requiring insurance companies to cover a wide range of preventive services, making these important services more affordable and accessible for millions of women. Before implementation of the law, women were more likely than men to go without necessary health care, including preventive care, because of cost.[7]

Plans must now cover these services—typically screenings, immunizations, patient education, and other proven preventive care—without cost-sharing, thus removing financial barriers to care and allowing women to stay healthy and address problems before they become untreatable. The law also requires that all new health plans cover a number of preventive services specific to women, including the full range of FDA-approved birth control methods, sterilization, and related education and counseling, well-woman visits, screening for gestational diabetes, breastfeeding support, supplies, and counseling, and domestic violence screening and counseling. These services, which plans must cover without cost-sharing, help women manage key aspects of their lives, such as determining when and if they become pregnant, recognizing and addressing unhealthy relationships, and ensuring healthy pregnancies and thriving newborns.

The ACA and its regulations prohibit discrimination in nearly all parts of the health care system. Section 1557 of the ACA protects individuals from discrimination based on race, color, national origin, sex, sex stereotypes, gender identity, age, or disability in health programs or activities operated by recipients of federal financial assistance; federally-administered programs or activities; or entities created under the ACA. Section 1557 is the first federal statutory protection that broadly prohibits sex discrimination in health care and applies to virtually all aspects of the health care system.

The ACA's reforms are historic for women's health. In order to ensure women are benefiting from the important reforms outlined here, issuers must comply with the ACA. Only through complete plan compliance can women be sure they are provided the full benefits and protections of the ACA.

Violations of the Affordable Care Act
Maternity Coverage that Fails to Comply with the ACA

FOURTEEN ISSUERS ACROSS SEVEN STATES OFFER MATERNITY COVERAGE THAT DOES NOT COMPLY WITH THE ACA.

Violations of maternity coverage requirements include:

- Excluding maternity coverage for dependent enrollees
- Restricting pregnant women's access to maternity services outside of the plan's service area
- Establishing arbitrary limits on maternity benefits, such as a single ultrasound

Fourteen issuers across seven states offer maternity coverage that does not comply with the ACA. To correct longstanding gaps in women's access to maternity coverage, the ACA requires all qualified health plans to cover maternity and newborn care as an essential health benefit. Before the ACA, the vast majority of individual market plans did not cover maternity care at all, while a limited number of insurers sold separate maternity coverage for an additional fee.[8] The high cost of maternity services was a major obstacle to women seeking critical prenatal care, which is proven to improve newborns' health outcomes.[9]

All QHPs must cover maternity care as part of the ten categories of Essential Health Benefits, and must extend this coverage to all enrollees, regardless of their status as dependents or spouses. The scope of maternity and newborn coverage can vary slightly by issuer and state, but a benchmark plan for each state sets the standard for coverage, meaning that states cannot create limits or exclusions on maternity care that go beyond the state's benchmark.

Violations of the requirements to provide maternity and newborn care pose serious threats to women and newborns. Early prenatal care is an essential element of good pregnancy care. While the United States has made progress on maternal and newborn health outcomes, infant mortality and preterm birth rates remain higher than in other developed countries.[10] Prenatal care helps providers identify and manage problems that can emerge throughout pregnancy and to mitigate risks associated with underlying chronic disease. Women who have little or no prenatal care are at increased risk for preterm labor, which is a leading factor in infant mortality and adverse health outcomes.[11]

Excluding Dependents from Maternity Coverage

Two issuers in two states exclude dependent enrollees from maternity coverage. A Tennessee insurance issuer explicitly excludes maternity coverage for dependent enrollees, stating that maternity expenses for dependents are excluded from coverage "unless there are life-threatening complications."[12] An issuer in Ohio had similar language that suggested dependents could be excluded from coverage by limiting maternity coverage to "the member or member's spouse."[13] Regulations defining the Essential Health Benefits, of which maternity care is one, clearly state that a plan cannot exclude an enrollee from any required coverage category.[14] Dependents can include spouses, domestic partners, and children under 26, which means that pregnant women who are covered as a dependent under a range of family relationships would not have insurance coverage for their pregnancy in this plan.

As a result of excluding dependent enrollees from maternity care, a pregnant woman could miss important prenatal screenings, ultrasounds, and regular check-ups throughout her pregnancy. She would also be expected to pay out-of-pocket for services she receives, as well as for her labor and delivery. The significant cost of pregnancy care would put her and her family at real financial risk, while missing important health services throughout her pregnancy could also threaten her health and the health of her newborn.

Impermissibly Limiting Maternity Benefits

Five issuers in three states create impermissible limits on maternity benefits. An issuer in Colorado and an issuer in South Dakota both limit the number of ultrasounds a pregnant woman can receive.[15] One issuer

ACA PROVISIONS ON MATERNITY COVERAGE

Maternity and newborn care is one of ten Essential Health Benefits. All qualified health plans are required to provide this coverage to all enrollees.

Key regulations:
The Essential Health Benefits are implemented through 45 CFR 156.115. Of special note for maternity coverage:

- Dependent enrollees cannot be excluded from maternity coverage.

- All qualified health plans must be substantially equal to the state's benchmark plan, meaning that plans cannot create new exclusions and limitations that were not approved as part of the selection of the state's benchmark.

The ACA also created new protections for women who need emergency coverage away from home or outside their plan's network. The implementing regulations at 45CFR 147.138 state that:

- Issuers must cover emergency services whether or not the provider is part of the plan network and without imposing coverage limits or other requirements that are "more restrictive" than the plan's coverage of emergency services delivered by in-network providers.

This is an important protection for all enrollees, but of particular importance to pregnant woman who may need emergency maternity coverage when away from home.

limits a woman to a single ultrasound and the other issuer only covers two routine ultrasounds. An issuer in Alabama limits the number of prenatal visits to six per year.[16] Three Colorado issuers impermissibly limit the scope of maternity coverage by excluding "preconception counseling, paternity testing, genetic testing, or testing for inherited disorders, screening for disorders, discussion of family history...."[17] A Wisconsin issuer impermissibly limits the services a pregnant woman can receive based on her age.[18]

These limitations violate the state's EHB-benchmark plan, which establishes the coverage parameters for the ten categories of EHB in each state. According to the federal rules implementing EHB, issuers must provide benefits that are "substantially equal" to the state's EHB-benchmark plan, including covered benefits and limitations.[19] However, in these cases, the issuers do not meet the maternity coverage requirements of the state EHB-benchmarks. The EHB-benchmark plans in Colorado, South Dakota, and Alabama do not include quantitative limits on ultrasounds or prenatal visits. In addition, the Colorado EHB-benchmark plan does not limit the scope of maternity coverage by excluding key counseling services and screenings, nor does the Wisconsin EHB-benchmark plan include an age limit for certain prenatal services.[20, 21]

These exclusions could result in fewer opportunities to receive important prenatal screenings or identify complications that can arise during pregnancy-and to intervene as early as possible to improve health outcomes for the woman and her newborn.

Limiting Women's Access to Maternity Care Outside of the Service Area

Six issuers across three states exclude coverage of maternity care or services related to labor and delivery outside the plan's service area. Depending on the issuer,

these exclusions cover the duration of pregnancy, the final trimester of pregnancy, or the final thirty days of pregnancy.[22] These unallowable coverage exclusions limit pregnant women's ability to travel outside of their service area by placing them at financial risk for the full cost of emergency maternity care, if needed. This restriction erodes the requirement that all plans must cover maternity care by creating unreasonable conditions whereby the issuer would not provide coverage.

Under the ACA, emergency services received outside of the service area or outside of the plan network must be covered for all enrollees, including pregnant women.[23] The coverage policies of these six issuers violate the emergency services protections of the ACA by creating circumstances where they could deny coverage for emergency maternity services. If a pregnant woman goes into early labor, she would likely seek immediate medical attention. With 98 percent of births occurring in hospitals, a pregnant woman would likely go to a hospital emergency department if she experienced labor symptoms outside of her service area.[24]

Under these restrictions on maternity coverage, a pregnant woman who seeks emergency maternity services outside of her service area could be denied coverage. Labor and delivery is the most expensive medical care most pregnant women are likely to receive. These unallowable provisions could leave women with the full financial responsibility for emergency maternity services, including labor and delivery.

Preventive Services Coverage That Fails To Comply With the ACA

Fifty-six issuers in 13 states offer preventive services coverage that does not comply with the ACA.

To encourage greater use of preventive services, address cost barriers to these services, and make sure all women have access to preventive health care, the ACA requires group and individual plans to cover certain preventive services with no cost-sharing requirements.[25] The law's emphasis on prevention and early detection represents a huge step forward for women's health. Preventive care helps women live longer, healthier lives. Because women are more likely than men to avoid needed care because of cost, the availability of preventive services without cost-sharing is especially crucial.[26]

These covered services are derived from four sets of expert recommendations: (1) services given an "A" or "B" recommendation by the U.S. Preventive Services Task Force (USPSTF); (2) all vaccinations recommended by the Center for Disease Control's Advisory Committee on Immunization Practices; (3) a set of evidence-based services for infants, children, and adolescents based on guidelines developed by the American Academy of Pediatrics and the Health Resources and Services Administration (HRSA); and (4) a set of additional evidence-based preventive services for women supported by HRSA.[27]

The ACA directed HRSA to address women's preventive health by identifying additional screenings and services needed to fill gaps in preventive care. HRSA enlisted the Institute of Medicine (IOM) to conduct a review of effective preventive health measures for women. In response, the IOM convened a committee of experts— including specialists in disease prevention, women's health, and evidence-based care—to develop a set of recommendations. The IOM recommended eight preventive services targeted to women, and HRSA adopted the IOM's recommendations in full.

As a result, QHPs are required to cover eight preventive services for women: the full range of FDA-approved birth control methods, sterilization procedures, and patient education and counseling for all women with reproductive capacity; well-woman visits; screening for gestational diabetes; breastfeeding support, supplies, and counseling; human papillomavirus testing; counseling for sexually transmitted infections; counseling and screening for human immunodeficiency virus; and domestic violence screening and counseling.

Of the many USPSTF recommendations and HRSA-required services, this analysis targets a sub-subset of services that are particularly important to women. These include: birth control, breastfeeding support and supplies, well-woman visits, and genetic testing. In addition, the Center examined all issuers' language on cost-sharing for preventive services.

ACA PROVISIONS ON PREVENTIVE SERVICES

The ACA requires coverage of certain preventive services, recommended by USPSTF and HRSA. This analysis reviewed coverage for: breastfeeding support and supplies, well-woman visits, genetic testing, and birth control.

Key regulations:
The preventive services are implemented through regulations at 45 CFR 147.130 and federal guidance from the U.S. Department of Labor, FAQs about Affordable Care Act Implementation (Part XII). Key points include:

- Issuers cannot impose cost-sharing on women's preventive health services.
- Issuers must permit women to use additional well-woman visits, without cost-sharing, to obtain all necessary preventive services, depending on a woman's health status, health needs, and other risk factors.
- Issuers must provide coverage of comprehensive lactation support and counseling and costs of renting or purchasing breastfeeding equipment, which extends for the duration of breastfeeding.

In addition, the Essential Health Benefits rules at 45 CFR 156.115 incorporate these requirements into EHB.

Imposing Cost-Sharing on All Women's Preventive Services

THREE ISSUERS IN TWO STATES REQUIRE COST-SHARING FOR PREVENTIVE SERVICES IN VIOLATION OF THE ACA.

Violations of preventive services coverage requirements include:

- Imposing cost-sharing on all of women's preventive services
- Subjecting preventive services to the plan deductible in some cases

Three issuers in two states offer coverage of preventive services that does not comply with the ACA by imposing cost-sharing on preventive services. Not only is this an explicit violation of the ACA, it also could deter women from obtaining important benefits.

Two issuers in Nevada impose cost-sharing on *all* women's preventive services.[28] One issuer in Minnesota that offers a catastrophic plan impermissibly limits coverage of preventive services to the three primary care visits that catastrophic plans must cover before the deductible.[29] This policy does not comply with the ACA because preventive services covered under § 2713 of the Public Health Service Act do not count towards the three primary care visits that catastrophic plans must cover before the deductible.[30]

Cost-sharing on preventive services could deter women from obtaining important benefits. Women would have to pay out-of-pocket for services their plan is required to cover—such as co-payments for preventive care visits or birth control prescriptions—or forgo services altogether. If her plan has a high deductible, a woman could be responsible for the full cost of her visit and medication, both of which should be provided without any cost-sharing.

WORKING TOWARDS BETTER COVERAGE

COST-SHARING FOR PREVENTIVE SERVICES

In 2014, Anthem BlueCross and Anthem BlueCross Multi-State Plan in Nevada imposed cost-sharing for required preventive services by stating, "[w]omen's Preventive Care services, as noted in the Health Resources and Services Administration guidelines, are covered but are subject to a cost share." This was a clear violation of the ACA's requirement to provide women's preventive services at no cost-sharing.

The Center contacted state advocates and collaborated on a joint letter to the Nevada Insurance Commissioner. In February 2015, the Insurance Commissioner responded and indicated that the issuer corrected this violation, and it does not appear in the 2015 coverage documents.

Creating Unallowable Limits on Breastfeeding Support and Supplies

TWENTY ISSUERS IN SIX STATES IMPOSE IMPERMISSIBLE LIMITS ON COVERAGE OF BREASTFEEDING SUPPORT, SUPPLIES, AND COUNSELING.

Violations of breastfeeding coverage requirements include:
- Limiting coverage of breast pumps
- Limiting coverage of lactation counselling and education

Twenty issuers in six states offer coverage of breastfeeding support and supplies that does not comply with the ACA. Violations include limitations on breast pumps and lactation counseling.

Breastfeeding benefits the mother and the child, but too often there is a gap between women's intent to breastfeed their babies and the support they need to successfully breastfeed. Although a majority of women plan to breastfeed, a much lower proportion actually do when they are discharged from the hospital after delivery.[31] After reviewing the clinical evidence, the Institute of Medicine recommended women receive comprehensive lactation support, counseling, and access to breastfeeding equipment. Based on this recommendation, the ACA requires coverage of breastfeeding support and supplies without co-payments, deductibles, or co-insurance for the duration of breastfeeding.

Limiting Coverage of Breast Pumps

Coverage of breast pumps varies by issuer and state, with coverage limitations falling into distinct patterns that unallowably limit the scope of coverage. Three issuers in three states explicitly exclude breast pumps from coverage.[32] Three issuers in two states only allow women to obtain a breast pump within 6 months of delivery.[33] Two issuers in one state limit rental of a breast pump to 12 months, while two issuers in two states indicate that the plan determines the duration of breast pump rentals.[34,35] One issuer in Ohio limits coverage of a breast pump to one purchase every three years.[36] All of these examples conflict with federal guidance requiring issuers to cover breastfeeding equipment and support for the duration of breastfeeding.[37]

Many women need access to breast pumps to maintain their milk supply, particularly when returning to work. In fact, one of the reasons the IOM recommended coverage of breastfeeding equipment was to ensure that women who return to work or have other obligations that separate them from their infant can continue to breastfeed, if they choose to, without cost barriers.[38]

Limiting Coverage of Lactation Counseling and Education

Coverage documents often say very little about lactation services. When it is mentioned, many issuers place significant limits on coverage that conflict with federal guidance. Nearly all issuers in Connecticut restrict access to lactation services to a narrow window, requiring women to get services within two months of delivery.[39] Three issuers in Connecticut go further by restricting coverage to a single lactation visit, also within two months of delivery.[40] Similarly, one issuer in Alabama limits breastfeeding education to two services per calendar year (for pregnant women) and three counseling sessions in conjunction with each birth.[41] In addition, one issuer in Tennessee limits breastfeeding education to one visit per pregnancy.[42]

All of these restrictions violate the ACA. Federal guidance clarifies that breastfeeding support and counseling extends for the duration of breastfeeding.[43] Furthermore, these restrictions could hamper women's ability to breastfeed successfully by significantly limiting access to lactation support.

Some women may need intensive lactation support to manage initial breastfeeding challenges such as insufficient milk supply or a newborn's difficulty latching. In other instances, women will need lactation support after breastfeeding has been established, but the woman needs treatment for medical issues associated with breastfeeding, such as thrush or mastitis, is returning to work, or experiences milk supply problems later in breastfeeding.

The IOM's breastfeeding recommendation encompasses the initiation and duration of breastfeeding. These coverage limits not only conflict with federal guidance but also undermine the intent of the IOM recommendation.[44]

Limiting Well-Woman Visits

Five issuers in four states limit coverage of well-woman visits by having frequency or service limitations that do not comply with the ACA. Well-woman visits are a crucial entry point for women to access recommended preventive services. The IOM recommends coverage for well-woman visits to close a long-standing gap in coverage for women, remove the cost barriers women face when seeking preventive services,

> ## FIVE ISSUERS IN FOUR STATES DO NOT COVER WELL-WOMAN VISITS AS REQUIRED BY THE ACA.
>
> Violations of well-woman coverage requirements include:
> - Limiting women to a single visit per year
> - Limiting the scope of services to gynecological exams

and address the fragmented nature of women's health care. These visits also create a unique opportunity for women to learn about their health risks, plan for preventive care, and receive education and counseling about maintaining or achieving healthy lifestyles throughout their lifespans.

> ## WELL-WOMAN VISITS
>
> Please visit www.nwlc.org/wellwoman for more information on well-woman care, particularly the education and counseling services that are a critical component of well-woman visits. These pages feature the Center's work in partnership with the Mary Horrigan Connors Center for Women's Health and Gender Biology at Brigham and Women's Hospital.

While the majority of coverage policies are silent on coverage of well-woman visits, some issuers limit well-woman visits in ways that conflict with federal guidance and the IOM recommendations. Three issuers in two states limit well-woman visits to a single visit per year.[45] One issuer in Alabama restricts coverage of a well-woman visit to two per calendar year.[46] One issuer in Rhode Island not only limits a well-woman visit to a single visit, but restricts the scope of that visit to a gynecological exam.[47]

Federal guidance notes that women may need more than one well-woman visit per year to obtain the full complement of recommended preventive services.[48] The HRSA guidelines recommend *at least* one well-woman preventive care visit annually so that a woman may access the USPSTF and HRSA-recommended preventive services that are appropriate to her age, health status, disease risk factors, and other criteria.[49] A one-visit-per-year limit and restrictions on the scope of services violate the ACA. Well-woman visits are also intended to be comprehensive and are not limited to a gynecological exam. According to HRSA, these visits may encompass a wide range of women's health needs, including cardiovascular health, mental health, and substance use screenings.

Coverage policies that restrict well-woman care could limit women's access to covered preventive services. For example, some preventive services, such as mammograms or genetic counseling, may require women to visit a provider or facility other than their primary care practice. A limit on the number of well-woman visits a woman may receive in a calendar year could therefore result in women paying inappropriate cost-sharing when they receive these services. While the issuer would likely still cover the preventive service without cost-sharing, women may be asked to pay a copayment or coinsurance for the visit itself—and decades of research have demonstrated that cost-sharing can depress use of necessary care.[50] Similarly, policies that impermissibly restrict well-woman care to gynecological services could lead to women going without other screenings and services that are appropriate to their age and health histories.

Excluding or Limiting Coverage for Genetic Testing

LIMITING COVERAGE OF STI COUNSELING

One issuer in Alabama places both service limitations and age restrictions on coverage of important services for women. The issuer only provides coverage for three sexually transmitted infections (STI) counseling sessions "per lifetime." This issuer also restricts the age limit for chlamydia screening to 15-24. USPSTF recommendations do not have this timeframe, rather they recommend screening for chlamydia in sexually active women age 24 years and younger, and in older women who are at increased risk for infection.

Further, the USPSTF makes recommendations about the effectiveness of specific clinical preventive services based on the benefits and risks associated with various screenings and tests. These recommendations sometimes include factors such as age, family history, and other risks for disease—however, all age and frequency-related recommendations are based on clinical evidence. All issuers must adhere to the USPSTF recommendations for age and frequency rather than creating any arbitrary limits.

The Center did not review all plans for violations related to STI screenings and counseling, but this issuer's violations are included because of their specific nature.

SEVEN ISSUERS IN THREE STATES OFFER COVERAGE OF GENETIC TESTING THAT DOES NOT COMPLY WITH THE ACA.

Violations of genetic testing coverage requirements include:
- Excluding genetic testing
- Limiting coverage of genetic testing to overly-narrow circumstances

Seven issuers in three states offer coverage of genetic testing that does not comply with the ACA. Genetic testing gives women the chance to learn if their family history of breast or ovarian cancer is due to an inherited gene mutation. Women who have a BRCA1 or BRCA2 mutation have a greatly increased risk of breast cancer and ovarian cancer, and may require more intensive and frequent screening for these cancers. In some circumstances women with these mutations may choose surgery or chemoprevention to reduce their risk.

All issuers are required to cover genetic counseling and testing for BRCA1 and BRCA2 mutations for women at high-risk for family-related breast or ovarian cancer. However, these issuers' plan documents prohibit coverage of these required services. For example, one issuer considers genetic testing only as part of a fertility evaluation.[51] Four issuers indicate that genetic testing is not covered unless it is used to diagnose a condition, or determine a treatment plan for an already-diagnosed patient.[52] Two issuers exclude all "genetic testing, counseling, or engineering" except for prenatal diagnosis of congenital conditions.[53]

The USPSTF has made a B recommendation for genetic counseling and genetic testing for these mutations for women with a high risk for family-related breast and ovarian cancer, which means that issuers are required to provide this coverage and these exclusions violate the ACA. Women whose plans do not cover genetic counseling and testing for BRCA mutations and cannot afford to pay for these expensive services may not have the information they need to manage their cancer risk.

Coverage of Birth Control, Sterilization, and Related Education and Counseling

33 ISSUERS IN 13 STATES OFFER BIRTH CONTROL COVERAGE THAT DOES NOT COMPLY WITH THE ACA.

Violations of birth control coverage requirements include:

- Failure to cover all FDA-approved methods
- Cost-sharing on birth control
- Limits on services associated with birth control
- Age limits on birth control

Thirty-three issuers in 13 states offer birth control coverage that does not comply with the ACA.

The IOM recommended that birth control coverage be included as a preventive service in the ACA because the health benefits of birth control are well-documented.[54] Birth control is highly effective at reducing unintended pregnancy, which can have severe negative health consequences for both women and children. It also allows women to space their pregnancies, which improves the health of both women and their children. Birth control is such a core part of women's lives that 99 percent of sexually active women have used birth control at some point.[55]

The ability of women to plan and space their pregnancies through access to birth control is linked to their greater educational and professional opportunities and increased lifetime earnings.[56] Access to reproductive health care can also benefit children later in life: a recent study shows that children whose mothers had access to birth control have higher family incomes and college completion rates.[57]

Failing to Cover All FDA-Approved Methods of Birth Control

Fifteen issuers in seven states fail to cover all FDA-approved methods of birth control. One issuer in South Dakota does not cover the contraceptive implantable rod.[58] An issuer in California fails to cover ella, a unique emergency contraceptive method, by defining "emergency contraceptive drugs" as those which have the same medication as "regular birth control drugs."[59] An issuer in Wisconsin excludes coverage of contraceptive sponges.[60] In these instances, a woman may not be able to get coverage for the method of birth control that she and her medical provider have determined is appropriate for her, and is required by law. This could lead to women forgoing birth control altogether or using an inappropriate method, which could lead to less effective or less consistent use.

ACA PROVISIONS ON BIRTH CONTROL COVERAGE

The ACA requires qualified health plans to provide coverage without cost-sharing of all FDA-approved birth control methods, sterilization procedures, and patient education and counseling for all women with reproductive capacity.

Key parts of this requirement include:

- All FDA-approved birth control methods must be covered.
- FDA-approved over-the-counter contraceptive methods, when prescribed for women, must be covered.
- Birth control-related services, such as follow-up visits, management of side effects, counseling for continued adherence, and device removal must be covered.

Issuers may use "reasonable medical management techniques" to determine the "frequency, method, treatment, or setting" for birth control, such as imposing costs on a branded drug when a generic equivalent is covered. However, these techniques are not without limits:

- If a generic version is not available, issuers must cover the branded drug without cost-sharing.
- Every plan must have a waiver process that would let women access the birth control method she and her provider determine is medically appropriate for her.

Eleven issuers in five states exclude over-the-counter (OTC) birth control methods.[61] These OTC exclusions raise particular concerns about women's access to some forms of emergency contraception (EC) which are available over-the-counter. According to federal guidance, plans must cover FDA-approved over-the-counter birth control methods without cost-sharing when prescribed.[62] Coverage of over-the-counter birth control methods is critical for women who rely on these methods to prevent pregnancy, and especially for access to EC so that a woman can prevent pregnancy if her primary birth control method fails or in cases of sexual assault.

Imposing Cost-Sharing on Birth Control

Seven issuers in three states require cost-sharing for birth control, some on all birth control methods while others impose cost-sharing on specific methods. A catastrophic plan in Maryland applies the deductible to "family planning services," including birth control.[63] Three issuers in Connecticut impose cost-sharing on sterilization services.[64] Two issuers in Ohio charge cost-sharing for IUDs and injectable contraceptives.[65] Another issuer in Ohio requires women to pay out-of-pocket for over-the-counter methods, but will reimburse women for those costs.[66]

All of these examples impermissibly require women to pay cost-sharing—which could have a significant financial impact that deters women from obtaining required benefits. Of particular concern are the costs imposed on the most effective forms of birth control, such as IUDs, whose upfront costs without insurance coverage are nearly a month's salary for a woman working full-time at minimum wage.[67] Cost-sharing for IUDs has been shown to be a significant barrier— only 25 percent of women who request an IUD have one placed after learning the associated costs.[68] Issuers that impose cost-sharing on IUDs violate the ACA, create a financial obstacle to women accessing these more effective methods, and could prevent a woman from using the birth control that is most appropriate for her.

Limiting and Imposing Cost-Sharing on Services Associated with Birth Control

Seven issuers in six states require cost-sharing for or place impermissible limits on services associated with birth control. Two California issuers require cost-sharing for the physician office visits for injectable contraception and for diaphragm fitting procedures.[69] An issuer in Alabama limits coverage of sterilization confirmation tests to two tests per lifetime.[70] An issuer in South Dakota will only cover IUD placement and removal once every five years.[71] The law does not allow these kinds of limitations.

Some plans require cost-sharing for, or impose impermissible limits on, birth control counseling. Multiple plans offered by one issuer in Colorado require cost-sharing, co-payments and/or deductibles, for birth control counseling.[72] An issuer in Florida requires office visit charges for preventive medicine services including "contraception management, patient education, and counseling."[73] An Ohio issuer limits contraceptive counseling to two visits per year.[74] These unallowable costs and coverage limits could prevent a woman from receiving the counseling she needs to find the birth control method that is right for her. Counseling is also critical to helping women use their birth control method correctly, such as knowing how often to apply a patch, take a pill, or return to the office for an injection.

Requiring Cost-Sharing for Brand-Name Birth Control Without Generic Equivalents

Eight issuers in five states cover generic oral birth control without cost-sharing, and impose cost-sharing on brand-name contraceptives.[75] An issuer in Ohio only covers generic injectable contraceptives, generic emergency contraceptives, and generic devices.[76] Any policy that limits coverage of birth control without cost-sharing only to generic forms is impermissible. Federal guidance specifies that issuers must cover brand name contraceptives without cost-sharing if a generic equivalent is not available.[77] In addition, where a generic equivalent is available, plans must have a waiver process for cases in which a provider has determined that the brand is the medically appropriate choice. Failure to cover brand-name birth control, when required, could leave women without access to the method of birth control best suited for them. Some women have adverse reactions to certain types of birth control and are unable to tolerate using that specific method. When this is the case for a generic and she is able to tolerate the brand-name version, she must have coverage of that version without cost-sharing.

Failing to Cover Sterilization for All Women of Reproductive Capacity

Five issuers in three states impose impermissible limitations on sterilization. Specifically, an issuer in South Dakota excludes sterilization for "dependent children"— which includes adults up to the age of 26.[78] This provision would leave many adult women without coverage for this procedure, even though the ACA's birth control benefit encompasses all women of reproductive capacity. In addition, two issuers exclude coverage of re-sterilization following a reversal of sterilization.[79] Another issuer limits coverage of sterilization to one procedure per lifetime.[80] If a prior sterilization procedure has been reversed, and a woman has reproductive capacity, the plan must cover a subsequent sterilization procedure under the ACA. Sterilization is the second-most used form of birth control, with 15.5 percent of all women relying on it.[81] Plans cannot limit coverage of this birth control method.

Imposing Age Limits on Birth Control Coverage

One issuer in one state denies coverage of birth control without cost-sharing based on a woman's age, regardless of her reproductive capacity. An issuer in Colorado limits coverage to women under age 50.[82] But, many women over the age of 50 continue to use birth control to prevent pregnancy.[83] Plans cannot arbitrarily limit coverage of birth control based on age because the ACA requires coverage for *all* women with reproductive capacity. If a woman's health care provider determines she needs birth control, the plan must provide that coverage.

WORKING TOWARDS BETTER COVERAGE

BIRTH CONTROL COVERAGE

After finding the violations in plans in Connecticut, the Center, along with Planned Parenthood of Southern New England, brought the problem to the attention of regulators in Connecticut. The state subsequently issued a clarifying bulletin about the birth control coverage requirements. Specifically, the bulletin directed issuers to ensure that sterilization and over-the-counter birth control is covered without any cost-sharing. The bulletin is an important step towards ensuring that issuers clearly understand the requirements of the law and are not inappropriately charging women cost-sharing.

Abortion Coverage that Fails to Comply with the ACA

One issuer in one state offers different abortion coverage to enrollees based on whether they receive financial help with their premiums, which is a violation of the ACA.

The ACA treats abortion differently from all other health care services, imposing limitations and rules that restrict women's access to insurance coverage of abortion.[84]

Currently, 25 states have laws prohibiting QHPs from covering abortion in some or all instances.[85] Of the 15 states includes in this report, six of them prohibit some

---

ONE ISSUER IN ONE STATE IMPERMISSIBLY LIMITS COVERAGE OF ABORTION.

This issuer offers different abortion coverage to enrollees based on whether they receive financial help with their premiums.

---

or all coverage of abortion in QHPs: Alabama, Florida, Ohio, South Dakota, Tennessee, and Wisconsin. These bans take a critical benefit away from women, endangering women's health. Abortion coverage is permitted in the remaining nine states reviewed for this report. In those states, coverage of abortion varied across plans.

ACA PROVISIONS ON ABORTION COVERAGE

The ACA treats abortion differently from other health care services.

- The ACA allows states to pass laws prohibiting abortion coverage in the Marketplaces.
- If a QHP covers abortion beyond certain limited circumstances, there are administrative requirements it must meet to ensure that federal financial assistance does not pay for those abortion services.

An issuer in Colorado offers different coverage to enrollees based on whether they receive financial help with their premiums. Specifically, it excludes coverage of abortion in any circumstance for individuals who receive help with their premiums, while offering other enrollees coverage for "non-elective procedures." [86] This differentiation is not allowed under the regulations implementing cost sharing reductions.[87] In addition, even within the severe limitations on abortion coverage in the ACA, QHPs are not authorized to treat enrollees receiving help with their premiums differently from those who are not in terms of abortion coverage within a plan. It is a violation of the ACA and would leave women receiving help with their premiums without the health care coverage that others in the plan receive. When it comes to a decision about whether or not to end a pregnancy, it's important that a woman has health coverage so that she can afford to make a real decision.

WORKING TOWARDS BETTER COVERAGE

TREATING ENROLLEES DIFFERENTLY FOR ABORTION COVERAGE

In 2014, the Center worked with advocates at Colorado Consumer Health Initiative to contact New Health Ventures because it provided different coverage of abortion based on whether an enrollee received federal financial assistance, in violation of the ACA. The issuer corrected the problem in the 2015 plans.

ACA PROVISIONS ON ESSENTIAL HEALTH BENEFITS

According to § 1301 of the Affordable Care Act, all qualified health plans must offer Essential Health Benefits (EHB). Section 1302 of the ACA defines EHB to include ten categories of services, and stipulates that EHB must:

- Be equal in scope to a typical employer plan;
- Reflect an appropriate balance across categories of benefits;
- Not discriminate based on an individual's age, expected length of life, disability, degree of medical dependence, or quality of life;
- Take into account the health needs of diverse populations, including women, children, persons with disabilities, and other groups.

45 CFR 156 establishes standards for EHB. These regulations include:

- Requiring QHPs to provide coverage that is substantially equal to the state EHB benchmark, including limitations on this coverage;
- Allowing issuers to substitute benefits within an EHB category, if the substitution is actuarially equivalent, unless the state prohibits substitution;
- Requiring QHPs to cover the greater of one drug in every category or class of the US Pharmacopeia, or the number of drugs in each category and class covered by the benchmark plan; and
- Prohibiting issuers from using benefit designs that discriminate against individuals based on age, expected length of life, disability, degree of medical dependence, quality of life, or other health conditions.

Additional Essential Health Benefit Coverage that Fails to Comply with the ACA

SEVEN ISSUERS IN FOUR STATES IMPERMISSIBLY LIMIT ESSENTIAL HEALTH BENEFITS IN WAYS THAT RESTRICT WOMEN'S ACCESS TO CRITICAL SERVICES.

Violations of Essential Health Benefits coverage requirements include:

- Establishing limits more restrictive than state benchmark coverage
- Imposing waiting periods for certain services

Seven issuers in three states impermissibly limit coverage of Essential Health Benefits in ways that are particularly critical for women.

All qualified health plans are required to cover the ten categories of EHB: ambulatory patient services; emergency services; hospitalization; maternity and newborn care; mental health and substance use disorder services, including behavioral health treatment; prescription drugs; rehabilitative and habilitative services and devices; laboratory services; preventive and wellness services and chronic disease management; and pediatric services, including oral and vision care.

The Essential Health Benefits are critically important to women. The EHB correct longstanding benefit gaps in the individual market and serve as the foundation of health coverage for QHPs sold in the Marketplaces. The EHB help ensure that women have the health coverage they need for a range of medical conditions, such as pregnancy, cancer, arthritis, and autoimmune conditions.

States can choose from a number of "typical employer plans" as the starting point for defining Essential Health Benefits. States identify one of these plans and then add additional coverage to ensure that it complies with federal regulation—creating an "EHB-benchmark plan" that serves as the basis for QHP coverage in that state.

Each issuer is required to use the EHB-benchmark plan to determine the scope of coverage they will offer on the Marketplaces. According to federal rules, issuers' covered benefits must be substantially equal to the state's benchmark plan. States may allow issuers to substitute benefits within the ten EHB categories, as long as the substitution is actuarially equivalent. Coverage of EHB cannot include discriminatory benefit designs and must be balanced across EHB categories.

Unallowable Restrictions on Essential Health Benefits

Improperly Limiting Drug Coverage

Three issuers in two states exclude self-injectable medications from coverage.[88] As a result, women may not have coverage for medication necessary to treat conditions such as rheumatoid arthritis, lupus, or multiple sclerosis—conditions that predominantly affect women. This exclusion improperly limits prescription drug coverage. All QHPs must cover the greater of one drug per category or class or the number of drugs per category or class covered by the benchmark. Given the design of the states benchmarks' pharmaceutical benefit, plans cannot meet this requirement for all categories and classes if they do not cover any self-injectable medications.

Failing to Cover Devices

A Colorado issuer unallowably excludes coverage of "permanent or temporary implantation of artificial, non-human or mechanical organs and devices."[89] This language would exclude breast implants used in breast reconstruction, which are regulated as devices by the Food and Drug Administration. This exclusion is not allowable. The law requires EHB to be equal to the

scope of benefits offered by a typical employer plan – which are required to cover breast reconstruction following mastectomy.[90] Similarly, the Colorado benchmark specifically covers breast reconstruction.[91] In addition, EHB regulations require plans to meet the health needs of women. Approximately two-thirds of breast reconstruction procedures use breast implants[92]; a woman whose QHP does not cover breast implants may not be able to choose the reconstruction technique most appropriate to her clinical circumstances and physique. An issuer who excludes breast implants from coverage therefore violates EHB.

Restricting Coverage of Maintenance Therapies

Two issuers in Connecticut improperly exclude coverage for maintenance therapy.[93] Depending on the issuer's interpretation of the exclusion, the restriction could exclude a broad array of treatments and services that are covered by the EHB. Connecticut does not allow substitution of EHB benefits, which means that the plans must cover all services included in the EHB.[94] This restriction could exclude many treatments that should be covered under the EHB, such as hormonal therapy following initial breast cancer treatment, maintenance therapies for lupus, and maintenance therapies that prevent opportunistic infections in people with HIV.[95] Women who do not have coverage for maintenance therapies may be at risk for cancer recurrence, accelerated progression of auto-immune disease, or unnecessary complications for other conditions.

Excluding Transplant Coverage for New Enrollees

In their 2014 plans, three issuers in two states exclude from coverage transplant services for new enrollees. Transplants are costly medical procedures but often provide life-saving results; limiting coverage of transplants in this way could be extremely dangerous for women's health. Two issuers in Washington State do not cover transplant services for individuals who had not been enrolled for the previous 90 days, thereby creating a three month waiting period for coverage.[96] A Colorado issuer goes further and restricts coverage to individuals enrolled for the previous year.[97]

Guidance from the Department of Health and Human Services clearly states that such benefit-specific waiting periods are not allowed in Marketplace plans. The guidance noted concerns that such waiting periods "discourage enrollment of or discriminate against individuals with significant health needs or present or predicted disability."[98] In addition to violating the EHB, these waiting periods— regardless of duration or limitations on the type of transplants that are excluded from coverage—also violate the ACA's ban on pre-existing conditions.[99]

Waiting periods for transplant services not only violate the ACA but also have the effect of excluding coverage for timely, life-saving treatment. Women may not be able to pay the full cost of an organ transplant without insurance coverage. Women may have to choose less effective treatment options or forgo care and potentially suffer poorer health outcomes because of this violation.

WORKING TOWARDS BETTER COVERAGE

COVERAGE OF TRANSPLANT SERVICES

The Washington State Office of the Insurance Commissioner began to look into transplant waiting periods after consumers contacted the office complaining about discriminatory waiting periods. While state regulators were reviewing these policies, HHS issued guidance clearly stating that waiting periods are not allowed on any EHB. Washington State regulators then ensured that all 2015 plans eliminated waiting periods for this critical service.

Discriminatory Benefit Design that Fails to Comply with the ACA

NINETY-SIX ISSUERS ACROSS 12 STATES OFFER COVERAGE THAT DOES NOT COMPLY WITH NON-DISCRIMINATION PROVISIONS OF THE ACA.

Some of these discriminatory provisions include:
- Denying or restricting maternity coverage
- Restricting coverage based on age
- Excluding coverage for chronic pain treatment
- Excluding coverage related to gender transition for transgender individuals

---

Ninety-six issuers across 12 states have explicitly discriminatory provisions in their plan documents.

Prior to the ACA, health insurance issuers engaged in a number of discriminatory and unfair practices. Women were routinely charged more than men for health insurance coverage, even coverage that excluded maternity care.[100] Health insurance issuers in the individual market denied coverage to anyone for almost any reason, and excluded coverage for pre-existing conditions.[101] Not only did insurance plans exclude coverage of maternity care—a health care service only women need—but they routinely treated being a woman as a pre-existing condition, making it hard, and sometimes impossible, for women to find coverage that would meet their needs.[102]

The ACA includes several provisions designed to correct this longstanding discrimination. QHPs must offer coverage to everyone, and cannot exclude those with pre-existing conditions.[103] Issuers are also prohibited from charging women more than men for insurance coverage.[104] Essential Health Benefits also cannot be denied to someone because of the individual's age, expected length of life, disability, degree of medical dependency, or quality of life.[105] This prohibition on discrimination in the EHB helps ensure that plans do not use plan design or other means to unlawfully deny or restrict coverage. The ACA also includes an anti-discrimination provision, § 1557, which contains broad prohibitions on discrimination in health care programs

---

ACA PROVISIONS TO PREVENT DISCRIMINATION

The ACA prohibits discrimination in the Essential Health Benefits. Specifically:

- An issuer does not provide EHB if its benefit design, or the implementation of its benefit design, discriminates based on an individual's age, expected length of life, present or predicted disability, degree of medical dependency, quality of life, or other health conditions.

- A QHP issuer must not, with respect to its QHP, discriminate on the basis of race, color, national origin, disability, age, sex, gender identity, or sexual orientation.

Section 1557 of the ACA prohibits discrimination in health care programs, including QHPs, on the basis of race, color, national origin, sex, sex stereotypes, gender identity, age, or disability.

on the basis of race, color, national origin, sex, sex stereotypes, gender identity, age, or disability.[106] This is the first time that federal law has prohibited sex discrimination in health care.

Despite these prohibitions some issuers continue to offer plans with discriminatory benefit designs that restrict women's access to health care services or exclude services on a discriminatory basis.

Denying or Restricting Maternity Care

As discussed previously in this report, two issuers in two states exclude dependent enrollees from maternity coverage and six issuers across three states exclude coverage of maternity care or services related to labor and delivery outside the service area.[107]

It is well-established civil rights law that discrimination based on pregnancy and pregnancy-related conditions is per se sex discrimination.[108] Section 1557 follows this precedent.[109] Thus, treating maternity coverage differently than other coverage is a violation of § 1557. This includes barring any beneficiary—including those who get their insurance through their parents or a spouse—from receiving maternity coverage. It also includes singling out maternity care as an excluded coverage outside of the plan service area.

Restricting Coverage Based on Age

Nine issuers in two states exclude coverage based on age. As mentioned previously in this report, one issuer in Wisconsin impermissibly limits the services a pregnant woman can receive based on her age. The issuer limits coverage of prenatal vitamins and folic acid to women under age 42.[110] Eight issuers in Connecticut impermissibly restrict coverage for infertility services based on age.[111] Connecticut includes infertility services in its EHB benchmark plan but also limits this coverage to individuals under age 40. Thus QHPs in the state must include this coverage and eight issuers in Connecticut also include the age limit in their benefit design. The age limit in the Connecticut benchmark is an arbitrary limit that denies women over the age of 40 a health service based solely on their age. Because the average age of menopause is 51, many women over 40 still have reproductive capacity and a medical need for prenatal care and infertility services.[112] Thus, the Connecticut benchmark itself, the QHPs offered in Connecticut with the age limit, and the Wisconsin QHP with the age limit violate the ACA.[113]

Excluding Coverage of Chronic Pain Treatment

Two issuers in Colorado exclude "[s]ervices or supplies for the treatment of intractable pain and/or chronic pain" and "[t]reatment at pain clinics and chronic pain centers."[114] Women report more frequent pain, more severe pain and pain of a longer duration than men.[115] Women are at least four times more likely than men to be diagnosed with four conditions associated with chronic pain: chronic fatigue syndrome, fibromyalgia, interstitial cystitis, and temporomandibular (TMJ) disorders.[116] About 6.3 million women are affected by endometriosis in the US and about 6 million women are affected by vulvodynia in the US, two chronic pain conditions impacting only women.[117]

Chronic pain conditions, such as arthritis or rheumatism, and back or spine problems are the two leading causes of disability. Untreated pain has a detrimental effect on quality of life.[118] Plans providing EHB cannot have benefit designs that discriminate based on disability or quality of life. HHS has interpreted this provision to mean that benefit designs that discourage enrollment by individuals based on a health condition are discriminatory benefit designs.[119] In addition, QHPs are prohibited by § 1557 of the ACA from discriminating against individuals with disabilities. The chronic pain exclusion discourages individuals that have chronic pain conditions from enrolling in plans with these issuers because the services to treat their pain are specifically excluded. These plans therefore discriminate against individuals with disabilities and reduced quality of life due to conditions with chronic pain in violation of the ACA.

Excluding Care for Transgender People

Ninety-two issuers in 12 states explicitly exclude care related to gender transition for transgender individuals. In some states, such as Ohio, the EHB benchmark excludes transition-related care. In some instances issuers broadly exclude all transition-related services, such as those services related to "sex transformation; gender dysphoric disorder; gender reassignment" or "treatment leading to or in connection with transsexualism."[120] Other issuers specifically exclude transition-related surgery, sometimes referred to as "transgender surgery" or "transsexual surgery," or exclude hormone therapy for transgender individuals.[121] In addition, some issuers specifically exclude transition-related services within the mental health benefit.[122]

These exclusions discriminate on the basis of sex, gender identity, and health condition in violation of EHB and § 1557 of the ACA. The exclusions apply only to transgender individuals. The majority of transition-related services fall within the EHB categories of ambulatory care, mental health services, prescription drugs, and laboratory services, and most if not all interventions excluded from coverage for transgender individuals are routinely covered for non-transgender people to treat other medical conditions.[123] For example, patients with hypogonadism and other endocrine disorders as well as menopausal symptoms may use hormone therapy. Likewise, psychotherapy is a medically necessary treatment for a wide variety of conditions. In addition, these exclusions discourage transgender individuals from enrolling in these plans. Excluding transgender services from coverage violates the ACA by denying access to coverage based on sex, gender identity, and health condition.

WORKING TOWARDS BETTER COVERAGE

EXCLUDING CARE FOR TRANSGENDER PEOPLE

In 2014, all issuers in Washington and Connecticut excluded transition-related care. Because of the work of state and national advocates, state regulators in Washington and Connecticut issued guidance ending discrimination based on gender identity in health insurance. The Washington State Insurance Commissioner issued a letter to health insurance carriers that cites § 1557 of the ACA, as well as the state's Law Against Discrimination, and clarifies that "broad exclusions of coverage on the basis of gender identity" and "denial of a medically necessary service on the basis of gender identity" are prohibited. The Connecticut Insurance Department issued guidance based on state nondiscrimination law.

Thanks to this guidance, no issuers in Washington or Connecticut explicitly exclude transition-related care in their 2015 plans.

The Colorado Division of Insurance issued similar guidance and most issuers removed explicit transition-related care exclusions; however two issuers continued to have discriminatory exclusions in 2015.

Recommendations

The ACA corrects longstanding problems with the individual health insurance market and makes significant improvements in coverage for the services women need to get and stay healthy. Federal and state officials, insurance issuers, consumer advocates, and women themselves must continue to push forward with these changes to fully realize the ACA's promise for women's health. All of these stakeholders have important roles to play to ensure that health plans in Marketplaces comply with the law and meet women's needs. The following recommendations will foster better plan compliance with the law's requirements, greater availability of plan information, more aggressive oversight, and better redress for consumers—with the end result of improving Marketplace coverage for women.

Issuers:

- Issuers **must know the law** and make sure the plans they offer **comply with the law**.
- Issuers must **correct identified problems** for the millions of women who hold QHP coverage today, and for those who will enroll in the future.
- Issuers must have **clear coverage policies** that reflect the scope of coverage within their plans and make these documents broadly available. Regulators who review and certify plans, and women who choose plans and use health services, need to know which services plans cover or do not cover.

State and Federal Regulators:

- State and federal regulators need to provide **stronger oversight** to ensure plans comply with the ACA, its implementing regulations, and related guidance. Most states are responsible for the initial certification of health plans on state and federal Marketplaces. States regulators must be diligent in their review of plan documents and determined in their efforts to bring plans into compliance with the law during the certification process. They must be similarly diligent about correcting violations as they arise throughout the plan year. As the managers of federally-facilitated Marketplaces, and as the first-line regulator for the states that rely on federal review for plan certification, federal regulators must be equally diligent and determined. They cannot presume that state oversight alone is sufficient to ensure plan compliance with the law, and they must assume an active role as the Marketplace manager.

- State or federal regulators (as applicable) should **open all proposed plans for public comment**. This would give advocates and consumers a chance to review plans, and provide comments to regulators, on any violations present prior to plan certification.
- Regulators in every state should ensure that **coverage documents are publicly available, beginning with open enrollment**. Greater availability of plan documents would ensure that women have the opportunity to know the details of the plans they are purchasing. Information is a key feature of a well-functioning Marketplace—it allows women to choose the plans that are best for them and their families, and it increases competition among issuers to offer plans that meet women's needs. In addition, women's health advocates will be able to review and monitor plans for compliance after certification.
- Regulators should **inform women** about the law and its coverage requirements for women's health. For example, states should work with stakeholders to develop and distribute informational bulletins on the ACA's insurance reforms and what qualified health plans must cover. Women need this information to be informed consumers, to advocate for the coverage they need, and to hold plans accountable when they violate the law.
- Federal regulators should **collect data on plan violations** to inform further rulemaking or guidance to issuers and state regulators on ACA requirements. This data would reveal trends in issuer policies and problems with particular issuers that arise in multiple states.
- Regulators should **broadly publicize the appeals process**. Women need to know the appropriate course of action when plans fail to provide the coverage the ACA requires, and plans need to be held accountable when they do not comply with the law.

Consumers and Consumer Advocates:

- Women and their advocates should **educate themselves about their coverage rights** and **contact state and federal regulators** when issuers violate these rights. This contact can include appealing an adverse coverage decision, or alerting state and federal regulators when health plan documents do not appear to comply with the law.

In several states where the Center identified violations in 2014 plans, the Center worked with local advocates to approach state regulators or plans directly to improve compliance with the ACA.

Thanks to the work of the Center and state advocates, women can now count on better benefits in a range of Marketplace plans. These successes include:

- Removing exclusions of certain contraceptive methods;
- Ensuring full coverage of breast pumps by an issuer that previously excluded them from coverage;
- Removing limits on prenatal services from a policy that limited women to a single ultrasound;
- Removing a provision that excluded care for dependents from maternity coverage;
- Eliminating cost-sharing for women's preventive services in a plan that inappropriately charged women for preventive services; and
- Correcting coverage that limited abortions to enrolees not receiving financial help with their premiums.

Conclusion

This review of plan documents in 15 states finds that a majority of these plans violate ACA requirements related to women's health coverage. These violations may relate to which services, drugs, or devices QHPs cover, whether—and how much—women will pay out-of-pocket for care that should be fully covered by their QHP, which women have coverage for critical health care services, and other limitations on the care women need. The extent of ACA violations in these 15 states suggests that women covered by other issuers, and in other states, may hold coverage that is also impermissibly limited.

Without question, insurance issuers are responsible for the plan documents they submit to regulators as they seek certification for plans they will offer in the Marketplaces. Issuers need to do better. At the same time, state and federal regulators must also do better by ensuring that QHPs offered in the Marketplaces meet the standards of the ACA and its implementing regulations and guidance.

The Center's experience working with issuers, state advocates, and state officials demonstrates that these violations can be identified and corrected. But without greater availability of plan information to inform this type of advocacy, and more systemic efforts to enforce the law, women's health coverage will remain at the mercy of insurance issuers whose previous practices drove the need for insurance reforms in the first place.

Appendix A   Number of Issuers with Violations of the ACA in Each State

Number of Issuers with Violations of the ACA in Each State: 2014 and 2015							
State	Maternity	Breast-feeding Support and Supplies	Birth Control	Other Preventive Services	Abortion	Essential Health Benefits	Discrimination
Alabama 2015	1	1	1	1			
California 2014			1	1			
California 2015			1	1			
Colorado 2014	3	3		2	1	1	10
Colorado 2015	1	1	2	2		1	2
Connecticut 2014		2	2			1	3
Connecticut 2015		5	1			2	5
Florida 2015			1				4
Maine 2014			2	2			3
Maryland 2014			1				6
Minnesota 2014			2	1			
Nevada 2014	1		3	2			5
Nevada 2015	1		2				6
Ohio 2014	2	2	7				12
Ohio 2015		3	4				13
Rhode Island 2014			1	1			2
South Dakota 2014	1		1				1
Tennessee 2014	1	2		1			4
Washington 2014						2	9
Washington 2015							
Wisconsin 2014	3	2		1			12

Appendix B: List of Issuers by State and Year

APPENDIX B		
Alabama		
Issuer	**2014**	**2015**
BlueCross BlueShield of AL	Plans were unavailable	Reviewed
Humana, Inc.	Plans were unavailable	Plans were unavailable
United HealthCare	Plans were unavailable	Plans were unavailable
California		
Issuer	**2014**	**2015**
BlueCross BlueShield	Plans were not offered or were unavailable	Plans were unavailable
Blue of California	Reviewed	Plans were unavailable
Chinese Community Health Plan	Reviewed	Reviewed
Contra Costa Health Plan	Reviewed	No longer offered
HealthNet	Reviewed	Plans were unavailable
Kaiser Permanente	Reviewed	Plans were unavailable
LA Care	Reviewed	Reviewed
Molina Healthcare	Reviewed	Plans were unavailable
Sharp	Plans were not offered or were unavailable	Plans were unavailable
Valley Health Plan	Reviewed	Reviewed
Western Health Advantage	Plans were not offered or unavailable	Plans were unavailable
Colorado		
Issuer	**2014**	**2015**
All Savers (UnitedHealthcare)	Reviewed	Plans were unavailable
Anthem BlueCross BlueShield	Reviewed	Reviewed
Anthem BlueCross BlueShield Multi-State Plan	Reviewed	Plan was available but not reviewed
CIGNA	Reviewed	Reviewed
Colorado Choice Health plans	Reviewed	Reviewed
Colorado Health OP	Reviewed	Reviewed
ELEVATE/Denver Health	Reviewed	Reviewed
Humana	Reviewed	Reviewed

Kaiser Permanente	Reviewed	Reviewed
New Health Ventures	Reviewed	Reviewed
Rocky Mountain Health Plans	Reviewed	Reviewed

Connecticut		
Issuer	**2014**	**2015**
Anthem BlueCross and BlueShield of CT	Reviewed	Reviewed
Anthem BlueCross and BlueShield Multi-State Plans	Plans were not offered or were unavailable	Reviewed
ConnectiCare	Reviewed	Reviewed
United Healthcare	Plans were not offered or were unavailable	Reviewed
Healthy CT	Reviewed	Reviewed
Healthy CT Multi-State Plans	Plans were not offered or were unavailable	Reviewed

Florida		
Issuer	**2014**	**2015**
Assurant	Plans were not offered or were unavailable	Reviewed
Humana	Plans were not offered or were unavailable	Reviewed
Molina	Plans were not offered or were unavailable	Reviewed
Preferred Medical Plan	Plans were not offered or were unavailable	Reviewed

Maine		
Issuer	**2014**	**2015**
Anthem BlueCross BlueShield	Reviewed	Plans were available but not reviewed
Anthem BlueCross BlueShield Multi-State Plan	Reviewed	Plan was no longer offered
Harvard Pilgrim	Plans were not offered or were unavailable	Plans were available but not reviewed
Maine Community Health Options CO-OP	Reviewed	Plans were available but not reviewed

Maryland		
Issuer	2014	2015
All Savers (UnitedHealthcare)	Reviewed	Plans were unavailable
CareFirst Blue Choice	Reviewed	Plans were unavailable
CareFirst of Maryland	Reviewed	Plans were unavailable
CareFirst of Maryland Multi-State Plan	Reviewed	Plans were unavailable
CIGNA	Plans were not offered or were unavailable	Plans were unavailable
Evergreen Health CO-OP	Reviewed	Plans were unavailable
Group Hospitalization & Medical Services, Inc.	Reviewed	No longer offered
Kaiser Permanente	Reviewed	Plans were unavailable

Minnesota		
Issuer	2015	2015
BlueCross BlueShield of MN	Reviewed	Plans were unavailable
HealthPartners	Reviewed	Plans were unavailable
Medica	Reviewed	Plans were unavailable
PreferredOne	Reviewed	No longer offered
UCare of MN	Reviewed	Plans were unavailable

Nevada		
Issuer	2014	2015
Anthem BlueCross Blue Shield	Reviewed	Reviewed
Anthem BlueCross Blue Shield Multi-State Plan	Reviewed	Reviewed
Nevada Health CO-OP	Reviewed	Reviewed
Prominence HealthFirst	Plans were not offered or were unavailable	Reviewed
Saint Mary's Health First	Reviewed	No longer offered
Time Insurance Company	Plans were not offered or were unavailable	Reviewed
Health Plan of NV	Reviewed	Reviewed

Ohio		
Issuer	**2014**	**2015**
Aetna	Plans were not offered or were unavailable	Reviewed
Anthem BlueCross Blue Shield	Reviewed	Reviewed
AultCare	Reviewed	Reviewed
Buckeye Community Health	Reviewed	Plans were unavailable
CareSource	Reviewed	Reviewed
Coordinated Health Mutual	Plans were not offered or were unavailable	Reviewed
Coventry Health America One	Reviewed	No longer offered
HealthSpan	Reviewed	Reviewed
Humana	Reviewed	Plans were unavailable
Kaiser Permanente	Reviewed	No longer offered
Medical Health Insuring	Reviewed	Reviewed
Molina	Reviewed	Reviewed
Paramount	Reviewed	Reviewed
Premier Health Plan	Plan was not offered or was unavailable	Reviewed
Summa	Reviewed	Reviewed
Time Insurance Company	Plan was not offered or was unavailable	Reviewed
UnitedHealthcare of Ohio	Plan was not offered or was unavailable	Reviewed

Rhode Island		
Issuer	**2014**	**2015**
BlueCross BlueShield of RI	Reviewed	Plans were available but not reviewed
Neighborhood Health Plan	Reviewed	Plans were available but not reviewed
United HealthCare	Plans were unavailable or not offered	Plans were unavailable

South Dakota		
Issuer	**2014**	**2015**
Avera Health Plans	Plans were unavailable or not offered	Plans were unavailable
DAKOTACARE/South Dakota State Medical Holding Company, Inc.	Plans were unavailable or not offered	Plans were unavailable
Sanford Health Plan	Reviewed	Plans were unavailable

Tennessee		
Issuer	**2014**	**2015**
Assurant	Plans were unavailable or not offered	Plans were unavailable
BlueCross Blue Shield of TN	Reviewed	Plans were unavailable
CIGNA	Reviewed	Plans were unavailable
Community Health Alliance	Reviewed	No longer offered
Humana	Reviewed	Plans were unavailable

Washington		
Issuer	**2014**	**2015**
BridgeSpan Health Company	Reviewed	Reviewed
Community Health Plan	Reviewed	Reviewed
Coordinated Care	Reviewed	Reviewed
Kaiser Permanente	Reviewed	No longer offered
LifeWise Health Plan	Reviewed	Reviewed
Moda Health Plan	Plans were not offered or were unavailable	Reviewed
Molina Healthcare	Reviewed	Reviewed
Premera Blue Cross	Reviewed	Plans were unavailable
Premera Blue Cross Multi-State Plan	Reviewed	Plans were unavailable

Wisconsin		
Issuer	**2014**	**2015**
Anthem BlueCross BlueShield	Reviewed	Plans were unavailable
Anthem BlueCross Blue Shield Multi-State Plan	Reviewed	Plans were unavailable

Arise Health Plan	Reviewed	Plans were unavailable
Common Ground CO-OP	Reviewed	Plans were unavailable
Dean Health Plan	Reviewed	Plans were unavailable
Gunderson Health Plan	Reviewed	Plans were unavailable
Health Tradition Health plan	Reviewed	Plans were unavailable
Medica Health Plans	Reviewed	Plans were unavailable
Molina Healthcare	Reviewed	Plans were unavailable
Physicians Plus	Reviewed	Plans were unavailable
Prevea 360 Health plan	Reviewed	No longer offered
Security Health Plan	Reviewed	Plans were unavailable
Unity Health Insurance	Plans were not offered or were unavailable	Plans were unavailable
United Healthcare	Plans were not offered or were unavailable	Plans were unavailable
Group Health Cooperative -SCW	Plans were not offered or were unavailable	Plans were unavailable
Ambetter from MHS Health WI	Plans were not offered or were unavailable	Plans were unavailable
MercyCare Health Plans	Plans were not offered or were unavailable	Plans were unavailable

"Access to Health Care for Women Living with HIV: A Reproductive Justice Issue"

By Ariel Tazkargy, Esq.

For the *National Women's Health Network*

Article taken from May/June 2015 Newsletter

This year, the Affordable Care Act (ACA) celebrated its fifth year of providing millions of people with health insurance. In 2015, 11.7 million Americans—including 6.2 million women—got covered thanks to the health reform law.[1] The ACA has been a *huge* advance for women's health, and has largely met its goals to increase the number of people with insurance, improve the overall quality of health care, and stem the tide of rising costs.

Yet, there have been kinks in implementing the ACA, and the most vulnerable Americans risk falling through the cracks. In particular, people living with HIV (PLHIV) have been hard-hit by problems with the ACA—especially women living with HIV (WLHIV), who need access to reproductive and sexual health care. For example, the ACA does not provide for any social support or case management services structured to meet WLHIV's unique needs and keep them engaged in life-saving care.

In commemoration of *National Women & Girls HIV Awareness Day* (March 10), the National Women's Health Network (NWHN), Positive Women's Network—USA (PWN), and SisterLove, Inc., published a paper about WLHIV's continued challenges in accessing health care. The paper, *Ryan White & the Affordable Care Act: Advocating for Public Healthcare for Women Living with HIV*,[2] analyzes how well the ACA and other publicly funded health care programs meet WLHIV's need for comprehensive, high-quality care delivered without stigma or discrimination, regardless of the ability to pay.

We believe that HIV services should be integrated into *all* comprehensive women's health care efforts. Yet, our review finds that WLHIV have been overlooked during the course of ACA implementation. In order for WLHIV to fully realize health care reform's benefits, women's health advocates must advocate for other public benefits programs that fill the gaps in ACA coverage. Until we have a robust health care system that adequately addresses the needs of *all* Americans, other publically funded programs continue to play an essential role in helping WLHIV met their sexual and reproductive health care needs.

The ACA & Women Living with HIV: More to Do

Over a quarter million U.S. women (280,000) are living with HIV, but women's infection risks are not uniform.[3] There are stark racial disparities among people with new HIV diagnoses. A White woman's likelihood of being diagnosed with HIV in her lifetime is 1 in 526, a Latina's likelihood is 1 in 106, and an African American woman's likelihood skyrockets to 1 in 32.[4] Latina women make up 16 percent of the U.S. female population and represent 19 percent of WLHIV; African American women, who comprise only 13 percent of the U.S. female population, represent 60 percent of WLHIV.[5]

The ACA has improved WLHIV's access to care. Women who work for most large employers can't be denied private health insurance or charged higher rates due to their HIV status. Insurers can no longer impose lifetime caps on coverage. And, many preventive services are now covered without cost—including well-woman visits, HIV screening and counseling, and screening and counseling for interpersonal and intimate partner violence (IPV).[6]

Yet, WLHIV still face significant barriers getting the full spectrum of health care they need. This is particularly true for women in the 22 states that did not expand Medicaid coverage (7 of these are debating expansion) in the wake of the 2012 Supreme Court decision striking down the ACA's Medicaid expansion requirement.[7]

Currently, an HIV diagnosis is not a "disability" that allows PLHIV to automatically qualify for Medicaid; PLHIV *only* qualify for disability-based Medicaid coverage when HIV progresses to AIDS. If all states expanded Medicaid, as the ACA originally required, PLHIV would have been able to access services based on an HIV (vs. AIDS) diagnosis; this makes good sense medically and helps PLHIV live longer, healthier lives. In states that refuse to expand Medicaid, the result is a devastating gap in coverage for PLHIV, especially for women who need reproductive health care. The problems are particularly acute for WLHIV's access to prescription drugs and affordable coverage.

In terms of prescription drug coverage, although preventive services must be provided without cost-sharing under the ACA, HIV treatment is *very* expensive. Some insurance companies discriminate against PLHIV by charging more for HIV-related prescriptions.[8] Some have placed all HIV medications (including generics) in their highest cost-sharing tiers. A recent study estimated that a person living with HIV could pay more than $3,000 out-of-pocket, annually, due to discrimination in HIV medication pricing.[9]

In terms of affordable care, the Supreme Court decision allowing states to not expand Medicaid eligibility pushed many low-income people into "the coverage gap." State Medicaid expansion generally lowers the income requirement levels and makes more people eligible for Medicaid coverage. The "coverage gap" occurs when a person's income is too low to qualify for health care subsidies,[10] but too high for state Medicaid.[11]

Unfortunately, almost half (43 percent) of PLHIV reside in states that didn't expand Medicaid, like Texas and Georgia.[12,13] For example, Masonia Traylor, a 28-year-old WLHIV pharmacy technician, makes less than $10 per hour (less than $1,000 per month, and less than $10,000 annually). Her schedule is capped at 30 hours per week, precluding her from getting employee benefits. At her current income, Masonia and her two children qualify for Medicaid in Georgia, but she's starting a part-time position as a health advocate. The second job will raise her income above Georgia's Medicaid qualification cut-off. And, even with her increase in income, she won't make enough to qualify for a subsidy on the marketplace. Without a subsidy, she can't afford to pay a private plan's monthly premiums for herself and her two children, as well as the out-of-pocket costs like deductibles and copays for her HIV

treatment. Without health insurance coverage, Masonia's and her family's health will be jeopardized due to a marginal shift in income.

Ryan White Program Helps WLHIV: Supplementing Gaps in the ACA

Until these problems can be addressed, it is critical that other public programs are supported to meet the identified needs of low-income Americans, including WLHIV. In particular, the Ryan White program is critical to ensure that WLHIV can access the full range of care services and medications needed to stay healthy.

Jacqueline Muther—long-time Atlanta HIV advocate and policy manager of the Grady Infectious Disease Program—notes that many of her clinic's patients make too much to qualify for Medicaid and cannot afford the costs associated with private plans. Muther comments: "The ACA isn't working in Georgia. It *will not work* in states that fail to expand Medicaid. That's the core of the thing." The clinic—like so many serving PLWHA—is often forced to pick up the tab for their care, which it does largely using Ryan White HIV/AIDS Treatment Extension Act funds.

Ryan White funding is distributed via complementary "parts," which together, provide primary care and wrap-around services to ensure that PLWHA receive uninterrupted care. "Part D" funds culturally relevant, family-centered services to help women, children, and youth living with HIV maintain continuous care. Part D services—which include case management, peer support, reproductive and mental health care, health education, and transportation for medical appointments—are indispensable for vulnerable PLHIV.

Without Part D services, people who fall into the "coverage gap" will have no way to get the care they need to stay healthy. This is especially true in states that did not expand Medicaid. These programs are essential to meeting the needs of women and others living with HIV.

Recommendations

There is much to do to fully realize the ACA's goals and protect Americans' health. Advocates and policymakers must ensure full access to treatment, without interruptions in care, so that PLHIV can lead long, healthy lives. Our document presents three key recommendations to ensure accessible, consistent, and affordable health care coverage is available for all people living with HIV through the ACA and other public programs:

- *ACA Regulations Must Address Discriminatory Prescription Drug Benefits.* Advocates must ensure that HIV medications stay affordable and accessible as the ACA is implemented. Advocates should act as watch-guards over instances of price and/or medication coverage discrimination and any resulting disruptions to care. Advocacy around discriminatory practices around HIV-related medications should also examine the role of the Ryan White CARE Act to meet WLHIV's needs.
- *Access to Ryan White Services Must Be Protected.* Since ACA implementation is still in its early stages, and many states failed to expand Medicaid, Ryan White must be supported as a critical tool to meet WLHIV's needs. Part D standards provide a model for the ACA, and should be preserved and/or expanded.
- *Ryan White Part D Services Must Be Expanded.* Advocates must remain vigilant in ensuring that WLHIV's needs are met by programs like Ryan White Part D services. Ryan White Part D services should be preserved, expanded, and used as a model for the required care provided through Marketplace insurance plans serving PLHIV.

The NWHN and our allies will continue to fight for truly universal health care for women and their families. With our partners in Raising Women's Voices (RWV), we will advocate for the remaining states to expand Medicaid as part of their ACA implementation. We will oppose high premiums, imbalanced pricing structures for HIV medications, and threats to vital social and medical services that provide care to WLHIV. We will keep working until the U.S. health care system finally meets the needs of all people, including those living with HIV.

Ariel Tazkargy is the NWHN's Law Students for Reproductive Justice (LSRJ) Reproductive Justice Law & Policy Fellow. She co-authored the policy paper and article with Melanie Medalle, LSRJ Fellow at Sister-Love, Inc. and Nerissa Irizarry, LSRJ Fellow at Positive Women's Network—USA.

REFERENCES:

1. Department of Health and Human Services, Office of the Assistant Secretary for Planning and Evaluation (ASPE), Issue Brief: Health Insurance Marketplaces 2015 Open Enrollment Period: March Enrollment Report, Washington, DC: Department of Health and Human Services, 2015, See Appendix Table A1. Retrieved March 12, 2015 from http://aspe.hhs.gov/health/reports/2015/marketplaceenrollment/mar2015/ib_2015mar_enrollment.pdf.

2. On the NWHN website (nwhn.org) or directly at: http://bit.ly/1E347we.

3. Centers for Disease Control and Prevention (CDC), HIV Surveillance Report, Atlanta, GA: CDC, February 2013. Retrieved March 10, 2015 from: http://www.cdc.gov/hiv/pdf/statistics_2011_HIV_Surveillance_Report_vol_23.pdf. See also Kaiser Family Foundation, HIV/AIDS Policy, Fact Sheet: Women and HIV/AIDS in the United States, Washington, DC: Kaiser, March 2013. Retrieved March 10, 2015 from: http://www.s-cap.org/events/documents/WomenHIVAIDSintheUS_KaiserFamilyFoundation3-2013.pdf.

4. Kaiser Family Foundation, HIV/AIDS Policy, Fact Sheet: Women and HIV/AIDS in the United States, Washington, DC: Kaiser, March 2013. Retrieved March 10, 2015 from: http://www.s-cap.org/events/documents/WomenHIVAIDSintheUS_KaiserFamilyFoundation3-2013.pdf.

5. Kaiser Family Foundation, HIV/AIDS Policy, Fact Sheet: Women and HIV/AIDS in the United States, Washington, DC: Kaiser, March 2013. Retrieved March 10, 2015 from: http://www.s-cap.org/events/documents/WomenHIVAIDSintheUS_KaiserFamilyFoundation3-2013.pdf.

6. U.S. Department of Health & Human Services (HHS), Family Violence Prevention & Services Program, The Affordable Care Act & Women's Health, Washington, DC: Family Violence Prevention & Services Program, Dec. 2013. Retrieved March 10, 2014 from: http://www.acf.hhs.gov/sites/default/files/fysb/aca_fvpsa_20131211.pdf. IPV screening is critical for WLHIV, who disproportionately experience it: more than 50 percent of WHLIV have experienced IPV, compared to 36 percent of women nationally. Positive Women's Network – USA, Healing Trauma and Ending Violence Against Women Are Crucial for Improving HIV Health Outcomes, Oakland, CA: PWN. Retrieved February 20, 2015 from: https://pwnusa.files.wordpress.com/2014/03/nwghaad-white-house-fact-sheet-final.pdf.

7. National Federation of Independent Business v. Sebelius: 132 S. Ct. 2566 (2012).

8. Jacobs D, Sommers B, "Using Drugs to Discriminate–Adverse Selection in the Insurance Marketplace," New England Journal of Medicine 2015; 372(5):399–402, http://www.nejm.org/doi/full/10.1056/NEJMp1411376.

9. Jacobs D, Sommers B, "Using Drugs to Discriminate–Adverse Selection in the Insurance Marketplace," New England Journal of Medicine; 372:399–402, http://www.nejm.org/doi/full/10.1056/NEJMp1411376.

10. In 2014, single adults had to make at least $11,670 to qualify for financial assistance to purchase a private plan on the Marketplace. A family of three, like Masonia's family, must make at least $19,970 to qualify for financial assistance.

11. Kaiser Family Foundation, The Coverage Gap: Uninsured Poor Adults in States that Do Not Expand Medicaid – an Update, Washington, DC: Kaiser, 2014. Retrieved March 10, 2015 from: http://kff.org/health-reform/issue-brief/the-coverage-gap-uninsured-poor-adults-in-states-that-do-not-expand-medicaid-an-update.

12. Kates J, Garfield R, Young K, et al., Assessing the Impact of the Affordable Care Act on Health Insurance Coverage of People Living with HIV, Washington, DC: Kaiser Family Foundation, 2014. Retrieved March 10, 2015 from: https://kaiserfamilyfoundation.files.wordpress.com/2013/12/8535-assessing-the-impact-of-the-affordable-care-act-on-health-insurance-coverage.pdf.

13. Southern AIDS Strategy Initiative (SASI), Georgia Ryan White Advocacy Two-Pager, Durham, NC: SASI, April 2014. Retrieved March 10, 2014 from: http://southernaidsstrategy.org/state-portal/georgia/.

"Challenging Unproven Medicine and Saving Lives"

By Amy Allina
For the *National Women's Health Network*

Article taken from July/August 2012 Newsletter

When the U.S. government invests more than $600 million in the largest study of older women ever conducted...

And, the study yields such definitive results that the scientists providing ethical oversight for the research decide that it should be halted years early because the questions it was designed to answer have been clearly and solidly answered...

And, as a result of people taking action based on the research results, the United States experiences the first significant drop in breast cancer rates—16,000 fewer women diagnosed in the first year alone...

You would think that the medical establishment would rejoice and celebrate this historic public health achievement: science giving women and their health care providers information that we can use to guide our behavior in a way that dramatically improves our health and saves lives.

But, in the case of the Women's Health Initiative (WHI), you'd be wrong. More than 10 years after the WHI announced the results of this unprecedented research effort—after a decade of lower breast cancer rates—the WHI's findings are still being questioned by hormone therapy (HT) defenders who continue to promote unproven theories about how taking hormones benefits women's health. And, they continue to urge women to look to hormone therapy for protection against age-related diseases and health concerns, despite the weight of evidence against these claims.

Money, money, money

Many factors contribute to this persistent commitment to counterfactual beliefs about hormone therapy, but the root cause is money from drug makers. It created the problem in the first place and shaped the conditions that encourage resistance to evidence-based health care practices. The pervasive influence of drug industry money over medical research and practice can be seen at every stage of the hormone therapy story.

A drug company paid for the earliest educational efforts to doctors, providing undisclosed grants and paying travel expenses for a doctor, Robert Wilson, who traveled the country in the 1960s lecturing about the glorious benefits of hormone therapy. In 1966, Wilson also published a book, *Feminine Forever*, touting his claims that HT would allow women to avoid the physical and emotional consequences of menopause, which he equated with the death of femininity. Comparing the effects of aging on men to that on women, he wrote:

> A man remains male as long as he lives. Age does not rob him of his sexual appetite nor of the means of satisfying it. Throughout life he retains his appreciation of a charming girl or a handsome woman and along with it, a certain liveliness of outlook and level of motivation in other areas that make him function fully and responsibly as a human being. [...] How different is the fate of woman. Though modern diets, cosmetics and fashions make her outwardly look even younger than her husband, her body ultimately betrays her. [...] At the very moment when she is most able and eager to enjoy her achievements, her femininity—the very basis of her selfhood—crumbles in ruin. But now, at last, medicine offers a practical escape from this fateful dilemma.

Wilson's loose relationship to facts and the fundamental sexism that this passage reveals are evident throughout the book and in much of the HT promotion of that era.

Over the following decades, the pharmaceutical industry continued to invest millions of dollars in corporate-sponsored medical education to promote HT to providers. It sponsored professional conferences and paid health care providers to attend lectures on HT's supposed benefits held at luxury resorts and gourmet restaurants. All with the goal of ensuring that generation after generation of prescribers would be indoctrinated in the gospel of hormone therapy.

For more than three decades, these prescribers routinely advised their female patients who were turning 50 that using hormone therapy, starting at menopause, would protect them from every age-related concern a woman might have. Worried about heart disease? Take hormones to protect your heart. Having trouble sleeping or remembering things? Hormones will help. Want to prevent hip fracture, wrinkles, dementia, and depression? Hormone therapy is the answer. Need the energy to keep up with your vigorous spouse? Here's your prescription.

Drug companies also paid for advertising campaigns aimed directly at women in order to drive home these messages. They produced educational materials touting claims about the benefits of HT that hospitals and medical practices could distribute to patients. And, they used their checkbooks to influence the production of clinical practice guidelines and standards used to evaluate quality of care for women at menopause, ensuring that routine prescription of hormone therapy to women at menopause was one of the key measures of whether older women's health care needs were being met.

Challenging Deeply Held Beliefs

By the early 1990s, routine prescription of hormone therapy for women at menopause was firmly established in medical practice. Even women who never experienced a single hot flash—one reason for taking HT that was well-established prior the WHI—were advised to start taking hormones when they reached menopause. By 1999, there were more than 90 million annual prescriptions written for these drugs1—a substantial revenue-producer for drug companies like Wyeth, which manufactured Premarin, the market leader in hormone therapy.

But some were concerned about troubling indications that HT drugs might not be as safe, or offer as many benefits, as their promoters claimed. Throughout this time, the National Women's Health Network produced independent information about HT for our members; asked tough questions about the unproven claims being made for the drugs; warned about research showing there might be risks that women weren't being informed about; and advocated for research to provide women with reliable answers to these important questions.

In 1990, when Wyeth asked the Food and Drug Administration (FDA) to add a heart disease prevention indication to the HT drug label, giving it approval to legally advertise the use of hormone therapy for that purpose, only two groups opposed the request: the National Women's Health Network and the Health Research Group at Public Citizen. Thankfully, the FDA held firm to its standards, rejecting Wyeth's application because it lacked adequate research evidence to back up the claim. This brave stand thwarted the company's promotion plans, but it didn't shake the medical community's belief in HT's preventive health benefits.

In 1991, the desire to provide the FDA with the evidence it demanded on HT's benefits—combined with political pressure from the newly expanded caucus of Congresswomen who sought to increase the nation's investment in women's health research—created the will to launch an HT clinical trial as part of the new Women's Health Initiative. As a whole, the WHI examined cardio-vascular disease, cancer, and osteoporosis, which are the leading causes of death, disability, and impaired quality of life, among post-menopausal women. The HT trial, involving more than 27,000 post-menopausal women at 45 clinical centers across the nation, was the most significant component of the multiple research studies that made up the WHI.

Still the drug-money fostered belief in HT had not flagged one bit, and the medical community fully expected the WHI to confirm its assumptions about the great benefits and safety of hormone use. So, in July 2002, when the National Institutes of Health halted part of the HT trial early and announced that using hormone therapy increased a woman's risk of getting breast cancer and her chance of experiencing a blood clot or stroke, the news was greeted with shock and disbelief in the medical community.

Hormone defenders scrambled to explain these results without accepting the obvious conclusion that HT wasn't all that it had been cracked up to be. They said that the women enrolled in the trial were too old, or had a pre-existing disease that kept them from gaining hormones' protective effect. But, none of that was true. (Read the Women's Health Activist article from May/June 2003, debunking those claims: "The Backlash Against the WHI: Myths and Facts About Menopause Hormone Therapy," available at: *http://nwhn.org/backlash-against-whi-myths-and-facts-about-menopause-hormone-therapy.*)

And women weren't persuaded. They heard about the WHI results and voted with their feet. The number of HT prescriptions that were filled dropped precipitously by about a third in the first year[1] and continued a slow decline after that.[2] The effect was dramatic: in the first year after the WHI results were released, U.S. breast cancer rates dropped by 16,000. This was the most significant reduction in breast cancer levels ever achieved in the United States.

Still, the argument continues. In May 2012, the U.S. Preventive Services Task Force (USPSTF) published an analysis affirming that the risks of hormone therapy for preventive health outweigh the benefits. Almost a decade after the announcement of the WHI findings this should hardly be a controversial claim. Yet, only a couple of weeks earlier, the journal Climacteric (a publication of the International Menopause Society, which receives substantial financial support from industry[3]) published an issue including several articles arguing that if women start taking HT at the "right age," its benefits would outweigh the risks.

This is known as the "window of opportunity" theory and, just like the previous theories about how all aging women could improve their health by taking hormones, it is not supported by reliable evidence. (Read the NWHN's analysis of the "window of opportunity" theory in our Fact Sheet, Menopause Hormone Therapy and Cardiovascular Protection, available at: *http:// nwhn.org/menopause-hormone-therapy-and-cardio-vascular-protection.*)

Both the USPSTF analysis and the Climacteric articles were covered by health journalists in the mainstream media, leaving readers to puzzle through the contradictions between the two. Many people understandably, although incorrectly, concluded that questions about whether or not hormone therapy prevents heart disease remain unanswered.

Learning from our mistakes

The National Women's Health Network views the WHI as an unprecedented and extraordinarily valuable public health victory. It not only provided women with essential answers to important questions about our health and led to changes that have already saved more than 150,000 women from breast cancer, but also demonstrated that independent advocacy can have a real and important impact on medicine.

At this 10-year anniversary of the WHI, we continue our independent advocacy for changes in policies and practices to better meet the health care needs of older women, and to prevent the repetition of past mistakes. These changes include:

- Stronger protections from misleading promotion of unproven and unsafe drugs, including better regulation of drug ads;
- Increased investment in research to develop safer alternatives to treat hot flashes;
- Inclusion of more women in heart disease prevention research; and
- An end to drug company funding for medical education.

Ten years later, the backlash against the WHI continues, to the detriment of women and our health. Prolonging the controversy risks depriving women of the important benefits of our public investment in that important research and potentially puts women who take HT for unproven reasons at unnecessary risk for disease.

But the positive legacy of the study lives on as well, growing every year that another 16,000 women are saved from breast cancer, and the legacy defines itself anew whenever another advocate, inspired by the example of the WHI, takes up a new campaign to challenge a dangerous or unproven medical practice.

Amy Allina is the Network's Program & Policy Director

REFERENCES

1. Hersh AL, Stefanick ML, Stafford RS, "National Use of Postmenopausal Hormone Therapy; Annual Trends and Response to Recent Evidence," JAMA 2004; 291(1): 47–53.

2. North American Menopause Society (NAMS), "Hormone Therapy Statistics," June 2011. Mayfield Heights, OH: NAMS. Avail-able online at: http://www.menopause.org/hormonetherapystats.aspx.

3. Website of the International Menopause Society, Ethical Codes of Conduct, accessed June 3, 2012. http://www.imsociety.org/ethical_ codes_of_conduct.php.

"Spreading My Legs for Womankind"

By Molly Kenefick

Ever wonder how doctors learn to do pelvic exams? Well, I can answer that question for more than six hundred medical students: I taught them—on my body.

At some medical schools, students learn to do the exam on cadavers, women under anesthesia, or with "pelvic models" (women who function simply as bodies for professors to demonstrate on). Students on the campuses where I teach learn from "pelvic educators," women who instruct students in anatomy, physiology, palpation techniques, and various emotional and cultural issues that arise in a clinical setting.

When I first heard about the job, it sounded amazing. I'd already been working to overcome negative feelings about my body (the same body-image crap most women internalize growing up in our culture), and this seemed like a good next step. More important, I felt that teaching future doctors to do sensitive, thorough pelvic exams could positively impact the lives of many female patients down the line. I thought of Joan Rivers's joke that there should be a commemorative stamp of a woman on an examining table, feet in the footrests, to honor those who keep their annual appointments. I remember thinking at the time, *Joan is right: Many women do dread the exam. But it shouldn't have to be horrible.* Now, years later, I take pride in teaching my students the many details that can make an exam a positive, comforting experience.

I was scared at first. I'd take the hospital gown into the bathroom to change, and then climb onto the table, holding the johnny tight to make sure nothing extra was exposed. I felt shy about opening my legs to strangers (especially without any foreplay!), so as I did this, I avoided looking students in the eyes. I steeled myself by acting nonchalant and businesslike, and held onto

the idea that this was important to women. Now, after six years, I simply turn my back to change (yes, in front of students), wrap a sheet around me, and casually hop onto the table.

Working with two to four students at a time, I first go over psychosocial issues. I tell them that though their patient may be an adult, it could be her first exam. I suggest they offer her a hand mirror so she can see what they are doing, and that they explain what they're doing as they do it. We discuss asking questions without making assumptions about a patient's sexual orientation or practices; looking for signs of sexual abuse, and, if they suspect it, how to handle it; words patients use to describe their anatomy; and culturally specific sexual customs.

Then it's time for the physical exam. I undress from the waist down and sit on the exam table, feet in the footrests ("Not stirrups; it's not a saddle"). I teach draping technique ("Expose only the area you will be examining"), the physician's first touch ("Put your hands by the outside of her knees, and ask her to bring her knees to meet your hands—that way she touches you first"), and subsequent touch techniques ("Clinical touch should feel as different from sexual touch as possible"). We start with the external exam, checking beneath the pubic hair for redness, lice, and scabies ("Don't mention lice and scabies unless she has them"). The external exam includes inspecting the vulva, perineum, and anus ("Always avoid touching the clitoris").

The internal exam is next. I teach them to insert an index finger to find my cervix and check my glands for infection and my vaginal walls for laxity. I demonstrate how to put in and open the speculum ("Warm it first, for patient comfort"). Then we view the cervix (a first sighting and a thrill for most students) and practice the Pap smear.

Next, the bimanual exam. With two fingers inside me, a student checks for cervical tenderness and feels for the uterus. The outside hand palpates the abdomen, pushing down toward the inside fingers. The most rewarding part for students is finding an ovary (yet another first), which feels like an almond hidden under layers of pastry dough ("The number of layers depends on how much pastry I've eaten"). Lastly, a student inserts one finger in my rectum, another in my vagina. They are often surprised at how much better they can feel my uterus from two angles.

In separate sessions with students, I also teach breast exams. The first time I did this, I looked at my 38-C breasts (heavy and pendulous: nipples soft, not pert) and wished they were perkier. Then I thought, *Who the hell looks like a centerfold in real life?* I'm a real woman, and this is what women look like. More important, this is what their patients will look like. My self pep talk ended with: *You're healthy. Get over it. Focus on the work.*

With up to eight students, we first practice on a silicone-filled model (with quite lumpy breasts). I show them the palpation technique: Fingers make circles of light, medium, and deep pressure as they move in a vertical stripe pattern (lawnmower versus zigzag). Then I take off my shirt and bra and we look for rashes, dimpling, and changes in the nipples (such as spontaneous discharge or inversion). I teach them to palpate my nodes along the clavicle and under the armpit ("No tickling!"). Then, one at a time, they practice the vertical stripe technique on my breast.

Most students have been a pleasure to teach. A few had terrible palpation skills (I can only hope they've gone into research). Two got noticeable erections (I sympathized, as they seemed mortified at this betrayal of their body). A couple were inappropriate (one kept asking if my parents and boyfriend knew I did this work), and one asked me out (though I thought, *Wouldn't this be a story to tell our grandkids?* I said *no*, of course). The majority of my students, however, have been respectful and grateful for the opportunity to learn from, and on, me.

I'm amazed by all the ways this job has impacted my life. As hoped (and as strange as it may sound), undressing in front of strangers has made me more comfortable with my body. Now, years into the job, I take off my shirt and bra, drop my pants, and often feel like a superhero. I'm not a "perfect 10," just a healthy, strong woman, unashamed of her body. I feel students' admiration and respect, and I deserve it because I am doing important work for women and women's health. In addition, I've become knowledgeable about my reproductive health. Knowing where my uterus is and what my cervix looks like makes me more in touch with being a woman. On the downside, as "party talk" goes, telling people I'm a pelvic educator can be a conversation starter—or stopper. And at times, no amount of kisses could summon my libido because it got lost earlier in the day during the third pelvic exam. In general, however, I've found this to be rewarding work, both because of the immediate positive changes I see in my students and because of the ripple effect I know my work will have on their future patients. Finally, a nice benefit is that every day when I go to work, I'm reminded that *Hey, I've got ovaries.*

MULTIPLE MARGINALIZATION AND HEALTH

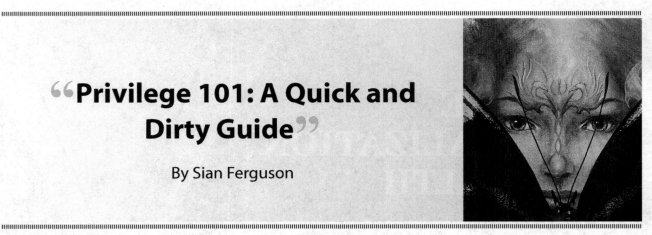

"Privilege 101: A Quick and Dirty Guide"

By Sian Ferguson

"**P**rivilege" is a word you'll hear often in social justice spaces, both offline and online.

Some people understand the concept easily. Others—*and I was like this*—find the concept confusing and need a little more help.

If you're willing to learn about privilege, but you don't know where to start, you've come to the right place!

Before we get started, I want to clarify that this article is not entirely comprehensive. That is to say, it's not going to explain everything there is to know about privilege. But it'll give you a good foundation on the basics.

Think of privilege not as a single lesson, but as a field of study. To truly understand privilege, we must keep reading, learning, and thinking critically.

Defining Privilege

The origins of the term "privilege" can be traced back to the 1930s,[1] when WEB DuBois wrote about the "psychological wage" that allowed whites to feel superior to black people. In 1988, Peggy McIntosh fleshed out the idea of privilege in a paper called "White Privilege and Male Privilege: A Personal Account of Coming to See Correspondences through Work in Women's Studies."[2]

We can define privilege as a set of unearned benefits given to people who fit into a specific social group.

Society grants privilege to people because of certain aspects of their identity. Aspects of a person's identity can include race, class, gender, sexual orientation, language, geographical location, ability, and religion, to name a few.

But big concepts like privilege are so much more than their basic definitions! For many, this definition on its own raises more questions than it answers. So here are a few things about privilege that everyone should know.

1. Privilege is the Other Side of Oppression.

It's often easier to notice oppression than privilege.

It's definitely easier to notice the oppression you personally experience than the privileges you experience since being mistreated is likely to leave a bigger impression on you than being treated fairly.

So consider the ways in which you are oppressed: How are you disadvantaged because of the way society treats aspects of your identity? Are you a woman? Are you disabled? Does your sexuality fall under the queer umbrella? Are you poor? Do you have a mental illness or a learning disability? Are you a person of color? Are you gender non-conforming?

All of these things could make life difficult because society disenfranchises people who fit into those social groups. **We call this oppression.**

But what about the people society *doesn't* disenfranchise? What about the people society empowers at our expense? We call that *privilege*.

Privilege is simply the opposite of oppression.

2. We Need to Understand Privilege in the Context of Power Systems.

Society is affected by a number of different power systems: patriarchy, white supremacy, heterosexism, cissexism,

---

[1] http://www.newyorker.com/books/page-turner/the-origins-of-privilege
[2] McIntosh's seminal work emphasizes how it can be easy to notice privilege that you lack, but easy to overlook what you have. If you haven't read it, it comes up easily on Google. As always, we strongly encourage you to seek out more information about material in this reader that interests or challenges you. *Ed.*

and classism—to name a few. These systems interact together in one giant system called the kyriarchy.

Privileged groups have power over oppressed groups.

Privileged people are more likely to be in positions of power—for example, they're more likely to dominate politics, be economically well-off, have influence over the media, and hold executive positions in companies.

Privileged people can *use* their positions to benefit people like themselves—in other words, other privileged people.

In a patriarchal society, women do not have institutional power (at least, not based on their gender). In a white supremacist society, people of color don't have race-based institutional power. And so on.

It's important to bear this in mind because **privilege doesn't go both ways.** Female privilege does not exist because women don't have institutional power. Similarly, black privilege, trans privilege, and poor privilege don't exist because those groups do not have institutional power.

It's also important to remember because people often look at privilege *individually* rather than *systemically.* **While individual experiences are important, we have to try to understand privilege in terms of systems and social patterns.** We're looking at the rule, not the exception to the rule.

3. Privileges and Oppressions Affect Each Other, but They Don't Negate Each Other.

I experience my queerness in relation to my womanhood. I experience these aspects of my identity in relation to my experience as a mentally ill person, as someone who's white, as someone who is South African, as someone who is able-bodied, as someone who is cisgender.

All aspects of our identities—whether those aspects are oppressed or privileged by society—interact with one another. We experience the aspects of our identities collectively and simultaneously, not individually.

The interaction between different aspects of our identities is often referred to as an *intersection.* The term *intersectionality* was coined by Kimberlé Crenshaw, who used it to describe the experiences of black women—who experience both sexism and racism.

While all women experience sexism, the sexism that black women experience is unique in that it is informed by racism.

To illustrate with another example, mental illness is often stigmatized. As a mentally-ill woman, I have been told that my post-traumatic stress disorder is "just PMS" and a result of me "being an over-sensitive woman." This is an intersection between ableism and misogyny.

The aspects of our identities that are privileged can also affect the aspects that are oppressed. **Yes, privilege and oppression intersect—but they don't negate one another.**

Often, people believe that they can't experience privilege because they also experience oppression. A common example is the idea that poor white people don't experience white privilege *because* they are poor. **But this is not the case.**

Being poor does not negate the fact that you, as a white person, are less likely to become the victim of police brutality in most countries around the world, for example.

Being poor is an oppression, yes, but this doesn't cancel out the fact that you can still benefit from white privilege.

As Phoenix Calida wrote:

> "Privilege simply means that under the exact same set of circumstances you're in, life would be harder without your privilege.
> Being poor is hard. Being poor and disabled is harder.
> Being a woman is hard. Being a trans woman is harder.
> Being a white woman is hard, being a woman of color is harder.
> Being a black man is hard, being a gay black man is harder."

Let's look at the example of people who are both poor and white. Being white means that you have access to resources which could help you survive. You're more likely to have a support network of relatively well-off people. You can use these networks to look for a job.

If you go to a job interview, you are more likely to be interviewed by a white person, as white people are more likely to be in executive positions. People in positions of power are usually the same race as you, so if they are racially prejudiced, it's likely that they would be prejudiced *in your favor.*

A poor black person, on the other hand, will not have access to those resources, is unlikely to be of the same race as people in power, and is more likely to be harmed by racial prejudice.

So once again: Being white and poor is hard, but being black and poor is harder.[3]

---

[3]Audre Lorde's classic piece "There Is No Hierarchy of Oppressions" (1983) is sometimes misinterpreted as evidence that one group of people cannot be said to be worse off than any other group. Her actual argument is that we cannot (or should not try to) fight one type of oppression while ignoring others, because they are all connected. While different marginalized identities certainly interact in different ways for different people, we can still look to social scientific research to see the severity and prevalence of particular negative outcomes based on different forms of marginalization, which can be important for addressing specific problems for specific groups. *Ed.*

4. Privilege Describes What Everyone Should Experience.

When we use the word "privilege" in the context of social justice, it means something slightly different to the way it's used by most people in their everyday environment.

Often we think of privilege as "special advantages." We frequently hear the phrase, "X is a privilege, not a right," conveying the idea that X is something special that shouldn't be expected.

Because of the way we use "privilege" in our day-to-day lives, people often get upset when others point out some of their privileges.

A male acquaintance of mine initially struggled to understand the concept of privilege. He once said to me, "Men don't often experience gender-based street harassment, but that's not a privilege. It's something everyone should *expect*."

Correct. Everyone should expect to be treated that way. Everyone has a *right* to be treated that way. **The problem is that certain people *aren't* treated that way.**

To illustrate: Nobody should be treated as if they are untrustworthy based on their race. But often, people of color—*particularly black people*—are mistrusted because of prejudice towards their race.

White people, however, don't experience this systemic, race-based prejudice. We call this "white privilege" because people who are white are free from racial oppression.

We don't use the term "privilege" because we don't think everyone deserves this treatment.

We call privilege "privilege" because we acknowledge that not everyone experiences it.

5. Privilege Doesn't Mean you Didn't Work Hard.

People often get defensive when someone points out that they have privilege. And I totally understand why—before I fully understood privilege, I acted the same way.

Many people think that having privilege means you have had an easy life. As such, they feel personally attacked when people point out their privilege. To them, it feels as if someone is saying that they haven't worked hard or endured any difficulties.

But this is not what privilege means.

You can be privileged and still have a difficult life. **Privilege doesn't mean that your life is easy, but rather that it's *easier* than others.**

I saw this brilliant analogy comparing white privilege and bike commuting in a car-friendly city,[4] and it inspired me to broaden the analogy to privilege in general.

So let's say both you and your friend decide to go cycling. You decide to cycle for the same distance, but you take different routes. You take a route that is a bit bumpy. More often than not, you go down roads that are at a slight decline. It's very hot, but the wind is at usually at your back. You eventually get to your destination, but you're sunburnt, your legs are aching, you're out of breath, and you have a cramp.

When you eventually meet up with your friend, she says that the ride was awful for her. It was also bumpy. The road she took was at an incline the entire time. She was even more sunburnt than you because she had no sunscreen. At one point, a strong gust of wind blew her over and she hurt her foot. She ran out of water halfway through. When she hears about your route, she remarks that your experience seemed easier than hers.

Does that mean that you didn't cycle to the best of your ability? Does it mean that you didn't face obstacles? Does it mean that you didn't work hard? No. **What it means is that you didn't face the obstacles she faced.**

Privilege doesn't mean your life is easy or that you didn't work hard. It simply means that you don't have to face the obstacles others have to endure. It means that life is more difficult for those who don't have the systemic privilege you have.

So What Now?

Often, people think that feminists and social justice activists point out people's privilege to make them feel guilty. This isn't the case at all!

We don't want you to feel guilty. We want you to join us in challenging the systems that privilege some people and oppress others.

Guilt is an unhelpful feeling: It makes us feel ashamed, which prevents us from speaking out and bringing about change. As Jamie Utt notes, **"If privilege guilt prevents me from *acting against oppression*, then it is simply another tool of oppression."[5]**

You don't need to feel guilty for having privilege because having privilege is not your fault: It's not something you chose. But what you *can* choose is to push back against your privilege and to use it in a way that

---

4 http://alittlemoresauce.com/2014/08/20/what-my-bike-has-taught-me-about-white-privilege/

5 http://everydayfeminism.com/2014/03/moving-past-privilege-guilt/

challenges oppressive systems instead of perpetuating them.[6]

So what can you—as a person who experiences privilege—do?

Understanding privilege is a start, so you've already made the first move! Yay!

There's a great deal of information out there on the Internet, so I'd firstly recommend that you read more about the concepts of oppression and privilege in order to expand your understanding. The links in this article are a good place to start.

But merely understanding privilege is not enough. We need to take action.

Listen to people who experience oppression. Learn about how you can work in solidarity with oppressed groups.[7] Join feminist and activist communities in order to support those you have privilege over. Focus on teaching other privileged people about their privilege.

Above all else, bear in mind that your privilege exists.

Sian Ferguson is a Contributing Writer at Everyday Feminism. She is a South African feminist currently studying toward a Bachelors of Social Science degree majoring in English Language and Literature and Gender Studies at the University of Cape Town. She has been featured as a guest writer on websites such as Women24 and Foxy Box, while also writing for her personal blog. In her spare time, she tweets excessively @sianfergs, reads about current affairs, and spends time with her gorgeous group of friends.

---

[6]http://www.blackgirldangerous.org/2014/02/4-ways-push-back-privi-lege/—This piece comes from a website specifically dedicated to "amplifying the voices of queer & transgender people of color." As Ferguson notes below, following links like this and actively listening to people who experience marginalization that you do not is an incredibly important first step in taking constructive social action. Websites like this can be especially useful

resources because they are designed to serve an educational purpose (so you are not demanding emotional or intellectual labor from someone who is unwilling or unable to provide it) and they also give you time to read and process at your own pace. *Ed.*

[7] http://everydayfeminism.com/2013/11/things-allies-need-to-know/

"Women's Health Disparities: Intersections of Gender and Other Forms of Marginalization"

By Jasmia Hamilton and Brooke Barnhart

There are many observable disparities in health outcomes and health care access among diverse demographics of women. Health disparities refer to the higher burden of disease, illness and death among certain populations, whereas health care disparities refer to inequities in access, quality, and insurance coverage in a population (Kaiser Family Foundation, 2012). There is a great deal of research on women's health disparities by race and ethnicity in particular. Over the last several decades, however, researchers have also taken the initiative to look at other population characteristics, including disability, immigration status, sexual orientation, gender expression, class, and geographic location to develop a more nuanced understanding of how individual people experience health inequalities in terms of both care and outcomes.

For example, while notable gender differences in life expectancy exist, such that in 2011, women lived to an average of 81.1 years and men lived to an average to 76.3 years (CDC, 2015d), there are other identity characteristics that exert greater influence on individual life expectancy, such as race. The life expectancy for White women and Black women in the United States is 81.3 and 78.2 years respectively (CDC, 2015d). Therefore, even though the average lifespan for women is greater than men, Black women's life expectancy is considerably lower than White women's. While Black women still outlive both White and Black men, their average life expectancy is only 1.6 years greater than that of White men (76.6), while White women's is 4.7 years greater (Ibid.).

As this broad measure of health shows, examining health by gender alone is inadequate because it conceals the health disparities that exist *between* different groups of women. The statistic of life expectancy illuminates how other social demographics, such as race, work in conjunction with gender to affect women's health. Therefore, it is important to complicate our knowledge of gendered health disparities and examine the ways in which the particular outcome of life expectancy has complex causes, but is certainly related to disparities in health care such as the increased likelihood of White non-Hispanic individuals, compared to Black non-Hispanic individuals, to have health insurance (Institutes of Medicine, 2009).

This article attempts to complicate how we study health disparities by starting a conversation on *why* these health disparities exist between women. In order to more fully understand the cause of these health disparities, we must interrogate the ways in which institutional oppression operates to influence these disparities. Social structures affect individuals by disadvantaging certain identities, systematically limiting specific group members' access to quality, life-sustaining health care. In this piece, we outline some of the health disparities that exist between women based on selected social markers.

Each one of these demographics represents a marginalized social and identity category within our society. We begin by examining education level and income and their effect on mortality rates for women. Then, we investigate geographic location and the ways in which each of these categories contribute to women's ability to obtain and maintain the health care they need throughout their lives. Although these categories are closely tied to one another, each one is important to examine as they reveal the complexities of socioeconomic class, for which absolute income is not the only significant marker. Additionally, this paper reviews differences in health outcomes based on women's sexuality, citizenship status, and dis/ability which all create significant disparities. Finally, we discuss some specific issues in healthcare that affect women disproportionately or in distinct ways: cancer, pain and pain management, and pregnancy and birth. It is important to note that while we try to examine each social category in this piece separately, in practice these categories intertwine and intersect, and we also touch on some such intersections identified in specific research studies.

Health Outcomes and Selected Demographic Characteristics

Education and Income

Despite the fairly well known fact that women generally outlive men, women's mortality rates have actually increased in recent years, narrowing that gender gap for many groups. From 1992 to 2006, mortality rates for women grew in over 40% of United States counties as compared to only 3% for men (Montez & Zacajova, 2014). These rates also vary by education level and race. For example, women who did not graduate high school have a higher mortality rate than women with a high school diploma, and additionally have a mortality rate that is more than *two and a half times higher* than the rate for women with a college degree (CDC, 2009). Furthermore, whereas mortality rates for more educated White women have decreased, they have steadily increased for White women of lower educational status (Montez & Zacajova, 2013). For example, between 1986 and 2006, White women with 0–11 years of education saw their mortality rates increase, while mortality rates for White women with a college education declined slightly. Yet over the same time period, mortality for men with lower educational attainment declined as well; women with less education seemed to be experiencing negative effects from which similarly educated men were somehow protected.

Researchers have largely explained this connection between increasing mortality rates and educational attainment via the latter's association with income (Montez & Zacajova, 2014). Although education is widely used as a proxy for income status by researchers, it is well documented that men earn more than women of the same racial category at every level of education (United States Department of Labor, 2015). This suggests that the relationship between education and income is complicated by gender, with less educated women experiencing more severe income penalties. For one thing, less educated women are more likely than men to be concentrated in low-wage or part-time work offering few benefits from employers. Increasingly, there are fewer job opportunities for low skilled

labor along with decreasing wages for these jobs. The effects of this can be seen on household income. Average household income (all figures adjusted to reflect 2012 dollars) for adults with nine to 11 years of education decreased from $45,531 in 1967 to $41,708 in 2000 (Montez & Zajacova, 2014, p. e6). Meanwhile, families in which at least one adult held a bachelor's degree saw an increase in their average income from $82,196 to $122,624 over the same time period. Over time, working class women are subsisting on an ever-decreasing real income while those around them have more. The negative psychological and physical effects of absolute poverty (below a specific income threshold) are thus compounded by those of relative poverty (a larger gap between people at the low and high ends of income/wealth distribution).

This increased gap between classes also exacerbates the geographic disadvantage experienced by working class women. As neighborhood segregation between high and low income people intensifies, working class women are increasingly concentrated in neighborhoods with poorer school systems, fewer parks and recreational activities, lower quality food choices, and higher crime rates (Montez & Zajacova, 2014, p. e6). These disparities deprive women of access to material goods and resources. Taken together, all of these factors negatively affect overall health and contribute to higher mortality rates for less educated, low-income women (Montez & Zajacova, 2014, p. e6).

Geographic Location

While many people assume that rural areas offer a higher quality of life than urban ones via stereotypical associations of "small town life" with healthy communities, there is evidence to suggest otherwise. To highlight health outcome differences based on geographic location we can return to life expectancy as an important marker of health. In recent years, life expectancy disparities have increased between rural and urban populations. Between 1969 and 1971, rural and urban women had roughly equivalent life expectancies; by 2005–2009, however, urban women were outliving rural women by an average of 1.6 years (Singh & Siahpush, 2014, p. e22). This disparity in life expectancy is comparable to other health disparities found between rural and urban populations. Women living in rural or nonmetropolitan places are more prone to experience psychological and mental health issues (American Psychological Association), disability and impairments (von Reichert et al, 2014), and injuries than are women living in urban areas (Eberhardt & Pamuk, 2004). Moreover, rural women are more likely to self-assess their health as fair or poor compared to their urban counterparts (Singh & Siahpush, 2014, p. e27).

These health disparities are likely linked to socio-economic disparities, such as income and employment, between rural and urban women. The wage gap between rural and urban families has increased significantly over time, from a $2,892 deficit for rural families in 1970 to a $16,842 deficit in 2009 (Singh & Siahpush, 2014, p. e28). Furthermore, compared to women living in urban areas, rural women are less likely to engage in paid employment at all, dramatically increasing the income gap between the two groups. Rural women's lack of financial stability, then, may be a primary barrier to health care by way of rendering it quite simply unaffordable.

Furthermore, lack of adequate transportation remains an additional barrier to rural women obtaining services even if they are technically available (e.g if one can afford insurance or has subsidized state health insurance) (Singh & Siahpush, 2014, p. e28). Health services are usually located in more metropolitan areas, and rural facilities that do exist must necessarily serve a much broader geographic area, resulting in generally longer commute times for rural women seeking health services. Lack of public transportation, cost associated with vehicle upkeep and gas, and being unable to afford to miss work for services may prevent rural women from accessing care. Thus, we can see that geographic location has a complex influence on one's ability to receive necessary health care, overall contributing to and shaping the health disparities that exist between rural and urban women. While these inequalities in education, income, and geographic location are major factors in health disparities among women, other social/identity factors discussed below may simultaneously prevent women from accessing the health care that they need.

LGBTQ+ Identity

LGBTQ+ identity plays a significant role in health disparities between women. Research shows that LGBTQ+ women experience more health problems and negative health outcomes than heterosexual and cisgender women because of a) economic marginalization, b) high risk of violence, c) general societal failures in recognizing the needs of people who are not heterosexual or cisgender, and d) stereotypical beliefs about what health problems do and do not impact the "LGBTQ+ community." As such, there are multiple dimensions that shape LGBTQ+ women's health outcomes.

Poorer health among sexual minorities is partially explained by decreased access to providers, which is in turn connected to a general negative association between LGBTQ+ status, particularly transgender status,[1] and income (in turn exacerbated for LGBTQ+ people of color). Particularly for women, sexual orientation affects income. Lesbian women are slightly more likely to live in poverty than heterosexual women and bisexual women are more than twice as likely to live in poverty as women in the general population (CAP & MAP, 2015). For transgender people, gender actually does not seem to significantly influence overall income. However, transgender people as a group are almost four times as likely to be living in extreme poverty (annual income <$10,000/year) compared to the general population (Grant et al, 2011, p.22), which has varied and significant impacts on health. In spite of the lower statistical influence of gender on overall income for transgender people, their observed higher rates of poverty can potentially be explained by cisnormativity and the continued absence of legislation that protects gender expression even when sexual orientation is protected.

Lack of financial resources and protective factors (e.g. consistent access to care providers, social support) contributes to increased behavioral health disparities for LGBTQ+ people. Lack of social support, for example, may reduce access to, and success with, interventions to correct risk-taking behaviors. Bisexual people, who report the least amount of emotional support among sexual identity groups, also report the highest amount of high-risk health behaviors such as excessive drinking and smoking (CAP & MAP, 2015). Perhaps contrary to expectations, bisexual people are often stigmatized by both heterosexual and gay and lesbian people. We can see the negative effects of social rejection interlocked with geographic location in Fredricksen-Goldsen et al's (2010) work on lesbian and bisexual women's mental distress levels. The two groups have similar mental distress levels in rural areas; however, in urban areas, lesbian women's distress levels significantly decrease while bisexual women's levels almost double compared to their rural counterparts (Fredriksen-Goldsen et al, 2010, p. 2258). This elevation in mental distress for bisexual women may be a consequence of bias against bisexual people within the "LGBTQ+" communities that are generally larger and more visible in urban areas.

This is one specific example of what has been more generally termed *minority stress*: frequent experiences of bias, discrimination, and other expressions of nega-

---

[1] For more information about transgender-specific health disparities, which tend to affect transgender women more severely than transgender men, see Kadin Henningsen's piece elsewhere in this section. Also keep in mind that transgender women may experience all of the disparities discussed throughout this chapter, since transgender women are women! *Ed.*

tive attitudes toward culturally denigrated LGBTQ+ identities, both from others and internalized (Meyer 2003). Minority stress has numerous negative health effects for LGBTQ+ people of various identities, but perhaps the most frequently identified consequence of minority stress is its association with suicide. The San Francisco Human Rights Commission's LGBT Advisory Committee provides disaggregated rates of *suicidal ideation* (thinking seriously about suicide, distinct from suicide attempts or completed suicide deaths) by gender and sexuality in their 2011 report "Bisexual Invisibility: Impacts and Recommendations" (p. 12):

Heterosexual men:	7.4%
Heterosexual women:	9.6%
Gay men:	25.2%
Lesbian women:	29.5%
Bisexual men:	34.8%
Bisexual women:	45.4%

For comparison, the rate of suicidal ideation among transgender people has been estimated in one study as 65.3% for transgender women and 83.0% for transgender men (Testa et al, 2012, p. 455). The same study reported a suicide attempt rate of 26.3% for transgender women and 30.4% for transgender men (ibid.); however, these estimates may actually be low. A 2014 report released by the Williams Institute, using data from the National Transgender Discrimination Survey, reported a suicide attempt rate of 42% for transgender women and 46% for transgender men, with 41% for the entire sample overall, which included people who identified with other categories such as non-binary (Haas et al, 2014, p. 2). For transgender people, suicide risk was heightened by lower levels of educational attainment and income, HIV+ status, mixed-race or Native identity,[2] prior experiences of physical or sexual violence, prior experiences of rejection (especially from family members *or* health care providers), harassment by law enforcement (which is particularly common for transgender women of color), and homelessness (Ibid.). Many of these exacerbating factors are related to violence, which LGBTQ+ people experience at high levels compared to the general population (Testa et al, 2012). Misconceptions about the type of violence that LGBTQ+ people are at risk for, however, may hamper attempts at intervention. The idea that sexual violence

is predominantly a problem perpetrated by (cisgender heterosexual) men against (cisgender heterosexual) women, for instance, conceals the impact of such violence on the LGBTQ+ community. The Centers for Disease Control and Prevention's 2010 National Intimate Partner and Sexual Violence Survey reported lifetime prevalence of rape, physical violence, or stalking by an intimate partner by sexual orientation for women (Walters et al, 2013, p. 18), revealing the following rates:

Heterosexual women:	35.0%
Lesbian women:	43.8%
Bisexual women:	61.1%

When the lifetime prevalence of sexual violence (including but not limited to rape) is reported, the numbers are even higher (Walters et al, 2013, p. 10):

Heterosexual women:	43.3%
Lesbian women:	46.4%
Bisexual women:	74.9%

While most studies still lack transgender-specific data, the National Transgender Discrimination Survey found that 64% of their participants reported experiencing sexual assault (Grant, 2011, p. 2). While this selection does not specifically cover the various negative health outcomes of sexual assault and IPV, they include disease transmission, unwanted pregnancy for people who can become pregnant, dramatically increased rates of post-traumatic stress disorder, and other lifelong psychological damage.

While sexual violence against LGBTQ+ people may be largely erased from public discourse, there are also negative consequences resulting from the stereotypical association of specific disease states with this group. In particular, HIV/AIDS continues to be associated in the public eye with gay men despite disproportionately affecting a number of marginalized groups. While men who have sex with men (MSM) are at increased risk of acquiring HIV, this risk is much higher for Black and Latino MSM than for White MSM. The risk for transgender women is higher still. It is estimated that globally, about 19% of transgender women are living with HIV (AVERT, 2015).[3]

These increased risks may be shaped by a variety of factors. For example, transgender women often must

---

[2]Native people have the highest rate of death by suicide in the United States, regardless of sexual orientation or transgender status; elsewhere in this piece, Hamilton & Barnhart mention the extremely high rate of sexual assault experienced by Native women, which as we see here is also an independent risk factor for suicide. *Ed.*

[3]Numbers for transgender men are difficult to find, but it should be noted that studies on MSM probably often include transgender men without identifying them as such, and at least one study suggests that transgender MSM are at elevated risk of acquiring HIV (CDC, 2016c).

engage in survival sex work due to widespread discrimination in housing and employment, and this puts them at almost twice the risk of acquiring HIV compared to transgender women who have not engaged in sex work (27% versus 15%) (AVERT, 2015). Other factors such as lack of stable housing (Fletcher et al, 2014), unmet need for gender affirmation and affection (Sevelius, 2013), and reliance on shared needles specifically related to use of black market hormones due to the inaccessibility of transition-related medical care (AVERT, 2015) also contribute to HIV risk. Similarly, drug use and low self-esteem induced by minority stress contribute to high-risk sexual behavior, which alone may influence high rates of HIV among transgender women (Sevelius, 2013). Finally, transgender women with HIV are less likely than cisgender people to know their diagnosis and receive timely, consistent, and culturally competent care (CDC, 2016c). LGBTQ+ women experience disproportionately negative health outcomes due to a variety of complex social causes.

Nationality and Citizenship

Nationality and citizenship status produce vast health disparities for women by way of stereotypes about who "deserves" care and assistance, and resulting structures that constrain access to appropriate resources. A broad variety of health care restrictions related to immigration status create complex disparities for foreign-born women in the United States. For example, Latina women born in the U.S. are about twice as likely as native-born White women to be uninsured, while Latina women born outside the U.S. are over four times as likely to be uninsured as native-born White women (Jones & Sonfield, 2016). In 2014, 42% of non-citizen immigrant women in the United States were uninsured compared to 13% of women who were native-born citizens, a more than threefold disparity (Guttmacher, 2016). When considering income level, these disparities are even greater. Over half (57%) of non-citizen women in the United States who fell right at or under the U.S. federal poverty level were uninsured compared to 22% of women born in the United States of comparable income. Between 2013 and 2014 many women did obtain coverage from health insurance due to the Affordable Care Act. However, the amount of uninsured non-citizen women fell by only 10% compared to 22% for women who were United States citizens.

This is partially the result of federal restrictions, which continue to block access to health care for many immigrant women in the United States. Following the Personal Responsibility and Work Opportunity Reconciliation Act of 1996, immigrant women are not eligible for Medicaid for the first five years after receiving legal United States citizenship (Hasstedt, 2013). Thus, immigrant women who achieve citizenship experience continuing health restrictions even though they are technically U.S. citizens. Additionally, after the time limit has passed and immigrant women become eligible for Medicaid, they still face additional barriers. As of 2006, in order to enroll, register for, or renew Medicaid coverage, eligible individuals must provide evidence of citizenship. Acceptable forms of documentation are ranked, with passports being the best form of proof, followed by birth certificates and photo identification such as a driver's license. Ironically, then, working class immigrant women's access to medical care is additionally reduced by the fact that the most readily accepted forms of documentation to access care are invariably also the most expensive.

Undocumented women in the United States have even less access to health care services. Immigrant women without documentation are completely denied access to health insurance coverage on both the federal and state level in the United States (Jones & Sonfield, 2016). This means they are unable to receive any governmental financial subsidies for health services, regardless of income. Even for women who have gained documentation, these restrictions may reduce access to care. For example, legal residents may be hesitant to sign up for health insurance coverage out of concern that to do so might expose undocumented family members and put them in jeopardy of deportation. Therefore, whether they have official documentation or not, women's access to health care in the United States is significantly impacted by both their national origin and their citizenship status.

Dis/ability

Dis/ability status greatly affects health outcomes for women; like sexuality and immigration status, it interacts with gender, race, and class in complex ways rather than producing predictable, additive effects. Women live with illness and disability more frequently than men. Although men have shorter life spans than women, women report being sicker more often (Tischler, 380–381). Intersections of race and class can exacerbate the health disparities suffered by people with disabilities; women of color are more likely to suffer from disabilities and experience negative health outcomes. Among racial groups in the United States, non-Hispanic Black people have the highest disability rate at approximately 23% compared to about 18% for both Hispanic and non-Hispanic White people and 14.5% for Asian people (Brault, 2012).

While aggregated statistics about Asian people often lead people to conclude that their outcomes are better than those of White people in the United States, there are major differences among Asian subgroups. Results from Singh and Lin (2013) reported the following disability prevalence among United States born and non-United States born Asian people as a general group, with more specific numbers for Cambodian, Chinese, and Vietnamese Asian people (for a more extensive list see full publication; we have selected three that tend to experience relatively poor outcomes):

United States Born

Asian 4.0
Cambodian 5.43
Chinese 5.49
Vietnamese 5.29

Non-United States Born

Asian 5.77
Cambodian 15.29
Chinese 7.33
Vietnamese 10.25

These higher rates of disability, disproportionately experienced by women, are associated with worse overall health. Of people living with disabilities, 40.3% self-report their health as poor or fair compared to 9.9% of people who do not have a disability (Krahn, Walker, & Correa-De-Araujo, 2015). Race affects the incidence and experience of disability in myriad ways. Self-reported limitations in daily activities and instruments of daily living (such as bathing, meal preparation, light housework, dressing, and grocery shopping) due to illness and disability are 4.4% and 2.0% for African American women and White women respectively (CDC, 2014 Table P-3a). These outcomes are further complicated by intersections with economic factors.

Unemployment and persistent poverty are economic factors that disproportionately affect people with disabilities, and they are more common among people whose disability status is classified as severe (Brault, 2012). Approximately 34% of people with disabilities have a household income below $15,000, compared to 15% of people without disabilities. Therefore, women with disabilities are more likely to be living in poverty, and this is compounded by women's higher poverty rates in general. Neely-Barnes et al (2004) note that this also affects the families of people with disabilities. Since families often have greater financial struggles while caring for dependents with specialized needs, they commonly face personal wellbeing issues

themselves, such as inadequate sleep. Furthermore, as Daly et al. (1995) note, families with greater financial means have better access to support services for dependents or children with disabilities compared to families of color or families with a lower income status. Since single-parent households are disproportionately headed by impoverished women of color in the United States (Entmacher et al., 2013), it is women, and particularly women of color, who are disproportionately affected by this lack of access to care for their dependents with disabilities, and whose own health is likely to be impacted from psychological, physical, and financial stress.

As a direct result of their economic marginalization, people with disabilities have significantly less access to both health insurance and health services. Roughly 75% of people without disabilities are insured under private health insurance companies, whereas fewer than 50% of people with severe disabilities have private health insurance; people with disabilities, and especially women (who are less likely to have access to employer-provided plans), have higher rates of insurance through government assistance (Krahn, Walker, & Correa-De-Araujo, 2015, p.s202). Although public health insurance will cover many people with disabilities, 28% of people with mental health issues, such as depressive disorders and anxiety, are uninsured. Women are more likely to be diagnosed with depression and anxiety, and they are also more likely to have chronic conditions such as fibromyalgia and chronic fatigue syndrome (CFS) that are still poorly understood and typically take years to diagnose and treat accurately (Arnold, Clauw, and McCarberg, 2011). Thus women with psychological or chronic illness may be particularly unlikely to have access to necessary care.

Furthermore, not only do women with disabilities have less access to health care, they may also be disproportionately subjected to unwarranted medical procedures. For example, women with disabilities are more likely to receive hysterectomies, a major surgery in which all or part of the uterus is removed. More than one third of women in the United States will undergo a hysterectomy by the age of 60 (National Women's Health Network, 2015), but the rate is much higher for women with multiple disabilities, who also tend to receive them at younger ages (Rivera Drew, 2013). These procedures are often performed unnecessarily while being framed as essential to ease the perceived burden for women with disabilities. For example, women with multiple disabilities may face more pressure to get hysterectomies in order to eliminate menstruation and the possibility of pregnancy. Additionally, working class women with disabilities who work low-income jobs are more likely to receive hysterectomies than those who have a higher socioeconomic status, possibly reflecting fewer resources to challenge medical authority or seek a second opinion.

Unnecessary hysterectomy is a particular problem since the procedure carries significant risk of serious complications. In fact, many health officials and organizations such as the American College of Obstetricians and Gynecologists now discourage hysterectomies for non-urgent purposes such as preventing pregnancy or to ease the job of caregivers (Rivera Drew, 2013, 162), a common justification for surgical procedures (sometimes quite extreme, as in the case of the so-called "Ashley Treatment") performed on developmentally or cognitively disabled female-assigned children and adults (Disability Rights Education and Defense Fund, 2007).[4] Therefore, it is important to not only interrogate women with disabilities' lack of access to most medical care, but also the specific types of medical care to which women with disabilities are subjected whether they choose it or not.

Specific Health Issues

Thus far we have examined health disparities among women in terms of the groups affected. Now, we will touch on three specific health issues, cancer, pain and pain management, and pregnancy and birth, in order to further demonstrate how women experience disparities in health outcomes based on different identity characteristics.

Cancer

Cancer remains an epidemic across the world and in the United States specifically. Despite the fact that cancer deaths in the United States are decreasing overall, there are significant gender and racial disparities in cancer incidence as well as treatment and survival outcomes. Incidence rates of cancer have decreased for men, yet have remained stable for women (CDC, 2016b); fewer men are developing cancer to begin with. From 1999 to 2012 cancer incidence rates for men decreased from 380 to 275 per 100,000 people, but remained steady at 280 per 100,000 people for women over the same time period (Ibid). These rates are impacted by race as well. In 2012, the incidence for combined cancer types was 446 for Blacks, 440 for Whites, 269 for American Indians/Alaska Natives, 340 for Hispanics and 285 Asians/Pacific Islanders (USCS, 2015).

Cancer death rates are also complicated by race. In 2011, the death rate for combined cancer types was "199 for African Americans, 169 for Whites, 112 for American Indians/Alaska Natives, 118 for Hispanics, and 106 for Asians/Pacific Islanders" (age adjusted) per 100,000 people (CDC, 2016a). In 2012, although White women were *diagnosed* with breast cancers at a higher rate than any other racial group, Black women were the most likely to *die* of the disease (CDC, 2015). While the two groups received similar preventative care, Black women were less likely than White women to receive appropriate follow-up care. For example, in 2010, Black and White women reported equal numbers of breast cancer screenings (CDC, 2012). However, while 83% of White women started treatment within 30 days, only 69% of Black women had done so (CDC, 2012). Additionally, Black women were less likely to receive medically indicated surgeries, radiation, and hormones necessary for treatment (CDC, 2012). Some of these disparities may be related to lack of medical coverage to help supplement the cost of treatment and unequal access to biomedical cancer treatment advancements (National Cancer Institute, 2008; Carey, et al., 2006).

Consider also the compounding role of race in mammogram screening numbers for lesbian, bisexual, and other queer women. LGB people are less likely than heterosexual people to have health insurance and are consequently more likely to delay medical care.[5] Lesbian and bisexual women are less likely to receive a mammogram than heterosexual women, but these disparities are compounded by race in different ways for different groups (Krehely, 2009: 2). While there is approximately an equal rate (69%) of heterosexual African American and White women receiving mammograms in the last two years, only 60% of LGB White women and 35% of LGB African American women received this care (Ibid.). For LGB White women, this was a relatively small decrease compared to their heterosexual counterparts; LGB Black women, however, were only about half as likely to receive a mammogram as theirs. For Latina women, on the other hand, there was little difference between heterosexual women receiving mammograms (53%) and LGB women receiving them (51%). However, both groups had significantly lower rates than the heterosexual Black and White women (ibid.). For some women, then, low mammogram rates may be best addressed through interventions targeted by race, while for others, sexual orientation is the key.[6]

---

[4]For more discussion of the Ashley Treatment, see s.e. smith's piece elsewhere in this volume. *Ed.*

[5]For discussion of other reasons LGBTQ+ people might delay care, see Kristin Puhl's piece on LGBTQ+ experiences of primary health care elsewhere in this volume. *Ed.*

[6]As Cynthia Pearson addresses elsewhere in this volume, however, there is some question about our current reliance on mammography as a diagnostic test. *Ed.*

Similar to racial disparities in breast cancer, racial disparities exist for cervical cancer as well. As of 2012, Hispanic women had the highest rate of cervical cancer incidence in the United States, with 9.5 per 100,000 women (U.S. Cancer Statistics Working Group, 2015). Black women's 2012 rate was 9.1, while the rate for White women was 7.1 per 100,000. However, once again, Black women had the highest death rate from the disease. The 2012 mortality rate from cervical cancer for Black women was 3.7, versus 2.7 per 100,000 for Hispanic women and 2.1 per 100,000 for White women (Ibid.). Black women are only about 25% more likely to be diagnosed with cervical cancer as White women, yet they are *75% more likely* to die from it. Differences in treatment may be responsible for this difference in outcomes between Black and White women. For example, Black women are less likely to receive medically indicated treatment such as radical hysterectomy and brachytherapy (Fleming et al, 2012).

Pain and Pain Management

Pain and pain management is a unique category of health to examine because most people in their life experience pain, be it acute or chronic. The topic's relationship with increased concerns regarding prescription opioids and home manufactured drugs creates a difficult conversation about demographic differences in access to efficient treatment because of the perception of widespread misuse of pain medications. Numerous studies over the last decade have highlighted disparities in management and acknowledgement of pain. Staton et al. found that doctors underrated pain ratings for Black patients nearly half of time compared to only one-third of the time for non-Black patients, using a numeric point scale (2007, Figure 1, 533). In contrast, physicians were more likely to perceive that patients who were not Black were in more pain (Staton et al., 2007, 535). In other studies, race was a "significant predictor of maltreatment with regards to pain management" after controlling for demographic characteristics like age and education (Ezenwa et al., 2012, 19). Health providers are more likely to consider chronic pain among women of color as a "symptom" to view with suspicion rather than a condition deserving treatment (Mossey, 2011).

This is a particular problem for women as there is evidence that women are more likely to experience clinical and post-operative pain compared with men (Fillingim et al, 2009). Again, however, providers treat patients differently based on the interplay of gender and race. Black women received lower doses of hydrocodone for persistent kidney stone pain than did Black men, but White women received higher doses of the same medication for treatment of kidney stones compared to White men (Weisse et al, 2003). Most studies highlight pain management differences among African Americans and Latinos compared to Whites. However, there is also evidence to suggest that Native Americans and the rural poor, regardless of race, are disproportionately undertreated for pain related to cancer treatment (Anderson, Green, and Payne 2009, 1192). Care provider recognition and understanding of pain, and adequate treatment for it, is an important factor to continue to monitor among different demographics for several reasons.

First, it is reasonably conceivable that if patients cannot receive adequate relief and/or medication monitoring from licensed practitioners, they will look to illegal/black-market sources of pain relief, which may have worse health outcomes and also contribute to existing racial and economic disparities in criminal justice. Secondly, histories of medical maltreatment of people of color in the United States[7] should serve as an ongoing reminder of the need for an ethical alertness on all aspects of health treatment. Pain management falls within the scope of medical ethics because it is inherently bad to allow certain groups to experience more pain on the basis of physical appearance or assumed group membership. Furthermore, monitoring is one of the primary ways to recognize disparities and perhaps create fewer instances of individual experiences of maltreatment or lack of treatment, which may set the stage for lifelong distrust in and disengagement from health services.

Pregnancy & Birth

Pregnancy and birth outcomes are embedded in a nexus of socially informed (and culturally specific) expectations about the role and experience of motherhood. A key issue with regards to birth and pregnancy among different demographics is the pregnancy rate for specific age brackets. Pregnancy rates are defined as the number of births per 1,000 women for the demographic being examined. Teen and adolescent pregnancy is an essential indicator of individual and community health because it reveals important information about who is vulnerable and how institutional resources are distributed.

Recent research shows Black girls with the highest pregnancy rate for the 15–19-year-old and 10–14-year-old age brackets (CDC- MMWR Report, 2013). Additionally, Black girls age 10–14 had the highest rate of fetal loss in the age bracket, while Hispanic girls age 15–19 had the highest rate of fetal loss in that bracket

---

[7]See "Under the Shadow of Tuskegee" elsewhere in this volume. *Ed.*

(CDC- MMWR Report, 2013). White girls in both age brackets had both the lowest pregnancy rate and the lowest incidence of fetal loss (CDC- MMWR Report, 2013). While policy debates about "teen pregnancy" often position it as solely the result of either individual irresponsibility or the unequal distribution of resources such as contraception, it is important to also consider the specific role of sexual violence and abuse. For infants born to girls age 15 or younger, 39% of fathers are between the ages of 20 and 29; for those born to girls age 11–12, *all* fathers are on average almost 10 years older than the mother (Nossel, 1996).

Moreover, in order to have a fuller understanding of pregnancy outcomes, it is important to look beyond pregnancy rates. Other outcome measures, such as infant mortality, preterm birth, and maternal mortality are also impacted by race as well. For example, the White infant mortality rate in the United States is 5.5 per 1,000 births. However, the rate for African Americans is more than *twice as high*, at 12.7 per 1,000 births (CDC, 2013). This is partially related to the higher rate of premature birth for Black babies (March of Dimes, 2015). Preterm birth is defined in the United States as a birth before 37 weeks; rates are calculated by dividing the number of preterm birth by the number of live births with known gestational age and multiplying by 100 (March of Dimes). The overall 2015 preterm birth rate in the United States was reported to be 9.5, yet the preterm birth rate for Black women was 13.4.[8] In contrast, White women's preterm birth was 9.1 and the lowest rate was among Asian women at 8.7 for this reporting year (March of Dimes, 2015).

Both of these problems are intensified by racial inequity in care for pregnant people. For instance, babies with a low birth-weight are just under twice as likely to be born to African American women (CDC, 2015a, Table 24, pg. 55). Furthermore, maternal mortality rates also reflect these racial disparities. The maternal mortality rate (people who die during pregnancy or within the following year) is three to four times greater for Black women than for White women (CDC, 2015c); it is also increasing overall for women in the United States, one of only eight countries in the world where this is the case (Kassebaum et al, 2014). These health issues are crucial to examine, as pregnancy and birth are causes of death that disproportionately affect women. Although it may seem counterintuitive that the United States' maternal death rate is increasing while the vast majority of countries in the world see maternal mortality decreasing, this serves as strong evidence that women,

especially women of color, are increasingly vulnerable in the current social context of the United States.

Conclusion

As we have discussed here, there are numerous health disparities that exist between women based on different demographic factors. Education, income, and geographic location all influence women's ability to access medical care. In addition, sexuality, gender, nationality, and dis/ability create different, yet similarly significant health disparities for women. An analysis of cancer, pain and pain management, and pregnancy and birth reveals some of the complex ways in which individual women's identities impact their health and experiences of care.

Reasons for the persistence of health and health care disparities are vast. Bias in health care is intensified by the fact that although many healthcare workers are people of color and nearly three quarters of all medical care workers are women, the majority of doctors (the primary decision makers) are White, male, and upper middle class (Tischler, 380). The absence of a diverse workforce at upper levels, compounded by a lack of cultural competency training in providers' education, allows the conditions for inappropriate health care to flourish even when marginalized group members are able to access physicians. For women, and especially women with multiple marginalized identities, lack of affordable health care/insurance, doctors' lack of cultural competence, and enduring structural sexism and racism are some of the greatest causes of health disparities within the United States. Therefore, it is important to further consider the ways in which social structures and institutions affect the health of women.

The information presented in this selection may leave the reader feeling grave discontent for the way things are and pessimism about the capacity of health care systems to do better for marginalized groups. However, health practitioners and potential future practitioners can use this knowledge to take pragmatic steps towards the alleviation and eventual elimination of the disparities we have covered. We believe that change requires awareness about the social context from which inequality arises; this awareness can then serve as a gateway for health professionals to gain cultural competency and a subsequent sense of activism within their work. We are optimistic about change when doctors and other care providers see their patients as 'people' rather than as strictly 'pathological bodies'. Cultural competence and activism among individual healthcare practitioners will allow for changes from within the health field itself

---

[8]See discussion of how the stress of racism may contribute to negative birth outcomes in Tanya Cook's piece elsewhere in this volume. *Ed.*

by placing greater emphasis on identifying, evaluating, and eventually solving problems with access to and delivery of care.

Although the eradication of these health disparities depends on societal changes, micro level interventions and compassion toward patients to enhance their health experiences and their livelihood is equally important to foster larger transformations. Individuals and organizations can have a more immediate impact in order to address healthcare inequalities by re-acclimating patients who have been disconnected from health services for various reasons. Similarly, these disparities should warrant questions about our health systems' structure (including but not limited to its for-profit status, modes of delivery, and access) and the impact of minimum diversity (of racial and gender composition of practitioners, of ideology and cultural experience, of sexuality etc). Lastly, one must consider: 1) how one can take ownership of one's own health experience by asking practitioners clarifying or new questions, 2) the potential positive impact of participating in local health education volunteer opportunities, and 3) the best practices for self-care if formal services are not available, adequate, or affordable.

WORKS CITED

Anderson, Karen O., Carmen R. Greeny, Carmen R., Payne, Richard. (2009, December) Racial and Ethnic Disparities in Pain: Causes and Consequences of Unequal Care. The Journal of Pain, 10(12): 1187–1204.

American Cancer Society. (2015). Facts About Cancer Pain. Retrieved from: http://www.cancer.org/treatment/treatmentsandsideeffects/physicalsideeffects/pain/facts-about-cancer-pain.

American Psychological Association (APA). THe Behavioral Health Needs of Rural Women. APA Committee on Rural Health Retieved from: https://www.apa.org/pubs/info/reports/rural-women.pdf

Arnold LM, Clauw DJ, & McCarberg BH. (2011). Improving the Recognition and Diagnosis of Fibromyalgia. *Mayo Clinic Proceedings* 86(5): 457–464.

AVERT (Averting HIV and AIDS). (2015). "Transgender People and HIV/AIDS." Retrieved from: http://www.avert.org/professionals/hiv-social-issues/key-affected-populations/transgender.

Behrman RE, Butler AS (editors). (2007) Preterm birth: causes, consequences, and prevention. Washington, DC: National Academies Press.

Brault, M. W. (2012, July). Americans with disabilities: 2010. United States Bureau of Census. Retrieved from: http://www.census.gov/prod/2012pubs/p70-131.pdf.

Breslau, Joshua; Marshall, Grant N. Marshall; Pincus, Harold A. & Brown, Ryan A. (2014) Are mental disorders more common in urban than rural areas of the United States?, Journal of Psychiatric Research, Volume 56, September 2014, Pages 50–55. Retrieved from:http://www.science-direct.com/science/article/pii/S0022395614001423

Carey, L., et al. (2006). Race, Breast Cancer Subtypes, and Survival in the Carolina Breast Cancer Study. *Journal of the American Medical Association 295(21)*. 2492–2502. doi: 10.1001/jama.295.21.2492.

Centers for Disease Control and Prevention (November 2012). Breast Cancer: Black Women Have Higher Death Rates from Breast Cancer from Other Women. *CDC Vital Signs*. Retrieved from: http://www.cdc.gov/vitalsigns/Breast-Cancer/index.html.

Centers for Disease Control and Prevention (CDC). (2013). Health Disparities and Inequalities Report—United States, 2013. Retrieved from: http://www.cdc.gov/mmwr/pdf/other/su6203.pdf.

Centers for Disease Control and Prevention (CDC). (2014). National Health Interview Survey 2014. Retrieved from: http://ftp.cdc.gov/pub/Health_Statistics/NCHS/NHIS/SHS/2014_SHS_Table_P-3.pdf.

Centers for Disease Control and Prevention (CDC). (2015a). National Vital Statistics Reports. CDC, National Vital Statistics System, 64(12). Retrieved from: http://www.cdc.gov/nchs/data/nvsr/nvsr64/nvsr64_12.pdf.

Centers for Disease Control and Prevention (CDC). (2015b). Cancer Rates by Race/Ethnicity and Sex. Retrieved from: http://www.cdc.gov/cancer/dcpc/data/race.htm.

Centers for Disease Control and Prevention (CDC). (2015c). At A Glance: Safe Motherhood. Retrieved from: http://www.cdc.gov/chronicdisease/resources/publications/aag/maternal.htm

Centers for Disease Control and Prevention (2015d). United States Life Tables, 2011 National Vital Statistics Reports, Vol. 64, No. 11. Retrieved from: http://www.cdc.gov/nchs/data/nvsr/nvsr64/nvsr64_11.pdf

Centers for Disease Control and Prevention (CDC). (2016a). At A Glance: Addressing the Cancer Burden. Retrieved from: http://www.cdc.gov/chronicdisease/resources/publications/aag/dcpc.htm.

Centers for Disease Control and Prevention (CDC). (2016b). Annual Report to the Nation on the Status of Cancer, 1975–2012. Retrieved from: http://www.cdc.gov/cancer/dcpc/research/articles/arn_7512.htm.

Centers for Disease Control and Prevention (CDC). (2016c). HIV Among Transgender People. Retrieved from: http://www.cdc.gov/hiv/group/gender/transgender/.

Daly, A., Jennings, J., Beckett, J. O., & Leashore, B. R. (1995). Effective coping strategies of African Americans. Social Work, 40(2), 240–248.

Disability Rights Education and Defense Fund. (2007). Modify the System, Not the Person. Retrieved from: http://dredf.org/public-policy/ethics/modify-the-system-not-the-person/.

Kaiser Family Foundation. (2012, November). "Disparities in Health and Health Care: Five Key Questions And

Answers." Disparities Policy. Retrieved from: http://kff.org/disparities-policy/issue-brief/disparities-in-health-and-health-care-five-key-questions-and-answers/.

Eberhardt, M. S., & Pamuk, E. R. (2004). The Importance of Place of Residence: Examining Health in Rural and Nonrural Areas. *American Journal of Public Health*, *94*(10), 1682–1686.

Ezenwa, Miriam O.; Fleming, Michael. F. (2012, Fall). Racial Disparities in Pain Management in Primary Care. Journal of Health Disparities Research and Practice, 5(3): 12–26.

Fillingim,Roger B.;. King, Christopher D; Ribeiro-Dasilva, Margarete C. ; Rahim-Williams, Bridgett; Riley III., Joseph L. (2009,May) Sex, Gender, and Pain: A Review of Recent Clinical and Experimental Findings, The Journal of Pain, 10(5): 447–485.

Fleming, S., Schluterman, N. H., Tracy, J. K., & Temkin, S. M. (2014). Black and White Women in Maryland Receive Different Treatment for Cervical Cancer. *Plos ONE*, *9*(8): 1–8. doi:10.1371/journal.pone.0104344.

Fletcher JB, Kisler KA, and Reback CJ. (2014). "Housing Status and HIV Risk Behaviors Among Transgender Women in Los Angeles." *Archives of Sexual Behavior* 43: 1651–1661.

Fredriksen-Goldsen KI, Kim HJ, Barkan SE, Balsam KF, and Mincer SL. (2010). "Disparities in Health-Related Quality of Life: A Comparison of Lesbians and Bisexual Women." *American Journal of Public Health* 100(11): 2255–2261.

Gorman, B., Denney, J., Dowdy, H., & Medeiros, R. (2015). A New Piece of the Puzzle: Sexual Orientation, Gender, and Physical Health Status. *Demography, 52(4)*. Retrieved from http://web.b.ebscohost.com.ezproxy.library.wisc.edu/ehost/pdfviewer/pdfviewer?sid=6ca949bc-eec4-46fb-a8dc-c766033ae289%40sessionmgr111&vid=1&hid=110.

Grant, Jaime M., Lisa A. Mottet, Justin Tanis, Jack Harrison, Jody L. Herman, and Mara Keisling. (2011). *Injustice at Every Turn: A Report of the National Transgender Discrimination Survey.* Washington: National Center for Transgender Equality and National Gay and Lesbian Task Force. Retrieved from: http://www.thetaskforce.org/static_html/downloads/reports/reports/ntds_full.pdf.

Guttmacher Institute. (2016, Feb. 22). *Health Coverage Trends Among U.S. Women of Reproductive Age Varied Considerably with ACA Implementation.* Retrieved from: http://www.guttmacher.org/media/inthenews/2016/02/22/NIC-ACA.html.

Haas AP, Rodgers PL, and Herman JL. (January 2014). "Suicide Attempts Among Transgender and Gender Non-Conforming Adults: Findings of the National Transgender Discrimination Survey." Retrieved from: http://williamsinstitute.law.ucla.edu/wp-content/uploads/AFSP-Williams-Suicide-Report-Final.pdf.

Hasstedt, K. (2013). Toward Equity and Access: Removing Legal Barriers To Health Insurance Coverage for Immigrants. *Guttmacher Policy Review, 16(1)*. Retrieved from: https://www.guttmacher.org/pubs/gpr/16/1/gpr160102.html.

Jones, R., & Sonfield, A. (2016). Health Insurance Coverage Among Women of Reproductive Age Before and After Implementation of the Affordable Care Act. *Contraception, 0(0)*. Retrieved from: http://www.contraception-journal.org/article/S0010-7824(15)30093-7/pdf.

Kassebaum et al. (2014). Global, regional, and national levels and causes of maternal mortality during 1990–2013: a systematic analysis for the Global Burden of Disease Study 2013. The Lancet. Volume 384: Pg 980–1004. Retrieved from: http://www.thelancet.com/pdfs/journals/lancet/PIIS0140-6736%2814%2960696-6.pdf.

Krahn, G., Walker, D., & Correa-De-Araujo, R. (2015). Persons With Disabilities as an Unrecognized Health Disparity Population. *American Journal of Public Health, 105(S2)*, S198-S206. doi: 10.2015/AJPH.2014.302182.

Krehely, Jeff. (2009). How to Close the LGBT Health Disparities Gap, Center for American Progress. Retrieved from: https://cdn.americanprogress.org/wp-content/uploads/issues/2009/12/pdf/lgbt_health_disparities.pdf.

March of Dimes. (2015). 2015 Premature Birth Report Card" Retrieved from: http://www.marchofdimes.org/materials/premature-birth-report-card-united-states.pdf.

McNeil, John M. (1993). Americans With Disabilities 1991–92: Data From the Survey of Income and Program Participation. U.S. Bureau of the Census. Current Population Reports. P.70–33. U.S. Government Printing Office, Washington D.C. 1993.

Meyer, I.H. (2003). Prejudice, social stress, and mental health in lesbian, gay and bisexual populations: Conceptual issues and research evidence. *Psychological Bulletin*, 129, 674–697.

Montez, J. & Zajacova, A. (2013). Trends in Mortality Risk by Educational Level and Cause of Death Among UW White Women from 1986 to 2006. *American Journal of Public Health, 103(3)*, 473–479. doi: 10.2105/AJPH.2012.301128.

Montez, J. & Zajacova, A. (2014). Why is Life Expectancy Declining Among Low-Educated Women in the United States. *American Journal of Public Health, 104(10)*, e5–e7. doi: 10.2105/AJPH.2014.302146.

Mossey, Jana M.(2011, July). Defining Racial and Ethnic Disparities in Pain Management. *Clinical Orthopaedics and Related Research* . 469(7): 1859–1870.

National Cancer Institute. (2008). Cancer Health *Disparities*. Retrieved from: http://www.cancer.gov/about-nci/organization/crchd/cancer-health-disparities-fact-sheet#q7.

National Coalition of Anti-Violence Programs (NCAVP). (2015). "Media Alert: An open letter from LGBTQ organizations in the United States regarding the epidemic violence that LGBTQ people, particularly transgender women of color, have experienced in 2015." Retrieved from: http://www.avp.org/storage/documents/webversion_ncavp_ma_national2015.pdf

National Coalition of Anti-Violence Programs (NCAVP). (2015b). "Media Alert: 2014 Report on Intimate Partner

Violence in Lesbian, Gay, Bisexual, Transgender, Queer and HIV-Affected Communities in the U.S. Released Today." Retrieved from: http://www.avp.org/storage/documents/2014_IPV_Report_Media_Release_Final.pdf.

National Women's Health Network. (2015). Hysterectomy. Retrieved from: https://www.nwhn.org/hysterectomy/.

Entmacher, Joan ;Gallagher Robbins, Katherine; Vogtman, Julie; Frohlich, Lauren. (2013). Insecure and Unequal: Poverty and Income Among Women and Families 200–2012. National Women's Law Center. http://www.nwlc.org/sites/default/files/pdfs/final_2013_nwlc_povertyreport.pdf.

Neely-Barnes, S.L. & Marcenko, M.O. (2004). Predicting impact of childhood disability on families: Results from the 1995 National Health Interview Survey Disability Supplement. *Mental Retardation, 4.,* 284–293.

Nossel, Ilana. (1996). Pregnancy and Childbearing Among Younger Teens. *Advocates for Youth.* Retrieved from: http://www.advocatesforyouth.org/publications/publications-a-z/467-pregnancy-and-childbearing-among-younger-teens.

Rivera Drew, J. (2013). Hysterectomy and Disability Among U.S. Women. *Perspectives on Sexual and Reproductive Health, 45(3).* 157–163. doi: 10.1363/4515713.

San Francisco Human Rights Commission LGBT Advisory Committee. (2011). *Bisexual Invisibility: Impacts and Recommendations.* Retrieved from: http://sf-hrc.org/sites/sf-hrc.org/files/migrated/FileCenter/Documents/HRC_Publications/Articles/Bisexual_Invisiblity_Impacts_and_Recommendations_March_2011.pdf.

Sevelius, JM. (2013). "Gender Affirmation: A Framework for Conceptualizing Risk Behavior Among Transgender Women of Color." *Sex Roles* 68: 675–689.

Singh, Gopal & Lin, Sue (2013). "Marked Ethnic, Nativity, and Socioeconomic Disparities in Disability and Health Insurance among US Children and Adults: The 2008–2010 American Community Survey". Hindawi Publishing Corporation BioMed Research International. Volume 2013, Article ID 627412 Retrieved from: http://www.ncbi.nlm.nih.gov/pmc/articles/PMC3819828/pdf/BMRI2013-627412.pdf

Singh, G. & Siahpush, M. (2014). Widening Rural-Urban Disparities in Life Expectancy, U.S., 1969–2009.

American Journal of Preventive Medicine, 46(2). e19–e29. doi: 10.1016/j.amepre.2013.10.017.

Staton LJ, Panda M, Chen I, Genao I, Kurz J, Pasanen M, Mechaber AJ, Menon M, O'Rorke J, Wood J, Rosenberg E, Faeslis C, Carey T, Calleson D, Cykert S.(2007). When race matters: disagreement in pain perception between patients and their physicians in primary care. Journal of National Medical Association, 99. 532–538.

Testa, RJ, Sciacca LM, Wang F, Goldblum P, Hendricks ML, Bradford J, and Bongar B. (2012). "Effects of Violence on Transgender People." *Professional Psychology: Research and Practice* 43(5): 452–459.

Tischler, Henry. (2011) Introduction to Sociology. Cengage Advantage. 11th Edition. 380–381. Print.

U.S. Cancer Statistics Working Group (USCS) . (2015). United States Cancer Statistics: 1999–2012 Incidence and Mortality Web-based Report. Atlanta: U.S. Department of Health and Human Services, Centers for Disease Control and Prevention and National Cancer Institute. Generated table : https://nccd.cdc.gov/uscs/cancersbyraceandethnicity.aspx Available at: www.cdc.gov/uscs.

United States Department of Labor. (2015). More education still means more pay in 2014. Retrieved from: http://www.bls.gov/opub/ted/2015/more-education-still-means-more-pay-in-2014.htm.

von Reichert, Christiane; Greiman, Lillie; Myers, Andrew; and Rural Institute, University of Montana. (2014). The Geography of Disability in America: On Rural-Urban Differences in Impairment Rates. *Independent Living and Community Participation*. Paper 7. Retrieved from: http://scholarworks.umt.edu/ruralinst_independent_living_community_participation/7

Walters, M.L., Chen J., & Breiding, M.J. (2013). The National Intimate Partner and Sexual Violence Survey (NISVS): 2010 Findings on Victimization by Sexual Orientation. Atlanta, GA: National Center for Injury Prevention and Control, Centers for Disease Control and Prevention. Retrieved from: http://www.cdc.gov/violenceprevention/pdf/nisvs_sofindings.pdf.

Weisse, Carol S; Sorum, Paul C; Dominguez, Rachel E. (2013, November) The influence of gender and race on physicians' pain management decisions, The Journal of Pain, 4(9). 505–510.

"Financially Vulnerable"

By Stephanie Rytilahti

This article places the reader in the position of a young woman I will call "Helena." Helena is a fictitious representation of the many clients I met with during my career in the financial industry. Although her story is untrue, her situation accurately reflects the financially vulnerable situation many Americans find themselves in when trips to the hospital are either uninsured or only partially covered by health insurance companies. In this narrative, I will optimistically guide Helena through a variety of options for dealing with her medical collections. None of these options will be without compromises, but, unlike many of the clients I assisted, she will have options. Her tale will be complicated by the same institutional hurdles many of my clients faced: gender, race, class, ethnicity, sexual orientation, parenthood, and limited educational and financial resources.

In a country where hospitals, financial institutions, and employment-based insurance are inextricably linked, many Americans face overwhelming and invisible obstacles on a daily basis. Helena largely represents the mythical norm. She is 25 years old, white, college-educated, and healthy. She works three different jobs to cover her expenses. None of her employers offers health insurance. She looks into a few different options after graduating from college, but the monthly premiums are beyond her financial resources. Thus far, she has avoided the need for major medical care. She knows her situation is risky, and eventually hopes to move into a position with full benefits. Unfortunately, a few months elapse and Helena is injured in a biking accident. The injuries are relatively minor, but without insurance she ends up owing the hospital over $1200. She sets up a payment plan to begin paying down the debt, but over the course of the next year she calls upon the healthcare system three additional times for strep throat, an ear infection, and a burn injury.

Two more years elapse, and Helena eventually finds a job that offers health insurance. She is delighted to have this aspect of her health covered. She has taken a total of seven trips to urgent care over the last two years, and knows there are still quite a few outstanding charges to pay. Her first priority is a new vehicle. Her new job is over thirty minutes from her apartment, and she walks a portion of the way every night in the dark because public transportation does not go directly to her office. It is not the safest part of town, and she is beginning to dread the walk each evening. She makes an appointment at her financial institution to apply for a loan, and the loan officer she meets with asks a few general questions about her employment, rent, and marital status. She lets Helena know it will take a few minutes to pull her credit report and determine her eligibility. Helena breathes a sigh of relief. She worked very hard, even during the months when illness kept her out of work, to keep up with her student loan payments and a small credit card bill. Thus, she is surprised when the loan officer begins to ask her about her outstanding collections. The names of the companies she owes money to do not make sense to her, and the loan officer explains that doctors regularly turn unpaid bills over to collection agencies for repayment, even if a patient has insurance and it is simply taking too long for bills to be reconciled. This strategy puts the pressure on the patient to cover unpaid expenses instead of hospitals arbitrating with insurance companies for past due bills.[1]

Now the intimidating calls from unknown collections agencies begin to make sense to Helena, but she is also relieved it is only medical collections appearing on her credit report. A friend told her a few years ago that these cannot hamper her ability to receive credit. Unfortunately, the loan officer goes on to explain that when a hospital chooses to turn over an unpaid medical bill to a collection agency, it has the same impact as any other unpaid debt. This situation is the same for those who lack insurance entirely, or when an insurance company makes a mistake and neglects to cover a bill. The overall effect can be devastating for a credit score. She indicates that advocacy groups have attempted to change the impact of medical collections in the past, but collection agencies are very lucrative businesses and have fought changes impeding debt collection.[2] She informs Helena that with twelve outstanding collections totaling over $8500.00, her request for a vehicle loan cannot be met. She hands Helena a copy of her credit report and the overwhelming number of unpaid medical bills jump off the page. The loan officer circles them in red, and Helena is suddenly very embarrassed. Her score is a 457, and she is kindly told that other lenders may work with consumers possessing "colorful" credit, but usually at a very high rate of interest. This makes the payments much higher and more difficult to manage monthly.

Similar to Helena, many of my clients never understood the ramifications of unpaid medical bills until a life event prompted a need for a vehicle loan, credit card, or mortgage loan. Most healthcare facilities will continue to send clients a bill for unpaid services, but after a period of time elapses; (in most states 45 days)[3] the debt is transferred to a state collection agency for repayment. Helena does not realize that medical collections will impact her credit score. She, like many others, has heard anecdotally that debts relating to medical services have little to no impact on her credit report. Although this is accurate in the initial stages of the billing process, when the medical establishment sells the debt to a collection agency it has the same devastating impact as any other outstanding bill. The 2003 Fair Credit Reporting Act allows for some consumer protections, but the reporting of any unpaid debt by a collection agency leaves the consumer in a financially precarious situation.[4]

Research relating to credit bureau reporting has found that over 50 percent of reportable collections are due to unpaid medical bills.[5] The conversation Helena has with her loan officer is very similar to others I had with clients in her situation. To obtain a loan with a reasonable interest rate, most lenders will require the consumer to have paid all or most of her collections.[6] Many consumers do not know where to start, because they did not receive or because they lost information from collection agencies stating an identification number for their unpaid account or even the appropriate number to call. Some financial institutions or debt counseling services will assist with this process, but the consumer can spend hours on the phone attempting to unravel years of financial history to no avail.

Based on my experience in the financial industry, it is safe to assume that Helena's situation will end in one of three ways. Faced with the inability to quickly conquer such a large amount of debt, she will simply go without a vehicle. This will decrease her physical safety during late hours, and also impact her mental health as she worries about walking alone to the bus stop at night. If she is a single parent, transporting children to and from school or daycare, purchasing groceries for a family, or dealing with unexpected trips to the hospital, it will be more difficult without her own vehicle. The stress of having no vehicle or "getting by" with something undependable is another unforeseen side effect of unpaid medical bills. Collections will stay on a credit report for seven years after they have been reported.[7] Thus, strep throat from five years ago could also impact Helena's ability to purchase her own home in the future. Many clients I worked with had no choice but to go without a credit card, new vehicle, or their own home because of unpaid medical debts.

Let's assume that going without a car is unthinkable to Helena. She is not willing to compromise her safety any longer, and her boss has intimated that she may be in line for some upcoming travel to other business sites. She investigates other options, and is pre-approved for a $20,000 vehicle loan! Helena is thrilled. This will allow her to buy a brand new vehicle, and not face the embarrassment of admitting to her employer that she is unable to get a car loan. When she sees the monthly payment amount of $618.00, she quickly understands how much her medical collections are costing her. Due to her credit problems, the alternative lender offers her a rate of 15.99% for her vehicle. The standard interest rate for new vehicles in her area is only 5.99%, and this would make monthly payments for the same vehicle only $490.00. However, due to her three years without insurance, Helena feels she has no choice but to accept the higher payments. Over the next few years, she will struggle greatly with this monthly requirement, and worry continually about her future financial picture.

Many of my clients would come to me after receiving these types of unfavorable loan terms, and hope to refinance the debt and escape unmanageable payments.

Even if they were successfully making payments at the higher amount, it was often impossible to assist them if medical bills were still unpaid or lowering a score. In this tale, Helena begrudgingly accepts and understands the relationship between healthcare and affordable credit in the United States. This allows her to rationalize a tough financial decision. Many of my clients in same-sex relationships lamented the unfairness of a system that provides joint medical coverage for heterosexual couples, but requires same sex partners to individually find their own forms of insurance. Additionally, many of my clients struggled with language barriers or were new to the United States. As I attempted to bridge both cultural and linguistic divides, it was sometimes nearly impossible to explain that a broken arm from three years ago prohibited a client from receiving an auto loan today. The client may have understood what I was saying, but the logic behind my explanation struck many as blatantly absurd and unimaginable. My office served a sizable Hispanic population, and the connection between access to healthcare and reasonable credit terms was often a tough lesson for newly arrived workers and their families.

Returning to Helena's final compromise, she may choose to pay down her collections based on her other available resources. She may have a modest sum in her savings account earmarked for unplanned expenses and a down payment on a house. Paying off her medical debt will significantly reduce her access to funds in an emergency, and delay home ownership by several years, but will make it easier for her to get more favorable loan terms in the present. If Helena were a few years older, she might have the option to withdraw funds from a retirement account to cover past medical debts. She will be required to pay a large penalty on the pre-retirement age withdrawal,8 and she will be less prepared for the staggering costs of prescription drugs, co-pays, and other expenses in her retirement years, but $8500.00 is a lot of debt to pay off without making other sacrifices. Helena may hedge her bets that she won't the miss the money in her retirement years, and finally pay off the sums for minor medical treatment from over six years ago. Although Medicare provides assistance to retirement age citizens, supplemental insurance and other long-term care policies are often needed to cover gaps. If this long-term planning was not conducted or was not financially viable, medical collections can also hamper the financial stability of ageing populations.

Overall, Helena's situation with her medical collections is not only inconvenient but also leaves her physically and mentally vulnerable. Based on my ability as a writer to manipulate her scenario to fit a variety of possible outcomes, I attempted to illustrate some of the compromises I witnessed clients making to overcome the repercussions of medical collections. Each option is not without its short and long-term consequences, and can impact one's access to safe housing and transportation. I only illustrated briefly the acute anguish medical collections can impart on one's mental health, and the guilt and humiliation that can result from needing to depend on family members for assistance, admit past debts to a partner, or deal with collection agencies on the phone. Helena was embarrassed to have her situation revealed to the lending officer and did not want her supervisor to find out about her situation. Her past indebtedness to the medical establishment probably also created stress-related issues that impacted her mental and physical well-being, job performance, and personal relationships.

In my lending experience, struggles relating to unpaid medical collections were significantly more common with non-Caucasian groups. According to a 2003 study conducted by the Office of Human Development, 45 million Americans lack health insurance. As a group, 13% of white Americans are without coverage. Hispanic Americans are more than twice as likely to be uninsured, at a rate of 34%, and 21% of black Americans are without insurance.9 Similar work undertaken by the Office of Minority Health and Health Disparities found that black Americans, Hispanics, American Indians, Alaska Natives, Native Hawaiians, and other Pacific Islanders all experienced additional barriers to receiving appropriate medical care based on a variety of factors, including insurance coverage.10 As a lender in Madison, Wisconsin, I began to understand the disparate racial impact this has on credit reports. Credit scores remain low because past and present medical debts go unpaid. This closes the door on affordable loans, and those loans granted tend to be under highly unfavorable terms, which can lead to additional delinquencies on unreasonable payments. As the above data supports, minority groups suffer disproportionately from this adverse situation, and, as a result, access to fair credit remains elusive.

The unfairness and inequities I witnessed in the financial industry prompted me to become an advocate for change. Lack of access, inadequate coverage, and discrimination-based barriers will continue to plague Americans seeking reliable healthcare unless more voices join the calls for reform. Listed below are steps you can take to protect your own health and financial future. Inaction and acceptance will only result in additional unpaid elbow fractures and fewer affordable car loans.

1. Learn more about the health insurance industry and how it impacts your physical, mental, and financial health. Visit the nearest locally owned feminist bookstore or library for books covering this topic.

2. Follow current political debates regarding healthcare coverage in the newspaper.

3. Use on-line networking connections and personal contacts to inform others about the health insurance industry and its link to financial wellness.

4. Write to your local and national representatives and let them know you care about this issue.

5. Track the voting record of your elected representatives on issues relating to affordable healthcare, and volunteer to support fundraisers, networking events, and other campaigns in support of candidates mobilizing for change.

6. Join or create a local organization to raise awareness and fight for a change in the current health insurance and/or financial industry.

REFERENCES

1. McDonald, Jay. "Medical Bills Can Make Your Credit Sick." *Bank Rate.* 7 July 2003. 17 July 2008. <http://www.bankrate.com/brm/news/insur/20020828a.asp>

2. Ulzheimer, John. "Medical Collections . . . Oh, What Trouble They Cause." *Credit.Com.* n.d. 16 July 2008. <http://www.credit.com/rs/vol20.jsp>

3. McDonald, Jay.

4. Hendricks, Evan. "Credit Scores and Credit Reports." *Veracity.* 2005. 17 July 2008. <http://www.veracitycredit.com/credit-scores-and-credit-reports-c-001.html>

5. Hendricks, Evan.

6. Hendricks, Evan.

7. Fair Isaac Corporation. "Managing Your Credit in Turbulent Financial Times." *My Fico Credit Education Center.* n.d. 22 July 2008. < http://www.myfico.com>

8. Orszag, Peter. "Penalties on Early IRAs and 401(k)s." *Tax Policy Center: Urban Institute and Brookings Institution.* 2007. 21 July 2008. <http://www.taxpolicycenter.org/publications/url.cfm?ID=1000812>

9. Rowland Diane, and Catherine Hoffman. "The Impact of Health Insurance Coverage on Health Disparities in the United States." *Human Development Reports.* 2005. 17 July 2008. <http://hdr.undp.org/en/reports/global/hdr2005/papers/hdr2005_rowland_diane_and_catherine_hoffman_34.pdf>

10. Centers for Disease and Control Prevention. "About Minority Health." *Office of Minority Health and Health Disparities.* 6 June 2007. 17 July 2008. < http://www.cdc.gov/omhd/AMH/AMH.htm>

Under the Shadow of Tuskegee "African Americans and Health Care"

By Vanessa Northington Gamble

Abstract   The Tuskegee Syphilis Study continues to cast its long shadow on the contemporary relationship between African Americans and the biomedical community. Numerous reports have argued that the Tuskegee Syphilis Study is the most important reason why many African Americans distrust the institutions of medicine and public health. Such an interpretation neglects a critical historical point: the mistrust predated public revelations about the Tuskegee study. This paper places the syphilis study within a broader historical and social context to demonstrate that several factors have influenced—and continue to influence—African Americans' attitudes toward the biomedical community. (*Am J Public Health*. 1997;87:1773–1778)

Introduction

On May 16, 1997, in a White House ceremony, President Bill Clinton apologized for the Tuskegee Syphilis Study, the 40-year government study (1932 to 1972) in which 399 Black men from Macon County, Alabama, were deliberately denied effective treatment for syphilis in order to document the natural history of the disease. "The legacy of the study at Tuskegee," the president remarked, "has reached far and deep, in ways that hurt our progress and divide our nation. We cannot be one America when a whole segment of our nation has no trust in America." The president's comments underscore that in the 25 years since its public disclosure, the study has moved from being a singular historical event to a powerful metaphor. It has come to symbolize racism in medicine, misconduct in human research, the arrogance of physicians, and government abuse of Black people.

The continuing shadow cast by the Tuskegee Syphilis Study on efforts to improve the health status of Black Americans provided an impetus for the campaign for a presidential apology. Numerous articles, in both the professional and popular press, have pointed out that the study predisposed many African Americans to distrust medical and public health authorities and has led to critically low Black participation in clinical trials and organ donation.

The specter of Tuskegee has also been raised with respect to HIV/AIDS prevention and treatment programs. Health education researchers Dr Stephen B. Thomas and Dr Sandra Crouse Quinn have written extensively on the impact of the Tuskegee Syphilis Study on these programs. They argue that "the legacy of this experiment, with its failure to educate the study participants and treat them adequately, laid the foundation for today's pervasive sense of black distrust of public health authorities." The syphilis study has also been used to explain why many African Americans oppose needle exchange programs. Needle exchange programs provoke the image of the syphilis study and Black fears about genocide. These programs are not viewed as mechanisms to stop the spread of HIV/AIDS but rather as fodder for the drug epidemic that has devastated so many Black neighborhoods. Fears that they will be used as guinea pigs like the men in the syphilis study have also led some African Americans with AIDS to refuse treatment with protease inhibitors.

The Tuskegee Syphilis Study is frequently described as the singular reason behind African-American distrust of the institutions of medicine and public health. Such an interpretation neglects a critic historical point: the mistrust predated public revelations about the Tuskegee study. Furthermore, the narrowness of such a representation places emphasis on a single historical event to explain deeply entrenched and complex attitudes within the Black community. An examination of the syphilis study within a broader historical and social context makes plain that several factors have influenced, and continue to influence, African Americans' attitudes toward the biomedical community.

Black Americans' fears about exploitation by the medical profession date back to the antebellum period and the use of slaves and free Black people as subjects for dissection and medical experimentation. Although physicians also used poor Whites as subjects, they used Black people far more often. During an 1835 trip to the United States, French visitor Harriet Martineau found that Black people lacked the power even to protect the graves of their dead. "In Baltimore the bodies of coloured people exclusively are taken for dissection," she remarked, "because the Whites do not like it, and the coloured people cannot resist." Four years later, abolitionist Theodore Dwight Weld echoed Martineau's sentiment. "Public opinion," he wrote, "would tolerate surgical experiments, operations, processes, performed upon them [slaves], which it would execrate if performed upon their master or other whites." Slaves found themselves as subjects of medical experiments because physicians needed bodies and because the state considered them property and denied them the legal right to refuse to participate.

Two antebellum experiments, one carried out in Georgia and the other in Alabama, illustrate the abuse that some slaves encountered at the hands of physicians. In the first, Georgia physician Thomas Hamilton conducted a series of brutal experiments on a slave to test remedies for heatstroke. The subject of these investigations, Fed, had been loaned to Hamilton as repayment for a debt owed by his owner. Hamilton forced Fed to sit naked on a stool placed on a platform in a pit that had been heated to a high temperature. Only the man's head was above ground. Over a period of 2 to 3 weeks, Hamilton placed Fed in the pit five or six times and gave him various medications to determine which enabled him best to withstand the heat. Each ordeal ended when Fed fainted and had to be revived. But note that Fed was not the only victim in this experiment; its whole purpose was to make it possible for masters to force slaves to work still longer hours on the hottest of days.

In the second experiment, Dr J. Marion Sims, the so-called father of modern gynecology, used three Alabama slave women to develop an operation to repair vesicovaginal fistulas. Between 1845 and 1849, the three slave women on whom Sims operated each underwent up to 30 painful operations. The physician himself described the agony associated with some of the experiments: "The first patient I operated on was Lucy. . . . That was before the days of anesthetics, and the poor girl, on her knees, bore the operation with great heroism and bravery." This operation was not successful, and Sims later attempted to repair the defect by placing a sponge in the bladder. This experiment, too, ended in failure. He noted:

> The whole urethra and the neck of the bladder were in a high state of inflammation, which came from the foreign substance. It had to come away, and there was nothing to do but to pull it away by main force. Lucy's agony was extreme. She was much prostrated, and I thought that she was going to die; but by irrigating the parts of the bladder she recovered with great rapidity.

Sims finally did perfect his technique and ultimately repaired the fistulas. Only after his experimentation with the slave women proved successful did the physician attempt the procedure, with anesthesia, on White women volunteers.

Exploitation after the Civil War

It is not known to what extent African Americans continued to be used as unwilling subjects for experimentation and dissection in the years after emancipation. However, an examination of African-American folklore at the turn of the century makes it clear that Black people believed that such practices persisted. Folktales are replete with references to night doctors, also called student doctors and Ku Klux doctors. In her book, *Night Riders in Black Folk History,* anthropologist Gladys-Marie Fry writes, "The term 'night doctor' (derived from the fact that victims were sought only at night) applies both to students of medicine, who supposedly stole cadavers from which to learn about body processes, and [to] professional thieves, who sold stolen bodies—living and dead—to physicians for medical research." According to folk belief, these sinister characters would kidnap Black people, usually at night and in urban areas, and take them to hospitals to be killed and used in experiments. An 1889 *Boston Herald* article vividly captured the fears that African Americans in South Carolina had of night doctors. The report read, in part:

The negroes of Clarendon, Williamsburg, and Sumter counties have for several weeks past been in a state of fear and trembling. They claim that there is a white man, a doctor, who at will can make himself invisible and who then approaches some unsuspecting darkey, and having rendered him or her insensible with chloroform, proceeds to fill up a bucket with the victim's blood, for the purpose of making medicine. After having drained the last drop of blood from the victim, the body is dumped into some secret place where it is impossible for any person to find it. The colored women are so worked up over this phantom that they will not venture out at night, or in the daytime in any sequestered place.

Fry did not find any documented evidence of the existence of night riders. However, she demonstrated through extensive interviews that many African Americans expressed genuine fears that they would be kidnapped by night doctors and used for medical experimentation. Fry concludes that two factors explain this paradox. She argues that Whites, especially those in the rural South, deliberately spread rumors about night doctors in order to maintain psychological control over Blacks and to discourage their migration to the North so as to maintain a source of cheap labor. In addition, Fry asserts that the experiences of many African Americans as victims of medical experiments during slavery fostered their belief in the existence of night doctors. It should also be added that, given the nation's racial and political climate, Black people recognized their inability to refuse to participate in medical experiments.

Reports about the medical exploitation of Black people in the name of medicine after the end of the Civil War were not restricted to the realm of folklore. Until it was exposed in 1882, a grave robbing ring operated in Philadelphia and provided bodies for the city's medical schools by plundering the graves at a Black cemetery. According to historian David C. Humphrey, southern grave robbers regularly sent bodies of southern Blacks to northern medical schools for use as anatomy cadavers.

During the early 20th century, African-American medical leaders protested the abuse of Black people by the White-dominated medical profession and used their concerns about experimentation to press for the establishment of Black controlled hospitals. Dr Daniel Hale Williams, the founder of Chicago's Provident Hospital (1891), the nation's first Black-controlled hospital, contended that White physicians, especially in the South, frequently used Black patients as guinea pigs. Dr Nathan Francis Mossell, the founder of Philadelphia's Frederick Douglass Memorial Hospital (1895), described the "fears and prejudices" of Black people, especially those from the South, as "almost proverbial." He attributed such attitudes to southern medicine practices in which Black people, "when forced to accept hospital attention, got only the poorest care, being placed in inferior wards set apart for them, suffering the brunt of all that is experimental in treatment, and all this is the sequence of their race variety and abject helplessness." The founders of Black hospitals claimed that only Black physicians possessed the skills required to treat Black patients optimally and that Black hospitals provided these patients with the best possible care.

Fears about the exploitation of African Americans by White physicians played a role in the establishment of a Black veterans hospital in Tuskegee, Ala. In 1923, 9 years before the initiation of the Tuskegee Syphilis Study, racial tensions had erupted in the town over control of the hospital. The federal government had pledged that the facility, an institution designed exclusively for Black patients, would be run by a Black professional staff. But many Whites in the area, including members of the Ku Klux Klan, did not want a Black-operated federal facility in the heart of Dixie, even though it would serve only Black people.

Black Americans sought control of the veterans hospital, in part because they believed that the ex-soldiers would receive the best possible care from Black physicians and nurses, who would be more caring and sympathetic to the veterans' needs. Some Black newspapers even warned that White southerners wanted command of the hospital as part of a racist plot to kill and sterilize African-American men and to establish an "experiment station" for mediocre White physicians. Black physicians did eventually gain the right to operate the hospital, yet this did not stop the hospital from becoming an experiment station for Black men. The veterans hospital was one of the facilities used by the United States Public Health Service in the syphilis study.

During the 1920s and 1930s, Black physicians pushed for additional measures that would battle medical racism and advance their professional needs. Dr Charles Garvin, a prominent Cleveland physician and a member of the editorial board of the Black medical publication *The Journal of the National Medical Association*, urged his colleagues to engage in research in order to protect Black patients. He called for more research on diseases such as tuberculosis and pellagra that allegedly affected African Americans disproportionately or idiosyncratically. Garvin insisted that Black physicians investigate these racial diseases because "heretofore in literature, as in medicine, the Negro has been written about, exploited and experimented upon sometimes not to his physical betterment or to the advancement of science, but the advancement of the Nordic investigator." Moreover, he charged that "in the past, men of other races have for the large part interpreted our diseases, often tinctured with inborn prejudices."

Fears of Genocide

These historical examples clearly demonstrate that African Americans' distrust of the medical profession has a longer history than the public revelations of the Tuskegee Syphilis Study. There is a collective memory among African Americans about their exploitation by the medical establishment. The Tuskegee Syphilis Study has emerged as the most prominent example of medical racism because it confirms, if not authenticates, long-held and deeply entrenched beliefs within the Black community. To be sure, the Tuskegee Syphilis Study does cast a long shadow. After the study had been exposed, charges surfaced that the experiment was part of a governmental plot to exterminate Black people. Many Black people agreed with the charge that the study represented "nothing less than an official, premeditated policy of genocide." Furthermore, this was not the first or last time that allegations of genocide have been launched against the government and the medical profession. The sickle cell anemia screening programs of the 1970s and birth control programs have also provoked such allegations.

In recent years, links have been made between Tuskegee, AIDS, and genocide. In September 1990, the article "AIDS: Is It Genocide?" appeared in *Essence*, a Black woman's magazine. The author noted "As an increasing number of African-Americans continue to sicken and die and as no cure for AIDS has been found some of us are beginning to think the unthinkable: Could AIDS be a virus that was manufactured to erase large numbers of us? Are they trying to kill us with this disease?" In other words, some members of the Black community see AIDS as part of a conspiracy to exterminate African Americans.

Beliefs about the connection between AIDS and the purposeful destruction of African Americans should not be cavalierly dismissed as bizarre and paranoid. They are held by a significant number of Black people. For example, a 1990 survey conducted by the Southern Christian Leadership Conference found that 35% of the 1056 Black church members who responded believed that AIDS was a form of genocide. A *New York Times/WCBS TV News* poll conducted the same year found that 10% of Black Americans thought that the AIDS virus had been created in a laboratory in order to infect Black people. Another 20% believed that it could be true.

African Americans frequently point to the Tuskegee Syphilis Study as evidence to support their views about

genocide, perhaps, in part, because many believe that the men in the study were actually injected with syphilis. Harlon Dalton, a Yale Law School professor and a former member of the National Commission on AIDS, wrote, in a 1989 article titled, "AIDS in Black Face," that "the government [had] purposefully exposed Black men to syphilis." Six years later, Dr Eleanor Walker, a Detroit radiation oncologist, offered an explanation as to why few African Americans become bone marrow donors. "The biggest fear, she claimed, is that they will become victims of some misfeasance, like the Tuskegee incident where Black men were infected with syphilis and left untreated to die from the disease." The January 25, 1996, episode of *New York Undercover*, a Fox Network police drama that is one of the top shows in Black households, also reinforced the rumor that the U.S. Public Health Service physicians injected the men with syphilis. The myth about deliberate infection is not limited to the Black community. On April 8, 1997, news anchor Tom Brokaw, on "NBC Nightly News," announced that the men had been infected by the government.

Folklorist Patricia A. Turner, in her book *I Heard It through the Grapevine: Rumor and Resistance in African-American Culture*, underscores why it is important not to ridicule but to pay attention to these strongly held theories about genocide. She argues that these rumors reveal much about what African Americans believe to be the state of their lives in this country. She contends that such views reflect Black beliefs that White Americans have historically been, and continue to be, ambivalent and perhaps hostile to the existence of Black people. Consequently, African-American attitudes toward biomedical research are not influenced solely by the Tuskegee Syphilis Study. African Americans' opinions about the value White society has attached to their lives should not be discounted. As Reverend Floyd Tompkins of Stanford University Memorial Church has said, "There is a sense in our community, and I think it shall be proved out, that if you are poor or you're a person of color, you were the guinea pig, and you continue to be the guinea pigs, and there is the fundamental belief that Black life is not valued like White life or like any other life in America."

Not Just Paranoia

Lorene Cary, in a cogent essay in *Newsweek*, expands on Reverend Tompkins' point. In an essay titled "Why It's Not Just Paranoia," she writes:

We Americans continue to value the lives and humanity of some groups more than the lives and humanity of others. That is not paranoia. It is our historical legacy and a present fact; it influences domestic and foreign policy and the daily interaction of millions of Americans. It influences the way we spend our public money and explains how we can read the staggering statistics on Black Americans' infant mortality, youth mortality, mortality in middle and old age, and not be moved to action.

African Americans' beliefs that their lives are devalued by White society also influence their relationships with the medical profession. They perceive, at times correctly, that they are treated differently in the healthcare system solely because of their race, and such perceptions fuel mistrust of the medical profession. For example, a national telephone survey conducted in 1986 revealed that African Americans were more likely than Whites to report that their physicians did not inquire sufficiently about their pain, did not tell them how long it would take for prescribed medicine to work, did not explain the seriousness of their illness or injury, and did not discuss test and examination findings. A 1994 study published in the *American Journal of Public Health* found that physicians were less likely to give pregnant Black women information about the hazards of smoking and drinking during pregnancy.

The powerful legacy of the Tuskegee Syphilis Study endures, in part, because the racism and disrespect for Black lives that it entailed mirror Black people's contemporary experiences with the medical profession. The anger and frustration that many African Americans feel when they encounter the healthcare system can be heard in the words of Alicia Georges, a professor of nursing at Lehman College and a former president of the National Black Nurses Association, as she recalled an emergency room experience. "Back a few years ago, I was having excruciating abdominal pain, and I wound up at a hospital in my area," she recalled. "The first thing that they began to ask me was how many sexual partners I'd had. I was married and owned my own house. But immediately, in looking at me, they said, 'Oh, she just has pelvic inflammatory disease.'" Perhaps because of her nursing background, Georges recognized the implications of the questioning. She had come face to face with the stereotype of Black women as sexually promiscuous. Similarly, the following story from the *Los Angeles Times* shows how racism can affect the practice of medicine:

When Althea Alexander broke her arm, the attending resident at Los Angeles County-USC Medical Center told her to "hold your arm like you usually hold your can of beer on Saturday night." Alexander who is Black, exploded. "What are you talking about? Do you think I'm a welfare mother?"

The White resident shrugged: "Well aren't you?" Turned out she was an administrator at USC medical school.

This example graphically illustrates that healthcare providers are not immune to the beliefs and misconceptions of the wider community. They carry with them stereotypes about various groups of people.

Beyond Tuskegee

There is also a growing body of medical research that vividly illustrates why discussions of the relationship of African Americans and the medical profession must go beyond the Tuskegee Syphilis Study. These studies demonstrate racial inequities in access to particular technologies and raise critical questions about the role of racism in medical decision making. For example, in 1989 *The Journal of the American Medical Association* published a report that demonstrated racial inequities in the treatment of heart disease. In this study, White and Black patients had similar rates of hospitalization for chest pain, but the White patients were one third more likely to undergo coronary angiography and more than twice as likely to be treated with bypass surgery or angioplasty. The racial disparities persisted even after adjustments were made for differences in income. Three years later, another study appearing in that journal reinforced these findings. It revealed that older Black patients on Medicare received coronary artery bypass grafts only about a fourth as often as comparable White patients. Disparities were greatest in the rural South, where White patients had the surgery seven times as often as Black patients. Medical factors did not fully explain the differences. This study suggests that an already-existing national health insurance program does not solve the access problems of African Americans. Additional studies have confirmed the persistence of such inequities.

Why the racial disparities? Possible explanations include health problems that precluded the use of procedures, patient unwillingness to accept medical advice or to undergo surgery, and differences in severity of illness. However, the role of racial bias cannot be discounted, as the American Medical Association's Council on Ethical and Judicial Affairs has recognized. In a 1990 report on Black-White disparities in healthcare, the council asserted:

Because racial disparities may be occurring despite the lack of any intent or purposeful efforts to treat patients differently on the basis of race, physicians should examine their own practices to ensure that inappropriate considerations do not affect their clinical judgment. In addition, the profession should help increase the awareness of its members of racial disparities in medical treatment decisions by engaging in open and broad discussions about the issue. Such discussions should take place as part of the medical school curriculum, in medical journals, at professional conferences, and as part of professional peer review activities.

The council's recommendation is a strong acknowledgment that racism can influence the practice of medicine.

After the public disclosures of the Tuskegee Syphilis Study, Congress passed the National Research Act of 1974. This act, established to protect subjects in human experimentation, mandates institutional review board approval of all federally funded research with human subjects. However, recent revelations about a measles vaccine study financed by the Centers for Disease Control and Prevention (CDC) demonstrate the inadequacies of these safeguards and illustrate why African Americans' historically based fears of medical research persist. In 1989, in the midst of a measles epidemic in Los Angeles, the CDC, in collaboration with Kaiser Permanente and the Los Angeles County Health Department, began a study to test whether the experimental Edmonston-Zagreb vaccine could be used to immunize children too young for the standard Moraten vaccine. By 1991, approximately 900 infants, mostly Black and Latino, had received the vaccine without difficulties. (Apparently, one infant died for reasons not related to the inoculations.) But the infants' parents had not been informed that the vaccine was not licensed in the United States or that it had been associated with an increase in death rates in Africa. The 1996 disclosure of the study prompted charges of medical racism and of the continued exploitation of minority communities by medical professionals.

The Tuskegee Syphilis Study continues to cast its shadow over the lives of African Americans. For many Black people, it has come to represent the racism that pervades American institutions and the disdain in which Black lives are often held. But despite its significance, it cannot be the only prism we use to examine the relationship of African Americans with the medical and public health communities. The problem we must face is not just the shadow of Tuskegee but the shadow of racism that so profoundly affects the lives and beliefs of all people in this country.

REFERENCES

A list of references is available in the original source.

"#BlackLivesMatter: Physicians Must Stand for Racial Justice"

From the White Coats for Black Lives (WC4BL) National Working Group

SECOND THOUGHTS American Medical Association Journal of Ethics October 2015, Volume 17, Number 10: 978–982. The viewpoints expressed in this article are those of the author(s) and do not necessarily reflect the views and policies of the AMA.

Racism is one of the major causes of health problems in the United States. Between 1970 and 2004, the Black-white mortality gap resulted in more than 2.7 million excess Black deaths [1], making racism[1] a more potent killer than prostate, breast, or colon cancer [2]. Physicians are intimately involved with institutions that contribute to the victimization of Black people and other people of color. As is widely documented, Black and Latino patients are less likely to receive the care they need, including adequate analgesia,[2] cancer screening, and organ transplants [3–6]. This is due both to physician bias and to the health care payment structure's financial disincentives for the care of people of color [7]—clinicians are paid less to care for patients who are uninsured, underinsured, or publicly insured, and these patients are disproportionately people of color. As a consequence, people of color are often denied access to the health care they need [8, 9].

These disparities in access to health care exacerbate the harm that social structures and policies cause to the health of people of color. Black and Latino people are disproportionately victimized by police violence, mass incarceration, and poverty [10–12]. Moreover, despite perceived improvements, rates of racial segregation across the country remain comparable to levels in the 1940s, and people of color face discrimination in their efforts to access adequate housing, quality education, and meaningful employment [13–16]. The harmful effects of structural inequity are augmented by the subjective experience of racism: for example, awareness of one's race[3] is correlated with increased diastolic blood pressure among Black patients [17].

Addressing racism and its consequences, therefore, should be a central task of American medicine; physicians must work both within and outside the health care system to eliminate inequities in access to and delivery of care. Health professionals and community organizations ranging from the Black Panther Party to the National Latina Institute for Reproductive Health have long proposed effective strategies for addressing racism to improve the health of people of color, including expansion of free clinics, increased research[4] on diseases affecting people of color, and legislative establishment of paid parental leave [18, 19]. Recent incidents and protests in Charleston, Baltimore, New York, and other cities across the country have reminded us of the urgency of acting on these and other proposals to address racism in medicine.

In particular, we, as members of the National Working Group of the medical student organization White Coats for Black Lives, suggest four ways that physicians and other health professionals can immediately pursue racial justice. The first is to more aggressively recruit,[5] support, and promote Black, Latino, and Native American people in medicine to ensure that the physician workforce reflects the diversity of the United States. Black and Latino people represent roughly 30 percent of our nation's population but make up only 8.5 percent of the physician workforce [20]. Physicians of color are more

[1] http://journalofethics.ama-assn.org/2011/02/msoc1-1102.html
[2] http://journalofethics.ama-assn.org/2015/03/medu1-1503.html
[3] http://journalofethics.ama-assn.org/2014/06/stas2-1406.html
[4] http://journalofethics.ama-assn.org/2014/06/stas1-1406.html
[5] http://journalofethics.ama-assn.org/2015/02/oped1-1502.html

likely to provide care for America's underserved communities, and patients of color report higher satisfaction when their doctor shares their racial background [21–23]. Despite the Association of American Medical Colleges' Project 3000 by 2000 [24], the past three decades have witnessed little growth in the population of Latino, Black, and Native American physicians [20]. Increasing the numbers of Black, Latino, and Native American doctors is a key step in eliminating health inequities.

Secondly, hospitals and practices must take action to eliminate the significant impact of implicit racial biases on the care of patients of color [7]. To counteract these subtle forms of racism, institutions must routinely administer implicit association tests to their medical staffs to make them cognizant of their unconscious biases and then train[6] their medical staffs to consciously overcome those biases when delivering care [25]. Furthermore, hospitals should create formal and informal structures to encourage accountability for incidents that may have involved racism. This can be done by fostering a work environment that makes it safe for colleagues to question each other's biased actions and by using structured venues such as morbidity and mortality conferences to discuss ways that racism may have impacted the quality of patient care.

Thirdly, physicians should join community members in advocating for a single-payer health care system[7] as a means of eliminating cost-associated barriers to care. In addition to improving access for all patients, a single-payer system would eliminate insurance-status discrimination and ensure that reimbursements for services provided to white patients and patients of color are equal.

Finally, health care workers must recognize that our responsibility[8] to our patients goes beyond physical exams, prescriptions, and surgical interventions; we must work to alter[9] socioeconomic and environmental factors, including structural racism,[10] that directly affect our patients' health. The manifestations of structural racism are varied and ubiquitous; addressing them will require joining movements to increase the minimum wage, end criminalizing school discipline practices, and develop mixed-income housing, among many others. In doing so, physicians will need to partner with and take direction from community members who have experienced systemic oppression and are dedicated to working to dismantle it. We will not be able to solve the problems of racism in our society and in our health care system without the input of those most affected by it. In working to combat structural racism, physicians must not only listen to people of color in their practices and communities, but also amplify those voices while advocating[11] for equitable social structures. The privilege[12] that physicians possess within society and within the professional hierarchy of medicine provides them with power that can be used to spearhead policy changes to advance racial justice locally and nationally. Using this "physician privilege" to advocate for social change is necessary if we are to eradicate the systemic illness that is racism.

REFERENCES

1. Rodriguez JM, Geronimus AT, Bound J, Dorling D. Black lives matter: differential mortality and the racial composition of the US electorate, 1970–2004. *Soc Sci Med.* 2015;136–137:193–199.

2. American Cancer Society. Estimated deaths for the four major cancers by sex and age group, 2015. http://www.cancer.org/acs/groups/content/@editorial/documents/document/acspc-044509.pdf. Accessed June 28, 2015.

3. Agency for Healthcare Research and Quality. 2014 National healthcare quality and disparities report. Rockville, MD: Agency for Healthcare Research and Quality; May 2015. http://www.ahrq.gov/research/findings/nhqrdr/nhqdr14/2014nhqdr.pdf.Accessed June 28, 2015.

4. Tamayo-Sarver JH, Hinze SW, Cydulka RK, Baker DW. Racial and ethnic disparities in emergency department analgesic prescription. *Am J Public Health.* 2003; 93(12): 2067–2073.

5. Agency for Healthcare Research and Quality. *2013 National Healthcare Quality Report.* Rockville, MD: Agency for Healthcare Research and Quality; May 2014. http://www.ahrq.gov/research/findings/nhqrdr/nhqr13/2013nhqr.pdf.Accessed June 28, 2015.

6. Churak JM. Racial and ethnic disparities in renal transplantation. *J Natl Med Assoc.*2005;97(2):153–160.

7. Chapman EN, Kaatz A, Carnes M. Physicians and implicit bias: how doctors may unwittingly perpetuate health care disparities. *J Gen Intern Med.*2013;28(11):1504–1510.

8. Hing E, Decker S, Jamoom E. Acceptance of new patients with public and private insurance by office-based physicians: United States, 2013. *NCHS Data Brief.*2015;(195):1–8.

9. Kaiser Family Foundation. Health coverage by race and ethnicity: the potential impact of the Affordable Care Act. March 13, 2013. http://kff.org/disparities-policy/issue-brief/health-coverage-by-race-and-ethnicity-the-potential-impact-of-the-affordable-care-act/. Accessed June 28, 2015.

10. Sadler MS, Correll J, Park B, Judd CM. The world is not black and white: racial bias in the decision to shoot in a multi ethnic context. *J Soc Issues.* 2012;68(2):286–313.

11. Kramer MR, Hogue CR. Is segregation bad for your health? *Epidemiol Rev.*2009;31(1):178–194.

12. The Sentencing Project. Reducing racial disparity in the criminal justice system: a manual for practitioners and policymakers. Washington, DC: The Sentencing Project;

---

[6] http://journalofethics.ama-assn.org/2014/06/medu1-1406.html

[7] http://journalofethics.ama-assn.org/2012/11/oped1-1211.html

[8]http://journalofethics.ama-assn.org/2014/09/oped1-1409.html

[9] http://journalofethics.ama-assn.org/2014/09/ecas2-1409.html

[10] http://journalofethics.ama-assn.org/2014/09/spec1-1409.html

---

[11] http://journalofethics.ama-assn.org/2014/09/coet1-1409.html

[12] http://journalofethics.ama-assn.org/2014/09/ecas1-1409.html

2008. http://www.sentencingproject.org/doc/publications/rd_reducingracialdisparity.pdf. Accessed June 28, 2015.

13. Shapiro T, Meschede T, Osoro S. Research and policy brief: the roots of the widening racial wealth gap: explaining the black-white economic divide. Waltham, MA: Brandeis University Institute on Assets and Social Policy; February 2013. http://iasp.brandeis.edu/pdfs/Author/shapiro-thomas-m/racialwealthgapbrief.pdf. Accessed June 28, 2015.

14. Fryer RG Jr, Pager D, Spenkuch JL. Racial disparities in job finding and offered wages. *J Law Econ.* 2013;56(3):633–689.

15. American Psychological Association Presidential Task Force on Educational Disparities. *Ethnic And Racial Disparities in Education: Psychology's Contributions to Understanding and Reducing Disparities.* August 3, 2012. http://www.apa.org/ed/resources/racial-disparities.pdf. Accessed June 28,2015.

16. Williams DR, Collins C. Racial residential segregation: a fundamental cause of racial disparities in health. *Public Health Rep.* 2001;116(5):404–416.

17. Brewer LC, Carson KA, Williams DR, Allen A, Jones CP, Cooper LA. Association of race consciousness with the patient-physician relationship, medication adherence, and blood pressure in urban primary care patients. *Am J Hypertens.*2013;26(11):1346–1352.

18. Nelson A. *Body and Soul: The Black Panther Party and the Fight Against Medical Discrimination.* Minneapolis, MN: University of Minnesota Press; 2013.

19. Center for Reproductive Rights; National Latina Institute for Reproductive Health; SisterSong Women of Color Reproductive Justice Collective. Reproductive injustice: racial and gender discrimination in US health care: a shadow report for the UN Committee on the Elimination of Racial Discrimination. 2014. http://www.reproductiverights.org/sites/crr.civicactions.net/files/documents/CERD_Shadow_US.pdf. Accessed July 24, 2015.

20. Association of American Medical Colleges. Diversity in the physician workforce: facts & figures 2014. http://aamcdiversityfactsandfigures.org. Accessed June 28,2015.

21. Marrast LM, Zallman L, Woolhandler S, Bor DH, McCormick D. Minority physicians' role in the care of underserved patients: diversifying the physician workforce may be key in addressing health disparities. *JAMA Intern Med.*2014;174(2):289–291.

22. Saha S, Komaromy M, Koepsell TD, Bindman AB. Patient-physician racial concordance and the perceived quality and use of health care. *Arch Intern Med.*1999;159(9):997–1004.

23. Cooper LA, Roter DL, Johnson RL, Ford DE, Steinwachs DM, Powe NR. Patient-centered communication, ratings of care, and concordance of patient and physician race. *Ann Intern Med.* 2003;139(11):907–915.

24. Nickens HW, Ready TP, Petersdorf RG. Project 3000 by 2000: racial and ethnic diversity in US medical schools. *New Engl J Med.* 1994;331(7):472–476.

25. Green AR, Carney DR, Pallin DJ, et al. Implicit bias among physicians and its prediction of thrombolysis decisions for black and white patients. *J Gen Intern Med.* 2007;22(9):1231–1238.

White Coats for Black Lives (WC4BL) is a national medical student organization devoted to safeguarding the lives of patients through the elimination of racism. The WC4BL National Working Group endeavors to raise awareness of racism as a public health concern that threatens the lives and health of people of color, end racial discrimination in the delivery of health care, and prepare future physicians to be advocates for racial justice. WC4BL encourages medical professionals to create a physician workforce that reflects the diversity of our nation by actively recruiting and supporting Black, Latino, and Native American people through medical school and into their careers.

Related in the *AMA Journal of Ethics*

Education to Identify and Combat Racial Bias in Pain Treatment,[13] March 2015

Structural Competency Meets Structural Racism: Race, Politics, and the Structure of Medical Knowledge,[14] September 2014

Complex Systems for a Complex Issue: Race in Health Research,[15] June 2014

Race: A Starting Place,[16] June 2014

"Vulnerable" Populations—Medicine, Race, and Presumptions of Identity,[17] February 2011

Race, Discrimination, and Cardiovascular Disease,[18] June 2014

A Call to Service: Social Justice Is a Public Health Issue,[19] September 2014

Advocacy by Physicians for Patients and for Social Change,[20] September 2014

The AMA *Code of Medical Ethics*' Opinion on Physician Advocacy,[21] September 2014

The viewpoints expressed in this article are those of the author(s) and do not necessarily reflect the views and policies of the AMA.

[13] http://journalofethics.ama-assn.org/2015/03/medu1-1503.html
[14] http://journalofethics.ama-assn.org/2014/09/spec1-1409.html
[15] http://journalofethics.ama-assn.org/2014/06/stas1-1406.html
[16] http://journalofethics.ama-assn.org/2014/06/msoc1-1406.html
[17] http://journalofethics.ama-assn.org/2011/02/msoc1-1102.html
[18] http://journalofethics.ama-assn.org/2014/06/stas2-1406.html
[19] http://journalofethics.ama-assn.org/2014/09/ecas2-1409.html
[20] http://journalofethics.ama-assn.org/2014/09/jdsc1-1409.html
[21] http://journalofethics.ama-assn.org/2014/09/coet1-1409.html

"Immigrant Women's Health A Casualty in the Immigration Policy War"

By Aishia Glasford and Priscilla Huang
For the *National Women's Health Network*
Article taken from March/April 2008 Newsletter

As the immigration policy battles rage in legislatures and presidential primaries and state elections throughout the country, there's been little attention to a serious casualty in these skirmishes: immigrant women's health. Immigrant women are facing serious threats to their health, and in the most dire cases, have even lost their lives as a result of problems in this broken system. Rosa Isela Contreras-Dominguez and Victoria Arrellano died in Federal custody awaiting deportation to Mexico; Contreras-Dominguez was 38 and pregnant at the time of her death, and Arrellano who had AIDS, deteriorated steadily in a San Pedro, California prison, eventually dying there at the age of 23.[1] In another tragic loss, Jiang Zhen Xing, pregnant with twins miscarried when Immigration and Customs Enforcement officials tried to forcibly deport her.[2] Among the estimated 37.5 million foreign-born people living in the United States, there are probably tens of thousands more women experiencing serious health and reproductive health problems that are being made worse by the violence, discrimination, and hurdles that U.S. immigration policy perpetuates.

The National Coalition for Immigrant Women's Rights (NCIWR) was formed in 2006 to bring a gender perspective to the immigration debate and to advocate for a truly comprehensive reform of the broken immigration system that is devastating the lives of women like Contreras-Dominguez, Arrellano, and Jiang and their families. One of NCIWR's goals is to bring to light the harm being done to immigrant women and their children's health as they attempt to secure the most basic rights, such as access to healthcare and reproductive health services.

Welfare, Immigration Reform and Immigrant Women's Healthcare

In 2006, approximately 12.5 percent of the total U.S. population was foreign-born.[3] (The term "foreign-born" describes anyone who is a naturalized citizen, legal permanent resident, or undocumented immigrant.[4]) About 53 percent of the U.S. foreign-born population immigrated from Latin America, 25 percent from Asia, and 14 percent from Europe.[5] Foreign-born women, who represent five percent of the total U.S. population, are twice as likely as their male counterparts to be widowed, divorced, or separated.[6] They are also more likely than U.S.-born women to live in poverty, be unemployed, and lack health insurance. Approximately 42 percent of immigrant women are of reproductive age (between 25–44 years of age), compared to 26 percent of native-born women.[6]

U.S. immigration laws and policies have restricted the mobility, status, and livelihood of immigrant women since the country began regulating its borders. In fact, the United States' first immigration law, the 1875 Page Law, targeted Asian women, particularly Chinese women. While the law specifically prohibited the entry of Chinese prostitutes, in practice it was intended to prevent wives and prospective brides of Chinese laborers from joining their husbands in the U.S. (Notably, many immigration scholars cite the 1882 Chinese Exclusion Act as the nation's first U.S. immigration law, however, the Page Law pre-dated this Act.)

Until the mid-1990's, immigrants were generally eligible for public benefit programs, such as Medicaid, on the same basis as their native-born counterparts. In 1996, however, the Welfare Reform Act (formally called the "Personal Responsibility and Work Opportunity Reconciliation Act of 1996," P.L. 104–193) and Illegal Immigration Reform and Immigrant Responsibility Act (IIRIRA) both made it increasingly difficult for immigrant women to flourish in their new homeland by creating barriers to accessing social services such as healthcare.

One of the Welfare Reform Act's most onerous provisions narrowed Medicaid eligibility criteria by imposing a "five-year bar" to access on most new immigrants. Thus, immigrant women who enter the country after August 22, 1996 must continuously reside in the U.S. for five years before becoming eligible for Federally funded health programs. Consequently, State and local governments which value the importance of a social net of services for both immigrant and U.S.-born residents must now use their own funds to extend public health programs to new immigrants. In addition, IIRIRA made it more difficult for immigrants to establish their income eligibility for Medicaid, even after reaching the five-year barrier. The law requires new immigrants with sponsors to include (or "deem") their sponsors' income when applying for Federal benefits. Thus, deeming and sponsor liability rules often render many immigrant women ineligible for services even after they have been in the U.S. for the required five years.

Both Acts restrict newly arriving, low-income immigrant women from accessing Federal benefits, and compound the financial strain and hardship that many immigrant families face when they first enter the country. (It is important to specify that neither welfare nor immigration "reform" laws changed the eligibility requirements for undocumented immigrants, who have always been ineligible for Medicaid and most other entitlement benefits.)

Impact on Immigrant Women

In 1996, when immigrants and native-born citizens had similar eligibility for public benefit programs, immigrants represented just 9 percent of the U.S. population and 15 percent of all welfare recipients.[7] By 1999, the number of immigrant welfare recipients dropped to 12 percent.[7] The number of low-income, immigrant children and parents receiving Medicaid fell by 7–8 percent between 1995–2000, while the same population experienced a 6–7 percent increase in un-insurance rates during the same period.[7]

The decline in welfare and Medicaid utilization by immigrant women was partly due to the increased restrictions imposed by the 1996 reforms. In addition, these policies created a chilling effect that discouraged Medicaid use even by immigrants who were eligible for, and needed, such services. As a result, thousands of eligible immigrant women and children have not accessed public programs and services for which they are eligible—including Medicaid and the State Children's Health Insurance Program (SCHIP)—and must either pay out-of-pocket for care or go without it altogether.[8]

The situation is far worse for undocumented immigrants. These individuals are eligible for services under Emergency Medicaid, but treatment is limited to serious health emergencies such as labor and childbirth. Therefore, most undocumented women forgo routine healthcare, including prenatal care and other preventive reproductive health services.

The Impact of Immigration Status, Economic Injustice, and Violence on Immigrant Women

Many immigrant women who wish to obtain a viable path of entry and citizenship to the U.S. face bleak prospects. Many U.S. citizens do not realize that obtaining a visa for entry to this country is a far more complicated and lengthy process than obtaining a passport or a driver's license. Applicants are routinely denied visas to travel to the U.S. Immigration procedures for both entry to the U.S. and citizenship are long, arduous, and extremely expensive. It takes many months of paperwork, large administrative and legal fees (up to thousands of dollars), and intense interviews with foreign consulate and immigration officers before one can get a visa or become a legal permanent resident (the first step to becoming a citizen). This process requires immigrant women to navigate a system that many trained immigration attorneys have difficulty fully understanding. The system's challenges mean that many immigrant women enter the U.S. without immigration documents (e.g., a visa).

Many other immigrant women enter the U.S. with some form of immigration status, such as a student, work, or tourist visa. Yet, they can easily lose this immigration status and become undocumented when their visa expires. This is common, because the U.S. immigration system is slow to notify visa holders and citizenship applicants of changes in their immigration status and/or relevant immigration rules.

For many immigrant women, the lack of documented immigration status and/or confusion over their status is a huge obstacle to accessing care, because access to publicly funded programs is now usually contingent upon one's immigration status. Moreover, lacking (or losing) immigration status endangers immigrant women because it makes them vulnerable to manipulation, coercion, and exploitation at the hands of employers, traffickers, smugglers, or intimate partners. Women who lack (or are unsure they have) immigration status are often forced to accept low-paying jobs where they are easily exploited. Domestic service, child care, agricultural work, nail salons, sweatshops, and forced sex work are a few industries in which exploitation can occur.

Immigrant women's working conditions are often deplorable and sometimes illegal, and may expose them to toxic chemicals, pesticides, poor ventilation, and dangerous equipment. Many immigrant women work long hours for little pay, without health benefits, and with no job security. For example, in 2001, 41 percent of immigrant women did not have health insurance.[9]

In 2000, 85 percent of migrant and seasonal farm worker women were uninsured,[10] of whom only 42 percent accessed prenatal care during their first trimester of pregnancy, compared to 76 percent of pregnant women nationally.[11] Exploitative working conditions are a covert form of violence, as these workers are exploited precisely because they tend to be undocumented. Immigrant women also experience overt violence including physical, emotional, and/or sexual abuse by their employers, traffickers, and/or intimate partners. Immigrant women may be raped or harassed by those who have power over them. Women may also be forced to remain in abusive relationships or employment when their undocumented status is used to intimidate them from reporting abuse to the authorities.

The Lack of Information on Immigrant Women's Reproductive Health Disparities

Compared to native-born women, immigrant women are more likely to have lower incomes, educational attainment, and acculturation levels; they are more likely to be uninsured and to lack awareness about preventative care and physician referrals. In addition, approximately 30 percent of immigrant households are linguistically isolated (defined by the U.S. Census Bureau as "a household in which all members 14 years old and over speak a non-English language and also have difficulty speaking English")[12] Linguistic isolation creates significant barriers to accessing reproductive and maternal health services. Studies have found that linguistically isolated individuals receive far fewer preventative services than English-speakers (including Pap tests, mammograms, and prenatal care).[13] These factors play important roles in if, how, and when immigrant women access healthcare.

While the consequence of the broken immigration system, economic exploitation, and violence is a multitude of reproductive health disparities for immigrant women, these negative outcomes remain hard to see because they are not adequately captured by current research. Statistical data on reproductive health disparities are not disaggregated by race, ethnicity and immigration status; thus, existing data are likely to be skewed and to underreport immigrant women's health problems. This means that an Afro-Latina immigrant woman may be categorized as African-American rather than as an immigrant or as Latina. The lack of specific information about foreign-born women is important because, as noted, immigrant women experience different constraints than native-born women, (including native born women of color) and require different strategies to increase their access to preventive and reproductive healthcare. Without such strategies we will continue to see in States, for example, with large Latina immigrant populations, disparities in access to services such as prenatal care: in 2002, 87.2 percent of White women in Arizona began prenatal care in the first trimester, compared to just 66.7 percent of Latinas who did so.[14]

The paucity of data on foreign-born women's health outcomes makes it hard to assess either the number of women who receive appropriate reproductive health services or strategies to improve their access to needed care. This problem is compounded by the fact that policymakers have failed to support funding and opportunities to study immigrant women's health in order to identify and address these disparities. Without such research, it is impossible to develop policies and programs that provide immigrant women with the care needed to protect their own and their children's health.

Policy Recommendations

In order to address the legal and reproductive health needs of immigrant women and their children, NCIWR advocates several policy recommendations:

- Comprehensive immigration reform must include legal and safe immigration options for undocumented men, women, and children; and a path to citizenship that allows immigrant women to obtain work permits, travel internationally, and access higher education and Federal financial aid.
- Reproductive healthcare coverage that is financed through public funds must be provided to all

immigrant women regardless of their legal or economic status.

- Equitable access must be guaranteed to confidential and non-coercive family planning services; and to linguistically, culturally competent, and medically accurate reproductive healthcare services.

- Funding must be provided to research specific data on the reproductive health disparities, needs, and services for immigrant women, as well as for outreach to engage immigrant women and their children in care.

- Federal policy should impose a moratorium on immigration raids, and ensure better access to medical and legal services for immigrant women held in detention centers.

The National Coalition for Immigrant Women's Rights is working to eradicate discriminatory practices in public policies that impact the reproductive health and well-being of immigrant women. As part of the Coalition's principles of defending and protecting the well-being of immigrant women, their children, and their communities, NCIWR will tackle immigration reform, reproductive health and wellness, and labor policies and practices. NCIWR seeks to highlight not only immigrant women's lives but also U.S. policies and practices that impact these women's lives. In doing so, the NCIWR will also confront a society that has, for too long, contributed to the violence perpetrated against immigrant women, and advocate for enforcement policies and a judicial system that treats immigrant women with respect and dignity.

For further information about the NCIWR, please contact Aishia Glasford at Aishia@latinainstitute.org, or Priscilla Huang at phuang@napawf.org.

REFERENCES

1. Fears D, "Three Jailed Immigrants Die in a Month," The *Washington Post*, August 15, 2007, page A02. Retrieved September 10, 2007 from http://www.washingtonpost .com/wp-dyn/content/article/2007/08/14/ AR2007081401690.html

2. Huang P, "Which Babies Are Real Americans?" Tom-Paine.com, February 20, 2007. Retrieved September 10, 2007 from http://www.tompaine.com/articles/2007/02/20/ which_babies_are_real_americans.php.

3. U.S. Census Bureau, 2006 American Community Survey Data Profile Highlights, Washington, DC: US Census Bureau, 2006. Retrieved September 12, 2007 from http:// factfinder.census.gov/servlet/ACSSAFFFacts?_event=& geo_id=01000US&_geoContext=01000US&_street=& _county=&_cityTown=&_state=&_zip=&_lang=en&_sse =on&ActiveGeoDiv=&_ useEV=&pctxt=fph&pgsl=010&_submenuId=factsheet_ 1&ds_name=DEC_2000_SAFF&_ci_nbr=107& qr_name=DEC_2000_SAFF_R1010®=DEC_2000_ SAFF_R1010%3A107&_keyword=&_industry=.

4. U.S. Census Bureau, The Foreign-Born Population in the United States: 2003, Washington DC: US Census Bureau, August 2004, page 1. Retrieved February 6, 2008 from http://www.census.gov/prod/2004pubs/p20-551.pdf.

5. U.S. Census Bureau, 2006 American Community Survey Origins and Language, Washington, DC: U.S. Census Bureau, 2006. Retrieved September 12, 2007 from http://factfinder.census.gov/servlet/ACSSAFFPeople?_ event=&geo_id=01000US&_geoContext=01000US&_ street=&_county=&_cityTown=&_state=&_zip=&_lang= en&_sse=on&ActiveGeoDiv=&_useEV=&pctxt=fph &pgsl=010&_submenuId=people_8&ds_name=null&_ ci_nbr=107&qr_name=DEC_2000_SAFF_R1010®=DEC_ 2000_SAFF_R1010%3A107&_keyword=&_industry=

6. Greico E, U.S. in Focus: Immigrant Women, Washington DC: Migration Policy Institute, May 2002. Retrieved January 6, 2008 from http://www.migrationinformation. org/USFocus/display.cfm?ID=2.

Primary Health Care and the LGBTQIA+ Patient Experience

By Kristin Puhl, M.S.,
University of Washington School of Medicine

Sexual minority patients, including but not limited to patients who are gay, lesbian, bisexual, asexual, transgender, intersex, are already negatively affected by social stigma. These patients have more difficulty accessing care than otherwise similar cisgender, heterosexual patients (Albuquerque et al., 2016). When they do access care, sexual minority patients have worse healthcare experiences and outcomes than patients who are cisgender and heterosexual (Elliott et al., 2014), and guidelines for their care are often absent or insufficient (McNair & Hegarty, 2010). The prevalence of sexual minority status in the population is notoriously difficult to ascertain, due to social pressures that discourage people from disclosing. Current estimates suggest that anywhere from 3 to 15 percent of people can be classified as sexual minority (Ellis, Robb, & Burke, 2005). In the United States, a country with a population of over 300 million, that means there is a minimum of 9 million patients to whom the issue of high-quality care for sexual minority patients is highly, personally relevant.

What does high-quality healthcare mean for a sexual minority patient? Gender identity and sexual orientation vary widely, and may result in healthcare issues unique to each patient. A gay man, a lesbian, a bisexual patient, a transgender patient—all may have unique concerns, not shared with each other or with other people who fall under the sexual minority umbrella. Risk profiles between different subgroups vary (Smalley, Warren, & Barefoot, 2015). Even within groups, there can be profound differences in healthcare needs. An intersex patient who was born with genitalia considered "ambiguous" may have a very different history from a patient who was assigned male at birth and had no cause to question the physiological assumptions carried by that gender assignment until the discovery of chromosomal variance later in life. The acronym LGBTQIA+ (lesbian, gay, bisexual, transgender, queer, intersex, asexual, and others), although widely used, does not necessarily capture all potential orientations or identities. People may identify as nonbinary, for example, or demisexual, relatively recent terms that have not made their way into the common cultural lexicon and that are virtually nonexistent in research literature. Research literature through the 1990s and into the 2000s rarely identified even bisexual participants as distinct from homosexual participants.

Healthcare providers can be helpful or harmful to sexual minority patients in many ways. Asexual patients often face disbelief from providers who were never educated about asexuality, and as a result, these patients may never disclose, or may face unwanted education about issues that are irrelevant to their health. Lesbian patients may be given education or testing that is inappropriate due to assumptions that "sexual activity" is synonymous with penile-vaginal intercourse. Bisexual patients may be denied education or testing that would be beneficial. Transgender patients may be forced to jump through bureaucratic hoops in order to obtain even basic care for transition, and unrelated medical problems may be interpreted as a result of transition, with consequent delay of appropriate care. This means that on a daily basis, doctors across the country are wasting time, both their patients' and their own, and at times actively harming their therapeutic relationships with patients. The consequences of lack of trust between providers and patients have meaningful consequences for patient health; for example, trans men are less likely to receive Pap smears than cis women (Petzmeier, Khullar, Reisner, & Potter, 2014). Sexual minority women have reported greater dissatisfaction with their primary care providers than non-sexual minority women, which undermines the quality of the therapeutic relationship (Mosack, Brouwer, & Petroll, 2013) and could result in delaying or avoiding care.[1]

High-quality care means that patients receive, or are at least offered, the care that is appropriate for them. Smokers should be offered counseling on quitting. People with prostates should be offered digital rectal exams. Individualizing patient care requires a trusting, high-quality therapeutic relationship, particularly with respect to sexual activity, which is a difficult topic for many patients and providers to discuss. Failure to individualize care leads to patients who have questions that are not answered during the course of a clinical encounter and issues that are never addressed. Sexual minority patients, from adolescence to adulthood, have worse health outcomes than cisgender heterosexual patients (Coker, Austin, & Schuster, 2010; Hutchinson, Thompson, & Cederbaum, 2006). Most medical research on health for sexual minority patients examines outcomes, but the patients themselves are rarely given a voice. Previous work specifically addressing this has been highly limited (Koh, Kang, & Usherwood, 2014). What does healthcare for sexual minority patients look like from the other side of the table?

In this study, sexual minority patients were asked to describe their experiences with the healthcare system—specifically, with primary care providers (PCPs). This includes a family doctor, an internal medicine doctor, or any other provider on the "front line" of medicine.

Developing guidelines and care strategies for PCPs that help effectively educate physicians and healthcare providers about the needs of sexual minority patients begins with finding out what sexual minority patients experience when they attempt to access primary care.

Methods

This study was designed as a cross-sectional survey of adult LGBTQIA+ patients, with both constrained and free response items. The proposal was approved by the University of Washington Institutional Review Board.

Recruitment was carried out through multiple online pathways. Posts linking to the survey were made on social media websites, including Twitter, Reddit, Facebook, and Tumblr. Repeated posting using tags or on boards relevant to the LGBTQIA+ community and/or healthcare yielded the largest number of partici-

pants. Outreach to chronically underrepresented sexual minority groups, most notably people of color, transgender individuals, and intersex individuals, included posting to message boards and tags specific to those groups.

Analyses included both quantitative analysis of constrained response items and qualitative textual analysis of free-response items.

Participants reported a diverse array of identities. Many identities were described as overlapping, with respondents describing themselves as "trans/genderqueer," or "queer/bisexual," for example. For coding numeric variables for use in analyses, if one term was given predominance (an alternate term in parentheses, for example), it was used. Otherwise, the first term listed was used.

Results

Descriptive Statistics. Recruitment efforts yielded a total of 980 respondents; 687 adult respondents identified as sexual minority and completed at least one question beyond consent. These participants were included in analysis, with 681 completing the entire survey. Mean age of participants was 27.82 years (SD = 8.47, min = 18, max = 78), and participants were primarily White (81.8%), with the remaining participants being mixed-race (5.5%), Hispanic/Latino (4.5%), Asian (3.8%), Black (2.6%), or other or unknown (1.7%). Participants were predominantly from urban areas (52%), with 38% percent from suburban and 10% percent from rural areas.

Sexual orientation and gender identity information was collected using free-text response options. For sexual orientation, participants reported self-identifying as homosexual (20.5%), bisexual (29.7%), pansexual (11.6%), asexual (17.2%), demisexual (4.8%), queer (12.8%), heterosexual (trans participants only; .9%), and other (2.5%). For gender identity, patients reported self-identifying as cis (53.3%), trans (11.6%), genderqueer or nonbinary (19.9%), or unknown (15.1%). Note that gender identity and sexual orientation variance might overlap (for example, a participant who identifies as both transgender and agender, or as biromantic asexual). Participants were roughly grouped according to whether they placed their gender somewhere within the binary spectrum or explicitly outside it based on their descriptions of themselves (cis women, trans women, and feminine-identified participants, 65.8%; cis men, trans men, and masculine-identified participants, 16.7%; non-binary or genderqueer participants, 15.1%; intersex, 0.4%; and unknown, 1.9%). Participant gender identity was not significantly associated with any other variables, although specific data on how participants believed their gender to be "read" by others were not collected.

---

[1]While this is still largely educated conjecture, consider the documented delay and avoidance of care that frequently results, especially for women, from experiences related to health care providers' weight bias, discussed elsewhere in this Ed.

Of respondents, 75.0% percent reported having a primary care provider, while 34.4% see a specialist for at least one specific health issue. A substantial proportion of patients see health care providers besides a doctor; 18.6% go to a specialized clinic for sexual health care; 23.4% percent see a nurse practitioner or other non-MD/DO healthcare provider; 8.9% see a provider for complementary and/or alternative medicine.

The majority of participants (70.2%) reported having a chronic medical condition. Patients were generally somewhat satisfied with care for their acute and/or chronic health problems. Fifty-four percent of the total, or 72.9% of those who had PCPs, responded that they felt they got adequate care from their primary care doctor for their acute or chronic health problems. Patients were also generally somewhat satisfied with care received for their reproductive and sexual needs (54.9% of the total sample, or 73.4% of those who had PCPs).

Most participants (67.8%) were out to most people in their life, 31.4% were not, and 0.7% did not respond to the question. With respect to their healthcare providers, 36.5% were out to their PCP, 39.6% were not, and 23.9% responded that it did not apply as they had no PCP. Of participants who had a PCP, therefore, 48.0% were out to them.

Of all patients, 37.6% reported having had a bad healthcare experience based on sexual orientation/gender identity; 61.7% had not, and 0.7% did not respond.

Patients overwhelmingly felt that medical students should receive training in sexual minority health issues, with 95.0% agreeing that medical students should have at least one class period devoted to LGBTQIA+ issues.

To help find appropriate care, 91.7% reported that they would want to know whether a provider was LGBTQIA+ friendly before scheduling an appointment. Specific actions that providers could take to increase patient comfort included (with percent of patients agreeing that it would help them feel more comfortable):

- Doctor's name badge has a rainbow sticker on it: **24.0%**
- Doctor's website has a section specifically for LGBTQIA+ patients: **62.0%**
- Doctor's office has flyers for LGBTQIA+ organizations, events, or issues posted: **64.5%**
- Doctor asks what your preferred name and pronouns are: **73.9%**
- Doctor's office intake forms have free text for gender and sexual orientation instead of checkboxes: **84.7%**
- Doctor is included in an online list of LGBTQIA+-friendly providers: **86.8%**

Chi-square. A chi-square test of independence was performed to examine the relationship between participant status as trans, cis, nonbinary, or unknown with likelihood of a negative physician experience. The relationship between these variables was significant, X^2 (3, $N = 682) = 16.26$, $p = .001$. Participants who identified as trans reported the highest percentage of having had at least one negative physician experiences (55.6%), followed by patients who identified as genderqueer, nonbinary, genderfluid, or agender (43.0%), then patients who identified as cis (33.2%). Patients whose gender identity was not specified were consistent with patients identifying as cis (33.6%).

An additional chi-square test of independence was performed to examine the relationship between being out to a primary care provider and having a negative experience with a physician. The relationship between these variables was significant, X^2 (1, $N = 522) = 28.9$, $p < .001$. More patients who were out to a primary care provider had had at least one negative experience with a physician (50.2%) than patients who were not out to a primary care provider (37.6%).

Textual analysis. Of the total number of participants, 273 (39.7%) described in their own words at least one negative experience with a physician. This number is greater than the percentage reporting at least one negative experience as a separate variable, because participants who were not out to their physicians and had had no negative experiences with them described their fear of a negative reaction as a negative experience in and of itself. Some participants described multiple events. Participants recounted a wide range of negative comments and behaviors from healthcare providers. Participants were asked about these experiences in general, not specifically restricted to primary care providers, but many of these experiences were in the context of seeking either primary or emergency care.

Some common themes emerged from analysis of text responses. The most common included:

- Providers failing to ask about, or give patients any chance to express, sexual minority status
- Providers expressing open disbelief about a patient's sexual orientation and/or gender identity
- Providers giving objectively inappropriate medical advice to patients
- Providers making openly bigoted statements to patients or within their hearing

Specific repeated issues involved physicians or other providers telling patients that women cannot transmit STDs through same-sex sexual contact. Patients with uteruses, whether cis, trans, or nonbinary, reported that physicians often assumed that they would desire to have children and would structure healthcare plans around this assumption without asking the patient or listening to the patient's own account of their goals. Participants from multiple groups reported that physicians sometimes over-disclosed or failed to protect their privacy, such as by loudly telling a nurse outside the exam room that the patient was trans or a lesbian.

Trans patients described repeated and sometimes openly malicious misgendering. Bisexual patients described providers assuming that they were unfaithful, promiscuous, and at high risk of STIs. People with trans partners who disclosed their partner's status to their physician reported misgendering of their partners and lack of acceptance on the part of the physician. There were few intersex participants, but those who responded to this question noted that doctors hid their intersex status from them until they were forced to disclose it, and that this had a negative impact on their ability to form trusting therapeutic relationships. Asexual patients reported that physicians did not believe them when they disclosed their sexual identity, called them "broken," or encouraged them to receive unnecessary medical care (e.g. STI testing for people who had never engaged in sexual activity; contraceptives for people who had no plans to engage in sexual activity).

Less frequent but more severe issues included providers associating sexual minority status with mental illness, making openly derogatory statements, or in some rare cases, engaging in behavior that threatened patient safety, such as refusing to provide care or, in the most extreme circumstance, committing sexual assault against the patient.

Some examples of specific patient statements included:

- "The few times I've told a doctor, typically someone I'm going to for reproductive healthcare, that I'm bisexual, I've felt judged. The response has typically been to move on right away—not necessarily rejecting, but certainly not a reaction that made me feel comfortable or confident."
- "I was told by a physician that it is not possible for two women to pass sexually transmitted diseases to one another."
- "My therapist didn't believe asexuality was a thing and I almost never came back. She believed me after I educated her but it's tiring."
- "Doctor refused to provide me birth control saying if I got pregnant I wouldn't be gay anymore."
- "I was reviewing my medical history with a specialist I had been referred to. He asked me why I had a vaginoplasty. I explained that I was a male-to-female transsexual. His manner completely

changed and after he left the examination room, I heard him through the door loudly referring to me by male pronouns."
- "Like most intersex people, my medical history was hidden from me as long as they could get away with it until abnormalities in puberty occurred. When it was revealed I felt lied to and still have trust issues and a fear of doctors."
- "My wife has had so many bad experiences with health care providers that just getting her to see one is a struggle. From incorrect pronouns to suggestions that she should take hormones, plus blatant anti-gay discrimination, healthcare is a permanent battle."
- "He slapped me."
- "I was raped by a doctor who discovered I was trans."

Discussion

Patients in the LGBTQIA+ community frequently find interaction with medical professionals to be fraught with challenges that are invisible to other patients. One example often used in teaching is the dysphoria trans patients may experience during a genital exam, which physicians can ameliorate or worsen, but there are dozens of ways for healthcare providers to express either support or discomfort during an encounter, and focusing on genitals even in sensitivity trainings may increase the perception that transgender issues can be reduced to genitals alone. Front-desk staff may be openly rude to patients who are not read as cisgender. Intake forms may constrain patients from reporting their identity fully and correctly unless they are willing to write it in, which may set up an adversarial dynamic from the start. More than a third (37.4%) of patients in this sample reported having had a negative experience with a healthcare provider that was specifically related to their sexual orientation and/or gender identity. That rate suggests that action is needed to decrease the stigmatization of sexual minority patients within the medical community.

Far fewer patients in this sample were out to their primary health care providers (48.0% of those who had a PCP) than to most people in their life (67.8%). The negative experiences that patients described with health care providers suggest a powerful rationale for this lower rate of disclosure, particularly in light of the relationship between disclosure of sexual minority status and negative provider experience. Sexual minority patients are essentially correct when they fear that coming out will increase their risk of being treated inappropriately or even abusively by providers.

Patients who have poor experiences with primary health care providers have had their trust in the therapeutic relationship shaken, and they often feel unsafe in what should be a deeply safe situation. Patients may also hear about negative healthcare encounters from friends within the community, and be hesitant to seek care or disclose to their physicians as a result of that.

Some patients described being out to their provider with respect to one aspect of their sexual identity (typically orientation), but not another (gender identity). This speaks to the fears that patients may have that providers may be accepting of some elements of their identity but not others, particularly when some identities (such as being trans) are more highly stigmatized.

The nature of sexual minority identity may be challenging for some providers. Identities may overlap or intersect. More participants in this survey identified as outside the gender binary—agender, bigender, genderfluid, or genderqueer—than identified within the better-known (and often heavily medicalized) model of trans identity, where the trans person feels a strong identification with a binary gender role (man or woman) other than the one to which they were assigned at birth based on their genitals. Patients outside the gender binary often feel that they are coerced into reporting that their own experiences fit the societally constructed narrative of trans-ness in order to receive care (Budge, Rossman, & Howard, 2014). This emphasizes the importance of active listening; providers who start by asking the patient open-ended, inclusive questions are likely to have more success in eliciting medically pertinent details, as well as building trust with patients.

Asexual patients reported high levels of doubt from providers. This is inappropriate in a therapeutic context, as it assumes that providers are better informed about the patient's internal experiences than the patient is—an assumption that is difficult to defend. Providers are not able to determine the reality of a patient's lived experience, and it is the responsibility of providers to give patients their trust. A patient who reports asexuality may still engage in sexual behavior, but that does not indicate that they are lying to the provider. Similarly, a patient who self-identifies as a lesbian may engage in sexual behavior with men; a patient who self-identifies as a gay male may engage in sexual behavior with women; a patient who self-identifies as transgender may choose not to begin hormone treatment. There are reasons for sexual minority patients to do all of these things that do not undermine the fundamental validity of their identities. Physicians should take none of these behaviors as contradictions of what the patient is telling them about their identity.

Patients responded positively to all proposed indicators that physicians would be LGBTQIA+-friendly, but several respondents also made the point that providers may consider themselves "friendly" but still lack the cultural competence to provide high-quality care. There are technical elements associated with providing appropriate care to sexual minority patients. A provider who considers themselves open-minded may still be unwilling to learn how to dose hormones and therefore would be an inappropriate clinician for a trans patient who desired hormonal treatment. Similarly, a provider who holds generally positive views about gay and lesbian people may still hold stereotyped views of bisexual people, assuming that a bisexual patient is necessarily promiscuous and at high risk of disease.

Even participants who self-identified as cisgender preferred to be asked what pronouns healthcare providers should use. This strongly suggests that sexual minority patients view providers who demonstrate concern for the comfort and safety of transgender patients as more likely to be sensitive to the needs of all sexual minority patients. Respondents favored all options for physicians to demonstrate openness to sexual minority patients, but the options that garnered the most support were requesting preferred pronouns, having free-text response options on intake forms, and being included in online lists of LGBTQIA+-friendly physicians. Currently, sexual minority advocacy groups are working on creating online lists of LGBTQIA+-friendly healthcare providers, but this again brings up the issue of whether a physician's belief that they are culturally competent to provide care to sexual minority patients reflects reality.

This is particularly an issue for patients from some sexual minority groups, such as trans patients or intersex patients, where physicians tend to be less familiar with both physiological and sociological issues. More objective measures, such as whether providers have completed continuing medical education courses (CMEs) specifically related to cultural competency with sexual minority patients, may be more reliable indicators for patients, especially those with previous negative experiences.

Some patients expressed confusion as to when it would be relevant for them to disclose their sexual orientation or gender identity to physicians. There are certainly many situations in which this information is unnecessary and physician attempts to elicit it may be experienced as invasive. However, sexual health encompasses a broad range of topics. Contraception and STI protection are classic examples, but thinking of contraception and STI protection in the classic heteronormative model of penile-vaginal intercourse between two (and only two) cisgender people only illuminates a small proportion of the reality of sexual life. Many people engage in sexual behaviors that have different risk profiles; oral sex and anal sex, for example, can take place between people of any gender or genital configuration, and pose risks that should be addressed separately. Patients should feel comfortable discussing not only risks but also their comfort and any pain they are having with their PCPs. PCPs should also be prepared to discuss hormones, conception, childbirth, and breastfeeding in the sexual minority population, which may differ substantially from the cisgender heterosexual population.[2]

When PCPs lack the knowledge base to answer patient questions, situations like those described by the patients in this study arise: physicians making blatantly factually incorrect statements, such as that lesbians cannot transmit STDs or that anal sex invariably leads to rectal prolapse; physicians ignoring patients' requests for information; patients refusing to see PCPs for future treatment of sexual or non-sexual healthcare needs. The minor embarrassment physicians may feel at being asked about sexual health practices, particularly those outside of what they perceive to be the norm,[3] is an insufficient reason to deny patients accurate and appropriate care.

Survey respondents reacted positively to a wide range of actions that providers could take. Cultural competence with the LGBTQIA+ community and other patients who may be sexual minority patients without self-identifying as such is critical for providers who want to provide high-quality care. Understanding, for instance, that a lesbian may still need or want a Pap smear, or that a trans patient may not desire gender affirmation surgery, helps providers initiate and guide discussions that are highly relevant to patient health and needs. Additional training and resources for primary care providers can help build trust and improve the health of sexual minority patients.

---

[2]For more specific discussion of some of these issues, see "Culturally Appropriate Doula Support for Queer and Transgender Parents" elsewhere in this volume. *Ed.*

[3]Unfortunately, many providers are uncomfortable discussing even sexual practices that fit well within cultural expectations of heteronormativity and cisnormativity, hence the need for many of the pieces included in the *Sexuality* section of this volume. *Ed.*

REFERENCES

Albuquerque, G. A., Garcia, C. L., Quirino, G. S., Alves, M. J., Belem, J. M., Figueiredo, F. W., . . . Adami, F. (2016). Access to health services by lesbian, gay, bisexual, and transgender persons: Systematic literature review. *BMC International Health and Human Rights, 16*(2). doi: 10.1186/s12914-015-0072-9.

Budge, S. L., Rossman, H. K., & Howard, K. A. (2014). Coping and psychological distress among genderqueer individuals: The moderating effect of social support. *Journal of LGBT Issues in Counseling, 8*, 95–117.

Coker, T. R., Austin, S. B., & Schuster, M. A. (2010). The health and health care of lesbian, gay, and bisexual adolescents. *Annual Review of Public Health, 31*, 457–477.

Elliott, M. N., Kanouse, D. E., Burkhart, Q., Abel, G. A., Lyratzopolous, G., Beckett, M. K., . . . Roland, D. M. (2014). Sexual minorities in England have poorer health and worse health care experiences: A national survey. *Journal of General Internal Medicine, 30*(1), 9–16.

Ellis, L., Robb, B., & Burke, D. (2005). Sexual orientation in United States and Canadian college students. *Archives of Sexual Behavior, 34*(5), 569–581.

Hutchinson, M. K., Thompson, A. C., & Cederbaum, J. A. (2006). Multisystem factors contributing to disparities in preventative health care among lesbian women. *Journal of Obstetric, Gynecologic, & Neonatal Nursing, 35*(3), 393–402.

Koh, C. S., Kang, M, & Usherwood, T. (2014). 'I demand to be treated as the person I am': Experiences of accessing primary health care for Australian adults who identify as gay, lesbian, bisexual, transgender or queer. *Sexual Heath, 11*, 258–264.

McNair, R. B., & Hegarty, K. (2010). Guidelines for the primary care of lesbian, gay, and bisexual people: A systematic review. *Annals of Family Medicine, 8*(6), 533–541.

Mosack, K. E., Brouwer, A. M., & Petroll, A. E. (2013). Sexual identity, identity disclosure, and health care experiences: Is there evidence for differential homophobia in primary care practice? *Womens Health Issues, 23*(6), e341–e346.

Petzmeier, S. M., Khullar, K., Reisner, S. L., & Potter, J. (2014). Pap test use is lower among female-to-male patients than non-transgender women. *American Journal of Preventative Medicine, 47*(6), 808–812.

Smalley, K. B., Warren, J. C., & Barefoot, K. N. (2015). Differences in health risk behaviors across understudied LGBT subgroups. *Health Psychology.* Advance online publication. http://dx.doi.org/10.1037/hea0000231

"Transgender and Trans Health 101"

By Kadin Henningsen

Transgender (often shortened to "trans") people have become increasingly more visible in the last few decades thanks to shows like *Orange is the New Black* (Netflix) and *Transparent* (Amazon). Although exact data has not been collected on the number of transgender people in the United States, the National Center for Transgender Equality estimates that between 1/4 and 1% of the population is transgender.[1] As more people become aware of the lived experiences of transgender people, highlighting trans specific health needs has also become increasingly important. But who are transgender people and what is "transgender"? The most common understanding of "transgender" is crossing (*trans-*) from one gender to another. Trans historian Susan Stryker defines "trans" as "*the movement across a socially imposed boundary away from an unchosen starting place—rather than any particular destination or mode of transition.*"[2] Therefore, transgender people move across the socially imposed boundary of sex/gender away from the gender assigned to them at birth. What exactly is the boundary of sex/gender that transgender people cross? Before discussing sex/gender boundary crossing, as well as the experiences and health needs of transgender people, it's important to become familiar with the terms and concepts we often use to talk about transgender people and trans experience.

Becoming Trans-Literate With Trans-Lingo

Sex (or sexed body): Sex is typically considered biological and is classified into two categories (male and female) according to the body's reproductive capacity or potential, meaning whether the body produces eggs (female) or sperm (male). Sex also includes genitalia, chromosomes, and other genetic factors that impact secondary sex characteristics like body hair, breasts, etc. It is important to note that sex, although generally associated with physiology, is still socially constructed and a cultural category. For this reason I prefer the term "**sexed body**" in order to call attention to the cultural creation of the category sex and the action of culturally ascribing this category to bodies. Put another way, we sex the body by ascribing meaning to different body morphologies using the categories male and female when a baby is born: a body with a penis (or sperm, or XY chromosomes, etc.) is sexed male, and a body with a vulva (or eggs, or XX chromosomes, etc.) is sexed female.[3]

Gender: Although often used interchangeably with "sex," gender is not the same as sex but is inextricably linked to sex. Like sex, gender is dichotomized into two categories (based on the sexed body): man and woman. Gender is generally considered to be socially constructed, meaning gender is the accumulation of actions, behaviors and roles, attached to and expected of certain sexed bodies within any given culture. Gender therefore is always culturally situated. When twentieth century

---

[1]National Center for Transgender Equality. "Understanding Transgender: Frequently Asked Questions about Transgender People." Washington: National Center for Transgender Equality, 2009. PDF.

[2]Stryker, Susan. *Transgender History*. Berkeley: Seal Press, 2008. 1. *Emphasis in the original.*

[3]As discussed elsewhere in this reader regarding intersex variations, the assumption that all "typical sex characteristics" (genitals, gametes, chromosomes, etc.) will align with a single sex category for every individual is incorrect.

French philosopher Simone de Beauvoir exclaimed "one is not born, but rather becomes, woman,"[4] she was calling attention to the social construction of gender. We learn from our parents, siblings, peers, the media, and the culture at large how to be women and men. Our sexed bodies often determine the lessons we receive. For instance, although we understand that a baby born with a vulva is sexed female, in practice we often proclaim: "It's a girl!" By proclaiming the baby a girl we begin to socially impose understandings and expectations of what it means to be a girl (gentle, passive, quiet, nurturing, etc.) and eventually a woman, all based on visible genitalia. In this way, gender and sex are hard to separate, and one of the reasons sex and gender are often used interchangeably. As a result, I prefer to use **"sex/gender"** in order to call attention to the way we culturally link sex and gender.

Gender Identity: How you understand your own gender or inner sense of being a woman, man, both, neither, or something else entirely.

Gender Expression: How you express your gender through clothing, mannerism, behavior, speech patterns, and social interactions. Gender expression is often understood along a spectrum of feminine and masculine. (Note: Masculinity and Femininity are also culturally linked to gender and thus sex: i.e. if you are sexed female you are expected to become or identify as a woman and express yourself in feminine ways, such as wearing dresses and make-up, keeping your hair long, etc. It's important to note as well that some deviation is acceptable so long as the overall identity of the person is cis- and heteronormative, for instance "tomboy" girls, or even sometimes women who present as "low maintenance" or "one of the guys." As such, deviation is often more permissible for women who incorporate some degree of "masculinity" into their gender expression than it is for men who deviate from socially acceptable forms of masculinity and incorporate "feminine" expressions of gender. This double standard is possible because of a current gender hierarchy in the U.S. that privileges masculinity over femininity, sometimes referred to as *androcentrism*.)

Transgender: A transgender person is someone who crosses (*trans-*) over from one sex/gender (usually the one assigned at birth) to another sex/gender, or someone who moves "across a socially imposed boundary away from an unchosen starting place"[5] and the meanings we culturally attach to that starting place. According to Finn Enke, professor of history and LGBTQ Studies at the University of Wisconsin-Madison, the term "trans-

gender" incorporates three distinct but overlapping arenas of social organization:

- An *identity* that people embrace for themselves. Transgender identity may include a gender identity that differs from the sex/gender assigned at birth; a gender expression that differs from that conventionally expected of people according to their sexed body; and/or a desire for alteration of the body's sex/gender characteristics.

- A *social category* or umbrella term that incorporates the broadest possible range of gender nonconformity for the purposes of movement building, organizing, and social recognition. In the US and Canada, this may include transsexuals, cross-dressers, drag queen and kings, persons with intersex variations, butches, studs, femmes, MTF, FTM, trans men, trans women, pangender people, third gender people, agender people, two-spirit people[6], and many, many more. People who place themselves in any of these categories, or other gender nonconforming categories, may or may not identity with the collective term "transgender." Many people who "do trans" or have "transed" their culture's gender expectations, meaning they continually cross ("do trans") or they've crossed (transed) the boundaries or borders of their culture's gender expectations, may not identify with the term "transgender."

- A *social movement* that insists on civil and social rights for all people regardless of gender identity, gender expression, and body type, as well as the right of all people to determine for themselves there own personal and legal gender status (gender self-determination), as well as freedom of gender identity and gender expression for all people (not just "trans" people).[7]

An important note about language: "transgender" is an adjective and therefore should always be used to describe someone: transgender person, transgender woman, etc.

---

[4]de Beauvoir, Simone. *The Second Sex*. Trans. Constance Borde and Sheila Malovany-Chevallier. New York: Vintage Books, 2011. 283.
[5]Styker, 1.

[6]Two-spirit is a term used by some Indigenous people. The term was coined in 1990 at an international conference of Indigenous gay and lesbian people in response to the use of the term *berdache* (literally meaning "passive partner in sodomy, boy prostitute") by predominantly White Europeans to describe cross gender and sexuality by Indigenous people. Two-Spirit is an identity often claimed by Indigenous people with a multitude of genders or those who embody both masculine and feminine expressions, but can be used by any Indigenous person who crosses social gender roles, gender expressions, and/or sexualities. In addition to the term Two-Spirit, most individual tribes also have their own terms to describe Indigenous people who cross gender or sexuality. For more information see: www.nativeout.com
[7]Enke, A. Finn. "Note on Terms and Concepts." *Transfeminist Perspectives In and Beyond Transgender and Gender Studies*. Philadelphia: Temple University Press, 2012. 18–19.

Many transgender people find it inaccurate and offensive to be referred to as "transgenders" or "transgendered" for a number of reasons. First, "transgenders" removes personhood and thus objectifies transgender people. Such objectification increases the likelihood of violence against trans people. Second, although the prefix "trans" operates as a verb (gender is "transed"), when attached to gender the word "transgender" no longer operates as a verb but as a descriptor, or adjective. Therefore "transgender" should not be articulated as a past-tense verb (transgendered), but as an adjective (transgender woman, transgender man, transgender people).

Transgender Woman (Trans Woman): A transgender person who identifies as a woman. (See also MTF)

Transgender Man (Trans Man): A transgender person who identifies as a man. (See also FTM)

Transsexual: Often a medical or clinical term, a transsexual person is a transgender person who has medically transitioned in some way. Who is considered transsexual is often contested within the transgender/transsexual community itself. Some people who have medically transitioned identify as transsexuals and some reject the label because of its attachment to medical and clinical institutions. There is also a generational shift in the use of the term transsexual. Older trans people who have medically transitioned are more likely to identify as transsexual, whereas younger generations of trans people often prefer to identify as transgender regardless of medical transition. (See also Transition)

Transition: The process of affirming one's own gender identity, often a movement away from the sex/gender assigned at birth. Transition can include a number of actions such as changing one's name, using new pronouns, dressing and grooming differently, changing legal documentation, or "medically transitioning" with processes such as taking hormones and/or undergoing gender affirming surgeries. Some transgender people choose to do all, some, or none of these actions. Some transgender people, because of other systems of oppression (such as class and race) do not have access to some transition options (especially legal and medical) regardless of their level of interest in those options.

FTM (or F2M): FTM stands for Female-to-Male and is sometimes used by people who are assigned female at birth (AFAB) and transition to male. Transition may or may not include legal and medical transition.

MTF (or M2F): MTF stands for Male-to-Female and is sometimes used by people who are assigned male at birth (AMAB) and transition to female. Transition may or may not include legal and medical transition.

Genderqueer: A term used by people who identify as both male and female, or neither entirely male nor female. Genderqueer people may also be interested in playing with gender and gender expression by pushing the boundaries of what masculinity and femininity look like. Some genderqueer people also use terms such as pangender (identify with all gender possibilities), agender (don't identify with any gender), nonbinary (identify with any form of gender that doesn't rely on binary gender), or gender-fluid (moves in, out, and across various expression of gender). In 2016, the term "genderqueer" was added to the unabridged Merriam-Webster dictionary along with "gender-fluid," "cis," and "cisgender."

Cisgender: The root *cis-* means "to be on the same side as" (as oppose to *trans-* which means "to cross over"). Therefore, a cisgender person is someone whose gender identity aligns with the sex/gender they were assigned at birth. This is the preferred term to refer to non-transgender people. The terms "real" and "biological" or "bio" (e.g. "real man" or "biological woman") are experienced by many transgender people as invalidating or denying their innate human identities. The rhetoric of "real" implies that trans men and women are not real men or women. They are. Furthermore, the rhetoric of "real" and "biological" assumes the sexed body as the location of reality and truth regarding sex/gender. As Tallia Bettcher, professor of philosophy and transgender studies, points out, we are able to recognize this assumption that the sexed body is the location of reality/truth because of the frequent use of expressions such as "really a man," "discovered to be female," or even the media's use of "born a man" or "born female," all of which are linked to genital status.[8]

Cis-privilege: The assumed and invisible advantages one receives because of being, or perceived as being, cisgender. Some of these privileges include not having to think about or be afraid to use gender specific spaces like bathrooms and locker rooms appropriate for your gender identity; not being asked by strangers about your genital morphology; people calling you by the name you provide them and not asking for your "real" name.

Cisnormativity: The assumption that all people are cisgender and meet (or should meet) normative expectations of masculinity and femininity based on the sexed body. Put another way, cisnormativity is the assumption that if you are assigned female at birth, you identify (or should) as a woman, and express yourself (or should) according to culturally defined expectations of femininity.

Passing: Within the context of the transgender community and transgender identities, passing occurs when a transgender person can appear in public as

---

[8]Bettcher, Talie Mae. "Evil Deceivers and Make-Believers: On Transphobic Violence and the Politics of Illusion." *Hypatia: A Journal of Feminist Philosophy*. 22.3 (2007). 48.

their affirmed gender and not as transgender. By definition, passing has historically meant to be perceived or accepted as something you are not.[9] For this reason, the concept of passing can be dangerous for transgender people because it implies that transgender people are engaged in secretive or deceptive behavior, and that transgender status should always be immediately apparent upon visual inspection. This definition, however, also shows us that passing is relational in that whether a transgender person passes is largely determined by whether they are perceived or accepted as male/men or female/women by *others*. In this way, it is not that the transgender person passes, or is passing, but is more accurately *passed by* others in public spaces based on culturally accepted and cisnormative understandings of what constitutes male/female or man/woman.

Boundary Crossing

If transgender is a movement across a socially imposed boundary, the primary boundary that transgender people cross is the "sex/gender binary." More broadly, binaries hold that there are two and only two options for any given identity category and that you must fit in one or the other. In addition, these two options must be oppositional. The sex/gender binary (male/female and man/woman) relies on a false assumption that you are either female (with a vulva, xx chromosomes, eggs, etc.) or male (with a penis, xy chromosomes, sperm, etc.) and that by being female, you identify as a woman and are feminine, or that if you are male you also identify as a man and are masculine. In this way, sex and gender are inextricably linked in that the sex/gender binary relies on the belief that sex=gender. As such, the sex/gender binary also assumes that all people are cisgender, erasing transgender and intersex identities and experiences.

We know, however, that there are many ways to be a woman or a man, and that femininity and masculinity take many forms. In this way gender is a spectrum. We also know that sex is a spectrum because of the prevalence of intersex variations. Although understanding sex/gender as a spectrum is incredibly useful in breaking down the sex/gender binary (as well as other binaries) there are two problems with spectrums.

First, because spectrums are comprised of the space between two poles (male and female in this case), people are still locked within an oppositional binary. People are still assumed to fall within any given binary, just to varying degrees along that spectrum. More specifically, within the sex/gender spectrum people are expected

to situate themselves somewhere along masculine or feminine expressions. Thus, a spectrum based on the sex/gender binary erases genderqueer people, including people who move away or cross over from an assigned gender at birth toward no gender at all (agender).

Second, we often understand binaries and spectrums as horizontal. This positions the two opposing parts of any given binary or spectrum as being on equal footing. For instance, the spectrum of masculinity and femininity, often written horizontally as masculine/feminine, implies that masculinity and femininity are equally valued in our culture. The systemic oppression of women (or feminine people) shows us that this is false. Therefore it is important to understand that when we talk about binaries and spectrums, they are not horizontal and equal (male/female), but vertical and hierarchical ($\frac{MALE}{FEMALE}$), meaning that one category is subordinate to the other. By understanding binaries and spectrums as vertical and hierarchical we can begin to see the power structures that impact our lives across many categories of difference:

$$\frac{MALE}{FEMALE} \qquad \frac{STRAIGHT}{GAY} \qquad \frac{ABLED}{DISABLED}$$

$$\frac{RICH}{POOR} \qquad \frac{WHITE}{PEOPLE\ OF\ COLOR} \qquad \frac{NON\text{-}BLACK}{BLACK}$$

All of these categories of difference also operate in relation to the binary cisgender/transgender, or more accurately $\frac{CIS}{TRANS}$.

Cisgender is privileged within this binary in part because cisnormativity privileges the sexed body as the "true" location of gender. In this way, we should understand sex/gender as also being hierarchical, i.e. $\frac{SEX}{GENDER}$.

Transgender people cross a culturally defined cisnormative boundary that requires that sex = gender = proper gender presentation. If we articulate this cisnormative boundary of sex/gender as a hierarchy, we can visually see this socially imposed boundary:

$$\frac{MALE = MAN = MASCULINE}{FEMALE = WOMAN = FEMININE}$$

Transgender people, thus, cross the boundary between man/woman and/or masculine/feminine (Male = Woman = Feminine or Female = Man = Masculine). Transsexual people who medically transition may also

---

[9]"passing, n.". OED Online. December 2012. Oxford University Press. 7 February 2013 <http://www.oed.com/view/Entry/138497?p=emailAa btc9hlq5iPs&d=138497>.

cross the socially imposed boundary between male/female:

$$\frac{MALE = WOMAN = FEMININE\ (= Transgender\ Womam)}{FEMALE = MAN = MASCULINE\ (= Transgender\ Man)}\ ^{10}$$

You can see then that gender and gender presentation have crossed the boundary separating male/female. Also notice, as a result of this boundary crossing, that the sex/gender hierarchy is less clear, or now unstable. Such boundary crossing threatens hierarchies because the people who occupy privileged positions within them need these boundaries to be clear and stable in order to retain their positions of power. As such, transgender people, by crossing the socially imposed boundary of sex/gender, throws the category of sex/gender into crisis. Once one category is in crisis, the very notion of categories is itself thrown into crisis.[11] The results of category crisis are often acts of verbal and/or physical violence against those (such as transgender people) who challenge socially imposed boundaries. Such violence, whether verbal or physical, interpersonal or institutional, can have a significant impact on health.

Trans Health

According to the World Health Organization, health is a person's overall mental, physical, and social well-being—not merely the absence of illness or disease.[12] There are many determinants of health, including environment and community, that can impact transgender people and their health. Stable employment and a safe home and environment can impact one's basic state of health. Employment and housing also impact one's ability to access healthcare, as healthcare is often only accessible to those who can afford a certain level of access to the healthcare system. Transgender people disproportionately experience hardship related to employment and housing, negatively impacting both their health and their access to appropriate and affordable healthcare.

For instance, according to the 2011 National Transgender Discrimination Survey[13] transgender people experience double the rate of unemployment compared to the general population. For transgender people of color, the rate is four times the national average. 90% of respondents reported harassment or mistreatment on the job, and 47% reported negative job outcomes, including being fired, not hired, or denied promotion because of their transgender status. Transgender people who had lost a job or were unemployed at the time of the survey also reported experiencing higher rates of incarceration and homelessness as well as negative health outcomes. This is compounded by the fact that many of the transgender people in this group (16%) engaged in underground employment (such as sex work or drug sales) for income that they could not generate legally.

Furthermore, employment is only one factor in transgender people's ability of find and secure affordable and safe housing. Transgender people also face high levels of housing discrimination, among other obstacles. Survey respondents reported being denied a home or apartment (19%) or evicted from a home (11%) because they are transgender. Because gender identity isn't included in most anti-discrimination laws regarding housing, transgender people have little to no legal recourse when experiencing housing discrimination due to their transgender status. As a result, 19% of transgender people have experienced homelessness at some point in their life. Those who experienced homelessness were 2.5 times more likely to have experienced incarceration and four times more likely to have engaged in sex work for income. In addition, they were more likely to be HIV-positive (7.12%), and were much more likely to have attempted suicide (69%) compared to those who had not experienced homelessness, showing the negative impact that a lack of safe and affordable housing has on individual health. Exacerbating the problem, transgender people experiencing housing instability or homelessness are especially likely to lack access to healthcare, which is essential to mental, physical and social well-being.

Healthcare is a fundamental right and transgender people face significant obstacles to accessing healthcare such as refusal of care, harassment and violence in medical settings, and lack of provider knowledge. These issues contribute both to lack of care and inappropriate care: 28% of transgender people postponed medical care when they were sick or injured, and 48% couldn't afford to access healthcare at all; 19% of survey participants reported being denied care because of their transgender status, with the highest numbers among trans people of color; 28% reported harassment and 2% were victims of violence perpetrated by medical practitioners; and 50% of transgender people surveyed reported having to teach their medical providers about appropriate care for

---

[10]Based on this diagram, we might be inclined to think that those assigned male at birth are still better off than those assigned female at birth, regardless of boundary crossing. Transmisogyny adds an additional layer here, and thus trans women, especially trans women of color, are often the most marginalized members of the trans community because of combined discrimination based on race, gender identity, and trans status.

[11]Garber, Marjorie. *Vested Interests: Cross-Dressing and Cultural Anxiety.* New York: HarperPerennial, 1993. 17.

[12]http://www.who.int/about/definition/en/print.html

[13]Unless noted otherwise, all statistics are from: Grant, Jaime M., Lisa A. Mottet, Justin Tanis, Jack Harrison, Jody L. Herman, and Mara Keisling. *Injustice at Every Turn: A Report of the National Transgender Discrimination Survey.* Washington: National Center for Transgender Equality and National Gay and Lesbian Task Force, 2011. PDF.

transgender people. Furthermore, disclosure of transgender status dramatically increased the likelihood of experiencing discrimination based on that status.

In addition to accessing healthcare, transgender people disproportionately face specific issues related to their health and wellbeing: survey participants reported over four times the national average of HIV infection (2.64% of the sample compared to .6% of the general population), with rates for transgender women at 4.28%, and those who are unemployed (4.67%) or who have engaged in sex work (15.32%) even higher. Over a quarter of participants reported misusing drugs and alcohol specifically to cope with mistreatment they faced due their gender identity, and 41% of transgender people report attempting suicide (compared to 1.6% of the general population). These numbers increase drastically for transgender people of color, those who experience unemployment and homelessness, and those who live in dire poverty (15% of respondents reported a household income under $10,000/year, nearly four times the rate of the general population living with such limited resources).

There is a lot of work to do to make employment, safe and affordable housing, and appropriate healthcare available to transgender people. Important changes have already been implemented on a national level, and in some cases also at the state level. For instance, in 2010 the Affordable Care Act (ACA) banned sex discrimination in many health care facilities and programs that receive federal funding, including discrimination based on gender identity. The ACA not only made health insurance more financially accessible for many people, including many transgender people who could not previously afford health insurance, it also provided new protections for patients. For instance, transgender people, like others, can no longer be denied health insurance for a pre-existing condition. Compared to the general population, we see higher rates of chronic conditions and disability among transgender people; many of these conditions would disqualify transgender people from obtaining insurance at a reasonable price or even at all without the protection of the ACA.

In addition, a diagnosis of Gender Identity Disorder (GID),[14] which is often required to access medical

transition, has previously been cited as a pre-existing condition in order to deny transgender people health insurance. By removing the barrier created by insurance companies under the language of "pre-existing conditions," transgender people have better access to affordable healthcare in order to treat and manage chronic conditions and disabilities. In addition, the ACA makes it easier to appeal coverage denials for any reason. It may now be illegal for a plan to deny coverage of services solely because of transgender status or because of the gender under which you are enrolled in the plan. This means, for instance, that it may now be illegal to deny coverage of pelvic exams for transgender men and prostate exams for transgender women.[15] In the Spring of 2016, President Barak Obama issued an executive order mandating that federally funded insurance programs such as Medicaid and Medicare also cover transition related medical expenses.

The ACA does not, however, require any group or individual insurance plans to cover transition related care. As of this writing, nine states and the District of Columbia have banned trans exclusions from both private and Medicaid insurance, with six states banning trans exclusions in either private or Medicaid but not both.[16] Access to transgender inclusive healthcare plans, however, is often dependent on access to the kind of employment that provides them. For those transgender people in a state that does not require trans inclusive insurance, relocating to a state that requires trans inclusive healthcare is both financially and physically difficult because of the obstacles already stacked against transgender people. Some transgender people don't have the option of relocating because they are minors and dependent on parents and legal guardians. Such dependence also requires the good will and understanding of parents and legal guardians to access care even if care is technically available. It should be noted that support of family can have a significant impact on trans youths' health beyond access to healthcare. Trans youth who are rejected by their families because of their trans status are more likely to experience homelessness or attempt suicide, with concomitant health issues.

Attending to the well-being of transgender people will require addressing various structural systems (employment, housing, etc.) that prevent transgender people from living and sustaining healthy lives. For instance, passing the Employment Non-Discrimina-

---

[14]The diagnosis of Gender Identity Disorder (GID) is a hotly contested issue. On the one hand, diagnosis is often needed for medical transition. Most insurance companies (if they cover trans related care at all) require that any transition-related care be "medically necessary," which often requires a specific diagnosis. On the other hand, such a diagnosis continues to pathologize and stigmatize trans people. For more information on the debate surround GID see Mary Burke's "Resisting Pathology: GID and the Contested Terrain of Diagnosis in the Transgender Rights Movement" in *Sociology of Diagnosis*.

---

[15]National Center for Transgender Equality. "Health Care Rights and Transgender People." Washington: National Center for Transgender Equality, 2014. PDF.

[16]"Map: Transgender Health Insurance Laws." *National Center for Transgender Equality*. National Center for Transgender Equality, 2015. Web. 18 May 2016.

tion Act (ENDA) would ensure that transgender people are able to find and keep employment providing them with the financial means to acquire housing and medical insurance, thus decreasing the negative health outcomes resulting from homelessness and lack of access to healthcare. Addressing the structural inequalities contributing to the ill health of transgender people, however, will not be enough. Incorporating the unique experiences of transgender, genderqueer, and gender nonconforming people in our histories, literatures, religions, and communities alleviates negative health outcomes as a result of bullying and discrimination. Affirming transgender identities, ensuring access to employment, safe and affordable housing, and healthcare allows transgender people to flourish and remain vital members of our communities.

BIBLIOGRAPHY

Bettcher, Talie Mae. "Evil Deceivers and Make-Believers: On Transphobic Violence and the Politics of Illusion." *Hypatia: A Journal of Feminist Philosophy*. 22.3 (2007): 43–65.

Burke, Mary. "Resisting Pathology: GID and the Contested Terrain of Diagnosis in the Transgender Rights Movement." *Sociology of Diagnosis*. Bingley, UK: Emerald Group Publishing Limited, 2011. 183–210.

de Beauvoir, Simone. *The Second Sex*. Trans. Constance Borde and Sheila Malovany-Chevallier. New York: Vintage Books, 2011.

Enke, A. Finn. "Note on Terms and Concepts." *Transfeminist Perspectives In and Beyond Transgender and Gender Studies*. Philadelphia: Temple University Press, 2012.

Grant, Jaime M., Lisa A. Mottet, Justin Tanis, Jack Harrison, Jody L. Herman, and Mara Keisling. *Injustice at Every Turn: A Report of the National Transgender Discrimination Survey*. Washington: National Center for Transgender Equality and National Gay and Lesbian Task Force, 2011. PDF. http://www.transequality.org/sites/default/files/docs/resources/NTDS_Report.pdf

National Center for Transgender Equality. "Health Care Rights and Transgender People." Washington: National Center for Transgender Equality, 2014. PDF. http://www.transequality.org/sites/default/files/docs/kyr/HealthCareRight_UpdatedMar2014_FINAL.pdf

___. "Map: Transgender Health Insurance Laws." *National Center for Transgender Equality*. National Center for Transgender Equality, 2015. Web. 18 May 2016. http://www.transequality.org/issues/resources/transgender-healthcare-insurance-laws

___. "Transgender Terminology." Washington: National Center for Transgender Equality, 2014. PDF. http://www.transequality.org/sites/default/files/docs/resources/Trans-Terminology_2014.pdf

___. "Understanding Transgender: Frequently Asked Questions about Transgender People." Washington: National Center for Transgender Equality, 2009. PDF. http://www.transequality.org/sites/default/files/docs/resources/NCTE_UnderstandingTrans.pdf

NativeOUT: Native American LGBT/Two-Spirit educational resources, multimedia, and news. NativeOUT. Web. 18 May 2016. www.NativeOUT.com

"passing, n.". OED Online. December 2012. Oxford University Press. 7 February 2013. http://www.oed.com/view/Entry/138497?p=emailAabtc9hlq5iPs&d=138497

Stryker, Susan. *Transgender History*. Berkeley: Seal Press, 2008.

"Transgender/Transsexual/ Gender Variant Health Care "

From the *American College of Nurse Midwives*

The American College of Nurse-Midwives (ACNM) supports efforts to provide transgender, transsexual, and gender variant individuals with access to safe, comprehensive, culturally competent health care and therefore endorses the 2011 World Professional Association for Transgender Health (WPATH) Standards of Care.

It is the position of ACNM that midwives

Exhibit respect for patients with nonconforming gender identities and do not pathologize differences in gender identity or expression;

Provide care in a manner that affirms patients' gender identities and reduces the distress of gender dysphoria or refer to knowledgeable colleagues;

Become knowledgeable about the health care needs of transsexual, transgender, and gender nonconforming people, including the benefits and risks of gender affirming treatment options;

Match treatment approaches to the specific needs of patients, particularly their goals for gender expression and need for relief from gender dysphoria;

Have resources available to support and advocate for patients within their families and communities (schools, workplaces, and other settings).

To facilitate these goals, ACNM is committed to

- Work toward the incorporation of information about gender identity, expression, and development in all midwifery educational programs;
- Make available educational materials that address the identities and health care needs of gender variant individuals in order to improve midwives' cultural competence in providing care to this population;
- Support legislation and policies that prohibit discrimination based on gender expression or identity;
- Support measures to ensure full, equal, and unrestricted access to health insurance coverage for all care needed by gender variant individuals.

Background

Gender variant people face multiple barriers to accessing health care and suffer disproportionate disparities in health outcomes. Gender variant individuals experience higher rates of discrimination in housing, education, and employment and lower rates of health insurance coverage than the general population.[1] As many as one-fourth of gender variant people avoid health care services due to concerns about discrimination and harassment.[2] HIV infection within the gender variant community is 4 times the rate of the general population; rates of drug, alcohol, and tobacco use, and depression and suicide attempts are also higher.[2,3] These outcomes disproportionately affect gender variant people of color.

When gender variant individuals are able to obtain health insurance, most find that their insurance providers specifically exclude gender affirming therapies (eg hormonal or surgical procedures), deny basic preventative care services on the basis of gender identity, and refuse to cover sex-specific services due to perceived gender incongruence (eg a man with a cervix may be refused coverage for a pap smear).[4-6] Few legal recourses exist because gender identity and expression are excluded from federal and most state non-discrimination protections.

In addition, the under-reported and under-researched reproductive health care needs of gender variant individuals are of particular interest to midwives. Qualitative studies and anecdotal evidence confirm that gender variant individuals desire parenting roles and can and do create biological families. [7]

Midwifery Practice and the Gender Variant Patient

As many as half of gender variant individuals report having to educate their health care providers about their health care needs, but gender variant people do not by default have unique or complicated health issues. Most members of this community require the same primary, mental, and sexual health care that all individuals need.[8] The most important thing all midwives can do to improve the health care outcomes of gender variant individuals is to use their skills to provide care that is welcoming and accessible.

Musculoskeletal, cardiovascular, breast, and pelvic care for individuals who have undergone hormonal and/or surgical therapy is typically straightforward but in some cases requires additional training. Similarly, administration of hormone therapy for gender affirmation is appropriate for primary care providers, including certified nurse-midwives/certified midwives (CNMs®/CMs®) who have undergone appropriate training. The World Professional Association for Transgender Health (WPATH) "strongly encourages the increased training and involvement of primary care providers in the area of feminizing/masculinizing hormone therapy."[9] Seeking hormone therapy is the entryway to health care for many gender variant individuals. According to WPATH, "medical visits relating to hormone maintenance provide an opportunity to deliver broader care to a population that is often medically underserved." [9]

CNMs/CMs should seek to provide evidence-based, welcoming, and accessible care for gender variant individuals in accordance with ACNM Standard of Practice VIII[10] and their state regulatory bodies.

REFERENCES

1. Grant JM, Mottet LA, Tanis J, Harrison J, Herman JL, Keisling, M. *Injustice at Every Turn: A Report of the National Transgender Discrimination Survey.* Washington, DC: National Center for Transgender Equality and National Gay and Lesbian Task Force; 2011.

2. Grant JM, Mottet LA, Tanis JT. (2010). National transgender discrimination survey report on health and health care. http://transequality.org/PDFs/NTDSReporton-Health_final.pdf. Published October 2010. Accessed November 13, 2012.

3. Dutton L, Koenig K, Fennie K. Gynecologic care of the female-to-male transgender man. *J Midwifery Womens Health.* 2008;53:331–337.

4. Transgender Law Center. Recommendations for transgender health care. http://www.transgenderlaw.org/resources/tlchealth.htm. Accessed November 13, 2012.

5. Gehi PS, Arkles G. Unraveling injustice: race and class impact of Medicaid exclusions of transition-related health care for transgender people. *Sex Res Social Policy.* 2007;4(4):7–35.

6. National Coalition for LGBT Health. An overview of U.S. trans health policies: a report by the Eliminating Disparities Working Group. http://transequality.org/PDFs/HealthPriorities.pdf. Published August 2004. Accessed November 13, 2012.

7. Wierckx K, Van Caenegem E, Pennings G, et al. Reproductive wish in transsexual men. *Hum Reprod.* 2012;27(2):483–487.

8. Feldman JL, Goldberg J. Transgender primary medical care: Suggested guidelines for clinicians in British Columbia. http://transhealth.vch.ca/resources/library/tcpdocs/guidelines-primcare.pdf. Published January 2006. Accessed November 13, 2012.

9. World Professional Association for Transgender Health. Standards of care for the health of transsexual, transgender, and gender nonconforming people. http://www.wpath.org/documents/Standards%20of%20Care%20V7%20-%202011%20WPATH.pdf . Accessed November 13, 2012.

10. American College of Nurse Midwives. Standards for the practice of midwifery. Published December 4, 2009. Accessed November 13, 2012.

RESOURCES

1. American Medical Association. (2008). Removing financial barriers to care for transgender patients. Resolution 122(A-08). http://www.gires.org.uk/assets/Medpro-Assets/AMA122.pdf. Accessed November 13, 2012.

2. Bernhard LA. (2011). Gynecologic health for sexual and gender minorities. In Schuiling KD, Likis FE, eds. *Women's Gynecologic Health.* 2nd ed. Burlington, MA: Jones & Bartlett Learning; 201: 185–208.

3. Brown Boi Project. *Freeing Ourselves: A Guide to Health and Self-Love for Brown Bois.* Oakland, CA: Brown Boi Project; 2011.

4. Fenway Institute. Understanding the T in LGBT: Caring for transgender patients. Fenway Guide to LGBT Health, Module 7 http://www.fenwayhealth.org/site/DocServer/Handout_7-A_Resources_final.pdf?docID=6221. Accessed November 13, 2012.

5. Gay & Lesbian Medical Association. Guidelines for care of lesbian, gay, bisexual, and transgender patients. http://www.glma.org/_data/n_0001/resources/live/GLMA%20

guidelines%202006%20FINAL.pdf. Accessed November 13, 2012.

6. Gorton RN, Buth J, Spade D. Medical therapy & health maintenance for transgender men: a guide for health care providers. http://www.nickgorton.org/Medical%20 Therapy%20and%20HM%20for%20Transgender%20 Men_2005.pdf. Accessed November 13, 2012.

7. Institute of Medicine. The health of lesbian, gay bisexual and transgender people: Building a foundation for better understanding. http://www.iom.edu/Reports/2011/The-Health-of-Lesbian-Gay-Bisexual-and-Transgender-People.aspx. Published March 31, 2011. Accessed November 13, 2012.

8. Lambda Legal. When health care isn't caring: Lambda legal's survey on discrimination against LGBT people and people living with HIV. http://data.lambdalegal.org/ publications/downloads/whcic-report_when-health-care-isnt-caring.pdf. Accessed November 13, 2012.

9. Steinle K. Hormonal management of the female-to-male transgender patient. *J Midwifery Womens Health*. 2011;56:293–302.

10. Tom Waddell Health Center: Protocols for hormonal reassignment of gender. http://www.sfdph.org/dph/comupg/ oservices/medSvs/hlthCtrs/TransGendprotocols122006. pdf. Revised December 12, 2006. Accessed November 13, 2012.

11. Center of Excellence in Transgender Health. Primary care protocol for transgender patient care. http://transhealth. ucsf.edu/trans?page=protocol-00-00. Published April 2011. Accessed November 13, 2012.

12. Vancouver Coastal Health. Transgender health program. http://transhealth.vch.ca/. Accessed November 13, 2012.

Note. The term "gender variant" is used throughout this document to reflect a broad range of gender non-conforming identities, expressions, and experiences. This term is used as an umbrella term for all individuals whose gender expression or identity differs from the sex assigned at birth.

Source: Task Force on Gender Bias; Clinical Standards and Documents Section DOSP

Developed: November 2012

Board of Directors Approved: December 2012

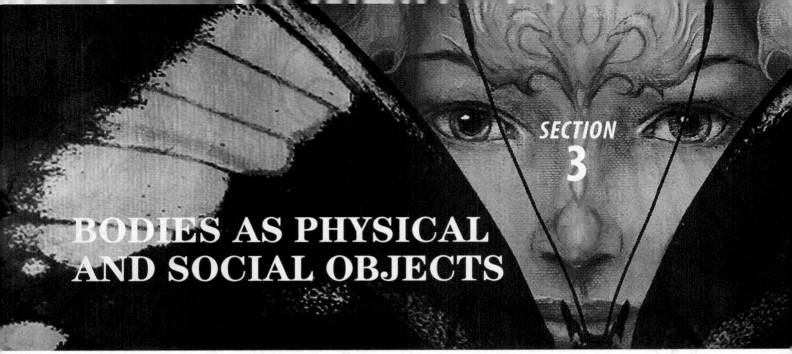

SECTION 3

BODIES AS PHYSICAL AND SOCIAL OBJECTS

"Take a Good Look"

By Megan Seely

We don't have to go very far back to find the origins of the modern feminist health movement. In 1971, the Feminist Women's Health Centers were founded by a group of Los Angeles women who wanted to know more about their bodies and their reproductive selves. At a time when pregnancy tests and yeast infection treatments were available only at physicians' offices and when libraries and bookstores were void of women's health books, the Feminist Women's Health Center provided a source of information and a place for women to gather to share experiences about their bodies, health, and lives.[4] They helped women across the country and around the world set up "self-help groups," where women came together to share information, learn from one another, and practice cervical self-exam. Yes, basically a group of women hangin' out and looking at their vaginas—despite the efforts of Eve Ensler to bring vaginas into fashion today, this still may sound a bit weird to people of my generation—but it was a real revelation to women then (and still is today!). The cervical self-exam was a way to gain control of one's body at a time when this domain belonged more to women's doctors and sexual partners. The practice continues to put women in touch with themselves and to assist in their awareness of their bodies—which returns our power to us. The Feminist Women's Health Centers' self-help is about understanding how our bodies work through our eyes; it is about making our bodily knowledge available and legitimate. Perhaps this is the first step in freeing ourselves from dependence on a medical system that does not value us. So, if you haven't done so, grab a mirror, and take a good look.

Vaginal and Cervical Self-Examination

Vaginal and cervical self-examination is one of the most useful health tools a woman can have. It enables us to see a vital part of our anatomy that is hidden from plain view—the vagina and cervix (the neck of the womb). By using a speculum, you can observe changes in your cervix and its secretions, the menstrual cycle, and indications of fertility; you can identify and treat common vaginal conditions such as yeast, trichomonas, or bacterial infections (which often cause itching or discharge);

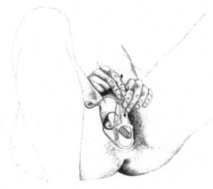

To insert a plastic speculum, spread the inner lips of the clitoris with two fingers of one hand, hold the bills of the speculum tightly together with the thumb and index finger of the other, and guide it into the vaginal canal. You can use a water-soluble jelly or just plain water to make insertion smoother. This woman is inserting her speculum with the handles upright, but some women prefer to insert it sideways initially. Inserting the speculum with the handles down is strictly for the doctor's convenience, and it requires that a woman put her feet into stirrups at the end of an exam table.

When the handles of the speculum are pinched together, they force the bills open, stretching the vaginal walls and revealing the cervix. With the handles held tightly together, the short handle slides down and the long handle slides up. When there is a sharp click the speculum is locked into place.

With the speculum locked, both hands are free to hold a mirror and a flashlight or gooseneck lamp. If a flashlight is used, shine the beam into the mirror, and it will, in turn, be reflected into the vagina, illuminating the vaginal walls and the cervix. The cervix won't always pop instantly into view. Sometimes you have to try several times. If it stubbornly refuses to appear, you can move around or jump up and down a few times. Sometimes it is also helpful to move to a firmer surface, like the floor or a tabletop. When the cervix is visible, you can see a rounded or flattened knob, between the size of a quarter and a fifty-cent piece, like a fat doughnut with a hole or slit in it. The hole, called the cervical os, is where the menstrual blood, other uterine secretions, and babies come out. Your cervix might be pink and smooth, or it might have a few reddish blemishes. It can also be uneven, rough, or splotchy. In any case, the only time to worry is when abnormal cells are found in a Pap smear.

*Material adapted from *A New View of A Woman's Body*, Federation of Feminist Women's Health Centers, Feminist Health Press, Los Angeles, CA. Suzann Gage created these beautiful illustrations, pp. 22–24. Reprinted with permission.

and you can learn what your cervix looks like day by day, rather than depending on a physician to look once a year to pronounce what is normal for you.

Beyond getting to know one's own vagina, a women-centered health agenda might also start at the beginning of our young lives and recognize the different ways that we are treated and taught to understand our own bodies. Little boys are often encouraged to be baseball players; little girls are encouraged to be fairy princesses. Little boys are encouraged to use their bodies in physical ways, whereas little girls are encouraged to dress their bodies in different clothes. When a little boy gets dirty, some say, "that's just a boy being a boy," but when a little girl does the same, she is a "tomboy" or "not acting like a nice little girl." While some of these tendencies may be biological, there is no doubting that society encourages these stereotypes. (Some might even say that this is how patriarchy continues itself.) Thankfully, there are now soccer leagues for both boys and girls, but there is still no doubting that there are many more athletic opportunities for boys than for girls and that, overall, boys are encouraged to be more physical and athletic than girls.

These bodily differences all but erupt at puberty. From the start, we are divided in gender-specific groups to see separate films about our changing bodies. Many of us struggle to pay attention during the coming-of-age video that highlights young girls that we barely recognize, while our curiosity wonders what the boys are learning about us—from someone else. We are both envious and fearful of the girls who begin menstruation before us—wanting to both be them and avoid the situation altogether. Very little if anything is shared ahead of time—as with most of our "education," we swap stories with our friends, trying to sort out this mess called *womanhood*. And then . . . the day—the day we see blood. We are indoctrinated into this new club, but usually with very little celebration. And our modern ritual begins—pads versus tampons, Midol versus heating pad—we learn the tortures of "the curse." We are bombarded with messages of fear—fear of someone knowing, fear of odor, fear of bloating, fear of leakage, fear of staining, fear of pain, fear, fear, fear. We are told that we need protection—but from what? Ourselves, our menstruating selves. The Solution: Deodorize, minimize, and hide the fact that we are women. Though this "secret" of womanhood is something that only women share as a rite of passage and though it may give us a certain sense of bonding (though the bonding over an "emergency" tampon gets you only so far), ultimately, this is a shameful secret to be kept, even from other women, in public. Even if we may want to, it is no wonder that we don't embrace and celebrate our femaleness; the messages that we should be ashamed are too strong.

We usually learn that menstruation and our cyclic bodily functions are disgusting. Just as quickly, we learn to judge these bodies harshly, and from another's point of view. As Emily Martin writes in *The Woman in the Body: A Cultural Analysis of Reproduction*,

> [b]ut because women are aware that in our general cultural view menstruation is dirty, they are still stuck with the "hassle": most centrally no one must ever see you dealing with the mechanics of keeping up with the disgusting mess, and you must never fail to keep the disgusting mess from showing on your clothes, furniture, or the floor.[5]

As a result, I argue that we gradually become disconnected from our bodies, particularly female bodies. And it is also no wonder that we are so disconnected—between the lack of adequate education and the widely endorsed negative attitudes about our bodies, our menstruation, and our sexuality—women learn early on to ignore, underemphasize, or keep quiet about the functions of our bodies. As Martin writes, ultimately, women are taught to see bodily functions such as menstruation, birth, and menopause as happening to them; they become an object to be dealt with and manipulated by the medical field.[6]

If we are to create a women-centered health agenda, we must recognize and appreciate the differentness of our bodies, perhaps even celebrate our female bodies. In addition to the Feminist Women's Health Centers, organizations like the Boston Women's Health Collective and the National Women's Health Network advocate for women's health so that we may have research that represents us and information that is accessible and comprehensible. Organizations like Good Vibrations and Babes in Toyland offer women a positive image and support for our sexuality. Authors like Christiane Northrup, Inga Muscio, Laura Owen, Geneen Roth, Eve Ensler, Laura Fraser, and Marilyn Wann encourage us to embrace and celebrate our bodies. It is from each of these that we find resources and support for a women-centered approach to our health and wellness. Or, as Eve Ensler has said, "I love the word *vagina*."

REFERENCES

A list of references is available in the original source.

Exposed at Last "The Truth about Your Clitoris"

By Jennifer Johnson

"At a witch trial in 1593, the investigating lawyer (a married man) apparently discovered a clitoris for the first time; he identified it as a devil's teat, sure proof of the witch's guilt. It was 'a little lump of flesh, in a manner sticking out as if it had been a teat, to the length of half an inch,' which the gaoler, 'perceiving at the first sight there of, meant not to disclose, because it was adjoining to so secret a place which was not decent to be seen. Yet in the end, not willing to conceal so strange a matter,' he showed it to various bystanders. The witch was convicted."

from The Vagina Monologues *by Eve Ensler [Villard].*

Pick up almost any medical, anatomy or biology text and you'll find something missing: the greater part of the clitoris.

The clitoris is like an iceberg; only the tip is visible on the outside, its larger mass is under the surface. The visible tip is the glans, or head of the organ. While modern medical science books stop there, the clitoris actually continues under the pelvic bone, then turns down to surround the vagina from above and on either side. The structure forms a dense pyramid of tissue, well-supplied with nerve and vascular network, and is comparable in size to the penis. Like the male organ, the clitoris is flaccid when unaroused and erect when aroused.

And yet, even in the most ponderous, detailed texts, the clitoris is described as a "vestigial organ," or "pea-sized." The diagrams typically show a diagram of a spread-legged female, with a little bulb arrowed "clitoris." The internal diagrams show her reproductive organs, but the bulk of the clitoris—the shaft (body), legs (crura), and bulbs—are missing. Next to the illustration showing the female sex organ as a bump usually appears a drawing of the male sex organ on an extremely well-hung man. Even *Gray's Anatomy*—the authoritative text of biologists—doesn't accurately depict the clitoris.

As a biologist, I first discovered this while doing an anatomical study (dissection) on a human subject. I was shocked to discover that the clitoris was far larger than I had been taught. I could not understand how such a basic—not to mention crucial—piece of biological information had been neglected. I searched textbooks, consulted doctors and professors and found all of them unaware of the actual size of the clitoris.

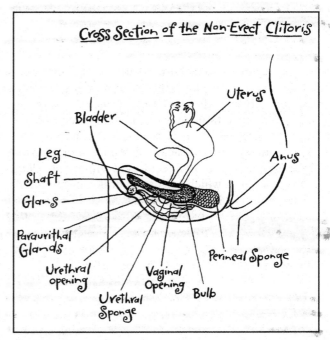

Cross Section of the Non-Erect Clitoris

Bladder
Uterus
Leg
Shaft
Glans
Anus
Paraurithal Glands
Perineal Sponge
Urethral opening
Vaginal Opening
Urethral Sponge
Bulb

Illustration: Noreen Stevens

Of course, I was not the only student of science to discover this. When Helen O'Connell became curious about why the female sex organ was "glossed over" in the texts, she made it her business to take a closer look when she became a doctor. Now a surgeon at the Royal Melbourne Hospital in Australia, she and her colleagues have been dissecting and measuring the clitoris; her findings were reported in a recent article in *New Scientist.* "Sometimes the whole structure is drawn as a dot," says Dr. O'Connell. In fact, the legs of the clitoris, called the crura, are five to nine centimeters long, extending from the body (shaft) of the clitoris and filling the space between its legs are two bulbs, one on either side of the vaginal cavity. Contrary to the belief that the urethra and clitoris are entirely separate, the clitoris actually encompasses the urethra. Dr. O'Connell believes the clitoris squeezes the urethra shut during sex, reducing the entry of bacteria.

Drawing a more accurate picture of the female sexual anatomy explains a few things. It helps explain why some women are not having orgasms, since women must first be erect before they can reach orgasm. It may also explain why Viagra appears to work for women even though it's not supposed to—suggesting that women may be impotent for the same physiological reasons as men. It also explains why women frequently report that their sex lives were damaged following some types of pelvic surgery—the nerves to the clitoris, and sometimes the organ itself, can be damaged or severed during surgery. It also sheds light on the controversy of the clitoral vs. vaginal orgasm that was debated a few years ago.

When seen as an entire complex organ, there is room for a wide range of experiences. Some women experience orgasm through stimulation of the outer glans of the clitoris; at other times they may experience a different orgasm when combined with penetration. An orgasm reached through external stimulation may feel quite different. For many women, orgasm is intense and relatively easy to reach with digital or oral contact because this is the most direct way to stimulate the large pudendal nerve which runs straight down into the tip of the clitoris (the glans). What has been referred to as "the vaginal orgasm" is a vaginal-induced orgasm, brought on by stimulating the clitoris indirectly through the vaginal walls. (Of course, it's common to add some direct pudendal stimulation on the outside.)

Then there is the G-spot. Part of the vaginal wall clinically known as the urethral sponge, the G-spot can be found by exploring the roof of the vagina. It's about a knuckle-length in—from one and a half to three inches inside. The easiest way to find it is to have your partner crook a finger or two and reach toward the belly button. The size varies from half an inch to 1.5 inches. When

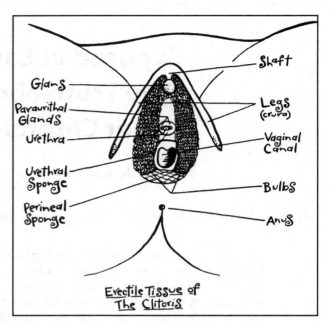

Illustration: Noreen Stevens

unaroused, it feels like the back of the roof of your mouth. If your partner presses up on this spot and you feel like you have to urinate, they've found it. When it is stroked, it will puff out and feel like a marshmallow.

While there are many differences between male and female sexual responses, there are unmistakably many similarities. When the clitoris is engorged and erect, endorphins are released and induce a 'high.' The long bands of the crura become hard and flare out along the pubic bones. Vaginal blood vessels widen and fill with blood and the perineal sponge thickens. The uterus balloons forward, the tubes and ovaries swell. The broad ligament tightens, pulling up the uterus and causing the vagina to enlarge. The neck of the cervix is flexible, like an accordion, and during orgasm, the cervix moves forward and down, dipping its head in the seminal pool if a male partner has ejaculated. As well, ejaculation fluid squirts from the woman's paraurithal glands, located on either side of the urethra. This may come as news to women who haven't had a female sexual partner and therefore may not have experienced a female ejaculation first hand. The ejaculate may be a small amount and not noticeable, or it may be a copious amount that 'soaks the sheets.'

The size of the clitoris is actually not a new 'discovery' but the revealing of a secret. The clitoris was more accurately described in some 19th century anatomy texts, but then it was mysteriously shrunk into a mere speck on the anatomical map. The French, however, have been more accurately depicting the clitoris since before the turn of the century.

While doing research for this article, I contacted many sex-related organizations, including the famous Kinsey Institute, the British Association for Sexual and Marital Therapy, even the German Society for Sex Research. None had accurate information on the clitoris, and most did not believe that the clitoris is larger and more complex than medical texts indicate. In bookstores, I found current sexology books that didn't have more than a paragraph on the clitoris, some only a few lines, many did not have "clitoris" indexed at all! Even the famous British 'feminist' scientist Desmond Morris's new book, *The Human Sexes,* contains no indexed references for clitoris. Without exception, every sex book gave 'penis' all kinds of room—entire sections, chapters and references.

What does it all mean? Dr. Jennifer Berman, director of the Women's Sexual Health Clinic at Boston University, predicts that knowing the proper female anatomy will lead to research in this area of female function and dysfunction, which she says has been "grossly neglected."

In an article published with her colleagues in *The Journal of Urology* in June 1998, Dr. O'Connell and her colleagues wrote, "Since the studies of Masters and Johnson, there has been surprisingly little investigation of basic female sexual anatomy or physiology." The article describes the intricate connection between the urethra and the clitoris and says that surgeons should be made aware of the damage that can be done to the organ during urethral surgery. O'Connell says anatomy texts should be changed to accurately depict the clitoris and perineal anatomy. She is now mapping the nerves to the pelvic region innervating the female sex organ.

"They were mapped in men a decade ago," says O'Connell, "but they've never been mapped in women."

It does beg the question doesn't it? Why not? One anthropologist I spoke to explained that the size of the clitoris may have been overlooked because "the size of the male phallus" is a symbol of power; admitting women have the same size organ would be like admitting they are equally powerful. Indeed.

Sex psychologist Dr. Micheal Bailey doesn't buy into the patriarchal conspiracy theory. "There's been very little scientific interest in female sexuality," he insists. Then adds, "It's possible *we* didn't look."

"Intersex Genitalia Illustrated and Explained"

By Dr. Cary Gabriel Costello

There is a lot of variation in how the genitalia develop from person to person in all of us. Nature provides us with a wide spectrum of forms, onto which our society imposes two absolute categories of male and female. In my last post, I described how all people start out with the same genitals in the womb, and how the phalloclitoris differentiates during development. In this post I will discuss the range of natural genital forms, explaining how they develop from the shared embryonic phalloclitoral structures.

I will illustrate this post with simple diagrams. I know that there is a lot of interest in what intersex genitals actually look like—most of the people who find this blog do so by searching for these words. I've discussed elsewhere[1] why I will not post medical photographs of intersex people's genitalia—these often picture children photographed without their consent, and I will not participate in their exploitation.[2] But I do support people's impulse to know more about the range of human forms. I want to help lift the veil of medically-enforced secrecy that makes our bodies invisible, so that intersex bodies can be demystified and accepted. So: diagrams it is.

I will start by reviewing the structures of our shared original genital form, and showing how they develop in what are deemed "normal" males and females.

The Embryo

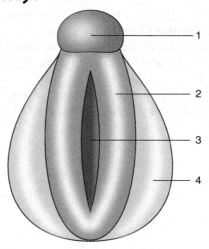

We all begin life with genitals that have four basic external elements. At the top is the part numbered 1 and colored pink on this illustration: the sensitive end of the phalloclitoris, which can differentiate into the head of the penis or clitoris. Below it is structure 2, drawn in orange, which is capable of differentiation into either a phallic shaft, or clitoral body and labia minora. In the center is structure 3, drawn in green: an inset membrane that can widen or can seal as the fetus develops. It will form the urethra, and the vagina, if any. And at the outside is the fourth part, colored blue: the labioscrotal swellings, which can develop into labia majora or a scrotum.[3]

---

[1] http://intersexroadshow.blogspot.com/2009/05/intersex-peep-show.html

[2] For an advanced discussion of photography in medical textbooks and its construction of some bodies as abnormal and pathological, with a specific focus on transgender and intersex people, see T. Benjamin Singer's "From the Medical Gaze to Sublime Mutations: The Ethics of (Re)Viewing Non-Normative Body Images" in The Transgender Studies Reader (eds. Susan Stryker and Stephen Whittle). *Ed.*

[3] This volume does not contain color illustrations or, obviously, allow the reader to click for an enlarged view. The illustrations in this reprint were created specifically for this volume. Costello's original drawings can be viewed with this piece online at his blog: http://intersexroadshow.blogspot.com/2011/04/intersex-genitalia-illustrated-and.html *Ed.*

"Normal Differentiation"

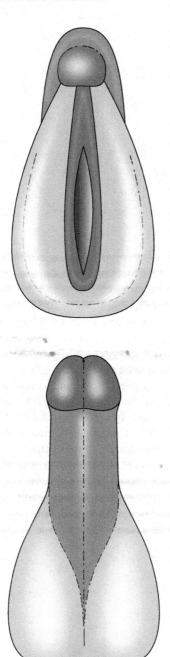

You can see how the four sectors of the embryonic genitalia differentiate in the diagrams of "typical" male and female genitals pictured here (illustrated without the foreskin or "hood"). Click on any illustration to see it larger. Notice that the pink phalloclitoral head points downward in typical female development and upright in typical male development. The orange body of the phalloclitoris separates and is buried beneath the labia in females, while it closes around the urethra and forms the penile shaft in males.

Sex variance occurs in many forms, but they are not random. Intersex conditions are produced by regular patterns of variation in development of one or more of the four parts of the embryonic genitalia. Let us consider a series of intersex conditions to see how these variations arise, and how they are framed by doctors.

"Aphallia"

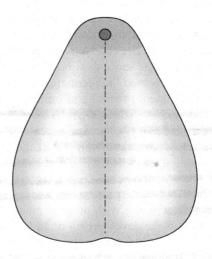

Aphallia the term given by doctors to a form of sex variance produced when the first two sections of the embryonic genitalia do not develop. While this is equally likely to occur in individuals with ovaries as those with testes, it is only generally commented upon medically when the individual has testicles and XY chromosomes. This illustrates how Western medicine is permeated by a strong gender bias. Having a large, erectile penis is considered a necessity for males, and its absence a tragedy of the highest order, to be addressed by somber medical articles. Having a clitoris capable of sensation and erection, however, is given little attention—so little that its congenital absence is treated as worthy of nothing more than a footnote.

The gendered beliefs that permeate Western medicine are further illustrated by the treatment plan for infants with testes who have aphallia. American doctors typically give these children sex reassignment surgery to remove the testes and create a vagina, it being apparently impossible to tolerate the idea of children being raised as boys without a penis. Without this surgical castration, the children could grow up to be fertile, but their fertility is medically sacrificed without their consent. What is particularly noteworthy is that doctors speak of the sex-reassigned patient with aphallia as growing up to have "normal female sexual function." "Normal," for a female, is thus medically defined as being capable of receiving a penis in a vagina, not having sexual pleasure.

"Microphallus"

Some people have large feet and some people have small ones; some have large noses and while others' are petite. When the phalloclitoris is quite small in a person with external testes and a male genital configuration, doctors say the individual has "microphallus." If the testes are deemed "inadequate," doctors often advise sex assignment to female in infancy as they do in the case of aphallia, because life as a man with tiny sex organs is deemed tragic. Again, the individual's fertility is sacrificed without consent. If the testes are considered normal the child may be treated instead with injections of testosterone, in effect triggering puberty in toddlerhood and leading to moderate enlargement of the clitorophallus (along with other premature pubertal effects such as the development of adult patterns of body hair).

Rarely considered as options by doctors are simply allowing the child to live life as a male with a small penis, or to decide for zirself[4] what course of action to take. Whether the sacrifice of some or all sexual sensation to have genitals that appear female is better than living life as a person with testes and a very small phallus is not a question that science can give a single "correct answer." It is a subjective and highly personal decision, and will be driven most strongly by the gender identity the child grows to develop. I and other intersex advocates believe that only the intersex person can make such a life changing decision, and that for doctors to force their choice upon an unconsenting child is both arrogant and cruel.

"Clitoromegaly"

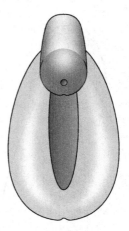

When a child with typically-male-configured genitals has a large phalloclitoris, the doctors make admiring jokes with the parents. But when the child is female, having a large phalloclitoris is deemed a "birth defect." Despite the lack of any functional harm from having a large clitoris, doctors perform surgery to "reduce" it to the "acceptable" female range. This often seriously impairs sexual sensation. Although today doctors like to brag that they preserve sexual sensation because they have abandoned the older surgical treatment of "clitoral amputation," usually some sensation is lost in "clitoral reduction," and sometimes the phalloclitoris loses all sensation, even though some of the tissue is permitted to remain. It is especially ironic that the removal of part of the clitoris in traditional female circumcision practices is renounced as "female genital mutilation" by Western doctors, yet they perform a similar procedure in cases of "clitoromegaly" without compunction.

"Chordee"

---

[4]This term is part of a set of gender-neutral pronouns used by some non-binary and genderqueer people: Ze/zir/zir/zirs/zirself. (Compare: She/her/her/hers/herself and he/him/his/his/himself.) For more discussion of various pronoun sets, see: https://genderneutralpronoun.wordpress.com/2010/01/24/the-need-for-a-gender-neutral-pronoun/ Note that this link dates from 2010; since then, gender-neutral singular they (they/them/their/theirs/themself) has gained popularity and acceptance despite continued linguistic prescriptivist pushback. In fact, singular they was named 2015 Word of the Year by the American Dialect Society. *Ed.*

The head of the phalloclitoris bends down in typical "female" configuration. When it does so in a person assigned male, it is termed "simple chordee." In some individuals, the only atypical characteristic is the folded-down head of the phallus, which is of typical penile size. Doctors present this status as a "malformation of unknown cause," rather than as a typically-female shape of the phalloclitoris in a male, because they are averse to terming any condition in a child assigned male "intersex." But chordee is not a random alternative shaping of the penis, as if the penile head might have been equally likely to spontaneously bend in an S-shape. Chordee arises when Sector 1 of the embryonic tissue develops in the "female" configuration, while the rest of the genital development is typically male. Doctors usually suggest surgical "correction" of the phalloclitoral bend, citing locker-room teasing and a purported challenge to fertility. Such surgery presents a serious risk to sexual sensation in the penile head. Furthermore, fertility is not impaired by having a bent or curved penis—the production of sperm is unaltered. Penetrating some partners may be more difficult, but there are many ways to engage in both sexual interaction and fertilization other than via penetrative sex, and only the possessor of the bent penis can decide whether it makes sense to risk the sacrifice of sensation in the phalloclitoral head to make it easier to engage in penetrative sex with partners who prefer a narrow penis. (Some partners may find the phallus with chordee to be more sexually stimulating than a typical penis.)

In other individuals with chordee, the phalloclitoris is of intermediate size. It appears as an intermediary form evenly balanced between the male and female manifestations of the phalloclitoris. Often the individual also has a shallow vagina (discussed below under "hypospadias").

Whether individuals assigned female at birth may have phalloclitoral heads that do not bend down like a typical clitoris but conform instead to the linear shape typical of males is not discussed in Western medical literature, with its obsession with penises and general disinterest in clitori. I consider it extremely likely that this unnamed counterpart to chordee does occur.

"Diphallia"

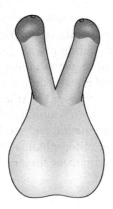

Section 2 of the embryonic genitalia is generally expected to fuse into a single penile shaft in male development, or to spread apart to form the two clitoral crura around the labia majora in female development. If the genitals devleop along male lines but the two sides do not fuse, the individual is born with two separate phalloclitori, side by side, each associated with one testis and having only one corpus cavernosum. Doctors remove one of the phalli (the one deemed smaller, no surprise there), though as in clitoromegaly there seems to be no functional danger involved in having two clitorophalli. This gential configuration can be associated with actual functional problems like an imperforate anus, obviously a true surgical emergency, but constructing an anus has nothing to do with removing half of the phalloclitoris. Doctors do not deem diphallia an intersex condition— the off-the-cuff reading is that the child is "doubly male"—but in fact the clitorophallus has developed in a manner intermediate between male and female norms.

A rarer bodily form than diphallia is phalloclitoral duplication, in which the embryo begins to twin in the genital region but ceases there—similar to what happens in the case of conjoined twins or people born with three legs. The individual is born with two penises or clitori, which may be located side-by-side or one above the other.

"Hypospadias"

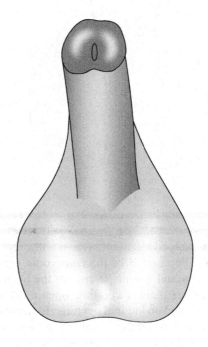

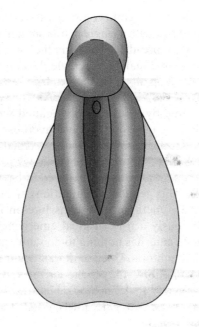

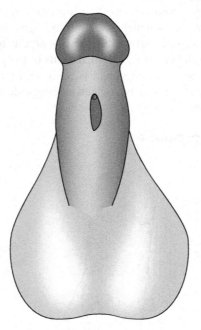

Physical statuses in which a child develops external testes while Sections 2 and 3 of the phalloclitoris develop atypically are grouped together under the medical term "hypospadias." Segment 3 of the embryonic genitalia forms the urethra and vagina, if any. In the normative male configuration, there is a urethral opening at the tip of phalloclitoris, and no vaginal opening. In individuals with hypospadias, the urethral opening is closer to the typically female location, and there may be some vaginal tissue. Individuals born with hypospadias in the U.S.

today are almost always assigned male, and doctors rarely call them intersex. This is an ideological choice rather than one driven by anatomical logic. The medical belief seems to be that if a child has external testes and the clitorophallus can be surgically reconstructed along penile lines, then the child should be assigned male and no question ever raised in the parents' minds about the child having an intersex status. Doctors believe being seen as less than "fully male" is untenable for a man.

The degree of difference between typical male morphology and the genital arrangement of individuals with hypospadias varies widely. In many, it is simply a displacement of the urinary meatus from the very tip of the penis, as shown in the first illustration above, so that the urinary orifice is located lower on the phallic head, which is of ordinary penile size. Doctors "correct" this in childhood, claiming that having a "displaced" urinary meatus is unacceptable, as it will lead to teasing, and ostensibly problems with urinating in a standing position and fertility. Loss of sensation in the head of the penis, fistulas, and problems with recurrent bladder infections are deemed a better outcome by doctors than perhaps needing to sit down to pee—though in adulthood, many who have had this surgery complain that the side effects outweigh any benefits in their lives. The idea that fertility is impaired by having semen emitted from a position slightly lower down on the penis is laughable.

Hypospadias is measured by doctors in degrees. The greater the degree, the more the phalloclitoris assumes a vaginal configuration. The urinary outlet takes the shape of a small vaginal slit if located further from the head of the phalloclitoris, becoming larger if located further down the shaft, as in the second illustration above. If the urethral opening is located at the base of the phalloclitoris, the condition is termed "perineal hypospadias." In people born with this configuration, the genitalia appear intermediate between the female norm and the male, with a vagina located in front of or between the labioscrota. Testes are located in the labioscrotum, with surface skin that can appear more close to typical labia majora or to scrotal skin. The clitorophallus is often intermediate in size and the head may bend down in the typical clitoral configuration called chordee. While children with "perineal hypospadias with chordee" have genitalia that look closer to the female norm than the male, they still may not be classified as "officially" intersex by American doctors, and surgery that closes their vaginas, dissects the clitorophallus from the perineum, and repositions the urethra to the head of the clitorophallus is termed a "repair" rather than sex assignment surgery. Such extensive surgery is painful, life-altering, and usually leads to loss of sensation. Furthermore, a substantial number of people born with this intermediate configuration grow up to identify as female, despite their infant surgical sex assignment to male, and bitterly resent having been given surgery that removed their vaginal tissue while forming their phallo-clitori into the sensation-impaired semblance of a penis.

Rarely mentioned by doctors in articles discussing hypospadias is that it can be accompanied by intermediate internal sex structures, particularly a large "prostatic utricle". (The embryonic structure that typically develops into a uterus in more female bodies forms a small "utricle" in the center of the prostate in bodies that are typically male.) In intersex bodies, this may exist as a small or average sized uterine structure within or aside a prostate—the greater the degree of the hypospadias, the more likely there is a utricle, and the larger it is likely to be. It fascinates me that the fact that people with hypospadias often have a uterine structure, evident in any literature search on the prostatic utricle, is rarely mentioned in medical descriptions of hypospadias, while much rarer associations between intersex conditions and cancer are often mentioned in articles on other intersex conditions. I believe it is not mentioned because discussing a uterine structure would undermine the medical framing of children with hypospadias as "boys with a penile malformation" rather than as intersex children.

"Vaginal Agenesis"

In some individuals, external genitalia are formed which appear close to the female side of the spectrum, but Section 3 only creates a shallow vagina or smooth patch of lubricating skin. Internally, such children may have no gonads, or may have ovaries but no uterus, or may have ovaries and an atypical uterus. Individuals with vaginal agenesis are always called female rather than intersex by doctors, even when they have no gonads and will develop no secondary sexual characteristics (such as breasts or facial hair absence/presence) without taking hormone medications. Again, Western medical ideology seeks to define away intersexuality as much as possible.

There is a lot of attention given by doctors to the creation of a vagina for children with genitals that otherwise appear female to them. This is framed as necessary for "sexual functioning," presuming that forms of sexual activity other than penetration of a vagina by a penis are "not really sex." As is the case with many intersex bodies, surgeries are often performed which sacrifice the capacity for sexual sensation out of an ideology that this is necessary for "normal sex."

"Female Pseudohermaphroditism"/ Congenital Adrenal Hyperplasia

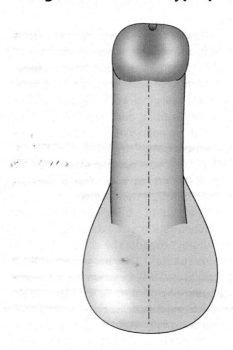

In some intersex conditions, the four zones of the external genitalia develop so that they look typically male (with urethral opening at the tip of the penis, scrotum, and no vaginal opening) but the individual possesses a uterus and ovaries, and the scrotum is empty. The most common diagnosis in people with such a bodily form is congenital adrenal hyperplasia or CAH in XX individuals. While most any person on the street would say that having both a penis and a uterus is an intersex bodily form, doctors hem and haw, and say instead that the child, while intersex, is a "pseudohermaphrodite," somehow really female. This is based on the move by doctors almost a century ago to define intersexuality out of existence by saying that only individuals with the very rare condition of having one ovary and one testis, or having intermediate ovotestes, are "true herm-paphrodites." An intersex person with testes was deemed "really male" and anyone with ovaries "really female" by the creation of the term "pseudohermaphrodite."

At the time doctors came up with the idea of the "pseudohermaphrodite," sex assignment surgery had not yet been developed. Today, however, doctors insist that babies with CAH should be surgically assigned female in infancy. The language of "female pseudo-hermphroditism" is used to sooth parents who are shocked at the idea of a doctor cutting off their baby's penis. Doctors tell them that it is not "really" a penis, but is "really a clitoris" that is malformed. The fact, of course, is that all babies have phalloclitori—and that their baby's is exactly like any other typical boy's penis. If doctors were consistent, they'd have to call all men's phalli "malformed clitori."

In any case, doctors in the U.S. routinely perform what they term "clitoral reduction" on children with CAH—that is, removal of almost all of the phallus—and cut apart the scrotum to give it the form of labia majora. In pressing this surgical sex assignment plan, doctors present parents with an odd assessment of the risks and benefits of such a course of intervention. They gloss over the fact that cutting off most of the phallus seriously impacts adult sexual sensation. They tell parents that this must be done to avoid the catastrophe of adult menstruation through the phallus. (Note that they do not inform parents of children with perineal hypospadias that menstruation is a "danger," or suggest that children with hypospadias be assigned female to avoid penile menstruation.) Doctors do not inform parents that an alternative would be hormone treatment to suppress menstruation, or that their children could grow up to identify as men and function sexually as males, albeit without semen production. (Some ejaculation could be possible, but it would not contain sperm.) Rather than warn parents that many children with CAH grow up not to identify as female and to despair over having been effectively castrated, they warn that the children "have a heightened risk of lesbianism," which is an eye-goggling assertion that is both homophobic and ignores the issue of gender identity.

"Male Pseudohermaphroditism"/ Androgen Insensitivity Syndrome

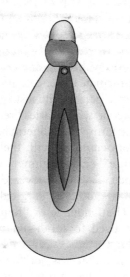

Children with complete androgen insensitivity syndrome or CAIS are the counterparts to XX CAH children. Their external genitalia take the typical female form, but internally they lack a uterus, and in the place where one would ordinarily find ovaries, they have internal testes. Because their bodies do not respond to testosterone, they grow up to develop very feminine secondary sexual characteristics at puberty, though they will never have menstrual periods. Despite their typically-female appearance, doctors call these individuals "male pseudohermaphrodites" because they have testes. However, in contrast to the treatment of children with CAH, doctors do not go on to say that they CAIS children have "malformed penises" that must be surgically altered to fit their "true sex." Instead of urging genital reconstruction, they tell parents to raise their CAIS children as girls, warn parents that their internal testes could possibly present a risk of cancer, and tell them to have the testes removed.

Unlike children with CAH, who often regret their sex assignment surgeries, individuals with CAIS seem to usually accept having been assigned female at birth. This is probably because of the contrast in the intersex individuals' experiences. Children with CAH are assigned female at birth via traumatic, scarring surgeries that impair sexual sensation, and then must take testosterone-suppressing drugs for life, while those with CAIS may not find out about their condition until puberty, retain uninjured and unaltered genitalia, and take no hormone-suppressant drugs. Nevertheless, despite typically identifying as female, these individuals are termed "male pseudohermaphrodites" on all of their medical records, and must live with the consequences of being deemed medically male throughout their romantic and sexual lives.

Some children have Partial Androgen Insensitivity Syndrome or PAIS. They are born with a wide range of phalloclitoral forms, from looking quite close to the male iconic form, to forms like that illustrated under "perineal hypospadias with chordee," to looking typically female. Most have an intermediate form and are given childhood sex assignment surgery to one dyadic norm or the other. As usual, such surgery is traumatic, scarring, does not result in genitalia of fully "normal" appearance, and puts sexual sensation at serious risk. This probably explains why a third to half of individuals with PAIS grow up not to live as the sex they were assigned, while 80% of individuals with CAIS identify as "fully female."

Those Not Pictured

Many bodies vary from sex-dyadic assumptions in ways that are not visible externally, so that they are rarely diagnosed at birth, such as variations in the sex chromosomes. We are told that "men are XY and women are XX," but there are XX men and XY women who are not visibly distinct in their bodily forms from those with typical chromosomes. There are many individuals with XXY chromosomes, termed Kleinfelter's syndrome, with a typical male genital configuration but small testes—about 1 in 500 of people raised male turn out to have this intersex karyotype. People often only discover they are XXY when undergoing tests due to infertility, or sometimes in cases where they develop substantial breasts ("gynecomastia"). Another fairly common genetic variation is to just have a single X chromosome with no second sex chromosome at all, which doctors term Turner Syndrome. Having only 45 chromosomes instead of the usual 46 is associated with a host of physical problems, and the fact that the individual's gonads never develop is treated as secondary to the many physical and mental challenges the individual faces.

Other intersex conditions exist on a more macro level than tiny chromosomes, but are internal and so may go undiagnosed for years or for an individual's entire life. Included among these, ironically, are the only conditions deemed to constitute "true hermaphroditism" under medical taxonomies: the presence of an intermediate ovotestis, or even more rarely, of an ovary and a testis in the same person. I'll write more about "true hermaphroditism" in a later post.

Also not pictured are the bodies of people with an atypical sex steroid balance between the feminizing hormones (estrogens, progesterone, etc.) and masculinizing hormones (testosterone and its byproducts).[5] Everyone produces all of these hormones, and requires both types for fertility and physical health, but those with bodies on the female size of the spectrum typically produce more feminizing hormones, and those with bodies on the male side typically produce more masculinizing hormones. Variations in this balance lead people with typically-female genitals to have higher levels of body and facial hair, muscle mass, likelihood of balding, and libido, and people with typically-male genitals to develop breast tissue, more curvaceous hips, etc. These variations are not

termed intersex by doctors, but there is no logical reason why they should not be. Their intersex character is denied because most adults with such conditions have normative gender identities that match their genitals but are challenged by their contrasting secondary sexual characteristics. They and doctors together strongly assert that their variations do not make them any less male or female. While I agree that no one's gender identity should be deemed undermined by their physical appearance, I believe it would help all sex and gender variant individuals if society and medicine would acknowledge the prevalence of physical sex variance while supporting individuals in their gender identity assertions. Some intersex activists disagree, wishing to limit the conditions that will make a person "count" as intersex, and patrolling the boundaries of the community to exclude others as "wannabes." Personally, I find this cruel and counterproductive. A woman with a beard lives a life in which her sex variance is very visible, and saying she can't be included in a community of those with sex variant bodies because she has typically-female genitalia does not make sense to me.

Another category of hormone-related variance includes individuals who produce low levels of sex steroids and whose bodies do not change much at the usual age of puberty. Such individuals are almost always treated with sex steroid therapy, without presenting them with the option of living in their androgynous bodies medically unaltered.

Finally, let me note that this catalog of intermediate bodily forms is not exhaustive. In my understanding, anyone whose body varies from the iconic male or female dyadic norms is sex variant, cannot be wished out of the intersex rubric by tricks of medical terminology, and should not be excluded from intersex community by gatekeepers.

We need society, the medical field, and intersex communities themselves to acknowledge that nature provides humanity with a wide range of forms, so that all of our bodies can be recognized as valid. Unless there is an actual rare functional problem, our bodies should not be altered in infancy, and only those functional problems should be addressed. Our genitals should be altered only if we ourselves request it, to make ourselves comfortable in our own skin, not to make society comfortable by our medical erasure. Society must come again to embrace the diversity that is nature's gift to us.

---

[5]For more discussion of sex hormones, see Mariamne H. Whatley's "Male and Female Hormones Revisited" elsewhere in this section. *Ed.*

About Dr. Cary Gabriel Costello: *I'm an academic and scaler of boundary walls, intersex by birth, female-reared, legally transitioned to male status, and pleased with my trajectory. Come journey with me! I blog about intersex issues at http:// intersexroadshow.blogspot.com/, and about trans issues at http://trans-fusion.blogspot.com/. If you are interested in contacting me or having me speak to your organization, please email intersexroadshow@ gmail.com.*

"Five Myths that Hurt Intersex People"

By Dr. Cary Gabriel Costello

I've had conversations with some intersex acquaintances recently about painful situations in which (non-intersex) people have accused my friends of not "really" being intersex. Besides revealing how rude people in our society can be about policing sex and gender, what these conversations have illustrated are some central myths about intersex status that come up over and over again. It's these that I will address in this blog post.

Myth 1: Intersex People All have Intermediate Genitalia

Imagine this: you're an intersex person, nervous about dating and finding a partner. You work up your courage to disclose your status to people you're interested in, and after a series of them seeming polite but disinterested in dating, you finally meet a guy who expresses interest. You date for a while, and get to the point where the clothes come off. Your boyfriend gets a good look at you naked, accuses you of "making up that story of being intersex" because your body looks female to him, and breaks off the relationship, leaving you feeling misunderstood and ill-used.

Many people are intersexed in ways that are not visible to their partners. For example, an individual with AIS (androgen insensitivity syndrome) is born with internal testes but genitalia that look typically female. Intersex people born with visibly intermediate genitals are often subject to infant sex assignment surgery, another reason why our bodies may not appear visibly intersex to others.

What disturbs me about incidents in which a partner seems interested in dating an intersex person until the clothes come off is that it generally reveals that the partner was fetishizing the intersex person—only interested in them for their "exotic" body. In the situation described here, the boyfriend wanted to have sex with someone who looked genitally intermediate generally. I've also heard stories from intersex people whose genitals are visibly atypical about how a partner lost interest in them when the clothes came off because they didn't see the kind of "hermaphrodite" genitals they'd dreamt of, with a big penis and a vagina (a configuration almost unheard of in real life, but popular in pornographic fantasy). It's depressing to find out your date wasn't really interested in *you*, but in playing with some fantasy set of genitalia.

Myth 2: Intersex Conditions are Always Diagnosed in Infancy

Here's another unfortunate scenario: a person is having infertility problems, so they visit some doctors. They receive a diagnosis and turn in shock to an online gender forum to post "I was just diagnosed as intersex." Somebody responds, "Stop trolling this blog. You're not really intersex—intersex people all know what they are from childhood. You probably have sick fantasies or think saying you're intersex will give you an excuse to gender transition without controversy." The non-intersex person is accusing the intersex individual of being a non-intersex person exploiting intersex individuals, which is pretty ironic.

As noted above, many intersex conditions aren't obviously visible in external genitalia. That means that people may not find out about their intersex status until quite late in life. While the experiences of late-recognized intersex people are different from those of intersex folks diagnosed in infancy, they are not "less" intersex, and have to deal with physical and psychological ramifications for which they need support.

Myth 3: All Infant Sex-Assignment Surgery is Aimed at Creating "Female" Genitalia

Imagine this situation: you were born with intermediate genitalia but surgically assigned male at birth. However, you grew up hating your male sex assignment, and so you transitioned to female. Your experience has given you a lot of empathy for people viewed as gender transgressive, so when you notice that a friend of a Facebook friend identifies as genderqueer, you write her a nice message and offer her friendship. She refuses your offer and writes you a nasty note back about how she knows you are lying about being intersex, since "all intersex children are made into girls." She accuses you of being a stalking, posing, creepy man-in-a-dress. Ironic and sad, isn't it—that a woman who identifies as breaking down the boundaries of sex and gender is policing those boundaries so rabidly and wrongheadedly?

It is true that intersex infants are disproportionately surgically assigned female, based on the appalling medical aphorism, "it's easier to make a hole than a pole." But some intersex infants are surgically assigned male—usually when they have at least one external testis, but sometimes under other conditions. The myth that this "never happens" leaves intersex people assigned male at birth open to constant suspicion and exclusion, increasing the difficulties they have to face.

Myth 4: Intersex People Should be Genderqueer

This myth comes up again and again in academic, activist and feminist circles: that intersex people, being neither male nor female in physical sex, must be genderqueer and androgynous. We're supposed to be standard-bearers for the fight to subvert artificial dyadic gender categories. Encountering an intersex person with an ordinary and "boring" masculine or feminine gender identity who doesn't look at all androgynous, these activists express puzzlement and disappointment—and in private, speculate that the person must have some minor, mild intersex condition, so they are not "intersex enough" to be insightful.

Intersex people face pressure from doctors and families and society at large to gender conform. Facing the opposite pressure to gender transgress—subversivism— is just as unfair. Yes, most intersex people open enough to disclose our sex status agree that it is damaging for our society to insist that everyone must identify as male or female. But we live in a society that understands gender as a dyad, and like non-intersex people, we commonly identify as masculine or feminine.

Myth 5: "Real" Intersex People are not Genderqueer

Frustrated and upset by pressure from gender activists to gender transgress, as descibed in Myth 4, some intersex people have created a reactionary opposite myth: that "real" intersex people have no interest in subverting dyadic gender understandings of male and female. These gender conservative individuals often don't actually identify as "intersex" but as "people with DSDs (Disorders of Sex Development)."[1] And they go around arguing to institutions that "real" intersex people don't identify as genderqueer—that people who say they are intersex and argue for third gender categories and the like are posers, probably crazed feminist zealots or deceptive trans people.

What makes the myth that intersex people are never genderqueer particularly painful to me is that it is spread by members of our community. To undermine your own intersex siblings and deny their identities is counterproductive, pathetic, and cruel. Many intersex people identify as typically masculine or feminine people, but there are plenty who do not do so, and like all genderqueer people, they face a lot of social bias. We have no duty as intersex people to be genderqueer, but I see a strong moral imperative for us to support people who do have genderqueer identities and manners of self expression. There are enough hurtful myths circulating about intersex people already. We don't need to add one of our own to the mix.

About Dr. Cary Gabriel Costello: *I'm an academic and scaler of boundary walls, intersex by birth, female-reared, legally transitioned to male status, and pleased with my trajectory. Come journey with me! I blog about intersex issues at http://intersexroadshow.blogspot. com/, and about trans issues at http://trans-fusion. blogspot.com/. If you are interested in contacting me or having me speak to your organization, please email intersexroadshow@gmail.com.*

---

[1]"Disorders of sexual development" (DSD) is a common term in medical literature. Some intersex people and activists have countered with the term "differences of sexual development" as a non-pathologizing alternative. You may also see the term "intersex variations" as a counter to "intersex conditions" for similar reasons. *Ed.*

"Trans and Intersex Children: Forced Sex Changes, Chemical Castration, and Self-Determination"

By Dr. Cary Gabriel Costello

Children's lives lie at the center of social struggles over transgender and intersex issues. If you talk with trans and intersex adults about the pain they've faced, the same issue comes up over and over again, from mirror-image perspectives: that of medical interventions into the sexed body of the child. Intersex and trans adults are often despairing over not having had a say as children over what their sexes should be, and how doctors should intervene. Meanwhile, transphobes and the mainstream backers of intersex "corrective" surgery also focus on medical intervention into children's bodies. They frame interventions into the sexual characteristics of intersex children as heroic and interventions into the bodies of trans children as horrific.

The Terms And Claims that Get Tossed Around in These Debates are Very Dramatic. Mutilation. Suicide. Chemical Castration. Forced Sex Changes.

We need to understand what's going on here, because it's the central ethical issue around which debates about intersex and trans bodies swirl. The issue here is the question of self-determination, of autonomy. Bodily autonomy is the shared rallying cry of trans and intersex activists, though we might employ it in opposite ways. Refusing it to us is framed as somehow in our best interests by our opponents.

In This Post[1] We Will Look at How Four Groups Frame The Issue: Intersex People, Trans People, the Mainstream Medical Professionals Who Treat Intersex People, and Opponents of Trans Rights.

If you talk to people who were visibly sex variant at birth, you hear a lot of pain and anger and regret about how their bodies were altered. This is crystallized in the phrase of intersex genital mutilation, or IGM. As a result of infant genital surgery, many intersex people suffer from absent or reduced sexual sensation—something mainstream Western medicine presents as unethical female genital mutilation (FGM) when similar surgeries are performed on girls in other societies. There are further sources of pain: as a result of "corrective" surgeries, intersex people can suffer a wide range of unhappy results, such as loss of potential fertility, lifelong problems with bladder infections, and/or growing up not to identify with the binary sex to which they were assigned. It is extremely painful to identify as female and to know one was born with a vagina that doctors removed with your parents' consent, or to identify as male and to know one's penis was amputated. Imagine if someone performed a forced change on you—would you not feel profoundly violated?

So the intersex perspective is that no one should medically intervene in a person's body without that person's full informed consent. **Bodily autonomy** is a fundamental right. Nobody except you can know how you will feel about your bodily form, whether you might want it medically altered, what risks of side-effects you'd consider acceptable. Routine "corrective" surgery performed on intersex infants is thus a great moral wrong.

---

[1]This piece was originally published on Dr. Cary Gabriel Costello's blog *The Intersex Roadshow*: http://intersexroadshow.blogspot.com/2012/05/trans-and-intersex-children-forced-sex.html

When you speak with trans people, childhood medical intervention again comes up with an air of great regret, but now the regret is that one was not permitted to access it. Almost every person I've ever spoken with who wants to gender transition medically, whether they're 18 or 75, has expressed the same fear to me: "I'm afraid I'm too old!" For a while this mystified me (how is 22 "old"?), until I realized what they meant was, "I'm post-pubertal." For many trans people, childhood was awkward but tolerable, as children's bodies are quite androgynous.[2] Puberty, however, was an appalling experience. Secondary sexual characteristics distorted the body—humiliating breasts or facial hair sprouting, hips or shoulders broadening in ways no later hormone treatments could ever undo. Many trans people live with lifelong despair over how so much maltreatment and dysphoria could have been avoided if they could just have been permitted to avoid that undesired puberty.

So for trans activists, advocating for trans children so that they might avoid this tragedy is vitally important. The child's autonomy is central, as it is for intersex advocates, but here the issue is getting access to medical treatment in the form of hormone suppressants, rather than fighting medical intervention. What trans activists seek is the right of children to ask for puberty-postponing drugs, to give the children's families and therapists time to confirm that the children truly identify as trans, and fully understand what a medical transition involves. Then the individual can medically transition to have a body that looks much more similar to that of a cis person than can someone who has developed an unwanted set of secondary sex characteristics.

So for trans and intersex people, children's autonomy is paramount when it comes to medical interventions into the sexed body. No child should have their sex (e.g. genitals, hormones, reproductive organs) medically altered until they are old enough to fully understand what is involved and actively ask for such intervention. Conversely, once a child is old enough to fully understand what is involved in medical interventions into the sexed body, and requests such intervention, then it should be performed—whether the child is born intersex or not.

This is not yet mainstream medical practice, however. Today, one in every 150 infants faces medical intervention into the sexed body to which they cannot object or consent. Doctors routinely perform such "cor-

rective procedures" on babies with genital "defects" and "malformations." Meanwhile, few trans-identified children are supported in their identities by families and medical practitioners—and great controversy and resistance swirls around them when it does happen.

So let's look at the arguments made by mainstream medicine and transphobic activists. How do they counter the cry for autonomy, given that self-determination and freedom are such central ideals in Western societies? What we'll see is that they employ two opposing claims based in medical ethics: the duty to save a life, and the duty to first do no harm. If we want to protect the rights of trans and intersex children, we have to understand these arguments and be able to counter them.

When intersex advocates try to fight the framing of intersex children's bodies as "defective" and somehow in need of surgical "correction," mainstream medicine responds with a claim of medical necessity. In some very rare cases, particular intersex conditions can be associated with actual functional problems such as an imperforate anus, clearly a serious medical problem that necessitates surgery. But the vast majority of medical interventions into intersexed bodies take place without any such functional, physical problem existing. They are responses to a social issue (discomfort with sex variance) rather than a physical one. What doctors do, however, is reframe social issues into medical ones. "If we don't do this surgery, this child will be mocked and humiliated— "he" won't be able to stand to pee, "she" won't be able to have "normal sex," "it" will never be able to marry. The child will be a social pariah and thus be at risk for suicide."

Through this line of argument, altering the body of the sex variant infant is cast as a noble act that doctors perform out of their duty to save lives. To counter this, what we need to do is point out that actual studies of intersex adults show that while we do have a heightened risk of depression and suicide, these are caused by unhappiness with our medical treatment rather than prevented by it. Loss of sexual sensation, feelings of having been humiliated by doctors, pain from years of "repair" surgery after "repair" surgery, and for those who do not identify with the binary sex to which we were assigned, the vast sense of betrayal that those who were supposed to care for us subjected us to a forced sex change—these are what lead to an increased risk of suicide. What would really help is would be for doctors to follow the precept of "first do no harm," to perform no procedures upon us without our full informed consent, and meanwhile, to provide intersex children and their families with social support.

Invocations of "primum non nocere," first do no harm, and of despicable medical impositions on the

---

[2]Consider, however, how much work goes into ensuring that children's bodies are "read correctly" as male or female, often with intensely gendered clothing—you could examine the separation of infant and child clothing at a store like Target or just observe pictures of babies and children on your Facebook feed. *Ed.*

lives of innocents are also raised by anti-trans advocates. Transphobic activists generally frame all medical transition interventions as mutilations, and this rhetoric rises to fever pitch when the issue of trans children arises. Recently, anti-trans rhetoric has framed the medical provision of puberty-postponing drugs as "chemical castration" (e.g. in this blog post).

"Chemical castration" is an odd concept. First off, if you read any medical article on the topic, you will find it starting by pointing out that the term is a misnomer, as none of the medications used in "chemical castration" destroy the gonads. The term is nevertheless employed due its specific history as a treatment being given by court order to "sexual deviants" to suppress their ability to have sex, where some prior courts had employed actual surgical castration. Today, some jurisdictions use "chemical castration" in cases of pedophilia, but it the past it was a treatment imposed on men convicted of sodomy—that is, to gay men in an era in which gay male sex was criminalized. Transphobic activists use the term "chemical castration" to evoke an aura of adult sexual deviance, in a manner calculated to frame doctors who provide puberty-suppressant drugs as sexually abusing children.

There is a curious twist in this matter of "chemical castration," in that universally when court-ordered in the past, and often still today, it did not consist of testosterone suppression drugs as you would expect. Instead, injections of estrogen and/or progesterone were (and are) given. In essence, it caused a forced sex change. Thus, for example, when codebreaking British war hero Alan Turing was convicted of homosexuality in 1952 and sentenced to "chemical castration," he found the unwanted sex changes in his body so horrifying and humiliating that he committed suicide two years into "treatment."

In the case of trans-identified kids today, the use of the term "chemical castration" is thus a double misnomer. Firstly, no child is castrated—instead, puberty is simply postponed so that if the child, family, and therapist all agree later that a medical transition is appropriate, unwanted secondary sexual characteristics will not have developed. Plenty of adolescents are "late bloomers" by nature; in fact, puberty today occurs many years earlier than it did through most of human history, when human diets lacked sufficient fats and nutrients to support early puberties. So postponing puberty carries no significant dangers.[3] Further, the point of hormone suppression is not to cause a sex change, in contrast

to court-ordered "chemical castration treatments." The point is merely to buy time to ensure that the trans child in question fully understands zir[4] gender identity and the implications of medical transition.

So: we've seen a lot of charged language, of claims and counterclaims regarding mutilation versus vital treatment, cruel withholding of medical assistance versus the imposition of sex changes on unconsenting children. How should trans and intersex advocates respond?

What I would do is to point out that strange and conflicting ideas about children's autonomy and free will are presented by our opponents. When specialists in intersex "corrective" treatments speak to parents or write in medical journals, they urge that genital surgery be performed in infancy, before age two and a half if at all possible. They claim that this way the child will not remember the treatment and will thus adjust well to the altered genitals and/or sex status. (As if medical monitoring and intervention did not often extend throughout the child's life, and the procedures left no scars and caused no loss of sensation, so the child would "never notice.") The age of two and a half came out of now largely-discredited ideas of a milestone of "gender constancy" occurring then, based upon notions of the developing brain that directly relate to autonomy.[5] Before age 2.5, it was basically argued, the baby is irrational and lacks agency, and thus thinks magically about bodily sex, including accepting the "crazy" idea that the sex of the body can change. So, in urging very early intervention into intersex bodies today, conventional medicine is urging the total avoidance of the child's rational thought and agency.

When it comes to treating trans children, on the other hand, instead of rushing things, all sorts of actors want to draw them out. Most doctors and clinics only provide transition services to legal adults. Those few who treat trans children are extremely cautious about providing any medical interventions other than the postponing of puberty.

Both of these approaches deny children autonomy over their bodies and their lives.

---

[3]Hormone suppression is also the established treatment for "precocious puberty" in cisgender children, defined by the Mayo Clinic as puberty before age 8 in female-assigned children and before age 9 in male-assigned children. *Ed.*

[4]This term is part of a set of gender-neutral pronouns used by some nonbinary and genderqueer people: Ze/zir/zir/zirs/zirself. (Compare: She/her/her/hers/herself and he/him/his/his/himself.) For more discussion of various pronoun sets, see: https://genderneutralpronoun.wordpress.com/2010/01/24/the-need-for-a-gender-neutral-pronoun/ Note that this link dates from 2010; since then, gender-neutral singular they (they/them/their/theirs/themself) has gained popularity and acceptance despite continued linguistic prescriptivist pushback. In fact, singular they was named 2015 Word of the Year by the American Dialect Society. *Ed.*
[5]For more information about John Money's discredited research on this topic, see John Colapinto's 2000 book As Nature Made Him: The Boy Who Was Raised as a Girl. *Ed.*

What we must urge is that society consistently respect the rights of children. No children should ever be subjected to sexual surgery without their consent. No children should be forced to have cosmetic surgery. But as children mature, they become able to consent to medical treatment that they do actively desire.

How old is "old enough" to agree to medical interventions into the sexed body? That answer depends on the given child—but 2.5 is certainly too young, and 18 is in most cases too old. What I suggest is that when addressing a medical practitioner urging genital surgery on an intersex infant, that we ask, "Would you perform a sex change on a child of this age who was not intersex?" Conversely, when facing transphobic activists saying that no one who is not a legal adult can be old enough to consent to medical transition services, we should ask if our opponent would say the same if the child were intersex. For example, a child with congenital adrenal hyperplasia may be born with a penis externally, and a uterus and ovaries internally. At around age 12 or 13, if there has been no medical intervention, that child can begin to menstruate through the penis, develop breasts, etc. Would the opponent argue that the child could not be old enough to say that he identifies as male and wants to take testosterone (or that she identifies as female and has decided that she wishes to have surgery to feminize her genitalia)? Would the opponent argue an intersex pubescent child should not at least be able to take puberty-postponing medications to avoid unwanted penile menstruation if they and their family and support professionals were still unsure whether to commit to any more permanent intervention?

What we must ask is that society treat intersex and trans-identified children consistently. We all raise our children to learn to make good decisions, so that they can lead good lives. We must nurture children's autonomy as they grow, understanding that there are some decisions only they can make for themselves. To force a person to live in a sex with which they do not identify is cruelty; to impose unwanted bodily alterations unconscionable. Wishing happiness for our children, we must nurture and then defer to their right to self-determination over interventions into the sexed body.

About Dr. Cary Gabriel Costello: *I'm an academic and scaler of boundary walls, intersex by birth, female-reared, legally transitioned to male status, and pleased with my trajectory. Come journey with me! I blog about intersex issues at http://intersexroadshow.blogspot.com/, and about trans issues at http://trans-fusion.blogspot.com/. If you are interested in contacting me or having me speak to your organization, please email intersexroadshow@gmail.com.*

"Boys and Girls Alike"
The Ethics of Male and Female Circumcision

An Un-Consenting Child, an Unnecessary, Invasive Surgery: is There Any Moral Difference Between Male and Female Circumcision?

By Brian D. Earp

I try not to talk about my research at dinner parties. I'll say "medical ethics" if pressed, which will sometimes trigger an unwelcome follow-up: "But what about medical ethics? That's a pretty big field."

"I study lots of things," I'll say—and that's true, I do. "But I focus on medically unnecessary surgeries performed on children."

"Like what?"

Like what, indeed. It's rarely a smooth ride from there.

The truth is: I study childhood genital surgeries. Female, male and intersex genital surgeries, specifically, and I make similar arguments about each one. As a general rule, I think that healthy children—whatever their sex or gender—should be free from having parts of their most intimate sexual organs removed before they can understand what's at stake in such a procedure. There are a number of reasons I've come to hold this view, but in some ways it's pretty simple. "Private parts" are private. They're personal. Barring some serious disease to treat or physical malfunction to address (for which surgery is the most conservative option), they should probably be left alone.

That turns out to be extremely controversial.

In the 1990s, when the Canadian ethicist Margaret Somerville began to speak and write critically about the non-therapeutic circumcision of infant boys, she was attacked for even addressing the subject in public. In her book *The Ethical Canary*, she says her critics accused her of "detracting from the horror of female genital mutilation and weakening the case against it by speaking about it and infant male circumcision in the same context and pointing out that the same ethical and legal principles applied to both."

She wasn't alone. The anthropologist Kirsten Bell has advanced similar arguments in her university lectures, provoking a reaction that was "immediate and hostile… How dare I mention these two entirely different operations in the same breath! How dare I compare the innocuous and beneficial removal of the foreskin with the extreme mutilations enacted against females in other societies!"

It's easy to see where these reactions are coming from. One frequent claim is that FGM is analogous to "castration" or a "total penectomy." Put that way, anyone who tried to compare the two on ethical (or other) grounds would be making a serious mistake—anatomically, at the very least.

You often hear that genital mutilation and male circumcision are *very different*. FGM is barbaric and crippling ("always torture," as the *Guardian* columnist Tanya Gold wrote recently), whereas male circumcision is comparatively inconsequential. Male circumcision is a "minor" intervention that might even confer health benefits, whereas FGM is a drastic intervention with no health benefits, and only causes harm. The "prime motive" for FGM is to control women's sexuality; it is inherently sexist and discriminatory and is an expression of male power and domination. That's just not true for male circumcision.

Unfortunately, there's a problem with these claims. Almost every one of them is untrue, or severely misleading. They derive from a superficial understanding of both FGM and male circumcision; and they are inconsistent with what scholars have known about these practices for well over a decade. It's time to re-examine what we "know" about these controversial customs.

The World Health Organization (WHO) defines FGM as any "non-medical" alteration of the genitalia of women and girls. What this is likely to bring to mind is the most extreme version of such "alteration," which is the excision of the external part of the clitoris followed by a narrowing of the vaginal opening, sometimes using stitches or thorns. It is rarely understood that this notorious form of FGM is comparatively rare: it occurs in a subset of the practicing communities, and makes up about 10 per cent of cases worldwide. More prevalent, but much less frequently discussed in the media, is a range of less extensive alterations, sometimes performed under anesthesia by medical professionals and with sterile surgical equipment. These include, among other interventions, so-called ritual "nicking" of the clitoral hood (common in Malaysia), as well as non-medically-indicated labiaplasty and even piercings that might be done for perceived cosmetic enhancement.

It should be clear that these different forms of FGM are likely to result in different degrees of harm, with different effects on sexual function and satisfaction, different chances of developing an infection, and so on. And yet *all* forms of non-therapeutic female genital alteration—no matter how sterilized or minor—are deemed to be mutilations in 'Western' countries. *All* are prohibited by law. The reason for this, when you get right down to it, is that cutting into a girl's genitals without a medical diagnosis, and without her consent, is equivalent to criminal assault on a minor under the legal codes of most of these societies. And, morally, I think the law is correct here. I don't think that a sharp object should be taken to any child's vulva unless it is to save her life or health, or unless she has given her fully informed permission to undergo such an operation, and wants to take on the relevant risks and consequences.

In that case, of course, she wouldn't be a "child" anymore, but rather an adult woman, who can make a decision about her own body.

The story is very different when it comes to male circumcision. In no jurisdiction is the practice prohibited, and in many it is not even restricted. In some countries, including in the United States, anyone, with any instrument, and any degree of medical training (including none) can attempt to perform a circumcision on a non-consenting child—sometimes with disastrous consequences. For a recent example, look up "Goodluck Caubergs" on the internet; similar cases happen every year. As the bioethicist Dena Davis has pointed out, "States currently regulate the hygienic practices of those who cut our hair and our fingernails... so why not a baby's genitals?"

Just like FGM, however, circumcision is not a monolith: it isn't just one kind of thing. The original Jewish form of circumcision (until about AD150) was comparatively minor. It involved cutting off the overhanging tip of the foreskin—whatever stretched over the end of the glans—thereby preserving (most of) the foreskin's

protective and sexual functions, as well as reducing the amount of erogenous tissue removed. The "modern" form is much more invasive: it removes between one-third and one-half of the movable skin system of the penis (about 50 square centimeters of richly innervated tissue in the adult organ), eliminates the gliding motion of the foreskin, and exposes the head of the penis to environmental irritation, as it rubs against clothing.

Male genital cutting is performed at different ages, in different environments, with different tools, by different groups, for different reasons. Traditional Muslim circumcisions are done while the boy is fully conscious, between the ages of five and eight, and sometimes later. American (non-religious) circumcisions are done in a hospital, in the first few days of life, with or without an anesthetic. *Metzitzah b'peh*, done by some ultra-Orthodox Jews, involves the sucking of blood from the circumcision wound, and carries the risk of herpes infection and permanent brain damage.

Subincision, seen primarily in aboriginal Australia, involves slicing open the urethral passage on the underside of the penis from the scrotum to the glans, often affecting urination as well as sexual function. And circumcision among some tribal groups in Africa is done as a rite of passage, in the bush, with spearheads, dirty knives, and other non-sterile instruments. Similar to female genital cutting rites performed under comparable conditions (and often by the very same groups), these operations frequently cause hemorrhage, infection, mangling, and loss of the sexual organ. In fact, between 2008 and 2014, more than half a million boys were hospitalized due to botched circumcisions in South Africa alone. More than 400 lost their lives.

But even "hospitalized" or "minor" circumcisions are not without their risks and complications, and the harm is not confined to Africa. In 2011, for example, nearly a dozen infant boys were treated for life-threatening hemorrhage, shock or sepsis as a result of their non-therapeutic circumcisions at a single children's hospital in Birmingham, England. Since this figure was obtained by a special freedom of information request (and otherwise would not have been public knowledge), it has to be multiplied by orders of magnitude to get a sense of the true scope of the problem.

When people talk about "FGM" they are usually thinking of the *most severe* forms of female genital cutting, done in the *least sterile* environments, with the *most drastic* consequences likeliest to follow—even though research suggests that these forms are the exception rather than the rule. When people talk about "male circumcision," by contrast, they are (apparently) thinking of the *least severe* forms of male genital cutting, done in the *most sterile* environments, with the *least drastic* consequences likeliest to follow—perhaps because this is the form with which they are culturally familiar.

One recurrent claim, recently underlined by the US Centers for Disease Control (CDC), is that male circumcision can confer a number of health benefits, such as a small reduction in the absolute risk of contracting certain sexually transmitted infections. This is not typically seen as being the case for FGM.

However, both parts of this claim are misleading. Certainly the most extreme types of FGM will not contribute to good health on balance, but neither will the spearheads-and-dirty-knives versions of genital cutting on boys. What about other forms of FGM? Its defenders (who typically refer to it as "female circumcision") regularly cite such "health benefits" as improved genital hygiene as a reason to continue the practice. Indeed, the vulva has all sorts of warm, moist places where bacteria or viruses could get trapped, such as underneath the clitoral hood, or among the folds of the labia; so who is to say that removing some of that tissue (with a sterile surgical tool) might not reduce the risk of various diseases?

Fortunately, it's impossible to perform this type of research in the West, because any scientist who tried to do so would be arrested under anti-FGM laws (and would never get approval from an ethics review board). So we simply do not know. As a consequence of this, every time one sees the claim that "FGM has no health benefits"—a claim that has become something of a mantra for the WHO—one should read this as saying, "we actually don't *know* if certain minor, sterilized forms of FGM have health benefits, because it is unethical—and would be illegal—to find out."

By contrast, a small and insistent group of (mostly American) scientists have taken it upon themselves to promote infant male circumcision as a form of partial prophylaxis against disease. Most of these diseases are rare in developed countries, do not affect children before an age of sexual debut, and can be prevented and/or treated through much more conservative means. Nevertheless—since it is not against the law for them to do so—advocates of (male) circumcision are able to conduct study after well-funded study to see just what kinds of "health benefits" might follow from cutting off parts of the penis.

Many European medical experts dispute these studies, and detect more than a whiff of cultural bias in favor of circumcision due to its peculiar status as a birth ritual in American society. The recent statement by the CDC is a case in point. This otherwise august organization contends that the benefits of circumcision outweigh the risks, where by "risk" they apparently mean "risk of surgical complications."

But in medical ethics, the appropriate test for a nontherapeutic surgery performed in the absence of disease or deformity is not benefit vs "risk of surgical complications" but rather benefit vs risk of *harm*. In this case, one relevant harm would be the involuntary loss of a healthy, functional, and erotogenic genital structure that one might wish to have experienced intact. Imagine a report by the CDC referring to the benefits of removing the labia of infant girls, where the only morally relevant drawback to such a procedure was described as the "risk of surgical complications."

It is often said that FGM is designed to "control" female sexuality, whereas male genital cutting is less symbolically problematic. But as the sociologist Lisa Wade has shown in her research, "attributing [the] persistence [of female genital altering rituals] to patriarchy grossly over-simplifies their social, cultural, and economic functions" in the diverse societies in which they are performed. Throughout much of Africa, for example, genital cutting (of whatever degree of severity) is most commonly performed around puberty, and is done to boys and girls alike. In most cases, the major social function of the cutting is to mark the transition from childhood to adulthood, and it is typically performed as part of an elaborate ceremony.

Indeed, in nearly every society that practices such coming of age rituals, the female half of the initiation is carried out by women (rather than by men) who do not typically view it as being a consequence of male dominance, but who instead see their genital-altering practices as being beautifying, even empowering, and as an important rite of passage with high cultural value. The claim that these women are all "brainwashed" is anthropologically ignorant. At the same time, the "rite of passage" ceremonies for boys in these societies are carried out by men; these are done in parallel, under similar conditions, and for similar reasons—and often with similar consequences for health and sexuality (as illustrated earlier with the example of South Africa).

In the US context, male circumcision was adopted by the medical community in the late 1800s in an effort to combat masturbation, among other dubious reasons. It has since persisted as a rationalized habit, long past the time when it was effectively abandoned by other developed nations. Of course, it is probably true that most contemporary Western parents who choose circumcision for their sons do not do so out of a desire to "control" their sexuality, but this is also true of most African parents who choose "circumcision" for their daughters. As the renowned anti-FGM activist Hanny Lightfoot-Klein has stated: "The [main] reasons given for female circumcision in Africa and for routine male circumcision in the United States are essentially the same. Both promise cleanliness and the absence of odors as well as greater attractiveness and acceptability."

Given that both male and female forms of genital cutting express different cultural norms depending upon the context, and are performed for different reasons in different cultures, and even in different communities or individual families, how shall we assess the permissibility of either? Do we need to interview each set of parents to make sure that their proposed act of cutting is intended as an expression of acceptable norms? If they promise that it isn't about "sexual control" in their specific case, but rather about "hygiene" or "aesthetics" or something less symbolically problematic, should they be permitted to go ahead?

But this is bound to fail. Every parent who requests a genital-altering surgery for their child—for whatever reason under the sun—thinks that they are acting in the child's best interests; no one thinks that they are "mutilating" their own offspring (whether female or male). So it is not the *reason* for the intervention that determines its permissibility, but rather the *consequences* of the intervention for the person whose genitals are actually on the line.

As the social anthropologist Sara Johnsdotter has pointed out, there is no one-to-one relationship between the amount of genital tissue removed (in males, females, or indeed in intersex people), and either subjective satisfaction while having sex, or a feeling of having been personally harmed because one's "private parts" were altered before one could effectively resist. Medically unnecessary genital surgeries—of whatever degree of severity—will affect different people differently. This is because each individual's relationship to their own body is unique, including what they find aesthetically appealing, what degree of risk they feel comfortable taking on when it comes to elective surgeries on their reproductive organs, and even what degree of sexual sensitivity they prefer (for personal or cultural reasons). That's why ethicists are beginning to argue that individuals should be left to decide what to do with their own genitals when it comes to irreversible surgery, whatever their sex or gender.

This article is adapted from a longer piece originally published at the University of Oxford's Practical Ethics website. Links to supporting research can be found in the original essay, available here: https://www.academia.edu/8817976/Female_genital_mutilation_FGM_and_male_circumcision_Should_there_be_a_separate_ethical_discourse

"Male and Female Hormones Revisited"

By Mariamne H. Whatley

In 1985 a chapter I wrote, "Male and Female Hormones: Misinterpretations of Biology in School Health and Sex Education," in which I examined in detail problems with both content and language in health and sexuality texts, was published in *Women, Biology, and Public Policy* (edited by Virginia Sapiro, Sage Yearbooks in Public Policy Studies, vol 10). Since then there have been a lot of changes in health education, sexuality education, and general knowledge about women's health and biology. However, when I reread the chapter to see how out-of-date it was, I was interested to find that the main points I made then are still very relevant.

One of central examples I presented was of the common use of the terms "male hormones" and "female hormones" to refer to androgens and estrogens respectively. By using this terminology, educators imply that men and women have two very different sets of hormones, which naturally could be seen as affecting development, behavior, and abilities, and could serve as the basis for believing incorrectly that there are biologically-determined sex roles, rather than culturally and socially influenced gender roles. In fact, men and women share the same hormones, but they appear in varying amounts. The average man will have higher levels of androgens than the average woman and the average woman will have higher levels of estrogen than the average man. However, just by looking at hormone levels a scientist could not determine with certainty whether an individual were male or female, because there is so much variation across individuals, across the lifespan, at different parts of the menstrual cycle for women, and even at different times of the day (Men's levels of androgens may vary more in a day than a woman's estrogen levels do over a month). There

are a number of reasons, therefore, why it is scientifically inaccurate to refer to male hormones and female hormones:

1. Both males and females produce both androgens and estrogens.
2. The adrenal glands and the gonads (ovaries, testes) produce both hormones in both sexes.
3. Both males and females need both androgens and estrogens for normal development.
4. Both hormones increase in both males and females at puberty.
5. Androgens and estrogens are steroids which are very similar in structure and can be interconverted (changed from one to the other) in our bodies.
6. Knowing hormone levels alone is not enough to determine whether an individual is biologically male or female.

In spite of these facts, much sexuality and puberty education material still refers to estrogens and androgens as very distinctly female or male. For example, in discussing female puberty, only estrogen will be discussed as a factor in changes in development, leaving out the fact that androgens do play a role in the development of girls, as well as of boys, in such changes as muscle growth, hair distribution, acne, and libido (sex drive). If androgen is presented as only a *male* hormone, then muscle development in girls is seen as abnormal. Boys on the other hand also normally produce estrogen, which sometimes reaches high levels at puberty, causing changes that may be seen as "female," such as temporary breast enlargement (gynecomastia) or more fat distribution on the hips. A boy with gynecomastia will undoubtedly feel uncomfortable no matter how sensitively the topic is handled, but it certainly won't help if he and his peers have all learned that breast enlargement is caused by estrogen, the *female* hormone. On the other hand, if the message is that all boys and men produce estrogens but that the levels can fluctuate, especially during puberty, and cause temporary breast enlargement, that boy might at least have some assurance that he is "normal."

At the other end of the reproductive cycle, there are often discussions of hormones in relationship to aging. Information on menopause may present postmenopausal women as becoming more "male" as their estrogen decreases and androgen becomes proportionately higher. Such changes may have to do with loss of breast size and density, growth of facial hair, and redistribution of body fat, so there is less on hips and thighs and more in the abdomen. Because her whole life, a woman has been told that she has "female hormones," the menopause literature which presents menopause as a total lack of estrogen or an "estrogen deficiency disease" is giving the message that the factor that makes her female is gone. She is, therefore, not really female any longer. When Robert Wilson wrote the book *Feminine Forever,* which extolled the virtues of exogenous estrogen to counter the effects of menopause, much of his focus was on the loss of estrogen as causing a loss in femininity and sexuality. While there has been much criticism of his work and, in recent years, there has been a decrease in the negative descriptions of menopause, these views do still persist. Discussing the fact that estrogen does not disappear after menopause and that androgens are actually converted to estrogens in fat and muscle cells can help give women a clearer view of what the real hormonal changes are. Also recognizing that their whole lives, they have gone through changing balances of hormones places menopause more in the context of ongoing biological processes rather than a new, completely different stage. Before puberty, girls and boys have very similar levels of hormones and the low estrogen in girls is certainly not considered an "estrogen deficiency disease" that needs to be treated with "estrogen replacement."

There are other implications of viewing estrogens and androgens as distinct hormones not shared by the sexes. If hormones are believed to have certain effects on behavior or abilities, then the association of a hormone with only one sex will imply biological limitations. For example, some scientists believe that androgen levels cause changes in aggression. There has been a long debate about this which includes such key opposing arguments as: the fact that behavior and environment can themselves alter hormone levels, so a high level of androgen may be a *result* of being in an aggressive position rather than a *cause* of it; the definition of aggression as very loose, ranging from rough and tumble play in primates to success in business and politics. If it were accepted that androgen levels cause aggression and aggression were loosely defined as meaning being able to compete in a highly competitive field, such as business or politics, then women would be seen as unable to compete in these areas. And, of course, women who are as aggressive (or assertive) as men may be seen as not really normal women. While we hope most people have discarded these outdated views, the basic misunderstanding of biology seeps into many discussions of women's abilities in general and in discussions of specific women. When someone refers to a woman as "ballsy," it may be seen as a compliment for her being a gutsy woman ready to take on challenges, but is also a backhanded compliment because it also implies she is not fully a woman, figuratively possessing testes—the major producer of androgens.

A discussion of changing the language which is used to describe hormones may seem trivial, as did attention to changing the generic male (e.g., mankind). However, a view of the world underlies choices we make in language and a change in language—however small—can cause a shift in perception. Just as we now refer to firefighters and police officers rather than firemen and policemen, to represent more accurately the status of women in the workforce, so must we also clean up our scientific language to reflect scientific reality, which is so often distorted and misrepresented.

SECTION 4

MENSTRUATION AND MENOPAUSE

"Period Products: Information About Tampons, Pads, and More"

From the *Center for Young Women's Health*

There are two basic types of period products: **external protection** and **internal protection**. External protection such as pads and panty liners attach to the crotch of underpants to absorb your menstrual flow after it leaves the body, while internal protection such as tampons are inserted into the vagina to catch or absorb menstrual flow before it leaves your body. Some people prefer internal protection because you can't feel it and it is easier to use when playing sports. Tampons[1] are the most common type of internal protection, but there are other choices available, too.

Using a tampon or other form of internal protection can be scary the first time, but after that it gets much easier! Some people worry that internal protection will change their hymen (a thin piece of tissue that partially blocks the entrance to your vagina), but this isn't true. Talk to your mom, older sister, or another adult that you trust about how to use a tampon, and you can also watch our video about using your first tampon.[2]

Both internal and external forms of protection are safe. There is a risk of *Toxic Shock Syndrome* with tampons, but the risk is very low when they are used correctly. You should read the directions on the package and change them frequently (every 4-8 hours). Make your decision about which type of period product to use based on whatever you feel most comfortable using! Talk about the different types of period products with an adult you trust. This will help you make your decision about which kind you will want to use.

[1]Using your first tampon: http://youngwomenshealth.org/2012/09/27/tampons/
[2]http://youtu.be/JbKkOd0LIpw

Can I Swim And do Normal Activities When I Have My Period?

Yes. People used to think that you shouldn't swim, play sports, or do other normal activities when you had your period. Now people know that this is not true. If you have the right type of menstrual protection, you can do anything! In fact, swimming and playing sports may make you feel better. Other girls prefer to be less active when they have a heavy flow or cramps. You will probably be most comfortable if you use a tampon rather than a pad when you swim or play sports.

Alternative and Environmentally Friendly Menstrual Products: If you're concerned about the chemicals and synthetic materials used to make regular pads and tampons, or you're looking for a more cost effective way to deal with your periods, you may want to consider using alternative products that are available in most pharmacies and grocery stores.

What are Some "Natural" Menstrual Products that are also Environmentally Friendly?

Reusable, absorbably period panties (Thinx) are the newest menstrual product on the market. The crotch is 4 layers thick and absorbs light to medium amounts of menstrual flow. Girls/young women can wear this type of underwear with or without a tampon. The cost of the underwear is pricey, starting at $24 for a thong style and up to $38 for high waste panties. However, they are washable and reusable and environmentally friendly. Users of this product say they are "thin but very absorbent and comfortable to wear, don't stain, and absorb normal menstrual flow all day."

Non-chlorine bleached all-cotton pads and tampons are available at many natural foods stores, some of the larger supermarket chains, and online. They're a bit more expensive than regular pads and tampons. They are disposable, so they aren't as environmentally friendly as reusable products, but they're not made using chemicals.[3] However, even 100% natural cotton can contain pesticides, so if you want to be sure that the product you're buying has no chemicals, it's best to choose a brand made with organic cotton.

Reusable, washable, cloth pads work just like regular disposable pads, but instead of throwing them away after use, you rinse them out, wash them, and use them again. Reusable pads usually come in two parts: a liner and a liner holder. The liner goes inside the holder, which has wings that snap around the crotch of your underwear to keep it in place. They come in different sizes and absorbencies and are usually less irritating because they are made of cotton, not plastic. Cloth pads are more expensive than disposables (when you first buy them) but they will save you money over time because they last for years. You change reusable pads as often as you would change disposable pads, except with reusable pads you hand or machine-wash them instead of throwing them away. Girls with sensitive skin or allergies may prefer cloth pads made with organic cotton.

Sea sponge tampons are a natural alternative to synthetic tampons that come in different sizes to absorb varying amounts of menstrual flow. On average they cost between $12-20 dollars (for a package of 2). These are not the same sponges that you might buy in a grocery store to wash dishes with. Sea sponges are actually harvested from the ocean floor and contain no synthetic materials. After harvesting them, they're naturally bleached with hydrogen peroxide; however, they're not sterile. One sea sponge will last about 6 months, but some may not last as long. A menstrual sea sponge should be thrown away and replaced if you notice that it rips apart while you're inserting or removing it from your vagina. You should follow the instructions that come with the product. Before using a sea sponge tampon, you'll have to dampen it, squeeze it tightly in your hand, and then gently insert it into your vagina. When the sponge is dry it's surprisingly hard, but once dampened it softens up immediately. Once in place, it works like a tampon to absorb menstrual flow.

A sea sponge needs to be rinsed out about every 3 hours and thoroughly cleaned, dried, and properly stored at the end of each menstrual cycle. Care must be taken to remove the sea sponge to avoid tearing it.

According to the manufacturer, Jade & Pearl Inc. the Sea pearl sponge can be left in place during intercourse, but it must be removed and rinsed/cleaned thoroughly afterwards. Check the manufacturer's website for instructions on how to disinfect your sponge. *As with tampons, it is possible to get toxic shock syndrome from sea sponges.*

Reusable Menstrual Cups: Menstrual cups are another alternative to tampons. The Keeper®, The Keeper Mooncup®, The DivaCup, Intimina Lily cup and one disposable cup (Instead Softcup) are examples of different kinds of menstrual cups. Most menstrual cups are made of rubber or medical grade silicone which makes the cup easy to fold so that it can be inserted into the vagina to "catch" menstrual blood rather than absorb it. The design is simple; a cup to collect menstrual blood and a "pull-tab" to remove it to make emptying it easy. A menstrual cup is placed inside the vagina a few inches below the cervix. When it is time to empty the cup, simply remove and empty the cup into the sink, or toilet then rinse with clean water then reinsert. Although it looks like a funnel, the blood does not drain out through the pull-tab (the tube is solid not hollow). Menstrual cups are not linked to TSS (Toxic Shock Syndrome) because they simply collect the blood rather than absorb it. They can be worn about 6-12 hours (depending on the amount of your flow). There are about ten different kinds of reusable menstrual cups available on the market today. The most popular menstrual cups come in two sizes. The bigger cup is recommended for women over 30 who have delivered a baby vaginally. The cup may not be the right choice if you are not sexually active or you have a heavy flow.

The Keeper®: The Keeper® menstrual cup is made of natural gum rubber from trees. It should NOT be used by women who are allergic to latex.

The Keeper Mooncup®: The Keeper Mooncup® is made of non-latex, medical-grade silicone.

Lunette Cup: Lunette cups are the only colored menstrual cups that the Federal Drug Administration has approved. They are made of the same medical-grade silicone as other cups and are approved by the U.S. Food and Drug Administration.

The DivaCup: The DivaCup is made of a medical-grade silicone, which makes it an alternative for women with latex allergies or who are sensitive to The Keeper®.

The DivaCup, The Keeper®, and The Keeper Mooncup® all sell for about $35 (a piece) which costs a lot more than a box of pads or tampons. However, with proper care they can last for years, making the cost reasonable over time. Some girls and women like to wear a panty shield when using the menstrual cup for extra protection.

---

[3]Here the authors are probably referring specifically to **dioxins**, rayon byproducts that raise health concerns for some users. *Ed.*

The Lily Cup™ is recommended for women who have not given birth or for those who have given birth by Caesarean. This cup folds easily so that it can be inserted into a woman's vagina. It is soft and thin and users say that they cannot "feel" the Lily cup while it is in their vagina. It collects rather than absorbs blood and it comes with a compact for easy storage.

Disposable Menstrual Cup:

The Instead Softcup is worn at the very back of the vagina and covers the cervix. It collects, rather than absorbs menstrual flow, and can be used for up to 12 hours at a time, depending on your flow. The manufacturer claims that it can be kept in place during any activity, including sexual intercourse (Note: Wearing the Instead Softcup during sex does NOT protect against pregnancy or STIs). The cup must be thrown away after a single use. Instead Softcups are sold in drug stores and supermarkets, but they can be hard to find and are more expensive than tampons.

Are Reusable Menstrual Products Safe and Healthy to Use?

Although it may be unacceptable for some girls and young women to handle their menstrual blood or place a menstrual cup in their vagina, it is important to know that they are safe and easy to use. There's nothing "dirty" about menstrual blood. It's important for reusable products to be properly cleaned and stored according to the manufacturer's instructions.

Of course, you should never share reusable menstrual products with anyone else, and you must follow the manufacturer's instructions about when and how to replace the product.

Where can I Learn More About Alternative Menstrual Products?

Because most women are not familiar with these products, their manufacturers are often willing to provide education and support to anyone interested in switching from the more popular menstrual products. Most manufacturers even offer a money-back guarantee to encourage uncertain consumers to give eco-friendly menstrual products a try.

When you think about all the tampons or pads that you would use over the course of your menstruating years, choosing a reusable product (instead of a throw-away one) would definitely have a positive impact on the environment. However, keep in mind that on average it takes 2-3 menstrual cycles of using these

products to get used to them and to see if you like them, especially if you've been using tampons and regular pads for a while. You might decide that you're happier using an alternative product or you might find that you'd rather stick with regular tampons and pads—and that's okay. There's no right or wrong choice! The best menstrual product is the product that you're most comfortable using.

Below you'll find some commercial web sites with FAQ's about alternative and environmentally friendly menstrual products. The CYWH does not necessarily endorse any of the following manufacturers of alternative menstrual products or their websites. Our goal is to provide our readers with links to the companies that make these reusable products, to learn more about them, and understand how to properly use them to lessen the risk of infection.

Commercial Websites:

- DivaCup: http://divacup.com/
- Lily Softcup & Instead Soft Cup: http://softcup.com/
- Thinx Period Panties: https://www.shethinx.com/pages/index[4]
- GladRags: http://gladrags.com/
- Lunapads: http://lunapads.com/
- Lunette Menstrual Cup: http://www.lunette.com/
- Sea sponge tampons: http://www.jadeandpearl.com/
- The Keeper: http://www.keeper.com/index.html

The Center for Young Women's Health (CYWH) is a collaboration between the Division of Adolescent and Young Adult Medicine and the Division of Gynecology at Boston Children's Hospital. The Center is an educational entity that exists to provide teen girls and young women with carefully researched health information, health education programs, and conferences.

All information is for educational purposes only. For specific medical advice, diagnoses, and treatment, consult your health care provider.

---

[4]Thinx has also run advertising specifically highlighting transgender men and non-binary people who menstruate, and offers a "boy short" style intended to be gender-neutral, although their website specifies that it is intended for "light flow": http://www.shethinx.com/pages/people-with-periods *Ed.*

"No, I Won't Ask About Your Period. Yes, You Can Tell Me About It."

By Kat Callahan (鮎川きお)

Trans women and menstruation: it's a touchy subject. For trans women, navigating conversations about menstruation can be difficult. If we come off as *too* interested, we also come off as *creepy* or even *fetishizing*. If we seem to be uncomfortable or uninterested in discussions involving Aunt Flo, then we can often make our cis friends uncomfortable with our presence in women only or women dominated spaces. Go too far in either direction, and you're bound to highlight your trans status in a way that is othering.

Most of my friends since starting (restarting?) my transition are women. This did not happen on purpose. In fact, it happened rather organically. I still have a number of male friends, but most of them are not in Japan or are fairly far from me in Japan. I honestly haven't been able to go three days without being involved in a conversation online or in person that involves menstruation, even as an offhanded comment, in months. The vast majority of these are not ones I start (although I do sometimes post amusing videos related to menstruation on my Facebook page). Instead, women often feel surprisingly free to discuss with me their particular circumstances quite openly. Sometimes this includes women who know I am a trans woman but to whom I am not particularly close.

I've spoken about my one coworker who is sort of a friend sort of not, and I've had some quite detailed conversations with her about the subject, at her instigation.

When I first discussed my idea of having an adult slumber party, my friend H immediately said, "Oooh, we can talk about boys and periods!" in a sing-song voice. I looked at her in horror, absolutely sure that she was making fun of me, or even accusing me of being terribly stereotypical about female socialization and upbringing. Luckily, she read my expression correctly and reassured me that, no, this really just was what teen girls talked about, and that the only difference with adult slumber parties is the addition of sex talk and booze. I wasn't entirely sure I believed her. But she wasn't lying. I had three friends over, H, SG, and R, two of who are members of the Diva Cup Army. We probably spent hours in conversation involving menstruation, and it carried over into our trip to downtown Tokyo the next day and later on the train ride home.

But do I *want* to discuss menstruation? That's a really odd question to ask. I guess, no, not particularly. But I also don't *not* want to discuss it if it comes up. I recognize it for what it is; a set of experiences nearly all women have. The exceptions don't just include trans women, but altogether, the exceptions are rare. To be part of a women's space, or even a circle of friends which is all women, means that discussions of the red tide are inevitable.

As for how I personally feel about my lack of uterus and ovaries and my inability to menstruate? Complicated feelings are complicated. Iron Mam recently asked me this:

> Do you lean more towards the "yay! At least I never have to deal with all that crap" mindset towards periods or is it more a matter of regretting not getting to have that experience that the majority of women have? I was wondering because I could imagine feeling both ways if I was not a cis-lady.

The simple, yet complicated answer is *both*.

I think it's possible to recognize what a shitty experience it often is, and yet still have lingering feelings of resentment that it seems so primary to the female experience. I don't think any rational trans woman *really* wants to experience the negative effects of menstruation. I am sure as hell positive no rational cis woman wants to experience those negative effects either. After this much time being in and around discussions, some of them complex and detailed, I can't say I much look forward to those effects.

That said, after a rather pointed discussion with a friend of mine who does not have issues with her own periods (they're apparently textbook regular, low flow, not terribly problematic, and other women despise her for it), and quite a lot of thinking, I realized in the event of an affordable, normalized transplant procedure for uteri (which I often point out is being developed, although we are just in the initial stages), I would probably choose to get one. I've actual cis friends who claim to be just as serious about getting rid of their uteri, that they seriously do not want them, will not have children, and think they would serve a much better purpose being given to trans and cis women without uteri. I think in some cases, we can take such comments with a grain of salt, but I am sure there are genuine examples. Not to mention trans men.

And maybe, just maybe, my mother would get off my back about kids.

So, no, ladies, I'm not going to ask about your period, but yes, I'm always willing to listen to you about it.

"Less Hormone Therapy, Less Breast Cancer"

By Adriane Fugh-Berman

For the *National Women's Health Network*
Article taken from January/February 2007 Newsletter

The exodus from menopausal hormone therapy after the Women's Health Initiative (WHI) proved that the risks of this therapy outweighed its benefits has resulted in a stunning drop in breast cancer rates. A new study shows that, in 2003, the year after the estrogen-progestin arm of the WHI was stopped, breast cancer rates plummeted by seven percent.[1] It was expected that about 200,000 women would develop breast cancer in 2003, so about 14,000 fewer women were diagnosed with the disease than expected.

The decrease was most pronounced in women who were older than 50: women who were the prime target audience for hormone therapy. Breast cancer rates dropped 11 percent for women in their 50s and 60s—and 7 percent for women in their 70s. In contrast, breast cancer rates dropped only 1 percent for women in their 40s, who are less likely than older women to take hormones.

The effects of hormone therapy are linked more strongly to estrogen-receptor (ER)-positive tumors than to estrogen-receptor-negative tumors. The decrease in cancer rates was twice as high (8 percent versus 4 percent) in ER-positive tumors than it was in ER-negative tumors. Among women 50–69 years of age, the reduction in ER-positive tumors was three times higher than the reduction in ER-negative tumors (12 percent versus 4 percent). This study provides dramatic confirmation that combined hormone therapy increases the risk of developing breast cancer, particularly of developing ER-positive tumors.

Normally, one has to be cautious in interpreting cause and effect from associations. For example, birth rates that go up in a location in which the number of storks is also increasing doesn't prove that storks bring babies. The dramatic drop in breast cancer rates, however, is extremely unusual—especially without a change in other cancer rates. The decrease was seen in every cancer registry that reports data to the federal government. The fact that there were so many people using, and then abandoning, hormone therapy makes this into a sort of large-scale natural experiment.

The wide use of hormone therapy, of course, was due to marketing. Menopausal hormones were heavily promoted as a way to prevent disease during the 1990s. In fact, gynecologists were so convinced of its benefits that they ranked hormone use above smoking cessation as a positive means to prevent disease.[2] Fifty-eight million prescriptions for hormone therapy were written in 1995; between 1999 and 2002, 90 million prescriptions were written annually.[3] That means about a quarter of all women over 40 were taking hormones during this time.

Six months after the WHI found that menopausal hormones increased breast cancer rates and did not prevent cardiovascular disease, hormone prescriptions dropped by two-thirds. A year later, hormone prescriptions were down by 80 percent, compared to the number written before the WHI results were announced.[4] Other studies have also found that hormone use has dropped. The National Ambulatory Medical Care Survey and the National Hospital Ambulatory Medical Care Survey found that visits to physicians that resulted in hormone prescriptions being written decreased 43.6 percent from 2001 to 2003.[5]

Fluctuations in breast cancer rates appear to closely follow the use of hormones. While hormones were being most heavily promoted, breast cancer rates increased: between 1990 and 1998, the incidence increased 1.7 percent per year. Breast cancer incidence began to drift down gradually after that, declining about 1 percent a year. Then, in 2003, the rates suddenly plummeted 7 percent. This is an astoundingly large drop; cancer rates just don't change that fast without something major going on.

Hormone therapy is effective for hot flashes, and its short-term use may be worth the risks for some women with severe symptoms. But at this point, many lines of evidence have proven that menopausal estrogen-progestin therapy increases breast cancer risk. Don't let anyone tell you otherwise.

REFERENCES

1. Ravdin PM, Cronin KA, Howlander N et al. "A sharp decrease in breast cancer incidence in the United States in 2003." Data from MD Anderson, the National Cancer Institute, and Harbor UCLA Medical Center, presented at the San Antonio Breast Cancer Symposium, December 14, 2006.

2. Saver BG, Taylor TR, Woods NF et al. "Physician policies on the use of preventive hormone replacement therapy." *Am J Prev Med* 1997: 13(5):358–365.

3. Hersh AL, Stefanick ML, Stafford RS. "National use of postmenopausal hormone therapy: annual trends and response to recent evidence." *JAMA*, 2004 Jan 7; 291(1): 47–53.

4. Majumdar SR, Almasi EA, Stafford RS. "Promotion and prescribing of hormone therapy after report of harm by the Women's Health Initiative." *JAMA*. 2004 Oct 27; 292(16):1983–8.

5. Hing E, Brett KM. "Changes in U.S. prescribing patterns of menopausal hormone therapy, 2001–2003." *Obstet Gynecol*. 2006 Jul:108(1):33–40.

"Menopause's Milder Side"

As answered by Margaret Lock
For the *National Women's Health Network*
Article taken from March/April 2004 Newsletter

Questions for Dr. Margaret Lock, the well-known Canadian anthropologist on Japanese women, cultural nuances and the eastward creep of the western medical model.

Women's Health Activist: Your work studying women in Japan in 1983 and 1984 was some of the first to document that women's experiences of the physical effects of menopause are not the same everywhere. Among your most striking findings was that less than 20 percent of menopausal and post-menopausal Japanese women had experienced hot flashes, compared to about two-thirds of American women. How else is menopause different in Japan than in North America?

Margaret Lock: One of the most obvious differences involves the concept of menopause itself. In North America, we equate the end of menstruation with menopause; in fact, we've conflated the two. The word used in Japan, *konenki*, simply means a change in life. *Konenki* is much closer to the term once used in Europe, the climacteric, meaning a gradual change in midlife that can extend for a decade or more.

In my study, at least 25 percent of women I interviewed said they had no sign of *konenki*, yet they had finished menstruating at least a year before. Instead, they were more likely to mention a whole range of changes, including weakened eyesight, a bit of hearing loss, shoulder stiffness, headaches and lumbago [pain in the lower back].

One lesson to be learned from cross-cultural research is that unless you are sensitive to language nuances, your findings are not reliable. For instance, there is no Japanese word that means only a menopausal hot flash, although you can use three words that are close. A colleague of mine, a very good linguist, and I went to a lot of trouble to give Japanese women all three options for

responding to questions about hot flashes. My impression when doing research in Japan was always that, if anything women were over-reporting, because they were trying so hard to be cooperative.

WHA: Your most recent trip to Japan was in 2003. Have things changed?

ML: Yes, things have changed because there's been an extensive effort on the part of Japanese gynecologists to medicalize menopause, with mixed success. There has been a massive amount of media coverage, with doctors appearing on television and publishing articles in popular magazines. I'm still in the process of analyzing these interviews, but my impression is that Japanese women are reporting more hot flashes than they did in the 80s, yet still many fewer than North American women reported at that time and presumably still are reporting.

I'm also finding, as I did in the earlier research, a very big difference in the severity and frequency of hot flashes. They're quite a bit milder in Japan than in North America, and for many women they simply don't happen at all. You would have to go a long way to meet a Japanese woman who needs to get up in the middle of the night to change her sheets. For the vast majority, hot flashes do not disrupt their daily activities much at all.

WHA: How are hot flashes treated in Japan?

ML: There are hormonal treatments, but most women don't want them; they're very concerned about the long-term side effects of medication and prefer to treat symptoms with herbals. Most Japanese gynecologists don't recommend lifetime usage [of hormone replacement therapy]; they start out recommending it for perhaps five years, then take women off it. Japanese women still do not routinely go to gynecologists, and family doctors usually don't do pelvic exams unless there's a problem. Japanese gynecologists want women to change their habits and come to see them regularly, but women are fairly resistant, it seems.

WHA: Where else is menopause treated differently than it is in North America, and is it always perceived in a negative light?

ML: Researchers have found consistently throughout Asia—in China, South Korea, India, Indonesia—that menopause is understood as a rather gradual midlife transition rather than simply as the end of menstruation. Low symptom reporting is also documented for many of these countries, and one group of researchers found no reporting of hot flashes among women in traditional Mayan society.

In rural India, this time seems to proffer increased status; women who are freed of the constraints of the modesty they had to have as younger, sexually active women can take greater part in the outside world. On the other hand, if you've had no children then it can be a terrible time because you have no one to look after you when you get old.

WHA: What do you think underlies the different perceptions and experiences of menopause around the world? Nutrition? Physical activity? Different attitudes toward aging women?

ML: Of course culture and attitudes contribute to differences and language does too, but I believe there's something biological going on as well. It could be to do with genetics; as we're learning from molecular genetics, even a small amount of genetic diversity can account for a significant difference in bodily experience. Or perhaps it's something to do with the destabilization of core body temperature when a woman has an FSH surge, and some women may be more vulnerable to this than others. Or, it could be to do with diet. The effect of soybeans is being checked out extensively in Japan, with mixed results.

It's also important to note that there is enormous concern about looking after one's health in Japan, particularly among women because they don't want to be a burden to someone else. Japanese women reported many fewer chronic problems than do North American women. They take herbal supplements, they're careful about dietary intake. On my last visit, I found that middle-aged women were reverting to traditional diets once their children had left the household and they no longer had to prepare western-style food for the younger

generation. Japanese women also exercise a great deal, and most of them have never smoked or been big caffeine drinkers.

WHA: Some researchers have argued that women's cultures lead them to describe their experiences differently, but that their experiences are actually similar. How do you respond to the implication that women's biology is universal, and the physical effects of menopause must be universal too?

ML: I disagree with this line of argument very strongly. I spent hours and hours talking with Japanese women about menopause, and they have no inhibitions about discussing their bodily experiences. Japanese language and culture encourage one to pay close attention to the rhythms and changes of the body. I would also respond by pointing to epidemiological findings. It is undeniable that there are major differences in the incidence of common diseases in different parts of the world. This geographical variation is due in part to environment and diet, and also as a result of socioeconomic status, age, gender and so on. So why do we make the assumption that women's bones are the same everywhere; that physical changes at menopause are the same everywhere? As an anthropologist, I cannot accept that a woman who says she does not have hot flashes is wrong; one must take subjective reporting seriously and not assume that women are duped by their culture.

Obviously, women everywhere stop having their menstrual cycle around the age of 50, when estrogen levels drop. Something very predictable and biological is going on. However, we know that the way in which estrogen levels drop is not uniform: in some women the drop is rapid, in others it seems to go up and down in spikes, and yet other women experience a slow, steady decline. These differences are mediated by individual biology and by diet. Again, these differences may well be related to genetics. Everything we're learning tells us to pay attention to the fact that even a little bit of genetic variation can be significant in interesting and surprising ways.

I think there are two reasons why such differences in symptom reporting make people uncomfortable. One is the pressure of the medical world, which trains health care practitioners to think in terms of universal models. The other reason, particularly in the United States, I believe, is resistance to thinking about possible biological differences because they are so readily associated with race and racism.

WHA: In the U.S., attitudes toward menopause have evolved from considering it a time of "living decay" to a time when women hear they need screening tests, drugs and medical management to prevent diseases of aging. NWHN has been critical of both of these responses. What hopes do you have for women who will reach menopause in the future?

ML: I would like people to think more about the life-cycle as a whole rather than picking out menopause as one distinct and difficult period. So much of what happens as we grow older depends in large part on what we do when we're younger. With bone loss, clearly genetics puts some people at greater risk, but many people who have exercised and built up good strong bones when younger have enough bone mass for there not to be a problem later. It isn't just a matter of doing something when you're 48.

Secondly, as researchers such as Sonja McKinlay and Patricia Kaufert have shown, menopause isn't a particularly difficult time for the majority of women. Studies that make use of samples drawn from the population at large in North America show no statistical correlation between depression and the end of menstruation. This research also found that the majority of menopausal women do not suffer from troublesome hot flashes and that 40 percent never have hot flashes. These positive experiences need to be publicized much more.

The medical vision of menopause has become the dominant way of understanding this midlife transition. But a physician's viewpoint tends to be skewed as a result of seeing patients, many of whom are indeed suffering and need help. While being fully sympathetic with women who have a hard time at menopause and with those who are at high risk for osteoporosis, for example, this is not the whole story. For many women the end of menstruation is unremarkable, and becoming older isn't at all bad. I'm 68 next month, and I have to say a lot of marvelous things are happening at this stage of my lifecycle, including becoming a grandparent.

SEXUALITY

"Education for Sexual Intimacy and Agency"

By Susan K. Pastor

Introduction: The Problem

When "sex" is defined for young children by parents, it is in terms of how babies are made. Schools also teach that sex is reproduction. Even where abstinence-only or abstinence-based curricula are used, this definition of sex is underscored. Public outcry about the scientific inaccuracies in and negative outcomes of abstinence-only curricula, while entirely legitimate, misses an important point. It is possible to add substantial information on contraception and an arsenal of facts about sexually transmitted infections to the fact of conception, leaving the definition of sex as reproduction unchanged. Teaching sex as reproduction contributes to the idea that a normal girl would not be interested in sex for its own sake and a normal boy always would. Erections and ejaculation are standard topics in school puberty education in fourth or fifth grade, but sex appears to be only about periods for girls. How would anyone know girls can become aroused? How would a girl realize her wetness is normal? No one learns the physical signs of female arousal. This silence supports beliefs held by many people, including some scientists, that the sexual double standard is "natural" and women are "wired" for monogamy. According to a neuroscientist writing in *Men's Health*, women mainly desire a good provider for their offspring (Amen and Bodegraven 2004).

A more viable explanation for the persistence of the sexual double standard today is that we teach it, in part by initially constructing female pleasure as irrelevant to partner sex, defined as heterosexual intercourse. One pamphlet produced by the federal government and used in elementary schools depicts a female figure with no external "parts" at all. A uterus, fallopian tubes and ovaries are shown, with an upper vagina leading nowhere. (Department of Health and Human Services 1981). Seeking extra-curricular materials will not help. The latest editions of the best-selling books on puberty, the *"What's Happening to My Body?"* books, include two chapters dedicated to the internal reproductive organs and menstruation for girls, while two chapters in the boys' book address the physiology of desire (Madaras 2007a;2007b). The chapter on "Erections, Sperm and Ejaculation" is followed by another on "Spontaneous Erections, Orgasms, Masturbation and Wet Dreams". In the entire book for girls, three paragraphs are devoted to female arousal and orgasm (Madaras 2007a:83). This topic is equally neglected in the boys' book. Both books discuss the clitoris and female orgasm only in connection with masturbation and give as much attention to the hymen as to the clitoris (Madaras 2007a:74–48; 2007b:172–173). In discussing intercourse, however, the books do mention that "fluid comes out of the vaginal walls when a female is sexually excited" (2007a:14; 2007b:12), so there is some indication that female sexual arousal is possible.

The author probably means to be complete, but what she chooses to emphasize is foundational to a pattern that continues into adult life. Female pleasure is so unnecessary in heterosexual encounters that popular writer John Gray counseled one married woman to have "fast food" sex with her husband, even though these encounters did not last long enough for her to become aroused. In the deal Gray negotiates, the man gets to have sex, but promises not to require his wife to pretend she enjoys it. This husband later reported that his wife did "lie there like a dead log" and "he didn't mind at all" (Gray 1995:80). Gray directs heterosexual couples to incorporate "quickies" into their sex lives, pointing out that the woman benefits in part by not having to fake interest and pleasure (ibid:141).

Gray's problem-solving is consistent with one use of medical and scientific authority since the development of gynecology, which has been to render women physically capable of satisfying men's desire for heterosexual intercourse. In the 19th century, the "father of modern gynecology" used anesthesia to accomplish this with patients experiencing vaginismus, a condition involving muscle spasms that make vaginal penetration impossible. Once these women were under anesthesia, their husbands could have intercourse with them (Kapsalis 1997:47). If you think no one has this kind of attitude today, consider the comments of sex therapist Drew Pinsky, M.D., in an interview with *O: The Oprah Magazine*. To illustrate men's lack of interest in an eager and knowledgeable female partner, Pinsky was quoted as saying "Now if a guy had slept with Claudia Shiffer, it wouldn't matter what the hell she did. She could have been dead and he'd be overjoyed" (Brody 2003).

Certainly Dr. Drew doesn't mean to suggest that men should be having sex with female corpses, but his comments reflect the history of sexual interaction between men and women as something considerably less than mutually satisfying. Dr. Drew's words also project that history onto the present and future, suggesting that male lack of regard for female pleasure (or even willing participation) is normal. Women's greater interest in "cuddling" and emotional closeness becomes normative too. Gray suggests that women can barter for cuddling by providing the "quickies" their male partners desire (Gray 1995:141). Commentators such as Pinsky and Gray most likely have good intentions and mean to smooth relations between the sexes. It is just that the usual formulas for smooth relations appear to be based mainly on women's accommodation of what everyone understands as men's greater need for sex—including sex that is not especially . . . relational.

Education and socialization also help explain the "orgasm gap" to which Douglas and Douglas (1997) refer, in which men are more likely to have an orgasm as a result of heterosexual partner sex, usually intercourse, than women are. These authors draw on data reported in *The Social Organization of Sex* (Laumann et al 1994:114). This same study reports that women have orgasms much more reliably from solo sex (ibid:82). Unless we see this part of the picture, we may fall back on the myth that women are just less sexual and harder to arouse than men. A male partner would have to know he was missing something and seek out information about female bodies and pleasure. Among the 40 young men I interviewed in the mid-1990s, no one had learned more than sex as reproduction. Nevertheless,

almost every man thought he had learned everything necessary. Only one said he would have liked to know something about pleasing a female partner.

Suggesting that men ask female partners what is pleasurable does not entirely solve the problem. Before puberty, girls have more knowledge of boys' genitals than of their own (Bem 1989), and less direct experience of touching themselves—since they don't have to hold themselves to urinate. Today the female genitalia have a name, but it is the wrong name. To call the female genitalia "vagina" instead of "vulva" is to render the other structures invisible and/or irrelevant. Add these circumstances to the official teaching only of reproduction and periods and some women might find "What should I do?" and "What do you like?" to be challenging questions. Growing up, girls hear mostly silence on female sexual anatomy and female pleasure. A now well-established literature in the social sciences has documented the confusion and inequality to which that silence leads (see for examples Tolman 2002 and Fine 1988). Based on the usual version of puberty and sex education, women in general will not be more knowledgeable about female pleasure than men in general, and neither will be encouraged to seek out more information. The usual version of knowledge is constructed as what there is to know (Pastor, undated).

At the same time, heterosexual girls in search of sexual agency may find it in pleasing boyfriends. Masters and colleagues quote a 17-year-old who seems to appreciate her capacity in this area. When her boyfriend wants sex but she isn't in the mood, she reports relying on oral sex: "I don't even have to take my clothes off and I can still get the job done" (Masters, Johnson and Kolodny 1994:445). The authors offer this quote as evidence for the casual attitude toward oral sex among young people, not to call attention to the young woman's sense of obligation to produce her partner's pleasure when she herself has no interest in sex. Nevertheless, the possibility that she takes pleasure in the control this strategy gives her, or in pleasing her boyfriend should not be overlooked.

Toward a More Egalitarian Understanding of Sexuality

What counts as knowledge about sex has been skewed toward what points to gender difference and justifies gender inequality. Certainly sex roles in reproducing are different. Yet beyond penises entering vaginas and ejaculating to make babies are biological facts that suggest more erotic possibilities for both partner and solo sex. This is definitely not to say that there is no erotic potential for penises and vaginas together. However, the exclusive focus on sex as reproduction through childhood and into adolescence limits both men's and women's spectra of erotic imagination and experience. The first president of the Sexuality Information and Education Council of the United States (SIECUS), Dr. Mary Calderone, believed that our failure to understand sexual response apart from reproduction, together with taboos against children's masturbation, explained the high rates of sexual dysfunction in American society. She argued that sexual response is a capacity that develops beginning at birth, and which our beliefs and practices impair (Calderone 1983). Since 1998, urologists and other professionals have hastened to define and treat "female sexual dysfunction" as a medical condition including lack of desire, impairment of arousal and difficulty with or inability to reach orgasm (anorgasmia). Lenore Tiefer has been foremost among feminist scholars criticizing this medicalization of sexuality and calling for more attention to cultural attitudes toward sexuality, women's early experiences and the conditions of women's intimate relationships (Tiefer 2001).

Embryonic Sex Differentiation

The belief that women and men are so sexually different by nature begins to unravel if one starts at the beginning. Before the sixth to eighth week of development, the genital and reproductive structures of human embryos are identical—regardless of male (xy) chromosomes and programming for male development or female chromosomes (xx). Testicles and ovaries develop from the same initially undifferentiated gonad and all embryos have a "genital tubercle", which will become either a penis or a clitoris. These structures will be approximately the same size, except that most of the clitoris lies below the skin and so is not visible. Similarly, the "labio-scrotal" folds in all embryos will fuse in normal male development, becoming the scrotum. In females, the labio-scrotal folds become the labia majora, or outer labia. The tissue that becomes the labia minora, or inner labia in females will form the underside of the penis in males (see Sloane 2002:145–151 for a thorough explanation).[1]

Women's bodies also have a structure analogous to the prostate gland in men. *A New View of a Woman's Body* calls this structure the urethral sponge, because its spongy tissue surrounds, cushions and protects the urethra (Federation of Feminist Women's Health Centers 1991). Like the prostate gland, the urethral sponge produces a clear fluid and a protease, prostate specific antigen, or PSA. While it was previously believed that only

male bodies produce PSA, it has now been identified in the vaginas of women, independent of sexual activity with men (Sundahl 2003). It is reasonable to say, therefore, that the structure that becomes the prostate gland in males becomes the urethral sponge in females. These facts explain female potential for ejaculation.

When this structure is finally recognized in medicine, it is likely to be called the "female prostate". The term has been in use in the sexology literature for some time, and reflects that this part of the anatomy is the same structurally in women and men (see Zaviacic and Whipple 1993). In terms of erotic significance, the urethral sponge is the anatomical structure to which the term "G-spot" refers. The prostate has erotic potential in men as well.

Perhaps the puberty education version of embryonic sex differentiation would be: "Girl parts and boy parts start out exactly the same and come from the same structures. These structures do different things when it comes to reproduction, but they respond similarly to sexual stimulation." Ejaculation could be explained in connection with the prostate gland. Some students in my classes have indicated that they did learn about embryonic sex differentiation in biology, while for others the information is new. However, very little biology education or sex education links similar morphology to erotic potential—even at the college level. Embryonic sex differentiation is therefore constructed as irrelevant to information about sexuality, although this knowledge is becoming somewhat more widespread as awareness of the conditions that lead to intersexuality increases (see Preves 2003).

Female Sexual Anatomy

The lack of information about female anatomy disadvantages girls as they begin to explore sexually. A girl who does not know her own anatomy cannot direct a partner. A girl who is self-conscious as to whether her genitalia are normal is less likely to enjoy exploring. Boys are also affected. Because of the stereotype that boys want sex and should initiate, they will be expected to know what to do with a female partner—though they have no more knowledge. The college students I interviewed consistently reported that they had learned "the basics" about sex, meaning only that penises enter vaginas. The following information points to ways in which the "basics" are in great need of expansion.

Labia   Puberty education assures boys that normal penises come in a range of sizes and shapes, although such assurances don't dispel anxiety. Men's anxiety about size is well-recognized and the subject of much email spam. Reassurance for women on the normal variation in labia has generally been absent—that is, until cosmetic surgery on the labia began growing in

---

[1] For more detailed discussion with useful illustrations, see Dr. Cary Gabriel Costello's piece "Intersex Genitalia Illustrated and Explained" elsewhere in this volume. *Ed.*

popularity (see Woods 2007). In anatomical drawings, labia are always of uniform size and hairless. They are often hairless in pornographic representations too. Anyone who has seen the range of sizes and shapes of labia knows that some are very pronounced. Sometimes the inner labia protrude and are larger than the outer labia. Labiaplasty reduces the inner labia and makes them more symmetrical. Failure to teach girls about normal variation makes them more likely to become customers for genital cosmetic surgery.

Perhaps the increasing number of labiaplasties performed has encouraged women's magazines to reassure their readers about genital variation, although such articles may also serve to call attention to labiaplasty as an option. Recent articles in *Seventeen* (Brodman-Grimm 2005), *Cosmopolitan* (Perron 2004) and *Redbook* (Graham and Lister 2003) tackled this subject. *Redbook* readers even learned that it is normal for there to be color variations in the labia of the same woman. The photographs in *Femalia*, edited by Joani Blank, are an excellent representation of normal variation. The *"What's Happening to My Body" Book for Girls* includes five drawings showing variation, described by a few lines of text. While this is a start, there are approximately six pages devoted to reassuring boys about penis shape and size in the boys' book (Madaras 2007a:74–75; 2007b:47–54).

Clitoris   Most girls probably cannot identify all the structures of the external genitalia, much less the normal variation. Most girls probably do not know that the clitoris is really as big as a penis. In terms of the visible parts of the clitoris, there is variability in how much of the shaft is visible and the extent to which the hood covers the glans. Examples of these variations can be seen in the photographs in *Femalia*. The high concentration of nerve endings in the glans make it the most erotically charged part of a woman's body. All of the structures of the clitoris under the skin are made up of erectile tissue and respond to stimulation. The spongiest and most erotically sensitive tissues, after the glans, are the "bulbs", which are located on either side of the vaginal opening, and the perineal sponge, which underlies the perineum. The legs, or crura, angling away from the front of the body are also made up of erectile tissue, though they are not as spongy as the bulbs and perineal sponge. *A New View of a Woman's Body* provides several different views of the entire clitoris.

Urinary Opening and Urethral Sponge   The area between the inner labia, officially called the vestibule, contains the urinary opening. A woman spreading her inner labia and looking at this area with a mirror might be able to see the urinary opening above the vaginal opening—how far above varies. As the photographs

in *Femalia* demonstrate, the opening is quite visible in some women. Other women may not be able to identify the opening at all. This range is normal. Whether visible or not, the opening is surrounded by the urethral sponge, or female prostate. The existence of this structure is not acknowledged in mainstream medical literature as of this writing. It is also not acknowledged in the *"What's Happening to My Body"* books. Girls are told experts disagree as to whether there is a G-spot and that ejaculate might really be urine (Madaras 2007a:83). Boys are assured that "females don't ejaculate when they have an orgasm" (2007b:173).

Milan Zaviacic has documented variance in the shape of the urethral sponge/female prostate. While the bulk of the structure is usually felt on the lower anterior wall of the vagina, some women may identify the structure deeper in the vagina, and some women may have a variation in which the tissue is more evenly spread—no bulky part can be felt. Therefore, instructing women to find their G-spot as though every woman would find it the same way and experience the same sensations may lead some only to frustration (Sundahl 2003:31–34). This is true also with regard to ejaculation. Now that ejaculation in women is becoming acknowledged, some particular experience of it need not come to define the success or failure of women's sexual expression.

Ejaculation   The best understanding available at this time suggests that all women have the anatomy to ejaculate, whether ejaculation is experienced or not. Glands within the urethral sponge produce a clear fluid in varying amounts from a few drops to as much as a cup or a cup and a half. *A New View of a Woman's Body* calls these the "paraurethral glands" but they are referred to as "Skene's glands" in medical literature, where their fluid-producing function is not necessarily acknowledged. It appears that ejaculation can occur with or without orgasm. It is probable that the ejaculate can seep through the vaginal wall (Sundahl 2003:34) and be experienced as lubrication. Ejaculate is not urine but it may contain some of the same compounds. It is not clear whether these compounds would normally be present in ejaculate or suggest, for example, that the pelvic floor muscles are not strong enough to seal off urine from the bladder. A woman who ejaculates in noticeable amounts and does not know about ejaculation may think she is incontinent (Boston Women's Health Book Collective 2005:197).

Vagina   Just inside the vagina, along each wall, are glands which *A New View of a Woman's Body* calls the vulvo-vaginal glands, and which are called Bartholin's glands in the medical literature. The extent to which a woman can feel these glands varies. In some women, it may be relatively easy to feel them as small, rounded bumps under the vaginal wall. A woman who does not know that these structures are normal may become alarmed when she feels them. The vulvo-vaginal glands are thought to produce a small amount of lubrication, which is generally considered to be insignificant.

The depth of the vagina also varies. A woman who has always believed she cannot use tampons because they won't go in, or they fall out, may be able to use shorter tampons. The protrusion of the cervix into the vagina creates a space called a fornix to the front, back and sides. The space between the cervix and the frontal wall of the vagina, toward the bladder, is the anterior fornix. Some researchers suggest that a triangular space in this area is the real location to which Grafenberg pointed in his documentation of an erotically sensitive area inside the vagina. The G-spot is named after him. Since understanding of the G-spot has now settled on the urethral sponge, the sensitive location within the anterior fornix has been named the "T-zone" (Wilhite 2005). Testimonies from women point to erotic sensitivity in this area, but as yet no systematic research has been published. The space between the cervix and the back wall of the vagina, toward the rectum, is the posterior fornix. The proximity of the posterior fornix to the rectum becomes significant when the erotic potential of anal penetration is considered. The bestselling puberty books do not describe erotic sensitivity within the vagina or acknowledge the erotic potential of the anus.

Erotic Response

The physiology of erotic response points to similarity between women and men. The two main processes of vasocongestion and mytonia are central to arousal and orgasm in both. Vasocongestion is the process in which new blood is drawn to spongy erectile tissue, such as the clitoris and the penis, causing the tissues to swell. Sensitivity to touch increases as the tissues become engorged. Vasocongestion is likely related to vaginal lubrication, though vaginal lubrication is not a well-understood process. It has been suggested that the cells in the vaginal walls secrete lubrication; based on an understanding of vasocongestion, a more specific understanding is plausible as well. The very spongy tissues of the bulbs of clitoris and the perineal sponge surround the lower vagina on both sides and across the bottom. As new blood fills those tissues, clear fluid may be pushed out of the old blood in the capillaries and through the permeable vaginal walls. *Our Bodies, Ourselves* attributes vaginal lubrication to "increased blood circulation" (Boston Women's Health Book Collective 2005:194; see also Sloane 2002:173). Any physical condition or medication that interferes with circulation can impair vasocongestion.

The second process is myotonia. Myotonia is the medical term for muscular contractions. Orgasmic response is characterized by muscle contractions in both women and men. Different orgasms can involve a different number of contractions. In women, the muscles that make up the outer third of the vaginal wall contract, producing throbbing sensations. The uterus, also a muscle, contracts. (Sloane 2002:175). Weak pelvic floor muscles can impair orgasmic response.

In addition to the similarity of erotic response, some structures with erotic potential are undifferentiated in women and men. Erotic sensitivity of the nipples and anus is present in both. The following discussion is organized around the best explanations available at this time for the potential erotic response of particular structures to stimulation. There is an important caveat to this discussion. Erotic potential is not the same as erotic experience. Potential does not define experience. Hysterectomy is a good example. From a biological perspective, there are a number of reasons why this surgery could reduce sexual functioning. Yet many women report improved sexual functioning. Most women reporting sexual problems post-hysterectomy have been those who enjoyed good sexual functioning before (Maas, Weijenborg and Kuile 2003). What is erotic may be based on what we *believe* will be erotic in some cases and on factors beyond biology.

Knowledge of erotic potential should not be used to conclude that any person *should* welcome or enjoy any particular form of stimulation. There appears to be individual variation in the sensitivity of particular structures and certainly there is variation in what people enjoy. While this discussion suggests ways in which stimulation of particular structures may trigger orgasm, it is important to note that some feminist writing on sexuality has criticized such a focus, with good reason. Erotic sensations do not reduce to orgasm and the range of erotic practices should not be reduced to the production of orgasm (Tiefer 2001). The term "orgasm" encompasses a range of physical sensation, intensity and emotion; orgasms may feel different based on the structure around which stimulation is centered. Sundahl suggests that physical and emotional sensations of orgasms centered around the clitoris, urethral sponge and deeper in the vagina may feel different from one another because different neural pathways are involved. Two different major nerves connect the female genital and reproductive anatomy to the brain (Sundahl 2003:46–47).

Most discussions of arousal and orgasm are based on the stage model of human sexual response—excitement, plateau, orgasm, and resolution, toward which feminist writers have also directed incisive criticism (Tiefer 1995). There are ample opportunities for individuals to learn about the model and decide for themselves whether it is useful (e.g. Sloane 2002:172–178). There are also ample opportunities to match the information provided here with information on safe sex practices widely available elsewhere. Finally, existing knowledge about erotic potential should not be seen as expressing the limits of that potential. For example, women with spinal cord injuries who have lost feeling in the pelvic area can develop erotic responses in other parts of the body (Whipple, Gerdes and Komisaruk 1996).

Clitoris   The high concentration of nerve endings in the glans of the clitoris account for its erotic sensitivity. Women's experiences of and preference for certain types of clitoral stimulation vary. Some women find direct stimulation of the glans uncomfortable and too intense. Direct stimulation of the glans can lead to orgasm, but the erectile tissue of the bulbs and perineal sponge are sensitive as well. This explains why some women might prefer stimulation of a larger area of the vulva. A woman might reach orgasm through this stimulation without directly touching the glans. The bulbs of the clitoris and the perineal sponge are in close proximity to the vaginal opening and lower vagina. Shallow vaginal penetration could stimulate those structures and may partly explain a woman's pleasure in vaginal penetration.

Urethral Sponge   Women also report variance in enjoyment of stimulation of the urethral sponge. While some women find the sensation highly erotic, others find it uncomfortable or unpleasant. Stimulation of the urethral sponge can also produce a sensation that feels like the urge to urinate (Boston Women's Health Collective 2005:197). This structure can be stimulated from the inside, through vaginal penetration, or outside, from pressure to the area below the glans of the clitoris and above the vaginal opening. Orgasm centered around stimulation of this structure can occur with ejaculation or without noticeable ejaculation, as with any orgasm. Ejaculation can also occur without orgasm.

In men, the prostate can similarly be stimulated externally by pressure to the area between the scrotum and the anus; it can also be stimulated internally through anal penetration angled toward the front of the body. As with women, some men enjoy the sensations, while others do not. Often for men the erotic potential of the prostate will remain unknown. If it is known, exploration of this potential may be considered inappropriate for heterosexual men. This is one of the ways in which the equation of sex with reproduction limits erotic expression. If "normal" sex is heterosexual intercourse, then sexual practices without the potential for reproductive outcomes can always be constructed as deviant, no matter who practices them. People can be made to experience shame and guilt in connection with their desires. One semester a vocal group of women in my advanced course on Women and Sexuality insisted that only gay men would desire anal penetration. As long as there remains a stigma attached to homosexuality, that stigma will also work to limit the erotic experience of heterosexuals.

Nipples   Some women and some men report pleasure from stimulation of the nipples, while others indicate that the nipples are not particularly sensitive. The nipples are made up of erectile tissue. Nipple stimulation can lead to erection in men and arousal in women. Some women can reach orgasm from nipple stimulation alone. Nipples are one anatomical location that can become highly charged erotically in women whose spinal cord injuries prevent sensation below the area of the injury. The pleasurable sensations can extend to breastfeeding an infant for some women. While many people might be shocked at the idea of the mother's pleasure in breastfeeding, the physiological reasons for that pleasure are clear, and clearly normal. Nipple stimulation can trigger release of the hormone oxytocin, which leads to uterine contractions (remember that the uterus contracts during orgasm). The limited knowledge of female anatomy and the physiology of erotic pleasure has had tragic consequences in some lives. One mother lost her child to the foster care system for nearly a year, because her call inquiring about the pleasurable sensations she was feeling during nursing was transferred to a rape crisis center, where staff contacted a sexual abuse hotline, instead of the La Leche League (Blum 1999:96–97).

Vagina and Vaginal Penetration   Studies have shown that most women do not achieve orgasm reliably from vaginal penetration by a male partner. In reports collected from women by Shere Hite beginning in the 1970s, about 30 percent could reach orgasm regularly in this way (Hite 1993:35). Groundbreaking feminist work on women's sexuality, such as "The Myth of the Vaginal Orgasm" (Koedt 1996) focused on the experience of most women and pointed to the centrality of clitoral stimulation for women's orgasm. This made sense. It was important to counter the assertion of medical and scientific authorities that the hallmark of a woman's sexual maturity and normalcy was the ability to have an orgasm as a result of heterosexual intercourse. By this standard, two-thirds of women were sexually immature or abnormal. But what of women in that last third, who reported regular orgasms as a result of vaginal penetration?

There is erotic potential in vaginal penetration, and it does not make one a dupe of the patriarchy to say so. *The Whole Lesbian Sex Book* devotes an entire chapter to vaginal penetration (Newman 2004). Perhaps there is now enough known about female anatomy to leave behind the need to pinpoint the epicenters of orgasms. Penetration can stimulate the clitoris and/or the urethral sponge, and potentially produce orgasm in this way. It makes sense that sensation will vary with the angle and depth of penetration. Deeper penetration angled to the anterior fornix may stimulate the T-zone, under which lies a concentration of nerves (Wilhite 2005), and lead to orgasm. Deeper penetration can also lead to orgasm through direct, rhythmic pressure on the cervix, triggering contraction of the uterus. In one study, women with spinal cord injuries were able to feel orgasms they experienced as a result of cervical stimulation, although they could not feel the stimulation itself (Whipple, Gerdes and Komisaruk 1996).

Anus and Anal Penetration   Nerve endings in the anus, although not concentrated to the extent of the nerve endings on the glans of the clitoris, account for its erotic sensitivity in both women and men. In women, the close proximity of the anus to the underlying perineal sponge may also account for the pleasure associated with touching and shallow penetration. This stimulation can lead to orgasm, as can deeper penetration. Depending on the angle and the depth, deeper penetration into the rectum will bring a finger, penis or sex toy close to the cervix, as the posterior fornix is adjacent to the rectum. Based on available research, anatomy and women's individual accounts of pleasure, it is likely that—as with vaginal penetration—the rhythmic pressure on the cervix, though less direct, could trigger uterine contractions and orgasm. In men, anal penetration can also lead to orgasm, including through internal stimulation of the prostate. Joannides provides a number of individual perspectives related to anal stimulation and penetration (2004:365–380), and *The Whole Lesbian Sex Book* includes a chapter devoted to anal penetration (Newman 2004).

Conclusion   Left to our own desires and inventiveness, some men and some women might be interested in sex all the time, and others might be interested rarely. We are not usually left to our own desires and inventiveness though. Beginning in childhood, lessons about sexuality profoundly shape our experience of sexuality and limit our potential. This was *exactly* the point of formal sex education, from its inception in the early 20th century. The first advocates of sex education in public schools wanted to teach only enough to blunt young people's curiosity, and they were quite clear that the only redeeming aspect of sex was reproduction

(Strong 1972). Rury (1987) identifies the way in which educators sought to repress female sexuality in particular. If we know this history, it is perhaps not so surprising that this trend continues today. What we teach still channels behavior and experience into gendered patterns, which many people believe are only natural. We even warp biology to make it fit social expectations of males who naturally want sex and females who naturally don't. Young people are misled to think that only males have "male" hormones and only females have "female" hormones (Whatley 1985).

Some current advocates of comprehensive sexuality education believe that sexuality education was better before the abstinence-only education movement achieved popularity. In truth, only information about contraception and sexually transmitted diseases was more thorough (McKay 1999; Sears 1992). Attempts to implement the comprehensive sexuality education curriculum developed by the SIECUS have been rare. This curriculum, now in its third edition, includes developmentally appropriate messages about pleasure and sexual anatomy, including the clitoris, from kindergarten on and acknowledges individuals who are intersexed (Sexuality Information and Education Council of the United States 2004).

Finding educational resources for young people that do not reduce sex to reproduction is challenging. An important exception is Joani Blank's *A Kid's First Book about Sexuality*, which seems to be directed at five to 11-year-olds. The idea that sex should be taught only as reproduction is so ingrained that some students in my classes have insisted that sharing this resource with a young person would be child abuse. Why should we not validate children's knowledge that touching certain parts of the anatomy produces particular feelings and explain cultural views about when touching is appropriate, as Calderone (1983) suggests? Teaching about sex only as reproduction is at best a distortion of reality and at worst a lie. Much of the time people engaging in sexual behavior are not trying to reproduce.

This is not to say that everyone would need or want the all information in this article. "If you had your way, sex would be boring," one student in Women and Sexuality said. His point has become increasingly compelling over time. Official language and knowledge have a limiting, circumscribing quality. It is hard to know what amount of knowledge is needed to address ignorance, heal shame or guilt and preserve a space for imagination, discovery and empowerment in individual practices. An enlightened culture would seek to find that amount, even knowing that the recipe could not be exactly the same for everyone. Schools and government are more likely to resist the conversations this process would require than to facilitate them, but we can look to ourselves to broaden the scope and veracity of sexual knowledge at the grassroots.

I am deeply indebted to the Women's Studies Program at the University of Wisconsin-Madison for the many opportunities to teach classes in which the insights from my research could be shared. I am also deeply indebted to the students in my Women's Studies classes since 2001. Special thanks to students in Women and Sexuality for engaging, challenging and extending those insights. Your work has made this article possible.

REFERENCES

Amen, Daniel G. and Amy Jo Bodegraven. 2004. Sex on the Brain. *Men's Health* 19(10, December):157–164.

Beland, Nikki. 1998. Does He Think You're a Labia Loser? *Cosmopolitan* 225(5):150.

Bem, Sandra Lipsitz. 1989. Genital knowledge and gender constancy in preschool children. *Child Development* 60(3): 649–662.

Blank, Joani. 1993. *Femalia*. San Francisco, CA: Down There Press.

Blank, Joani. 1983. *A Kid's First Book About Sexuality*. San Francisco, CA: Yes Press.

Blum, Linda M. 1999. *At The Breast: Ideologies of Breastfeeding and Motherhood in the Contemporary United States*. Boston: Beacon Press.

Boston Women's Health Book Collective. 2005. *Our Bodies, Ourselves*. New York: Touchstone.

Brodman-Grimm, Karen. Your Body Questions Answered. 2005. *Seventeen* 64(4):100.

Brody, Liz. 2004. How Sex is Like Pizza . . . and Other Startling Features of the Male Mind. *O: The Oprah Magazine* 5(6):190–193.

Calderone, Mary S. 1983. Above and Beyond Politics: The Sexual Socialization of Children. Pp. 131–137 in Vance, Carole S. (Ed.), *Pleasure and Danger: Exploring Female Sexuality*. London: Pandora.

Department of Health and Human Services. 1981. *Changes—Sex and You*. Publication Number HSA 81–5648. Washington D.C.: United States Government Printing Office.

Douglas, Marcia and Lisa Douglas. 1997. *Are We Having Fun Yet?* New York: Hyperion

Federation of Feminist Women's Health Centers. 1991. *A New View of a Woman's Body*. Los Angeles, CA: Feminist Health Press.

Fine, Michelle. 1988. Sexuality, Schooling and Adolescent Females: The Missing Discourse of Desire. *Harvard Educational Review* 58:29–53.

Graham, Janis and Pamela Lister. 2003. Her Most Secret Sex Question. *Redbook* 200(1):62.

Gray, John. 1995. *Mars and Venus in the Bedroom*. New York: HarperCollins.

Hite, Shere. 1993. *Women as Revolutionary Agents of Change: The Hite Reports 1972–1993*. London:Bloomsbury.

Joannides, Paul. 2004. *Guide to Getting It On*. Waldfort, OR:Goofy Foot Press.

Kapsalis, Terri. 1997. *Public Privates: Performing Gynecology from Both Ends of the Speculum*. Durham, NC: Duke University Press.

Koedt, Annette. 1996. The Myth of the Vaginal Orgasm. Pp. 111–116 in Jackson, Stevi and Sue Scott (Eds.) *Feminism and Sexuality*. New York: Columbia.

Laumann, Edward O., John H. Gagnon, Robert T. Michael, and Stuart Michaels. 1994. *The Social Organization of Sexuality*. Chicago: Univ. of Chicago.

Maas, Cornelis P., Philomeen Th. M. Weijenborg and Moniek M. Ter Kuile. 2003. The Effect of Hysterectomy on Sexual Functioning. *Annual Review of Sex Research* 14:83–114.

Madaras, Lynda. 2007a. *"What's Happening to My Body?" Book for Girls*. New York: Newmarket Press.

Madaras, Lynda. 2007b. *"What's Happening to My Body?" Book for Boys*. New York: Newmarket Press.

Masters, William H., Virginia E. Johnson and Robert Kolodny. 1994. *Heterosexuality*. New York: HarperCollins.

McKay, Alexander. 1999. *Sexual Ideology and Schooling: Towards Democratic Sexuality Education*. Albany, NY: State University of New York Press.

Newman, Felice. 2004. *The Whole Lesbian Sex Book* (Second Edition). San Francisco, CA: Cleis Press.

Pastor, Susan K. Unpublished Research. Learning the Basics: The Social Construction of Knowledge about Sexuality. Madison, WI.

Perron, Celeste. 2004. My Labia Are Long and Uneven—Am I a Freak? *Cosmopolitan* 237(5):158.

Preves, Sharon E. 2003. Intersex and Identity: The Contested Self. New Brunswisck, NJ: Rutgers University Press.

Rury, John L. 1987. 'We Teach the Girl Repression, the Boy Expression': Sexuality, Sex Equity and Education in Historical Perspective. *Peabody Journal of Education* 64(4, Fall):44–58.

Sears, James T. 1992. Dilemmas and Possibilities of Sexuality Education: Reproducing the Body Politic. Pp. 5–33 in Sears, James T. (Ed.), *Sexuality and the Curriculum: The Politics and Practices of Sexuality Education*. New York: Teachers College Press.

Sexuality Information and Education Council of the United States National Guidelines Task Force 2004. *Guidelines for Comprehensive Sexuality Education Kindergarten Through 12th Grade*. New York: Sexuality Information and Education Council of the United States.

Sloane, Ethel. 2002. *Biology of Women* (Fourth Edition). Albany, NY: Delmar/Thomson Learning.

Strong, Bryan. 1972. Ideas of the Early Sex Education Movement in America, 1890–1920. *History of Education Quarterly*. Summer: 129–161.

Sundahl, Deborah. 2003. *Female Ejaculation and the G-spot*. Alameda, CA: Hunter House.

Tiefer, Lenore. 2001. Arriving at a 'New View' of Women's Sexual Problems: Background, Theory and Activism. Pp. 63–98 in Kaschak, Ellyn and Lenore Tiefer (Eds.) *A New View of Women's Sexual Problems*. New York: Haworth.

Tiefer, Lenore. 1995. *Sex Is Not a Natural Act and Other Essays*. Boulder, CO: Westview. Pp. 41–58, Historical, Scientific, Clinical and Feminist Criticism of the Human Sexual Response Cycla Model.

Tolman, Deborah. 2002. *Dilemmas of Desire*. Cambridge, MA: Harvard University Press.

Whatley, Mariamne H. 1985. Male and Female Hormones: Misinterpretations of Biology in School Health and Sex Education. Pp. 67–88 in Sapiro, Virginia (Ed.) *Women, Biology and Public Policy*. Newbury Park, CA: Sage Publications.

Whipple, Beverly, Carolyn A. Gerdes and Barry R. Komisaruk. 1996. Sexual Response to Self-Stimulation in Women with Complete Spinal Cord Injury. *The Journal of Sex Research* 33(3):231–241.

Wilhite, Myrtle. 2005. T-zone and G-spot. (Pamphlet) Madison, WI: A Woman's Touch Sexuality Resource Center.

Woods, Stacey Grenrock. 2007. Sex. *Esquire* 148(5):78.

Zaviacic, Milan and Beverly Whipple. 1993. Update on the Female Prostate and the Phenomenon of Female Ejaculation. *Journal of Sex Research* 30(2):148–151.

"Sexual Health Education in Wisconsin and the United States: Current Issues & Future Possibilities"

By Erica R. Koepsel, MA

Many of us can recall vivid memories (good or bad) of our time in sex education classes. Likely, many of us would have comparable experiences: perhaps we would have similar stories about the eccentric teacher who was uncomfortable talking about sex, or maybe we experienced comparable fear-based lessons about sexually transmitted infections (STIs) and childbirth, or it is possible that we both felt invalidated due to the limited representation of sexuality. However, for every similar experience we might have had in our sexual health education, there is likely more variation than we will ever really understand.

This inconsistent dissemination of sexual health information among adolescents prepares some individuals to become sexually healthy adults, but leaves many others dangerously uninformed and invalidated. The root of the problem does not lie strictly in what topics are or are not covered, but comes from an inequitable overall approach to sexual health, which excludes underserved and minority populations (Trudell, 1993; McKay, 1999; Fields, 2008; Connell & Elliot, 2009; Lamb, Lustig, & Graling, 2012). Most students are inadequately prepared for healthy sexual futures, but the particular exclusion of some students leads to further inequalities. Although the introduction of additional topics could make sex education more inclusive, the real solution lies in reframing our approach. We need to move away from education that emphasizes negative messages about sex and sexuality, toward programs with truly sex-positive foundations.

Throughout this article I will discuss some faults in our current approach to sex education and offer ways for advocates and instructors to improve the experiences of all students. First, I will define sexual health education and explore the current state of sex education in Wisconsin and the United States. Then, we will examine the ways in which sex education classrooms are exclusive. Finally I will suggest ways to make sexual health education more inclusive, accessible, and sex-positive.

Defining the Field: What is Sexual Health Education Anyway?

The debates surrounding sexual health education tend to be framed in absolutist terms, pitting Abstinence-Only supporters against proponents of Comprehensive Sexuality Education in disputes about morality, religion, and effectiveness. In reality, this argument, though politically convenient, provides an inadequate representation of sexual health education in America. As we look at the four overarching approaches to sexuality education, existing federal and state laws, and local systems that control sexual health curricula, we should consider how educators and advocates might navigate the many barriers to developing new curricula or improving existing ones.

Although some sexual health curricula operate outside of the public school system, this article will focus on those approaches being used within public secondary schools. Ideally, sexuality education would be a life-long learning process starting at a young age with the introduction of anatomically correct language and general concepts like autonomy and consent (De Melker, 2015). In our current reality, however, students typically receive most sexual health education in high school, so this will be our focus. While there are challenges to implementing a quality, inclusive, school-based sexual health curriculum, it is important to note that we cannot know what information students are getting from home (Trudell, 1993; FoSE, 2011; Planned Parenthood, 2014). We know for some adolescents, "a safe space for discussion, critique, or construction of sexualities is not something they find in their homes. Instead, they relied on school, the spot they chose for safe exploration of sexualities" (Fine, 1997), indicating that school-based sexual health education is an important facet of sexuality education and the sole source for some students.

There are four "types" of sexual health curricula being used throughout the United States: Abstinence Only Until Marriage, Abstinence Plus, Comprehensive Sex Education, and Sex Positive Education (Advocates for Youth; Sexuality Information and Education Council of the United States [SIECUS], 2016a).

In general, **Abstinence-Only Until Marriage** (AOUM) teaches that abstinence is the "only morally correct option of sexual expression for teens" (Advocates for Youth, 2001). AOUM tends to censor information about contraception and condoms for prevention of pregnancy and STIs. If prevention methods are discussed, it is generally with misinformation or misrepresentation of scientific facts, e.g. "condoms fail to prevent HIV transmission as often as 31 percent of the time," "pregnancy occurs one out of every seven times that couples use condoms," and "HIV can be spread via sweat and tears" (Advocates for Youth, 2001; United States House of Representatives Committee on Government Reform, 2004). Most research suggests that an abstinence only approach is not effective at delaying initiation of sex or increasing safe sex behaviors (Trenholm, 2007; Kirby, 2002).

Abstinence Plus education complicates abstinence-based approaches. Although these curricula are accompanied by strong messages about abstinence, they do provide generally accurate information about condoms and contraception. At times the line between these programs and comprehensive ones can blur, making categorization more difficult (Advocates for Youth, 2001).

A true **Comprehensive Sexuality Education** curriculum highlights abstinence as the best method for preventing STIs and pregnancy, but also consistently educates students on proper condom use, contraceptive options, and communication skills. Comprehensive programs are often rooted in an exploration of values, goals, and options as they relate to sexual decision-making. Research indicates that comprehensive courses are effective at reducing risk behaviors and increasing contraception and condom use among sexually active teens (Kirby, Laris, & Rolleri, 2006; Kirby, Laris, & Rolleri, 2007; Kirby, 2007).

Sex Positive Education is very similar to comprehensive education, but rather than focusing on the risk factors of sexual activity, it approaches sexuality as a healthy aspect of human life, which tends to make it more inclusive overall (Recapp, 2016; Center for Positive Sexuality, 2016). This approach is often used at the university level, but rarely within high schools, so there is little research on its efficacy.

While we may separate programs into these broad types, it is important to acknowledge that there can be incredible variation between curricula within the same category, and similar information may be shared via all methods of education. Even if we are able to identify which type a given curriculum most resembles, we still do not know the specific content and messages that are being delivered in the classroom.

Further complicating matters, there are no federal laws regulating sexual health education. The availability of curricula depends upon federal and state funding, with the majority of legislative efforts regarding sexual health education taking place at the state level (SIECUS, 2015; Guttmacher, 2016). While this might seem preferable to a uniform national curriculum, allowing individual states to develop guidelines that are culturally situated, the reality of this practice is that state laws often fail to offer adequate guidance to those teaching sex education, resulting in enormous discrepancies in the information students receive both between and within individual states.

The Guttmacher Institute distributes a frequently updated fact sheet summarizing related state laws (Guttmacher, 2016)[1]. This fact sheet clearly indicates that each state has their own matrix of requirements (or lack thereof); some states have requirements that look out for the best interests of students (like medical accuracy) and others have requirements that demean specific student populations (such as by mandating a negative representation of homosexuality). As of March 2016, only the District of Columbia and 24 states mandate sex education, and Wisconsin is not one of them.

Twenty-seven states, plus the District of Columbia, mandate that sex and HIV education, when provided, must meet certain general criteria such as: medical accuracy, cultural competency (without bias against any race, sex, or ethnicity), age appropriate instruction (information is developmentally appropriate for the students receiving it), and religious neutrality. Once again, Wisconsin is not one of those states.

In fact, in Wisconsin, when sex or HIV education is provided, it does not have to be medically accurate, culturally appropriate, age appropriate, or unbiased. It can promote religion, and is required to stress abstinence and discourage sex outside marriage. There are no sex

---

[1]A good visual of these data can be found in a Huffington Post article from 2014 (Klein, 2014): http://www.huffingtonpost.com/2014/04/08/sex-education-requirement-maps_n_5111835.html

education guidelines in Wisconsin regarding sexual orientation, healthy decision-making, family communication, or avoiding coercion, and there is no requirement to teach about condom use (Guttmacher, 2016; Wisconsin State Legislature, 2011). When it comes to Wisconsin state law and sexual health education, nearly anything goes. In one sense, this lack of structure can allow great leeway for educators who are willing and able to approach sexuality from a positive perspective. On the other hand, however, it leaves students across the state with wildly varying levels of sexual health knowledge.

In practice, the content of specific sexual health education classes comes down to the local government and individual educator. The process for getting a given sex education curriculum into classrooms includes school boards, Parent Teacher Associations, and state organizations like the Department of Public Instruction or Department of Health Services. The process of curriculum development, approval, and review are different for each school district, making a streamlined approach to curriculum improvement daunting (Wisconsin Department of Public Instruction, 2014).

Similarly, the person teaching sexual health varies so much from district to district that it can be difficult to identify 'the' sex educator (DeCoste, 2011). Sex education can be a single class taught by the physical education teacher, a week of classes from a local organization (such as a Title X clinic, community center, or religious group), or a month of an intensive sex education course delivered by a dedicated health teacher (DeCoste, 2011). Even using the same curriculum, different instructors will sometimes deliver drastically different information. The end result is that we have no real way to know what students actually learn in their sexual health courses.

This alarming lack of consistency across the nation leaves students even in the same cities with disparate levels of sexual health knowledge. Such inconsistent dissemination of information does a disservice to all youth by inhibiting our ability to talk about sexuality openly and honestly. Most concerning, however, is that this inconsistent approach clearly allows some students to access high-quality information in an inclusive way, while many others learn about sexual health in negative, exclusionary environments. We cannot know what exactly particular students are or are not learning, but we know that our current approach to sexual health education has measurable negative outcomes.

The Need for Change: Inclusive Sex Education or Bust

While lack of support makes it difficult to deliver truly comprehensive and inclusive sexual health curricula, it is the common cultural dialogue surrounding sexuality that leads to the most alienating approaches to sex education. While it might not be immediately apparent, the tenets that make up many sexual health curricula (even those that are quite comprehensive) such as abstinence/virginity, morality, and reproduction are often reflective of the mythical norm (McKay, 1999; Bay-Cheng, 2003; Connell & Elliott, 2009; Schalet, 2011; Preston, 2013; Lorde, 1984). This means sex education is founded upon an understanding of sameness that favors the experiences of individuals who are young, White, heterosexual, male, Christian, thin, and financially secure. By building curricula upon only one understanding of sexuality, sexual health education ultimately reflects sexist, cis-sexist, heterosexist, racist, and ableist thinking. While this approach does a disservice to all individuals in the classroom, it has a greater negative effect upon those who already experience oppression in their day-to-day lives, as common sexual health narratives fail to recognize their lived experiences (Trudell, 1993; McKay, 1999; Fields, 2008; Connell & Elliot, 2009; Lamb, Lustig, & Graling, 2012).

When populations are excluded from a classroom for any reason, it inhibits their access to necessary information and hinders open communication about sensitive health topics. When students feel targeted or invalidated they often shut down or retreat from classroom involvement, much like those who have experienced trauma or other adverse childhood experiences (Fava & Bay-Cheng, 2012; CDC, 2014). This increases stress and anxiety levels for students (Mutchler, Ayla, & Neith, 2005) and leaves them highly unlikely to retain new information. A relationship between high rates of victimization and additional health risk behaviors has been observed, suggesting that underserved youth's everyday experiences of bullying, harassment, and violence, along with resulting lowered self-esteem and depression, affect their future decision-making (Bontempo & D'Augelli, 2002). Daily microaggressions, like exclusion from sex education curricula, may put these youth at further risk as they explore aspects of their own sexuality that were not addressed in their sexual health education (Botsford, 2013). These exclusions and inequalities, as they exist in sexual health classrooms, will become more apparent as we examine a series of cultural assumptions about sex and sexuality.

Both mainstream cultural discourse and the majority of sex education classrooms define sex through reproduction and prioritize body parts, sex acts, and relationships that contribute to that reproduction (McKay, 1999; Bay-Cheng, 2003; Connell & Elliott, 2009; Schalet, 2011; Preston, 2013). While this "definition" of sex is rarely explicit, we can see examples of this sex—reproduction narrative in various classroom teachings.

For example, a number of sexual health curricula begin with lessons about bodies and body parts and heavily emphasize reproductive functions over sexual pleasure (Planned Parenthood of Wisconsin [PPWI], 2011; Milwaukee Public Schools [MPS], 2012; Seattle and King County Public Health, 2013; Johnson, 2009; Pastor, 2009; Douglass & Douglass, 2009). The frequent titling of these lessons with terms like "Reproductive Anatomy" demonstrates how bodies have been constructed as only reproductive beings, rather than sexual ones. Wisconsin guidelines are not unique in their requirement that all sexual health curricula "address the positive connection between marriage and parenting" (Wisconsin State Legislature, 2011). This requirement not only reifies sex as solely reproductive, but also strictly limits the relationships in which sex belongs. Though the sex for reproduction definition is certainly limiting in itself, it also produces a foundation for several assumptions that amplify the exclusive character of many sexual health classrooms.

The first such assumption is that penile-vaginal intercourse (PVI) is the only "real" sex because it is the only "natural" way to reproduce (McGarry, 2013; Gowan & Winges-Yanez, 2014). This belief is mirrored when all other sexual acts are considered foreplay or when sex is equated to bases; in both examples, all acts ultimately lead up to PVI as the "main event." We tend to link reproductive PVI with heterosexuality and therefore validate this act and this sexual orientation. At the same time, we link other sex acts with non-heterosexual identities, thereby labeling both the acts and identities as "wrong" because they are not reproductive (Foucault, 1996; Rasmussen, 2004). Even though we know people of any orientation can and do engage in a wide variety of acts, we automatically label lesbian, gay, and bisexual (LGB) people as deviant because some of their sexual practices are not reproductive. This validation of some activities and rejection or erasure of others leads to incomplete or incorrect information in sex education classrooms and makes it difficult for educators to lead open, positive discussions about sexual orientation (McKay, 1999; Fine & McClelland, 2006). This also sends a message to LGB youth that they have no value in our society and further reinforces feelings of invisibility and invalidation, which may inhibit their ability to absorb or retain the information being communicated (Mutchler, Ayla, & Neith, 2005; Fava & Bay-Cheng, 2012; CDC, 2014).

Finally, when we promote abstinence in sex education classrooms without defining sexual activity more broadly, we risk not fully communicating risks associated with sexual activity that is not PVI (Blake, et al., 2001). In the moments when sex education does move beyond conversations of abstinence to talk about STI prevention, we still often fail to fully address preventative methods for anal sex, manual stimulation, use of toys, or other sex acts. Together with negative messages about LGB identity, this inadequate coverage of a full range of sexual activities may contribute to the high rates of unintended pregnancy and STIs among sexual minority populations (Saewyc, Bearinger, Blum, & Resnick, 1999; Blake et al., 2001; Bontempo & D'Augelli, 2002; Goodenow, Szalacha, Robin, & Westheimer, 2008; Mustanski et al, 2011; CDC, 2015).

Second, when we assume PVI is the end-all be-all of sexual activity, we also assume that sex should "look" a certain way. The underlying assumption that PVI is "natural" leads to a belief that folks who are unable to engage in sex as it is commonly depicted must be "doing it wrong." The sexual experiences of people with physical disabilities, who may need additional tools or position aids due to chronic pain, mobility issues, or other impairments, are ignored and delegitimized (Kaufman, Silverberg, & Odette, 2003). Once again, if we do broaden beyond a focus on PVI, it is typically only to allow three additional acts as sexual: oral sex, anal sex, and manual stimulation (Goldfarb & Casparian, 2000; PPWI, 2011; MPS, 2012; Seattle and King County Public Health, 2013). This is an understanding of sexuality focused exclusively on the genitals, perpetuating beliefs that other activities are less legitimate forms of sexual expression. Thus, sex education curricula do not capture the experiences of individuals who are unable to engage in such activities due to illness, injury, or impairment.

Furthermore, people with physical, cognitive, or developmental disabilities are often not just excluded through course content, but are physically removed from sexual health education classrooms in many school districts (Kim, 2011). This is particularly troubling considering that people with disabilities are especially vulnerable to sexual abuse and violence (Sullivan & Knuton, 2000; Harrell & Rand, 2010) and could greatly benefit from sexual health-enhancing skills and related information. The lack of inclusive content and removal of students from classrooms reflect the cultural belief that individuals with disabilities lack sexual desire and agency, and fails to prepare students with disabilities to engage in healthy, pleasurable, and safe sexual activity (Galler, 1984; Tepper, 2000).

A third assumption that might lead to exclusion from sexual education is the belief there are only two sexes and that reproductive ability/anatomy corresponds with gender identity. We've been socialized to assume a "natural" gender/sex binary that is foundational to most sexual health curricula (Fausto-Sterling,

2000). For example, students often learn about men and women as "opposites" and explore the inherent differences between their bodies through lessons titled "female anatomy" and "male anatomy" (Wilson, 1999; Goldfarb & Casparian, 2000; PPWI, 2011; MPS, 2012, Seattle and King County Public Health, 2013). Sex education further solidifies this binary by gendering body parts and bodily functions, e.g. a woman's menstrual cycle, a man's erection, or a woman's pregnancy (PPWI, 2011; MPS, 2012; Goldfarb & Casparian, 2000; Seattle and King County Public Health, 2013). These lessons reify assumptions that reproductive anatomy consists of EITHER a penis or a vulva (ignoring the reality of intersex variation) and that those body parts then determine gender identity (disregarding the existence of trans people). In both cases sex education pays no attention to the complexity of sexual physiology or gender identity.

Sexual health education also often uses images of anatomy that portray a single "ideal" size, shape, length, and color for external genitalia, a practice that fails to recognize the diversity among bodies and the variation that can occur during development (Gowen & Winges-Yanex, 2014). When educators use only one "representative" image or gender body parts they fail to educate about intersex and trans bodies and erase the young people who inhabit them. This exclusion from the sex education classroom sends a clear message, echoing many similar messages present in mainstream culture: deviant bodies and the experiences of trans people and intersex individuals do not matter (Bettcher, 2014).

The emphasis on abstinence within an understanding of sex for reproduction leads to a fourth assumption: that all people will be interested in sex some day. By constructing sexual desire as something everyone will have to work to "overcome" and by valorizing those who "choose" abstinence, sexual health education classes erase folks who identify as asexual and practice abstinence outside of this context. People are generally expected to engage in sexual activity one day, and those youth who do not experience desire will likely feel neglected or somehow deficient when asexuality is not recognized (The Asexual Visibility and Education Network [AVEN], 2012). Our culture tends to construct asexuality as something bad; when someone is deemed undesirable or incapacitated for some reason (age, body size/shape, ability status, etc), they are considered 'asexual'. By ignoring the real experiences of people who identify as asexual, we are continuing to reinforce these negative beliefs. It is important to understand that asexual people, like people of other sexual orientations, identify along a spectrum, and while some will never engage in sexual activity, others do have physi-

cal relationships with partners for a variety of reasons (Kim, 2011; AVEN, 2012). If asexual students are not engaged in classroom conversations, they will not gain the skills needed to safely express their desires or communicate their boundaries.

The final assumption, which we have previously touched upon, is that some bodies and populations are more desirable, because their reproduction is valued more. Specifically, the moral messages surrounding sexuality are based around a White, middle-class understanding of sex (Froyum, 2010; Connell & Elliott, 2009; Fields, 2008). Rarely do we address the ways in which sexuality is experienced differently based on culture or race. The narratives provided in classroom settings for practicing safer sex and preventing unintended pregnancies or STIs may not seem attainable to many students of color because they either do not reflect what has been modeled within those students' communities, or they depend on interaction with a healthcare system that has repeatedly failed people of color (Fields, 2008; Bay-Cheng, 2008). Additionally, sex education does not take into account that White bodies have historically been valued, while bodies of color have been hypersexualized and commodified (Fields, 2008; Connell & Elliot, 2009). This simultaneous commodification and hypersexualization interferes with a healthy sense of sexual agency for young students of color, as assumptions are always being made about their sexuality before they are able to identify it for themselves (Springer, 2008).

As we neglect to address how racial identity and experience may shape sexual activity, we fail to include students of color in the classroom and provide them with relevant, relatable, reliable information, which may contribute to disproportionate rates of negative sexual health outcomes among people of color (Augsutine, 2010). For example, approximately half of African American men who have sex with men (MSM) and 1 in 4 Hispanic MSM are expected to be diagnosed with HIV in their lifetime, rates significantly higher than for White MSM. Similarly, the lifetime HIV risk for all African American men is 1 in 20 and for women 1 in 48. When we compared these with the estimated rates for White Americans (1 in 132 and 1 in 880, respectively), the clear racial disparity indicates a need for improved, inclusive sex education.

In just this one foundational understanding of sex as solely reproductive we have seen several instances where individuals (and whole populations) have been excluded from sex education courses. I encourage you to consider which other populations might also experience exclusion in sexual health education classrooms and how a lack of attention to intersectional identities might further impact students' learning about sexual health. Sex education can and should have positive outcomes for a healthy sexual future, but when students are not validated, useful information is overshadowed by messages of inferiority. As discussed, this exclusion may interfere with students' ability to access or absorb necessary information, reinforce stereotypes, encourage risk taking, and ultimately result in negative health outcomes. The students who are excluded from sexual health classrooms belong to populations that already experience the highest rates of STIs, HIV, unintended pregnancy, and victimization (Fine, 1988; Weinstock, Berman, & Cates, 2004; Kost & Henshaw, 2014). These underserved populations need more support to live happy, healthy sexual lives and adults who teach in sexual health education classrooms can be one of those resources. It may feel like there are overwhelming barriers to changing our approach to sex education, but change *is* possible and *you* can help facilitate it.

Transforming Education: Sex Positive, Pleasurable, and Inclusive

Sex-positive approaches to sexual health education present the most promise for both improvement of public health outcomes and inclusion of diverse individuals. According to social work practitioners affiliated with the *Center for Positive Sexuality*, "[f]rom a sex-positive perspective, people have more options to enjoy and express consensual sexuality, with less fear of negative judgment, in ways that best fit them," making it a promising approach for the resolution and prevention of sexual 'problems' (Williams, Prior, & Wegner, 2013). Many public health researchers suggest that sex education approaches that acknowledge sexual pleasure, independence, and acceptance are also effective for encouraging positive sexual health outcomes (Holland & Ramazanoglu, 1992; Ingham, 2005; Philpott, Knerr, & Boydell, 2006; Higgins & Hirsch, 2007; Schalat, 2011). A key effort in sex-positive curriculum that will likely improve efficacy is the move away from limiting definitions of sex. Engaging students in discussions that address the complexity of sexuality as it relates to race, ability status, sexual orientation, gender identity and other lived experiences makes sexual health education inclusive, explorative, and perhaps most importantly, *collaborative.*

While this may seem like a desirable but distant goal, individual sexual health educators can begin with some immediate changes to cultivate a classroom environment where all students are welcome. The impact an individual educator can have on a student's classroom experience is immense. Instructors have the ability to deliver information in a way that does not shame or make assumptions about students. Further, sexual health educators' impact is not limited to only the students in their classrooms. Over time, classrooms where sexuality is discussed positively and openly will also affect larger cultural narratives about sexuality.

One of the first actions an educator can take in transforming the culture surrounding sexual health education is to change the language they use to talk about sex and sexuality. First, educators can stop using the words "all," "most," "typical," and "normal" to avoid reinforcing beliefs that some activities/bodies are normal and others abnormal, and instead promote recognition of natural variation. Educators can also be more inclusive of all sexual orientations by using "partner" rather than terms like "boyfriend"/"girlfriend," or by assigning gender-neutral names during role play scenarios to better represent diverse relationships (Botsford, 2013; Bishop, Personal Communication 2013; McGarry, 2013). An even more direct approach would be to explicitly include diverse sexual identities in scenarios throughout the curriculum.

It is also possible for health educators to develop a more inclusive classroom without assumptions about gender identity by introducing gender-neutral pronouns and speaking about "people who menstruate" or "people with penises" rather than assuming that body parts mandate gender (Frantz, 2012). As educators model inclusive language change for their students, they also need to intervene when other students use biased or stereotypical language (McGarry, 2013). Finally, sexual health educators need to speak about sex as more than PVI, something that happens for reproduction, or something that occurs between able-bodied men and women. Rather, they must present sex as something that is culturally situated and socially influenced and redefine sexual activity as something healthy, natural, and even pleasurable. More than anything else, health educators need to create a space in which students collectively can articulate and challenge sexual stereotypes, and where each student can see their lived experiences reflected in the examples provided and topics discussed.

While individual educators may work effectively within existing structures, for a widespread cultural shift to occur, we need changes in policy at the state and national level. The only way to ensure equitable access to information is to advocate for sexual health education requirements that are sex-positive, medically accurate, inclusive, and age-appropriate. As advocates, it's important to be aware of positive movement in the field of sexual health education, because we can look to these effective guidelines, laws, and/or programs for guidance within our own communities.

Nationally, two organizations in particular, Sexuality Information and Education of the United States (SIECUS) and the Future of Sex Education (FoSE), have released great sets of guidelines for sex-positive, inclusive, and comprehensive sex education (SIECUS, 2004; Future of Sex Education, 2011). Advocates for Youth also released a 2015 curriculum that is inclusive and follows both national guidelines and CDC recommended topics (Schroeder, Goldfarb & Gilpern, 2015). All of these are available for free online to any district or educator seeking a more comprehensive curriculum.

In individual states, a number of bills mandating inclusive, comprehensive sexual health education have been introduced, considered, or passed between 2006 and 2016 (SIECUS, 2016b). As of January 2016, California requires all schools to teach comprehensive and unbiased sexual health education at least once in middle school and once in high school (Tucker, 2015) and in 2016 several states introduced or continued attempts to require age-appropriate sexual health education from kindergarten through 12th grade (National Conference of State Legislatures, 2016). This represents important progress for the movement towards accessible and positive sex education, though there are still many legislative barriers to overcome.

In Wisconsin, a comprehensive mandate existed for two short years under the *Healthy Youth Act*, but was unfortunately overturned following changes in governmental leadership (SIECUS, 2012). However, despite little governmental support for sexual health education, community organizations in Wisconsin are actively training educators in a new comprehensive, culturally appropriate, sex-positive, and inclusive curriculum (Stern, 2016). Change is happening, and as advocates, our job is to support those health educators working to improve the system from within, stay informed about approaches to sexual health education, start conversations with leaders in our community, and cast our vote for representatives and organizations that will support sex-positive, inclusive sexual health education.

BIBLIOGRAPHY

Advocates for Youth. (2001). Sex education programs: Definitions & point-by-point comparison. *Transitions 12*(3). Retrieved from http://www.advocatesforyouth.org/publications/937?task=view

The Asexual Visibility and Education Network. (2012). *Overview*. Retrieved from http://www.asexuality.org/home/overview.html

Augustine, J. (2010). Youth of color—At disproportionate risk of negative sexual health outcomes. *Advocates for Youth*. Retrieved from http://www.advocatesforyouth.org/storage/advfy/documents/youth_of_color.pdf

Bay-Cheng, L.Y. (2003). The trouble of teen sex: The construction of adolescent sexuality through school-based sexuality education. *Sex Education: Sexuality, Society and Learning, 3*(1), 61–74.

Bettcher, T. M. (2014). Trapped in the wrong theory: Rethinking trans oppression and resistance. *Signs, 39*(2), 383–406.

Bishop, T. (personal communication, October 23, 2013).

Blake, S., Ledsky, R., Lehman, T., Goodenow, C., Sawyer, R., & Hack, T. (2011). Preventing sexual risk behaviors among gay, lesbian, and bisexual adolescents: The benefits of gay-sensitive HIV instruction in schools. *American Journal of Public Health, 91*(6), 940–946.

Bontempo, D. E., & D'Augelli, A. R. (2002). Effects of at-school victimization and sexual orientation on lesbian, gay or bisexual youths' health risk behavior. *Journal of Adolescent Health, 30*, 364–374.

Botsford, J. (October 18, 2013). *Planned parenthood: Creating inclusive practice & policy*. Lecture presented at Knowledge in the Making: 37th Wisconsin Women's Studies Conference, Madison, WI.

Centers for Disease Control. (2015). *HIV among youth*. Retrieved from http://www.cdc.gov/hiv/risk/age/youth/

Centers for Disease Control. (2014). *Injury prevention & control: Division of violence prevention*. Retrieved from http://www.cdc.gov/violenceprevention/acestudy/

Center for Positive Sexuality. (2016). *Sex positive education & research*. Retrieved from http://positivesexuality.org/

Connell, C., & Elliott, S. (2009). Beyond the birds and the bees: Learning inequality through sexuality education. *American Journal of Sexuality Education, 4*, 83–102.

DeCoste, J.M. (2011). Queering sex education: Rural sex educators' perceptions of queer issues. (Doctoral Dissertation). The Pennsylvania State University, State College, PA.

De Melker, S. (2015). The case for starting sex education in kindergarten. *PBS Newshour*. Retrieved from http://www.pbs.org/newshour/updates/spring-fever/

Douglass, M., & Douglass, L. (2009). The Orgasm Gap. In N. Worcester & M. H. Whatley (Eds.), *Women's health: Readings on social, economic and political issues* (pp. 466–479). Dubuque, IA: Kendall Hunt.

Fausto-Sterling, A. (2000). *Sexing the body: Gender politics and the construction of sexuality*. New York, NY: Basic Books.

Fava, N.M., & Bay-Cheng, L.Y. (2013). Trauma-informed sexuality education: Recognizing the rights and resilience of youth. *Sex Education, 13*(4), 383–394.

Fields, J. (2008). *Risky lessons: Sex education and social inequality*. New Brunswick, NJ: Rutgers University Press.

Fine, M. (1988). Sexuality, schooling, and adolescent females: The missing discourse of desire. *Harvard Educational Review, 58*(1), 29–53.

Fine, M. (1997). Sexuality, Schooling, and Adolescent Females. In M.M. Gergen, & S.N. Davis (Eds.), *Toward a new psychology of gender: A reader*. New York, NY: Routledge.

Fine, M., & McClelland, S.I. (2006). Sexuality education and desire: Still missing after all these years. *Harvard Educational Review 76*(3), 297- 338.

Frantz, O. (2012). On trans-inclusive language. *The good men project.* Retrieved from http://goodmenproject.com/noseriouslywhatabouttehmenz/on-trans-inclusive-language/

Froyum, C. M. (2010). Making 'good girls': sexual agency in the sexuality education of low-income black girls. *Culture, Health, & Sexuality, 12*(1): 59–72.

Foucault, M. (1996). The end of the monarchy of sex. In S. Lotringer (Ed.), *Foucault live: (Interviews, 1961–1984)* (pp. 214–225). New York, NY: Semiotext(E).

Future of Sex Education Initiative. (2011). *National sexuality education standards: Core content and skills, K-12.* Retrieved from http://www.futureofsexed.org/nationalstandards.html

Galler, R. (1984). The myth of the perfect body. In C. Vance (Ed.). *Pleasure and danger: Exploring female sexuality* (pp. 165–172). Boston, MA: Routledge & Kegan Paul.

Goldfarb, E. S., & Casparian, E. M. (2000). *Our whole lives: Sexuality education for grades 10–12.* Boston, MA: Unitarian Universalist Association.

Goodenow, C., Szalacha, L. A., Robin, L. E., & Westheimer, K. (2008). Dimensions of sexual orientation and HIV-related risk among adolescent females: Evidence from a statewide survey. *American Journal of Public Health, 98*(6), 1051–1058.

Gowen, L. K., & Winges-Yanez, N. (2014). Lesbian, gay, bisexual, transgender, queer, and questioning youths' perspectives of inclusive school-based-sexuality education. *Journal of Sex Research, 51*(7), 788–800.

The Guttmacher Institute. (2016). *State Policies in Brief: Sex and HIV Education.* Retrieved from http://www.guttmacher.org/statecenter/spibs/spib_SE.pdf

Harrell, E., & Rand, M. R. (2010). Crime against people with disabilities, 2008. *U.S. Department of Justice.* Retrieved from http://www.bjs.gov/content/pub/pdf/capd08.pdf

Higgins, J., & Hirsch, J.S. (2007). The Pleasure Deficit: Revisiting the "sexuality connection" in reproductive health. *Perspectives on Sexual and Reproductive Health 39*(4), 240–247.

Holland J., & Ramazanoglu, C. (1992). Risk, power and the possibility of pleasure: Young women and safer sex. *AIDS Care, 4*(3), 273.

Ingham, R. (2005). "We didn't cover that at school"": Education *against* pleasure or education *for* pleasure? *Sex Education, 5*(4), 375–388.

Johnson, J. (2009). Exposed at last: The truth about your clitoris. In N. Worcester & M.H. Whatley (Eds.), *Women's health: Readings on social, economic and political issues* (pp. 454–456). Dubuque, IA: Kendall Hunt.

Kaufman, M., Silverberg, C., & Odette, F. *The ultimate guide to sex and disability: For all of us who live with disabilities, chronic pain & illness.* San Francisco, CA: Cleis Press.

Kirby, D. (2007). *Emerging answers 2007: Research findings on programs to reduce teen pregnancy and sexually transmitted diseases.* Washington DC: National Campaign to Prevent Teen and Unplanned Pregnancy.

Kirby, D., Laris, B. A., & Rolleri, L. (2006). *Sex and HIV education programs for youth: Their impact and important characteristics.* Scotts Valley, CA: Family Health International.

Kirby, D., Laris, B. A., & Rolleri, L. (2007). Sex and HIV education programs: Their impact on sexual behaviors of young people throughout the world. *Journal of Adolescent Health, 40*, 206–217.

Kirby, D. (2008). The impact of abstinence and comprehensive sex and STD/HIV education programs on adolescent sexual behavior. *Sexuality Research & Social Policy, 5*(3), 18–27.

Kirby D. (2002). *Do abstinence only programs delay the initiation of sex among young people and reduce teen pregnancy?* Washington DC: National Campaign to Prevent Teen Pregnancy, 2002.

Kim, E. (2011). Asexuality in disability narratives. *Sexualities, 14*(4): 479–493.

Kline, R. (2014). These maps show where kids in America get terrifying sex ed. *Huffington Post.* Retrieved from http://www.huffingtonpost.com/2014/04/08/sex-education-requirement-maps_n_5111835.html

Kost K., & Henshaw S. (2014). *U.S. teenage pregnancies, births and abortions, 2010: national and state trends and trends by age, race and ethnicity.* Retrieved from http://www.guttmacher.org/pubs/USTPtrends10.pdf

Lamb, S., Lustig, K., & Graling, K. (2012). The use and misuse of pleasure in sex education curricula. *Sex Education, 13*(3), 305–318.

Lorde, A. (1984). Age, race, class, and sex: Women redefining difference. In A. Lorde, (Ed.), *Sister Outsider.* Freedom, CA: The Crossing Press.

McGarry, R. (2013). Build a curriculum that includes everyone. *Kappan Magazine, 94*(5), 27–31.

McKay, A. (1999). *Sexual ideology and schooling: Towards democratic sexuality education.* Albany, NY: State University of New York Press.

Milwaukee Public Schools Wellness and Prevention Office. (2012). *Human Growth & Development Curriculum High School Lessons.*

Mustanski, B. S., Newcomb, M. E., Du Bois, S. N., Garcia, S. C., & Grov, C. (2011). HIV in young men who have sex with men: A review of epidemiology, risk and protective factors, and interventions. *Journal of Sex Research, 48*(2–3), 218–253.

Mutchler, M., Ayla, G., Neith, K. (2005) Safer sex stories told by young gay men: Building resiliency through gay-boy talk. *Journal of Gay and Lesbian Issues In Education 2*(3), 37–51.

National Conference of State Legislatures. (2016). *State policies on sex education in schools.* Retrieved from http://www.ncsl.org/research/health/state-policies-on-sex-education-in-schools.aspx

Pastor, S. K. (2009). Education for sexual intimacy and agency. In N. Worcester & M.H. Whatley (Eds.), *Women's health: Readings on social, economic and political issues* (pp. 440–446). Dubuque, IA: Kendall Hunt.

Philpott, A., Knerr, W., & Boydell, V. (2006). Pleasure and prevention: When good sex is safer sex. *Reproductive Health Matters, 14*(28), 23–31.

Planned Parenthood of Wisconsin. (2011). *Safe, Healthy, Strong: A Comprehensive Sexuality Education Curriculum.*

Planned Parenthood. (2014). *Implementing Sex Education.* https://www.plannedparenthood.org/educators/implementing-sex-education

Preston, M. (2013). "'Very very risky': Sexuality education teachers' definition of sexuality and teaching and learning responsibilities." *American Journal of Sexuality Education 8,* 18–35.

Rasmussen, M. L. (2004). Wounded identities, sex and pleasure: 'Doing it' at school. NOT! *Discourse: studies in the cultural politics of education, 25*(4), 445–458.

Recapp. (2016). *Topics In Brief: Positive Sexuality.* Retrieved from http://recapp.etr.org/recapp/index.cfm?fuseaction=pages.TopicsInBriefDetail&PageID=61

Saewyc, E. M., Bearinger, L. H. Blum, R. W., & Resnick, M. D. (1999). Sexual intercourse, abuse and pregnancy among adolescent women: Does sexual orientation make a difference? *Family Planning Perspectives, 31*(3), 127–131.

Schalet, A.T. (2011). *Not under my roof: Parents, teens, and the culture of sex.* Chicago, IL: University of Chicago Press.

Schroeder, E., Goldfarb E.S., & Gilpern, N. (2015). *Rights, respect, responsibility: A K-12 sexuality education curriculum.* Retrieved from http://www.advocatesforyouth.org/3rs-curric-lessonplans

Seattle and King County Public Health. (2013). *Family Life and Sexual Health, 3rd Ed.*

Sexuality Information and Education Council of the United States. (2004). *Guidelines for comprehensive sexuality education, 3rd ed.* Retrieved from http://www.siecus.org/_data/global/images/guidelines.pdf

Sexuality Information and Education Council of the United States. (2012). *Wisconsin legislature repeals healthy youth act, continues attack on sexual health and women's rights.* Retrieved from http://www.siecus.org/index.cfm?fuseaction=Feature.showFeature&featureID=2160

Sexuality Information and Education Council of the United States. (2015). *A brief history of federal funding for sex education and related programs.* Retrieved from http://www.siecus.org/index.cfm?fuseaction=page.viewpage&pageid=1341&nodeid=1

Sexuality Information and Education Council of the United States. (2016a). *Sexuality Education Q & A.* Retrieved from http://www.siecus.org/index.cfm?fuseaction=page.viewpage&pageid=521&grandparentID=477&parentID=514

Sexuality Information and Education Council of the United States. (2016b). *Policy Updates.* Retrieved from http://www.siecus.org/index.cfm?fuseaction=feeds.list&categoryid=27&publishdate=3/01/2016&pageid=483

Springer, K. (2008). Queering black female heterosexuality. In J. Friedman & J. Valenti (Eds.), *Yes means yes: Visions of female sexual power & a world without rape* (pp. 77–92). Berkeley, CA: Seal Press.

Stern, L. (2016). *General Session.* Lecture presented at Great Lakes Institute for Community Health Educators, Green Lake, WI.

Sullivan, P.M., & Knuton, J.F. (2000). Maltreatment and disabilities: A population-based epidemiological study. *Child Abuse & Neglect, 24*(10), 1257–1273.

Tepper, M. (2000). Sexuality and disability: The missing discourse of pleasure. *Sexuality and Disability, 18*(4), 283–290.

Trenholm, C., Davaney, B., Fortson, K., Quay, L., Wheeler, J., & Clark, M. (2007). *Impacts of Four Title V, Section 510 Abstinence Education Programs Final Report.* Princeton, NJ: Mathematic Policy Research; submitted to U.S. Dept. Health & Human Services, Assistant Secretary for Planning and Evaluation.

Tucker, (2015). Governor signs bill mandating sex ed in schools across California. *SF Gate.* Retrieved from http://www.sfgate.com/education/article/Governor-signs-bill-mandating-sex-ed-in-schools-6551585.php

United States House of Representatives, Committee on Government Reform. (2004). *The content of federally funded abstinence-only education programs, prepared for Rep. Henry A. Waxman.* Washington, DC: The House.

Weinstock, H., Berman, S., & Cates, W. (2004). Sexually transmitted diseases among American youth: incidence and prevalence estimates, 2000. *Perspectives on Sexual and Reproductive Health, 36*(1), 6–10.

Williams, D.J., Prior, E., Wegner, J. (2013). Resolving Social Problems Associated with Sexuality: Can a 'Sex-Positive' Approach Help? *Social Worker 58*(3), 273–277.

Wilson, P. M. (1999). *Our whole lives: Sexuality education for grades 7–9.* Boston, MA: Unitarian Universalist Association.

Wisconsin Department of Public Instruction. (2014). *Human growth and development: A resource guide to assist school districts in policy and program development and implementation.* Retrieved from http://dpi.wi.gov/sites/default/files/imce/sspw/pdf/hgdedition5.pdf

Wisconsin Human Growth and Development Instruction, Wisconsin State Legislature § 118.019 (2011).

"Adolescent Sexual Health in Europe and the U.S.— Why the Difference?"

From *Advocates for Youth*

Regularly since 1998, Advocates for Youth has sponsored study tours to France, Germany, and the Netherlands to explore why adolescent sexual health outcomes are more positive in these European countries than in the United States.

Rights. Respect. Responsibility.® The study tour participants—policy makers, researchers, youth serving professionals, foundation officers, and youth—have found that this trilogy of values underpins a social philosophy regarding adolescent sexual health in France, Germany, and the Netherlands. Each of the three nations has an unwritten social contract with youth: "We'll respect your right to act responsibly and give you the tools you need to avoid unintended pregnancy and sexually transmitted infections, including HIV."

In France, Germany, and the Netherlands, two things create greater, easier access to sexual health information and services for *all* people, including teens. They are: (1) societal openness and comfort in dealing with sexuality, including teen sexuality; and (2) *pragmatic* governmental policies. The result—better sexual health outcomes for French, German, and Dutch teens when compared to U.S. teens.

Adolescent Pregnancy, Birth, and Abortion Rates in Europe Outshine Those in the United States*

Pregnancy

The United States' **teen pregnancy rate** is over five times that of the Netherlands, over four times that of Germany, and over three times that of France.[1,2,3]

Birth

U.S. teens account for about 71 percent of all teenage births occurring in all developed countries.[4] The United States' **teen birth rate** is nearly nine times higher than the Netherlands', four and a half times higher than France's, and over four times higher than Germany's.[1,3,5]

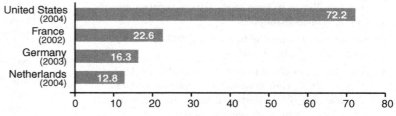

Pregnancy rate per 1,000 women ages 15 to 19, latest year available

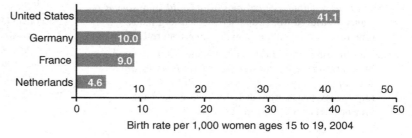

Birth rate per 1,000 women ages 15 to 19, 2004

---

*Throughout this fact sheet, data are the most recent available for France, Germany, and the Netherlands. Pregnancy data do not include fetal losses. N/A means not available.

Abortion

In the United States, the **teen abortion rate** is more than twice that of Germany and nearly twice that of the Netherlands.[3,6,7]

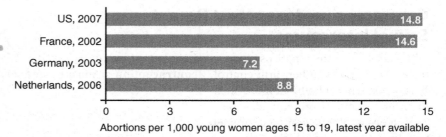

Abortions per 1,000 young women ages 15 to 19, latest year available

U.S. HIV/STI Rates Also Compare Poorly

HIV

The proportion of the United States' adolescent and adult population that has been diagnosed with HIV or AIDS is six times greater than in Germany, three times greater than in the Netherlands, and one and a half times greater than in France.[8,9]

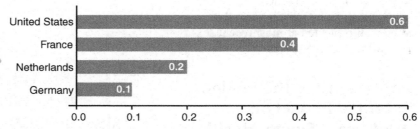

Proportion of the total adolescent and adult population of the country diagnosed with HIV or AIDS

Syphilis

Among teens, syphilis rates are more than 70 percent higher in the United States than in the Netherlands.[10,11,12]

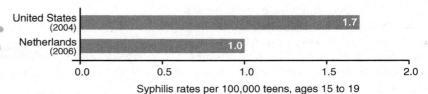

Syphilis rates per 100,000 teens, ages 15 to 19

Gonorrhea

Gonorrhea is the second most commonly reported infectious disease in the United States, and the U.S, adolescent rate is 28 times greater than teen rates in the Netherlands.[10,11,12]

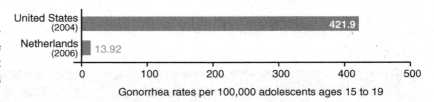

Gonorrhea rates per 100,000 adolescents ages 15 to 19

Chlamydia

Chlamydia infection is more than 15 times more common among U.S. teens than Dutch teens.[10,11,12]

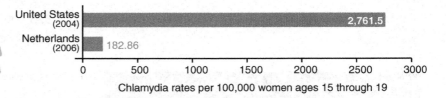

Chlamydia rates per 100,000 women ages 15 through 19

Contraceptive Use at Most Recent Sexual Intercourse

Although U.S. teens report using contraception (usually either birth control pills or condoms or both) far more often than their peers of previous decades, U.S. teens still use contraception or condoms much less consistently than their peers in Europe. When measuring use of highly effective hormonal contraception, condoms, or both, researchers found that German, French, and Dutch youth were significantly more likely to be well protected at most recent sex than were their U.S. peers.[13,14,15,16]

Percent of sexually active 15 year old youth reporting use of contraception at most recent sex.

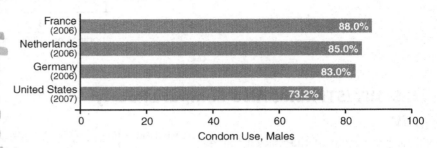

Condom Use, Males

Implementing the Model: Potential Impact on Adolescent Sexual Health in the U.S.

If society in the United States were to become more comfortable with sexuality and *if* governmental policies were to create greater and easier access to sexual health information and services, *then* US. teens' sexual health outcomes would improve markedly. Imagine that the United States' teen pregnancy, birth, and abortion rates would improve to match those of the Netherlands, Germany, and France. Improved *rates* would mean large reductions in the *numbers* of pregnancies, births, and abortions to US. teens each year.

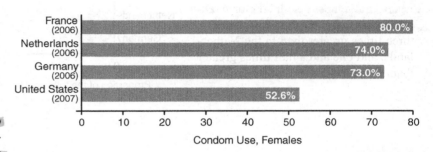

Condom Use, Females

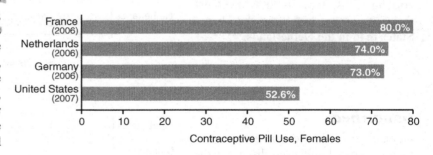

Contraceptive Pill Use, Females

If U.S. Rates equaled those in:	The number of U.S. teen pregnancies would be reduced by:	The number of U.S. teen births would be reduced by:	The number of U.S. teen abortions would be reduced by:
France	515,000	333,000	8,000
Germany	581,000	323,000	83,000
Netherlands	617,000	379,000	75,000

If the U.S. birth rates in 2004 equaled those in:	U.S. annual public savings in 2004 would have equaled:
France	$476,190,000
Germany	$461,890,000
Netherlands	$541,970,000

It has been estimated that the public costs associated with teen birth in the United States were at least **$9.1 billion** in 2004, an annual average cost of $1,430 per child born to a teen mother.[17]

Therefore, if the U.S. could reduce its teen birth rate to equal that of France, Germany or the Netherlands, it would save significantly on public funds expended to support families begun by a teen birth.

The Lessons Learned: A Model to Improve Adolescent Sexual Health in the United States

So, if Dutch, German, and French teens have better sexual health outcomes than U.S. teens, what's the secret? Is there a 'silver bullet' solution for the United States that will reduce the following statistics?

- *Nine million* new cases of sexually transmitted infections among 15- to 24-year-old. youth;[18]
- *Five thousand* new HIV infections among 13- to 24-year-old youth;[19]
- Estimated *750,000* pregnancies among U.S. teens;
- *125,000* abortions among U.S. teens; and
- *435,000* births among 15- to 19-year-old women.[20]

Unfortunately, there is no single, 'silver bullet' solution! Yet, the United States can use the experience of people in the Netherlands, Germany, and France to guide its efforts to improve adolescents' sexual health. The United States can achieve social and cultural consensus that sexuality is a normal and healthy part of being human and of being a teen. It can do this by using the lessons learned from the European study tours.

- Adults in France, Germany, and the Netherlands view young people as assets, not as problems. Adults value and respect adolescents and expect teens to act responsibly. Governments strongly support education and economic self-sufficiency for youth.
- Research is the basis for public health policies to reduce unintended pregnancies, abortions, and sexually transmitted infections, including HIV. Political and religious interest groups have little influence on public health policy.
- A national desire to reduce the number of abortions and to prevent sexually transmitted infections, including HIV, provides the major impetus in each country for ensuring easy access to contraception and condoms, consistent sex education, and widespread public education campaigns.
- Governments support massive, consistent, long-term public education campaigns, through the Internet, television, films, radio, billboards, discos, pharmacies, and health care providers. Media is a respected partner in these campaigns. Campaigns are direct and humorous and focus on both safety and pleasure.
- Youth have convenient access to free or low-cost contraception through national health insurance.

- Sex education is not necessarily a separate curriculum and is usually integrated across school subjects and at all grade levels. Educators provide accurate and complete information in response to students' questions.
- Families have open, honest, consistent discussions with teens about sexuality and support the role of educators and health care providers in making sexual health information and services available to teens.
- Adults see intimate sexual relationships as normal and natural for older adolescents, a positive component of emotionally healthy maturation. At the same time, young people believe it is 'stupid and irresponsible' to have sex without protection. Youth rely on the maxim, 'safer sex or no sex.'
- Society weighs the morality of sexual behavior through an individual ethic that includes the values of responsibility, respect, tolerance, and equity.
- France, Germany, and the Netherlands struggle to address issues around cultural diversity, especially in regard to immigrant populations whose values related to gender and sexuality differ from those of the majority culture.

Rights. Respect. Responsibility.® A National Campaign to Improve Adolescent Sexual Health

In October 2001, Advocates for Youth launched a long-term campaign—*Rights. Respect. Responsibility.®*—based on the lessons learned from the European study tours. The Campaign works to shift the current U.S. societal paradigm of adolescent sexuality away from a negative emphasis on fear and ignorance and towards an acceptance of sexuality of healthy and normal and a view of adolescents as valuable and important.

- Adolescents have the right to balanced, accurate, and realistic sex education, confidential and affordable health services, and a secure stake in the future.
- Youth deserve respect. Today they are often perceived as part of 'the problem'. Valuing young people means they are part of the solution to societal issues and participate in developing programs and policies that affect their well-being.
- Society has the responsibility to provide young people with the tools they need to safeguard their sexual health and young people have the

responsibility to protect themselves from too early childbearing and sexually transmitted infections, including HIV

Advocates develops and disseminates campaign materials for specific audiences, such as the entertainment industry and news media professionals, policy makers, youth-serving professionals, parents, and youth activists. Advocates will continue its thought-provoking European study tours. Advocates will also collaborate with key national and statewide organizations to promote *Rights. Respect. Responsibility.*® through Campaign materials, workshops, presentations, and technical assistance. For additional information on the Campaign or to become a partner in this important initiative, contact Advocates for Youth at 202.419.3420 or visit www.advocatesforyouth.org

REFERENCES

A list of references is available in the original source at www.advocatesforyouth.org.

"How Being a Good Girl Can Be Bad for Girls"

By Deborah L. Tolman and Tracy E. Higgins

Women's sexuality is frequently suspect in our culture, particularly when it is expressed outside the bounds of monogamous hetero-sexual marriage. This suspicion is reflected in the dominant cultural accounts of women's sexuality, which posit good, decent, and normal women as passive and threatened sexual objects. When women act as sexual agents, expressing their own sexual desire rather than serving as the objects of men's desire, they are often portrayed as threatening, deviant, and bad. Missing is any affirmative account of women's sexual desire. Yet, even while women's sexuality is denied or problema-tized, the culture and the law tend to assign to women the responsibility for regulating heterosexual sex by re-sisting male aggression. Defined as natural, urgent, and aggressive, male sexuality is bounded, both in law and in culture, by the limits of women's consent. Women who wish to avoid the consequences of being labeled "bad" are expected to define the boundaries of sexual behavior, outlined by men's desire, and to ignore or deny their own sexual desire as a guide to their choices.

The cultural anxiety precipitated by unbounded female sexuality is perhaps most apparent with regard to adolescent girls. Coming under scrutiny from across the political spectrum, girls' sexuality has been deemed threatening either to girls themselves (potentially result-ing in rape, sexually transmitted diseases, unwanted pregnancy), or to society (as evidenced by the single mother, school dropout, welfare dependent). Although none of these issues is limited to teenage girls, all fre-quently arise in that context because of society's sense of entitlement, or, indeed, obligation, to regulate teen sexuality. Accordingly, the cultural and legal sanctions on teenage girls' sexuality convey a simple message: good girls are not sexual; girls who are sexual are either

(1) bad girls, if they have been active, desiring sexual agents or (2) good girls, who have been passively vic-timized by boys' raging hormones. Buttressed by the real concerns that girls themselves have about preg-nancy, AIDS, and parental as well as peer disapproval, the good-girl/bad-girl dichotomy organizes sexuality for young women. This cultural story may increase girls' vulnerability to sexual coercion and psychologi-cal distress and disable them from effectively seeking legal protection.

The Cultural Story of Girls' Sexuality in the Media and in Law

Sexually assertive girls are making the news. A dis-turbed mother of a teenage boy wrote to Ann Landers, complaining of the behavior of teenage girls who had telephoned him, leaving sexually suggestive messages. After publishing the letter, Landers received twenty thousand responses and noted, "If I'm hearing about it from so many places, then I worry about what's going on out there. . . . What this says to me is that a good many young girls really are out of control. Their hormones are raging and they have not had adequate supervision" (qtd. In Yoffe 1991). What were these girls doing? Call-ing boys, asking them out, threatening to buy them gifts, and to "make love to [them] all night." In the *Newsweek* story, "Girls Who Go Too Far," in which the writer described this Ann Landers column, such girls were referred to as "obsessed," "confused," "emotionally disturbed," "bizarre," "abused," "troubled." Parents described the girls' behavior as "bewilder[ing]" or even "frighten[ing]" to boys. A similar, more recent story in the *Orlando Sentinel* noted that "girls today have few qualms about asking a boy out—and they have no qualms about calling a boy on the telephone" (Shrieves 1993). Describing late-night telephone calls from girls to their teenage sons, the adults interviewed characterized the situation as "frustrating" and "shocking" and suggested that "parents should be paying more attention to what their daughters are doing." Girls' behavior, including "suggestive notes stuck to a boy's locker or even outright propositions," was deemed "obsessive."

In contrast, media accounts of boys' sexuality tend to reflect what Wendy Hollway has called the "discourse of male sexual drive," wherein male sexuality is portrayed as natural, relentless, and demanding attention, an urge that boys and men cannot help or control (Hollway 1984). Media coverage of the so-called Spur Posse in Lakewood, California, reflects this discourse. Members of the Spur Posse, a group of popular white high school boys in a middle-class California suburb, competed with one another using a point system for their sexual "conquests" (Smolowe 1993). When girls eventually complained, several boys were charged with crimes ranging from sexual molestation to rape. Although many criticized the incident as an example of unchecked adolescent sexuality, others excused or even defended the boys' behavior. One father explained, "Nothing my boy did was anything any red-blooded American boy wouldn't do at his age." Their mother commented, "What can you do? It's a testosterone thing."

A comparison of the different boundaries of acceptable sexual behavior for girls and boys illustrates the force of the cultural assumption of female passivity and male aggression. Although the Spur Posse incident was covered as a troubling example of male sexuality out of control, the point at which adolescent sexual aggression becomes suspect is strikingly different for girls and boys. For girls, it's phone calls; for boys, it's rape. The girls' suggestive phone calling is described as shocking to the parents and even threatening to the sons, not because the desire expressed was unusual in the realm of teen sexuality, but because the agents were girls and the objects were boys. In the Spur Posse incident, the possibility of girls' sexual agency or desire shifted responsibility from the boys' aggression to the girls' failure to resist. For some observers, whether or not the boys in the Spur Posse were considered to have acted inappropriately depended upon an assessment of the sexual conduct of the girls involved. If the girls were shown to have expressed any sexual agency, their desire was treated by some as excusing and justifying the boys' treatment of them as objects or points to be collected. As one mother, invoking cultural shorthand put it, "Those girls are trash." The boys' behavior was excused as natural, "a testosterone thing," and the girls were deemed culpable for their failure to control the boys' behavior.

Through these cultural stories, girls are simultaneously taught that they are valued in terms of their sexual desirability and that their own desire makes them vulnerable. If they are economically privileged and white, they become vulnerable because desiring (read "bad") girls lose credibility and protection from male aggression. If they are poor and/or of color, or bisexual or lesbian, they are assumed to be bad, as refracted through the lenses of racism, classism, and homophobia that anchor the cultural story (Tolman forthcoming). While in some communities girls' and women's sexuality is acknowledged and more accepted (Omolade 1983), the force of cultural stories permeating the dominant culturel presses upon all girls. This constant pressure often inflames the desire of marginalized girls to be thought of as good, moral, and normal, status denied them by mainstream standards.[1] Moreover, all girls' vulnerability is compounded by the extraordinary license given to adolescent boys regarding the urgency of their sexuality. Perhaps more than any other group of men, teenage boys are assumed to be least in control of their sexuality. The responsibility for making sexual choices, therefore, falls to their partners, usually teenage girls, yet these "choices" are to be enacted through passivity rather than agency. Girls who attain good girlhood are at constant risk of becoming bad girls if they fail in their obligation to regulate their own sexual behavior and that of their partners. It is during adolescence, then, that girls are both most responsible for sexual decision making and most penalized for acting on their own sexual desires. It is also during adolescence that girls are socialized into cultural stories about being sexual and being women (Brown and Gilligan 1992; Tolman 1994a and 1994b).

The power of these cultural norms to mediate the interpretation of teen sexuality is perhaps most vividly revealed in the comments of those who would defend "aggressive" girls. Teenage girls interviewed in the *Sentinel* story explained their peers' behavior in terms of girls giving boys what the boys wanted. One suggested that "sometimes girls, in order to get certain guys, will do anything the guy wants. And that includes sex." That would include propositioning a boy "[I]f that's what she thinks *he wants*." The girl's actions are reinterpreted in terms of satisfying the boy's desire rather than her own. Explaining away the possibility of the girls' sexual desire, one counselor suggested that the girls may not really be "sex-crazed." Rather, they are probably simply "desperate for a relationship" (Shrieves 1993). Describing the girls as trading sex for relationships, the counselor reinterprets their actions in a manner that is consistent with the cultural story of male aggression and female responsibility, which is devoid of female desire. The girl gives the boy what he (inevitably or naturally) wants, negotiating her need only for a relationship by managing his drive for sexual pleasure.

The contrasting media coverage of teenage girls' and teenage boys' sexuality stands as one manifestation of a broader cultural message about gendered norms of sexual behavior. Feminists have documented and discussed this message as a theme present throughout literature, law, film, advertising, and general sources of cultural wisdom on sexuality such as self-help books, advice columns, and medical treatises. The story of male aggression and female responsibility suffuses the culture and operates to regulate human sexuality on conscious and subconscious levels in a gender-specific way. By discouraging women's sexual agency and men's sexual responsibility, these cultural norms undermine communication and encourage coercion and violence. This effect is perhaps nowhere more clear than in the legal regulation of sexuality through rape statutes and the media coverage of rape trials.

Premised on the notion of male sexual aggression and irresponsibility, the law of rape incorporates cultural norms that place upon the woman the burden of regulating sexual activity and, at the same time, penalize her for acting as a sexual subject (Henderson 1992). In so doing, the law of rape incorporates both sides of the good girl/bad girl dynamic. The good girl's attempt to exercise her responsibility to regulate male sexuality is encoded in the requirement of nonconsent to sexual intercourse. Proof of nonconsent, however, frequently depends upon establishing an absence of desire. To be a victimized good girl and therefore entitled to protection, a girl or woman must both resist *and* lack desire. A desiring bad girl, on the other hand, is often deemed deserving of the consequences of her desire.

In cases of nonstranger (acquaintance) rape, rape trials frequently hinge upon whether nonconsent is established, a standard which, as feminists have noted, takes little account of women's sexuality. As Carol Smart has argued, the consent/nonconsent dyad fails to capture the complexity of a woman's experience (Smart 1989). A woman may seek and initiate physical intimacy, which may be an expression of her own sexual desire, while not consenting to intercourse. Nevertheless, by imposing the consent/nonconsent interpretive framework, rape law renders a woman's expression of any desire immediately suspect. Expression of desire that leads to intimacy and ultimately submission to unwanted sex falls on the side of consent. As the "trashy" girls who were the victims of the Spur Posse illustrate, to want anything is to consent to everything. The woman has, in effect, sacrificed her right to refuse intercourse by the expression of her own sexual desire. Or, more precisely,

the expression of her desire undermines the credibility of her refusal. Evidence that the rape victim initiated sexual interaction at any level operates to undermine her story at every stage of the process—police disbelieve her account, prosecutors refuse to press the case, and juries refuse to convict. At trial, the issue of consent may be indistinguishable from the question of whether the woman experienced pleasure. Thus, within rape law, a woman's behavior as a sexual subject shifts power to the aggressor, thereby maintaining the power hierarchy of the traditional story of male aggression and female submission. As in pulp romance, to desire is to surrender.

The centrality of the absence of female desire to the definition of rape cuts across racial lines, albeit in complicated ways. As African American feminists have pointed out, rape and race are historically interwoven in a way that divides the experiences of women of color from white women (i.e., Collins 1990 and Harris 1990; see also Caraway 1991). Nevertheless, whatever the woman's race, the absence of female desire stands as a prerequisite to the identification of a sexual act as rape. The difference emerges as a product of the interlocking elements of the cultural story about women's sexuality which segregate white women and women of color. For example, a key element in the cultural story about women's sexuality is that African American women are sexually voracious, thereby making them unrapable—as distinguished from white women, who are asexual and thus in a constant state of rapability. The absence-of-desire standard is still applied to women of color but presumed impossible to meet. Conversely, when white women accuse African American men of raping them, the required absence of female desire is simply presumed.

If, under ordinary rape law, expression of female sexual desire takes women and girls outside the protection of the law, rendering them unrapable, statutory rape law defines female sexuality as outside the law in a different way. By criminalizing all intercourse with minors, statutory rape laws literally outlaw girls' expression of their own sexuality.[2] In terms of female sexual desire, statutory rape laws represent a complete mirroring of rape law regulating men's access to adult women—with statutory rape, absence of desire is presumed. Instead of rendering a woman unrapable or fully accessible to men, the law simply makes young women's expression of sexual desire illegal.

Both rape law and statutory rape law reinforce cultural norms of female sexuality be penalizing female sexual desire. The coverage of rape in the media, in turn, frequently heightens the focus on the sexuality of the victim, casting her as either good (innocent) or bad (desiring). For example, in the coverage of the Mike

Tyson rape trial, the media referred repeatedly to the fact that Desiree Washington taught Sunday school, as though that fact were necessary to rebut the possibility that she invited the attack by acting on her own sexual desire. In an even more extreme case, the mentally disabled adolescent girl who was raped by a group of teenage boys in her Glen Ridge, New Jersey, neighborhood was portrayed both by her lawyers and by the media as largely asexual. To establish nonconsent, the prosecution argued explicitly that she was incapable of knowing or expressing her sexuality.[3] Although she was not sexually inexperienced, this strategy rendered her sexually innocent. Coverage of these two trials stands in sharp contrast to another highly publicized rape trial at the time, that of William Kennedy Smith, in which the media revealed not only the victim's name but her sexual history and her driving record. Much was made in the media of the victim's sexual history and her apparent willingness to accompany Smith home that night. Her desire to engage in flirtation and foreplay meant that her alleged refusal of intercourse could never be sufficiently credible to convict. Smith was acquitted.

As illustrated by the coverage of rape trials, the media and the law interact to reinforce the cultural story of male aggression and female passivity, reinforcing the good girl/bad girl distinction. With the suffusion of this story throughout our culture, girls and women come to understand the norms of acceptable sexual behavior— that good girls are those who are sexually innocent, meaning without sexual desire, although not necessarily without sexual experience. These girls are sexual objects, not subjects, charged with defending the boundaries of their own sexual activity by resisting male aggression. In contrast, bad girls are girls who express their desire, acting as sexual subjects on their own behalf. They are assertive girls, "girls who go too far." Vilified by the media and the culture more broadly as deviant and threatening, these girls are rendered far less likely than good girls to be able to invoke the protection of rape laws and are thus made doubly vulnerable.

Problem of Desire for Adolescent Girls

In this section, we turn to the voices of adolescent young women speaking about their experiences. We rely on a feminist method of analyzing interviews to understand how cultural stories about girls' sexuality may create vulnerability for girls rather than protect them from it.[4] This method takes women as authorities on their own experiences. We listen to what they say and how they say it so that our role as interpreters of their words is clear; that is, we do not claim the authority to say what they are saying but convey how we understand the stories they tell, given our perspective on these issues. We have drawn two case studies from a psychological study of adolescent girls' experience of desire (Tolman 1994a and 1994b),[5] and one from the legal literature. We selected the cases from the study because each of these girls chose to speak about a sexual experience with a boy who was not her boyfriend. Although each associated her experience with sexual violence, the two girls differ profoundly in their understanding of these experiences and also in their critical perspective on gender relations, the cultural story about male and female sexuality, and the good girl/bad girl dynamic. In Jenny's case, a lack of a critical perspective on these issues disables her from feeling outraged or empowered to act on her own behalf. For Pauline, such a perspective appears to enhance her sense of entitlement and ability to act. Through this contrast, we demonstrate how being a good girl can be bad for girls and, conversely, how challenging the terms of the good girl/bad girl dichotomy can be enabling. Finally, we selected the case of Sharon from the legal literature to underscore our point that denying desire in the name of good girlhood can diminish girls' ability to garner protection under the law.

Jenny: When Bad Things Happen to Good Girls

Sixteen-year-old Jenny, who lives in a suburb of a large city, looks like the quintessential good girl. She is white, has long, straight, blond hair framing a lightly freckled, fair face. She is slim, dressed fashionably yet unassumingly. She sits with her legs tensely crossed; she is polite and cooperative and smiles often. Like many girls in this study, throughout the interview Jenny describes how she lives her life by trying to stay carefully within the boundaries of good girl. She and her mother are "very close," and it is very important to her to be "nice" and a "good friend"—even if it means silencing her own displeasure or dissent in relationships.[6] Complying with conventional norms of femininity, Jenny explains that she has never experienced feelings she calls sexual desire: "I actually really don't think I've ever like, wanted anything, like sexually that bad. I mean I don't think I've ever been like sexually deprived or like saying, oh I need sex now or anything, I've never really felt that way before, so, I don't know. I don't really think that there's anything that I would, I mean want." Given Jenny's concern about and success at being a good girl in other domains of her life, it is not surprising that she does not report feeling desire. Having a "silent body" is a psychological response to the belief that good girls are not sexual (Tolman 1994a).

The vulnerability of this silence in her life is tangible in the narrative she tells about the first time she had sexual intercourse, which occurred just prior to our interview. This experience was not what she had hoped it would be:

> We got alone together, and we started just basically fooling around and not doing many things. And then he asked me if I would have sex with him, and I said, well I didn't think I, I mean I said I wanted to wait, 'cause I didn't want to. I mean I like him, but I don't like him so, and I mean he sorta pushed it on me, but it wasn't like I absolutely said no, don't, I—it was sort of a weird experience. I just, I sort of let it happen to me and never like really said no, I don't want to do this. I mean I said no, but I never, I mean I never stopped him from doing anything. . . . I guess maybe I wanted to get it over with, I guess . . . I don't know. I, I just, I mean I could've said no, I guess and I could've pushed him off or whatever 'cause he, I mean, he wasn't, he's not the type of person who would like rape me or whatever, I mean, well I don't think he's that way at all. . . . I was always like, well I want to wait, and I want to be in a relationship with someone who I really like, and I want it to be a special moment and everything, and then it just sort of like happened so quickly, and it happened with someone who I didn't like and who I didn't want a relationship with and who didn't want a relationship with me, and it was just sort of, I don't, I don't know, I regret it. . . . I wish I had just said no. I mean I could've, and I did for once but then I just let it go. And I wish that I had stood up for myself and really just like stood up and said no, I don't want to do this. I'm not ready or I want it to be a different experience. I mean I could've told him exactly how I felt. . . . I don't know why I didn't.

In this story, Jenny is unsure about how to understand her first experience with sexual intercourse. In listening to her, we, too, are unsure. When she begins this story, Jenny knows that she did not want to have sexual intercourse with this boy, although she did want to "fool around." She, in fact, said "no" when the boy asked her if she would have sex with him. There is a clarity to her no that she substantiates with a set of compelling reasons for not wanting to have sex with this boy: she "wanted to wait," she didn't "like him" or "want a relationship with him." After the fact, she is again clear that she did not want to have sex with this boy. She "regrets it." But we notice that this clarity gives way to a sense of confusion that colors Jenny's voice and gains momentum as her narrative, itself an interplay of description and assessment, unfolds. Cleaving to the convention that girls are ultimately responsible for boys' sexual behavior, she attempts to make sense of the fact that this boy behaved as though she had not said no. Assuming responsibility, Jenny suggests that she had "never stopped him from doing anything," implying, perhaps, that she had not meant the no that she had said.

Jenny's suggestion that she might have said *no* and meant *yes* raises a troubling issue for feminists who have rallied around the claim that "no means no." Although "no means no" is effective as an educational or political slogan or perhaps even as a legal norm, such norms protect girls only at the margin. Within the broader context of adolescent sexuality, girls' no must be credible both to girls and to their partners. Yet the cultural story that good girls do not have sexual desire undermines the credibility of their no, not only to others but also to themselves. When girls cannot say yes, no (or silence) is their only alternative and must express the range of their choices. Some have suggested that girls can ameliorate the problem by simply taking responsibility for communicating their desire (e.g., Roiphe 1993). This answer falls short and, in fact, leaves girls in the lurch by failing to account for the cultural sanctions on girls' expression of their sexuality. Leaving those sanctions unaddressed, so-called power feminists reinforce the assignment of responsibility to girls for sexual decision making without criticizing the constraints under which such decisions are made.

Jenny struggles within those constraints as she attempts to take seriously the possibility that she may have wanted to have sex with the boy despite having said no; the possibility that her no meant yes. Yet her reflection, "I guess maybe I wanted to get it over with, I guess" is literally buttressed by doubt. While this statement stands as a potential explanation of why she had sex even though she said no, Jenny herself does not sound convinced. The explanation sounds even less plausible when compared to the clarity of her elaborated and unambiguous statements about why she did not want to have sex. She explains, "I want to be in a relationship with someone who I really like, and I want it to be a special moment and everything."

As her story progresses, we hear Jenny's confusion about what she wanted intensify. This confusion seems to undermine Jenny's knowledge that she had actually said no to this boy. Eventually, Jenny seems to forget that she ever said no at all. Despite having just explained that she had not wanted to have sex with this boy and had told him so, Jenny starts to speak as if she had not said no. "I said no" becomes "I sort of let it happen to me and never like, really said no, I don't want to do this." She progressively undoes her knowledge that she articulated her wish not to have sex. "I mean I could've said no, I guess, and I could've pushed him off or whatever," finally becomes "I wish I had just said no." Thus, when this boy behaved as though Jenny had not said no, Jenny loses track of her knowledge and her voice, becoming confused not only about what she wanted but also about what she said.

The conditions Jenny gives for an appropriate sexual encounter—"a special relationship," someone she "really like[s]"—resonate with the cultural story that girls' sexuality is about relationships and not desire. Because the encounter she describes did not meet these conditions, she decided that she did not want to have sex and told the boy no. Yet these conditions did not supply an adequate framework for Jenny either to make a clear decision and insist that it be respected, or, if it was not respected, to identify the incident as one of violation. In this context, it is significant that Jenny makes no reference to her own sexual desire. It is only later in the interview, in response to a direct question, that Jenny reports that she "hadn't felt desire for the person I was with." She notes, however, that this absence of desire does not distinguish this encounter from any other: "I've never like had sexual feelings to want to do something or anything." We wonder whether, in the moment, Jenny was not able to hold onto her knowledge that she did not want to have sex because her own desire has never been available as a guide to her choices. We suggest that not feeling desire is one way to cope with the good girl/bad girl dichotomy. Were Jenny not subject to the good girl standard that prevents her from attending to her own sexual feelings, perhaps she would feel desire in some situations, and her lack of sexual desire could operate as a clear signal to her, perhaps leaving her less vulnerable to such confusion.

The consequences of Jenny's confusion include physical and psychological vulnerability. Her difficulty in holding on to her no and insisting that her no be respected leaves her physically vulnerable to sexual encounters that she does not in any clear way want. Jenny's confusion makes her vulnerable psychologically as well. By discounting her own thoughts and feelings, she risks becoming dissociated from her own experience and from reality. Such dissociation makes it difficult for Jenny to be able to know and name sexual exploitation. Accustomed to being the object of someone else's sexual desire, not considering that her own sexual desire might be relevant or significant, Jenny pastes over the complexity of what did, in fact, happen with the phrase

"it just sort of like happened." This "cover story" symbolizes and sustains Jenny's vulnerability in a culture that leaves out her sexual desire.

At the same time, Jenny's suggestion that "it just sort of like happened" keeps another story at bay, a story of a girl whose spoken wish was not heeded, who was coerced. Was Jenny raped? Jenny herself brings the word "rape" into her story: "I mean I could've said no, I guess and I could've pushed him off or whatever 'cause he, I mean, he wasn't, he's not the type of person who would like rape me, or whatever. I mean, well I don't think he's that way at all." She seems to wonder whether this experience might somehow be connected to rape. She may associate this experience with rape because the word signifies something about what it felt like for her, a violation. Although she stopped saying no and apparently assented nonverbally to the act, this sexual experience was not related to any feeling of yes on Jenny's part. Jenny's experience of having passively consented and of having been violated suggests the disjuncture between consent and desire in women's experience, a disjuncture that likely heightens Jenny's confusion over how to interpret what happened to her. Such confusion prevents Jenny from speaking clearly in the first instance about her desire and from later interpreting what happened in a way that acknowledges her own resistance.

Nonetheless Jenny is an astute observer of the social landscape of adolescent heterosexual relationships. She identifies some imbalances in how girls and boys behave and in how they are treated by others in response to their behavior. Later in the interview, she notes that "whenever like a girl and a guy do something and people find out, it's always the girl that messed up or, I mean, maybe the guy messed up, but the guys like get praise for it [laughing] and the girl's sort of like called, either a slut or something, or just like has a bad reputation. Which is sort of [laughing] awful." Jenny believes that "it is just as much the guy's fault as it is the girl's fault. . . . It's just like the guys and the girls make fun of the girls but no one makes fun of the guys [laughing]." What Jenny needs is an analytic framework that links the inequities she observes to cultural stories about sexuality. She suspects, but does not know, that these stories operate in a way that creates gendered power differences. Identifying the good girl/bad girl divide, Jenny tries without success to make sense of the contradiction she observes, that both girls and guys may be at "fault" in sexual situations like hers, but only girls are chastised. We notice that she does not say what she thinks about this contradiction. When she is asked directly, her constant confusion about gender relations is audible: "I really don't know."

Sharon: The Slippery Slope off Good Girlhood

The legal vulnerability created when girls become confused about their own desire is illustrated by the testimony of Sharon, the victim in the U.S. Supreme Court's statutory rape case *Michael M.* v. *Sonoma County*. In her portion of the trial transcript reproduced in the Supreme Court's opinion, Sharon, who, like Jenny, is sixteen and white, is being questioned by the defendant's lawyer about whether she wanted to have sex with the defendant, a boy who was not her boyfriend. Ordinary rape law requires that she make a clear claim that she did not want to have sex with the defendant in order to gain legal recourse. The confusion that emerges as she testifies not only renders the case problematic under ordinary rape law but also calls into question the legitimacy of the statutory rape prosecution. The lawyer's questions about Sharon's desire subtly garner the good girl/bad girl dynamic as part of a strategy to undermine the credibility of her claim that she did not want to have sexual intercourse. In the face of these questions, Sharon appears to lose her clarity about the exact parameters of her desire:

Q: Now, after you met the defendant, what happened?

A: We walked down to the railroad tracks.

Q: What happened at the railroad tracks?

A: We were drinking at the railroad tracks and we walked over to this bus and he started kissing me and stuff, and I was kissing him back, too, at first. Then I was telling him to stop—

Q: Yes.

A: —and I was telling him to slow down and stop. He said, "Ok, Ok." But then he just kept doing it. He just kept doing it and then my sister and two other guys came over to where we were and my sister told me to get up and come home. And then I didn't. . . . We were laying there and we were kissing each other, and then he asked me if I wanted to walk with him over to the park. We walked over to the park, and then we sat down on a bench, and then he started kissing me again, and we were laying on the bench. And he told me to take my pants off. I said "No," and I was trying to get up and he hit me back down on the bench, and then I just said to myself, "Forget it," and I let him do what he wanted to do and he took my pants off and he was telling me to put my legs around him and stuff.

Q: Did you have sexual intercourse with the defendant?

A: Yeah.

Q: Did you go off with [the defendant] away from the others?

A: Yeah.

Q: Why did you do that?

A: I don't know. I guess I wanted to. (Michael M. *v.* Sonoma County 450 U.S. 464 [1980]: 483–488)

Sharon begins by speaking clearly about what she did and did not want to do with the boy. She wanted to kiss him back, she wanted him to slow down and stop, and she also wanted to walk over to the park with him. However, when the sexual interaction turned from kissing or "fooling around" to "tak[ing] off [her] pants," she said "no," unequivocally and clearly and "tri[ed] to get up." We hear that her desire had specific contours: while she had wanted to "fool around," she did not want to have sexual intercourse. Nevertheless, like Jenny, she stopped saying no and "let him do what he wanted to do." In so doing, she may have given her consent legally although not emotionally or psychologically.

Initially Sharon maintains clarity about the limits of her desire. Confusion creeps into her previously straightforward account, however, as she is asked about her motives for having gone to the park with the defendant. Implicit in the lawyer's question "[why] did you go off with [the defendant] away from the others?" is the unspoken condemnation of the actions of a bad girl, the conditional phrase *"unless you wanted to have sexual intercourse with him?"* So understood, the question is really about her desire. Having been asked to speak about her own desire, Sharon loses the clarity of her earlier explanation. She seems to suspect (along with the lawyer) that there is an inconsistency between having wanted to go to the park and having not wanted to have sex with the boy.

Confronted with the threat of bad girl status, Sharon retreats from the earlier articulation of her desire. Following on the heels of an unequivocal account that portrays the parameters of her desire, Sharon's statement of ambivalence makes her seem confused and uncertain. By responding that she does not know what she wanted, that she "guess[es]" that she "wanted to," Sharon undermines the credibility of her previous testimony. As a witness, Sharon becomes trapped within the good girl/bad girl dichotomy. Her admission of her desire to go to the park with the boy undermines the credibility of her claim that she was coerced. At this point, her reiteration of her direct statement that she wanted to go to the park coupled with her retreat from that statement render her testimony unreliable. Her mistake, as she seems to realize, was to relinquish good girl status by confessing her desire.

Paulina: Empowerment through Rejecting the Good Girl/Bad Girl Dichotomy

Paulina, a white girl who lives in an urban environment, tells stories that offer a counterpoint to Jenny's. Seventeen-year-old Paulina looks like the other adolescent girls in this study: long, dark hair frames her pretty, open face; stylish jeans and sweater clothe a slim figure. Despite her appearance, Paulina does not sound like the other girls: having immigrated from Eastern Europe several years prior to the interview, Paulina speaks with a strong accent. It is the content of her narrative, however, that distinguishes her from most other study participants. Like Jenny, Paulina is also a competent consumer of cultural stories about girls and sexuality, and can recite them without a moment's hesitation:

They expect the woman to be pure, I mean, she has to be holy and everything, and it's okay for a guy to have any feelings or anything, and the girl has to be this little virgin who is obedient to the men. . . . usually a guy makes the first move, not the girl, or the girl's not supposed to do it, the girl's supposed to sit there going, no, no you can't. I can't do that. . . . I mean the guy expects the girl to be a sweet little virgin when he marries her, and then he can be running around with ten other women, but when he's getting married to her, she's not supposed to have any relationship with anybody else.[7]

Paulina echoes Jenny's observation about how the label "slut" is—and is not—used: "Guys, they just like to brag about girls. Oh she does this, and she's a slut because she slept with this guy, and with this guy, but they don't say that about guys. It's okay for them to do it, but when a girl sleeps with two guys it's wrong, she shouldn't do that, she automatically becomes a slut."

In contrast to Jenny's ambivalence and uncertainty, Paulina has strong opinions about the sexual double standard: "I just don't agree with it. . . . I just don't think so." A sense of entitlement, accompanied by outrage, suffuses her well-articulated view of female sexual agency: "Woman can do whatever they want to, why shouldn't they? . . . . I think that women have the same feelings as men do, I mean, I think it's okay to express them too. . . . I mean, they have the same feelings, they're human, why should they like keep away from them?" While Jenny seems unable to make sense of this inequity, Paulina grounds her dissension in an analysis linking gender and power: "I think males are kind of dominant, and they feel that they have the power to do whatever they want, that the woman should give in to them." Paulina also parts from Jenny in her detailed knowledge about her own sexual desire.

Perhaps not coincidentally, Paulina speaks of this embodied experience with an ease that reflects and underscores her belief that girls' sexual desire is normal or, in her words, "natural": "I feel really hot, like, my temperature is really hot. . . . I felt like a rush of blood like pumping to my heart, my heart would really beat fast, and it's just, everything are combined, you're extremely aware of every touch, and everything, everything together . . . you have all those feelings of want." Paulina is clear that this desire can guide her choices and that it should be respected: "To me if you have like a partner that you're close to, then it's okay. And if you feel comfortable with it, 'cause if you don't, then you shouldn't do it. You just don't want to." Thus, Paulina grounds her sexual decisions in her own feelings and beliefs—she can identify and is able to account for the presence and absence of her own desire. As a result, Paulina appears to be less vulnerable to becoming confused about what she feels and what she has said.

Like Jenny, Paulina has had a "bad" sexual experience with a boy whom she thought of as a friend. In the interview, she describes a time when this male friend tried to force her to have sex with him:

There was one experience, the guy wanted to have sexual intercourse and I didn't. I didn't have sex with him. He, he like pulled me over to the couch, and I just kept on fighting. . . . I was just like begging him to like not to do anything, and like, I really did not have like much choice. Because I had my hands behind me. And he just like kept on touching me, and I was just like, just get off me. He goes, you know that you want to, and I said no I don't. Get off me, I hate you. . . . So he's like, well, I'll let you go if you're gonna kiss me. So I kissed him, and I'm like well I can go now. And he was like no. But um, the phone rang later on, I said I have to answer this, it's my mother. . . . So he let me answer the phone. So. And it was my friend and I just said, oh can you come over? And, since I'm Polish I spoke Polish, so I'm like oh just come over, come over as soon as you can.

Ultimately, when her friend arrived, she was able to convince the boy to leave. Paulina's assailant attacked her both physically and psychologically, telling her, "You know that you want to." However, because Paulina had a clear understanding of her sexual feelings, she is able to speak clearly about not feeling sexual desire. In response to his coaxing, Paulina's retort is direct and unequivocal: "No, I don't. Get off me. I hate you." Unlike Jenny and Sharon, Paulina does not become confused: she has no doubt in her mind about the parameters of her own sexual feelings; she did not want any sexual interaction with this young man. Her sense of entitlement to her feelings and choices empowers her to resist the attack.

It must be emphasized that Paulina was very lucky in this situation. She was able to think clearly and take advantage of an opportunity—her friend's phone call—to protect herself from being raped. The critical point is not that she was able to avoid assault in this case, but that she was clear about the threat of violence. Had Paulina not escaped attack, it seems likely that she would have maintained her clarity about her own actions and desires, a clarity that would enable her to claim the protection the law offers.

Conclusion

In listening to three adolescent girls voice experiences with their own sexuality, we hear both how the good girl/bad girl dynamic becomes embodied and embedded in girls' psyches and relationships and how it can be resisted. We suggest that Paulina's ability to know her desire and know its absence, in contrast to Jenny's "silent body" and Sharon's confusion, is linked to her critical consciousness about how male power and dominance underpin the good girl/bad girl dichotomy. Because she rejects a cultural story about her sexuality that makes her own desire dangerous, we think she is less vulnerable to the confusion that Sharon and Jenny voice and more empowered to know and to speak with clarity about her sexual interactions and the social landscape of gendered relationships.

The voices of these three girls living (with) the good girl/bad girl dynamic suggest the necessity of what Michelle Fine terms an affirmative discourse of desire (Fine 1988) for adolescent girls. Such a discourse must recognize, reveal, and then reject the good girl/bad girl categories as patriarchal strategies that keep girls and women from the power of their own bodies and their bonds with one another. It should center on all girls' entitlement to their sexuality, rather than focus solely on the threat of lost status and respect or diminished safety. With the words and analysis to interrupt the good girl/bad girl dynamic, girls and women can identify and critique cultural stories that impair them psychologically and under the law.

The task for feminists, then, is to help adolescent girls and women to analyze the complexity of living in women's bodies within a culture that divides girls and women within themselves and against each other. It is true that the threat of sexual violence against girls and women, as well as social isolation, is real and constant, effectively keeping girls' and women's bodies and psyches filled with fear, rendering sexual desire difficult and dangerous. Yet it is also true that girls and women at this moment in history can feel profound pleasure and desire and should be entitled to rely on their own feelings as an important aspect of sexual choices. By holding the contradiction of pleasure and danger, girls and women can expose and loosen the tight weave seamlessly worked by the good girl/bad girl dynamic in society and in their individual lives.

Notes

1. Some young women are able to resist such norms by anchoring their sexual self-concept in their culture of origin (Robinson and Ward 1991).

2. Although the modern reinterpretation of the purpose of statutory rape laws is that such legislation is designed to prevent teen pregnancy, the historical justification was the protection of female virtue. For example, in 1895, the California Supreme Court explained:

   The obvious purpose of [the statutory rape law] is the protection of society by protecting from violation the virtue of young unsophisticated girls. . . . It is the insidious approach and vile tampering with their persons that primarily undermines the virtue of young girls, and eventually destroys it; and the prevention of this, as much as the principal act, must undoubtedly have been the intent of the legislature. (People *v.* Verdegreen, 106 Cal. 211, 214–215, 39 P. 607, 607–609 [1895]

   In 1964, the same court explained that "an unwise disposition of her sexual favor is deemed to do harm both to herself and the social mores by which the community's conduct patterns are established. Hence the law of statutory rape intervenes in an effort to avoid such a disposition" (People *v.* Hernandez, 61 Cal. 2d 531, 393 P. 2d 674 [1964]).

   As Professor Fran Olsen has argued, although the boy's conduct is punished by criminal sanction, it is the girl who is denied the capacity to consent. Under gender-specific statutory rape laws, the boy may legally have intercourse with women who are over the age of consent (Olsen, 1984).

3. The prosecution's strategy to portray the victim as asexual was controversial among advocates for people with mental disabilities. (See Houppert 1993, citing Leslie Walker-Hirsch, president of the American Association on Mental Retardation's special interest group on sexual and social concerns). Nevertheless, in this, as in many other rape trials, the surest means of establishing lack of consent was to establish the sexual innocence of the victim.

4. This method adopts the psychodynamic concept of the layered psyche in interpreting girls' and women's narratives in individual interviews conducted by women (Brown et al. 1991). Importing this clinical construct into empirical research is not by fiat a feminist act. But requiring the interpreter to focus actively on her own subjectivity and theoretical framework in the act of interpretation subverts the tendency in psychology of an authoritative, expert "voice over" of a girl or woman's words. This psychological method, called the Listening Guide, enables an exploration of ways in which internalized oppression may operate to constrain what a girl or woman says, thinks, or knows, and how she may resist such oppressions. This method asks us to consider what is not said as well as what is said

and how power differences embedded in the brief research relationship may circulate through the narrative. The method obligates the interpreter to ask herself persistently how a woman's structural position in society or individual relational history may contribute to layered ways of understanding her voice—what she says, where she falters, when she is silent. The use of this method yields multiple interpretations of women's narratives by highlighting different voices or perspectives audible in a single story. Using this method means creating a dialectic between the way one girl or woman speaks and how another woman, from a distinctly feminist point of view, hears her story.

5. The study was designed to fill in a gap in the psychological literature on adolescent girls' sexuality: how girls experience their own sexual feelings, particularly their bodies. This feminist question challenged the belief that girls' sexuality is essentially a response to boys' sexual feelings and began to flesh out how sexual desire is a part of adolescent girls' lives. For her dissertation, Tolman interviewed a random sample of thirty girls from two different social contexts: they were juniors, aged fifteen to eighteen, at a suburban and an urban public high school. These girls were black, Hispanic, and white and represented a range of religious backgrounds, sexual experiences, and ethnicities. The interviews often had a conversational tone because the feminist approach used emphasizes listening to girls, in contrast to the traditional procedure of strict adherence to a preset questionnaire. Overall these girls reported that their own desire was a dilemma for them because they were not supposed to experience sexual feelings but, in fact, did. For more on this study see Tolman 1994a, 1994b, and forthcoming. The analyses of this data have focused on class rather than race differences, due to the demographics of the sample. Both qualitative and quantitative analyses revealed similarities across class, such as in the proportion of girls who reported an absence of or confusion about desire and those who reported an awareness of their own desire, and significant class differences in the association of desire with vulnerability and pleasure. Urban girls' narratives were more likely to be about vulnerability and not about pleasure, while suburban girls' narratives were more likely to be about pleasure rather than vulnerability.

6. Brown and Gilligan 1992 and Jack 1991 describe these qualities of the "tyranny of nice and kind" and the tendency to silence or sacrifice the self's disruptive feelings as characteristic of girls' and women's descriptions of their relationships.

7. Paulina's responses have been reported previously in Tolman 1994b.

REFERENCES

Brown, Lynn, and Carol Gilligan. 1992. *Meeting at the Crossroads.* Cambridge, MA: Harvard University Press.

Brown, Lynn, Elizabeth Debold, Mark Tappan, and Carol Gilligan. 1991. "Reading Narratives of Conflict for Self and Moral Voice: A Relational Method." In *Handbook of Moral Behavior and Development: Theory, Research and Application,* ed. William Kurtines and Jacob Gewirtz. Hillsdale, NJ: Lawrence Erlbaum.

Caraway, Nancie. 1991. *Segregated Sisterhood.* Knoxville: University of Tennessee Press.

Collins, Patricia Hill. 1990. *Black Feminist Thought.* New York: Routledge.

Fine, Michelle. 1988. "Sexuality, Schooling, and Adolescent Females: The Missing Discourse of Desire." *Harvard Educational Review* 58 (10: 29–53).

Harris, Angela. 1990. "Race and Essentialism in Feminist Legal Theory." *Stanford Law Review* 42: 581–592.

Henderson, Lynne. 1992. "Rape and Responsibility." *Law and Philosophy* 11 (1–2): 127–128.

Hollway, Wendy. 1984. "Women's Power in Heterosexual Sex." *Women's Studies International Forum* 7 (1): 63–68.

Houppert, Karen. 1993. "The Glen Ridge Rape Draws to a Close." *Village Voice* (March 16): 29–33.

Jack, Dana. 1991. *Silencing the Self.* Cambridge, MA: Harvard University Press.

Michael M. v. Sonoma County, 450 U.S. 464 (1980).

Olsen, Frances. 1984. "Statutory Rape: A Feminist Critique of Rights Analysis." *Texas Law Review* 63: 387.

Omadale, Barbara, 1983. "Hearts of Darkness." In *Powers of Desire: The Politics of Sexuality,* ed. Ann Snitow, Christine Stansell, and Sharon Thompson. New York: Monthly Review Press.

Robinson, Tracy and Janie Ward. 1991. "A Belief in Self Far Greater than Anyone's Disbelief: Cultivating Resistance Among African American Female Adolescents." In *Women, Girls, and Psychotherapy: Reframing Resistance,* ed. Carol Gilligan, Annie Rogers, and Deborah Tolman. New York: Haworth Press.

Roiphe, Katie. 1993. *The Morning After: Sex, Fear, and Feminism on Campus.* Boston: Little, Brown.

Shrieves, Linda. 1993. "The Bold New World of Boy Chasing." *Orlando Sentinel* (22 December): E1.

Smart, Carole. 1989. *Feminism and the Power of the Law.* New York: Routledge.

Smolowe, Jill. 1993. "Sex with a Scorecard." *Time* (5 April):41.

Tolman, Deborah. Forthcoming. "Adolescent Girls' Sexuality: Debunking the Myth of the Urban Girl." In *Urban Adolescent Girls: Resisting Stereotypes,* ed. Bonnie Leadbetter and Niobe Way. New York: New York University Press.

———. 1994a. "Daring to Desire; Culture and the Bodies of Adolescent Girls." In *Sexual Cultures: Adolescents, Communities and the Construction of Identity,* ed. Janice Irvine. Philadelphia: Temple University Press.

———.1994b. "Doing Desire: Adolescent Girls' Struggle for/with Sexuality." *Gender and Society* 8(3): 324–342.

Yoffe, Emily. 1991. "Girls Who Go Too Far." *Newsweek* (22 July): 58.

"The Gender Orgasm Gap"

By Mona Chalabi

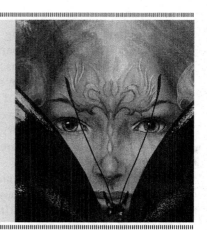

Sex appears in my inbox at least once a month. We all occasionally wonder if we're normal, especially when it comes to the most private parts of our lives. This week, after I received two questions from readers about their masturbation habits (something I've quantified before by age, frequency,[1] and relationship status[2]), I decided to return to the original data source to see if I had missed anything.

I had—statistics on what makes women and men reach orgasm.

In 2009, the National Survey of Sexual Health and Behavior[3] (NSSHB) asked 1,931 U.S. adults ages 18 to 59 about their most recent sexual experience. The topline findings show that men are more likely to orgasm than women—91 percent of men said they climaxed during their last sexual encounter, compared with 64 percent of women.

But there seems to be a perception gap, too—at least among men. Eighty-five percent of men said their partners in that recent sexual encounter had

How Come?

Share of respondents who achieved orgasm during their last sexual encounter, by type of sex act performed during encounter

SEX ACT	RESPONDENTS		SHARE REACHING ORGASM
	MEN	WOMEN	50% 60 70 80 90 100
Partner masturbation	301	199	
Gave oral	377	315	
Received oral	457	263	
Penile-vaginal	830	730	
Received anal	25	31	
Gave anal	66	–	

FIVETHIRTYEIGHT   SOURCE: NATIONAL SURVEY OF SEXUAL HEALTH AND BEHAVIOR

reached climax, far higher than the percentage of women who said they orgasmed. That can't simply

[1] http://fivethirtyeight.com/datalab/dear-mona-i-masturbate-more-than-once-a-day-am-i-normal/

[2] http://fivethirtyeight.com/datalab/dear-mona-p-s-do-single-people-masturbate-more/

[3] http://www.nationalsexstudy.indiana.edu/

be explained away by saying that the men were referring to different sexual partners. Most of these sexual encounters were heterosexual—92 percent of men and 98 percent of women said their last sexual encounter was with someone of the opposite sex. So it seems like some of those men were wrong when they said their partners had orgasmed—either their egos are causing them to overestimate, or some of those women are faking it.

The survey also asked which sexual acts people had engaged in and whether they had experienced an orgasm during that encounter. It's worth mentioning at this point that only people who reported a sexual experience in the previous 12 months were included in the survey—presumably because it might get tricky to accurately recall sexual encounters after a while, especially the forgettable ones.

For men, the results don't vary much—they orgasmed around 90 percent of the time regardless of which sexual acts the encounter included. But for women, there were some big differences—64 percent of women reported orgasms in encounters that included partnered masturbation (defined in the study as "mas-turbating with a partner, rubbing genitals together, dry sex, or humping"), while 81 percent orgasmed during encounters in which they received oral sex.

Anal sex appears to be the hands-down winner for both sexes—100 percent of men and 94 percent of women say they orgasmed during encounters in which they received anal sex. However, these numbers are less reliable than the others cited in the chart because only 25 men and 31 women interviewed said they received anal sex during their last sexual encounter.

That's not to say that anal sex, or any other sex act, worked on its own. Generally speaking, the more sexual acts that were performed during the last sexual encounter, the higher the probability that respondents would say they had climaxed. By the time they experienced five sexual acts in one session, both men and women said they had orgasmed more than 89 percent of the time. I should bloody well hope so after all that effort.

Mona Chalabi (Twitter: @monachalabi) is data editor at the Guardian US, and a columnist at New York Magazine. She was previously a lead news writer for FiveThirtyEight.

Variety Is The Spice of Life

Share of respondents who achieved orgasm during their last sexual encounter, by the number of sexual acts performed

NUMBER OF SEX ACTS	RESPONDENTS		SHARE REACHING ORGASM
	MEN	WOMEN	
1	384	381	
2	181	149	
3	118	90	
4	185	128	
5	99	64	

FIVETHIRTYEIGHT   SOURCE: NATIONAL SURVEY OF SEXUAL HEALTH AND BEHAVIOR

"12 Reasons Why There's Orgasm Inequity (And No, It's Not That Women Are 'Harder to Please')"

By Suzannah Weiss

I was young when I came to discover masturbation, and I had orgasms long before I knew what they were.

Nothing about it seemed complicated. I just rubbed "down there" for a few minutes, and it happened. But later, magazines, comedy routines, and sitcoms taught me that my body—and vaginas in general—were mysterious and complex, often too complex for those without them to figure out.

Confirming what I'd been taught, orgasms weren't as simple with partners as they were by myself. This is to be expected to some extent. There's a learning curve when you're getting to know someone new. But what confused me was that not everyone seemed eager to learn.

"Sorry," I (unnecessarily) apologized to a partner for taking what I thought was too long.

"It's okay. I know it's harder for girls," he said—and then stopped.

Compounding the lack of effort I encountered from some (though not all) partners, it became harder for me to orgasm when I started SSRI antidepressants. When I told my doctor, she said, "Oh, that's hard for a lot of women anyway."[1]

I knew my body long and well enough to know being a woman wasn't to blame, but others didn't share my view that the problem was fixable. I grew hesitant to bring it up with partners out of fear that asking them to perform the supposedly impossible feat of getting a woman off was too demanding.

Orgasm doesn't have to be the focus of sex, but if a woman wants one, she should have as much of a right to request it as anyone else does.

When people say that women's bodies are more difficult—and these generalizations typically refer to cis women and are accompanied by rants about how complicated vaginas are—they teach cis women that an orgasm is too tall an order.

Trans women also have a slew of sexual stigmas attached to them, which Kai Cheng Thom describes here,[2] though they're beyond the scope of this article. In addition, though most research on orgasm inequity has studied cis women, trans and non-binary people with vaginas may relate to the frustrations of being taught their genitals are impossible to decode, too.

The view that cis women are hard to please maintains what sociologists call the orgasm gap,[3] in which men have three orgasms for every one a woman enjoys, and 57% of women orgasm[4] during all or most of their sexual encounters, but 95% say their partners do.

These statistics may appear to confirm the stereotype that women's bodies are more complicated, but there are other forces at work.

As sociologist Lisa Wade points out, the orgasm gap is conditional. Lesbians report orgasming 74.7% of the time,[5] only 10 percentage points lower than gay men.

[1] As we frequently discuss in this course, a good doctor is a **partner** in your healthcare. A doctor who dismisses a side effect that is causing you distress, without brainstorming possible alternatives or offering to investigate them and actually following up on that offer, may not be a good doctor for you. For tips on how to discuss marginalized aspects of your identity and experience with doctors, some of which may also transfer to discussion of sensitive health issues, see Marianne Kirby's work elsewhere in this volume. *Ed.*

[2] http://everydayfeminism.com/2015/10/men-who-date-trans-women/
[3] http://www.alternet.org/sex-amp-relationships/orgasm-gap-real-reason-women-get-less-often-men-and-how-fix-it
[4] http://www.cosmopolitan.com/sex-love/news/a37812/cosmo-orgasm-survey/
[5] http://www.huffingtonpost.com/2014/08/19/lesbians-more-orgasms-straight_n_5691470.html

In addition, women take under four minutes on average to masturbate to orgasm.[6]

If these statistics don't convince you that there's more to the orgasm gap than biology, here are twelve cultural factors that contribute to it.

1. People Believe Women Are Less Sexual

Women, the story goes, aren't *that* into sex.

They may enjoy it, but they do it partially in exchange for validation, commitment, or financial support, popular wisdom says. As long as a woman is getting one of those things, she doesn't need much out of the sex itself.

To the contrary, a lot of research[7] and lived experiences[8] indicate that women are as capable of wanting and enjoying sex as men.

Until we acknowledge this, we won't prioritize making sex as enjoyable as possible for women because we'll believe sexual pleasure isn't as important to them.

It may *not* be because women themselves may buy into myths about their gender, neglecting their desires because they're not supposed to have them. If they do, they and their partners miss out on balanced sexual interactions, not to mention fun.

2. Pornography Privileges Male Pleasure

Most people who have watched porn videos know they typically culminate with a "money shot" in which the man comes, and then the scene ends. Most woman-focused orgasms depicted in porn are merely incidental events on the path to a man's pleasure.

Additionally, most mainstream porn scenes feel incomplete without blow jobs, while cunnilingus is less common.

All in all, the message is clear: It's imperative that a man gets off, and if a woman manages to in the process, props to him,[9] but it's just an added bonus.

3. The Myth of 'Blue Balls' Persists

Blue balls, according to Urban Dictionary, is "the excruciating [sic] pain a man receives when his balls swell to the size of coconuts because of lack of sex,

unfinished bjs, and just not cummin when he knows he should."

The entitlement reflected in this description is characteristic of most uses of the term "blue balls." While vasocongestion,[10] the accumulation of blood flow to the genitals, can occasionally cause mild pain in people with *any* genitals, this is not what men are usually referring to when they complain about blue balls. And whether they're experiencing this or just sexual frustration, it's never anyone else's duty to relieve it.

Even though most women know no medical condition results from an erection that doesn't lead to an orgasm, many of us feel guilty for not providing one. So, in addition to some men's lack of effort to pleasure women, the pressure many women feel to pleasure men maintains the orgasm gap.

4. There's More Information in the Media About Pleasing Cis Men Than Women

As a teenager, my secret guilty pleasure was buying copies of *Cosmo* from the drugstore and hiding them under my pillow to read at night.

I read all their sex articles just because I found anything sex-related titillating, but along the way, I learned all about different tricks to please men—and cis men, specifically. By the time I encountered a real-life penis, I already knew all the basic tricks in the book, plus some out-there ones my dude friends urged me *not* to try.

I don't know what most teenage boys' secret reading material was, but there aren't many mainstream men's magazines as obsessed with pleasing women as women's are with pleasing men. If anything, I've heard it's common for boys to sneak glimpses of *Playboy*, which is *also* geared toward pleasing men.

Maybe this explains why 25% of men and 30% of women can't locate the clitoris on a diagram.[11,12]

Amid all the advice we read about different ways to hold and touch a penis, many remain in the dark about vulvas and vaginas.

5. Hookup Culture Privileges Male Pleasure

"I will do everything in my power to, like whoever I'm with, to get [him] off," one woman said in a study by Elizabeth Armstrong on college hookups. But when it

---

[6]http://www.brown.edu/Student_Services/Health_Services/Health_Education/sexual_health/sexuality/female_orgasm.php#8

[7]http://www.smh.com.au/lifestyle/life/family-relationships-and-sex/women-think-about-sex-more-than-men-do-according-to-new-survey-20141118-11pffg.html

[8]http://www.glamour.com/sex-love-life/blogs/smitten/2015/09/questions-about-sex-penis-men

[9]http://everydayfeminism.com/2015/12/focusing-on-her-pleasure/

[10]http://www.soc.ucsb.edu/sexinfo/article/epididymal-hypertension-blue-balls

[11]https://lisawadedotcom.files.wordpress.com/2011/02/wade-kremer-brown-2005-the-incidental-orgasm.pdf

[12]Fortunately, after taking this class, you'll be part of this (unfortunately) elite group! We hope that you won't keep this life-changing knowledge to yourself. *Ed.*

came to their own pleasure, women held different expectations.

"The guy kind of expects to get off, while the girl doesn't expect anything," a woman in another study by Lisa Wade said.

Accordingly, one man in Armstrong's study boasted, "I'm all about making her orgasm," but when asked to clarify the word "her," he added, "Girlfriend *her*. In a hookup *her*, I don't give a shit." Perhaps he sensed that women don't expect much from their hookups.

Statistics about women's orgasms reflect these attitudes.

The ratio of men's and women's orgasms is 3.1:1 for first-time hookups, but only 1.25:1 for relationships.[13] For whatever reason, hookup culture appears to have embraced the message espoused by the media that women's orgasms are optional, while men's are obligatory.

6. Sex Education Doesn't Teach Us About Pleasure, Especially Female Pleasure[14]

Like many schools in the US,[15] mine only had a couple of days a year dedicated to sex education in middle and high school. During the initial classes on puberty, the portion about women was on periods and the portion about men was on erections, ejaculation, and wet dreams. Already, our bodies were associated with making babies, while boys' were associated with sexual arousal and pleasure.

Later on, we learned how to use a condom—along with how to complete a very normative sequence of events. You put it on, we were told, and then you have intercourse, and then someone ejaculates, and then you pull out and take it off. Men's orgasms, but not women's, were built into our safer sex lesson.

Nobody said "then you stop whenever you feel like it" or "your partner may need you to pull out" (because, contrary to what we see in porn, not every woman is multi-orgasmic and many have a refractory period,[16] so we can't all comfortably keep going until our partner wants to stop).

This is one sneaky way we learn to prioritize men's pleasure without ever really learning about pleasure at all.

7. Self-Evaluative Thoughts Can Disrupt Women's Arousal Process

Due to the emphasis on women's appearances in mainstream porn and throughout the media, women learn to picture themselves during sex.[17]

"How does my stomach look from this angle," "Does my face look sexy or silly in this expression," and "Would it be sexier if I made more noise?" are a few thoughts that have distracted me in the bedroom.

And I don't think I'm alone: 32% of women say that when they don't orgasm, it's often because they're stuck in their heads or focused on their looks.[18] Orgasm itself can become a source of performance anxiety.

Because the women's orgasms are dramatized in porn and the media, with exaggerated moans and calculated facial expressions, some women feel so much pressure that fear of *not* coming keeps them from coming. This pressure can also lead women to fake orgasms instead of sticking it out for a real one.

Once again, women's magazines don't help.

Cosmo even provides a guide on "how to look even hotter naked."[19] Though "even" implies the reader looks hot already, the pre-bedroom workout routine and self-tanner application tips make it clear we don't look as hot as we could—and even if we do, the focus is still on our partner's pleasure, not what *we* see or feel.

Thoughts about partners' perceptions place women outside their bodies, looking in, rather than inside them, feeling the sensations the sexual activity is causing. It's hard to have an orgasm when you're not even thinking sexual thoughts.

8. Sexual Trauma Can Impede Arousal and Orgasm

It's extremely common for women to experience sexual trauma within their lifetimes. One out of six women[20] has been the victim of attempted or completed rape.

---

[13]http://www.alternet.org/sex-amp-relationships/orgasm-gap-real-reason-women-get-less-often-men-and-how-fix-it

[14]For more on this important issue, see Susan K. Pastor's and Erica Koepsel's work elsewhere in this section. *Ed.*

[15]https://www.plannedparenthood.org/files/3713/9611/7930/Sex_Ed_in_the_US.pdf

[16]http://www.xojane.com/sex/i-dont-care-if-you-havent-come-yet

[17]Social scientists refer to this phenomenon as **spectating**. *Ed.*

[18]http://www.cosmopolitan.com/sex-love/news/a37812/cosmo-orgasm-survey/

[19]http://www.cosmopolitan.com/health-fitness/advice/g2021/how-to-look-good-naked/—This could be a great piece to consider with a critical lens, but on the other hand, maybe you don't want to/need not to read it, and that is okay. *Ed.*

[20]https://rainn.org/get-information/statistics/sexual-assault-victims—Note that these numbers do not separate women by racial category; RAINN reports much higher numbers for mixed-race women (1 in 4) and Native women (1 in 3). Disabled women are also at significantly higher risk, particularly when their disabilities are cognitive or developmental in nature. *Ed.*

According to sex therapist Vanessa Marin,[21] this trauma can have lasting effects on one's sex life.

"Sexual assault can rob your enjoyment of sex and can make any type of intimacy feel scary," she said. "Some survivors experience feelings of disconnect or dissociation when they're having sex. Others can easily get triggered by being touched in certain places or in specific ways."

Marin recommends that survivors seek out therapy or a support group so they don't have to deal with the effects of their pasts alone.

In the short-term, Marin has written that reminding yourself you're with your partner, not the person who assaulted you, can quell trauma-related sexual problems.[22] "Of course your brain knows that it's [them], but this exercise can help the more subconscious parts of your psyche start to relax," she writes.

Other emotions women disproportionately experience around sex, such as guilt and shame, may also lead to **anorgasmia** (ed. note: difficulty reaching, or the inability to reach, orgasm, such that the person experiences distress).[23]

9. More Women Than Men Are on Antidepressants

SSRI antidepressants,[24] like Prozac and Zoloft, can cause anorgasmia. This side effect isn't gender-specific, but antidepressants themselves are.

Between 2001 and 2010, 25% of American women (but only 15% of men) had been prescribed medication for mental health conditions.

This may occur because women are more likely to suffer from anxiety and depression,[25] both frequently treated with SSRIs, the medication class most commonly known to cause anorgasmia. There are many theories as to why [women suffer higher rates of anxiety and depression in the first place], but one possible source of this difference is societal misogyny.

As Ally Boghun writes of her anxiety, "A lot of the stressors that impact me the most are actually stressors put upon women by society to look and act in certain ways."[26]

In addition, women are more likely to seek therapy,[27] since toxic standards of masculinity deter men from discussing their emotions.

This is one case where the orgasm gap may be related to biological differences, but the sources of these differences[28] are still societal.

10. Women Are Discouraged from Asking for What They Want

Women are taught to accommodate others' wishes and put their own on the back burner, to be pleasant and polite and grateful and not ask for more, whether that's food, payment, or sexual pleasure.

To bring back Armstrong's research,[29] one woman said she didn't have the "right" to request an orgasm and "felt kind of guilty almost, like I felt like I was kind of subjecting [guys] to something they didn't want to do and I felt bad about it."

I can relate: I've said "sorry" many times for requesting or giving myself the stimulation I wanted, for taking what I thought was too much time, and for receiving pleasure without immediately returning it.

The same fear that keeps women from voicing their opinions in work meetings[30] or negotiating salaries[31] also keeps us from speaking up in bed.[32]

But until we can "lean in" without bumping into hostility, women can't singlehandedly solve this problem in any domain. It's also up to our partners, coworkers, and others to make it clear they want to hear and accommodate our wishes.

11. The Normative Definition of Sex Isn't Optimal for Many Women's Orgasms

When someone says "sex," most people think of penis-in-vagina intercourse, even though it means many different things to different people.

---

[21]http://www.vmtherapy.com/how-to-orgasm

[22]http://www.bustle.com/articles/61205-cant-orgasm-during-sex-7-ways-to-let-go-and-let-your-partner-pleasure-you

[23]http://anorgasmia.net/causes/

[24]http://www.currentpsychiatry.com/home/article/sex-and-antidepressants-when-to-switch-drugs-or-try-an-antidote/86749671080867876b2bfa80e8aa18a6.html—This article provides detailed information about the prevalence of sexual side effects for specific psychiatric medications, and also discusses different strategies for dealing with those side effects, including drug substitutions and combinations. It could be a useful resource in conversation with a psychiatric health provider. *Ed.*

[25]http://www.hcp.med.harvard.edu/ncs/ftpdir/NCS-R_12-month_Prevalence_Estimates.pdf

[26]http://everydayfeminism.com/2014/05/feminism-and-anxiety/

[27]http://www.apa.org/monitor/jun05/helping.aspx

[28]http://everydayfeminism.com/2015/08/science-supports-feminism/

[29]http://asr.sagepub.com/content/early/2012/04/19/0003122412445802.abstract

[30]http://www.nytimes.com/2015/01/11/opinion/sunday/speaking-while-female.html?_r=0

[31]http://www.inc.com/flash-steinbeiser/women-less-likely-to-negotiate-starting-salary.html

[32]See Suzannah Weiss's other work in this volume specifically connecting the gender wage gap to women's higher rates of anxiety and depression! *Ed.*

For example, some couples may see oral sex as sex. Some may also put oral or manual sex on the same level as penetrative sex, but this is still not the norm.

When someone talks about losing their virginity, for instance, we usually assume they're talking about the first time they had penis-in-vagina intercourse. **This assumption can be problematic for women who get off more easily through other activities.**

In one survey,[33] 20% of women said they seldom or never had orgasms during intercourse. Only 25% said they consistently do. In another,[34] 38% said that when they don't orgasm, a common obstacle is "not enough clitoral stimulation."

Since penetrative sex often doesn't directly stimulate the clitoris, this could explain why other types of sex—or clitoral stimulation during intercourse, which women considered the most common way they got off with a partner—may be more optimal.

When we consider the activities that often help women reach orgasm as warmup or extra, we deprioritize women's pleasure.

12. People Think the Orgasm Gap Is Biological

Orgasm inequity is a self-fulfilling prophecy.

When men believe women's bodies are an impossible puzzle, they don't try to solve it. Neither do women who are taught their own pleasure is inaccessible.

That's why it's important we acknowledge all the societal factors that contribute to this discrepancy. Genetics can't be fixed, but a lot of these problems can, which means that closing the orgasm gap *is* possible.

***

If you're a woman having trouble orgasming, it's likely not you. It may not be the result of any carelessness on your partner's part either. You may just need to talk about it, challenge the myths you've learned about sexuality, and, if necessary, seek help for any psychological or medical conditions that could be contributing to the problem.

Or maybe it's not a problem at all. Maybe orgasming isn't important to you, and that's your choice as well. But if it is something you would like, you have the same right to ask for it as your partner. If he expects orgasms from you, he shouldn't mind you wanting one.

It's not too much to ask, and your anatomy isn't too complicated. The only thing that's complicated is the toxic set of messages we're taught about sexuality. But that's not on you or your body.

Suzannah Weiss is a Contributing Writer for Everyday Feminism and a New York-based writer whose work has appeared in The Washington Post, Salon, Seventeen, Buzzfeed, The Huffington Post, Bustle, and more. She holds degrees in Gender and Sexuality Studies, Modern Culture and Media, and Cognitive Neuroscience from Brown University. You can follow her on Twitter @suzannahweiss.

---

[33] https://www.psychologytoday.com/blog/all-about-sex/200903/the-most-important-sexual-statistic

[34] http://www.cosmopolitan.com/sex-love/news/a37812/cosmo-orgasm-survey/

"Kegel Exercises"

By Nancy Worcester and Mariamne H. Whatley

The pubococcygeus (P.C.) muscles support the walls of the vagina, the urethra, and rectum. Good, strong P.C. muscles can be important for childbirth, and for preventing stress incontinence (loss of urine when coughing or sneezing), and can enhance sexual enjoyment. Kegel exercises (developed by Dr. Arnold Kegel) are designed to strengthen the P.C. muscles. Unlike most exercises, no special clothes, gyms, and the like are required. These exercises can be done anywhere and no one else will even know you are doing them.

1. Find your P.C. muscles. When you are urinating, stop the flow of urine in midstream. The muscles you are feeling are your P.C. muscles, the muscles you want to strengthen.

2. Examples of Kegel exercises:

Flicks: Do a series of contractions as rapidly as possible. It has been suggested that one does this in time to the car's turn signals.

Squeeze and hold for as long as possible, trying to work up to holding for 8–10 seconds.

Take a slow, deep breath, squeezing the P.C. muscles as you are breathing in. Pretend you are slowly drawing something into your vagina. Imagine you are lifting weights in your vagina!

From *Women's Health: Readings on Social, Economic, and Political Issues*, Fifth Edition by Nancy Worcester and Mariamne H. Whatley.

SECTION
6

MEDICALIZATION AND MARKETING

"The Picture of Health"
How Textbook Photographs Construct Health

By Mariamne H. Whatley

Photographs in textbooks may serve the roles of breaking up a long text, emphasizing or clarifying information in the text, attracting the buyer (the professor, teacher, or administrator who selects texts), and engaging the reader. But photographs cannot be dismissed merely as either decorative additions or straightforward illustrations of the text. Photographs are often far more memorable than the passages they illustrate and, because they are seen as objective representations of reality, rather than artists' constructions (Barthes, 1977), may have more impact than drawings or other forms of artwork. In textbooks, photographs can carry connotations, intentional or not, never stated in the text. The selection of photographs for a text is not a neutral process that simply involves being "realistic" or "objective"; selection must take into account issues such as audience expectations and dominant meanings in a given cultural/historical context (Whatley, 1988). In order to understand the ideological work of a textbook, a critique of the photographs is as crucial as a critique of the text itself.

Using ideological analysis to identify patterns of inclusion and exclusion, I examined photographs in the seven best-selling, college-level personal health textbooks. This chapter presents the results of that research. In the first part of the analysis, I examined the photographs that represent "health," describing who and what is "healthy," according to these representations. In the second part of the analysis, I determined where those excluded from the definition of health are represented in the approximately 1,100 remaining photographs in the texts.

Selling Health in Textbooks

Generally, textbook authors do not select specific photographs but may give publishers general descriptions of the type of photographs they wish to have included (for example, a scene showing urban crowding, a woman in a nontraditional job). Due to the great expense involved, new photographs are not usually taken specifically for texts. Instead publishers hire photo researchers to find appropriate photographs, drawing on already existing photographic collections. The result is that the choice of photographs depends on what is already available, and what is available depends to some extent on what has been requested in the past. In fact, because the same sources of photographs may be used by a number of different publishers, identical photographs may appear in competing books. Although authors may have visions of their books' "artwork," the reality may be limited by the selection already on the market. In addition, editors and publishers make decisions about what "artwork" will sell or is considered appropriate, sometimes overruling the authors' choices.

Photographs, especially cover-photos and special color sections, are considered features that sell textbooks, but they also can work as part of another selling process. Textbooks, in many cases, sell the reader a system of belief. An economics text, for example, may "sell" capitalism, and a science text may "sell" the scientific method, both of which help support dominant ideologies. Health textbooks may be even more invested in this selling process because, in addition to convincing readers to "believe" in health, their "success" depends on the readers' adoption of very specific personal behavioral programs to attain health. Health textbooks hold up the ideals of "total wellness" or "holistic fitness" as goals we can attain by exercising, eating right, reducing stress, and avoiding drugs. The readers' belief in health and their ability to attain it by specific behaviors is seen by many health educators as necessary to relevant educational goals; the belief in a clearly marked pathway to health is also part of a process of the commodification of health.

In North America and Western Europe, health is currently a very marketable commodity. This can be seen in its most exaggerated form in the United States in the proliferation of "health" clubs, in the trend among hospitals and clinics to attract a healthy clientele by advertising their abilities to make healthy people healthier (Worcester & Whatley, 1988), and in the advertisements that link a wide range of products, such as high fiber cereals and calcium rich antacids, to health. In a recent article in a medical journal, a physician examined this commercialization of health:

> Health is industrialized and commercialized in a fashion that enhances many people's dissatisfaction with their health. Advertisers, manufacturers, advocacy groups, and proprietary healthcare corporations promote the myth that good health can be purchased; they market products and services that purport to deliver the consumer into the promised land of wellness. (Barsky, 1988, p. 415)

Photographs in health textbooks can play a role in this selling of health similar to that played by visual images in advertising a product in the popular media. According to Berger (1972), the role of advertising or publicity is to

> make the spectator marginally dissatisfied with his present way of life. Not with the way of life of society, but with his own place within it. It suggests that if he buys what it is offering, his life will become better. It offers him an improved alternative to what he is. (p. 142)

The ideal of the healthy person and the healthy lifestyle can be seen as the "improved alternative" to what we are. It can be assumed that most of us will be dissatisfied with ourselves when measured against that ideal, just as most women are dissatisfied with their body shapes and sizes when compared with ideal media representations.

In effective advertising campaigns the visual image is designed to provoke powerful audience responses.

In health textbooks the visual representation of "health" is calculated to sell, and it is likely to have a greater impact on the reader than discussions about lengthened life expectancy, reduction in chronic illness, or enhanced cardiovascular fitness. The image of health, not health itself, may be what most people strive for. In the attempt to look healthy, many sacrifice health. For example, people go through very unhealthy practices to lose "extra" weight that is in itself not unhealthy; being slim, however, is a basic component of the *appearance* of health. A recent survey found that people who eat healthy foods do so for their appearance and *not* for their health. "Tanning parlors" have become common features of health and fitness centers, though tanning in itself is unhealthy. As with being slim, having a good tan contributes to the appearance of what is currently defined as health.

The use of color photographs is particularly effective in selling the healthy image, for, as Berger (1972) points out, both oil painting and color photography "use similar highly tactile means to play upon the spectator's sense of acquiring the *real* thing which the image shows" (p. 141). The recent improvement in quality and the increase in number of color photographs in textbooks provide an opportunity to sell the image of health even more effectively than black and white photographs could.

Selection of Textbooks

Rather than trying to examine all college-level personal health (as opposed to community health) textbooks, I selected the best-selling ones, since those would have the widest impact. Based on the sales figures provided by the publisher of one popular text, I selected seven texts published from 1985 to 1988. Sales of these textbooks ranged from approximately 15,000 to 50,000 for each edition. (Complete bibliographic information on these textbooks is provided in the Appendix. Author-date information for these textbooks refer to the Appendix, rather than the chapter references.) Obviously, the sales figures depend on the number of years a specific edition has been in print. For one text (Insel & Roth, 1988), I examined the newest edition (for which there could be no sales figures), based on the fact that its previous editions had high sales. A paper on the readability of personal health textbooks (Overman, Mimms, & Harris, 1987), using a similar selection process, examined the seven top-selling textbooks for the 1984–85 school year, plus three other random titles. Their list has an overlap with mine of only four texts, which may be due to a number of factors, including differences in editions and changing sales figures.

Analysis I: Healthy-Image Photographs

The first step in my analysis was a close examination of the photographs that I saw as representing "health," the images intended to show who is healthy and illustrate the healthy lifestyle. These included photographs used on covers, opposite title pages, and as openers to units or chapters on wellness or health (as opposed to specific topics such as nutrition, drugs, and mental health). While other pictures throughout the texts may represent healthy individuals, the ones selected, by their placement in conjunction with the book title or chapter title, can be seen as clearly connoting "health." I will refer to these as healthy-image photographs. I included in this analysis only photographs in which there were people. While an apple on a cover conveys a message about health, I was interested only in the question of who is healthy.

A total of 18 different photographs fit my criteria for representing health. I have eliminated three of these from discussion: the cover from Insel and Roth (1988) showing flowers and, from Dintiman and Greenberg (1986), both the cover photograph of apples and the health unit opener of a movie still from the *Wizard of Oz*. (This textbook uses movie stills as openers for all chapters; this moves the photograph away from its perceived "objective" status toward that of an obvious construction.)

There are a number of points of similarity in the 15 remaining photographs. In several photographs (windsurfing, hang gliding), it is hard to determine race, but all individuals whose faces can clearly be seen are white. Except for those who cannot be seen clearly and for several of the eight skydivers in a health unit opener, all are young. No one in these photographs is fat or has any identifiable physical disability. Sports dominate the activities, which, with the exception of rhythmic gymnastics and volleyball played in a gym, are outdoor activities in nonurban settings. Five of these involve beaches or open water. All the activities are leisure activities, with no evidence of work. While it is impossible to say anything definitive about class from these photographs, several of the activities are expensive (hang gliding, skydiving, windsurfing), and others may take money and/or sufficient time off from work to get to places where they can be done (beaches, biking in countryside); these suggest middle-class activities, whether the actual individuals are middle class or not. In several photographs (windsurfing, hang gliding, swimming) it is hard to determine gender. However, excluding these and the large group of male runners in a cross-country race, the overall balance is 23 males to 18 females, so it does seem that there is an attempt to show women both as healthy individuals and in active roles.

How Health Is Portrayed

A detailed analysis of three photographs can provide insight into how these text photographs construct health. The first is a color photograph of a volleyball game on a beach from the back cover of *Understanding Your Health* (Payne & Hahn, 1986). As with most of these images of health, the setting is outdoors, clearly at a distance from urban life. The steep rock walls that serve as a backdrop to the volleyball game additionally isolate the natural beach setting from the invasion of cars[1] and other symbols of "man-made" environmental destruction and ill health. The volleyball players appear to have escaped into a protected idyllic setting of sun, sand, and, we assume, water. They also have clearly escaped from work, since they are engaged in a common leisure activity associated with picnics and holidays. None of them appears to be contemplating the beauty of the natural setting, but merely using it as a location for a game that could go on anywhere in which there is room to set up a net.

The photograph is framed in such a way that the whole net and area of the "court" are not included, so that some players may also not be visible. On one side of the net are three women and a man, on the other two women and a man. While this is not necessarily a representation of heterosexual interactions, it can be read that way. Two players are the focus of the picture, with the other five essentially out of the action. The woman who has just hit the ball, with her back toward the camera, has her arms outstretched, her legs slightly spread, and one foot partly off the ground. The man who is waiting for the ball is crouched slightly, looking expectantly upward. Her body is partially superimposed on his, her leg crossed over his. This is essentially an interaction between one man and one woman. It would not work the same way if the key players were both female or both male, since part of the "healthiness" of this image appears to be the heterosexual interaction. For heterosexual men, this scene might be viewed as ideal—a great male-female ratio on an isolated beach; perhaps this is their reward for having arrived at the end of this book—this photograph is on the *back* cover—attaining their goal of health.

All the volleyball players are white, young, and slim. The woman farthest left in the frame appears slightly heavier than the others; she is the only woman wearing a shirt, rather than a bikini top, and is also wearing shorts. Besides being an outsider in terms of weight, dress, and location in the frame, she is the only woman who clearly has short hair (three have long hair tied back in ponytails, one cannot be seen completely). Perhaps she can move "inside" by losing weight and changing her image. As viewers, we are just a few steps beyond the end of the court and are also outsiders. As with pick-up games, there is room for observers to enter the game—if they are deemed acceptable by the other players. By achieving health, perhaps the observer can step into the game, among the young, white, slim, heterosexual, and physically active. But if the definition of health includes young, white, slim, heterosexual, and physically active, many observers are relegated permanently to the outside.

If this photograph serves as an invitation to join in the lifestyle of the young and healthy, the second photograph, facing the title page of another book, serves the same function, with the additional written message provided by the title of the book—*An Invitation to Health* (Hales & Williams, 1986). The photograph is of six bicycle riders, three women and three men, resting astride their bicycles. This photograph is in black and white, so it is perhaps not as seductive as the sunny color of the first cover. However, the people in this photograph are all smiling directly at the viewer (rather than just leaving a space in back where the viewer could join in). Two of the women, in the middle and the right, have poses and smiles that could be described as flirtatious. They are taking a break from their riding, so it is an opportune moment to join the fun of being healthy.

As with the volleyball players, all the bicycle riders are young, slim, white, and apparently fit. Another similarity is the amount of skin that is exposed. Playing volleyball on the beach and riding bikes in warm weather are activities for which shorts and short-sleeved shirts are preferable to sweatpants and sweatshirts. The choice of these types of activities to represent health results in photographs in which legs and arms are not covered. Appearing healthy apparently involves no need to cover up unsightly flab, "cellulite," or stretch marks. A healthy body is a body that can be revealed.

The bikers are in a fairly isolated, rural setting. While they are clearly on the road, it appears to be a rural, relatively untraveled road. Two cars can be seen far in the distance, and there may also be a house in the distance on the right side of the frame. Otherwise, the landscape is dominated by hills, trees, and grass, the setting and the activity clearly distance the bike riders both from urban life and from work.

In a third photograph, a health unit chapter opener (Levy, Dignan, & Shirreffs, 1987), we can see a possible beginning to alternative images of health. The players in this volleyball game are still slim, young, and apparently white. However, the setting is a gym, which could be urban, suburban, or rural. While four players

are wearing shorts, one woman is wearing sweatpants; there are T-shirts rather than bikini tops, and gym socks rather than bare legs. The impression is that they are there to play a hard game of volleyball rather than to bask in the sun and each other's gaze. Two men are going for the ball from opposite sides, while a woman facing the net is clearly ready to move. Compared with the other volleyball scene, this photograph gives more of a sense of action, of actual physical exertion, as well as a sense of real people, rather than models.

It is interesting to imagine how healthy the volleyball players and bike riders actually are, underneath the appearance of health. The outdoor groups, especially the beach group, are susceptible to skin cancer from overexposure to the sun. Cycling is a healthy aerobic sport, though it can be hard on the knees and back. It is particularly surprising, however, to find that the bikers represented in a health text are not wearing helmets, thus modeling behavior that is considered very risky. Compared with biking, volleyball is the kind of weekend activity that sends the enthusiastic untrained player home with pulled muscles, jammed fingers, and not much of a useful workout. The question also arises as to how the particularly thin women on the beach achieved their weight—by unhealthy weight-loss diets, by anorexia, by purging? The glowing image of health may have little to do with the reality.

Similarities to Advertising

Shortly after I began the research for this chapter, I was startled, while waiting for a movie to begin, to see a soft drink advertisement from which almost any still could have been substituted for a healthy-image photograph I had examined. There were the same thin, young, white men and women frolicking on the beach, playing volleyball, and windsurfing. They were clearly occupying the same territory: a never-never land of eternal sunshine, eternal youth, and eternal leisure. Given my argument that these textbook photographs are selling health, the similarities between soft drink advertising images and textbook healthy images are not surprising. They are appealing to the same groups of people, and they are both attempting to create an association between a desirable lifestyle and their product. You can enjoy this fun in the sun if you are part of the "Pepsi generation" or think "Coke is it" or follow the textbook's path to health. These can be considered one variant of the lifestyle format in advertising, as described by Leiss, Kline, and Jhally (1986).

> Here the activity invoked in text or image becomes the central cue for relating the person, product, and setting codes. Lifestyle ads

commonly depict a variety of leisure activities (entertaining, going out, holidaying, relaxing). Implicit in each of these activities, however, is the placing of the product within a consumption style by its link to an activity. (p. 210)

Even a naive critic of advertising could point out that drinking a carbonated beverage could not possibly help anyone attain this lifestyle; on the other hand, it might be easier to accept that the same lifestyle is a result of achieving health. However, the association between health and this leisure lifestyle is as much a construction as that created in the soft drink ads. Following all the advice in these textbooks as to diet, exercise, coping with stress, and attaining a healthy sexuality will not help anyone achieve this sun-and-fun fantasy lifestyle any more than drinking Coke or Pepsi would.

These healthy-image photographs borrow directly from popular images of ideal lifestyles already very familiar to viewers through advertising[2] and clearly reflect the current marketing of health. The result is that health is being sold with as much connection to real life and real people's needs as liquor ads that suggest major lifestyle changes associated with changing one's brand of scotch.

Analysis II: Where Are the Excluded?

For each textbook, the next step was to write brief descriptions of all other photographs in the books, totaling approximately 1,100. The results of the analysis of the healthy image photographs suggested a focus on specific aspects of the description of the individuals and activities in examining the remaining 1,100 photographs. The areas I selected for discussion are those in which "health" is linked to specific lifestyles or factors that determine social position/power in our society. I described the setting, the activity, and a number of observable points about the people, including gender, race, age, physical ability/disability, and weight. These photographs were all listed by chapter and when appropriate, by particular topic in that chapter. For example, a chapter on mental health might have images of positive mental health and also images representing problems such as severe depression or stress. These descriptions of photographs were used to establish whether there were images with characteristics not found in the healthy images and, if so, the context in which these characteristics were present. For example, finding no urban representations among the healthy images, I identified topic headings under which I did find photographs of urban settings.

White, young, thin, physically abled, middle-class people in the healthy images represent the mythical norm with whom the audience is supposed to identify. This not only creates difficulties in identification for whose who do not meet these criteria, but also creates a limiting and limited definition of health. I examined the photographs that did not fit the healthy-image definition to find the invisible—those absent from the healthy images: people of color, people with physical disabilities, fat people, and old people. I also attempted to identify two other absences—the urban setting and work environment. Because there were no obvious gender discrepancies in the healthy images, I did not examine gender as a separate category.

People of Color

After going through the remaining photographs, it was clear that there had been an attempt to include photographs of people of color in a variety of settings, but no obvious patterns emerged. In a previous paper, I examined representations of African-Americans in sexuality texts, finding that positive attempts at being nonracist could be undermined by the patterns of photographs in textbooks that, for example, draw on stereotypes and myths of "dangerous" black sexuality (Whatley, 1988). Rather than reviewing all the representations of people of color in these health textbooks, I will simply repeat what I pointed out earlier—that there is a strong and clear *absence* of photographs of people of color in the healthy-images category. People of color may appear as healthy people elsewhere in the text, but not on covers, title pages, and chapter openers. If publishers wanted to correct this situation, they could simply substitute group photographs that show some diversity for the current all-white covers and title pages.

People with Disabilities

From the healthy-image photographs, it is apparent that people with visible physical disabilities are excluded from the definition of healthy. Therefore, I examined the contexts in which people with disabilities appear in the other photographs. Out of the approximately 1,100 photos, only 9 show people with physical disabilities, with 2 of these showing isolated body parts only (arthritic hands and knees). One shows an old woman being pushed in a wheelchair, while the six remaining photographs all are "positive" images: a number of men playing wheelchair basketball, a man in a wheelchair doing carpentry, a woman walking with her arm around a man in a wheelchair, a man with an amputated leg walking across Canada, children with cancer (which can be seen both as a disease and a disability) at a camp (these last two both in a cancer chapter), and a wheelchair racer. However, three of these six are from one textbook (Payne & Hahn, 1986), and two are from another (Levy, Dignan, & Shirreffs, 1987), so the inclusion of these few positive images is over-shadowed by the fact that three books show absolutely none. In addition, none of these positive images are of women, and the only disabilities represented are those in which an individual uses a wheelchair or has cancer.

This absence of representation of disabled people, particularly women, clearly reflects the invisibility of the physically disabled in our society.

> It would be easy to blame the media for creating and maintaining many of the stereotypes with which the disabled still have to live. But the media only reflect attitudes that already exist in a body-beautiful society that tends to either ignore or ostracize people who don't measure up to the norm. This state of "invisibility" is particularly true for disabled women. (Israel & McPherson, 1983, pp. 4–15)

In a society that values the constructed image of health over health itself, a person with a disability does not fit the definition of healthy. In addition, since the person with a disability may be seen as representing a "failure" of modern medicine and healthcare (Matthews, 1983), there is no place for her or him in a book that promises people that they can attain health. The common attitude that disability and health are incompatible was expressed in its extreme by a faculty member who questioned the affirmative action statement in a position description for a health education faculty member; he wanted to know if encouraging "handicapped" people to apply was appropriate for a *health* education position.

Looking at the issue of health education and disabilities, it should be clear that it is easier for able-bodied people to be healthy, so more energy should be put into helping people with disabilities maximize their health. Able-bodied people often have more access to exercise, to rewarding work (economically[3] as well as emotionally), to leisure activities, and to healthcare facili- ties. Healthcare practitioners receive very little training about health issues relating to disability (self-care, sexual health), though they may receive information about specific pathologies, such as multiple sclerosis or muscular dystrophy. The inability to see, hear, or walk need not be the impairments to health they often are considered in our society. Health education is an obvious place to begin to change the societal attitudes toward disability that can help lead to poor physical and emotional health for disabled people. Health textbooks could present possibilities for change by showing ways that both disabled and able-bodied people can maximize health, and this could be done in both the text and the photographs. For example, one of those color chapter openers could include people with disabilities as healthy people. This might mean changing some of the representative "healthy" activities, such as windsurfing. While there are people with disabilities who participate in challenging and risky physical activities, there is no need for pressure to achieve *beyond* what would be expected of the able-bodied.[4] Showing a range of healthy activities that might be more accessible to both the physically disabled and the less physically active able-bodied would be appropriate.

Fat People

There are no fat people in the healthy-image photographs. Some people who agree with the rest of my analysis may respond here, "Of course not!" because there is a common assumption in our society that being thin is healthy and that any weight gain reduces health. In fact, evidence shows that being overweight (but not obese) is *not unhealthy*. In many cases, being very fat is a lot healthier than the ways people are encouraged to attempt to reduce weight—from extreme low-calorie diets, some of which are fatal, to stomach stapling and other surgeries (Norsigian, 1986). In addition, dieting does not work for 99 percent of dieters, with 95 percent ending up heavier than before they started. Repeated dieting stresses the heart, as well as other organs (Norsigian, 1986).[1] Our national obsession with thinness is certainly one factor leading to an unhealthy range of eating behaviors, including, but not limited to, bulimia and anorexia. While health textbooks warn against dangerous diets and "eating disorders," and encourage safe, sensible weight-loss diets, they do nothing to counter the image of thin as healthy.

Defining which people are "fat" in photographs is obviously problematic. In doing so, I am giving my subjective interpretation of what I see as society's definition of ideal weight. The photographs I have identified as "fat" are of people who by common societal definitions would be seen as "needing to lose weight." In the United States most women are dissatisfied with their own body weight, so are more likely to place themselves in the "need to lose weight" category than to give that label to someone else of the same size.

Not counting people who were part of a crowd scene, I found 14 photographs that clearly showed people who were fat. One appeared in a chapter on the healthcare

---

[1]For more on our cultural obsession with thinness and the lack of compelling evidence that fat itself is unhealthy, see Anna G. Mirer and Lacey Alexander's work elsewhere in this volume, as well as Michaela Null's piece in which she argues that the health of fat people is irrelevant to how they should be treated in society. *Ed.*

system with a caption referring to "lack of preventive maintenance leading to medical problems" (Carroll & Miller, 1986, p. 471), one in a chapter on drinking, and one under cardiovascular problems. The remaining 11 appeared in chapters on weight control or diet and nutrition. Of the 11, one was the "before" of "before and after" weight-loss photographs. One showed a woman walking briskly as part of a "fat-management program" (Mullen, Gold, Belcastro, & McDermott, 1986, p. 125); that was the most positive of the images. Most of the photographs were of people doing nothing but being fat or adding to that fat (eating or cooking). Three of the photographs showed women with children, referring by caption or topic heading to causes of obesity, either genetic or environmental. Only 3 of the 11 photographs were of men. In these photographs, it seems we are not being shown a person or an activity, but a disease—a disease called obesity that we all might "catch" if we don't carefully follow the prescriptions for health. Fat people's excess weight is seen as their fault for not following these prescriptions. This failure results from a lack of either willpower or restraint, as implied by the photographs that show fat people eating and thus both draw on and lend support to the myth that fat people eat too much. The only health problem of fat people is seen as their weight; if that were changed, all other problems would presumably disappear. As pointed out earlier, the health problems of losing excess weight, particularly in the yo-yo pattern of weight loss/gain, may be greater than those created by the extra weight. In addition, the emotional and mental health problems caused by our society's fatphobia may be more serious than the physical problems (Worcester, 1988). These texts strongly reinforce fatphobia by validating it with health "science."

Health educators who consciously work against racism and sexism should carefully reevaluate how our attitudes help perpetuate discrimination against all groups. As Nancy Worcester (1988) points out,

> The animosity towards fat people is such a fundamental part of our society, that people who have consciously worked on their other prejudices have not questioned their attitude towards body weight. People who would not think of laughing at a sexist or racist joke ridicule and make comments about fat people without recognizing that they are simply perpetuating another set of attitudes which negatively affect a whole group of people. (p. 234)

An alternative approach would be to recognize that people would be healthier if less pressure were put on them to lose weight. Fat people can benefit from exercise, if it is accessible and appropriate (low impact aerobics, for example), without the goal needing to be weight loss (Sternhell, 1985). Photographs of "not thin" people, involved in a variety of activities, could be scattered throughout the text, and the pictures of those labeled obese could be eliminated completely. We all know what an obese person looks like; we do not need to have that person held up as a symbol of both unhealthiness and lack of moral character.

Old People

The healthy-image photographs show people who appeared to be predominantly in their teens and twenties, which is the age group toward which these college texts would be geared. Rather subjectively, as with the issue of weight, I will describe as old[5] those who appear to be about 65 or older. Obviously I probably judged incorrectly on some photographs, but since the representations seem to be skewed toward the young or the old, with the middle-aged not so prominent, my task was relatively easy. I identified 84 photographs that contained people I classified as old. Of these, 52 appeared in chapters specifically on aging or growing older, 10 appeared in chapters on death and dying, and the remaining 22 were distributed in a wide range of topics. Of these 22, several still focused on the issue of age. For example, a photograph of an old heterosexual couple in a chapter entitled "Courtship and Marriage" is captioned, "While some people change partners repeatedly, many others spend their lifetime with a single spouse" (Carroll & Miller, 1986, p. 271). One text showed a similar photo and caption of a heterosexual couple, but also included an old gay male couple on the next page (Levy, Dignan, & Shirreffs, 1987). This represents an important step in terms of deghettoization of gay and lesbian images, and a broadening of views about sexuality and aging. Two photos showed old people as "non-traditional students;" another depicted a man running after recovering from a stroke; and yet another featured George Burns as a representative of someone who has lived a long life. In others of the 22, the age is incidental, as in a man painting (mental health), people shopping in an open market (nutrition), people walking (fitness), a man smoking.

As the societally stereotyped *appearance* of health diminishes, as occurs with aging, it is assumed that health unavoidably diminishes. In fact, while there is some inevitable biological decline with age, many health problems can be averted by good nutrition, exercise, and preventive healthcare. Many of the health problems of aging have economic, rather than biological, causes, such as lack of appropriate health insurance coverage (Sidel, 1986). In a society that is afraid to face aging, people may not be able to accept that they will experience the effects of aging that they so carefully avoid (if they are lucky enough to live that long). In addition, as with disability, the people who may need to do more to maintain health are those being most ignored.

It is significant that these texts have sections on aging, which contain many positive images, but it is also crucial that health be seen as something that can be attained and maintained by people of all ages. The attempt to include representations of aging in these books must be expanded so that people of all ages are seen to be able to be healthy—a state now seemingly, in those images of health, to be enjoyed only by the young.

Urban Setting

The healthy-image photographs showing outdoor scenes are situated at the beach or in other nonurban settings; it is possible some were set in city parks, but there are no urban markers in the photographs. Bike riding, running, kicking a soccer ball, playing volleyball can all be done in urban settings, though the hang gliding and sky diving would obviously be difficult. Considering the high percentage of the U.S. population that lives in cities (and the numbers of those that cannot easily get out), it seems that urban settings should be represented in the texts. Of the 28 other photographs I identified as clearly having urban settings, I could see only 4 as positive. Two of these showed outdoor vegetable/fruit markets, one showed bike riding as a way of both reducing pollution and getting exercise in the city, and one showed a family playing ball together. Of the rest, 9 appeared in chapters on the environment, with negative images of urban decay, smog, and crowded streets; 10 were in chapters on mental health or stress, showing scenes representing loneliness, stress, or anger, such as a crowded subway or a potential fight on a street corner. Drinking and drug chapters had two urban scenes: "skid row" alcoholics and an apparently drunk man unconscious on the street. There were also three urban scenes in sexuality chapters—two of streets with marquees for sex shows and one showing a "man 'flashing' Central Park" (Payne & Hahn, 1986, p. 348).

There is a clear message that it is unhealthy to live in the city. While this is partly true—that is, the city may have increased pollution of various kinds, specific stresses, less access to certain forms of exercise, and other problems—there are healthy ways to live in a city. One of the roles of health education should be to help us recognize healthier options within the limits imposed on us by economic or other factors. Rather than conveying the message that urban dwelling inevitably condemns

people to ill health (unless they can afford to get away periodically to the beach or the mountains), scenes showing health within the city could be presented.

Options for positive images include scenes of outdoor activities in what are clearly city parks, people enjoying cultural events found more easily in cities, gardening in a vacant lot, or a neighborhood block party. Urban settings are excellent for representing walking as a healthy activity. City dwellers are more likely to walk to work, to shopping, and to social activities than are suburbanites, many of whom habitually drive. Urban walking can be presented as free, accessible, and healthy in terms of exercise, stress reduction, and reducing pollution. More indoor activities could be shown so that the external environment is not seen as a determinant of "healthy" activity. These might give a sense of the possibilities for health within what otherwise might appear to be a very dirty, dangerous, stressful place to be.

Work and Leisure

The healthy-image photographs I analyzed were all associated with leisure activities, so I tried to establish how these texts represent work in relationship to health. For this analysis, all photographs of healthcare workers were excluded, since these are used predominantly to illustrate health or medical issues. Of the 16 other photographs showing people at work, 4 were related to discussions of sex roles and women doing nontraditional work (phone "lineman," lawyer). This seems part of a positive trend in textbooks to reduce sexism. An obvious next step would be to show women in nontraditional work roles without commenting on them, as is done with a number of photographs of women as doctors. Six of the photographs of work accompany discussions of stress. Besides stress, there are no illustrations of health hazards at work except for one photograph of a farm worker being sprayed with pesticides. Three positive references to work show someone working at a computer (illustrating self-development), a man in a wheelchair doing carpentry, and an old man continuing to work.

Overall, the number of photographs representing work seems low, considering the amount of time we put into work during our lifetime. Blue-collar work is represented by trash collectors in an environmental health section, police officers in a weight control chapter, firefighters under stress, a construction worker in the opener for a stress chapter, the farm worker mentioned above, and women in nontraditional work. Blue-collar work is seen in terms of neither potential health hazards beyond stress nor the positive health aspects of working. The strongest connection between health and work presented involves the stress of white-collar jobs (symbolized by a man at a desk talking on the phone).

The message seems to be that health is not affected by work, unless it is emotionally stressful.

The photographs in this book seem to be aimed at middle-class students who assume they will become white-collar workers or professionals who can afford leisure activities, both in terms of time and money. Those who work in obviously physically dangerous jobs, such as construction work, or in jobs that have stress as only one of many health hazards, are rarely portrayed. These people are also likely not to be able to afford recreation such as hang gliding (and also might not need the stimulus of physical risk taking if their job is physically risky in itself). These photographs serve to compartmentalize work as if it were not part of life and not relevant to health.

Rather than selecting photographs that reinforce the work-leisure split and the alienation of the worker from work, editors could include photographs that show the health rewards of work and the real health risks of a wide variety of work. For example, a photograph of a group of workers talking on a lunch break could be captioned, "Many people find strong support networks among their co-workers." Another photograph could be of a union meeting, illustrating that work-related stress is reduced when we have more control over the conditions of our work. In addition the mental health benefits of a rewarding job might be emphasized, perhaps in contrast with the stress of unemployment. Health risks, and ways to minimize them, could be illustrated with photographs ranging from typists using video display terminals to mine workers. A very important addition would be inclusion in the healthy-image photographs of some representation of work.

Conclusion

The definition of health that emerges from an examination of the healthy-image photographs is very narrow. The healthy person is young, slim, white, physically abled, physically active, and, apparently, comfortable financially. Since these books are trying to "sell" their image of health to college students, the photographs presumably can be seen as representing people whom the students would wish to become. Some students, however, cannot or may not wish to become part of this vision of the healthy person. For example, students of color may feel alienated by this all-white vision. What may be most problematic is that in defining the healthy person, these photographs also define *who can become healthy*. By this definition many are excluded from the potential for health: people who are physically disabled, no longer young, not slim (unless they can lose weight, even if in unhealthy ways), urban dwellers, poor people,

and people of color. For various social, economic, and political reasons, these may be among the least healthy groups in the United States, but the potential for health is there if the healthcare and health education systems do not disenfranchise them.

The healthy-image photographs represent the healthy lifestyle, not in the sense of the lifestyle that will help someone attain health, but the white, middle-class, heterosexual, leisure, active lifestyle that is the reward of attaining health. These glowing images imitate common advertising representations. An ice chest of beer would not be out of place next to the volleyball players on the beach, and a soft drink slogan would fit well with the windsurfers or sky divers. It must be remembered, however, that while college students may be the market for beer, soft drinks, and "health," they are not the market for textbooks. Obviously, the biggest single factor affecting a student's purchase of a text is whether it is required. The decision may also be based on how much reading in the book is assigned, whether exam questions will be drawn from the text, its potential future usefulness, or its resale value.

The market for textbooks is the faculty who make text selections for courses (Coser, Kadushin, & Powell, 1982). While the photographs may be designed to create in students a desire for health, they are also there to sell health educators the book. Therefore, health educators should take some time examining the representations in these texts, while questioning their own definitions of who is healthy and who can become healthy. Do they actually wish to imply that access to health is limited to young, white, slim, middle-class, physically abled, and physically active people? If health educators are committed to increasing the potential for health for *all* people, then the focus should not be directed primarily at those for whom health is most easily attained and maintained. Rethinking the images that represent health may help restructure health educators' goals.

It is an interesting exercise to try to envision alternative healthy-image photographs. Here is one of my choices for a cover photograph: An old woman of color, sitting on a chair with a book in her lap, is looking out at a small garden that has been reclaimed from an urban backlot.

Acknowledgments   I would like to thank Nancy Worcester, Julie D'Acci, Sally Lesher, and Elizabeth Ellsworth for their critical readings of this chapter and their valuable suggestions.

NOTES

1. Cars appear in health textbook photographs primarily in the context of either environmental concerns or the stresses of modern life.

2. Occasionally, photographs used were actually taken for advertising purposes. For example, in a chapter on exercise there is a full-page color photograph of a runner with the credit "Photo by Jerry LaRocca for Nike" (Insel & Roth, 1988, p. 316).

3. Examining the wages of disabled women can give a sense of the potential economic problems: "The 1981 Census revealed that disabled women earn less than 24 cents for each dollar earned by nondisabled men; black disabled women earn 12 cents for each dollar. Disabled women earn approximately 52 percent of what nondisabled women earn" (Saxton & Howe, 1987, p xii).

4. "Supercrip" is a term sometimes used among people with disabilities to describe people with disabilities who go beyond what would be expected of those with no disabilities. It should not be necessary to be a one-legged ski champion or a blind physician to prove that people with disabilities deserve the opportunities available to the able-bodied. By emphasizing the individual "heroes," the focus shifts away from societal barriers and obstacles to individual responsibility to excel.

5. I am using "old" rather than "older" for two reasons that have been identified by many writing about ageism. "Older" seems a euphemism that attempts to lessen the impact of discussing someone's age, along with such terms as senior citizen or golden ager. The second point is the simple question: "Older than whom?"

REFERENCES

A list of references is available in the original source.

Appendix: Textbooks Examined for This Chapter

Carroll, C., & Miller, D. (1986). *Health: The science of human adaptation* (4th ed.). Dubuque, IA: Wm. C. Brown.

Dintiman, G. B., & Greenberg, J. (1986). *Health through discovery* (3rd ed.). New York: Random House.

Hales, D. R., & Williams, B. K. (1986). *An invitation to health: Your personal responsibility* (3rd ed.). Menlo Park, CA: Benjamin/Cummings Publishing Company.

Insel, P. M., & Roth, W. T. (1988). *Core concepts in health* (5th ed.). Mountain View, CA: Mayfield Publishing.

Levy, M. R., Dignan, M., & Shirreffs, J. H. (1987). *Life and health.* (5th ed.). New York: Random House.

Mullen, K. D., Gold, R. S., Belcastro, P. A., & McDermott, R. J. (1986). *Connections for health.* Dubuque, IA: Wm. C. Brown.

Payne, W. A., & Hahn, D. B. (1986). *Understanding your health,* St. Louis: Times Mirror/Mosby.

"Finding Good Health Information on the Web"

By Electra Kaczorowski

For the *National Women's Health Network*

Article taken from March/April 2006 Newsletter

When looking for health formation on the Internet, most of us type the name of a condition or procedure into Google or another search engine, then wait for the results to pop up onto the screen.[1] While this method immediately yields many results, it also can generate inaccurate, unreliable, or biased health information. This is of particular concern to women, who are more likely than men to seek health information on-line.[1] There are several women's health topics that are currently controversial, but are hard to find evidence-based, feminist information about. This makes it even harder for women to rely on web resources when making healthcare decisions. Nevertheless, the Internet can be a great tool for becoming more informed about your health. But, to get the best information, you have to take a critical look at your search results and use the best information available. Here are our guidelines for becoming a web-savvy health researcher:

Beware of Drug Ads

When a health site includes drug advertisements it's an obvious red flag that the health information is, at best, biased, and at worst, factually incorrect. This is because the drug companies who run ads on the site are also likely to sponsor site's health information. The information presented will have been reviewed and selected to ensure it meets the standards of the drug companies rather than the consumer. It's not always easy to spot the advertisement on health sites, though. Drug ads are often ingeniously placed to be as unobtrusive as possible; sometimes they even merge seamlessly with the site itself. This is especially true on mainstream, general health websites heavily promoted on TV and in other media. While it is usually easy to access basic information

on these large, popular sites, it is difficult to avoid the barrage of ads that come with it. Be on the lookout for product promotions that are disguised as health information, an essential skill in conducting good web research. Being aware of the presence of drug ads will help you review the site's information carefully and with a critical eye.

Look Behind the Scenes

Even if a website has no overt advertisements, the agency that runs it may be sponsored or supported by the pharmaceutical industry. Creating and maintaining a website costs money, so many companies seek support from drug and device manufacturers. Just like in politics, these financial contributors have a say in the information and research their money supports. It can be hard to tell if an agency or organization (and, thus, its website) has corporate ties, as the information may be hidden well within the site. Try looking for links to "sponsors," "partners," or "advisory boards" to get more information. A long list of pharmaceutical companies or medical device manufacturers indicates that the site's content is subject to corporate influence. Even if the information you're looking for is factually correct, there's an excellent chance that other information (e.g., alternate, non-pharmacological treatments or risk factors and complications) has been downplayed or omitted.

Read Between the Lines

When looking at web-based information, it is important to identify the intended purpose of the information provided. Is the site trying to sell a specific treatment, or convince the viewer that one particular procedure is the best way to go? Is the information provided in a way that informs and educates the reader? Reliable health information should help individuals make informed decisions, not to promote specific health procedures. If a website includes numerous mentions of one specific approach without also discussing risks, side-effects, or alternatives, it may not be the best tool to use in making a health decision.

For example, one popular menopause site features Q&A sessions with a physician who essentially prescribes specific regimens of bioidentical hormones to women who write in, complete with dosage information and referrals to specific businesses. This is clearly intended to be a substitute for a doctor's visit, and leaves no room for questions that do not end with a specific recommendation. The women who write in are encouraged to follow this particular doctor's orders in lieu of gathering information to make their own informed decision. Look for information that is balanced, well-organized, and comprehensively addresses all aspects of the topic.

Check the Address

Before going to a link, it's a good idea to assess if the website is a commercial site (ending in *.com* or *.net*), a non-profit site (ending in *.org*), an educational institution site (ending in *.edu*), or a governmental site (ending in *.gov*). (Internet addresses are expanding, but these are the most common suffixes.) Commercial sites aim to sell products and may contain many ads. Or, they may be simply trying to promote one type of treatment over another, as do many commercial sites on fibroids. Organizational sites are run by an agency and reflect the group's perspective and that of any sponsors. Finding out more about the agency's philosophy and approach to women's health can help visitors take a critical look at the site's health information. Governmental sites on women's health generally contain accurate information, but may not always be comprehensive, and often lack analysis. Knowing the kind of website from which the information is coming is helpful in making informed decisions and learning more about a health topic.

Watch for Hype

Health information on the web is just like any other kind of information: subject to bias and inaccuracies. Some hot-button women's health topics have been getting a lot of attention recently, the most prominent being menopause hormone therapy, bioidentical or 'natural' hormones, hysterectomy, osteoporosis, and infertility. Websites that cover any of these topics should be looked at very carefully to ensure that their information is based on scientific evidence (with clear references), not just testimonials or theories. Information on these hot-button

issues abounds; even TV stations may have auxiliary websites featuring 'experts' on these topics. While consumer education is important, the views represented on these sites usually reflect those of corporate sponsors and the information is rarely presented in a balanced way. The more controversial a health topic is, the more essential it is for the reader to be vigilant and discerning.

Keep an Eye on the Evidence

There are places out there that are committed to providing individuals with the information they need to make decisions about their healthcare. Supporting individual decision, making is very important to the NWHN, and we plan to expand our website to make even more information available on-line. Other sites with feminist, evidence-based health information are www.bcaction.org (Breast Cancer Action), www.ourbodiesourselves.org (Our Bodies, Ourselves), www.stopbreastcancer.org (National Breast Cancer Coalition), www.desaction.org (DES Action), www.susanlovemd.org (Susan Love's website, and www.center4research.org (National Research Center for Women and Families), to name just a few. The Network also appreciates the good work of the Cochrane Collaboration (www.cochrane.org), which produces and disseminates reviews on evidence-based healthcare interventions. For a more comprehensive list of sites NWHN likes, please visit the *links* section of our website.

Women can also access journal articles and studies on their own through www.pubmed.gov or www.medlineplus.gov (both services of the National Institutes of Health), although it is essential to be aware that even these sources are subject to bias and industry influence.

A Final Word

Being aware of all of these factors is the key to solid web research. Sometimes it's impossible to find information on a certain topic that is free of product promotions or pharmaceutical-sponsored studies. Just knowing about these potential influences can make a big difference when sifting through information, however. The Internet is a wonderful way for individuals to quickly and privately become more informed and educated about their health. As with any tool, it is important to know how to use it well and to the best advantage.

NOTES

1. Fox, S., Rainie L. 'Vital Decisions: How Internet Users Decide What Information to Trust When They or Their Loved Ones Are Sick.' Pew Internet and American Life Project, May 2002. On-line at http://www.pewinternet.org/pdfs/ PIP_Vital_Decisions_May2002.pdf.

"Women Need Better Medical Tests, Not More Treatment"

By Cynthia Pearson

No woman diagnosed with ductal carcinoma in situ, or D.C.I.S., should make decisions about what to do next without knowing the findings of this new study.

Surgical and medical oncologists now have a duty to tell women with D.C.I.S. that most of them have a very low chance of dying from breast cancer, and that aggressive treatment doesn't improve their odds. Once women know this, they can feel confident that they are making a safe choice if they decide to simply remove the D.C.I.S. via lumpectomy,[1] or to possibly not treat it at all, depending on the characteristics of the lesion.

But feeling confident isn't the same as feeling comfortable. It's extraordinarily difficult for most people to do nothing when given a diagnosis—look at how few men make the safe choice of watchful waiting when they're given a diagnosis of prostate cancer;[2] or how few women make the safe choice to turn down drug therapy when given a diagnosis of osteopenia,[3] which is only a risk factor, not a disease state.

Women with D.C.I.S., like men with P.S.A.-detected prostate cancer, and women with osteopenia, are all too often faced with a diagnosis as a result of the over-use of screening tests. These types of screening tests — bone mineral density,[4] P.S.A.[5] and mammography[6] starting at age 40 — all make individuals, trying to cope on their own, face frightening information and potentially dangerous treatments.

Better information and decision-making tools can be somewhat helpful to women with D.C.I.S. But what women really need is better screening tests, and they need a health care system that doesn't encourage the over-use of tests and treatments that haven't been shown to save lives. Instead of mammography, which finds many lesions that will never spread, women need tests that find disease that truly needs to be treated. That kind of screening test for breast cancer doesn't exist right now, but it will never exist if we don't try to create it.

Cynthia Pearson is the Executive Director of the National Women's Health Network.

---

[1]http://www.breastcancer.org/treatment/surgery/lumpectomy/what_is
[2]http://www.nytimes.com/health/guides/disease/prostate-cancer/overview.html?8qa
[3]http://www.webmd.com/osteoporosis/tc/osteopenia-overview

[4]http://www.nytimes.com/health/guides/test/bone-mineral-density-test/overview.html
[5]http://well.blogs.nytimes.com/2011/10/06/answering-questions-about-the-p-s-a-test/
[6]http://www.nytimes.com/2015/05/19/health/study-finds-dense-breast-tissue-isnt-always-a-high-cancer-risk.html

Originally published in the newsletter of the National Women's Health Network. Reprinted by permission.

A Dangerous Combination
"Direct-to-Consumer Advertising, Abstinence-Only Education, and Young Women's Health"

By Ronna Popkin

In recent years, advertisements for hormonal contraceptives have become an increasingly noticeable presence in popular women's magazines. These ads are colorful, multi-page spreads with catchy slogans and images of attractive women or couples, and they often include coupons, special offers, or information on obtaining free samples. The explosion in contraceptive advertising is part of a larger, overall increase in direct-to-consumer (DTC) prescription drug advertising that began in 1997, when the U.S. Food and Drug Administration (FDA) loosened drug ad regulations through the FDA Modernization Act. As many health advocates and media critics have argued, all DTC drug advertising has the potential to impact consumer health negatively (Laurence & Weinhouse, 2000; Pearson, 1995; Wilkes et al., 2000). However, DTC hormonal contraceptive advertising, far more than other DTC drug advertising, raises specific concerns and has potentially serious implications for young women's health.

Since 1997, prescription drug advertising has become the fastest growing segment of the advertising industry (Headden & Melton, 1998). Spending on drug advertising has increased exponentially—drug manufacturers spent $791 million on DTC drug ads in 1996, but by 2001 spending had risen to nearly $2.7 billion (Kaiser Family Foundation, 2003a; Levitt, 2001). A study conducted by the National Institute for Healthcare Management (NIHCM) found that DTC advertising of prescription drugs is heavily concentrated on about 50 drugs, and that consumer spending on just these 50 drugs accounted for almost half—$9.9 billion—of the overall $20.8 billion increase in retail prescription drug spending in 2000. Furthermore, the sales growth of these 50 drugs in 2000 was over 32%, more than double the 14% sales growth for all other drugs, and doctors

wrote nearly 25% more prescriptions for these 50 most heavily advertised drugs in 2000 than in 1999, while they wrote only 4% more prescriptions for all other drugs (National Institute for Healthcare Management, 2001). What these statistics demonstrate is that DTC advertising of prescription drugs works—it increases prescription rates, sales growth, and consumer spending on drugs.

While the FDA technically requires that DTC ads provide a fair balance of risk and benefit information in the main copy of the advertisement, the agency neither requires prior approval of DTC ads nor monitors the ads once they are released. As a result, drug companies often fail, or do the bare minimum required, to comply with this regulation. Several content analyses of DTC ads have demonstrated that they frequently contain vague, misleading, confusing, and unbalanced messages and present information in a manner that makes the benefits of using the drugs appear to outweigh the risks (Bell *et al.*, 2000; Roth, 1996; Welch Cline & Young, 2004; Woloshin *et al.*, 2001).

The misleading and manipulative messages in DTC drug ads could negatively impact any individual's health; however, they have a disproportionate potential to influence young women because teens often cite the media as important sources of sexual health information. In a recent survey conducted by the Kaiser Family Foundation on teen sexuality, 74% of teenage girls reported that they got "a lot" or "some" information on birth control and STD protection from magazines, and 68% reported getting "a lot" or "some" information on those topics from product advertising. Furthermore, those numbers were higher than the percentage of young women who reported learning "a lot" or "some" about birth control and STD protection from their healthcare providers (64%), teachers (53%), and siblings (47%) (Kaiser Family Foundation, 2004). These statistics illustrate that young women view magazines and advertising as important sources of sexual health information, and since hormonal methods of birth control are some of the most widely promoted drugs in the U.S. (Wilkes et al., 2000), young women are likely to be heavily influenced by DTC ads for hormonal contraception.

Another reason DTC ads might be more likely to impact young women is that since 1997, the same year the FDA loosened prescription drug advertising restrictions, the federal government has poured over 1.5 billion dollars into abstinence-only sexuality education programs (Sexuality Information and Education Council of the United States, 2008). These programs, which several recent studies have found to be ineffective, provide young people with absolutely no information about contraception or protection against STDs except for potential—and often exaggerated—side effects and failure rates (Bennett & Assefi, 2005; Hauser, 2004; Kirby, 2002; Trenholm *et al.*, 2007; Waxman, 2004). The increases in abstinence-only sexuality education in schools means that many young women are being denied, at an institutional level, access to accurate and objective information on the health effects of taking hormonal contraception, which may make them more likely to believe and trust the potentially misleading messages in the ads.

As media critic Douglass Kellner explains, the promotional strategy of highlighting benefits and downplaying risks is used in all advertising: "Ads form textual systems with basic components which are interrelated in ways that positively position the product" (Kellner, 1995). However, manipulating and influencing consumers to buy a specific product is not that damaging when the choice is between buying Revlon or L'Oreal mascara. But when young women are being targeted and influenced to demand and use drugs that have widespread, systemic bodily effects, and they are simultaneously denied, in their schools, objective, unbiased information about the potential health consequences of taking those drugs, this manipulation has serious, dangerous implications.

An Unparalleled Presence

To more effectively assess the potential impact of DTC birth control advertising on young women's health, I tracked and examined the prevalence and content of ads for hormonal contraception printed in *Cosmopolitan, Essence,* and *Glamour* between 2001 and 2004. This detailed analysis revealed that hormonal contraceptives are, by far, the category of drugs most heavily promoted to young women. During this period, pharmaceutical companies printed a total of 148 advertisements for nine brands of hormonal contraception in the magazines, with the contraceptive ads occupying a total of 418 pages. Drugs that treat mood disorders were the second most heavily advertised category of drugs, with 44 advertisements occupying 106 total pages. Thus, hormonal contraception was advertised at more than three times the rate of the next most heavily advertised category of drugs.

The consistent and dominating presence of birth control ads in these magazines is one reason why these DTC ads have the potential to impact young women's health. Over the four year period, young women interested in treating their asthma would have come across only 13 DTC asthma drug ads: two in *Glamour*, six in *Cosmopolitan*, and five in *Essence*. Most of these ads had only one page of graphic content, and no issue of any magazine contained more than one DTC asthma drug ad. The DTC advertising for asthma drugs is therefore sporadic enough that women are not likely to be heavily influenced by the ads.

In contrast, over the same period of time, women would have been exposed to 148 hormonal contraceptive ads: 70 in *Glamour*, 53 in *Cosmopolitan*, and 25 in *Essence*. More than 2/3 of these ads had two or more pages of graphic content and many contained postcard or special offer inserts that encouraged the magazines fall open to those pages. Furthermore, approximately 1/3 of the issues of *Cosmopolitan* and *Glamour* printed DTC ads for two or more brands of hormonal contraceptives. Issues with several birth control ads and advertisements occupying multiple page spreads are far more likely to effectively capture readers' attention than shorter or less frequently printed ads. Clearly DTC hormonal birth control advertisements are a consistent presence in women's magazines that is significantly larger and more captivating than that of DTC ads for other drugs, and this presence enables the messages in DTC birth control ads to have a much greater impact on women and their health. But what messages are these ads sending to young women?

Ortho Tri-Cyclen: Skin Medication or Birth Control?

Ortho Tri-Cyclen was the first hormonal contraceptive to be heavily marketed to women through DTC ads, and advertisements for the brand heavily stressed and promoted the potential beauty benefits of using this form of hormonal contraception. "It's the #1 prescribed birth control pill. And it's clinically proven to help your skin look better," was the slogan plastered boldly across all 30 of the Ortho Tri-Cyclen advertisements. Thus, the first piece of information that readers were likely to absorb about Ortho Tri-Cyclen had nothing to do with contraception, its primary use and purpose; rather, women were likely to learn that that the drug has a positive effect on appearance. In fact, the emphasis on beauty in the Ortho Tri-Cyclen ads was so pervasive that none of the highlighted information on the main page of one of their most frequently used advertisements directly, clearly, or explicitly related to its use as a contraceptive. Instead, highlighted and bolded phrases emphasized that "nearly 9 out of 10 women saw significant improvements in their skin," conveyed that women taking the drug "showed no change in weight," and explained that the drug may work to make women's "periods shorter and more regular, and to reduce cramps."

Ortho McNeil, the manufacturer of Ortho Tri-Cyclen, also downplayed any health risks associated with taking the drug. None of the phrases in bold type were about major risks, side effects, or contraindications to the drug. Instead, the information about health risks that the FDA requires was printed in extremely small type at the very bottom of the page. In this brief section on risks and side effects, the first thing mentioned was that "most side effects of birth control pills are not serious. Those that are occur infrequently." Leading with this statement softens the impact of the subsequent information, which explained that the serious risks include blood clots, stroke, and heart attacks. While fewer than 5% of women do experience such serious side effects, these can be life threatening, so it is vital that women considering taking the drug be clearly alerted to these potential health issues (Boston Women's Health Book Collective, 1998). Yet the only risk information in the ad that was even remotely highlighted was a lightly underlined phrase printed at the bottom of the page that warned smokers over 35 not to take oral contraceptives. This phrase, however, was nowhere near as visible as the health and beauty benefit phrases printed in bold type. Because the information in the ad on beauty and health benefits outnumbered and was far more visible than the information on risks, the ad leaves women with the impression that taking hormonal contraceptives has many benefits and few health consequences.

Reading the Fine Print?

In contrast to the primary page of the ad, the back page, which contains the full product-labeling insert that comes with the drug, makes the actual potential dangers of using Ortho Tri-Cyclen eminently clear. This page lists 12 major warnings about using Ortho Tri-Cyclen, 13 serious precautions to consider, and over 50 adverse reactions that have been demonstrated in conjunction with the use of hormonal contraceptives. These risks and contraindications include milder problems like nausea and headaches, and more severe health issues like breast cancer, cervical cancer, and gallbladder disease. Only one short sentence amidst the sea of information on this page is the only place where the ad explains that the pill does not protect against the spread of HIV or STDs.

Alarmingly, research demonstrates that the majority of consumers do not read the important information printed on the back of DTC ads. When the FDA asked consumers in a 2002 survey how much of this small print information they usually read, only 16% said they read almost all or all of the information, while 73% said they read little to none of the small print information (Aikin, 2003). In addition, a recent study revealed that the literacy demands of the information on these summary pages is at a college or graduate level (Kaphingst *et al.*, 2004), so even if younger women were attempting to read this information they might not have the literacy skills to fully comprehend it.

These studies demonstrate that ads for birth control are not clearly and explicitly giving women all of the information they need to consider when deciding whether or not they want to use the pill. Technically the ads follow FDA regulations because the information on risks is printed somewhere in the advertisement; however, information on benefits is stressed and highlighted, while the risk information is presented in a manner that seriously discourages women from reading it. As a result, a majority of physicians surveyed by the FDA have noticed a dramatic difference in their patients' comprehension of drug benefits vs. risks after viewing DTC ads. While 78% of doctors felt that their patients were somewhat or very clear on the possible benefits and positive effects of advertised drugs, 60% felt that patients understood little or none of the risks and negative side effects (Aikin, 2003).

Seasonale: A False Sense of Freedom

Ads for Seasonale, another brand of hormonal contraceptives, also tended to highlight benefits while downplaying risks. Seasonale was approved by the FDA in 2004, and it is not a new formulation of birth control pills, but rather is a repackaging of traditional birth control pills that only includes placebo pills once every three months instead of once a month. Because it is the brief withdrawal of hormones during the placebo week that creates a pseudo-menstruation when women are on oral contraceptives, women taking Seasonale will have, as the advertisements state, "just four periods a year." There is absolutely no increased contraceptive benefit to Seasonale—birth control pills are just as effective at protecting against pregnancy whether or not a placebo week is included on a monthly basis.

Since the only advantage to Seasonale is that women taking it will menstruate less frequently, this is what advertisements for the drug promoted. Yet Barr Laboratories, the manufacturer of Seasonale, didn't just promote the drug to women who would most benefit from using it, like those who were already heterosexually active and experienced severe menstrual pain or difficulties. Instead, they glorified the notion of fewer periods for *all* women, conveying through both the imagery and copy that women will be happier and freer if they have fewer periods. For example, every Seasonale ad contained a wildly dancing woman with a beaming smile and hair soaring in the wind. These women appeared absolutely ecstatic about the fact that they were menstruating less frequently. The copy in the ads reinforced the notion that Seasonale could liberate women, as the trademarked slogan for the product is "Fewer periods. More possibilities." This statement makes it perfectly clear that reducing the frequency of menstruation will provide women with more freedom and options, which adds to the widespread cultural notion that menstruation is a shackle and burden for women. These negative messages about menstruation could have a stronger impact on younger women who are still learning about, and becoming comfortable in, their changing bodies.

Many of the other messages in Seasonale ads, like those in Ortho Tri-Cyclen ads, were misleading and downplayed the negative side effects of the drug. First, the main copy in the ad touted the fact that Seasonale is "the only FDA-approved birth control pill that lets you have just 4 periods a year." Technically this is true, as Seasonale is the only contraceptive pill packaged with twelve weeks of active hormones and one week of placebo pills. However, women actually can use any birth control pill in the same manner as Seasonale and they will get the same main result: fewer periods. All they have to do is skip the placebo pills at the end of one package and then immediately begin taking the active pills from their next pack. So while the ads for Seasonale portrayed it as an innovative concept in contraceptives that "has changed the way you take the Pill," women can make this change whether or not they buy this specific product.

Another very misleading statement printed in every ad for Seasonale was that "leading women's healthcare experts agree you don't need a monthly period when you're on the Pill because you're not ovulating." First, this statement is scientifically inaccurate. Ovulation is a physiological process that occurs in the ovaries and has little bearing on the build up of women's uterine lining, which is the main tissue that is shed during menstruation. In fact, women not taking hormonal contraceptives sometimes have anovulatory cycles in which they still menstruate, so clearly a lack of ovulation does not make menstruation unnecessary. But even more misleading is the fact that women's health experts do *not* agree on this issue—there is actually widespread debate among healthcare providers about the safety of continuously suppressing menstruation, not only because they are unsure of what changes it might cause in women's endometrial tissue, but also because it requires significant additional hormone exposure (Rabin, 2004).

Having only four periods a year means that women will annually be exposed to nine additional weeks of hormones, a potentially risky aspect of Seasonale that was heavily downplayed in ads for the product. When using regular birth control pills, women take active hormones for 39 weeks a year, so the extra nine weeks of hormones in Seasonale amounts to a 23% annual increase in women's hormone exposure. Ads for Seasonale did, in the small copy at the bottom of the page, present this information by stating that "Seasonale users receive 9 more weeks of hormones every year than with a same-dose 28 day pill." Yet, immediately after that statement, Barr Laboratories also claimed that, "While this may increase the chance of serious health risks, current studies have not shown an increased risk." This statement is extremely misleading because it falsely implies that studies of the long-term health effects of the additional annual hormone exposure have been done and showed no increased risks. However, in reality, Seasonale was only studied for one year on a total of 261 women (Rabin, 2004), so the reason "current studies have not shown an increased risk" is that adequate studies have not been completed. Barr Laboratories leaves women with the impression that their product has been proven safe, when all that's really been proven about Seasonale is that it is an effective contraceptive.

The fact that the Seasonale ads played on and reinforced women's negative attitudes toward menstruation is also incredibly ironic, because, while women taking the drug may get only four official "periods" a year, they are much more likely to frequently spot or experience heavy breakthrough bleeding between periods. This information, like the most serious risk and side effect information in the Ortho Tri-Cyclen ads, was displayed non-prominently at the bottom of the page, and the alarming frequency of the intermenstrual bleeding wasn't at all clear. The main study done on Seasonale found that, during their first 13-week cycle on the drug, 65% of women experienced at least 7 days of bleeding between periods and 35% bled for a total of 20 or more days. While, as the primary page of the ad claimed, this frequency did "decrease over time," at the end of the year 42% of women still experienced at least 7 days of bleeding between periods and 15% experienced 20 or more days. Yet these statistics were only presented on the back page of the ad that people are very unlikely to read. Given that Seasonale is being primarily promoted as a product that will free women from the burden of menstruation, it is highly misleading to conceal the fact that over half of the women taking the drug are actually bleeding more than just four times a year.

Ortho Evra: Feigning Cultural and Racial Sensitivity

Out of the seven pharmaceutical companies who printed contraceptive advertisements in *Cosmopolitan, Glamour*, and *Essence* between 2001 and 2004, only Barr Laboratories and Ortho McNeil used women of color in their ads. In fact, in stark contrast to the other manufacturers who made little or no attempt to reflect the racial and ethnic diversity of women in the United States, Ortho McNeil actually printed more ads with images of black women than with white women. Ortho McNeil also was one of only two contraceptive manufacturers to advertise in *Essence*, and ads for the company's three different contraceptive products accounted for 23 of the 25 birth control ads printed in *Essence* over the four year period.

Given their consistent use of women of color in their promotional materials and their choice to purchase advertisements in *Essence*, it appears that Ortho McNeil is more sensitive to women's diversity and is targeting black women more than other contraceptive manufacturers. Yet, while their marketing approaches and strategies indicate greater sensitivity to racial and ethnic diversity in the United States, one of their major products does not. Ortho Evra, the transdermal birth control patch developed by Ortho McNeil and released in the U.S. market in 2002, is available *only* in a beige color. Not surprisingly, a number of African-American women have cited the patch's visibility on their skin as the main reason they have chosen not to use Ortho Evra (Kaiser Family Foundation, 2003b).

Ortho McNeil's choice to manufacture Ortho Evra, a product that they market as concealable, in a shade that will match relatively few women's skin obviously greatly lacks cultural and racial sensitivity, but it is also radically incongruent with the company's

marketing approach for the product. Over 60% of the ads printed for Ortho Evra in *Essence, Cosmopolitan*, and *Glamour* between 2001 and 2004 contained images of black women. Furthermore, with 13 advertisements in *Essence*, Ortho Evra was by far the most frequently advertised contraceptive product in the magazine and was the second most heavily advertised drug overall.

The possible motivation behind Ortho McNeil's contradictory approach of targeting young, African-American women with a product that illustrates insensitivity toward them was, initially, baffling. In order to justify the company's racially insensitive choice of patch colors, a vice president of Ortho McNeil claimed that the company had attempted to make the patch clear, but that it looked "grimy" in clinical trials. She also claimed that their manufacturing technology at the time they released the patch did not give them "color options" (Kaiser Family Foundation, 2003b). While their justification is suspect, even if one accepts the company's statements as true, they do not explain why or how executives felt that young, African-American women would still be a lucrative market for their product.

However, Ortho Evra is a longer-acting contraceptive than either Ortho Tri-Cyclen or Ortho Tri-Cyclen Lo, which may help explain why it is being marketed more heavily to black women than other contraceptive products. Unlike the various formulations of birth control pills, which women should take at the same time every day, Ortho Evra slowly releases hormones into a woman's body over the course of a week. Women using the patch need to change it only once a week for three consecutive weeks, and then wear no patch on the fourth week so that they will still get their periods. The convenience of a longer acting hormonal method like Ortho Evra is certainly something that is likely to please a number of women, as many women find it challenging to remember to take a pill at the same time every day.

Yet, for many women of color and poor women, Ortho Evra might raise some concerns, as there is a well-documented history of other longer acting hormonal contraceptive methods, such as Norplant and Depo-Provera, being inappropriately promoted or distributed within their communities. The disproportionate promotion of long acting contraceptives to poor women and women of color has mostly been due to grossly inaccurate racist and classist stereotypes that they cannot be relied upon to use contraceptives that require daily effort, yet need to limit their reproduction because they have too many children who become dependent on social services (Collins, 2004; Roberts, 1997). While none of these stereotypes are true—poor women and women of color do not have more children, on average, than wealthy or white women, nor have they ever been proven to have higher failure rates with other contraceptive devices—these notions continue to circulate in public ideology. These stereotypes were also reflected in the rates at which longer acting methods were promoted within *Cosmopolitan, Glamour,* and *Essence,* and therefore might help explain Ortho McNeil's choice to target black women in their promotion of Ortho Evra. Ads for longer acting methods accounted for 60% of the contraceptive ads printed in *Essence,* but only 27% of those printed in *Glamour* and 36% of those in *Cosmopolitan.*

Because Ortho Evra contains similar hormones to daily birth control pills, its longer acting nature is its primary advantage over other hormonal products, and therefore the convenience of using weekly birth control is what Ortho McNeil chose to emphasize in their marketing campaign. The trademarked slogan for Ortho Evra, printed in every advertisement for the product, is "On your body. Off your mind." This message required marketing it directly as a contraceptive device, which might also help explain Ortho McNeil's choice to target black women more heavily with the patch. As the content in Ortho Tri-Cyclen and Seasonale ads shows, many hormonal methods of contraception are promoted mostly for their non-contraceptive advantages. But advertisements for Ortho Evra, unlike ads for nearly every other contraceptive product promoted in *Cosmopolitan, Essence,* and *Glamour,* did not highlight a single non-contraceptive benefit of the patch, despite the fact that it possesses the same advantages of most other hormonal products. Ortho McNeil's choice to market Ortho Evra only for its role as a contraceptive, combined with the fact that they promoted it in *Essence* far more heavily than any of their other contraceptive products, sends a subtle, disturbing message that both reflects and reinforces existing stereotypes: black women are more likely to need and use birth control to prevent pregnancy and limit their reproduction, while white women are more likely to use hormonal contraceptives for a whole host of other reasons.

Operating from stereotypes similar to those about women of color and poor women, some public health and health education professionals have suggested that Ortho Evra and other longer acting methods of contraception might be especially beneficial for younger women, whom they speculate might be more likely to have increased rates of user error with other contraceptives. If preventing pregnancy were our only public health goal with young women, this might be a valid assessment. However, little testing has been done regarding the long-term safety of the use of hormonal methods by young women. Furthermore, while teen pregnancy rates have been consistently dropping, rates of most sexually transmitted infections in young people have been slowly climbing (Centers for Disease Control and Prevention, 2004, 2004b). Thus, disassociating sexual activity from the risks it presents and responsibilities it requires might not be the soundest approach for young women. Encouraging them to use a contraceptive product that they can "take off their minds" might make them even more likely to also take disease protection measures "off their minds." In fact, research suggests that this is true, as longer-acting hormonal contraceptives have a stronger inverse relationship with condom use than daily oral contraceptive pills (Cushman et al., 1998).

The Dangers Revealed

The misleading and persuasive messages in these contraceptive advertisements are likely to have a disproportionately negative impact on the nearly 1/3 of young American women who are being taught about sexuality through abstinence-only programs. When students are openly taught about different contraceptive methods in schools, they learn accurate and valuable information about each method that they can use whenever they become sexually active: what it is; how it works; how to use it; and its benefits, drawbacks, efficacy, and safety. Abstinence-only approaches to sexuality education not only restrict such information on contraception in the classroom, but also convey to young people that they should not be sexually active at all, which could discourage them from actively seeking out other reliable sources of contraceptive information.

Without alternate sources of information on birth control, the advertisements that young women regularly see in magazines are likely to be one of their primary sources of sexual health information. In fact, in a recent survey of teens about birth control and sexual health, product advertising was the second most frequently cited source of information about birth control and STD-protection, surpassing parents, siblings, teachers, healthcare providers, partners, television, the internet, and even magazine articles; only friends were cited more frequently (Kaiser Family Foundation, 2004). Other studies have shown that individuals with lower levels of education are more likely to seek information from media sources and have more positive attitudes toward advertising (Robinson *et al.,* 2004). Yet abstinence-only programs leave young women ill equipped to understand and critically evaluate the benefit and risk information in DTC birth control ads. These programs rarely teach media literacy skills, so young women educated through these programs might be even more likely to be influenced by the ads' misleading messages and choose to take hormonal products to clear up their skin or eliminate their periods without being fully informed of the potential risks the drugs pose to their health.

In addition, because abstinence-only programs often use scare tactics and exaggerate the risks of using contraceptives, these programs might actually lead young women to disregard the minute amount of risk information that is presented in the ads. Research has repeatedly indicated that, in any area of health education, scare tactics are ineffective, because once students discover that adults have exaggerated risk information, they become very skeptical of any other warnings they are issued (Hedgepeth & Helmich, 1996; Telljohann *et al.*, 2004). Young women educated through abstinence-only programs who are actively reading or seeking information about birth control are also likely to be, or soon become, sexually active. These young women, therefore, may already feel lied to or misled by the greatly exaggerated dangers of sexual activity and safer sex measures that are presented in these programs. As a result, even if these women read the finely printed risk information in birth control ads, they might also be more likely to disregard these warnings.

The failure of several manufacturers of hormonal contraceptives to clearly and explicitly present the lack of STD protection is also particularly dangerous for young women. Given that one out of four sexually active teenagers contracts an STD before the age of 20 (Centers for Disease Control and Prevention, 2004), STD protection is clearly a crucial component of young people's sexual health. Using a method of birth control that does not provide STD protection also disproportionately affects young women. Women are twice as likely as men to contract an STD in an unprotected act of heterosexual intercourse, and they are far more likely to go undiagnosed for longer because initial symptoms of STDs in women are often internal. When STDs go untreated in women, the consequences, such as pelvic inflammatory disease and infertility, are far more severe than those for men (Sloane, 2002). In addition, the cervixes of women in their teens and early twenties are still undergoing changes that make them more susceptible to infection than those of older women (Centers for Disease Control and Prevention, 2004).

Yet, despite these greater risks, many young women are unaware that hormones do not protect against STDs. In one recent survey, nearly half of teens who felt knowledgeable about hormonal methods of contraception also believed that these methods conferred some protection against disease transmission (Kaiser Family Foundation, 2004). Due to their lack of access to accurate education about contraception, young women educated through abstinence-only sexuality education programs may be especially likely to have misconceptions about hormones and STD protection. Thus, many teen girls could be unknowingly putting themselves at risk because they incorrectly believe that hormonal contraceptives also provide them with disease protection, and unfortunately the DTC ads they see often fail to clearly inform them otherwise.

The lack of STD information in hormonal birth control ads might not be so problematic if there were also a similar quantity of advertisements for condoms, which don't pose any serious health risks and do protect against STD transmission. However, not a single condom advertisement was ever printed in *Essence* during the four years of my analysis, and from 2001 through 2003, none were printed in either *Cosmopolitan* or *Glamour*. In fact, Trojan, the only condom manufacturer to advertise in the magazines, printed only three ads in total: one in the May and July 2004 editions of *Glamour*, and one in the August 2004 edition of *Cosmopolitan*. Compared to the 148 ads for hormonal contraception printed in the magazines over the same four-year period, the Trojan ads were an insignificant presence.

The Trojan advertisements also failed to provide factual information about condoms' effectiveness at protecting against both pregnancy and STDs. Abstinence- only programs that make references to condoms often present inaccurate and greatly exaggerated information about condom failure rates (Waxman, 2004). Since nothing printed in the Trojan ads countered those erroneous teachings, even young women who saw these three condom advertisements would not have learned about the benefits of using condoms over the hormonal methods that are so pervasively being marketed to them. Teens taught inaccurate information about condom failure rates might, in fact, be more heavily persuaded by ads for hormonal birth control since these ads consistently stress hormones' high rates of effectiveness. Incorrectly believing that condoms will not effectively protect them against pregnancy could lead them to choose products that they have been assured will.

Conclusion

DTC ads for hormonal contraception occupy many more pages and are far more prevalent than ads for other drugs in women's magazines. Hormonal birth control ads, like all advertisements, are primarily designed to increase sales of products and to generate profits, not to educate consumers, and they therefore contain misleading and manipulative messages designed to favorably position the products in consumers' eyes. The pharmaceutical manufacturers of these drugs do abide by FDA regulations and print serious risks, contraindications, and side effects associated with the drugs, but they do so in a manner that downplays these risks and strongly highlights other potential benefits. Therefore, the dominating presence of DTC hormonal birth control ads, coupled with the dramatic increase in abstinence-only sexuality education, poses serious risks to young women's health.

Young women adequately educated about the risks and benefits of hormonal contraception through school or community programs are better equipped to critically evaluate these misleading messages because they can negotiate the information that the ads provide with information they already have about sexual health. However, nearly one-third of young American women are taught sexuality in schools through an abstinence-only model, and therefore the birth control ads that are consistently and widely printed in women's magazines are likely to become primary sources of sexual health information for these women. Women who don't readily have access to non-promotional sources of information about contraception can't adequately evaluate the accuracy of the information provided in these ads and are therefore more susceptible to the misleading and persuasive messages in them.

DTC advertisements for hormonal birth control are relatively new, yet increasingly prevalent, voices in the sea of mixed messages and blurry information that young women receive about their sexuality and bodies. If, as a society, we want young people to safely navigate through those mixed messages and grow into sexually healthy adults, we have to model and teach them the principles of healthy relationships; help them build communication, critical thinking, decision-making, and media literacy skills; and provide them with accurate and current information about safer sex practices and sexual health. Both abstinence-only sexuality education programs and DTC birth control advertising fail on most of the above accounts, so the combination of distorted information from both of these sources poses a serious potential threat to young women's health. Yet, despite research illustrating their negative effects, funding for abstinence-only programs and spending on DTC advertising have both continued to increase annually at dramatic rates, and this is unlikely to change in the near future. Thus, it is vital that media critics, health researchers, sexuality educators, and youth advocates further investigate and address the joint impact of DTC birth control advertising and abstinence-only education on young women's sexual knowledge, behavior, and health.

REFERENCES

Aikin, K. J. (2003). The impact of direct-to-consumer prescription drug advertising on the physician-patient relationship. *Presentation at Direct-to-Consumer Promotion Public Meeting* Retrieved April 5, 2005, from http://www.fda.gov/ cder/ddmac/aikin/sld001.htm

Bell, R. A., Wilkes, M. S., & Kravitz, R. L. (2000). The educational value of consumer-targeted prescription drug print advertising. *The Journal of Family Practice, 49*(12), 1092–1098.

Bennett, S. E., & Assefi, N. P. (2005). School-based teenage pregnancy prevention programs: A systematic review of randomized controlled trials. *Journal of Adolescent Health, 36*(1), 72–81.

Boston Women's Health Book Collective. (1998). *Our bodies, ourselves for the new century.* New York: Simon & Schuster.

Centers for Disease Control and Prevention. (2004). *Sexually transmitted disease surveillance, 2003.* Atlanta: U.S. Department of Health and Human Services.

Centers for Disease Control and Prevention. (2006). Youth risk behavior surveillance: United States, 2005. *Morbidity and Mortality Weekly Report, 55*(SS–5).

Collins, P. H. (2004). *Black sexual politics: African Americans, gender, and the new racism.* New York: Routledge.

Cushman, L. F., Romero, D., Kalmuss, D., Davidson, A. R., et al. (1998). Condom use among women choosing long-term hormonal contraception. *Family Planning Perspectives, 30*(5), 240–243.

Hauser, D. (2004). *Five years of abstinence-only-until-marriage education: Assessing the impact.* Advocates for Youth.

Headden, S., & Melton, M. (1998, July 20). Madison Ave. loves drug ads. *U.S. News and World Report,* 56.

Hedgepeth, E., & Helmich, J. (1996). *Teaching about sexuality and HIV: Principles and methods for effective education.* New York: New York University Press.

Kaiser Family Foundation. (2003a). *Impact of direct-to- consumer advertising on prescription drug spending.* Menlo Park, CA.

Kaiser Family Foundation. (2003b). Some African-American women avoid Ortho Evra birth control patch citing patch's visibility on skin. *Kaiser Daily Reproductive Health Report* Retrieved January 23, 2005, from http://www .kaisernetwork.org/daily_reports/rep_index.cfm?hint=2&DR_ID=19141

Kaiser Family Foundation. (2004). Birth control and protection. *SexSmarts* Retrieved April 13, 2005, from http:// www.kff .org/entpartnerships/7106.cfm

Kaphingst, K. A., Rudd, R. E., DeJong, W., & Daltroy, L. H. (2004). Literacy demands of product information intended to supplement television direct-to-consumer prescription drug advertisements. *Patient Education and Counseling, 55*(2), 293–300.

Kellner, D. (1995). Reading images critically: Toward a post-modern pedagogy. In G. Dines & J. M. Humez (Eds.),

Gender, race, and class in the media: A text-reader (pp. 126–132). London: Sage Publications.

Kirby, D. (2002). *Do abstinence-only programs delay the initiation of sex among young people and reduce teen pregnancy?* Washington D.C.: National Campaign to Prevent Teen Pregnancy.

Laurence, L., & Weinhouse, B. (2000). Drug marketing: Selling women out. In N. Worcester & M. H. Whatley (Eds.), *Women's health: Readings on social, economic, and political issues* (3rd ed., pp. 166–174). Dubuque, IA: Kendall/Hunt Publishing Company.

Levitt, L. (2001). *Prescription drug trends.* Menlo Park, CA: Henry J. Kaiser Family Foundation.

National Institute for Health Care Management. (2001). *Prescription drugs and mass media advertising, 2000.* Washington, D.C.: National Institute for Health Care Management.

Pearson, C. (1995). Direct-to-consumer promotion of prescription drugs. Retrieved November 18, 2002, from http://www .womenshealthnetwork.org/advocacy/fulltext/tdtc.htm

Rabin, R. (2004, February 9). A hard pill to swallow: Menstrual suppression worries many. *Milwaukee Journal Sentinel*, pp. 1G, 16G.

Roberts, D. (1997). *Killing the black body: Race, reproduction, and the meaning of liberty.* New York: Random House, Inc.

Robinson, A. R., Hohmann, K. B., Rifkin, J. I., Topp, D., Gilroy, C. M., Pickard, J. A., et al. (2004). Direct-to-consumer pharmaceutical advertising: Physician and public opinion and potential effects on the physician-patient relationship. *Archives of Internal Medicine, 164*(4), 427–432.

Roth, M. S. (1996). Patterns in direct-to-consumer prescription drug print advertising and their public policy implications. *Journal of Public Policy & Marketing, 15*(1), 63–75.

Sexuality Information and Education Council of the United States. (2008). Spending for abstinence-only until marriage programs. Retrieved April 9, 2008, from http://www.siecus.org/policy/states/2006/federalGraph.html

Sloane, E. (2002). *Biology of women* (4th ed.). Albany: Delmar Publishing.

Telljohann, S. K., Symons, C. W., & Pateman, B. (2004). *Health education: Elementary and middle school applications* (4th ed.). Boston: McGraw Hill.

Trenholm, C., Devaney, B., Fortson, K., Quay, L., Wheeler, J., & Clark, M. (2007). *Impacts of Four Title V, Section 510 Abstinence Education Programs: Final Report.* Princeton, NJ: Mathematica Policy Research, Inc.

Waxman, H. A. (2004). The content of federally funded abstinence-only education programs (pp. 1–22): Committee on Government Reform—Minority Staff, United States House of Representatives.

Welch Cline, R. J., & Young, H. N. (2004). Marketing drugs, marketing healthcare relationships: A content analysis of visual cues in direct-to-consumer prescription drug advertising. *Health Communication, 16*(2), 131–157.

Wilkes, M. S., Bell, R. A., & Kravitz, R. L. (2000). Direct-to-consumer prescription drug advertising: Trends, impact, and implications. *Health Affairs, 19*(2), 110–128.

Woloshin, S., Schwartz, J. T., & Welch, H. G. (2001). Direct-to-consumer advertisements for prescription drugs: What are Americans being sold? *Lancet, 358*(9288), 1141–1146.

"The Marketing and Politics Behind the Promotion of Female Sexual Dysfunction and its "Pink Viagra""

From the *National Women's Health Network*

Female Sexual Dysfunction

The cultural impact and multi-billion dollar profitability of male impotence drugs has accelerated the race to develop and market a parallel drug treatment for women. The overnight success of Viagra, which was developed quite incidentally in an English lab in 1998 when clinical trial volunteers testing a high blood pressure medication reported a suspicious number of erections, prompted drug manufacturers to wonder if Viagra would have a similar effect on women.[1] It didn't. However, drug companies immediately attempted to create and market an expectation for a "pink Viagra." Soon thereafter, a new disease category called "Female Sexual Dysfunction" was created. Despite over a decade of research and millions of dollars spent on drug development, the U.S. Food and Drug Agency (FDA) has yet to approve a single drug treatment for women dealing with sexual problems.

This reality has promoted the pharmaceutical industry to launch a campaign headlined by many prominent women's health advocates in an effort to persuade the FDA to approve of a female sexual dysfunction drug for women. Members of the campaign called "Even the Score" are challenging the FDA on what they claim is a perpetuation of a gender bias by virtue of the claim that the FDA is holding drugs that treat women's sexual problem to a higher standard than those for erectile dysfunction. Even the Score has engaged prominent women's rights organizations, health care providers, the media and members of Congress in a public relations misinformation campaign to criticize the FDA.

There are Female Sexual Dysfunction drugs currently under FDA review, and Even the Score is attempting to move the discussion away from the safety and effectiveness of these drugs and towards controversy about gender bias.[2]

The reality is that no amount of public relations or slick marketing can get around the fact that the drugs currently being proposed for Female Sexual Dysfunction simply don't work and may be quite dangerous. Poor efficacy, a strong placebo effect, and valid safety concerns have plagued all of the drugs that have been tested so far.[3] There are many reasons why the proposed drugs may not have been effective in increasing women's sexual enjoyment; chief among them is the heterogeneity of female sexuality and, of course, research demonstrating that sexual problems are mostly shaped by interpersonal, psychological, and social factors. Nevertheless, pharmaceutical executives will continue to drum up hype over the possibility of a "pink Viagra" because the profit market for this type of drug is estimated to be over $2 billion a year.[4]

Even the Score's petition and attempts to make this a conversation about gender equality is misleading and dangerous; while the FDA should be held accountable for gender equality, it should not compromise the safety of women's health by approving a drug that is not effective and not safe. The FDA should continue to balance a serious and respectful incorporation of patient input while maintaining a rigorous, uncompromised science-based review standard for drugs and devices they approve for women.

Below are some Myths and Facts to Know about Female Sexual Dysfunction (FSD) and the Even the Score Campaign

Myth: There is a norm of female sexual function.

- **Fact:** The implied parallel between female sexual dysfunction and male impotence is actually very deceptive. The word "dysfunction"—medical jargon for anything that doesn't work the way it should — suggests that there is an acknowledged norm for female sexual function. That norm has never been established. Unlike erection, which is a quantifiable physical event, a woman's sexual response is qualitative. It reflects desire, arousal, and gratification — which are utterly subjective and rather difficult to quantify in objective clinical terms. As we all already know, sexual desire differs over time and between people for a range of reasons largely related to relationships, life situations, past experiences and personal and social expectations.

Myth: FSD is a defined disease category.

- **Fact:** Without an empirical standard by which to assess female sexual function, it is extremely difficult, if not impossible, to come up with criteria for female sexual dysfunction. But that hasn't stopped drug manufacturers from trying. Insidiously, every time a new drug sponsor touts a solution for women's sexual concerns, the purported cause of female sexual dysfunction changes. For example, when drugs affecting blood flow were being tested, the notion that women had an "insufficiency of vaginal engorgement" had scientific currency. When testosterone was proposed, claims were made that a vast number of women were suffering of a hormone deficiency. Most recently, as drugs that affect the neurotransmitters are being tested for female sexual dysfunction–we are being told that low libido is due to a chemical problem inside a woman's brain.

Myth: Drug developers are searching for a solution for women's sexual concerns.

- **Fact:** The pharmaceutical industry is driven by profit, and as such, if a solution is not found at the bottom of a pill bottle, they are simply not interested. If product-development-driven research was happening in a balanced context with proportionate attention being paid to the myriad of causes of women's sexual concerns, the focus on biomedical causes might not be so damaging. The focus on pharmaceutical rather than emotional solutions has serious limitations. The way the industry has shaped the FSD discussion threatens to make women's sexual experience, no less than men's, a performance issue. Also, without downplaying the significance of any woman's pain or distress, there can be real danger in defining *difference* as "dysfunction". There are many provocative research questions that don't attract pharmaceutical industry funding but yet would hold very important answers for women facing problems with sex, some of these include: What are the effective strategies for couples who are dealing with the impact of a major life crisis and how that affects sexual desire. What's the effect of exercise on sexual desire and does it differ by gender? How does a history of physical and sexual and gender based trauma impact women's sexual satisfaction through the course of their lives.

Myth: 43% of women suffer from FSD.

- **Fact:** There is a perception that Even the Score is trying to advance which suggests that up to 43 percent of women suffer from FSD. The disorder is so widespread that American women are breaking down drug manufacturers' doors desperately pleading for solutions for their sexual problems. The making and marketing of FSD as a distinct disease category was amplified by a 1999 Journal of American Medical Association piece which claimed that 43 percent of American women suffer from a sexual dysfunction. As should come as no surprise, the authors of the paper had financial ties to pharmaceutical companies. The 43 percent figure emerged from an analysis of responses by 1,749 women to a set of questions. Women who reported any of the following "symptoms" within the last two months — lack of sexual desire, difficulty in becoming aroused, inability to achieve orgasm, anxiety about sexual performance etc. — were considered to have sexual dysfunction. The study also found that women were more likely to suffer from sexual dysfunction if they were single, had less education, had physical or mental health problems, had undergone recent social or economic setbacks, or were dissatisfied with their relationship with a sexual partner.[5] In the years since the report's publication, researchers have revisited it and rightly challenged its conclusions.

Myth: The standard for FDA review of male impotence drugs should be the same for FSD drugs.

- **Fact:** Even the Score's gender equity argument ignores the real safety difference between FSD drugs that are currently being tested and the drugs approved for men: a different indication for use, specifically the dosage and administration. All but one of the drugs approved for men are taken on an as-needed basis, whereas the most recent drug being tested for women is a central nervous system serotonergic agent with effects on adrenaline and dopamine in the brain; it requires chronic — daily, long-term — administration. This raises toxicological concerns that make it appropriate for the FDA to subject that type of drug to an elevated safety scrutiny. Substantial adverse events reports and drop-out rates in the latest FSD trials also rightly require serious consideration.

Myth: There are 24 drugs approved for men, and none approved for women.

- **Fact:** Because several drugs have been approved for male sexual dysfunction, groups have asked whether the FDA is holding women's sexual satisfaction to a different standard. A recent blog titled "The FDA, Sexual Dysfunction and Gender Inequality" inaccurately claimed that there are 24 drugs approved for men, and zero for women.[6] This claim perpetuates a miscalculation. It counts each brand name drug and its identical generic counterparts or different formulations as unique treatment options, which artificially inflates the number of drugs available for men. In fact, there are only six different FDA-approved drugs available for male sexual dysfunction, including erectile dysfunction.[7] Nevertheless, the inflammatory claim of gender bias produced press and political attention.

More Resources

The National Women's Health Network is a non-profit advocacy organization that works to improve the health of all women. We are supported by our members, and do not take financial contributions from drug companies, medical device manufacturers, insurance companies or any other entity with a financial stake in women's health decision-making. Since the Network's founding almost 40 years ago, we have brought the voices of women to the FDA, advocating for safe and effective medical products that meet women's real life needs and a drug development process that reflects women's lived experience.

Contact Us

The National Women's Health Network is committed to ensuring that women have access to accurate, balanced information about the marketing and politics of Female Sexual Dysfunction and "Pink Viagra". For more information, email us at *healthquestions@nwhn.org* or call the Women's Health Voice at (202) 682–2646. Stay informed by connecting with us on Facebook (TheNWHN) and Twitter (@thenwhn).

REFERENCES

1. CNN Website, *Viagra: The little blue pill that could*, New York, NY: CNN, 2013. Retrieved on June 22, 2015 from: http://www.cnn.com/2013/03/27/health/viagra-anniversary-timeline/index.html.

2. Even the Score Website, *The Problem*: Even the Score, no date. Retrieved on June 22, 2015 from: http://eventhescore.org/the-problem/.

3. Food and Drug Administration Website, *Summary Minutes of the Advisory Committee for Reproductive Health Drugs Meeting*, Silver Spring, MD: Center for Drug Evaluation and Research, 2010. Retrieved on June 22, 2015 from www.fda.gov/downloads/AdvisoryCommittees/CommitteesMeetingMaterials/Drugs/ReproductiveHealthDrugsAdvisoryCommittee/UCM248751.pdf.

4. ABC News Website, *"Pink Viagra?" Drug Promises to Boost Female Sex Drive*, New York, NY: ABC News, 2010. Retrieved on June 22, 2015 from: http://abcnews.go.com/GMA/OnCall/female-viagra-pill-promises-enhance-female-libido/story?id=10731882.

5. Laumann EO, Paik A, Rosen RC, "Sexual Dysfunction in the United States: Prevalence and Predictors," *JAMA* 1999; 281(6):537-544. doi:10.1001/jama.281.6.537. Retrieved on June 22, 2015 from: http://jama.jamanetwork.com/article.aspx?articleid=188762.

6. Clayton, Anita, HuffPost Website, *The FDA, Sexual Dysfunction, and Gender INequality*, New York, NY: HuffPost, 2014. Retrieved on June 22, 2015 from: http://www.huffingtonpost.com/anita-h-clayton-md/the-fda-sexual-dysfunctio_b_4724459.html.

7. Bloom J, *Is The FDA Really Sexist?*: Science 2.0, 2014. Retrieved on June 22, 2015 from: www.science20.com/pfired_still_kicking/fda_really_sexist-130694.

Updated: 2015

"I Tried the Bleach and Failed"

By Shannon Barber

I was just reading this bit from xoJane on skin bleaching.[1]

So let me tell you a very sad story.

As a teenager I became violently self-conscious about how dark my skin was.

Outside of the usual Whiteness, beauty ideals etc. that played into it some other stuff was going on. I had some scarring from acne that turned into the deep brown to black marks I battle with to this day, I didn't know to use sunscreen (it was the 90s I believed Black skin was invincible), I couldn't find foundation or colored powder to use on my face and worst for me at the time I got rejected for a date because someone said I was just too dark.

In a perfect confluence of teenage mortification I had decided to go to some stores to look for foundation because obviously that would have fixed everything.

I remember going to three drug stores and nada. When I went to K-Mart with my parents I bought the one shade of Fashion Fair foundation they had and it was about four shades too light. I bought a stick foundation by Black Opal out of a discontinued bin and it was way the wrong color and dried out.

So I saved up about 20 or so dollars and went to the mall. I figured that if it was a fancy brand, of course I would be able to get make up.

Off I went to the mall. I went alone and y'all—I went to the fancy counters and maybe 10% (I'm being generous) of the time they had something close to my color but generally not my actual color.

At one counter the girl felt so bad she gave me this make over and I remember when I looked in the mirror I looked like an ashy faced Claire Huxtable in the worst kind of way. Frosty fuchsia lips, frosty weird brown eye shadow, my face was weird and greasy and ashy. I went into the bathroom and cried my eyes out.

I very vividly remember trying to use the hand soap to wash the shit off of my face while pretending I wasn't crying my eyes out and having people stare at me. One woman remarked to her friend that I must have gotten caught stealing.

I was fifteen or sixteen and I felt the weight of racism and racist beauty ideals weigh so heavily on me I thought I was wrong. I was made wrong and ugly and there was nothing I could do about it.

I fully believed that I was ugly because I was too Black. I did not have the bone straight silky locks I saw on Black women on TV, my face had dark marks, my knees and elbows were dark, I don't have a small button nose and I was certain I was the fattest fat girl who ever fat girled in the world.

I knew it.

Cut to a few months later I was at the dirt mall beauty supply store and came upon a skin lightening product. The woman told me if I used it I could be "fairer" and my skin would look pretty.

I went for it.

Of course I did.

I bought and used it twice a day for months.

At first I only used it on my dark spots but when those faded I used it on more of my face.

[1] http://www.xojane.com/issues/nigerian-singer-releases-whitenicious-skin-lightening-cream-and-its-sold-out—This article from 2014 discusses a celebrity endorsed skin lightening cream sold in Nigeria, where 77% of women use skin lightening products on a regular basis. While most White people in the United States may be unaware of their prevalence, these products are sold in the U.S. and many European and American companies do big business the international market for them as well. This includes Dove's parent company, Unilever, which produces the skin lightener Fair & Lovely, sold across Africa and Asia; it is particularly popular in India. *Ed.*

You know what happened?

First my skin was kind of okay and then it just really wasn't. I burned my cheeks, my little Ashanti style side-burns were burnt off, I got darker marks on my chin and a scar by my left ear that did not fade for almost a decade.

I was so ashamed of myself. And I wasn't ashamed because I had tried to bleach my face I was ashamed because I failed.

I wound up uglier than I was to begin with. I let my parents think it was just teenaged acne and to cover it I would cake on this "translucent" (read: still way too light for me) powder. When I was able to get that coveted Cover Girl OG Shade Soft Sable anything I would use it as much as I could. Unfortunately it was very hard to find even that where I lived.

I learned to pretend that I didn't care that I was ugly. I held my tongue when the White girls said disgusting things about Black girls. I never expected or was comfortable with anyone thinking I was at all attractive. I stopped caring and decided to do something about my body instead. I was yearning to be a "butterface."[2]

I tried to wear my hair so that it looked "nicer" which at the time meant to me anything but like Black hair.

I thought that if my body was good enough I could somehow transcend my ugly Blackness.

And then a few years later it all came crashing down on me when I realized that my Blackness was not the problem. This time after another attempt at bleaching my face, and more burns and scars someone finally had the sense to tell me I didn't have to do that.

A grown Black woman in Sally's Beauty supply almost slapped a jar of skin lightener out of my hands and she read me to filth and then gave me a hug.

The fact is before it dawned on me that I did not have to participate in my own oppression I had no idea.

I wish I had known her name, I have her to thank for my years and years of social justice stuff. I have her to thank for that seed of rebellion that has led to me preaching the gospel of look how the fuck you want to look.

So the lesson today my darlings is that sometimes all it takes to get someone out of a destructive set of behaviors or pattern of beliefs is to tell them that there are other options.

So this is me telling you.

You don't have to do it.

You don't have to participate in your own subjugation, in your own oppression or in these destructive systems of belief. It is so hard to break away from them but if I, wee little scared baby Shannon could do it without the internet or any support you can do it right here, with the rest of the homies with you.

We can.

We can because we need to survive and we don't want to be hurt anymore.

Homo Out.

---

[2]This term refers to a girl or woman who has a conventionally attractive body but a conventionally unattractive face: everything "but-her-face" is attractive. Barber has also written extensively about bodies and fat, including a piece written specifically for this volume. *Ed.*

REPRODUCTIVE JUSTICE AND TECHNOLOGY

The Color of Choice
"White Supremacy and Reproductive Justice"

By Loretta J. Ross[1]

> [T]he regulation of reproduction and the exploitation of women's bodies and labor is both a tool and a result of systems of oppression based on race, class, gender, sexuality, ability, age and immigration status.[2]

It is impossible to understand the resistance of women of color to the reproductive politics of both the Right and the Left without first comprehending how the system of white supremacy constructs different destinies for each ethnic population of the United States through targeted, yet diffuse, policies of population control. Even a cursory examination of the reproductive politics dominating today's headlines—such as debates on abortion and welfare—reveals that some women are encouraged to have more children while others are discouraged. Why are some women glorified as mothers while others have their motherhood rights contested? Why are there obstacles for women who seek abortions while our society neglects mothers and children already here? As we move toward "designer babies" made possible by advances in assisted reproductive technologies, does anyone truly believe that all women will have an equal right to benefit from these "new reproductive choices," that children of all races will be promoted, or that vulnerable women will not be exploited?

Women of color reproductive justice activists oppose all political rationales, social theories, and genetic justifications for reproductive oppression against communities of color, whether through blatant policies of sterilization abuse or through the coercive use of dangerous contraceptives. Instead, women of color activists demand "reproductive justice," which requires the protection of women's human rights to achieve the physical, mental, spiritual, political, economic and social well-being of women and girls.[3] Reproductive justice goes far beyond the demand to eliminate racial disparities in reproductive health services, and beyond the right-to-privacy-based claims to legal abortion made by the pro-choice movement and dictated and limited by the U.S. Supreme Court. A reproductive justice analysis addresses the fact that progressive issues are divided, isolating advocacy for abortion from other social justice issues relevant to the lives of every woman. In the words of SisterSong president Toni Bond, "We have to reconnect women's health and bodies with the rest of their lives."[4] In short, reproductive justice can be described as reproductive rights embedded in a human rights and social justice framework used to counter all forms of population control that deny women's human rights.

White Supremacy and Population Control on the Right, and Left

> Population control is necessary to maintain the normal operation of US commercial interests around the world. Without our trying to help these countries with their economic and social development, the world would rebel against the strong US commercial presence.[5]

Although the United States does not currently have an explicit population control policy, population control ideologies march from the margins to the mainstream of reproductive politics and inform policies promoted by the Right and the Left. Fears of being numerically and politically overwhelmed by people of color bleach meaning from any alternative interpretations of the constellation of population control policies that restrict immigration by people of color, encourage sterilization and contraceptive abuse of people of color, and incarcerate upwards of 2 million people, the vast majority of whom are people of color.

The expanded definition of white supremacy as I use it in this essay is an interlocking system of racism, patriarchy, homophobia, ultranationalism, xenophobia, anti-Semitism, and religious fundamentalism that creates a complex matrix of oppressions faced by people of color in the United States. As a tenacious ideology in practice, it is evidenced on both the Right and the Left—in the Far Right, the Religious Right, paleoconservatives, neoconservatives, neoliberals, and liberals. Abby Ferber, a researcher on the intersection of race, gender, and white supremacy, writes that "defining white supremacy as extremist in its racism often has the result of absolving the mainstream population of its racism, portraying white supremacists as the racist fringe in contrast to some non-racist majority."[6]

White supremacy not only defines the character of debates on reproductive politics but it also explains and predicts the borders of the debate. In other words, what Americans think as a society about women of color and population control is determined and informed by their relationship to white supremacy as an ideology, and these beliefs affect the country's reproductive politics. Both conservatives and liberals enforce a reproductive hierarchy of privatization and punishment that targets the fertility, motherhood, and liberty of women of color.

Population control policies are externally imposed by governments, corporations, or private agencies to control—by increasing or limiting—population growth and behavior, usually by controlling women's reproduction and fertility. All national population policies, even those developed for purportedly benign reasons, put women's empowerment at risk. Forms of population control include immigration restrictions, selective population movement or dispersal, incarceration, and various forms of discrimination, as well as more blatant manifestations, such as cases in which pregnant illegal immigrants and incarcerated women are forced to have abortions. According to a 1996 study by Human Rights Watch, abuses of incarcerated women not only include denial of adequate health care, but pressure to seek an abortion, particularly if the woman is impregnated by a prison guard.[7]

Meanwhile, impediments are placed in the way of women who voluntarily choose to terminate their pregnancies. The only logic that explains this apparent moral inconsistency is one that examines precisely who is subjected to which treatment and who is affected by which reproductive policy at which time in history. Women of color have little trouble distinguishing between those who are encouraged to have more children and those who are not, and understanding which social, political, and economic forces influence these determinations.

Population control policies are by no means exclusively a twentieth-century phenomenon. During the Roman Empire, the state was concerned with a falling birthrate among married upper-class couples. As has been the case for elite classes throughout history, procreation was seen as a duty to society. Emperor Augustus consequently enacted laws containing positive and negative incentives to reproduction, promoting at least three children per couple and discouraging childlessness.[8] Augustus probably knew that the falling birthrate was not a result of abstention among Roman men and women, but rather of contraceptive and abortifacient use by Roman women to control their fertility. Through legislation, he asserted the state's interest in compelling citizens to have more children for the good of society.[9] Because no ancient Roman texts offer the perspectives of women on this issue, it is difficult to ascertain what women thought of this territorial assertion of male privilege over their private lives. However, the Roman birthrate continued to decline despite the emperor's orders, suggesting that Roman women probably did what most women have done throughout the ages: make the decisions that make sense for them and refuse to allow men to control their fertility. As historian Rickie Solinger points out, "The history of reproductive politics will always be in part a record of women controlling their reproductive capacity, no matter what the law says, and by those acts reshaping the law."[10]

Despite the Roman failure to impose the state's will on individual human reproductive behavior, many governments today have refused to recognize the virtual impossibility of regulating human reproductive behavior through national population policies. China and Romania have instituted population control measures with catastrophic results. Even governments seeking to achieve their population objectives through more benign policies, such as offering financial incentives for women to have children, can only report negligible results. Despite government and moralistic pronouncements, women perceive their reproductive decisions as private, like their periods and other health concerns. Even when the law, the church, or their partners oppose their decisions, they tend to make the decision about whether or not to use birth control or abortion, or to parent, for themselves.

This lived reality has not stopped lawmakers from trying to assert control oven women's reproduction. Who gets targeted for positive, pronatalist policies encouraging childbirth versus negative, antinatalist policies that discourage childbirth is determined by powerful elites, informed by prejudices based on race, class, sexual identity, and immigration status. Policies that restrict abortion access, distort sex and sexuality education, impose parental notification requirements for minors, allow husbands to veto options for abortion, and limit use of emergency and regular contraception all conspire to limit access to fertility control to white women, especially young white women. Meanwhile, women of color face intimidating obstacles to making reproductive choices, including forced contraception, sterilization abuse, and, in the case of poor women and women of color on social assistance, welfare family caps. These population control policies have both domestic and international dimensions, which are rarely linked in the minds of those who believe that the struggle is principally about abortion.

Internationally, the fertility rate of women of color is the primary preoccupation of those determined to impose population controls on developing countries. According to the United Nations, in 2000, more than one hundred countries worldwide had large "youth bulges"—people aged fifteen to twenty-nine accounted for more than 40% of all adults. All of these extremely youthful countries are in the developing world, where fertility rates are highest, and most are in sub-Saharan Africa and the Middle East. Many of the young people who make up these "youth bulges" face dismal prospects because of deliberate underdevelopment. Over the past decade, youth unemployment rates have risen to more than double the over-all global unemployment rate. In the absence of a secure livelihood, many experts believe that discontented youth may resort to violence or turn to insurgent organizations as sources of social mobility and self-esteem. Recent studies show that countries with large youth bulges were roughly two and a half times more likely to experience an outbreak of civil conflict than countries below this benchmark.[11]

To respond to these alarming trends, many on the Right and the Left want to restrict the growth of developing world populations, and in this context, "family planning" becomes a tool to fight terrorism and civil unrest. Some on the Left want to increase access to family planning, economic development, and education as a way to curb population growth, even if achieved through the coercive use of contraceptives and sterilization. Some on the Right prefer military interventions and economic domination to achieve population control.

The Bush administration's family planning and HIV/AIDS policies are also having the impact of serving as tools of population control in the Global South. The US government's "ABC program" (A is for abstinence, B is for being faithful, and C for condom use) is purportedly designed to reduce the spread of HIV/AIDS. Critics of the policy point out that the ABC approach offers no option for girls or women coerced into sex, for married women who are trying to get pregnant yet have unfaithful husbands, or for victims of rape and incest who have no control over when and under what conditions they will be forced to engage in sexual activity. As a result, instead of decreasing the spread of HIV/AIDS, some suspect the ABC policy of actually increasing the ravages of the disease. In combination with the US government's failure to provide funding for and access to vital medications for individuals infected with HIV, the effects are deadly.

Meanwhile, right-wing policies that appear to be pro-natalist—such as the Global Gag Rule which prohibits clinics in developing countries that receive USAID funds from discussing abortion—are, in fact, achieving the opposite result. Catering to its radical antiabortion base, the Bush administration has withdrawn funds from programs for family planning for women around the world, withholding $136 million in funding for the United Nations Population Fund (UNFPA) since 2002. This money could have prevented at least 1.5 million induced abortions, 9,400 maternal deaths, and 154,000 infant and child deaths.[12] In September 2005, the U.S. State Department announced that it was denying funding to UNFPA for the fourth year.

One might ask why staunch conservatives are opposed to family planning in developing countries when family planning so clearly limits population growth and reduces the need for abortions. One of the leading causes of death for women in developing countries is maternal mortality—death from childbirth. The UN estimated a worldwide total of 529,000 maternal deaths in the year 2000, with less than 1% of deaths occurring in developed nations.[13] Women of color cannot help but observe that family planning is not nearly as efficient in reducing populations of color as factors such as maternal mortality, infant mortality, and AIDS. We are also not oblivious to the wealth of natural resources like oil, gold, and diamonds in the lands where these populations are shrinking—after all, a depopulated land cannot protect itself.

Overt and covert population control polices are also at play on the domestic front. In October 2005, former secretary of education William Bennett declared on his radio talk show that if "you wanted to reduce crime . . . if that were your sole purpose, you could abort every Black baby in this country, and your crime rate would go down." While Bennett conceded that aborting all African American babies "would be an impossible, ridiculous, and morally reprehensible thing to do," he still maintained that "the crime rate would go down."

Bennett is merely echoing widespread perceptions by many radical and moderate conservatives in the United States who directly link social ills with the fertility of women of color. The Heritage Foundation, a right-wing think tank influential in the national debates on reproductive politics, offers the following analysis: "Far more important than residual material hardship is behavioral poverty: a breakdown in the values and conduct that lead to the formation of healthy families, stable personalities, and self-sufficiency. This includes eroded work ethic and dependency, lack of educational aspiration and achievement, inability or unwillingness to control one's children, *increased single parenthood and illegitimacy* [emphasis added], criminal activity, and drug and alcohol abuse."[14]

This mainstream white supremacist worldview is based on the notion that people are poor because of behaviors, not because they are born into poverty. In reality, according to Zillah Eisenstein, "poverty is tied to family structures in crisis. Poverty is tied to the unavailability of contraceptives and reproductive rights. Poverty is tied to teenage pregnancy. Poverty is tied to women's wages that are always statistically lower than men's. Poverty is tied to the lack of day care for women who must work. Poverty is tied to insufficient health care for women. Poverty is tied to the lack of access to job training and education."[15]

It would be logical to assume that people who claim to value all human life from the moment of conception would fiercely support programs that help disadvantaged children and parents. Sadly, this is not the case. Surveys show that, on average, people who are strongly opposed to abortion are also more likely to define themselves as political conservatives who do not support domestic programs for poor families, single mothers, people of color, and immigrants.[16] They are also opposed to overseas development assistance in general, and to specific programs for improving women's and children's health, reducing domestic violence, helping women become more economically self-sufficient, and lowering infant mortality.[17]

Perspectives from the Left are hardly more reassuring to women of color. Is Bennett, a member of the Heritage Foundation, any worse than an environmentalist who claims that the world is overpopulated and drastic measures must be taken to address this catastrophe? Betsy Hartmann writes about the "greening of hate," or blaming environmental degradation, urban sprawl, and diminishing natural resources on poor populations of color. This is a widely accepted set of racist myths promoted by many in the environmental movement,

which is moving rather alarmingly to the right as it absorbs ideas and personnel from the white supremacist movement, including organizations such as the Aryan Women's League.[18]

The reality is that 20% of the world's population controls 80% of the global wealth. In other words, it is not the population growth of the developing world that is depleting the world's resources, but the overconsumption of these resources by the richest countries in the world. The real fear of many in the population control movement is that the developing world will become true competitors for the earth's resources and demand local control over their natural wealth of oil and minerals. Rather than perceiving overconsumption by Americans, agricultural mismanagement, and the military-industrial complex as the main sources of environmental degradation, many U.S. environmentalists maintain that the fertility of poor women is the root of environmental evil, and cast women of color, immigrant women, and women of the Global South as the perpetrators, rather than the victims, of environmental degradation.[19] This myth promotes alarmist fears about overpopulation, and leads to genocidal conclusions such as those reached by writers for *Earth First! Journal* who said, "The AIDS virus may be Gaia's tailor-made answer to human overpopulation," and that famine should take its natural course to stem overpopulation.[20]

Population control groups on the Left will often claim that they are concerned with eliminating gender and economic inequalities, racism, and colonialism, but since these organizations address these issues through a problematic paradigm, inevitably their efforts are directed toward reducing population growth of all peoples in theory and of people of color in reality.[21] In fact, these efforts are embedded within the context of a dominant neoliberal agenda which trumps women's health and empowerment. And some prochoice feminists have supported the neoliberal projects of "privatization, commodification, and deregulation of public health services that . . . have led to diminished access and increasing mortality and morbidity of women who constitute the most vulnerable groups in both developing and developed countries."[27]

Similarly, the prochoice movement, largely directed by middle-class white women, is oblivious to the role of white supremacy in restricting reproductive options for all women, and, as a result, often inadvertently colludes with it. For instance, a study published in 2001 in the *Quarterly Journal of Economics* by John J. Donohue III, a professor of law at Stanford University, and Steven D. Levitt, a professor of economics at the University of Chicago, claimed that the 1973 legalization of abortion prevented the birth of unwanted children who were likely to have become criminals. Of course, the authors state that these children would have been born to poor women of color. They also disingenuously and incorrectly assert that "women who have abortions are those most at risk to give birth to children who would engage in criminal activity"[23] and conclude that the drop in crime rates approximately eighteen years after the *Roe v. Wade* decision was a consequence of legal abortion. Despite the quickly revealed flaws in their research, some prochoice advocates continue to tout their findings as justification for keeping abortion legal, adopting a position similar to Mr. Bennett's.[24]

Indeed, the prochoice movement's failure to understand the intersection between race, class, and gender led leaders of the movement to try their own "Southern Strategy" in the 1980s. Central to this strategy was an appeal to conservative voters who did not share concerns about women's rights, but who were hostile to the federal government and its public encroachment on individual choice and privacy. Some voters with conser-vative sympathies were pruned from the anti-abortion movement for a while, uneasily joining the ranks of the prochoice movement in an admittedly unstable alliance based on "states' rights" segregationist tendencies.[25] Not surprisingly, on questions of abortion policy—whether the government should spend tax money on abortions for poor women or whether teenagers should have to obtain parental consent for abortions—the alliance fell apart. And this appeal to conservative, libertarian Southern voters drove an even deeper wedge in the pro-choice movement, divorcing it from its original base of progressive white women and alienating women of color.

Meanwhile, the Right pursued its population control policies targeting communities of color both overtly and indirectly. Family planning initiatives in the Deep South in the 1950s encouraged women of color (predominantly African American women) to use contrceptives and sterilizations to reduce the growth of our populations, while obstacles were simultaneously placed in the paths of white women seeking access to these same services. A Louisiana judge, Leander Perez, was quoted as saying, "The best way to hate a nigger is to hate him before he is born."[26] This astonishingly frank outburst represented the sentiments of many racists during this period, although the more temperate ones disavowed gutter epithets.

For example, conservative politicians like Strom Thurmond supported family planning in the 1960s when it was used as a racialized form of population control, aimed at limiting Black voter strength in African American communities.[27] When it was presented as a race-directed strategy to reduce their Black populations, North Carolina and South Carolina became the first states to include family planning in their state budgets in the 1950s. One center in Louisiana reported that in its first year of operation, 96% of its clients were Black. The proportion of white clients never rose above 15%.[28] Generally speaking, family planning associated with women of color was most frequently supported; but support quickly evaporated when it was associated with white women.

Increased federal spending on contraception coincided with the urban unrest and rise of a militant Civil Rights movement in the late 1960s. In 1969, President Nixon asked Congress to establish a five-year plan for providing family planning services to "all those who want them but cannot afford them."[29] However, the rationale behind the proposed policy was to prevent population increases among Blacks—this would make governance of the world in general, and inner cities in particular, difficult. Reflecting concerns strikingly similar to those driving U.S. population policies overseas, Nixon pointed to statistics that showed a "bulge" in the number of Black Americans between the ages of five and nine. This group of youngsters who would soon enter their teens—"an age group with problems that can create social turbulence"—was 25% larger than ten years before.[30] This scarcely disguised race—and class-based appeal for population control persuaded many Republicans to support family planning.

Today the U.S. government's less obvious—but no less effective—approach of promoting policies overseas that contribute to high maternal mortality rates and devastation as a result of HIV/AIDS was also recently revealed to have a counterpart on the domestic front. Images of chaos and death as Hurricane Katrina's floodwaters engulfed Black neighborhoods shocked many Americans. But according to Jean Hardisty, a researcher on white supremacy in America, these pictures of poor New Orleans residents, many of them Black women and their children, revealed some essential truths:

> Much of the white public will never understand that those images were more than the result of neglected enforcement of civil rights laws, or the "failure" of the poor to rise above race and class. They were images of structural racism. In one of the poorest cities in the country (with 28% of New Orleanians living in poverty—over two times the national poverty rate), the poor were white as well as African American. But, the vast majority (84%) of the poor were Black. This is not an accident. It is the result of white supremacy that is so imbedded in US society that it has become part of the social structure. Structural racism is not only a failure to

serve people equally across race, culture and ethnic origin within private and government entities (as well as "third sector" institutions, such as the print, radio and TV media and Hollywood). It is also the predictable consequence of legislation at the federal, state, and local level.[31]

This racial illiteracy on the part of white people is part of the hegemonic power of whiteness. Through a historical mythology, white supremacy has a vested interest in denying what is most obvious: the privileged position of whiteness. For most people who are described as white, since race is believed to be "something" that shapes the lives of people of color, they often fail to recognize the ways in which their own lives and our public policies are shaped by race. Structural or institutionalized racism is not merely a matter of individual attitudes, but the result of centuries of subordination and objectification that reinforce population control policies.

Politicians have continuously used policies of population control to conquer this land, produce an enslaved workforce, enshrine racial inequities, and preserve traditional power relations. For just as long, women of color have challenged race-based reproductive politics, including the forced removal of our children; the racialization and destruction of the welfare system; the callousness of the foster care system that breaks up our families; and the use of the state to criminalize our pregnancies and our children. These become an interlocked set of public policies which Dorothy Roberts calls 'reproductive punishment.' She observes that the "system's racial disparity also reinforces negative stereotypes about . . . people's incapacity to govern themselves and need for state supervision."[32]

Reproductive politics are about who decides "whether, when, and which woman can reproduce legitimately and *also* the struggles over which women have the right to be mothers of the children they bear."[33] Entire communities can be monitored and regulated by controlling how, when, and how many children a woman can have and keep. This is particularly true for women on Native American reservations, incarcerated women, immigrant women, and poor women across the board, whose reproductive behavior is policed by an adroit series of popular racist myths, fierce state regulation, and eugenicist control. The use of the "choice" framework in the arena of abortion, as Rhonda Copelon points outs, underwrites "the conservative idea that the personal is separate from the political, and that the larger social structure has no impact on [or responsibility for] private, individual choice."[34]

For the past thirty years, women of color have urged the mainstream movement to seriously and consistently support government funding for abortions for poor women. The 1977 Hyde Amendment prohibited the use of taxpayer funds to pay for abortions for women whose health care is dependent on the federal government, and it affects women on Medicaid, women in the military and the Peace Corps, and indigenous women who primarily rely on the Indian Health Service for their medical care. Yet despite its obvious targeting of poor women of color, prochoice groups have not made repealing the Hyde Amendment a priority because polling data has indicated that the majority of Americans do not want taxpayer money used to pay for abortions.

When the Freedom of Choice Act was proposed by prochoice groups in 1993, it retained the provisions of the Hyde Amendment. According to Andrea Smith, one NARAL Pro-Choice America (formerly known as the National Abortion Rights Action League) petition in favor of the act stated that, "the Freedom of Choice Act (FOCA) will secure the original vision of *Roe v. Wade*, giving *all* women reproductive freedom and securing that right for future generations [emphasis added].[35] As Smith wryly points out, apparently poor women and indigenous women did not qualify as "women" in the eyes of the writers of this petition.

In a 1973 editorial, the National Council of Negro Women pointed out the link between civil rights activism and reproductive oppression that mitigated the concept of choice for oppressed communities:

> The key words are "if she chooses." Bitter experience has taught the Black woman that the administration of justice in this country is not colorblind. Black women on welfare have been forced to accept sterilization in exchange for a continuation of relief benefits and others have been sterilized without their knowledge or consent. A young pregnant woman recently arrested for civil rights activities in North Carolina was convicted and told that her punishment would be to have a forced abortion. We must be ever vigilant that what appears on the surface to be a step forward, does not in fact become yet another fetter or method of enslavement.[36]

Yet currently the hard-core Right has begun to demand the political disenfranchisement of people receiving public assistance. For example, in 2005 a law was proposed in Georgia that would have required voters to have driver's licenses or other forms of state identification to vote; right-wing proponents complained that the bill didn't go far enough, and that the vote should be taken away from welfare recipients.[37] And while linking political enfranchisement to population control is blatantly coercive and antidemocratic, it has not been unusual in the United States. In 1960, when the city of New Orleans was ordered to desegregate its schools, local officials responded by criminalizing the second pregnancies of women on public assistance; after they were threatened with imprisonment and welfare fraud, many of these African American women and children disappeared from the welfare rolls.[38] The Right is often blatant in its determination to restrict the fertility of women of color, and thus control our communities. They endlessly proffer an array of schemes and justifications for intruding on the personal decisions of women of color and for witholding the social supports necessary to make healthy reproductive decisions.

On the other hand, in its singular focus on maintaining the legal right to abortion, the prochoice movement often ignores the intersectional matrix of race, gender, sovereignty, class and immigration status that complicates debates on reproductive politics in the United States for women of color. The movement is *not* the personal property of middle-class white women, but without a frank acknowledgement of white supremacist practices in the past and the present, women of color will not be convinced that mainstream prochoice activists and organizations are committed to empowering women of color to make decisions about our fertility, or to reorienting the movement to include the experiences of *all* women.

Mobilizing for Reproductive Justice

Prior to the 1980s, women of color reproductive health activists organized primarily against sterilization abuse and teen pregnancy, yet many were involved in early activities to legalize abortion because of the disparate impact illegal abortion had in African American, Puerto Rican, and Mexican communities. Most women of color refrained from joining mainstream pro-choice organizations, preferring instead to organize autonomous women of color organizations that were more directly responsive to the needs of their communities. The rapid growth of women of color reproductive health organizations in the 1980s and 1990s helped build the organizational strength (in relative terms) to generate an analysis and a new movement in the twenty-first century.

This was a period of explosive autonomous organizing.[39] Women of color searched for a conceptual framework that would convey our twinned values—the right to have and not to have a child—as well as the myriad ways our rights to be mothers and parent our children are constantly threatened. We believed these values and concerns separated us from the liberal pro-choice movement in the United States, which was preoccupied with privacy rights and maintaining the legality of abortion. We were also skeptical about leaders in the pro-choice movement who seemed more interested in population restrictions than women's empowerment.

Some promoted dangerous contraceptives and coercive sterilizations, and were mostly silent about economic inequalities and power imbalances between the developed and the developing worlds. Progressive women of color felt closest to the radical wing of the women's movement that articulated demands for abortion access amd shared our class analysis, and even closer to radical feminists who demanded an end to sterilization and contraceptive abuse. Yet we lacked a framework that aligned reproductive rights with social justice in an intersectional way, bridging the multiple domestic and global movements to which we belonged.

We found an answer in the global women's health movement through the voices of women from the Global South. By forming small but significant delegations, women of color from the United States participated in all of the international conferences and significant events of the global feminist movement. A significant milestone was the International Conference on Population and Development in 1994 in Cairo, Egypt. In Cairo, women of color witnessed how women in other countries were successfully using a human rights framework in their advocacy for reproductive health and sexual rights.

Shortly after the Cairo conference, drawing on the perspectives of women of color engaged in both domestic and international activism, women of color in the United States coined the term "reproductive justice." In particular, we made the link between poverty and the denial of women's human rights, and critiqued how shared opposition to fundamentalists and misogynists strengthened a problematic alliance between feminists and the population control establishment.

The first step toward implementing a reproductive justice framework in our work was taken two months after the September Cairo conference. A group of African American women (some of whom became cofounders of the SisterSong Women of Color Reproductive Health Collective) spontaneously organized an informal Black Women's Caucus at a national pro-choice conference sponsored in 1994 by the Illinois Pro-Choice Alliance in Chicago. We were attempting to "Bring Cairo Home" by adapting agreements from the Cairo program of action to a US-specific context. In the immediate future, we were very concerned that the Clinton administration's health care reform proposals were ominously silent about abortion rights, which appeared to renege on the promises the Administration made at Cairo. Even without a structured organization, we mobilized for a national signature ad in the *Washington Post* to express our concerns, raising twenty-seven thousand dollars and collecting six hundred signatures from African American women to place the ad in the *Post*. After debating and rejecting the choice framework in our deliberations, we called ourselves Women of African Descent for Reproductive Justice. We defined reproductive justice, at that time as "reproductive health integrated into social justice," bespeaking our perception that reproductive health is a social justice issue for women of color because healthcare reform without a reproductive health component would do more harm than good for women of color. Three years later, using human rights as a unifying framework and reproductive justice as a central organizing concept, the SisterSong Women of Color Reproductive Health Collective was formed in 1997 by autonomous women of color organizations.

SisterSong maintains that reproductive justice—the complete physical, mental, spiritual, political, economic, and social well-being of women and girls—will be achieved when women and girls have the economic, social, and political power and resources to make healthy decisions about our bodies, sexuality, and reproduction for ourselves, our families, and our communities in all areas of our lives. For this to become a reality, we need to make change on the individual, community, institutional, and societal levels to end all forms of oppression, including forces that deprive us of self-determination and control over our bodies, and limit our reproductive choices to achieve undivided justice.[40]

An instructive example of how the reproductive justice framework employed by SisterSong has influenced the mainstream movement is the organizing story behind the March for Women's Lives in Washington, D.C., on April 25, 2004. The march, which mobilized 1.15 million participants, was the largest demonstration in US history. Originally organized to protest anti-woman policies (such as the badly named Partial Birth Abortion Ban Act) and to call attention to the delicate pro-choice majority on the Supreme Court, it also exposed fissures in the pro-choice movement that have not been fully analyzed.

Mobilizing for the march uncovered cleavages on the Left. The event's original title, the "March for Freedom of Choice," reflected a traditional focus on a privacy-based abortion rights framework established by the Supreme Court. At the same time, the dominant issue on the American Left was the illegal war against Iraq, not abortion politics. Tens of millions of people had marched around the globe to protest Bush's invasion in February 2003. As the initial organizing for the march progressed in 2003, it became clear that targeted supporters would not turn out in sufficient numbers if the march focused solely on the right to legal abortion and the need to protect the Supreme Court. Abortion isolated from other social justice issues would not work.

Ultimately, in order to broaden the appeal of the march and mobilize the entire spectrum of social jus-

tice activists in the United States, organizers sought a strategic framework that could connect various sectors of US social justice movements. They approached SisterSong in the fall of 2003, asking for endorsement of and participation in the march. SisterSong pushed back, expressing problems with the march title and the then all-white decision-makers on the steering committee. SisterSong demanded that women of color organizations be added to the highest decision-making body, and counteroffered with its own "reproductive justice" framework. (The original March organizers were the Feminist Majority Foundation, the National Organization for Women, Planned Parenthood Federation of America, and NARAL Pro-Choice America. Eventually, the National Latina Institute for Reproductive Health, the Black Women's Health Imperative and the American Civil Liberties Union were added to the march steering committee.) Reproductive justice was a viable way to mobilize broader support for the march. It also had the potential to revitalize an admittedly disheartened pro-choice movement. The central question was: were pro-choice leaders ready and willing to finally respect the leadership and vision of women of color?

Through the leadership of Alice Cohan, the march director, the March for Freedom of Choice was renamed in the fall of 2003, and women of color organizations were added to the steering committee. Using the intersectional, multi-issue approach fundamental to the reproductive justice framework, march organizers reached out to women of color, civil rights organizations, labor, youth, antiwar groups, anti-globalization activists, environmentalists, immigrants' rights organizations, and many, many others.

The success of the march was a testament to the power of reproductive justice as a framework to mobilize and unite diverse sectors of the social justice movement to support women's human rights in the United States and abroad. Just as importantly, it also showed how women of color have to take on the Right and the Left when asserting control over our bodies, our communities, and our destinies.

> I am not wrong: Wrong is not my name
> My name is my own my own my own
> and I can't tell you who in the hell set things up
>   like this
> but I can tell you that from now on my resistance
> my simple and daily and nightly self-
>   determination
> may very well cost you your life.
>
> —**June Jordan**

NOTES

A list of end notes is available in the original source.

"The Need for Different Voices: Revisiting Reproductive Justice, Health and Rights"

By Grace Adofoli

For the *National Women's Health Network*

Article taken from November/December 2013 Newsletter

As an African woman, I come from a place where sexual and reproductive health is not explicitly discussed or confronted like it is here. I've long struggled to understand the ways that issues and concepts like Reproductive Justice, Reproductive Health, and Reproductive Rights fit together and interact within the women's health movement. So, I was delighted to have the opportunity, as a NWHN intern, to attend the United Nations' 57th session of the Commission on the Status of Women (CSW57), and participate in the dialogues about these issues and women's rights. (CSW57 was held in March 2013, at the United Nations' headquarters in New York City.)

I am very interested in women's health research and advocacy to end sexual violence. My career goal is to help change policies and create global networks that improve women's status around the world, specifically on the African continent. What I learned at CSW57 is that you cannot impact sexual violence without considering Reproductive Justice, reproductive health, and reproductive rights—they are all intertwined.

These terms—"Reproductive Justice," "Reproductive Health," and "Reproductive Rights"—are often used interchangeably, but they are rooted in "different analyses, strategies, and constituencies.[1] Reproductive Justice (often just called "RJ") is defined as the physical, spiritual, political, economic, and social wellbeing of women and girls. It merges the concepts of reproductive health and social justice.[2] RJ "is based on the human right to make personal decisions about one's life, and the obligation of government and society to ensure that the conditions are suitable for implementing one's decisions."[2] Proponents say that it "will be achieved when women and girls have economic, social, and political power and resources to make healthy decisions about our bodies, sexuality, and reproduction for ourselves, our families and our communities in all areas of our lives."[2]

"Reproductive Health" (RH) specifically promotes people's ability to "have a responsible, satisfying and safe sex life and . . . the capability to reproduce and the freedom to decide if, when and how often to do so."[3] RH is about helping people access reproductive health information and services—including contraception and childbirth care. Reproductive and sexual health problems (like HIV/AIDS, maternal mortality, lack of contraception access, and teen pregnancy) are much worse in low-income communities and communities of color, due to factors like the high cost of services, lack of transportation, and restrictive laws and policies. RH is about overcoming these barriers to affordable, accessible, and culturally competent services.[1]

"Reproductive Rights" (RR) refers to efforts to ensure people have the legal and political ability to make their own sexual and reproductive choices. The term, coined by the pro-choice movement in the 1980s, focuses on creating the legal protection, laws, and/or enforcement of laws that ensure an individual's (usually women's) "legal right to reproductive health care services" and information.[2, 4]

These frameworks—Reproductive Justice, Reproductive Health, and Reproductive Rights—encompass different aspects of the lives of women from all backgrounds. At CSW57, different organizations and groups connected these frameworks to sexual violence. Sexual violence is costly and harmful to woman, particularly for 16-to-24-year-olds, who are at a greater risk. It limits the woman's ability to manage her life (and her reproductive health) and exposes her to sexually transmitted infections (STIs). According to Future Without

Violence, girls who are abused by their boyfriends are five times as likely to be forced into having sex without a condom, and eight times more likely to be pressured to become pregnant.[4]

After participating in CSW57, I've concluded that collaboration between sexual violence prevention and reproductive frameworks is needed to address the issues of violence against women. A broad view is needed because, when it comes to these issues, no one-size-fits-all solution exists; understanding the individual's unique personal situation is imperative when addressing violence against women. The different frameworks of RJ, RH, and RR can impact sexual violence in multiple ways—by addressing oppression, poverty and economic status, lack of social support, negative legal systems, cultural stigma against rape, immigration, and barriers to services. One can focus on one framework or another, but only by affecting all three will real change occur.

I attended CSW57 eager to learn about applying these frameworks in the international context to promote women's health. While attending CSW57, I found myself in conversations that made me uncomfortable, because I realized that not everyone was on the same page about Reproductive Justice, Health, and Rights. For example, an older African woman asked: "Do they want our kids to get pregnant and abort the babies? I need someone to explain to me what 'reproductive' means." This just reminded me that the frameworks have to be clearly expressed and the goals communicated as part of promoting them.

While attending CSW57, I realized that the heterogeneity of these frameworks can be prioritized in different ways in different countries. For example, Africa has 54 countries and countless tribes, traditions, cultures, and languages—but people tend to group Africa into one category and discount its diversity. Hence, in the African context, efforts to advance Reproductive Justice, Reproductive Health, and Reproductive Rights will vary depending on the specific country. For example, in Sudan and Congo, the major reproductive and sexual health issue might be combating violence against women, protecting women from rape, and providing access to clinics in times of conflict and war. On the other hand, in countries like Zambia and Ghana, which are more stable, the main focus might be reducing the very high rates of maternal mortality.

All of these efforts fit into the larger framework of women's reproductive justice, rights, and health. From a rights perspective, it is important to pass laws that defend women who have been abused and encourage stern prosecution of abusers. In relation to reproductive rights, policies are needed to expand women's access to services (like contraception and abortion) that help them avoid unplanned pregnancies and STIs. Providing reproductive health services that cater to women's needs enables them to act upon the best decisions about their bodies. Each community and country must determine which issues are most significant to them and where they want to put their energies.

The RJ, RR, and RH frameworks all provide a lens through which to understand, and work on, women's health problems that range from sexual violence to pregnancy prevention. In order to be successful, these movements have to be grounded in specific cultures and respond to issues that are that community's top priority.

For more information, follow organizations like Every Mother Counts; Our Bodies, Ourselves; the United Nations; Ipas; Amnesty International; Madre; and NWHN—just to mention a few. They are taking the lead on expanding the work and conversations within Reproductive Justice, Reproductive Health, and Reproductive Rights frameworks internationally.

Grace Adofoli is a graduate from University of Wisconsin-River Falls. She interned at NWHN in the spring of 2013 and plans to pursue her graduate degree in women's health and policy. She also hopes to receive her PhD in Public Health after the completion of her Master's.

REFERENCES

1. Silliman J M, Undivided Rights: Women of Color Organize for Reproductive Justice, Cambridge MA: South End Press, 2004.

2. Forward Together (formerly Asian Communities for Reproductive Justice), A New Vision for Advancing Our Movement for Reproductive Health, Reproductive Rights and Reproductive Justice, Oakland CA: Forward Together, 2005.

3. World Health Organization (WHO), Health Topics: Reproductive Health, Geneva: WHO, 2013. Available online at: http://www.who.int/topics/reproductive_health/en/

4. Futures Without Violence, The Facts on Reproductive Health and Partner Abuse. San Francisco: Futures Without Violence, no date. Available online at: http://www.futureswithoutviolence.org/userfiles/file/Children_and_Families/Reproductive.pdf

"Contraceptive Options and Decision Making"

By Kristin M. Ryder, MPH, CHES

No current method of contraception is "perfect." Though availability of reliable and effective contraceptive methods has reduced the rate of unintended pregnancies to a 30-year national low, the fact remains that 45% of pregnancies in the United States are still unintended.[1, 2]

Contraceptive users must make complex tradeoffs between desirable or undesirable method features and a multitude of additional factors when considering available contraceptive options.[3–7] A method that meets a user's needs increases the probability of consistent use; consistent and *correct* use results in fewer unintended pregnancies.[8, 9] Here, I discuss the different contraceptive method options currently available in the United States, as well as factors that can influence decision making regarding method choice.

Definitions and Contraception Basics

Contraceptive User (CU)

I will use 'CU' to denote 'contraceptive user.' People who identify as female and/or women are not the only users of contraception, nor do all women use contraceptives. CU is thus the most inclusive and accurate term for people using contraception or making decisions about contraceptive methods.

Other Frequently-Used Abbreviations

HCP = healthcare provider
IUD = intrauterine device
OTC = over-the-counter (i.e., does not require a prescription)
STI = sexually-transmitted infection

What are Contraceptives, and How Do They Work?

Medically and legally, pregnancy or "conception" is defined as "implantation" of a fertilized egg in the uterine wall.[10, 11] Therefore, contraceptives are any "agent which prevents fertilization of an egg or prevents implantation of a fertilized egg, preventing a pregnancy from taking place."[12] This also includes contraceptives that prevent ovulation as they ultimately prevent conception by ensuring that an egg is not released.

There are three main ways that different contraceptive methods "work":

- Prevent ovulation (release of egg from ovary)
- Prevent fertilization (joining of egg and sperm)
- Prevent or interfere with implantation (embedding of fertilized egg in uterine wall)

Hormonal methods (pills, patch, ring, shot, implant, hormonal IUDs) work primarily by preventing ovulation and/or fertilization. Synthetic forms of estrogen and/or progesterone 'override' the normal hormonal cues present in the menstrual cycle, disrupting signals to the brain. This prevents the growth or release of an egg from the ovary and may also thicken the cervical mucus, reducing the mobility of sperm.[13] Hormonal methods can also cause changes in the lining of the uterus to prevent or interfere with implantation.[13]

The non-hormonal IUD does not prevent ovulation but instead emits copper ions that reduce the mobility of sperm, thereby preventing fertilization. It also prevents implantation by altering conditions within the uterus, making pregnancy unlikely.[14]

Barrier methods (condoms, cervical caps, diaphragms, sponges, spermicide) work by creating a physical or chemical barrier that prevents fertilization.[13]

Failure Rates

A contraceptive method's effectiveness, or how *well* it "works," is calculated with two kinds of failure rates[13]:

The "typical user failure rate" refers to the percentage of users (number of users out of 100) who experience an unintended pregnancy while using the method inconsistently (i.e., not every single time) *or* incorrectly over the course of a year.

The "perfect user failure rate" refers to the percentage of users who experience an unintended pregnancy while using the method consistently (i.e., every single time) *and* correctly over the course of a year.

As shown in Chart 1, the typical user failure rates for user-controlled methods such as condoms and pills are noticeably higher than the perfect user failure rates since it is more difficult to use these methods consistently *and* correctly. In contrast, with provider-controlled methods such as the implant or IUD, the typical user failure rate is nearly equal to the perfect user failure rate.

Available Contraceptive Options

In this section, I discuss two categories of contraceptive methods: methods for bodies that produce eggs and methods for bodies that produce sperm. I present basic information[1] on how the methods are used and note key considerations related to each method choice.

Important considerations as you read:

- Unless it is noted that the method is available OTC, visits to and coordination with an HCP are required. For these methods, the HCP conducts an exam and collects health history to determine medical eligibility. This is true for *all* hormonal methods, the ParaGard IUD, and methods that require fitting (i.e., cervical caps and diaphragms).
  - State laws regarding OTC hormonal contraception change frequently—at the time of publication, CUs in Oregon (over 18) or California can get pills, the patch, or the ring from qualified pharmacists, without a HCP's prescription.[15]

  - Methods with refills (e.g., patch, pill, ring) may also require monthly or tri-monthly trips to the pharmacy, depending on one's insurance coverage.

- For more information about side effects of and eligibility for specific methods, and the most recent information about methods, I recommend visiting reliable online resources like *plannedparenthood. org* or *bedsider.org*, or speaking with a HCP or contraceptive counselor.
  - Side effects associated with combined hormonal contraceptives (some pills, the patch, the ring)—which contain both estrogen and progesterone—can include: irregular bleeding or spotting, controlled or decreased menstrual bleeding/cramping, breast tenderness, nausea, or bloating. The risk of blood clots is also increased with use of combined hormonal contraceptives, but it is low, with about 1–3 out of 10,000 CUs experiencing this complication in a given year.[16]

Options for Bodies that Produce Eggs (ordered from most-used to least-used)

Oral contraceptive (Pill)

There are three main oral contraceptives: *combined oral contraceptive pills (COCs)* and *"continuous"/"extended" pills* contain synthetic estrogen and progesterone, whereas *progestin-only mini-pills* contain synthetic progesterone. There are many different brands of each of these types, as well as generic formulas.

With COCs and mini-pills, the CU ingests one "active" (containing hormones) pill every day for three weeks, ingests "inactive" (placebo) pills for one week, and then begins a new pack to start the cycle again. They may also choose to skip the inactive pills and take active pills continuously, in order to stop menstrual bleeding.

Another way to stop menstrual bleeding and side effects associated with menstruation is to choose continuous/extended pills. Packs of these pills do not contain inactive pills so CUs take three months to a year of active pills.

Key consideration: Must take pill at same time every day

Female sterilization

Female sterilization is also called tubal ligation or occlusion and is popularly known as getting one's "tubes tied." The HCP performs one of three different

---

[1]Unless otherwise noted, the reference for this information is: Association of Reproductive Health Professionals. (2011). Choosing a Birth Control Method. *A Quick Reference Guide for Physicians.*

procedures to render the fallopian tubes nonfunctional and thereby prevent fertilization:

- With **hysteroscopy** (non-surgical), small devices are placed in tubes to form scar tissue.
- With **minilaparatomy** (surgical), a small section is removed from each tube.
- With **laparoscopy** (surgical), instruments are inserted via a laparoscope to close off tubes.

The choice of procedure depends upon the provider's training, the patient's medical history and anatomy, and the availability of supplies.[17]

Key consideration: Procedure is permanent

Intrauterine device (IUD)

The HCP measures the distance to top of uterus and inserts a small "T"-shaped device:

- Mirena, Skyla, and Liletta devices release synthetic progesterone to prevent ovulation and/or fertilization for 3 years (Sklya, Liletta) to 7 years (Mirena).
- ParaGard device, which is hormone-free, emits copper ions to prevent fertilization and/or implantation for up to 12 years. Ovulation is unaffected.

It is possible for CUs to remove their own IUDs, though many CUs still choose to return to their provider to have the device removed, either at the end of its approved use span or if/when they want to stop the method.[18]

Key considerations:
- Device's strings hang down through cervix to facilitate removal
- Insertion can be painful; OTC pain relief recommended to reduce discomfort
- ParaGard can cause increased bleeding/cramping during menstrual periods
- Mirena, Sklya, and Liletta can cause unpredictable or decreased bleeding/cramping

Injectible (Shot)

The HCP administers Depo-Provera, a shot of synthetic progesterone (depot medroxyprogesterone acetate or DMPA) that prevents ovulation and/or fertilization for up to 3 months. The CU must return to receive additional shots in this pattern for as long as they want to use the method.

Key considerations:
- Most private contraceptive method option available
- Can cause unpredictable or decreased bleeding/cramping, temporary & reversible bone mass density loss, and weight gain
- Delayed return to fertility (on average, 10 months) after one discontinues use

Vaginal Ring

The CU inserts a flexible plastic ring into the vagina, where it releases synthetic estrogen and progesterone to prevent ovulation and/or fertilization. The CU leaves the ring in for three weeks, removes it for one week, and inserts a new ring to start the cycle again.

Key considerations:
- Can cause increased vaginal secretions

Fertility awareness-based methods (FAMs)

There are four main types of fertility awareness-based methods, sometimes referred to as natural family planning:

- CUs choosing the *ovulation/rhythm method* or the *Two Day method* observe changes in cervical mucus to determine when they are ovulating and avoid having sex during that time.
- CUs who have regular menstrual cycles may choose the *Standard Days method* and avoid having sex on days 8 through 19 of their menstrual cycle.[16]
- CUs using the *Symptothermal method* observe changes in their cervical mucus to determine the first fertile day and observe mucus changes and basal body temperature (BBT) changes to determine the last fertile day, in order to plan sexual activity during non-fertile days.[16]

Key considerations:
- Must know how to accurately observe and interpret cervical mucus, BBT changes
- Must have a regular menstrual cycle

Implant

The HCP makes an incision and inserts a small rod into the upper arm that releases etonogestrel, a synthetic progestogen, preventing ovulation and/or fertilization for up to 3 years. The CU must return to the provider to have the device replaced at the end of the activity period or removed if they choose to stop the method.

There are currently two different brands of implants available, Nexplanon and Implanon. Nexplanon is slightly easier to insert than Implanon, and it can be detected with medical imaging technology (e.g., X-rays).

Key considerations:
- Temporary pain and/or bruising at insertion/removal site
- Can cause unpredictable or decreased bleeding/cramping, weight gain, mood changes, headache, or acne in some CUs

Patch

The CU applies a beige-colored adhesive patch to the upper arm, upper torso, buttocks, or abdomen where it releases synthetic estrogen and progesterone through the skin to prevent ovulation and/or fertilization. The CU leaves the patch on for three weeks, removes it for one week, and applies a new patch to start the cycle again.

Key considerations: Can cause skin irritation at application site

Emergency contraception (EC)

Depending on when ingested or inserted—up to 5 days (120 hours) after unprotected sex—EC can prevent ovulation, fertilization, or implantation. EC will **not** interfere with an established pregnancy (i.e., fertilized egg implanted in the uterine wall) and thus it **cannot** cause an abortion.

Method choice will depend on contraceptives previously used, when unprotected sex occurred, the CU's weight/size (measured using Body Mass Index or BMI), and which method is most accessible/affordable for the CU.

Hormonal options ("morning-after pill"):

Levonorgestrel pills (Brand names: Plan B One Step, Next Choice One Dose, AfterPill, Take Action, My Way)

Levonorgestrel is a synthetic form of progesterone, similar to the synthetic progesterone found in other hormonal contraceptive methods. As described earlier, this hormone can disrupt signals to the brain in order to prevent ovulation, or it can prevent fertilization or implantation.

Key considerations:
- Most effective when taken up to 3 days (72 hours) after unprotected sex
- Most effective with BMI <25; may not be effective with BMI >30

Also note: At time of publication, federal law dictates that levonorgestrel EC be available OTC to CUs over 16 years old (though they must pay out-of-pocket). In some states and under some plans, EC pills may not be covered by insurance even with a prescription.[19]

Ulipristal pill (Brand name: Ella)

Ulipristal acetate is a selective progesterone receptor modulator that can also prevent ovulation, fertilization, or implantation.

Key considerations:
- Most effective when taken up to 5 days (120 hours) after unprotected sex

- Effective with BMI ≤ 35
- Not compatible with breastfeeding
- Requires a prescription

Non-hormonal/intrauterine option

The HCP can insert the ParaGard IUD up to 5 days after unprotected sex (see *Intrauterine device*). This method of EC is effective regardless of body size or composition.

Lactational amenorrhea method (LAM)

This method prevents pregnancy via lactation-induced amenorrhea, that is, the absence of menstruation that typically occurs while breastfeeding an infant.

Prior to the first menstruation after giving birth, the CU begins breastfeeding (or pumping) continuously, naturally releasing hormonal signals to indicate to the body that another ovulation should not occur, thereby preventing pregnancy. LAM is a highly effective, though *temporary*, form of contraception.

Key consideration: Another contraceptive method must be used once menstruation resumes, the CU reduces frequency or duration breastfeeds and/or introduces bottle feeds, or the baby reaches 6 months of age.[16]

Use estimates of the following methods—all considered "barrier" methods—were combined in latest available data[20] so they are listed here alphabetically:

Cervical cap

The HCP fits the CU for the cap, a small disc (cap) that is meant to fit tightly over the cervical opening to prevent fertilization. Spermicide must be applied to the cap and inserted into the vagina up to 6 hours prior to sexual activity, then removed after at least 6 hours following sexual activity. The cap must be cleaned and stored after every use.

Key consideration: Less effective for CUs who have previously given birth

Diaphragm

The HCP fits the CU for a diaphragm, a latex or silicone disc that is slightly larger than the cervical cap. The CU applies spermicide and inserts it into the vagina as close to the cervix as possible to cover it, up to 2 hours prior to sexual activity, thereby preventing fertilization. The CU must remove the diaphragm at least 6 hours after sexual activity, but not more than 24 hours. The diaphragm must be cleaned and stored after every use.

Key consideration: Only water-based lubricants are safe to use with this device

Female condom

The CU inserts one end (flexible plastic ring) of a polyurethane condom into the vagina, close to the cervix, and covers the vulva with a slightly larger flexible plastic ring on the opposite end, up to 8 hours prior to sexual activity to prevent fertilization and STI transmission.

Key considerations:
- Only option that can prevent STIs for bodies with vulvas/vaginas
- Cannot be re-used; new condom should be applied prior to every sex act

Spermicide

There are numerous forms of spermicide—substances that kill or immobilize sperm to prevent fertilization—including foams, jellies/gels, creams, vaginal suppositories, and vaginal films. Jellies/gels or creams are most often used with the cervical cap or diaphragm, although CUs can choose to use spermicide alone as well.

Spermicide should be inserted into the vagina, near the cervix, no more than 30 minutes before sexual activity. It should remain in place for 6–8 hours after sex and be reapplied with each sex act.

Key considerations:
- Should only be used if CUs are at low risk of HIV infection; frequent use can increase risk of transmission from HIV-positive partners
- Can cause allergic reactions
- Can increase risk of urinary tract infections and/or vaginitis

Sponge

The CU moistens and inserts a doughnut-shaped foam sponge containing spermicide into the vagina to cover the cervical opening, preventing fertilization. The device must be used up to 2 hours prior to sexual activity. After sexual activity, the sponge should be left in the vagina for at least 6 hours, but no longer than 24 hours, and then discarded.

Key considerations:
- Less effective for CUs who have previously given birth
- Not-reusable

Under investigation

Methods for bodies that produce eggs which are currently in research and development include:

- Contraceptive vaccines, such as one that targets human chorionic gonadotropin (hCG); the goal of this method is to use the immune system to prevent implantation, causing bodies that produce eggs to generate "anti-hCG" antibodies overcoming immunological tolerance to hCG[21]
- Transdermal (through the skin) hormonal gels and sprays to prevent ovulation and/or fertilization[22]

Options for Bodies that Produce Sperm (ordered from most-used to least-used)

Male condoms

The CU places a latex or polyurethane condom over an erect penis prior to inserting it in the vagina, leaves it on during the entire sex act, ejaculates inside the condom, and removes it away from the vulva and vagina so that contents do not come into contact with them.

Key considerations:
- Only option that can prevent STIs for bodies that produce sperm/semen
- Cannot be re-used; new condom should be applied prior to every sex act

Vasectomy (Male sterilization)

With this procedure, the HCP either uses a needle to inject anesthesia ("no-scalpel method") or uses a piston-like instrument to force anesthesia into scrotal tissues ("no-needle/no-scalpel method").

After anesthesia is administered, the HCP makes an incision in the scrotum, then locates and closes or cauterizes the vas deferens, the tubes which facilitate transportation of sperm from the testicles to the urethra.

Key considerations:
- Permanent method
- Temporary pain, tenderness, or bruising at incision site
- Back-up methods should be used until HCP confirms no sperm present in semen sample
- Slightly more effective, and much less invasive, than female sterilization

Withdrawal ("pull-out method," "coitus interruptus")

The CU removes the penis from the vagina prior to ejaculation and ejaculates away from the vulva and vagina so the ejaculate does not make contact with them.

Contrary to popular belief, and the sentiment that withdrawal is not a "real" method of contraception, withdrawal is about as effective as male condoms at preventing pregnancy.[23]

Key considerations:

- Does not prevent STIs
- Requires some degree of concentration and practice

Under Investigation

Methods for bodies that produce sperm that are currently in research and development include:

- Injection of a polymer substance called Vasalgel into the vas deferens to block sperm traveling from the testicles to the urethra; procedure known as RISUG, Reversible Inhibition of Sperm Under Guidance[24]
- Therapeutic ultrasound used on testes to interfere with spermatogenesis (sperm development)[25]
- Testosterone injections to interfere with spermatogenesis[26]
- Transdermal hormonal (testosterone and progesterone) gel to suppress spermatogenesis[24]

Options for Bodies that Produce Eggs and Bodies that Produce Sperm

Abstinence

Abstinence, or not engaging in sexual activity that involves exposure to bodily fluids or unclothed genital contact, is the most effective way to prevent pregnancy and STI transmission.[14]

Dual method and multiple method use

Dual method use refers to concurrent use of a hormonal method to prevent pregnancy and condoms to prevent STIs.[27] Multiple method use, also called "buttressing" methods, refers not only to the use of a hormonal method and condom, but can include a hormonal method and withdrawal or any other combination of contraceptive methods.[28]

Many CUs choose dual or multiple method use to "reassure" themselves and their partners that they are preventing pregnancy, or to feel more confident that they are preventing both pregnancy and STI transmission.[28]

Method Features That Influence Decision Making

Contraceptive methods are often categorized according to specific method features or attributes, such as effectiveness (see Chart 1). However, in order to provide appropriate care, it is critical to understand that each individual CU has different contraceptive priorities: what they personally consider to be the most important or relevant method features.[3, 29]

For example, a CU who is uncomfortable with unpredictable bleeding may prefer a method that allows them to menstruate regularly and might care more about this feature than effectiveness. Similarly, a CU who intends to become pregnant in the relatively near future might care more about return to fertility as a feature than effectiveness.

However, few CUs choose a method based upon one feature alone.[4] Private, public, and medical factors that affect CUs must all be considered together. The pros and cons of particular methods may differ based upon an individual's situation and experience.[4] Further, values and assigned importance to features can change as one ages, gains experience and increases knowledge of one's body, or as health status, relationship or family status, income, or living situation changes.[9, 30–32]

Client-centered contraceptive counseling, which focuses on and is guided by the client, can help CUs determine how they prioritize different method features and assist with the complex process of considering tradeoffs to select a particular method for use.[4, 33] Contraceptive counseling can also be used to correct misinformation and clarify understanding of method features, potential side effects, costs, etc.[6]

Chart 1 presents some important features and questions for CUs to consider as they make contraceptive decisions:

Method Feature	Also known as	Questions to Consider
Accessibility	Availability	- Does the method require trips to the pharmacy? To the clinic/doctor's office? If so, how many or how often? - Does my local pharmacy carry the method of my choice? - Do I have to be a certain age to use this method? - Can I get this method where I live? - Am I able to get transportation to the pharmacy or to the clinic/provider's office? - How many visits are required to *start* or *stop* the method?

(continued)

Control	–	- Who controls the start/stop of the method: me or the HCP? - Can I start or stop using the method whenever I want? - Do/can I apply/insert and/or remove the method on my own? - What is involved with removal if I don't like this method or I want to get pregnant? - Will I face pressure from my HCP to start a certain method? - Will I face resistance from my HCP if I want to stop/remove the method?
Cost	Affordability	- How much does the method cost? - Are there clinic visits required? If so, how much do they add to cost (including lost pay, childcare, etc.)? - Is there any testing/screening that needs to be done in order for me to get the method? If so, how much does it cost? - Will prescription refills be required? - Do I have insurance that covers the method? - Do I have the necessary resources to use the method consistently *and* correctly? - Are there additional costs associated with starting or stopping the method?
Covertness	Ability to hide; Privacy; Concealability	- Can I easily hide the method from others? - Does the method need to be stored where others could access it? - Is the method visible? - Can the method be felt by myself or others? - Where is the method applied or inserted?

Ease of Use	–	- How easy or hard is it to use the method correctly *and* consistently?
		- Do I have to:
		  ◦ Stop what I'm doing in the heat of the moment to insert or apply the method before I have sex?
		  ◦ Apply and remove the method every time I have sex?
		  ◦ Remember to take the method at the same time every day?
		  ◦ Remove and replace the method once a month?
		  ◦ Return to the clinic every three months for another dose?
		  ◦ Leave the method in place for 3–12 years?

Effectiveness	–	- What is the perfect-user failure rate? Typical-user failure rate? - How likely is it that I will get pregnant if I use the method correctly *and* consistently?
Length of Activity	Duration	- For how long will the method prevent pregnancy?

Mechanism of Action	Mode of Action	- How does the method "work"?
		- Is the method's mechanism of action consistent with my beliefs?
		- Is the method hormonal or non-hormonal?
		  ◦ Have I ever used a hormonal method before? If so, what type was it, and how did it affect me?
		  ◦ If the method is hormonal, what hormone(s) are involved and what is the dosage?
		- How can I know/be sure the method is "working"?

Return to Fertility	Reversibility	- Is the method reversible, so I can choose to become pregnant in the future? - How long do I have to wait to become pregnant after I stop the method?
Safety	–	- How long has the method been on the market? - How was the method tested? - How common are any adverse side effects or complications associated with the method? - Is the method recommended to certain CUs over others? - Is the method safe for *me*? - Do I have any pre-existing conditions that may make me a poor candidate for certain methods? - Do I meet medical eligibility criteria for the method(s) of my choice? - Does the method offer any protection against STIs? - How painful is the insertion and/or removal of the method?
Side Effects	–	- What are *positive* side effects that may increase my interest in the method? - What are *negative* side effects that may decrease my interest in the method? - How will the method's side effects impact my sex life?

Factors That Influence Decision Making

The decision to use a particular contraceptive method is often made with input from partners, family members, friends, healthcare professionals, and even strangers on the internet. Methods chosen also tend to reflect personal priorities and awareness, and they are often dependent upon variables such as age, race/ethnicity, and socioeconomic status.[8]

In this section, I divide some factors impacting contraceptive decision making into three broad categories: private, public, and medical circumstances.

Private Circumstances

Pregnancy desires

Desires regarding pregnancy differ between CUs and evolve for individual CUs based on factors such as employment or educational stability and relationship or marital status.[9, 30–32] However, *intentions* about pregnancy may not always align with pregnancy *planning*.[34]

Pregnancy ambivalence, or conflicted desire to have a baby, can impact contraceptive method choice as well as the correct and consistent use of the chosen method(s).[35, 36] For instance, how one feels about pregnancy at the time of method choice may influence whether a CU opts for longer-lasting methods, such as an IUD, or less effective methods, such as a diaphragm or withdrawal, that may be stopped independently at any time and allow for pregnancy to occur.

Sexual acceptability

How a method impacts sexual activity is critically understudied in contraceptive research.[37] Method features and side effects can significantly impact sexual activity and experience, affecting the acceptability of a method to a CU and their partner(s), as well as impacting their ability to use the method consistently and correctly.[37]

For example, some CUs don't mind inserting or applying barrier methods prior to sexual activity, whereas others are unlikely to use a method "perfectly" if it means they have to stop what they're doing "in the heat of the moment" and insert or apply a method.

Side effects associated with certain methods can also impact sexual acceptability. Some hormonal methods can cause mood and libido-related changes in CUs, which may impact desire to have sex or vaginal lubrication prior to and during sex.[37]

Relationship status, type, and/or length

How long CUs have been dating or seeing each other, whether or not they are in a relationship, and expected duration of the relationship can all impact method choice/use.[9, 30–32] Some CUs may have previously chosen the pill for many years, but after meeting someone and dating them for a couple of months, they decide that they want an IUD or implant because that person is "worth it." Other CUs choose methods independent of relationship type or partner inputs.

Prior Experience with Method or Method Type

CUs consider prior experiences with methods when making future contraceptive decisions.[8] For example, if a CU previously had difficulty inserting barrier methods such as cervical caps or diaphragms, they may consider methods applied or inserted elsewhere, such as the patch or implant. Similarly, if CUs had positive experiences with a hormonal method in the past, they may be more likely to "stick with" hormonal methods.

Public Circumstances

Trusted Others

Trusted others include family members, friends, neighbors, and anyone else whose input is valued by the CU. Anecdotes, experiences, or opinions shared by these trusted others may weigh more heavily in some CUs' considerations of methods.[8, 38] For example, if a CU's sibling had a negative experience with a method, that may discourage the CU from choosing that method, even if its features are consistent with the CU's reproductive goals and lifestyle.

"Horror Stories"

"Horror stories," or worst-case scenarios, tend to be shared more widely and "stick" in CUs' minds more than positive experiences when making a decision about contraception.[5] Horror stories can include hearing about emergency surgeries due to complications, disastrous side effects, or even method recalls.

Media

It is yet unknown what impact contraceptive information and experiences with methods portrayed through media outlets (e.g., magazines, advertising, blogs, forums, TV, movies) can have on contraceptive choice. Some researchers have found, however, that use of sites such as Facebook could improve contraceptive knowledge.[39]

Medical Circumstances

Contraindications

Contraindications are reasons why a method should not be used because it may be harmful to the CU.[40] HCPs utilize contraceptive medical eligibility criteria to determine contraindications and which CUs may or may not be good candidates for a particular type of method.

Contraindications vary according to method and individual CU, but some include:

- Known allergy or hypersensitivity to materials used in device or procedure
- Scar tissue from past surgeries involving uterus, fallopian tubes, or ovaries
- Hypertension (high blood pressure) or cardiovascular disease risk factors
- Smoking (particularly for CUs over 35)
- Breastfeeding
- Breast cancer history

Provider Inputs

Trust in a HCP can impact contraceptive choice. If a CU has had positive experiences with the healthcare system, has known their HCP for an extended period of time, or has had no reason to doubt a HCP in the past, they may be more likely to choose a method based on HCP recommendation.[38]

Conversely, if a CU has had negative experiences with the healthcare system, does not know their HCP well, has had reason to doubt a HCP in the past, or comes from a population which has been abused or victimized by health systems/institutions in the past (e.g., women of color, low-income women, immigrant women, LGBTQ-identified individuals, drug-using women), they may be leery of HCP method recommendations, especially regarding long-acting reversible contraceptive methods (e.g. IUDs and implants).[41–45]

Concluding Remarks

A key takeaway related to contraceptive decision making is that *the choices we make are limited by the choices we have*. There is still no "perfect" method available for any given CU. The choice of method for each CU is weighed against private, public, and medical factors, specific method features, and general pros and cons in order to find and use—consistently and correctly—the best available method for them.

Further, improvement and expansion of the methods available, as well as increased accessibility to the current range of options—for bodies that produce eggs as well as bodies that produce sperm—is needed, for three key reasons:

1. Negative side effects, costs, and other "drawbacks" associated with currently available methods are overwhelmingly experienced by bodies that produce eggs, such that

2. Doing so can promote gender equity, and

3. There is no "perfect" method currently available.

Until such a range of method options is available *and* accessible, the goal of finding each CU's "perfect" contraceptive method will remain unattainable.

REFERENCES

1. Finer, L. B. & Zolna, M. R. (2016). Declines in unintended pregnancy in the United States, 2008–2011. *New England Journal of Medicine 374*(9):843–852.

2. Guttmacher Institute. (2016, Mar.). Unintended Pregnancy in the United States.

3. Lessard, L. N., Karasek, D., Ma, S., Darney, P., Deardoff, J., Lahiff, M., Grossman, D., & Foster, D. G. (2012). Contraceptive Features Preferred by Women at High Risk of Unintended Pregnancy. *Perspectives in Sexual and Reproductive Health, 44*(3):194–200.

4. Madden, T., Secura, G. M., Nease, R. F., Politi, M. C., Peipert, J. F. (2015). The role of contraceptive attributes in women's contraceptive decision making. *American Journal of Obstetrics and Gynecology, 213*(1):46.e1–46.e6.

5. Higgins, J. A., Ryder, K., Skarda, G., Koepsel, E., & Bennett, E. A. (2015). The sexual acceptability of intrauterine contraception: A qualitative study of young adult women. *Perspectives on Sexual and Reproductive Health, 47*:115–122.

6. Dehlendorf, C., Levy, K., Kelley, A., Grumbach, K., & Steinauer, J. (2013). Women's preferences for contraceptive counseling and decision making. *Contraception, 88*(2):250–256.

7. Wyatt, K. D., Anderson, R. T., Creedon, D., et al. (2014). Women's values in contraceptive choice: a systematic review of relevant attributes included in decision aids. *BMC Women's Health, 14*(28).

8. Rosales, C., Mansour, D., & Cox, M. A. A. (2012). Does current contraceptive choice correspond with user satisfaction? *Journal of Obstetrics and Gynaecology, 32*(2):166–172.

9. Frost, J. J. & Darroch, J. E. (2008). Factors associated with contraceptive choice and inconsistent method use, United States, 2004. *Perspectives on Sexual and Reproductive Health, 40*(2):94–104.

10. American College of Obstetricians and Gynecologists. (1998, Jul.). Statement on Contraceptive Methods.

11. Gold, R. B. (2005). The Implications of Defining When a Woman is Pregnant. *The Guttmacher Report on Public Policy 8*(2).

12. American College of Obstetricians and Gynecologists. (2014). Facts are Important: Emergency Contraception (EC) and Intrauterine Devices (IUDs) are Not Abortifacients.

13. Hatcher, R. A., Trussell, J., Nelson, A., & Cates, W. (2011) *Contraceptive Technology*. 20th ed. New York, NY: Ardent Media.

14. Boston Women's Health Collective. (2011). *Our Bodies, Ourselves*. Touchstone: New York, NY.

15. Belluck, P. (2016, Jan.). Birth Control Without Seeing a Doctor: Oregon Now, More States Later. *The New York Times*.

16. Trussell, J. (2011). Contraceptive failure in the United States. *Contraception 83*(5):397–404.

17. Bartz, D. & Greenberg, J. A. (2008). Sterilization in the United States. *Reviews in Obstetrics and Gynecology, 1*(1):23–32.

18. Foster, D. G., Karasek, D., Grossman, D., Darney, P., & Schwarz, E. B. (2012). Interest in using intrauterine contraception when the option of self-removal is provided. *Contraception, 85*: 257–262.

19. Guttmacher Institute. (2016). Emergency Contraception. *State Policies in Brief (Mar. 2016)*.

20. Daniels, K., Daugherty, J. & Jones, J. (2014). Current contraceptive status among women aged 15–44: United States, 2011–2013. *National Health Statistics Reports 173*.

21. Talwar, G. P., Gupta, J. C., Rulli, S. B., Sharma, R. S., et al. (2015). Advances in development of a contraceptive vaccine against human chorionic gonadotropin. *Expert Opinion on Biological Therapy, 15*(8):1183–1190.

22. Bahamondes, L. & Bahamondes, M. V. (2014). New and emerging contraceptives: a state-of-the-art review. *International Journal of Women's Health, 6*:221–234.

23. Jones, R. K., Lindberg, L. D., & Higgins, J. A. (2014). Pull and pray for extra protection? Contraceptive strategies involving withdrawal among US adult women. *Contraception, 90*:416–421.

24. Payne, C. & Goldberg, E. (2014). Male Contraception: Past, Present and Future. *Current Molecular Pharmacology, 7*:175–181.

25. Tsuruta, J. K., Dayton, P. A., Gallippi, C. M., O'Rand, M. G., et al. (2012). Therapeutic ultrasound as a potential male contraceptive: power, frequency and temperature required to deplete rat testes of meiotic cells and epididymides of sperm determined using a commercially available system. *Reproductive Biology and Endocrinology, 10*(7).

26. Plana, O. (2015). Male Contraception: Research, New Methods, and Implications for Marginalized Populations. *American Journal of Men's Health*.

27. Berer, M. (2006). Dual Protection: More Needed than Practised or Understood. *Reproductive Health Matters, 14*(28):162–170.

28. Frowirth, L., Blades, N., Moore, A. M., & Wurtz, H. (2016). The Complexity of Multiple Contraceptive Method Use and the Anxiety That Informs It: Implications for Theory and Practice. *Archives of Sexual Behavior*.

29. Donnelly, K. Z., Foster, T. C., Thompson, R. (2014). What matters most? The content and concordance of patients' and providers' information priorities for contraceptive decision making. *Contraception, 90*(3):280–287.

30. Reed, J., England, P., Littlejohn, K., Bass, B. C., Caudillo, M. L. (2014). Consistent and Inconsistent Contraception Among Young Women: Insights from Qualitative Interviews. *Family Relations, 63*:244–258.

31. Musick, K., England, P., Edgington, S., & Kangas, N. (2009). Education differences in intended and unintended fertility. *Social Forces, 88*:543–572.

32. Sassler, S., Miller, A., & Favinger, S. M. (2009). Planned parenthood: Fertility intentions and experiences among cohabiting couples. *Journal of Family Issues, 30*:206–232.

33. Dehlendorf, C., Fox, E., Sobel, L., & Borrero, S. (2016). Patient-Centered Contraceptive Counseling: Evidence to Inform Practice. *Current Obstetric and Gynecology Reports, 5*: 55–63.

34. Borrero, S., Nikolajski, C., Steinberg, J. R., et al. (2015). It just happens: A qualitative study exploring low-income women's perspectives on pregnancy intention and planning. *Contraception, 91*(2):150–156.

35. Higgins, J. A., Popkin. R. A., & Santelli, J. S. (2012). Pregnancy Ambivalence and Contraceptive Use Among Young Adults in the United States. *Perspectives on Sexual and Reproductive Health, 44*(4):236–243.

36. Askelson, N. M., Losch, M. E., Thomas, L. J., & Reynolds, J. C. (2015). "Baby? Baby Not?": Exploring Women's Narratives About Ambivalence Towards an Unintended Pregnancy. *Women & Health, 55*(7):842–858.

37. Higgins, J. A. & Smith, N. K. (2016). The Sexual Acceptability of Contraception: Reviewing the Literature and Building a New Concept. *Journal of Sex Research, 53*(4–5):417–456.

38. Melo, J., Peters, M., Teal, S., & Guiahi, M. (2015). Adolescent and young women's contraceptive decision-making processes: Choosing the best method for her. *Journal of Pediatric and Adolescent Gynecology, 28*(4):224–228.

39. Kofinas, J. D., Varrey, A., Sapra, K. J., Kanj, R. V., Chervenak, F. A., & Asfaw, T. (2014). Adjunctive Social Media for More Effective Contraceptive Counseling: A Randomized Control Trial. *Obstetrics & Gynecology 123*:763–770.

40. World Health Organization. (2015). Medical Eligibility Criteria for Contraceptive Use, 5th Ed.

41. Gomez, A. M., Fuentes, L., & Allina, A. (2014). Women or LARC first? Reproductive autonomy and the promotion of long-acting reversible contraceptive methods. *Perspectives on Sexual and Reproductive Health, 46*(3): 171–175.

42. Dehlendorf, C., Ruskin, R., Grumbach, K., Vittinghoff, E., Bibbins-Domingo, K., et. al. (2010). Recommendations for intrauterine contraception: a randomized trial of the effects of patients' race/ethnicity and socioeconomic status. *The American Journal of Obstetrics and Gynecology, 203*(4):319e.1–8.

43. Downing, R. A., LaVeist, T. A., & Bullock, H. E. (2007). Intersections of ethnicity and social class in provider advice regarding reproductive health. *American Journal of Public Health, 97*(10):1803–1807.

44. Higgins, J. (2014). Celebration meets caution: LARC's boons, potential busts, and the benefits of a reproductive justice approach. *Contraception, 89*(4):237–41.

45. Borrero, S., Schwarz, E. B., Creinin, M., & Ibrahim, S. (2009). Impact of Race and Ethnicity on Receipt of Family Planning Services in the United States. *Journal of Women's Health, 18*(1): 91–96.

"The Future of Sex?"

By Emily Anthes

Once derided as being like a plastic bag with the erotic appeal of a jellyfish, the female condom is being reinvented as the next big thing in safe sex.

1. Excitement

In 1987, an American pharmaceutical executive called Mary Ann Leeper flew to Copenhagen to get a firsthand look at what she thought might be the world's next great health innovation. She didn't expect to find it tucked away inside an old cigar box.

When she arrived at the old farmhouse owned by Danish doctor and inventor Lasse Hessel, he opened the door with a cigar in his mouth. Then he fetched the box. "Inside were all these bits and pieces—metal, plastic, all different kinds of stuff," Leeper recalls. "I took a deep breath and thought, 'Holy mother—what have I gotten myself into?'" Somehow, these bits and pieces fit together to form a contraption that women could wear during sex to prevent pregnancy and sexually transmitted infections—the world's first female condom.

The presentation may have been unconventional, but Leeper and her colleagues at Wisconsin Pharmacal had high hopes for Hesse's invention. "The AIDS crisis in the United States was just fully being recognized, and it was clear to us that for women to have a product that they could use to help protect themselves would be a good thing," Leeper says.

Indeed, when Wisconsin Pharmacal finally introduced the female condom to the USA in 1993, public health experts hailed it as a game-changer. The condom, a polyurethane pouch inserted into the vagina before sex, would protect women from sexually transmitted infections even if their male partners refused to wear condoms.

Technically, the female condom works. When used correctly, it reduces a woman's risk of contracting HIV by around 94–97 per cent each time she had sex, accord-ing to estimates. Studies show that making female condoms available alongside the male version increases the percentage of sexual acts that are protected, and decreases the prevalence of sexually transmitted infections.

Yet, two decades after its much-celebrated introduction, the female condom still isn't living up to its potential. Less intuitive and familiar than the male condom, the device simply never caught on. Journalists mocked it, clinicians ignored it, and women shunned it, claiming that the condom was aesthetically unappealing and technically difficult to master. Today, only 1.6 per cent of all condoms distributed worldwide are female condoms.

There may finally be an opening to change the female condom's fate. For years, a handful of researchers, engineers and entrepreneurs have been quietly tinkering with the device. Their efforts are now maturing and an assortment of redesigned and reinvented female condoms are beginning to make their way onto the market. The introduction of new, more user-friendly products—coupled with renewed efforts to promote the technology around the globe—may finally be positioning the female condom for a breakthrough.

2. Plateau

From the start, the female condom was a difficult project —far more difficult than Leeper had bargained for. After buying the rights to the technology, Leeper and her colleagues at Wisconsin Pharmacal needed to turn Hessel's prototype into a marketable product. After some tweaking, they ended up with a thin polyurethane pouch with a flexible ring at each end. A woman would insert the device by squeezing the ring that sits in the closed end of the pouch and pushing it into her vagina. Once expanded inside the vagina, this inner ring would keep the condom in place. The larger ring at the open end of the pouch would sit outside the vagina, covering the external genitalia. When a man ejaculated, the internal condom pouch would trap his semen, preventing pregnancy and sexually transmitted infections.

But before Wisconsin Pharmacal could put the condom on the market, they needed approval from the US Food and Drug Administration (FDA). Because the female condom was an utterly new kind of product, the FDA decided to regulate it as a class III medical device, a category that is generally reserved for "high-risk" medical equipment—such as pacemakers and certain lasers—and that requires the highest level of regulatory scrutiny. (The FDA classifies male condoms as class II medical devices, so they are subject to fewer controls and do not require pre-market approval.)

It took six years for the female condom to wind its way through the regulatory system, and when the government finally approved it, in 1993, Leeper breathed a sigh of relief. "I thought that the hardest part was going to be getting it through FDA because it was *really* difficult and they kept changing the specifications, the requirements, the clinical studies," she says. But she was wrong. The hard part was just beginning.

As Wisconsin Pharmacal prepared to launch the Reality female condom[1] in the USA (it would go by other brand names in other countries), they made all the standard arrangements, hiring sales reps to visit medical practices and commissioning a big advertising firm to market the product directly to consumers. "We did all the checklist things that you're supposed to do," Leeper says. "And we fell flat on our face."

The challenge, in part, was the era, and the public's squeamishness about a sex-related product. "In those days, you couldn't talk 'condom' out loud," Leeper recalls. "Male condoms were referred to as 'rubbers.' You said them in a whisper and they were held behind the counter by the pharmacist." And although the AIDS crisis was raging, for many American women, the risk of contracting HIV was abstract, something that happened to other people and not to them.[2] While women in

focus groups had said they liked the *idea* of the condom, according to Leeper, "when push came to shove, when they were in that bedroom, the female condom was out on the dining-room table."

There were other barriers, too. The condoms cost as much as $5 a piece, compared to male condoms, which can typically be had for $1 or less. Krissy Ferris recalls hearing about female condoms when she was a student at Oberlin College in Ohio, but the price was a deterrent. "I didn't actually try one until I got free samples," recalls Ferris, who now works at a medical practice in Cleveland, Ohio. "Am I going to buy $6 worth of condoms to try this out a couple times? It seems like maybe not. You're getting male condoms for free everywhere when you're in your 20s."

What's more, the female condom was, frankly, strange. Unlike the male condom, which is sold rolled up and compressed, the female condom came fully open. Women and men alike were turned off by the unfamiliar, big, plastic-bag-like device they found when they undid the packet. Though some women did eventually come to like the condoms, there was a definite learning curve and as many as one-third to one-half of women had difficulty inserting them. Once in place, the condom had a tendency to squeak or rustle during sex.

The media pounced on these complaints, and utterly skewered the female condom. They ridiculed its aesthetics with seemingly limitless creativity. As sociologist Amy Kaler recounts in her 2004 paper on the condom's introduction,[3] journalists compared the product to: "a jellyfish, a windsock, a fire hose, a colostomy bag, a Baggie, gumboots, a concertina, a plastic freezer bag, something to line Boston's Inner Harbor with, a cross between a test tube and a rubber glove, Edvard Munch's *The Scream*, something designed for a female elephant, something out of the science-fiction cartoon *The Jetsons*, a raincoat for a Slinky toy, or a 'contraption used to punish fallen virgins in the Dark Ages.'"

Though the media treatment was especially harsh, journalists "were picking up on what were genuine design issues of the first generation of the female condom," says Kaler, an assistant professor at the University of Alberta in Canada. "It wasn't the most beautiful thing in the world. It was easy to make fun of. It was kind of laughed out of existence before it really got a chance to take off."

Still, there were signs that Wisconsin Pharmacal was onto something. In 1995, two years after bringing the condom to market, Leeper got a call from an official at

---

[1] http://brown.edu/Student_Services/Health_Services/Health_Education/sexual_health/safer_sex_and_contraceptives/reality_condom.php

[2] In fact, in 1988, *Cosmopolitan* published an article by Dr. Robert E. Gould claiming that women could not become infected with HIV through "ordinary sexual intercourse" with male partners, which was completely false and obviously posed a serious health risk for people who believed this misinformation. For an interesting history of HIV/AIDS that further discusses the public reaction to this case, and emphasizes the role of women in AIDS activism overall, look for the 2011 documentary *Sex In An Epidemic* (directed by Jean Carlomusto). *Ed.*

[3] http://www.ingentaconnect.com/content/routledg/cjgs/2004/00000013/00000002/art00004

Zimbabwe's Ministry of Health and Child Welfare. The health worker had received a petition demanding that the government of Zimbabwe bring the female condom into the country. It had been signed by 30,000 women.

Though Leeper had initially envisioned selling the female condom in America's private sector, the call from Zimbabwe, coupled with the condom's poor reception in the USA, prompted the company to shift course.

International nonprofit groups and aid organisations have long been big buyers of male condoms. The United Nations Population Fund (UNFPA), the US Agency for International Development, Population Service International and others regularly purchase male condoms in bulk and then donate them—or sell them at a deeply subsidised price—to clinics and programmes that serve particularly high-risk populations.

In 1996, Wisconsin Pharmacal changed its name to the Female Health Company[4] and began to focus on this global public sector, working with governments, global health organisations and aid agencies to get the condoms into the hands of at-risk women in low-income countries. The female condom became a particularly important tool in several countries in sub-Saharan Africa, where, in the early 2000s, 60 per cent of new HIV diagnoses were made in women, who often contracted the virus through their long-term partners.

Patience Kunaka, who was teaching nursing and midwifery students in Zimbabwe when she first heard about female condoms, knew these risks all too well. Two of her cousins had died of AIDS-related causes, and three additional family members were infected with HIV. Like many other women, she was not initially impressed by the female condom. "When I first saw one my immediate reaction was, 'Wow! How does it remain inside with penile movement?'" she recalls. "I thought it would be sliding in and out and what a messy act! I also thought the plastic would crumble inside me causing discomfort."

But Kunaka suspected her partner at the time of being unfaithful and was—in her own words—"obsessed about sexual hygiene", so she decided to give the female condom a shot. It didn't go well at first. "I had problems inserting it and felt discomfort from the inner ring," she says. Slowly, after some practice, she got the hang of it. Kunaka even came to like the device, especially "the fact that I don't have to beg my partner to use a condom."

She became a female-condom convert. "In my African context, where men are at liberty to have as many partners as they can have, they give me power to negoti-ate for safer sex," she says. She even went on to get a job as the condoms and training manager for Population Service International Zimbabwe, and now spends her days spreading the word about female condoms to men and women throughout the country.

The female condom received a better reception in Africa than it had in the USA, and as the Female Health Company sought to expand its global reach, it tweaked its original product, switching from a polyurethane condom to one made of nitrile, the same material used in many medical gloves. The nitrile condom, called the FC2,[5] is significantly cheaper than its polyurethane predecessor, now commonly referred to as the FC1, and also less noisy during sex. In 2007, the UNFPA 'prequalified' the FC2, making it eligible for bulk purchasing by public-sector agencies, and between 2007 and 2010, the number of female condoms distributed globally doubled from 25 million to 50 million.

Not bad for a contraceptive device that's been likened to *The Scream,* but it's still a drop in the ocean compared to male condoms. For every female condom that the major donor organizations purchase, they buy 71 male condoms. And although female condoms have got cheaper, price remains a limiting factor. An aid agency purchasing the FC2 in bulk will pay anywhere from $0.55 to $0.88 per condom but can get male condoms for as little as $0.02 apiece.

In many clinics in low-income countries, the supply of female condoms can be inconsistent, and the situation's not much better in the private sector. While pharmacy shelves overflow with male condoms of every imaginable kind—ribbed, studded, ultrathin, warming, aloe-enriched, neon pink, glow-in-the-dark, bubble-gum-flavored—it can be difficult to find female condoms for sale at all.

In some places, the condoms are stigmatized, thanks to clinical trials and distribution programs that initially focused on sex workers. Elsewhere, the devices are still saddled with the baggage of the product's first, failed introduction. In March 2013, for instance, a writer for Jezebel, a popular feminist blog and news site, published a post titled "Stop Trying to Make Female Condoms Happen."[6] She expressed scepticism that "women will change their minds about wanting to line their vaginas like a waste paper basket," and concluded by noting that "female condoms are just ew."

More than two decades after the first female condom hit the shelves, this is not exactly the revolution that public health experts had in mind.

---

[4]http://www.femalehealth.com/

[5]http://www.fc2femalecondom.com/
[6]http://jezebel.com/5989171/stop-trying-to-make-female-condoms-happen

3. Orgasm

For nearly 40 years, PATH,[7] a global health nonprofit based in Seattle, Washington, has been radically re-inventing basic medical technologies. The group's designers and engineers, for instance, created the Uniject: a disposable syringe pre-loaded with a single dose of vaccine. They built a one-size-fits-all diaphragm, removing the need for women to visit a doctor to have one specially fitted. And they invented a portable, hand-held scale that health workers can bring to home deliveries. The scale requires no electricity, can be read in the dark, and is decipherable even to birth attendants with low literacy, making it easy to identify under-weight infants.

In the late 1990s, PATH turned its attention to the female condom. "The Female Health Company did an incredible thing," says Maggie Kilbourne-Brook, a programme officer at PATH. "They created a product that had never existed, and they got it approved, and they got it registered and marketed in more than 100 countries. They actually changed people's perceptions of what barrier protection could be." But as it became apparent that the condoms weren't quite living up to their potential, some experts began to think that perhaps a radical makeover was in order. "In product development," says Kilbourne-Brook, "We always expect first-generation devices will need to be improved."

PATH prides itself on its user-centred design process, and so, in an effort to create a female condom that women would want to use, those at PATH decided to do something both radical and obvious: consult actual women. In 1998, PATH began convening focus groups in four countries—South Africa, Thailand, Mexico and the USA—asking women and men what they thought about female condoms and what they wanted from them.

From Durban to Seattle, it turns out that users' desires were pretty basic: "a product that was going to be easy to use, easy to insert, stable during use," says Kilbourne-Brook. Plus, "if it was possible, they wanted something that was more aesthetically pleasing."

These requests became the guiding principles for the designers and engineers working at PATH's product development laboratory in Seattle. The team ran an iterative, multi-step design process, building prototypes of potential new condoms in the lab and then sending them out to heterosexual volunteers in each of the four countries. These women and men handled and examined each model, sharing their impressions with researchers, and couples received samples of some of the more advanced prototypes to try out in their bedrooms. The product designers used the feedback to refine—and sometimes utterly rethink—their designs and then sent new, tweaked models back for further testing.

Early generations of female condoms had relied on a ring-based design. One of PATH's first prototypes was similar, with a polyurethane pouch anchored between two fixed rings. But some women reported that it was difficult to push the inner ring into the vagina—the same complaint often made about the FC1 and FC2—and that it was painful once inside. "Device is stable but uncomfortable," one Mexican tester reported. So PATH decided to scrap the rings entirely. They briefly tested a prototype that could be inserted using a tampon tube applicator, but the condom didn't deploy reliably.

They spent a lot of time talking about how to improve insertion. "We know from a user perspective, if you have a difficult time the very first time you try to use a device, a woman may never come back," says Kilbourne-Brook. "We wanted this to be not only easy to use, but it needed to be easy to use for someone who's never used it before."

According to Kilbourne-Brook, the ultimate break-through was inspired by feedback from testers and researchers in Thailand, who said, "Wouldn't it be won-derful if you had some kind of insertion device that helped you insert it and then it got out of the way?"

By 2003, they had hit on the solution: a dissolving applicator. The engineers created a condom that looked like a funnel, with a thin sheet of polyurethane that nar-rowed into a rounded tip. This tip contained the main pouch of the condom, collapsed inside a dissolving cap-sule. To insert the condom, women would simply push the capsule inside, much the same way they'd insert a tampon. Once it came into contact with the moisture of the vagina, the capsule would melt away—often within 30 to 60 seconds—releasing the full condom pouch.

The product designers gave the condom stability by attaching four small, thin pieces of polyurethane foam to the outside of the condom. Once the pouch expanded, these foam pieces nestled up against the vaginal wall, keeping the condom in place. Like other female con-doms, the model also featured a flexible outer ring to cover the external genitalia.

Between November 2003 and January 2004, 60 couples received samples of this prototype to try at home. They were impressed. Eighty-eight per cent of the women said it was easy to insert and 97 per cent said the pouch was stable during sex. The vast major-ity of men and women asked said the condom was comfortable, and 98 per cent of women and 100 per cent of men said it allowed for satisfactory sensation during sex.

---

[7]http://www.path.org/

It had taken six years and more than 300 unique prototypes, but by early 2004, PATH had found its female condom.

The final product, which PATH named the Woman's Condom, is "just a brilliant design," says Kaler, who was not involved in its creation. "When you look at it visually, it isn't huge. It's clear what you do with it. And the way that it's been designed with these foam pads means that it doesn't move around."

A series of larger clinical trials—conducted in Mexico, South Africa, Thailand, China and the USA—has reinforced what PATH found in its initial testing, with users reporting that the Woman's Condom is comfortable, stable and easy to insert. Several studies have found that both men and women tend to like the Woman's Condom better than the FC1 and FC2. Users' main complaint was that it does not come pre-lubricated, as the FC2 does. Instead, each condom comes with a packet of lubricant that users can apply themselves.

In 2011, the Woman's Condom received the stamp of approval from the Shanghai Food and Drug Administration and is currently under review by the UNFPA; approval is expected in 2014. In the meantime, limited quantities are already being sold in China and South Africa.

The Woman's Condom isn't the only new female condom on the scene. In 2012, the UNFPA pre-qualified the Cupid, which is manufactured by an Indian condom company. The Cupid relies on a ring-shaped foam sponge tucked into the closed end of the condom pouch for internal stability. Made of natural latex, the Cupid may be the cheapest female condom yet, and is now available for purchase in both the public and private sectors.

Several other condoms, each slightly different in design, are currently under UNFPA review. For instance, the Phoenurse, which is currently sold in China, comes with an optional insertion stick. Then there's the panty condom, in which a condom pouch is affixed to a pair of reusable panties with an opening over the vagina. Before sex, a woman can push the condom inside with her finger—or a man can with his penis—without her having to take off the undergarment.

And there are still more designs in the early stages of development. Origami Condoms,[8] based in Los Angeles, California, has developed a silicone female condom that unfolds like an accordion as it's pushed into the vagina. The company just completed a small phase I acceptability study—overall, participants preferred the Origami condom to the FC2, though they said the

FC2 felt more stable during sex. The company plans to conduct a larger clinical trial this year.

Not every product will be right for every woman or couple, but that's precisely the point. "In the studies we've done, we've found that some women will say, 'I really love this one and I don't like this one at all'," says Mags Beksinska, research director at the division of maternal, adolescent and child health at the University of the Witwatersrand, South Africa. "There are different aspects that appeal to different women in the different designs. So it would be good if there was a wider choice."

Krissy Ferris, the woman who was initially turned off by the cost of female condoms, came to see their advantages while dating a man who had trouble maintaining an erection with a male condom. "It was definitely a barrier to male condom use, and I was not ready to compromise on using a barrier method," she says. The female condom was a "low-stress" solution.

Over the years, Ferris has tried several different products, including the FC1, the FC2 and the VA w.o.w.,[9] which, like the Cupid, uses an internal sponge to hold the condom pouch in place. Ferris found that she preferred the VA w.o.w. because the sponge made it feel more secure during sex. "If you're using something with this desire for safety, having this extra measure of security was definitely a positive for me," she says. But the FC1 and FC2 felt more natural, she acknowledged, and for some women, that may be more important.

There is some evidence to suggest that women are more likely to have safe sex—and less likely to become pregnant or contract sexually transmitted infections—when a larger selection of contraceptive and barrier products is available. Giving women a greater choice in female condoms may increase the odds that they choose any female condom at all.

Meanwhile, male condoms are also getting a redesign. In November 2013, the Gates Foundation[10] awarded 11 grants of $100,000 to designers, engineers and scientists with ideas for a 'next-generation condom'—male or female—that would be easier and more pleasurable to use. The winning proposals include a male condom that is packaged with a built-in applicator, allowing the condom to be removed from its foil wrapper and donned in a single smooth motion, and a one-size-fits-all male condom designed to tighten during sex.

4. Resolution

Of course, upgrading a product is merely a first step. While the FC1 certainly had its flaws, they weren't the only reason that female condoms didn't take off. "Some

---

[8]http://www.origamicondoms.com/

[9]http://www.inspiral.tv/
[10]http://www.gatesfoundation.org/

technologies are harder than others," says Laura Frost, a partner at Global Health Insights,[11] a research and consulting firm. "Compared to other products where there's one huge issue, like affordability or awareness, this one had those barriers at every stage."

That's why, for the female condom to truly break through, advocates will need to invest in comprehensive marketing and education campaigns at the local, national and global levels. "It takes more than just putting it on the shelf," says Susie Hoffman, an associate professor of epidemiology at Columbia University in New York.

Female condoms remain less straightforward than male condoms, and one of the major lessons of the last two decades is that women often need a little bit of training to use them correctly. That means that clinicians and counsellors may have to do more than simply tell women that female condoms exist—they'll need to give them the opportunity to practice inserting one, either on a pelvic model or on themselves.

In addition, women may need help figuring out how to broach the subject with their male partners. Though the condoms have won praise for being female-initiated, they're not entirely invisible, and most men will notice if their partners are wearing them. "In many cases, she's probably going to want to mention to her partner before having sex that this is a new product that she's going to try," Hoffman says. "Ideally there's going to be some kind of a conversation about it, and women need help in figuring out how to do that."

Male partners are also a potential market. "Men probably feel, when it's called the 'female condom', that it's not something that's for them," Mags Beksinska says. But "there's no reason that a man shouldn't take one and bring it home and introduce it to his partner." In fact, she adds, once men get used to the female condom, they often prefer it to the more constricting male version. Female condoms even enhance sex for some people: the outer ring can be used to stimulate the clitoris, while the inner ring of some designs can bump up pleasurably against the tip of the penis.

The female condom may remain a tough sell, but the good news, experts say, is that there are now more organizations trying to make the pitch. "Now we're seeing a much bigger coalition of advocates, which is what we need," Frost says. Some existing agencies, most notably the UNFPA, have stepped up their support, while champions have created a variety of new advocacy and awareness groups, including the National Female Condom Coalition[12] in the USA, and the Universal Access to Female Condoms Joint Program, based in the Netherlands.

Alongside this, the condom's supporters are getting more creative in their promotion efforts, establishing Global Female Condom Day—the first one was held on 12 September 2012—and holding female-condom-themed fashion shows and film festivals. Several organizations have turned salons and barbershops in Zimbabwe, Malawi, Cameroon and elsewhere into female condom distribution centers, training hairdressers to promote and sell the product to both male and female clients. And all-out media blitzes in Africa—in which the condoms are promoted on billboards, television and the radio—have fed a sharp increase in demand.

"I think people had kind of written off the female condom," says Beth Skorochod, a senior technical adviser at Population Service International. "But now people are beginning to say, 'OK, with more competition and more interest, maybe this deserves another look.'"

There may even be hope for the hard-to-crack private sector in higher-income countries. After winning FDA approval for the FC2 in 2009, the Female Health Company relaunched the female condom in the USA, creating female condom campaigns and programs in a handful of major American cities, including New York, San Francisco and Washington, DC.

Some local US groups are also beginning to lay the groundwork for the future. Staff members at the Chicago Female Condom Campaign[13] now show off samples of some of the newest products—including the Cupid[14] and the Woman's Condom[15]—in their training and education sessions. The goal is to make sure that healthcare providers and consumers will be familiar with the products if and when they appear in the USA. But there's an added benefit. "Frankly what this also does is it helps to cultivate new female condom advocates," says Jessica Terlikowski, who coordinates the Chicago Female Condom Campaign and the National Female Condom Coalition. Seeing other products, she says, can prompt women to ask, "'How can I get that?' 'Why don't we have that here?' People can't ask for or demand what they don't know about."

Women may soon have choices beyond the conventional condom. Scientists have been developing interventions that would be truly invisible to women's partners: oral antiretroviral pills and vaginal gels that prevent HIV. Despite the enormous excitement surrounding these drugs, they won't be magic bullets either, and the public health community will still have to grapple with the thorny issues of education, access and adherence. In 2013, for instance, researchers announced that a clinical trial of two different HIV prevention

---

[11]http://www.glohi.org/
[12]https://www.facebook.com/NationalFCCoalition

[13]http://ringonit.org/
[14]http://www.cupidltd.com/toc_female.php
[15]http://www.path.org/projects/womans_condom.php

pills and one vaginal gel,[16] conducted among women in three African nations, failed because women weren't using the medications regularly.

Such outcomes are making it increasingly obvious that the global fight against HIV and other sexually transmitted infections is unlikely to be won with any one technology, no matter how elegantly designed. Instead, it will require an arsenal of weapons, a diverse array of tools that allow women and men to protect themselves. The female condom may never be as cheap or as popular as the male condom, but that doesn't mean it has no role to play.

Among those optimistic about the female condom's future is Lasse Hessel, the Danish doctor who started it all. The condom's champions made some mistakes in the early years, Hessel says, but he's encouraged by the recent resurgence of interest and the new products that are hitting the shelves. In fact, he wishes other inventors had redesigned his condom sooner, especially because there was so much room for improvement: "How can my ugly, clumsy female condom get any worse?" Hessel says. "It can only get much better."

- Author: Emily Anthes
- Editor: Chrissie Giles
- Copyeditor: Tom Freeman
- Fact checker: Audrey Quinn
- Photographer: Giles Revell
- Art director: Madeleine Penny
- Art director: Madeleine Penny

EXTRA: A condom for anal sex?

Male condoms are more likely to break during anal sex than vaginal sex, so some health clinics and workers have been promoting female condoms as an alternative. A handful of studies have found that 35–48 per cent of gay men surveyed in the USA have heard of using female condoms for anal sex and about 13–21 per cent say they've actually done so.

The hitch is that female condoms have only been approved for vaginal sex and there isn't yet convincing evidence supporting their use during anal sex. "Our

[16]http://www.nytimes.com/2013/03/05/health/african-trial-of-hiv-drugs-fails.html

group did a review of the studies around anal sex and found that there really just weren't enough solid studies to say whether it was safe or effective," says Susie Hoffman, an associate professor of epidemiology at Columbia University in New York.

Certain design elements may, in fact, make female condoms inappropriate for anal sex. As a team of researchers wrote in a 2009 review, "The female condom has features specifically designed for insertion into the vagina, most notably a flexible inner ring secured by the cervix. When used in the anus, the female condom may not be easy to insert, comfortable, or even safe." (Indeed, a small study of gay men conducted in 2003 suggests there may be reason for concern; female condoms slipped more during anal sex than male condoms and men using female condoms were more likely to experience pain, discomfort and rectal bleeding.)

Still, some female-condom advocates recommend the female condom for anal sex because they believe it's preferable to using no protection at all. "The Chicago Female Condom Campaign does promote it as a risk reduction strategy," says Jessica Terlikowski, the director of prevention technology education at the AIDS Foundation of Chicago, which is the coordinating partner of the campaign. "We're very clear about what information does and does not exist," she says.

While some state health departments agree with Terlikowski and recommend the female condom for anal sex, others specifically caution against it. Among the health departments that endorse the use of the female condom for anal sex, there is disagreement about whether users should remove the inner ring before inserting the device.

These mixed messages highlight the need for more research specifically into how the female condom performs during anal sex, as well as better options for couples, gay and straight, that want to engage in it. The anal condom may be the next frontier—Origami Condoms currently has one in development. If approved, it would become the first method of barrier protection designed explicitly for use during anal sex. "We're all really excited to see that come out," Terlikowski says.

Author: Emily Anthes

"State Of Birth Control Coverage: Health Plan Violations Of The Affordable Care Act"

Introduction

The affordable care ACT's (ACA) requirement that insurance companies cover birth control without out-of-pocket costs is already positively affecting the lives of millions of women and families across the country. Prior to the ACA's birth control coverage benefit, cost was a significant barrier to women getting preventive services like birth control.[1] This contributed to the nation's unintended pregnancy rate, and had consequences for women and their families' long-term health and economic well-being.

Since the ACA's birth control benefit went into effect, more than 48 million women no longer face cost barriers to accessing birth control.[2] Research shows that two-thirds of women using oral birth control and nearly three quarters of women using the vaginal contraceptive ring are no longer paying out-of-pocket for these methods.[3] In 2013, women saved more than $483 million in out-of-pocket costs for birth control, or an average of $269 per woman.[4] And, women have told the National Women's Law Center (the Center) that this change has significantly affected their lives. They are no longer choosing between birth control and paying for other necessities, like groceries, and are continuing their education and advancing their careers because of this landmark law. Indeed, access to birth control has benefits for the health of women and children, improves women's ability to control whether and when they will have a child, and fosters women's ability to participate in education and the workforce on an equal footing with men. It is also an incredibly popular part of the ACA, with nearly 70% of people supporting the requirement.[5]

There are some women, however, whose insurance companies are still charging them out-of-pocket costs for their birth control in ways that do not comply with the ACA.[6] The National Women's Law Center operates a nationwide hotline, CoverHer, which women can call when they face problems accessing the birth control benefit to which they are entitled. Through this hotline, the Center has heard from women in *every state in the country*. These women have spent hours on the phone with their insurance company trying to find out why they still have to pay for their birth control. They often are given conflicting information about their coverage by the insurance company. And, too often, the insurance company tells them their method of birth control simply is not covered, or that they should switch birth control methods if they do not want to pay out-of-pocket for the method prescribed for them. These women should be benefiting from the ACA already, but their insurance companies' impermissible coverage policies are preventing them from doing so.

In addition to reports received through the CoverHer hotline, the National Women's Law Center reviewed over 100 plan documents from issuers in the new marketplaces in 15 states, reviewed publicly-available documents on insurance company websites, and corresponded with insurance companies. This research has uncovered three major trends in the ways insurance companies are not complying with the birth control benefit:

Reprinted by permission of National Women's Law Center. Full report with end notes is available online from their website: http://nwlc.org/wp-content/uploads/2015/08/stateofbirthcontrol2015final.pdf

- Insurance companies are still not providing coverage for *all* FDA-approved methods of birth control, or they impose out-of-pocket costs on them;

COVERHER HOTLINE

The Center has been collecting stories from women since the ACA's birth control benefit first went into effect in August 2012. Through the CoverHer hotline and associated website (1-866-745-5487, coverher@nwlc.org or www.coverher.org), the Law Center assists women who are having trouble securing coverage for birth control without out-of-pocket costs. CoverHer provides resources that help women understand the birth control coverage requirement, as well as information and resources to assist women in filing appeals with their insurance company and filing complaints with the government agency that regulates their plan. To date, nearly 2,800 individuals have contacted CoverHer, and over 75,000 individuals have accessed the related online resources.

Women who have contacted CoverHer and used its resources have succeeded in getting their birth control covered. Some women have used the information to work with their employer's benefits staff and insurance broker to fix the coverage. Often, the benefits staff has been instrumental in assisting women with appeals, communicating with the issuer or third-party administrator, and ultimately fixing the coverage violation. Some women have used the CoverHer template appeal letters to successfully change their plan's coverage policy and get reimbursed for past charges. Some women have filed successful complaints with the government agency that regulates their plan to change the plan's policy and obtain reimbursement.

All hotline calls are confidential. Not every person who contacts the hotline discloses their location. Records for specific women's experiences referenced in this report are on file with the National Women's Law Center.

The Center gratefully acknowledges Bayer HealthCare's support of the CoverHer project.

- Insurance companies limit their coverage to generic birth control; and,
- Insurance companies fail to cover the services associated with birth control without out-of-pocket costs, including counseling or follow-up visits.

In addition to these three major trends, the research and review of CoverHer contacts have unearthed several other violations of the ACA's birth control benefit, such as plans not having a required waiver process, failing to cover sterilization for dependents, imposing age limits on coverage, and other policies that in effect deny coverage of birth control.

The goal of this report is to highlight these problems so that all stakeholders—insurance companies, the federal government, state regulators—are aware of the barriers women still face in getting the preventive health care services they need and to which the ACA guarantees them coverage. It will take attention and effort to make sure this critical new benefit is implemented properly. To that end, this report includes recommendations for various stakeholders. Insurance companies must closely examine their policies and be sure that they are in compliance. Additionally, the federal government must issue further clarifying guidance about the birth control benefit. And, both state and federal agencies must enforce the ACA, both in approving insurance companies' plans and in handling consumer complaints about insurance company practices. These steps will go a long way to ensuring that the promise of the birth control benefit becomes a reality for women across the country.

The Affordable Care Act's Birth Control Coverage Benefit

The health benefits of birth control are well-documented. Birth control is highly effective at reducing unintended pregnancy, which can have severe negative health consequences for both women and children.[7] It also allows women to space their pregnancies, which improves the health of both women and their children.[8] Additionally, improving women's ability to control whether and when they will have a child fosters women's ability to participate in education and the workforce on an equal footing with men. Birth control is such a core part of women's lives that 99% of sexually active women have used birth control at some point.[9] However, prior to the ACA's requirement, many women found cost an insurmountable barrier to getting access to birth control or the birth control method recommended by their health care provider.[10]

The ACA's birth control coverage benefit is part of the law's preventive health services coverage provision, which is designed to enable individuals to avoid preventable conditions and improve health overall by increasing access to preventive care and screenings.[11] This provision requires health insurance plans to provide coverage for certain preventive services without out-of-pocket costs, including a set of preventive services for women.[12] To determine which women's preventive services would be covered without out-of-pocket costs, the Health Resources and Services Administration (HRSA) of the Department of Health and Human Services commissioned the Institute of Medicine (IOM) to study gaps in coverage of women's preventive services and to recommend which additional women's preventive services should be included. After conducting its analysis, the IOM recommended eight preventive services for women, including well-woman visits, breastfeeding support and supplies, and "the full range of Food and Drug Administration-approved con-

traceptive methods, sterilization procedures, and patient education and counseling for women with reproductive capacity."[13]

HRSA adopted the recommendations set forth in the IOM Report.[14] The ACA's birth control coverage requirement means that plans cannot charge out-of-pocket costs for birth control, sterilization, and related education and counseling.

All FDA-Approved Methods of Birth Control Must Be Covered Without Out-of-Pocket Costs

There are currently twenty unique FDA-approved birth control methods, delineated in the FDA's Birth Control Guide, and each of these unique methods for women must be covered under the ACA.[15] The federal government has reiterated in guidance that plans must cover all of the FDA-approved birth control methods for women.[16] The guidance clarifies that health insurance plans and issuers cannot limit their birth control coverage to only oral contraceptives.[17] It explicitly states that plans and issuers must cover FDA-approved intrauterine devices (IUDs) and implantable contraceptives.[18] The guidance is also clear that FDA-approved over-the-counter contraceptive methods, when prescribed for women, must be covered without out-of-pocket costs.[19] The Department of Health and Human Services has also publicly acknowledged that plans and issuers must cover the vaginal contraceptive ring and the contraceptive patch.[20]

Counseling and Other Birth Control-Related Services Must Be Covered Without Out-of-Pocket Costs

The benefit covers not only the cost of a birth control drug or device, but also the services related to receiving the birth control—such as office visits, counseling, or medical services related to insertion of a birth control method or to a sterilization procedure. The guidance makes clear that other related services, such as follow-up visits, management of side effects, counseling for continued adherence, and device removal must be covered without cost sharing.[21]

Insurance Companies May Use Limited "Reasonable Medical Management"

Under the regulations implementing the preventive health services, insurance companies are allowed to use "reasonable medical management techniques" to

---

IN THEIR OWN WORDS: WHY BIRTH CONTROL WITHOUT OUT-OF-POCKET COSTS MATTERS TO WOMEN

Expanding birth control options "I am grateful for the ability to choose the form of contraception that works best for me. I could not afford the up-front cost of an IUD without health care reform. Since the IUD is much more effective than the pill, I am able to more effectively manage my reproductive health."—*Woman in New York*

Financial security "Thanks to zero copay birth control, I can get the medication I need without having to go without groceries for a week."—*Woman in Virginia*

Advancing education and career "Now that birth control is free under Obamacare, my husband and I have a lot more security. We know that we'll be able to decide when to start a family at a time that's good for both of our studies and careers."—*Woman in Illinois*

Benefiting the whole family "I am thankful that my husband and I can have the children we can afford to love and invest in, at the appropriate time of our choosing, when we are financially stable and emotionally ready."—*Woman in Michigan*

determine the "frequency, method, treatment, or setting for which a recommended preventive service will be available without cost sharing requirements to the extent not specified in a recommendation or guideline."[22] But these medical management techniques are not unlimited. For example, the Administration has stated that an allowed "reasonable medical management technique" is imposing out-of-pocket costs on a branded drug when the insurance company covers an available generic equivalent.[23]

If a generic version is not available, however, the guidance requires the insurance company to provide coverage for the branded drug without out-of-pocket costs.[24]

The guidance also requires every insurance company to have a waiver process that would enable women to have insurance coverage of the birth control method—at no out-of-pocket costs—that she and her provider determine is medically appropriate.[25] Additionally, if the insurer does not have a provider in its network that can provide a preventive service, including birth control, it cannot impose out-of-pocket costs when a person accesses the service from an out-of-network provider.[26]

Insurance Companies Fail to Comply With the Birth Control Benefit

Unfortunately, not every woman who should be getting coverage of her birth control without out-of-pocket costs has been able to access this import ant benefit. The Center has documented this through the review of publicly available documents from some of the nation's largest health insurance issuers, and correspondence with some of these companies about their coverage policies. In addition, since the birth control benefit went into effect on August 1, 2012, the Center has received calls and emails through our CoverHer hotline from women whose plans continue to impose cost sharing on their birth control.[27]

The Center has identified three major categories of insurance plan non-compliance:

- Some plans are not providing coverage for *all* FDA-approved methods of birth control, or they impose out-of-pocket costs on them;
- Some plans will only cover generic birth control; and,
- Some plans impose costs on the services associated with birth control methods.

In addition, the Center has identified several other policies which deny coverage of birth control without out-of-pocket costs. Insurance companies using these practices are violating the ACA's birth control benefit

and leaving women without full access to a critical benefit.

Plans Fail to Cover All FDA–Approved Birth Control Methods or Impose Out-of-Pocket Costs

The FDA has approved 20 unique birth control methods, and the ACA requires that insurance companies cover each unique method without out-of-pocket costs. However, several major insurance companies' birth control coverage policies are violating the law. In some cases they are imposing costs on birth control, and in some cases, they are denying coverage completely.

Most commonly, the coverage problems are for the vaginal contraceptive ring, the contraceptive patch, and long-acting reversible contraceptive methods, such as an IUD. It is notable that in many of these cases, the insurance plans cover other birth control methods without out-of-pocket costs, and sometimes even suggest that a woman switch methods if she does not want any out-of-pocket costs. However, birth control methods are not interchangeable. When a plan places a cost barrier between a woman and her prescribed method of birth control, she is less likely to use birth control consistently or correctly, thereby increasing her risk of unintended pregnancy. Furthermore, a particular method is prescribed for a woman by her health care provider based on health needs. When insurance companies impermissibly fail to cover all FDA-approved birth control methods or impose out-of-pocket costs on some birth control methods, it can interfere with health care providers' decisions about the best care for a woman.

The coverage policies detailed below not only fail to comply with the ACA, but recreate the cost barriers that existed prior to the ACA that contribute to increased risk of unintended pregnancy.

Plans Fail to Cover Birth Control Methods

The Center's review of plan documents found multiple instances of plans that simply did not cover all FDA-approved birth control methods:

- An issuer in South Dakota does not cover the contraceptive implantable rod.[28]
- An issuer in California fails to cover ella, a unique emergency contraceptive method.[29]
- An issuer in Wisconsin specifically excludes coverage of contraceptive sponges.[30]
- Two issuers in Nevada and one issuer in Alabama fail to cover sterilization by imposing impermissible limits on coverage.[31]

- Ten issuers in Maine, Minnesota, Ohio, Rhode Island, and Wisconsin exclude all over-the-counter (OTC) contraceptive methods.[32] The FDA identifies several types of over-the-counter methods of birth control as unique birth control methods, and plans must cover them without out-of-pocket costs when prescribed. These OTC exclusions raise particular concerns about women's access to forms of emergency contraception which are available over-the-counter.

Plans Impose Out-of-Pocket Costs on Birth Control Methods

CoverHer contacts and the Center's investigation identified several instances of plans imposing out-of-pocket costs on birth control methods, in violation of the ACA:

- A major insurance company did not include the contraceptive patch or the vaginal contraceptive ring on its list of drugs covered without out-of-pocket costs in 2014.[33] In explaining why it failed to cover these two unique FDA-approved methods of birth control as required by the ACA, the company noted that it divides birth control into five "methods": barrier; hormonal; implantable; emergency; and, permanent methods. Under this categorization, the company includes the vaginal contraceptive ring and the contraceptive patch in their "hormonal methods" category. Because the company covers other "hormonal methods" without out-of-pocket costs—most notably oral contraceptives—it refused to cover the ring and the patch.[34] In 2014, several women used CoverHer resources to appeal the company's refusal to cover the ring. In the first weeks of January 2015 these women contacted the hotline again to say that they had finally gotten the coverage required by the ACA. In 2015, the company has started to cover the ring without out-of-pocket costs, creating a sixth "method" on its list: vaginal ring.[35] However, it continues to fail to cover the contraceptive patch.[36]
- A second major insurance company's list of drugs covered without out-of-pocket costs did not include the contraceptive ring or the contraceptive patch in 2014. Publicly available documents on the company's website in 2014, including the company's "No Cost Preventive Medications by Drug Category" pamphlet, simply do not include these methods on the list.[37] In 2015, the company's

"No Cost Preventive Medications by Drug Category" pamphlet indicates that it continues to deny coverage of the vaginal contraceptive ring.[38]

- A third major insurance company's lists of drugs covered without out-of-pocket costs do not include the vaginal contraceptive ring or the contraceptive patch. In explaining why it fails to cover these two FDA-approved methods of contraception as required by the ACA, the company stated that it divides birth control into five "methods": barrier; hormonal; implantable; emergency; and, permanent methods. Because the company covers other "hormonal methods"—most notably oral birth control—it refuses to cover the ring and the patch. Currently,[39] this insurance company maintains three lists of preventive drugs covered without out-of-pocket costs. It has not added coverage of the vaginal contraceptive ring to any of those lists to comply with the ACA.[40] Two of the three lists include the contraceptive patch.[41]

- Some independently operated plans across the country refuse to cover the vaginal contraceptive ring without out-of-pocket costs. Women who contact the CoverHer hotline routinely report that customer service representatives at these insurance companies tell them that they have the option of having the pill covered without out-of-pocket costs or paying to get the ring.[42]

- Women also report that some independently operated plans fail to cover certain long-acting reversible contraceptive methods. One woman reported that her plan would not cover the IUD with copper without out-of-pocket costs.[43] For some women, the IUD with copper is one of only a few birth control options they can use because of underlying health conditions for which taking hormones are contraindicated.

The Center's review of plan documents uncovered additional examples of plans impermissibly imposing out-of-pocket costs on birth control.

- Plan documents from Ohio show that one plan requires women to pay out-of-pocket for over-the-counter birth control methods, but will reimburse women for those costs.[44]
- Two insurance companies in Connecticut impose out-of-pocket costs on sterilization services.[45]
- Two insurance companies in Ohio impose out-of-pocket costs on IUDs and injectable contraceptives.[46]

- An insurance company in Maryland applied the deductible to birth control in its catastrophic plan.[47]

Plans Wrongly Limit Their Coverage to Generic Birth Control

Many women have reported to the CoverHer hotline that their insurance plan will only cover generic birth control. This is an impermissible coverage exclusion that has two major effects on women's access to the birth control prescribed for her. First, there are several birth control methods for which there is no generic equivalent, including the IUD with copper, the IUD with progestin, and the vaginal contraceptive ring. Second, there are certain types of oral birth control that do not yet have a generic equivalent, and must be covered under the ACA. In both instances, the "generic only" policy bars women from getting coverage of an "FDA-approved method of contraception" without cost-sharing. As noted above, federal guidance addresses this by allowing plans to only cover generics, except in cases in which no generic equivalent is available. In that case, plans must cover the brand-name birth control.

These types of "generic only" policies mean that a cost barrier between women and some birth control methods continues to exist, contrary to the ACA's requirement. Failure to cover birth control that doesn't have a generic equivalent can leave women without access to the method of birth control best suited for them and specifically prescribed by their health care provider. Women in plans with this type of impermissible coverage policy are not fully benefiting from the ACA.

The plans below impermissibly limit coverage to generics only:

- There are several examples of independently operated insurance companies that have "generic only" coverage policies, including in Alabama and Florida. The company in Alabama indicates that for pharmacy contraceptive methods only generics are covered. The plan in Florida only provides coverage of birth control without out-of-pocket costs for "certain *generic* contraceptive medications or devices (e.g., oral contraceptives, emergency contraceptive, and diaphragms.)"[48]
- Five other insurance companies in the 15 states examined in the Center's plan document review have similar impermissible "generic only" coverage policies.[49]

Plans Fail to Cover Services Associated With Birth Control and Sterilization

Women who contact the CoverHer hotline have reported that insurance plans refuse to cover services associated with birth control and sterilization without imposing out-of-pocket costs. The Center's review of plan documents confirmed this impermissible practice in several plans. Services that plans have refused to cover without out-of-pocket costs include birth control counseling services, follow-up visits and services, and necessary tests. If a plan denies coverage without out-of-pocket costs for these types of services, it can put the woman at risk for complications, for example if she is unable to have a follow-up appointment after her IUD insertion to confirm it has been placed correctly. These types of policies can even prevent a woman from accessing her birth control altogether, such as if she cannot afford to pay for the office visits that are required every 12 weeks for birth control injections. When insurance companies impermissibly impose costs on the services necessary to obtain birth control, they recreate the cost barriers that existed prior to the ACA. As a result, while a woman may have coverage of the specific birth control method her health care provider prescribes, it can remain out of reach.

Birth Control Counseling Services

Despite the fact that the birth control coverage benefit explicitly includes coverage of "patient education and counseling," some plans impose out-of-pocket costs for these services or place impermissible limits on them. The Center's plan document review discovered these examples of plans refusing to fully cover birth control education and counseling:

- Multiple plans offered by one insurance company in Colorado in 2015 require out-of-pocket costs, copayments, and/or deductibles for family planning counseling.[50]
- An insurance company in Florida requires office visit charges for birth control management, patient education, and counseling.[51]
- An insurance company in Ohio limits birth control counseling to two visits per year.[52]

Services Associated with Provider-Administered Birth Control

Prior to the ACA, some of the most effective birth control methods that are administered by health care providers were out of reach for many women because of their high upfront costs. Women have reported to the Center that removing cost barriers to long-acting reversible contraceptives (LARCs), like IUDs, has enabled them to choose this very effective method, which would not have been possible prior to the ACA. LARCs have higher upfront costs than other birth control. Without insurance coverage, IUDs can cost between $500 and $1000 upfront, which can be nearly a month's salary for a woman working a minimum wage job.[53] Prior to the ACA, these costs prevented some women from choosing a LARC.[54] However, even after the birth control benefit removed the cost barriers to these more effective methods, some women are still being billed for costs associated with LARCs. Women then face hundreds of dollars in unexpected and unallowable medical costs.

Women have reported this problem to CoverHer, and the Center's review of plan documents confirms this problem:

- An insurance company in Missouri required a woman to pay $228.31 in out-of-pocket costs for her follow-up visit, including a routine ultrasound, after she received an IUD.[55] The plan covered the device and insertion, but when she returned for the follow-up visit to ensure the IUD was properly placed, her plan imposed a co-pay on the follow-up visit and required her to meet her deductible before covering the costs of the ultrasound.
- An insurance company in South Dakota will only cover IUD placement and removal once every five years.[56] This could result in impermissible charges for women, such as a woman who removes her IUD in order to become pregnant, and wants an IUD after the birth of her child.
- An insurance company in California requires out-of-pocket costs for the physician office visits for injectable contraception.[57] These visits must occur every 12 weeks, which could become a financial burden for a woman.
- This same insurance company in California requires office visit costs for diaphragm fitting.[58]

Services Associated with Sterilization

Other women have reported being charged for services associated with sterilizations, such as the test to confirm that a sterilization procedure was successful. The non-surgical sterilization procedure is not considered complete, and women must continue using other birth control methods, until testing confirms the initial procedure was successful. Women have told the CoverHer hotline that they are shocked by these unanticipated costs, and some women have told the CoverHer hotline that they did not undergo the confirmation test because of the out-of-pocket costs. These women are left in limbo with a procedure that "may or may not be complete," as one woman told CoverHer.

Reports to the CoverHer hotline and the Center's review of plan documents have found that plans continue to charge women for services associated with sterilizations:

- After covering one woman's sterilization procedure completely, a major insurance company required her to pay $1,600 for her follow-up confirmation test.[59]
- An insurance company applied a total of $8,600 to a woman's deductible and subjected her to co-payments for her sterilization.[60] While the plan covered the charges for a woman's gynecologist to perform a sterilization procedure, it imposed out-of-pocket costs on the other items and services associated with it, including the necessary anesthesia.
- An issuer in Alabama limits coverage of sterilization confirmation tests to two tests per lifetime, even though multiple tests may be needed for the procedure to be confirmed as successful.[61]

Plans Have Other Impermissible Policies

In addition to the three major trends discussed above, the Center's review of plan documents, reports received on CoverHer, and correspondence with insurance companies identified other violations of the birth control coverage benefit:

Failure to Have a Process to Waive Out-of-Pocket Costs

No plan that was reviewed for this report had a clear process to waive out-of-pocket costs when a woman's medical provider has determined a specific method or brand is medically appropriate for her. This is reflective of the experiences of women who contact the CoverHer hotline. For example, when a woman needs a brand-name birth control because she has had adverse reactions to a generic equivalent, the plan must have a waiver process so that she can access the brand-name version that is medically appropriate for her. Women are sometimes told by their insurance company that the plan does not need a waiver process, and she is left without coverage. Often, women are told to go through

a prior authorization process, but when their health care provider submits the form, there is no record of it at the insurance company, or the coverage is approved, but she still has out-of-pocket costs.

Failing to Cover Sterilization for Dependents

An insurance company in South Dakota excludes sterilization for "dependent children"—which includes adults up to the age of 26.[62] The ACA's birth control benefit encompasses all women of reproductive capacity. This provision violates the law and would leave many women without coverage of this procedure.

Imposing Age Limits on Birth Control Coverage

An insurance company in Colorado limits coverage of birth control to women under 50.[63] Many women over the age of 50 continue to need birth control to prevent pregnancies.[64] Women who contact the CoverHer hotline with this problem often previously had coverage of their birth control without out-of-pocket costs, but when they turned 50 suddenly had a copay, had to meet a deductible, or had no coverage of their birth control. The ACA requires coverage of *all* women with reproductive capacity—these types of age restrictions violate that requirement.

Policies That in Effect Delay or Deny Coverage of Birth Control

When a plan uses medical management techniques that have the effect of delaying or denying coverage of a birth control method, the plan does not comply with the ACA. For example, an insurance company in Nevada requires a health practitioner to determine that oral contraceptive drugs are not medically appropriate before it will provide coverage for other FDA-approved birth control methods.[65] An insurance company in Connecticut requires prior authorization for all birth control, which adds an improper barrier to all birth control so that no birth control is available without additional steps by a provider.[66] Two insurance companies in Minnesota create similar obstacles to access all methods through step-therapy and medical necessity tests.[67] In these instances, a woman may not be able to get coverage for the method of birth control that she and her medical provider have determined is appropriate for her, and is required by law. This could lead to women forgoing birth control altogether or using an inappropriate method, which could lead to less effective or less consistent use.

IN THEIR OWN WORDS: WOMEN WHO STILL PAY OUT-OF-POCKET FOR BIRTH CONTROL

"So far they said they only have to cover 'Tier One' prescriptions. So, I asked what that meant and they said generic. They said she can be put on another generic medication so it's paid for but on 'my plan' they only cover part of the prescription. They suggested again I have her prescription switched. [My daughter is] only 15 and the first time to be on birth control. I don't feel I should have to 'experiment' with other medications because they are trying to sideskirt the law."
—*Woman in Iowa*

STATES ENSURING WOMEN GET THE COVERAGE THEY DESERVE

After finding violations in plans in Connecticut, the Law Center, with Planned Parenthood of Southern New England, notified regulators in Connecticut. The state subsequently issued a clarifying bulletin about the birth control coverage requirement. Specifically, the bulletin directed issuers to ensure that sterilization and over-the-counter birth control are covered without out-of-pocket costs. The bulletin is an important step towards ensuring that insurance companies clearly understand the requirements of the law and do not impose inappropriate costs on women.

Recommendations

While many women are receiving coverage of birth control without out-of-pocket costs, the Center's documentation of insurance companies' practices shows that not all plans are complying with the law. To make certain that every woman gets the coverage guaranteed to her under the ACA, insurance companies and state and federal governments can take several steps to guarantee that plans comply with the law.

Issuers: Bring Coverage into Compliance

- Insurance companies should carefully **examine the coverage they provide to ensure it complies** with the ACA's birth control benefit.
- Specifically, plans and issuers must carefully examine their birth control coverage to **ensure that they are covering all FDA-approved birth control methods for women without out-of-pocket costs** as required by the law. Based on the Center's findings, they should pay particular attention to their coverage of the contraceptive patch, the contraceptive ring, over-the-counter methods, brand name methods, and services associated with birth control.

Federal Regulators: Enforce the Law and Educate the Public

- The Departments of Health and Human Services and Labor and the Treasury must **issue**

regulations that make unmistakably clear what plans must do to comply with the ACA's birth coverage requirement. For example, the Departments must **specify that *all* birth control methods for women** identified in the FDA's Birth Control Guide must be covered without out-of-pocket costs. The Departments should **reiterate that plans must cover without out-of-pocket costs brand-name birth control without a generic equivalent**. The Departments should also reiterate that **plans must cover all services associated with birth control**.

- The Departments must **robustly enforce** the ACA's birth control requirement. For example, women in self-funded coverage regulated by the Department of Labor reported to the CoverHer.org hotline that the Department was unable to resolve their complaints about coverage of the vaginal contraceptive ring. The federal government can **improve its enforcement at two critical points**. First, when the Departments take on the role of reviewing plan documents, the Departments must ensure that the plans provide coverage of every FDA-approved birth control method without cost sharing. Also, where the Departments are tasked with enforcing the birth control coverage requirement, such as in states that have declared they will not enforce the ACA or for self-funded health plans, the Departments must do so.

- The Departments should **undertake greater efforts to ensure that every woman guaranteed coverage of birth control without out-of-pocket costs under the ACA knows about the**

requirement. Without knowledge of this part of the law, women will not have the information they need to make the Departments aware of implementation problems. The Departments must ensure that the public has the knowledge it needs to report violations of the ACA.

State Regulators: Enforce the Law

- **Prior to approving** any plan to be offered as insurance coverage in the state, either on the marketplace or through an employer, the state agency tasked with reviewing the plan must ensure that the plan provides coverage of every FDA-approved birth control method without out-of-pocket costs. This would ensure that women would never enroll in a plan that is not compliant with the law. States should be doing this already.
- Should a woman be charged inappropriate cost sharing for birth control and file a complaint with the state, the state **must deal with her complaint swiftly and appropriately**. Several women reported to the CoverHer.org hotline that they

had filed complaints with their state insurance commissioners about their plans' failure to cover the vaginal contraceptive ring or the contraceptive patch. However, in several states, the commissioner simply reiterated a health plan's coverage policy without consideration of the ACA's birth control requirement. These commissioners have not addressed the women's complaints or resolved the issue as it should be resolved under the ACA.

Conclusion

The ACA's birth control benefit is critical to making sure that women are able to access the preventive health care they need. Millions of women across the country are already benefiting from the law, in terms of their health and the impact it has on their families and lives. But some plans are not fully in compliance, leaving women without the coverage to which they are entitled. Identifying problems is the first step, but it is attention and dedicated efforts by various stakeholders that will guarantee that every woman receives the full promise of the ACA's birth control coverage benefit.

"Challenges to the Contraceptive Coverage Rule: What's at Stake?"

By Jennifer Lee and Sarah Lipton-Lubet

For the *National Women's Health Network*

Article taken from May/June 2013 Newsletter

Since the Obama Administration announced in August 2011 that health insurance plans would be required to cover contraceptive care without charging co-pays, over 50 lawsuits have been filed across the country claiming that requiring employers to provide insurance coverage for contraception violates employers' religious beliefs. The lawsuits may be making headlines, but the Administration's rule for implementing this policy, which includes a narrow exemption for institutions such as houses of worship, is fully consistent with religious freedom law and principles—not to mention that it is a major advance for women's health and equality. Nonetheless, with this many cases at play, it is almost certain that at least one of the lawsuits will be heard by the Supreme Court, and the outcome could affect far more than the future of the contraceptive coverage rule.

Challenges Brought by Non-Profit Organizations

Many of the challenges have been brought by religiously affiliated non-profit organizations, including universities and social service agencies. As we explain below, these cases should fail on the merits because requiring health plans to cover contraception doesn't harm religious liberty. For the most part, however, courts have dismissed these cases as premature. That's because the administration put in place a two-part system to respond to objections from religiously affiliated employers.

Part one was a "safe harbor" provision that means the rule won't be enforced against non-profits with religious objections to contraception until August 1, 2013. Part two is an "accommodation" whereby employees who work for non-profits that hold themselves out as reli-

gious can get contraceptive coverage directly from their insurance companies, allowing their employers to opt out of contributing to that part of their insurance. The Obama Administration issued a proposed rule laying out this accommodation on February 1, 2013, and it is due to be finalized before the safe harbor expires in August.

The non-profit challenges never had a leg to stand on, and in light of the accommodation, their cases are even weaker. Nonetheless, some plaintiffs are likely to continue to press their claims.

Challenges Brought by For-Profit Companies

A substantial number of these cases, however, have been filed by *for-profit* companies, including a mining company in Missouri, a wastewater treatment company in Minnesota, and, most famously, the national craft supply chain store, Hobby Lobby, headquartered in Oklahoma. The lawsuits claim that providing contraceptive coverage "substantially burdens" both the companies' and their owners' religious beliefs. All this despite the fact that many of these companies had been covering—and continue to cover—contraceptives in their health insurance.

These cases are moving at a faster clip than the cases brought by non-profits, and are making their way through the courts. Most decisions in the for-profit cases have been preliminary—responding to requests to temporarily block the rule while the litigation proceeds—as opposed to a final decision as to whether the rule violates religious liberty and therefore whether employers need to comply with it and provide coverage in the long run. The courts have been divided in these cases with roughly half temporarily blocking the rule, and the other half declining to do so. The one court to actually reach a final decision dismissed the case altogether, reasoning that it is clear that the contraceptive coverage rule doesn't violate any religious liberty protections.

Some of these cases have already been appealed to higher courts. Four appellate courts and U.S. Supreme Court Justice Sotomayor (acting as the Circuit Justice for the 10th Circuit) refused to temporarily block the rule, reasoning either that the connection between a business and its employees' use of birth control is too remote to violate religious liberty protections, or that a for-profit company cannot exercise religion.

In contrast, two other appellate courts, wagering that the plaintiffs might prevail in the end, granted preliminary relief blocking the rule, meaning that it won't be enforced against those plaintiffs until their entire case has played out. Such splits are likely to continue as the cases wind their way through the appellate courts and up to the U.S. Supreme Court.

Here's How We See It

While this country ardently embraces the fundamental right of religious freedom, that right is not limitless. The Supreme Court has long recognized that "[w]hen followers of a particular sect enter into commercial activity as a matter of choice, the limits they accept on their own conduct as a matter of conscience and faith are not to be superimposed on the statutory schemes which are binding on others in that activity."[1] In other words, religious liberty protects your right to believe whatever you want, but it does not mean you can impose your religious beliefs on others to their detriment.

What's more, the contraception rule simply does not "substantially burden" religious exercise, as the plaintiffs claim. Purchasing health insurance that covers a wide range of medical care, including contraceptives, which an employee might decide to use or not use, does not substantially burden the *employer's* religious beliefs about contraception.

Health insurance is another form of employee compensation, similar to one's salary. An employer could not refuse to pay an employee's salary on the grounds that the employee might use that money to purchase alcohol, or rent an apartment shared with a non-marital partner—even if those actions are contrary to the employer's beliefs. Similarly, we all pay taxes, and our money might eventually fund a war that we oppose, or contraceptive coverage through programs like Medicaid. But we cannot refuse to pay taxes as a result, and the courts have recognized that a chain of events like this is too attenuated to violate religious freedom.

Fundamentally, an employer is free to believe and say whatever she wants about contraception. She can refuse to use it and try to discourage others from doing so, but she must still comply with the law and give her employees the option to obtain affordable preventive health care through their insurance. Whether an employee makes the independent choice to use her health insurance to obtain contraception is, frankly, none of the boss's business.

We believe the contraception rule should survive the lawsuits for another reason as well. Even when a law substantially burdens religious exercise, it can stand as long as it furthers a "compelling government interest." In the past, courts have found that such interests include combating discrimination. The contraceptive coverage rule does just that by promoting women's health and equality.

Women pay substantially more than men do in out-of-pocket medical expenses, and much of those costs are related to reproductive health care. Studies show that cost is a significant barrier to accessing necessary health care.[2] By making contraceptives more affordable—and more accessible—the ACA's contraceptive coverage rule ensures that more women can get the health care they need, improving both their own health and their future children's.

Broadly speaking, increasing contraceptive access is an important step towards promoting women's equality. Contraceptive availability has played a critical role in allowing women to attend college and graduate school by allowing them to decide whether and when to become parents.[3] It has also improved women's ability to advance in the workplace through education or on-the-job training, which has narrowed the wage gap between men and women.[4] These are exactly the kinds of interests courts have, in the past, considered to be "compelling."

Blast From the Past

The spate of challenges to the contraception rule is not the first time we've seen religious freedom claims invoked to oppose laws designed to advance equality. After passage of the Civil Rights Act of 1964, owners of a restaurant chain in South Carolina argued that the law violated their religious beliefs opposing integration, and that they should be allowed to exclude African-Americans from their restaurant.[5]

Decades later, religiously affiliated schools argued that they should be allowed to pay men more than women—despite the Equal Pay Act—because the Bible designated men as the heads of households.[6] In all of these cases, the courts rejected the argument that religious beliefs can be used to discriminate and to justify violating civil rights and labor laws.

While those examples might sound outmoded, the same reasoning is being revived today—and not just in the context of contraceptive coverage. When the Supreme Court decides one of the contraception rule cases, it will also weigh in on how far the mantle of religious freedom can be used to discriminate and to impose one person's religious beliefs on others.

If your employer can withhold contraceptive coverage, can he also deny coverage for HIV/AIDS treatment due to religious beliefs about how the disease is transmitted? Can he fire you for becoming pregnant outside of marriage because of his religious opposition to non-marital sex?[7] The issue goes beyond the context of employment. Can a hotel refuse to host a gay couple's wedding because the owners believe the Bible limits marriage to a man and a woman?[8] Can a pharmacy refuse to fill prescriptions for fertility drugs because he is opposed to *in vitro* fertilization? Can a police officer refuse to protect a mosque?[9]

Like other significant laws that promote equality by prohibiting discrimination, ensuring equal treatment, or rectifying systemic inequalities, the contraception rule is a huge step forward for our society. It ensures that millions of women can decide for themselves, based on their own beliefs, whether and when to use birth control. As the Supreme Court put it in 1961, we live "in a cosmopolitan nation made up of people of almost every conceivable religious preference."[10] It is important that our commitment to religious freedom ensures that *no* single set of religious beliefs is privileged, imposed on others, or used as a license to discriminate.

Learn more about the contraception rule and lawsuits at: *http://www.aclu.org/reproductive-freedom/ challenges-federal-contraceptive-coverage-rule*

Jennifer Lee is a staff attorney in the ACLU's Center for Liberty and Sarah Lipton-Lubet is a policy counsel in the ACLU's Washington Legislative Office.

REFERENCES

1. United States v. Lee, 455 U.S. 252, 261 (1982).

2. Liang SY, Grossman D, Phillips KA, et al., "Women's Out-of-Pocket Expenditures and Dispensing Patterns for Oral Contraceptive Pills between 1996 and 2006," *Contraception* 2011; 83: 528–36.

3. Goldin C and LF Katz, "The Power Of The Pill: Contraceptives And Women's Career And Marriage Decisions," *Journal of Political Economy* 2002; 110: 730–770.

4. Bailey MJ, Hershbein B, Miller AR, "The Opt-In Revolution? Contraception and the Gender Gap in Wages," *American Economic Journal* 2012: 4(3); 225–54.

5. Newman v. Piggie Park Enter., Inc., 256 F. Supp. 941 (D.S.C. 1966), aff'd in relevant part and rev'd in part on other grounds, 377 F.2d 433 (4th Cir. 1967), aff'd and modified on other grounds, 390 U.S. 400 (1968).

6. Dole v. Shenandoah Baptist Church, 899 F.2d 1389 (4th Cir. 1990).

7. See, e.g., Katherine Bindley, "Teri James, Pregnant Woman, Allegedly Fired for Premarital Sex, Sues Christian School," Huffington Post (Mar. 1, 2013), available at http://www.huffingtonpost.com/2013/03/01/teri-james-pregnant-woman-fired-premarital-sex-christian-school_n_2790085.html (last visited Mar. 22, 2013).

8. See, e.g., Dave Gram, "Vermont's Wildflower Inn Settles Gay Marriage Lawsuit with Lesbian Couple," Associated Press (Mar. 23, 2012), available at http://www.huffington-post.com/2012/08/23/wildflower-inn-vermont-gay-marriage-lawsuit_n_1826218.html (last visited Mar. 22, 2013).

9. See, e.g., David Harper "Judge Rules for Tulsa in Police Captain's Suit Over Event at Mosque," Tulsa World (Dec.14, 2012), available at http://www.tulsaworld.com/news/article.aspx?subjectid=14&articleid=20121214_14_A1_CUTLIN548215 (last visited Mar. 22, 2013).

10. Braunfeld v. Brown, 366 U.S. 599, 606 (1961).

"The Battle for Reproductive Justice: Denying Indian Women Plan B Affects All Women"

By Chloe Haimson
For *Indian Country Today Media Network* (1/3/13)

As the presidential election approached, we heard plenty of political rhetoric about reproductive rights. From abortion laws to "legitimate rape," everyone seems to have an opinion about women's bodies.

It's time we refocus the conversation and stand back to examine the effect these decisions are having on real women—not merely characters featured in politicians' talking points.

As a recent female college graduate, entering into the professional world, I often hear the debate regarding whether women can have it all: career, kids, and a healthy marriage. It's an important question but there's an inherent privilege that's implied by asking it. What about this question—forget "having it all" for a moment—*can women even have Plan B?*

To answer the question, I spoke with Charon Asetoyer, a health activist working with young women on the Yankton Indian Reservation in South Dakota. She is leading the battle for reproductive justice in the Native American community and, ultimately, for women everywhere.

Charon Asetoyer

"Native women cannot get Plan B through their primary healthcare provider, Indian Health Service (IHS). We're looking at more than 1 in 3 Native women being raped in her lifetime and Indian Health Service is doing absolutely nothing to address these residual effects of rape. That is a human rights violation being committed against Native women every day in this country," says Asetoyer.

Very few IHS pharmacies administer over-the-counter Plan B (the morning after pill) and many do not carry it at all. Asetoyer says that what 26-year-old Lakota Sunny Clifford experienced is all too common.

"I wasn't even aware I could get Plan B from IHS," Clifford, who lives on the Pine Ridge Reservation, tells me. This past July, Clifford called her local clinic to request the emergency contraceptive. In the United States, every woman 17 and older is legally entitled to access Plan B over the counter. However, Clifford's clinic in Kyle, South Dakota told her that she would have to get a prescription from the midwife who was not in the office. Her other options were to drive to Wanbli Health Center or Pine Ridge, both of which are about 50 miles away.

"I sat there and cried a little bit. It was really frustrating for me. I was sitting there and I didn't have a dollar to my name. I didn't have a car. I felt powerless," says Clifford.

Remember the beginning of this post, when I told you I wanted to talk about the effect reproductive rights policies are having on REAL women. Well, here's an example: Asetoyer explains that often mothers will walk into her office, wanting to know when Plan B will be widely accessible. "They want more information about Plan B so they can talk to their daughters so that when they are sexually assaulted, they'll know about it and be able to request it."

It's frightening to consider how something so horrific becomes the norm. There is no question; rather, it's an expectation for these women that one day their daughter may be sexually assaulted. Asetoyer adds, "That's shocking when a mother says *when my daughter is sexually assaulted.* And that is absolutely unacceptable in every other community and the government is doing little of anything to help address this."

Indian Country Today Media Network (http://indiancountrytodaymedianetwork.com/article/battle-reproductive-justice-denying-indian-women-plan-b-affects-all-women-146721),

It is an outrage that not only may it be difficult to physically access Plan B but also the lack of information regarding emergency contraceptives can serve as an obstacle for young women who have been sexually assaulted.

Sunny Clifford

Most women living in non-rural areas can simply walk into their local pharmacy and request Plan B. So what does all this have to do with the vast majority of women in America? As Asetoyer explains, "These issues are not only affecting Native women but anytime a woman is denied a right, it affects all women. Because if they can get by with it with a small segment of the population in the country then they're gonna be able to get by with it with another group."

We need to be careful when we discuss this question of "having it all." What does it mean? Who are we talking about it? Many of us can walk into a pharmacy and request Plan B without the worry of whether the person at the counter will tell us to travel hours away. For some women, justice does not simply begin at economic opportunities equal to men but also encompasses a human right to control our reproductive systems that more privileged women, myself included, take for granted every day. The truth is no woman can count on "having it all" as long as some women continue to be denied even the basics.

For more information, please visit http://www.native-shop.org/images/stories/media/pdfs/Plan-B-Report.pdf for the Roundtable Report on the Access of Plan B as an Over the Counter (OTIC) Within Indian Health Service.

[Editor's note: This piece follows as the next selection in this volume.]

Chloe Haimson, a recent graduate of Princeton University, lives in New York City. This piece is the first in a series she is working on funded by Native American Public Telecommunications. The series, Sovereign Bodies, focuses on Native women reproductive health issues and is being produced in conjunction with the documentary film Young Lakota, airing on PBS Independent Lens in November 2013 as part of the Women and Girls Lead initiative.

"Roundtable Report On The Accessibility of Plan B® As An Over The Counter (OTC) Within Indian Health Service"

From the *"Native American Women's Health Education Resource Center Indigenous Women's Dialogue"*

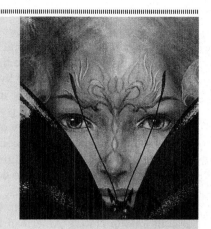

Introduction By Charon Asetoyer, MA

What does it mean for a Native American woman to be denied information after a sexual assault that could prevent an unwanted pregnancy; to not be informed of, or offered, Emergency Contraception and at a later date be faced with the dilemma of a pregnancy from a rape? What kind of a Government would impose such a trauma on a woman, to force her to experience such a cruel and emotional life event? For thousands of Native American women this is reality.

Although Plan B® is legal as an "over the counter" (OTC) contraceptive for women age 17 years old and up, Native American women do not have consistent access to it from our primary health care provider, the Indian Health Service. For land based (reservation) Native American women the only pharmacist on most reservations is within the local Indian Health Service. Other options would be to travel to the nearest city to a mainstream pharmacy to access Plan B®, which could be as far away as one hundred miles. Does a woman have the resources to travel that hundred miles to find a pharmacy that carries Plan B®? Does she have a car, gas money, and the $50.00 to purchase Plan B®? Native women need far more resources then other women to access Plan B®. These barriers prevent access to Plan B® for Native American women.

Unfortunately statistics tell us that Native American women are sexually assaulted at a higher rate then all other women in the United States and receive less health care services and less "due process" after a sexual assault. This situation is unacceptable and must be resolved in order to bring some relief and equality in treatment to Native American women.

As the country debates the access to Plan B® as an OTC for women 16 years and younger, Native American women 17 years and older have yet to receive access to Plan B® as an OTC by their primary health care provider, the Indian Health Service. No one but Native American women are concerned about this denial of service. As Native American women we are the only race of women that is denied this service based on race. To make an exception to a legal form of contraception based on race is not acceptable. To deny a Native American woman access to Plan B® as an OTC when every other woman in this country can access it is a denial to a basic health care service, which violates her human rights. It is a direct violation to her sovereign right to make decisions for her own health care, it removes her from the decision making process concerning a potential pregnancy resulting from a rape and puts that responsibility of decision in the hands of a government agency.

On a late Saturday night our office called the Sioux San Indian Health Service Emergency room in Rapid City, South Dakota to ask if they would provide Plan B® for a rape victim, the response was "no we do not, if you want it go buy it", that response was cold, lacking compassion and judgmental. For an advocate to hear a response like that from an Indian Health Service health care provider was very offensive. This situation is not the only incident of denial of Plan B® (EC) within the Indian Health Service system.

Within this report you will hear the voices of Native American women from a diverse number of Tribes discuss their own personal experience with sexual assault either as a victim or as a service provider.

It is important to understand that the issue of access to Plan B® is not a matter to be decided by the predominately male led leadership of our communities, but is a matter of equal access to a legal contraceptive that is to be made by a woman. To use the excuse that access to Plan B® needs to be decided by Tribal leadership is extremely oppressive and is not in the best interest of Native American women. The issue of access to Plan B® has been approved for every other demographic of women in this country, so why continue to deny Native American women access. Traditionally the maters of women were left up to women to decide and not thrown into the political arena.

Taking into consideration the high rates of sexual assault among Native American females, rural isolation and lack of resources to access Plan B® we ask the current Administration to respect our rights, to let actions speak louder then words and take the necessary steps to ensure that Native American women are no longer denied Plan B® as an OTC within the Indian Health Service.

Charon Asetoyer, MA, Executive Director
Native American Women's Health Education Resource Center

Indigenous Women's Dialogue

"Let us learn from each other and not be afraid to speak. Let us take the time to share with each other, and be strong because that's what we need to do to ensure that we get our work done. What we do today has a connection with the other women doing this work and to the people in our communities."—Peggy Bird

> ### DID YOU KNOW?
>
> Native American Women experience sexual assault at a higher rate then all other U.S. populations.
>
> - 34.1% or more than 1 in 3 Native American women will be raped in their lifetime.
> - 92% of Native American girls who had sexual intercourse reported having been forced against their will to have sexual intercourse on a date.

Background

The Declaration on the Rights of Indigenous Peoples sets out the individual and collective rights of Indigenous Peoples, as well as their rights to culture, identity, language, employment, health, education and other issues.

It also emphasizes the rights of Indigenous Peoples to maintain and strengthen their own institutions, cultures and traditions, and to pursue their development in keeping with their own needs and aspirations. It prohibits discrimination against Indigenous Peoples, and it promotes their full and effective participation in all matters that concern them and their right to remain distinct and to pursue their own visions of economic and social development.

Taking note of the recommendation of the Human Rights Council by which the Council adopted the text of the United Nations Declaration on the Rights of Indigenous Peoples, the General Assembly formally adapted the Declaration on September 13, 2007. You may view the full text here: http://www.worldinbalance.net/intagreements/2007-indigenouspeoples.php

The United States of America was the last of the four nations who opposed the Declaration in 2007. Eventually, the United States of America endorsed the United Nations Declaration on the Rights of Indigenous Peoples on December 16th, 2010. During the White House Tribal Nations Conference on December 16, 2010, President Obama made the following statement:

> *"The aspirations it affirms—including respect for the institutions and rich cultures of Native Peoples—are ones we must always seek to fulfill." "But I want to be clear: What matters far more than words—what matters far more than any resolution or declaration—are actions to match those words."*
>
> **—President Barack Obama**

Article 23

Indigenous peoples have the right to determine and develop priorities and strategies for exercising their right to development. In particular, Indigenous peoples have the right to be actively involved in developing and determining health, housing and other economic and social programs affecting them and, as far as possible, to administer such programs through their own institutions.

Article 24

1. Indigenous peoples have the right to their traditional medicines and to maintain their health practices, including the conservation of their vital medicinal plants, animals and minerals. Indigenous individuals also have the right to access, without any discrimination, all social and health services.
2. Indigenous individuals have an equal right to the enjoyment of the highest attainable standard of

physical and mental health. States shall take the necessary steps with a view to achieving progressively the full realization of this right.

Our Work—Our Impact

The Native American Women's Health Education Resource Center (NAWHERC) provides direct services to Native American women in South Dakota and advocates for Native American women at the local, national and international levels to protect our reproductive health and rights. Internationally, we organize Indigenous women and participate in coalitions working on reproductive health and rights policies. As a long-lived "pathfinder" organization, NAWHERC has become the leader in addressing Indigenous women's reproductive health and rights issues in the country. NAWHERC focuses its programs on serving reservation & land based Native American women with ongoing outreach to urban Native American women throughout the United States.

NAWHERC's reports have been submitted to and used by Congress, the United Nations, the World Health Organization and university and policy institutes to bring awareness of the reproductive health issues facing Indigenous women, and by Amnesty International's *Maze of Injustice* (released April 2007 and updated in spring 2008), a report that shows the failure to protect Native American women from sexual violence in the United States. NAWHERC's work has resulted in policy changes such as: improvements in informed consent; providing patients with results for abnormal pap tests; treatment of HIV+ patients; patient confidentiality; and the discontinuation of Norplant. NAWHERC has brought to the forefront Indian Health Services' (IHS) treatment of rape/incest victims and has documented IHS's violations of Native American women's right to health care and to pregnancy prevention/choice. NAWHERC has linked Native American women to federal policies affecting their daily lives, and has promoted their voice and activism to decision makers at the highest levels. NAWHERC works with a national, broad-based and diverse coalition of Native American, women's health and civil liberties organizations.

Challenges Faced By Native American Women

The potential for Native American women to need reproductive choice or emergency contraception (EC) because of a violent incident statistically far exceeds that of the general population. Native Americans are raped at a rate nearly double that of rapes reported by all races annually—34.1%, or more than 1 in 3, of Native American women will be raped in their lifetime. Three-fourths of Native American women have experienced some type of sexual assault in their lives.

> *"I've heard women ask for information about Emergency Contraceptives so they can talk to their daughters about what to do when they are sexually assaulted, not if they are sexually assaulted, but when."*
>
> **—Charon**

For most Native Americans, IHS serves as our primary health care provider. IHS is subject to federal policies, including the Hyde Amendment, that exclude abortion from the comprehensive health care services provided to low-income people by the federal government, except in cases of rape, incest, or endangerment of the woman's life.

From 1973—2001 throughout its 157 IHS and Tribal managed Service Units, IHS performed only 25 abortions under the Hyde Amendment. Due to the sexual violence statistics cited above, it is **highly unlikely** that in nearly 30 years, only 25 Native American women nationwide who were victims of rape or incest or whose lives were endangered by pregnancy sought an abortion from IHS. In fact, our documented research revealed that the vast majority—85%—of IHS Service Units were not in compliance with the official IHS abortion directive, which supports the Hyde Amendment. Despite the existence of directives, services and procedures are not standardized at each IHS unit. The standard of abortion counseling, abortion information provided to interested women and referrals to abortion providers are often left to the discretion of IHS personnel.

Over the years, IHS has denied Native American women the same options of birth control that are afforded to mainstream women. EC and Plan B® (or their generic forms) are still not adequately available at IHS facilities as an OTC (over the counter). NAWHERC's January 2009 research, *"Roundtable Report on the Availability of Plan B® and EC within the IHS"* found that: 1) Only 10% of IHS unit pharmacies surveyed have Plan B® available over the counter (OTC); 2) 37.5% of pharmacies surveyed offer an alternative form of emergency contraception; and 3) The remaining have no form of EC available at all.

The minimal availability of Plan B® is due, based on pharmacists' responses to our survey, to Pharmacy and Therapeutics Committees neglecting to put the drug on approved lists (formularies), medical staff deciding Plan B®'s inclusion on the formulary is not necessary, the expense of the drug, the existence of another method of EC of the same efficacy, pharmacies not handling "symptoms" of this nature (despite carrying daily oral contraceptive pills), the drug not being requested by doctors and to the low overall number of requests for EC. The low number of requests for EC despite the high incidence of rape of Native American women indicates that *women are unaware of the existence of EC*. It also illustrates that IHS doctors and nurses are not informing women of its existence although it is IHS's duty to provide women with this information.

Many Native American women are not receiving the services to which they are legally entitled. IHS's failure to provide these services to women who are entitled is a violation of our legal right to access abortion/pregnancy prevention services and of our fundamental human rights. These violations have been further highlighted in Amnesty International's *Maze of Injustice* report mentioned above.

Our study illustrates the fact that some IHS units provide EC and some do not, that some use Plan B®, but most use the old formula of several high dose birth control pills. This provides a clear picture of the need for standardized care within IHS Service Units. A women should be able to go into an IHS Service Unit and get the same standard of care no matter where she is being seen. The inconsistency of services from one service unit to another creates a situation that lowers the standard of health care for Native American victims of sexual assault. It violates our right to health services, permits discrimination against Native Peoples and is in direct violation of Article 23 & 24 of the United Nations Declaration on the Rights of Indigenous Peoples.

---

[1] American Indian Women's Chemical Health Project report.

[2] NAWHERC's January 2005 report, "A Survey of Sexual Assault Policies and Protocols within IHS Emergency Rooms," documented the huge gap in IHS services for Native American women who have been sexually assaulted. A national roundtable in June 2005 brought together Native, health and women's organizations, tribes, violence shelter advocates and Native rape/incest victims. A fall 2005 report published the Roundtable's recommendations and was sent to 350+ organizations, tribes and legislators.

[3] Consisting of two pills, Plan B® is a method of EC that is an extremely safe, simple, and effective way to reduce unwanted pregnancy and the possible need to have an abortion. Plan B® is not an abortificent. Plan B® is safer, easier to use and more effective than the off-label use of birth control pills or other older EC methods. If started within 24 hours of unprotected sex, Plan B® reduces the risk of pregnant by 95% (and if taken within 72 hours reduces pregnancy by 89%). Plan B® was approved by the U.S. Food and Drug Administration (FDA) in 1999 for prescription use. A 2006 FDA ruling made Plan B® available OTC for adult women and available with a prescription for women under 18. An April 2009 ruling by a U.S. District Court judge lowered the OTC age to 17. (Women under 17 still need a prescription to access the drug. Therefore it must be kept behind the counter. This creates two potential barriers to access, as proof of age must be presented and buyers must interact with a pharmacist (who could refuse to provide the medication on "moral" grounds) in order to obtain the drug.)

Indigenous individuals have an equal right to the enjoyment of the highest attainable standard of physical and mental health. States shall take the necessary steps with a view to achieving progressively the full realization of this right.

History of Standardized Sexual Assault Policies and Protocols

The Native American Women's Health Education Resource Center (NAWHERC) staff is victorious with this objective. Although it did not occur overnight, it is now reality. Some historical facts: we started working on Standardized Sexual Assault Policies and Protocols within Indian Health Service Emergency Rooms in 2004 and released a report in January of 2005. The report Sexual Assault Policies and Protocols within the Indian Health Emergency Rooms revealed that 30 percent of the service units have no protocol in place for the care of women who have been raped or sexually assaulted; although 70 percent of the units report that they have a protocol, only 56 percent of those indicate that the protocol is posted and accessible to staff members.

- In 2005, we convened our Roundtable and released the Roundtable Report on Sexual Assault Policies and Protocols within Indian Health Service Emergency Rooms in October of 2005. Over the course of 2005—2010, we formed a coalition of allied organizations and individuals to help us work on this issue. On November 4, 2005, the National Congress of American Indians passed a Resolution in support of our work. NCAI passed Resolution #TUL-05-101 in support of adoption and implementation of these Standardized Sexual Assault Policies and Protocols. When Indian Health Service was asked about Standardized Sexual Assault Policies and Protocols their repeated response is that they respect the sovereignty of tribes and IHS does not impose standardized policies. With the passage of this resolution, which is a collective decision of sovereign Tribes, IHS still did not implement Standardized Sexual Assault Policies and Protocols. This is not respecting the decision or the sovereignty of Tribes; it is undermining the sovereignty of Tribes to work together.
- During 2006–2007, we worked with Amnesty International on the development of the Maze of Injustice Report that documents the failure of the U.S. Government to protect Indigenous women from sexual violence in the United States. NAWHERC Executive Director Charon Asetoyer

was appointed to IHS's National Native American Women's Health Advisory Committee that allowed us some influence on developing and advising on the implementation of IHS' Standardized Sexual Assault Policies and Protocols along with developing guidelines for national level pilot projects for SANEs. NAWHERC and Coalition members met with IHS representatives at IHS Headquarters.

- In 2009, Charon Asetoyer, Executive Director of NAWHERC, was invited to testify in front of the U.S. House Interior and Environment Appropriations Subcommittee on the issue. What was to be a five-minute statement on the issues turned into twenty-minutes of questions and answers by the Subcommittee members. Each question proving farther into the issues of sexual assault against Native American women and the lack of services available for reservation based women through IHS, establishing the need for Standardized Sexual Assault Policies and Protocols within IHS Emergency Rooms.

- In 2009, NAWHERC Executive Director Charon Asetoyer and members of the Amnesty International's *Maze of Injustice* committee met with White House staff to continue with top-level discussions on the issue of sexual assault against Native American women. Issues of priority included but were not limited to the following; standardized sexual assault policies and protocols within IHS, the need for changes in the IHS witness approval process for sexual assault victims and the issues related to EC / Plan B® access for Native American women within IHS.

- In 2008 a call from Senator Tim Johnson's office (D-SD) came into the NAWHERC requesting Charon Asetoyer to recommend four items of need that would improve the health care services within IHS for victims of sexual assault. It was to be added onto the Indian Health Care Improvement Act. It didn't take long for Charon to contact Attorney Sarah Deer, a coalition member and an expert on the topic of IHS witness approval process. Between the two coalition members four recommendations were sent back to Senator Johnson's office recommending; Standardized Sexual Assault Policies and Protocols within IHS Emergency Rooms, a change in the witness approval process for the health care provider that do the "rape exam", funding for Sexual Assault Nurse Examiner programs, and modifications in the IHS method of collecting statistics on sexual assaults victims. The recommendations were put

into the Bill. However, due to a poison bill provision slipped in by Sen. David Vitter (R-La) that explicitly restricts abortion under IHS programs the bill passed the Senate but did not pass the House. With quick thinking staff from Senator Tim Johnson's office some of the recommendations were able to get into the 2009 Omnibus Appropriations Act.

- On March 11, 2009, President Obama signed the Omnibus Appropriations Act of 2009. Included in the Act there is language that provides the following: "In order to provide the IHS with additional tools to better address child and family violence in American Indian/Alaska Native communities, the bill includes $7,500,000 to implement a nationally coordinated domestic violence prevention initiative. With these funds, the IHS is encouraged to further expand its outreach advocacy programs into Native communities, expand the Domestic Violence and Sexual Assault Pilot project already in operation, and use a portion of the funding for training and the purchase of forensic equipment to support the Sexual Assault Nurse Examiner program . . . The report [required of the IHS] should address the Service's progress in developing standardized sexual assault policies . . . " This was a step forward in terms of the Government not only acknowledging there are sexual assault issues in Indian Country that need to be addressed but taking steps to assist in addressing some of these issues.

Through an impressive ground swell of public interest brought on by all of the hard work, community education and advocacy done by the NAWHERC and coalition members, major language was included into the Tribal Law and Order Act of 2010. This bill, when fully implemented, will make major improvements in the way Native American women receive reproductive health services from the Indian Health Service and will give Tribes more control over law enforcement on Tribal land.

On July 29, 2010, Lisa Iyotte introduced President Obama during the bill signing at the White House, there was not a dry eye in the House when she told her story of being raped in front of her children; "No one asked me about the rape and I had to wait all night for someone to collect the DNA evidence from the attack." Iyotte said. No federal investigators interviewed Lisa Iyotte. Lisa went on to say in her speech, "The Tribal Law and Order Act will prevent cases like mine from slipping through the cracks, now that we have Standardized Sexual Assault Policies and Protocols within the Indian Health Service." NAWHERC Executive Director Charon Asetoyer was sitting in the audience when Lisa Iyotte made that statement, at that moment all she could think about was all the years of hard work that NAWHERC put into getting people to understand the importance of those few words "Standardized Sexual Assault Policies and Protocols within Indian Health Service Emergency Rooms". Now the real work begins- we must ensure that these policies are implemented within IHS.

Tribal Law and Order Act of 2010

Subtitle F—Domestic Violence and Sexual Assault Prosecution and Prevention

SEC. 17. POLICIES AND PROTOCOL

''The Director of the Indian Health Service, in coordination with the Director of the Office of Justice Services and the Director of the Office on Violence Against Women of the Department of Justice, in consultation with Indian Tribes and Tribal Organizations, and in conference with Urban Indian Organizations, shall develop standardized sexual assault policies and protocol for the facilities of the Service, based on similar protocol that has been established by the Department of Justice."

Purpose of the Indigenous Women's Dialogue

The Indigenous Women's Dialogue brought together Native American women from three states, South Dakota, Oklahoma and New Mexico—all with large Native populations and considered to be bellwether states targeted to be used as springboards by "the opposition" for national level influence. The activism supplied by Native American women can mean the difference between a restrictive policy being passed or defeated. By meeting "the opposition" on their own territory, Native American women and our allies can prevent their efforts from escalating to the national level. Fortunately, many of these bellwether states also have large Native populations, presenting the Native American Women's Health Education Resource Center with the opportunity to organize Native American women—and catalyze our allies—in response. Issues addressed by the Indigenous Women's Dialogue examined the accessibility of emergency contraception (EC) as an OTC (over the counter) by sexual assault victims through Indian Health Service, what understanding women have in terms of what EC is and the impact "the opposition" has had in terms of it's purpose and accessibility.

Indigenous Women's Dialogue:

Accessibility of Emergency Contraception for Native American Sexual Assault Victims

Over the course of the spring and summer of 2011, we convened and listened to over fifty Native American women's voices joining together in conversation, laughter and tears. They were mainly workers in domestic abuse, women's shelters and tribal sexual assault programs, and ironically, many were victims of sexual assault themselves. Overwhelmingly, we found evidence of a worsened situation for Native American women (since our 2009 report) in their attempts to gain access to emergency contraception through the Indian Health Service, and that very little is known about the improved type of emergency contraception (EC) known as Plan B®. Women shared their stories of facing an interlocked system of barriers between themselves and equitable and fair health care. These barriers relate to the control of women's bodies and lives by government policies and under-funded health care services, coupled with racist, sexist and religious attitudes embedded within those services.

Education, outreach and open discussion on the facts about sex, sexual violence, incest, birth control, emergency contraception and abortion are minimal. Unless the women have jobs with insurance or live in an urban area, there is scant information available or offered— much less actual services provided.

> *"A lot of our women in our communities aren't aware that Plan B® even exists or they associate it with the abortion pill RU486, they don't realize the difference because the media and the opposition have projected this: it's an abortion pill, when it really is a contraceptive."*
> —**Charon**

> *"I think there is confusion, because the media did speak on RU486 here in Oklahoma. Then, they put it together with Plan B®, where doctors didn't want to prescribe it because of their faith. The doctors had the option to not provide RU486, but Plan B® went out with it. That's what I got from the media here in Oklahoma, and that's what I hear arguments about."*
> —**Maya**

Access to safe, state of the art, emergency contraceptives (Plan B®) for Native American sexual assault victims at their primary health care provider (Indian Health

Service, through its parent DHHS/PHS) is more than a legal right in the United States, but a global Human Right as described earlier.

Human Rights are created and adopted to be applicable across the board, but we continue to hear Native American women's stories of restrictive and inconsistent policies, un-funded health care needs, difficulty in accessing preventive and emergency services—whether the institutions are run by the Indian Health Service, a treaty tribe or non treaty tribe, a PL 638 situation, or a "self-governed" tribe. The complexities of sovereignty and the collision of the Indian Health Services with Tribal Nations provision of some or part of those services is a labyrinth too hard to navigate, especially during a crises such as assault, violence and fear.

In many situations pertaining to Native American women's health, religious groups control access and unduly influence policy making through their long-standing and systematic advocacy and control of restrictive contraception uses by owning clinics, and in some cases entire health care systems, etc.

> *"In South Dakota, the Benedictine nuns are shrewd businesswomen. They own just about every clinic and health care facility. Even in Lake Andes, which is like a dot on the map— the whole southeast quarter of South Dakota they've bought almost every hospital and every clinic so that they can have control of family planning services. IHS contracts with some of these facilities because they don't have a choice, they shouldn't be allowed to accept federal dollars if they don't provide services."*
> **—Charon**

In Native American communities women face the added burden of "traditional Native American" roles being played out as women being silent and living in servitude to their husbands and sons. The role of boarding schools operated by churches, especially the Catholic church, means that "sexual abuse may be 'traditional' to the Catholics, but not to Native Americans" as one participant put it. This is a learned attitude that many women reported as the "norm" for tribal communities—don't talk about the sexual abuse within your family and do not speak out against it. It is frowned upon, even for the sexual assault workforce, to talk about the extremely high levels of sexual abuse in our communities, as it becomes a black eye on the Tribe itself. After listening to the women in the first two roundtables, Charon Asetoyer said, *"Sexual assault is happening all the time and we need to do something!"* These patriarchal and co-dependent or shameful

attitudes are creating the climate for unchecked sexual abuse to spawn serial rapists, who are never brought to justice. Plan B® can prevent abortions through emergency contraception, but this information must be conveyed in language that is "understood and in laymen's terms".

The statistics tell us that one in three Native American women are molested, but the women in our roundtables cautioned that rape statistics are higher in their communities and that young girls have to watch for it, taking the "not if, but when" attitude toward self protection. Many women in our discussions revealed that a lot of molestations happen within the family and they feel it is important to learn from these mistakes and put a stop to the incest by examining root causes and teach our young ones to not let anyone touch them.

The discussions and findings of the 2011 Indigenous Women's Dialogue are illustrated in the following five areas of concern:

- Inadequate Systems and Resources Perpetuate the Oppression
- Inconsistency Equals Inequality
- Indigenous Women's Bodies are Sovereign
- Laws Do Not Change Attitudes
- Women's Rights are Human Rights

1. Inadequate Systems and Resources Perpetuate the Oppression

There was resounding agreement by roundtable participants that Native American women have never received the same type or quality of health care that other American women receive. Due to the complexities of the tribal and government health care provision, each Native American community has a different set of rules and resources to access. Many of our women's shelters are not tribal shelters- they may be Native run and operated, but are generally local nonprofit organizations who may also be serving the general public.

We heard from women in four different IHS regions about the barriers in access to safe, emergency contraception through the Indian Health Service and tribal clinics. The inconsistencies, even within the Albuquerque Area were startling. A survey of 15 hospitals and clinics revealed that only two of them dispensed Plan B® as an over the counter medication. Most Native American women, and their service providers, are not aware of emergency contraception like Plan B®, or they have heard of it but have been confused by media coverage to believe it is the abortion pill RU486. Only a few of the health care workers and service providers attending the Roundtables fully understood the difference between the two pills, depending upon their area of services or expertise.

> *"The next alternative in over-the-counter access comes only if you have the financial resources to purchase Plan B® at a commercial pharmacy, generally for fifty dollars, which is a huge barrier for most Native American women. "If you are living on the reservations or one of the Pueblos without insurance, or money to pay for EC, or transportation to get you to town you are out of luck because you do not have accessibility through our own health care provider."*
>
> **—Charon**

> *" It's important to point out that we have to be concerned about forcing women to jump through so many hoops to provide health care for themselves in crises. If you are forced to undergo a rape exam to prove you have been raped before you can get this medication, which in itself is a tremendous barrier. We should have policies and procedures in place to safeguard the woman who comes to the pharmacy and says, "I was raped" . . . or she can just say "I had unwanted sex," because there are so many stereotypes and prejudices associated with sex."*
>
> **—Evelyn**

We heard from the participants that in general, the IHS providers do not want to go to court and be forensic witnesses in sexual assault cases, and generally it is impossible to obtain a conviction without a rape kit being performed in the proper way and in a timely manner, and to have a primary provider testify in court. We believe this presents an enormous challenge to Native American women's health and safety.

> *"Why should the FBI come to the reservation to investigate a rape or sexual assault? Especially, if there is no forensic witness, no forensic test, no health care provider to back it up? They will not get a conviction in court. So why come down to the reservation to investigate. We've been written off. Doctors don't want to get involved in local politics at all. IHS has a very complicated process of approving an employee to testify in court, even with the policy changes that came about with the Tribal Law and Order Act. By the time they approve a subpoena it's too late. And the perpetrators know this; these rapists walk around free to commit*

> *crimes again. So we have serial rapists. IHS staff just doesn't want to have to deal with testifying. IHS is preventing us from our right to due process and we continue to be victimized."*
>
> **—Charon**

> *"It's a cost issue. Everything is with IHS I have no health insurance and a lot of health problems. I have been on a waiting list for a heart monitor, but they can't pay it, so I'm still waiting. That's what I hear from everybody—it's a cost issue."*
>
> **—Maya**

> *"You want to talk about cost effective? What's the cost of having an unwanted child? What's the cost of having a child to a mother who's drinking or drugging? The list goes on and on and on . . . . The fact that President Obama signed an order stating that women 17 years and older can access Plan B as an "over the counter", why are we being denied Plan B® as on "over the counter" through our primary healthcare provider, when it was the President, who signed the order?"*
>
> **—Charon**

2. Inconsistency Equals Inequality

It has been shown in a recent National Congress of American Indian's (NCAI) task force report that thirty percent of Indian Health Care Service Units do not have standardized protocols. We continue to hear this complaint from Native American women as they describe the maze of bureaucracy they must navigate. In each region, the participants were very savvy about the services and how to access them, but we were speaking with health care providers, non-profit directors and law enforcement workers who know the lay of the land much more than the victim of a crime. And yet, most participants were victims of sexual assault in one form or another.

If quality health care is provided, women will receive much more than a rape kit that is collected during a rape exam—the staff are providing women with information about STDs, pregnancy, emergency contraception and abortion options. These are essential services that Native American women are not currently receiving from their primary health care providers.

> *"All IHS hospitals and clinics are required to have their policies and medications in place. There was a lot of resistance because IHS does*

not standardize anything—every Service Unit does their own. We said, "This is of utmost importance, and here are suggested standardized policies and protocols." If this is the first time, then this will be the first time they have standardized protocols. Now they are required to do this—they received a directive: It has to be standardized and it has to be across the board. If we stay within the norms of what we think is impossible, nothing happens. The need for this was so great we just moved forwa rd, without fear. We did not allow the ever-present government budget concerns limit our vision."

—Donna

"Our tribal EMT said doctors can give patients lifesaving meds before we take them in the ambulance, but won't do it. We have had rape victims given prescriptions to get EC, but at IHS they wouldn't administer it, because the Pharmacy Director and her staff didn't believe in it, so she wouldn't administer EC. The only way for our victims to get it was to go to a drug store pharmacy to get it in person and pay for it."

—Lisa

"We need to ask why they aren't giving our women the same level of care that other women are getting and why they aren't doing everything they can to help a woman prevent an unwanted pregnancy after a sexual assault? Are women being informed that have been sexually assaulted or raped that they're entitled to be able to access an abortion in the event that they are pregnant? No, they do not getting that info from IHS. What about EC? No, some were and some weren't, all women should be getting that information—whether they decide to use it or not it is their choice but at least inform them about it."

—Charon

"When men talk to you about abortion or these pills, you have to say, "Do you have a daughter? What if she is, ten, or eleven? If she was raped, would you want her to have that baby or could it have been taken care of at the hospital? Plan B® is non-invasive, she doesn't have to think about it again and she can start to heal."

—Catherine

Participants agreed that someone else's personal values should not be involved in the process of assisting women during a criminal process. We discussed the drawbacks of the "Conscience Clause" where physicians can refuse to provide contraceptives and doctors can also refuse to work in facilities that provide abortions. In rural areas, this affects women who may receive a referral that might mean a hundred miles of travel, creating further barriers and burdens. Most tribal and IHS clinics are closed over the weekend, virtually shutting the seventy-two hour time frame a woman has to work within if she is going to be able to use EC.

"It's not illegal for someone to deny serving you EC because of religious practices, that doctor has to refer you to someone who will provide that service. If that is not done it is ILLEGAL."

—Charon

3. Indigenous Women's Bodies are Sovereign

Native American women are blessed with a recent history of strong, women leaders and clan mothers who were wise in the ways of the natural world and the world of healing and health. Our grandmothers, midwives and healers knew the women's ways and the medicines available to us for our use. The women in these roundtables remember their grandmothers and know their role in carrying forth women's knowledge within their tribes.

"I keep telling my 5-year-old granddaughter to 'have respect for yourself'. And she didn't know what that meant." I said, "Don't let anybody yell at you, don't let anybody blame you, and don't you blame anybody else. Try to be nice to people even when they are mean to you."

—Cheryl

"Even if you're a poor tribe, you have a substantial voice. I see how the efforts of organizations like NCAI and the NACB have made on violence against women."

—Heather

"Oklahoma is not pro-choice by any means if you look at it from the legislative standpoint and our laws. We are the Bible belt. I mean "birth control" is like a bad word, heaven forbid you want to get your daughter on birth control at a young age. I made my daughter

get on birth control right before she turned 16, and she was mortified. She said, "I'm not even having sex! Why do I have to get on birth control?" and I said, "Because! We want to beat the rush before we have to deal with it. We want to be proactive, not reactive." When we went to IHS, they weren't empathetic about her situation at all. They didn't believe her at all when she said she wasn't sexually active. The doctor asked her twice how many partners she's had and then asked, "If mom left the room if you would feel more comfortable?" She said, "No." I think it's just the mindset. I'm not even talking about Plan B® or emergency contraceptive or anything—just general birth control for young girls. It is frowned upon from the get go in Oklahoma in general and how women are viewed."

—Renee

"I'm southern Baptist so I can talk about it, though after they voted in that a woman cannot be head of the church that's when I stopped going. Lord, there wouldn't be a man in church if a mom hadn't grabbed him, scrubbed him up, and dragged him there. What was that about? I don't get it!"

—Catherine

"I currently go to different programs and trainings and share my story of what happened to me down to the very detail. My family does ministry work. I'm not for abortion—I'm southern Baptist—but I think it's important that women hear that it's not okay, and even if it's your husband they can be charged and convicted of those crimes. I wasn't aware of the morning after pill. In a previous marriage, we'd been having problems with our marriage—I told him no and I didn't want him to be a part of my life anymore after he had beat me up and attempted to take my life by strangulation and then raped me. After escaping and while at the hospital, the nurse had offered me the Morning after Pill. My sister was there and she encouraged me not to take it, but I didn't want this man to be a part of my life anymore. She thought it was OK since he was my husband. Well, so what? To this day, I have flashbacks. It's taken me years to build my self-esteem back up to where it is today. From the time of being a teenager all the way up to adulthood I saw abuse within

our family, whether it was in our immediate family such as aunts, uncles—always looked the other way. Then I got into relationships to where I accepted that. They tell you you're ugly and you're nothing and you don't amount to anything and you start to believe it. I'm realizing that I am somebody. I'm not stupid, I'm not ugly, I'm not fat, I'm not dumb, it's just finally getting to that point to realizing that. A light goes on. We've got to save our children to where our little girls and little boys will see that, and then that cycle can be broken. That's one great thing we push at our tribe—the culture camps and teaching our young women and our young men how to treat women, and how boys should be treated as young men within their families, and their roles in their families. I'm going to go back and share with my colleagues, friends, family and my tribe and tell the IHS coordinating director that this needs to be that choice we offer. It's not an abortion pill. Plan B is something that can prevent an abortion down the line at a later date. Plan B is an emergency contraceptive. This discussion today is a growing experience for me; it's another step that I can share in my testimony, my own story, because it was a horrible story. When your ex-husband's charged with assault and battery and attempted first-degree murder, it's something you don't move on from. Seven years later and that night is just like it was yesterday, it's still there and little things will bring on flashbacks all these years later."

—Ramona

"I have three generations of family who have either died, been murdered, or committed suicide. That's three generations affected in my immediate family. My mother died when I was fifteen from cirrhosis; my sister was running away from an attacker and was hit by a car on the highway; her son a few years ago committed suicide; and her daughter who has a child gave the child away. We believe her daughter is now a prostitute in Las Vegas. That's four generations of my immediate family that has almost been wiped out. It's so overwhelming—I have to take it, look at it and get some perspective. How did this happen? When and why? Where did this all come from? It's from assimilation, government policy, religion, culture, loss of language, subjugation, everything. I have to look at that and see how all that hap-

pened. It has led up to today, to my kids and me, and how I have stopped the cycle."
—**Maya**

"I got pregnant at sixteen and got married and went through 20 yrs of abuse and I'm ill because of it. I've been diagnosed with a rare disease called Raynaud's, which is offset by stress and cold air. But, I knew I needed to break that cycle and I fought back every time. I had told him before we got married, "Don't think you're going to beat on me because I will fight back, I grew up fighting." I would fight him back, but it was a lot of verbal and mental abuse that you go through along with the physical abuse and it destroyed me health wise. Even to this day. I have two children with him. I've apologized to them for making them stay in our home, having to experience that abuse, and now my daughter is in the same situation with an abusive relationship."
—**Billie**

"When I work with the counseling agency here in Norman, the therapists asked me why Indian men are sexually abusing children, and overall, the answer was boarding schools—they were taught those behaviors and they were abused. These workers were trying to say that it was part of the way we do things in our culture and I had to inform them, "No we don't."
—**Bernice Armstrong**

4. Laws Do Not Change Attitudes

As our discussion deepened into the unique situations that Native American women find themselves in, it became clear that federal laws do not change the attitudes of families or communities. Native American women hold their men and sons in high regard and respect their fathers, uncles and husbands. But, sometimes this means standing back and keeping quiet. Native communities are very spiritual and religious communities, but once again, mixing of these attitudes can make change hard and put women's health issues on the back burner of priorities.

"A lot of these girls are having children at 14, 15 years of age. In the Cochiti Pueblo, the girls are pregnant at 12 and 13 years old. The fact is, even before these girls are 18, they're on their second or third child. I just found out the CHR program doesn't even hand out condoms."
—**Yvette**

"Our organization operates support groups for boys and girls who are in middle school and high school. We have found that there is no conversation with their parents with other responsible adults around HIV/AIDS. . . . and they have no idea what HIV/AIDS is; what their risks are; or how to avoid the risks. So, we are offering a huge educational piece for our community around all of those different issues. Its not just our area that opens us up to risk, it's the drug use, the needle sharing, the unprotected sex—these kids need someone to be able to talk with them openly and honestly—to figure out what they're at risk for and to have adults in their life who are willing to have that conversation with them. Through our Doula program, we know youth who have gotten pregnant and came to us after hiding their pregnancy from their parents. We know that there is that strong family influence of, 'they're going to beat me; they're going to disown me; they're going to do all these things to me.' So they are risking their health and the health of their babies because they are still trying to hide that pregnancy from their parents. We offer them support and mediation and talk to them about the risks that not telling their parents puts their babies and themselves at."
—**Corrine**

"Incest and sexual abuse is something that's not talked about. It's like DV—something that you don't talk about. I know that's something that won't be talked about in our tribe; it's like a bad word. The church, abortion, and morning after pill, all of that is not talked about."
—**Ramona**

"We have to deal with the religious right. Religion comes up very conveniently when it's needed to control us. It's just another form of getting people geared up, something people are passionate about: their beliefs, their god. If they can latch onto that and get a vote, they do it."
—**Catherine**

"The woman was with an older man and they lived way out in the country in a mobile home. He didn't allow her off the land, and he didn't allow her to go in town without him. She had no car and never had any money. She came from up north, lived out there and nobody

knew she even existed. They home schooled their two children and he would beat her if she tried to leave off their strip of land. He had her fenced in. She was telling me this and I didn't believe it until I went out there with the tribal police and she met us by the gate. She said she thought she was pregnant. "I can't have another baby with this man. He's going to keep impregnating me—that's his way of putting a hold on me, how he controls me". We created a safety plan, so she had choices available to her. She literally had to hide this pregnancy from him until we could get her out of that home, out of state and into a shelter with the children. Then he was charged with domestic assault and battery, and kidnapping."

—**Ramona**

"Part of the reason I don't go in a traditional way is that I know in my own family, our male leader was molesting children."

—**Leslie**

"They'll preach against it, but it's not written. They definitely do preach against it. They come right out and say abortion is like drinking, drugs—it's a sin. The fetus—they call it a baby. As soon as the seed's been planted the pastor says that it's already a human being. It's talked about, and especially when you see something about it on the news there's discussion about it, but it's not like that's the main topic. It's brought up in a quiet way because usually in most Southern "Baptist churches the majority of the population that attend are elders and that goes back into the respect thing—you don't talk about those kinds of things with your elders. They don't talk about birth control, but they openly talk about abortion."

—**Ramona**

"I'm from Santa Clara and there's a lot of Catholics there. I'm also a devoted Catholic but I don't believe in someone telling me if I was raped or anything else, that I can't abort that child. There is no one who is going to tell me that, because I think, "My body is my body. And whatever I want to do is what I'm going to do," but I am Catholic."

—**Laura**

"I find myself holding back things I want to say because both sides—mother and father—hold very traditional roles in different parts of the government within our tribe and if I were to say something, I could get either side of my family into trouble, and that plays a big role for women, and for me to speak truly what I feel just because there is that fear of what if somebody else hears . . . It's going to go back and my parents, my grandparents, my uncles are going to get in trouble. I held a royalty position for New Mexico State and there were people who asked me questions on what my view was and my response was, "I cannot comment on that". Because my father was standing behind me—because if I were to say something, I don't want to make him upset. I have that fear, and, for me, I call it respect, because I respect his views and how he raised me, but I also disagree with him on some issues . . . and I find that difficult for myself."

—**Yvette**

"I work with young women, especially teenagers. They're afraid to go to IHS, because they know Grandma or Auntie's going to be sitting in the waiting room. They're going to say, "Well, what are you here for?" It also appears that almost anyone can access IHS medical records—there is no confidentiality!"

—**Maya**

"Prayer is so important no matter what religion it is . . . I don't think there is anything wrong with that. But, it's the place where it becomes institutionalized and prevents other people's voice in that process that bothers me. For instance, in the state police there is a Chaplin, so who decided that? How did that get institutionalized? In hospitals, they have prayer rooms or churches and some are non-denominational. We know that prayer is really powerful—it heals you and it moves us through dark times, but, as native people we do not try to convert other people to our way of being—that is a different way of dividing and conquering. We are moving towards prayer because we need it; the world needs it as earthquakes are happening, governments are falling, and chaos is going on all around. So how do you counter that but through mediation and prayer? What do we offer young people but ourselves?"

—**Corrine**

5. Women's Rights are Human Rights

"It's not an aspirin; it's not cold tablets, its withholding services from a victim."

—**Charon**

This series of discussions with Native American women was interwoven with threads of ongoing human rights violations throughout Indian country. It became very clear that the Indian Health Service must standardize their sexual assault policies and protocols, and they should take the lead in working with, not only tribal governments in creating some standardized policies among all of the facilities, but with consumers, in this case Native American women. When the disparity of care among tribal members becomes detrimental to women's health, it becomes a treaty violation. Native American women should have clear expectations of what types of emergency contraception and care they can access.

With the Indian Health Service as our primary provider of health care to Native American women, then the standardized sexual assault manual becomes our insurance policy that explains our benefits and rights as Native American women. The same policies should be followed in all facilities and they should be adequately funded to provide basic services. When a Native woman is assaulted, family members and care givers should be able to assist any woman in obtaining optimum health care. We have heard that half of all pregnancies are unplanned, so Native American women wonder why they are not entitled to have medical facilities that treat them fairly.

The group discussed the importance of putting their focus and efforts on young people and teaching the young women about "women's body sovereignty". The participants were very interested in creating options and maintaining a choice for women. All three roundtables discussed the truly traditional roles for women and to remember the importance of building our Women's Society as opposed to reacting to a male dominated political arena ("we need to demand sovereignty") and to keep these two realms separate. Participants affirmed the need to "keep our realm and knowledge as Native American women" and to continue as advocates for women's health and human rights by sharing their stories of healing and survival and teaching the young ones.

"Our work as advocates is about stopping violence against women. That frames the way you do the work. If it's about specific crimes, the major response is after the crime is committed,

and it's not about social change. But as a coalition we are trying to look at root causes . . . We need to continue to make the connections between root causes, domestic and sexual violence, reproductive rights and other forms of gender-based violence."

—**Brenda**

"If a woman has been sexually assaulted Plan B® is an ideal thing to have access to. Every woman in the country can access it, except Native American women, who have to see a doctor and then go to the pharmacist. Most IHS will give you the old regime of higher dose birth control, which requires a prescription. It would be much easier to have access to Plan B® as an OTC."

—**Charon**

"In Oklahoma we're either self-governing tribes, which means we are not under the BIA's thumb at all—we govern ourselves by our own tribal codes, our own policies, our own laws, and then we have tribes that are on 638 contracts who have to abide by the code of federal regulations and they are still governed somewhat by the BIA. I'm also a citizen of the United States and I'm a citizen of Oklahoma, but when I step outside of my tribal boundaries and I'm not in my 8 county jurisdiction, at that point, my voice doesn't hold a whole lot of water."

—**Renee**

Exercising our Right to Vote

At the Oklahoma roundtable, we heard from Maya Torrelba, a young Comanche woman who had recently ran for a county political position. She was eventually defeated by the incumbent, "a white, middle aged rancher", but Maya learned a lot and had her whole family working for her campaign. She was one of the first Native's to post campaign signs all around the area, but she said, "Everyone is doing it now"! Participants shared that they are able to encourage their immediate family to vote in tribal elections now and then, but rarely does anyone they know vote in mainstream state or national elections.

In New Mexico, we heard of an even more complicated political landscape for the Pueblo women. Some of the Pueblos do not elect their leadership at all; in others only the men vote for leaders, while women may vote on issues; and in a few Pueblos everyone votes for all seats and issues, including the women. We found an extremely high level of political awareness and activism among the women in New Mexico compared to other regions, with active voting in state and federal elections. Their knowledge of bills and propositions affecting women's health was deep and inspirational!

> *"At Santo Domingo Pueblo nobody votes for leadership. Zia Pueblo has no voting—this idea of choosing leadership is a very new idea to Pueblo people . . . it's very new, and a lot of older people say that we don't choose our leaders. But, then we have people in there who you hope a re not power hungry and will do it for your people as a sacrifice, not as a career."*
> **—Frances**

> *"My clients don't think they can make a difference when they vote—they're so busy surviving from day to day that they don't think about things like that . . . Natives are so downtrodden that it's hard to get them moving. The professional women and men do vote, but not our clients—the people in poverty or people who just survive day to day, do not vote."*
> **—Bernice**

> *"The first people to vote are the elders . . . some elders watch TV and understand, but we have an interpreter. The hard thing about that is how do you explain some things in Indian, or in English? There are some things you cannot interpret . . . so us younger ones have to help out. My first language is Navajo, so English was second, but the elders kind of get mad because you use words that you have to makeup yourself. . . .it hard trying explain to the elders about anything political or like Plan B®!"*
> **—Chastity**

Actions and Solutions

In the three states we visited, there was consensus on many issues, but generally discussions about action steps were bound by various threads relating to education and sharing stories. Education of all women, but especially the younger ones, care givers, tribal leaders and women's health advocates and allies—about the barriers for Native American women to emergency contraceptives. As a group, they agreed it will require

a community groundswell to activate a set of national policies that will be applicable and affordable throughout Indian Country. The leaders at the roundtables understand the importance of creating strong allies, and the critical networking to be done. Participants felt that if they could pool their resources they would get more accomplished, and to this end the New Mexico group selected a point person, committees, a strategy and timeline for actions. Their immediate plans included setting up a Navajo tribal council presentation with follow up question sessions. These ladies encourage others to "educate your tribal First Lady" as a beginning strategy!

Participants agreed that it is critical to educate and empower the Native youth to understand and make healthy choices for themselves. They discussed the importance of building "resiliency" for young people and their families by sharing information and personal stories. Our stories are very powerful and Native American women learn from each other in this way. We must be up to the minute with the technology utilized in getting women's health information out there where young people will see and share it. As one participant said, "Do this for the young people—there are too many children having children, and too many rapes".

Some of the young women are advocating the creation of their own systems, operating outside of the Indian Health Service. They are operating non-profit organizations and providing unique services to Native people who are falling through the cracks in urban areas, especially where there is no tribal affiliation in the regions.

> *"We have to be watchdogs and stay in their face, continually asking them, "Where are the protocols? Are they posted? When will they be posted?" We have to really make sure that we talk to our health boards at the local level, our health representatives, our doctors, our tribal leadership, about making sure these Standardized Sexual Assault Policies and Protocols are in place, and going beyond that and talking to our area Tribal Health Boards as well."*
> **—Charon**

> *"We haven't made the connections between sexual assault and reproductive rights. We should have those discussions . . . The downside of VAWA if you read the act is it has been de-gendered. The word "women" is ra rely used. Rather than the emphasis on ending violence against women, it is now focused on specific crimes—reactive, rather than proactive."*
> **—Brenda**

Key Points For Gaining Access on Demand

- Lower the cost with generic options for Plan B® and purchase in bulk through Indian Health Service
- Debate the economics argument by presenting the cost of an unwanted pregnancy
- Promote the adoption of national Standardized Sexual Assault Policies (SAPPS)
- Create an alliance with physicians—have and attend group meetings especially with the educators and allies
- Ensure Medicare coverage for women who cannot afford Plan B® over the counter
- Educate tribal leaders so they understand the options for women in crises

- Advocate for "Reproductive Safety"—it's a powerful concept that should be included in assault victims' procedure manuals.
- Conduct community education campaigns to inform community members about Plan B®.
- Demand that Indian Health Service include consumers in the process of consultation in the development of Standardized Sexual Assault Policies and Protocols and other health issues of Native American women by restating the Native American Women's Health Advisory Committee.
- Demand that Indian Health Service use the process of consultation with the inclusion of consumers and review the Standardized Sexual Policies and Protocols every 3–5 years for updates.

"Billboards, Women of Color, and Politics"

By Shaniqua Seth and Malika Redmond

For the *National Women's Health Network*

Article taken from May/June 2012 Newsletter

Accentuated and airbrushed, often young and Caucasian, female body parts are displayed on billboards throughout the U.S. as a staple marketing technique to attract consumers' attention and dollars. Feminists have long critiqued the way this advertising strategy objectifies women, but the strategy took a twist when a controversial billboard made national news after it was erected in New York City in 2011. The ad used a woman of color's body not to sell a product, but to promote an anti-choice message. The young African-American girl in the billboard was both the object and subject of the message, which read: "The Most Dangerous Place for an African-American is in the Womb."

Last year, nearly 200 similar anti-choice billboards were displayed in major cities across the country, including Atlanta, Georgia; Jacksonville, Florida; Austin, Texas; and Los Angeles, California. (The Los Angeles billboards targeted Latinas rather than African American women, stating: "The most dangerous place for a Latino is in the womb.") Despite the number of ads, many people were unaware of the billboards, in part because most were strategically placed in low-income, Southern, communities of color. The New York City ad garnered national media attention as much for where it was placed—the affluent art and cultural SoHo district—as for the distasteful words written near the African-American girl pictured in the billboard.

While New York City reproductive rights activists were faced with challenging one offensive billboard, Atlanta became a hub for the vicious ads with tailored anti-choice rhetoric. These messages conflated abortion with genocide and compared abortion to the deaths of thousands of African-American people due to the inhumane conditions of 300 years of chattel slavery.

Anti-choice activists also staged a protest in 2010 at the renowned Martin Luther King, Jr. Center for Nonviolent Social Change, where they used civil rights language to argue that abortion is discrimination against a fetus.[1]

These campaigns are the creation of anti-choice groups—including the Radiance Foundation, Life Always, and Issues4Life—which focus on reducing access to abortion in the African-American community. Anti-choice activists promoting these billboards and messages believe that African-American women's abortions have the same devastating impact on the Black community as do critical socio-economic and health issues like high unemployment and heart disease.

Sadly, this stated concern for the wellness of the Black community by the anti-choice groups obscures their ultimate goal: to distort the facts about abortion in order to promote their anti-choice agenda and shame women of color from utilizing abortion services.[2] Understanding, detangling, and responding effectively to the convoluted messages are vital to our work as women's health advocates.

Abortion has been a legal right in the U.S. for 39 years, and is just one part of the full range of reproductive health and family planning options that all women need—including Latinas and African-American women. According to the well-respected Guttmacher Institute,[1] "About one-third of all abortions are obtained by white women, and 37% are obtained by Black women. Latinas comprise a smaller proportion of the women who have abortions."[2] Although white women have the greatest number of abortions, the rates of abortions for African-American women and Latinas

---

[1] See national and Wisconsin state fact sheets on abortion from the Guttmacher Institute immediately following this piece. *Ed.*

are disproportionately higher than their white counterparts based on their overall population size. Guttmacher notes, "These patterns of abortion rates mirror the levels of unintended pregnancy seen across these same groups. Black women are three times as likely as white women to experience an unintended pregnancy; Hispanic women are twice as likely—sharply disproportionate to their numbers in the general population."[2]

Women's health and reproductive justice advocates do not dispute these numbers, and agree that women of color have higher abortion rates. They consider the factors that are driving the numbers of higher-than-average abortion rates and find it reflects a crisis in access to high-quality, culturally appropriate reproductive health care, including effective contraception choices and education. Specific groups that face such barriers include our society's most vulnerable populations: women who are poor, young, rural, uneducated, undocumented, and/or women of color. The Institute of Medicine (IOM) has noted "minorities are less likely than whites to receive needed services, including clinically necessary procedures." The IOM also notes that minority communities have a higher level of mistrust in the health care system, which also creates a barrier to care.[2]

The billboard campaigns misrepresent what's driving the data on women of color's abortion rates and scapegoats Latina and African-American women for the very socio-economic conditions faced by their communities that impact their disproportionate use of abortion services. As California Latinas for Reproductive Justice (CLRJ) notes, "The problem in our communities is not abortion. What Latinas/os truly need to thrive is access to quality health care, good paying jobs to support their families, and quality education to provide positive life opportunities."3 Loretta Ross, SisterSong's National Coordinator (and former NWHN board member),[2] astutely counters their claims that abortion is genocide by noting, "The best way to fight genocide is to make sure the objects of that genocide or control make these decisions for themselves."

Women of color have always been a vital part of efforts for women to gain full bodily integrity and have been speaking, writing, and organizing around issues of race and gender since the mid-19th century. In 1851, Sojourner Truth famously asked, "Ain't I a Woman?" In 1970, Frances Beal, head of the Black Women's Liberation Committee of the Student Non-violent Coordinating Committee (SNCC), declared that: "Black women have the right and the responsibility to determine when it is in the interest of the struggle to have children or not to have them and this right must not be relinquished."[4]

Today's activists are building on this long history and saying: "Trust Black Women!" Advocates and activists with women of color reproductive justice organizations have challenged these anti-choice billboard initiatives— and won! The Trust Black Women Partnership (TBW) was born from a commitment to protect Black women's dignity and dismantle the billboard campaigns. TBW, comprised of 20 founding partners who are both for and against legal abortion, but unanimously support women's right to make their own decision about reproductive health. TBW seeks to "develop a strong network of African American women organizations and individuals mobilized to defend our human right to make abortion and family planning decisions for ourselves."5 TBW also works "to counter the growing anti-abortion movement in African American community and defeat race—and gender-based campaigns and legislation that limits abortion access for Black women."[5]

TBW hit the ground running and coordinated street protests and mass media campaigns (including blogs, documentaries, and online protests) that saturated communities where the billboards appeared. At the 2011 SisterSong Reproductive Justice Conference, TBW premiered the film *"We Always Resist: Trust Black Women"*, which describes how Black women have always fought for reproductive rights and considered these rights to be essential. *"We Always Resist"* is part of TBW's long-term strategy to combat anti-choice messages that women of color are incapable of making appropriate reproductive choices. To date, TBW and its allies have been successful in taking down many of the anti-choice billboards! [5]

We proudly stood for the dignity of women, and won! We must proactively work towards change and must not become complacent because of victories over specific billboards or anti-choice initiatives. We invite you to join the effort and stay connected by following the organizations that founded the TBW Partnership and their allies. You can find out more about TBW and the founding organizations by going to *www.trustblackwomen.org*. Most importantly, put your money where your heart and mind are because TWB and its allies need our support. We encourage you to continue to make a difference by becoming an ally, organizer, or advocate to any of the TBW member organizations.

Shaniqua Seth is the NWHN Health Communications Manager. Malika Redmond, M.A., is a Feminist Researcher/Writer and Women's Advocate for the Women's Resource Center to end Domestic Violence, Atlanta GA and NWHN Board Member.

---

[2]See Ross's work on White supremacy and reproductive justice elsewhere in this section. *Ed.*

REFERENCES

1. Ross L "Trying to Hijack the Civil Rights Legacy: What's Behind the Anti-choice Freedom Rides", *Conscience 2011,* Vol. XXXII(2: 17–20.

2. Cohen, S. "Abortion and Women of Color: The Bigger Picture", *Guttmacher Policy Review* 2008; 11(3). Available online at: http://www.guttmacher.org/pubs/gpr/11/3/gpr110302.html

3. Valle G, "California Latinas for Reproductive Justice (CLRJ) Denounces Racist Billboard Campaign Attacking California Latinas' Reproductive Justice", Los Angeles: CLRJ, 2011. Available online at: *http://www.california-latinas.org/news/downloads/CLRJ_Press_Release_Anti_Latina_RJ_6.9.11.pdf*

4. Nelson J, Women of Color and the Reproductive Rights Movement. New York: New York University Press, 2003.

5. Trust Black Women, "Our Story", Available online at: http://www.trustblackwomen.org/about-trust-black-women/our-story

"Induced Abortion in the United States"

From the *Guttmacher Institute* (May 2016)

- Nearly half of pregnancies among American women in 2011 were unintended, and about four in 10 of these were terminated by abortion.
- Twenty-one percent of all pregnancies (excluding miscarriages) in 2011 ended in abortion.
- In 2011, approximately 1.06 million abortions were performed, down 13% from 1.21 million in 2008. From 1973 through 2011, nearly 53 million legal abortions occurred.
- The abortion rate in 2011 was 16.9 per 1,000 women aged 15–44, down 13% from 19.4 per 1,000 in 2008. This is the lowest rate observed since abortion became legal in the United States in 1973.
- In 2011, 1.7% of women aged 15–44 had an abortion. Half of these women had had at least one previous abortion.
- At 2008 abortion rates, almost one in 10 women will have an abortion by age 20, one in four by age 30 and three in 10 by age 45.

Who has Abortions?

- Twelve percent of U.S. abortion patients in 2014 were teenagers: Those aged 18–19 accounted for 8% of all abortions, 15–17-year-olds for 3% and teenagers younger than 15 for 0.2%.
- More than half of all abortion patients in 2014 were in their 20s: Patients aged 20–24 obtained 34% of all abortions, and patients aged 25–29 obtained 27%.
- White patients accounted for 39% of abortion procedures in 2014, blacks for 28%, Hispanics for 25% and patients of other races and ethnicities for 9%.

- Seventeen percent of abortion patients in 2014 identified as mainline Protestant, 13% as evangelical Protestant and 24% as Catholic; 38% reported no religious affiliation.
- In 2014, some 46% of all abortion patients had never married and were not cohabiting.
- Fifty-nine percent of abortions in 2014 were obtained by patients who had had at least one previous birth.
- Forty-nine percent of abortion patients in 2014 had incomes of less than 100% of the federal poverty level ($11,670 for a single adult with no children).*
- Twenty-six percent of abortion patients in 2014 had incomes of 100–199% of the federal poverty level.
- The reasons patients gave for having an abortion underscored their understanding of the responsibilities of parenthood and family life. The three most common reasons—each cited by three-fourths of patients—were concern for or responsibility to other individuals; the inability to afford a child; and the belief that having a baby would interfere with work, school or the ability to care for dependents. Half said they did not want to be a single parent or were having problems with their husband or partner.
- Fifty-one percent of abortion patients had used a contraceptive method in the month they got pregnant, most commonly condoms (27%) or a hormonal method (17%).

---

*Poverty guidelines are updated periodically in the Federal Register by the U.S. Department of Health and Human Services under the authority of 42 USC 9902(2).

Guttmacher Institute, Induced Abortion in the United States, *Fact Sheet*, New York: Guttmacher Institute, 2016, http://www.guttmacher.org/pubs/fb_induced_abortion.html

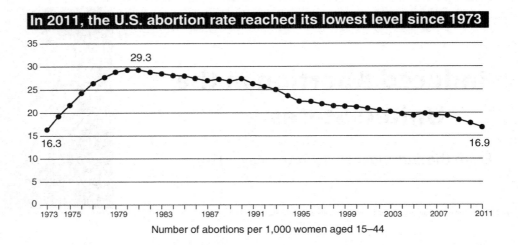

In 2011, the U.S. abortion rate reached its lowest level since 1973

Number of abortions per 1,000 women aged 15–44

Providers and Services

- The number of U.S. abortion providers declined 4% between 2008 and 2011 (from 1,793 to 1,720). The number of clinics providing abortion services declined 1% over this period (from 851 to 839). Eighty-nine percent of all U.S. counties lacked an abortion clinic in 2011, and 38% of women of reproductive age lived in those counties.
- Forty-six percent of abortion providers offer very early abortions (before the first missed period), and 95% offer abortion at eight weeks from the last menstrual period. Sixty-one percent of providers offer at least some second-trimester abortion services (at 13 weeks or later), and 34% offer abortion at 20 weeks. Only 16% of all abortion providers perform the procedure at 24 weeks.
- In 2011–2012, the average amount paid for a nonhospital abortion with local anesthesia at 10 weeks' gestation was $480. The average paid for an early medication abortion before 10 weeks was $504.
- Eighty-four percent of clinics reported at least one form of antiabortion harassment in 2011. Picketing was the most common form of harassment (80%), followed by phone calls (47%). Fifty-three percent of clinics were picketed 20 times or more in a year.

Early Medication Abortion

- In September 2000, the U.S. Food and Drug Administration approved mifepristone to be marketed in the United States as an alternative to surgical abortion.

- In March 2016, the Food and Drug Administration updated the mifepristone label to reflect the scientifically proven regimen that was already being used by most health care providers. The new regimen allows patients to take lower doses and make fewer provider visits, and also allows for medication abortion up to 10 weeks' gestation.
- In 2011, some 59% of abortion providers—1,023 facilities—provided one or more early medication abortions. At least 17% of providers offered only early medication abortion services.
- Medication abortion accounted for 23% of all nonhospital abortions in 2011, and for 36% of abortions before nine weeks' gestation.
- Early medication abortions increased from 6% of all aborti\ons in 2001 to 23% in 2011, even while the overall number of abortions continued to decline. Data from the Centers for Disease Control and Prevention show that the average time of abortion has shifted earlier within the first trimester; this is likely due, in part, to the availability of medication abortion services.

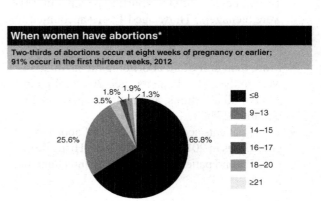

When women have abortions*

Two-thirds of abortions occur at eight weeks of pregnancy or earlier; 91% occur in the first thirteen weeks, 2012

1.8% 1.9% 1.3%
3.5%
25.6%
65.8%

≤8
9–13
14–15
16–17
18–20
≥21

*In weeks from the last menstrual period.
*In weeks from the last menstrual period.

Safety of Abortion

- A first-trimester abortion is one of the safest medical procedures and carries minimal risk— less than 0.05%—of major complications that might need hospital care.
- Abortions performed in the first trimester pose virtually no long-term risk of problems such as infertility, ectopic pregnancy, spontaneous abortion (miscarriage) or birth defect, and little or no risk of preterm or low-birth-weight deliveries.
- Exhaustive reviews by panels convened by the U.S. and UK governments have concluded that there is no association between abortion and breast cancer. There is also no indication that abortion is a risk factor for other cancers.
- Leading experts have concluded that among women who have an unplanned pregnancy, the risk of mental health problems is no greater if they have a single first-trimester abortion than if they carry the pregnancy to term.
- The risk of death associated with abortion increases with the length of pregnancy, from 0.3 for every 100,000 abortions at or before eight weeks to 6.7 per 100,000 at 18 weeks or later.

Insurance Coverage and Payment

- Most abortion patients had health insurance in 2014. Thirty-five percent reported that they had Medicaid coverage, while 31% had private insurance. However, insurance does not necessarily cover abortion services, and even if it does, patients may not use their coverage for a variety of reasons (e.g., because they do not know their plan covers it, they are concerned about confidentiality or their provider does not accept their plan).
- Overall, 53% of abortion patients paid out of pocket for their procedure in 2014.
- Medicaid was the second-most-common method of payment, reported by 24% of abortion patients. The overwhelming majority of these patients live in the few states that allow state funds to be used to pay for abortion.
- Fifteen percent of patients used private insurance to pay for the procedure. Most patients with private insurance (61%) paid out of pocket.

- In 2004, 58% of abortion patients said they would have liked to have had their abortion earlier in the pregnancy. Nearly 60% of women who experienced a delay in obtaining an abortion cited the time it took to make arrangements and raise money.

Law and Policy

- In the 1973 *Roe v. Wade* decision, the Supreme Court ruled that women, in consultation with their physician, have a constitutionally protected right to have an abortion in the early stages of pregnancy—that is, before viability—free from government interference.
- In 1992, the Court reaffirmed the right to abortion in *Planned Parenthood v. Casey*. However, the ruling significantly weakened the legal protections previously afforded women and physicians by giving states the right to enact restrictions that do not create an "undue burden" for women seeking abortion.
- Congress has barred the use of federal Medicaid funds to pay for abortions, except when the woman's life would be endangered or in cases of rape or incest. States can fund abortion with state dollars, and about one-third of states do so voluntarily or by court order.
- As of April 1, 2016, at least half of the states have imposed excessive and unnecessary regulations on abortion clinics, mandated counseling designed to dissuade a woman from obtaining an abortion, required a waiting period before an abortion, required parental involvement before a minor obtains an abortion or prohibited the use of state Medicaid funds to pay for medically necessary abortions.
- In 2000, a total of 13 states had at least four types of major abortion restrictions and so were considered hostile to abortion rights; by 2015, this category included 27 states. The proportion of women of reproductive age living in hostile states rose from 31% to 56% during this time period.
- In contrast, the number of states that were supportive of abortion rights fell from 17 to 12 between 2000 and 2015. The proportion of women of reproductive age living in supportive states declined from 40% to 30% over this period.

"State Facts About Abortion: Wisconsin"

From the *Guttmacher Institute* (2014)

National Background and Context

Abortion is a common experience: At current rates, about three in ten American women will have had an abortion by the time she reaches age 45. Moreover, a broad cross section of U.S. women have abortions. 58% of women having abortions are in their 20s; 61% have one or more children; 85% are unmarried; 69% are economically disadvantaged; and 73% report a religious affiliation. No racial or ethnic group makes up a majority: 36% of women obtaining abortions are white non-Hispanic, 30% are black non-Hispanic, 25% are Hispanic and 9% are of other racial backgrounds.

Contraceptive use is a key predictor of women's recourse to abortion. The very small group of American women who are at risk of experiencing an unintended pregnancy but are not using contraceptives account for more than half of all abortions. Many of these women did not think they would get pregnant or had concerns about contraceptive methods. The remainder of abortions occur among the much larger group of women who were using contraceptives in the month they became pregnant. Many of these women report difficulty using contraceptives consistently.

Abortion is one of the safest surgical procedures for women in the United States. Fewer than 0.5% of women obtaining abortions experience a complication, and the risk of death associated with abortion is about one-tenth that associated with childbirth.

In the 1973 *Roe v. Wade* decision, the U.S. Supreme Court ruled that a woman, in consultation with her physician, has a constitutionally protected right to choose abortion in the early stages of pregnancy-that is, before viability. In 1992, the Court upheld the basic right to abortion in *Planned Parenthood v. Casey*. However, it also expanded the ability of the states to enact all but the most extreme restrictions on women's access to abortion. The most common restrictions in effect are parental notification or consent requirements for minors, limitations on public funding, and unnecessary and overly burdensome regulations on abortion facilities.

Pregnancies and Their Outcomes

- In 2011, there were 6 million pregnancies to the 63 million women of reproductive age (15–44) in the United States. Sixty-seven percent of these pregnancies resulted in live births and 18% in abortions; the remaining 15% ended in miscarriage.
- In Wisconsin, 89,800 of the 1,092,349 women of reproductive age became pregnant in 2011. 76% of these pregnancies resulted in live births and 9% in induced abortions.
- In 2011, 1.1 million American women obtained abortions, producing a rate of 16.9 abortions per 1,000 women of reproductive age. The rate is a decrease from 2008, when the abortion rate was 19.4 abortions per 1,000 women 15–44.
- In 2011, 7,640 women obtained abortions in Wisconsin, producing a rate of 7 abortions per 1,000 women of reproductive age. Some of these women were from other states, and some Wisconsin residents had abortions in other states, so this rate may not reflect the abortion rate of state residents. The rate decreased 6% since 2008, when it was 7.4 abortions per 1,000 women 15–44. Abortions in Wisconsin represent 0.7% of all abortions in the United States.

Guttmacher Institute, Induced Abortion in the United States, *Fact Sheet*, New York: Guttmacher Institute, 2016, https://www.guttmacher.org/fact-sheet/state-facts-about-abortion-wisconsin

Where Do Women Obtain Abortions?

- In 2011, there were 1,720 abortion providers in the United States. This is a slight (4%) decrease from 2008, when there were 1,787 abortion providers. Thirty-five percent of these providers were hospitals, 19% were abortion clinics (clinics where more than half of all patient visits were for abortion), 30% were clinics where fewer than half of all visits were for abortion, and 17% were private physicians' offices. Sixty-three percent of all abortions were provided at abortion clinics, 31% at other clinics, 4% at hospitals and 1% at private physicians' offices.
- In 2011, there were 8 abortion providers in Wisconsin; 4 of those were clinics. This represents a 11% decline in overall providers and a no change in clinics from 2008, when there were 9 abortion providers overall, of which 4 were abortion clinics.
- In 2011, 89% of U.S. counties had no abortion clinic. 38% of American women lived in these counties, which meant they would have to travel outside their county to obtain an abortion. Of women obtaining abortions in 2008, one-third traveled more than 25 miles.
- In 2011, 96% of Wisconsin counties had no abortion clinic. 67% of Wisconsin women lived in these counties.

Restrictions on Abortion

- A woman must receive statedirected counseling that includes information designed to discourage her from having an abortion and then wait 24 hours before the procedure is provided. Counseling must be provided in person and must take place before the waiting period begins, thereby necessitating two separate trips to the facility.
- Health plans that will be offered in the state's health exchange under the Affordable Care Act can only cover abortion when the woman's life is endangered, her physical health is severely compromised, rape or incest.
- The parent of a minor must consent before an abortion is provided.
- Public funding is available for abortion only in cases of life endangerment, rape, incest or when necessary to prevent longlasting damage to the woman's physical health.
- A woman must undergo an ultrasound before obtaining an abortion; the provider must show and describe the image to the woman.

Definitions and Data Sources

References for information contained in this fact sheet are available at http://www.guttmacher.org/pubs/sfaa/sfaa-sources.html

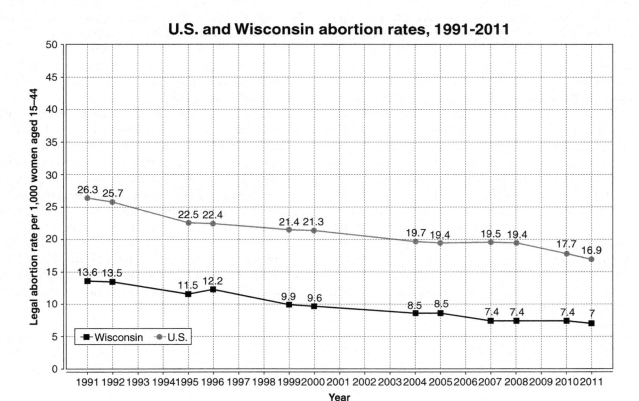

U.S. and Wisconsin abortion rates, 1991-2011

What Kind of Mother Is Eight Months Pregnant and Wants an Abortion?

By Rachel Bertsche for *Yahoo Parenting*

Kate, already mom to one daughter, terminated her second pregnancy at 36 weeks. She named the daughter she lost Rose.

When Kate, a 29-year-old mom outside Boston, found out she was pregnant with a second daughter, she was elated. Then, at 36 weeks along, she got the news that is every expecting parent's worst nightmare: Her baby, whom she would later name Rose, had two brain malformations. Kate decided to have an abortion, and eventually found solace in a support group on the website Ending a Wanted Pregnancy.1 The online community is for parents who terminate pregnancies for medical reasons (pregnancies they wanted, but chose to end after a severe prenatal diagnosis or maternal health issue) and who often feel alone or ashamed, and suffer in silence. Kate, one of the site's administrators, shares her story with Yahoo Parenting's Rachel Bertsche.

My husband and I always wanted a big family. We wanted to have a lot of kids and to start young and have them close together. In 2010, we had our first. A healthy baby girl. But when we were ready for number two, getting pregnant—or, rather, staying pregnant—was harder. I had three miscarriages before a pregnancy finally stuck. I was expecting a second little girl in the summer of 2012, and everyone around me said everything looked great.

Well, almost everyone. At my 18-week fetal scan, a technician thought she saw something—she wasn't sure what, exactly—so they sent me for a Level 2 ultrasound at a local teaching hospital. "Level 2" meant that it would be more detailed than the standard sonogram, and a maternal fetal medicine (MFM) specialist would look at it. When I went for that test, the MFM specialist said the baby was healthy. I was worried, but when I expressed my concern to the hospital's genetic counselor, she said, "His job is on the line. He must be completely confident."

That whole pregnancy was hard for me. I was sick for much longer than most people are. I had sleep apnea. When I was pregnant with my first daughter, she would kick responsively, and then she would take naps. It seemed logical. This baby never stopped moving, but she never did anything responsive, either. The movements were so random. I remember telling a friend, "This baby is already different than my first." I don't know if it was that, or my history of miscarriages, or having that seed planted that something might be wrong, but I was uneasy.

Because of that worry, at 35 weeks, my midwife sent me for a "peace of mind" ultrasound. I was eight months pregnant—huge!—and I went to the hospital thinking I was being silly. The rational side of me knew everything was fine. I figured they would tell me all was good, put my mind at ease, give me a picture and send me home.

I went to the appointment alone, on a Wednesday in May. I was so chatty with the technician while I was lying on the table. Towards the end, I said to her, "It's funny, I keep picturing the baby I already have, but I know this one will be different." And she looked right at me, with these serious eyes, and said, "This baby will be different. They are all different."

---

[1] http://endingawantedpregnancy.com/

While I waited for the doctor, I worked on the sweater I was knitting for my little girl. When two doctors came in, one of them asked me about it. Was I making it for the baby? I told her I was, and, with tears in her eyes, she said, "It's beautiful."

Then she continued. "The things they couldn't find the last time you were here, we are seeing those things today. Your baby has brain malformation." Right away, she said, "We might be able to arrange an abortion, we just don't know. We can arrange an adoption if that's what you want."

I'm grateful that she led with that. It told me it was safe to talk to her about options, and it told me that something was very wrong. That was the only thing she said that got through to me. Everything else came up against that denial wall. Of course, she told me about keeping the baby, too.

I know she said the words "Dandy-Walker," which I know now is a brain syndrome that has varying degrees of severity. I remember asking, "Are babies with this ever normal?" and she said that sometimes they were. She told me they couldn't know the severity of the situation until after I had an MRI. That's how they would determine if my baby would be OK or if she would be "incompatible with life." Those are the words they used. Incompatible with life.

I was in total shock. I wasn't even crying. I picked up the phone to call my husband, and all at once, I completely fell apart. By the time he got to the phone, I was unintelligible. "Where are you?" he said. I named the hospital and he said, "I'm on my way."

***

We couldn't get the MRI for two days. My parents took my daughter so that my husband and I could be miserable alone. Waiting was awful. I imagined every possibility: What would it be like to have the miracle baby who was OK and exceeded all expectations? What if she died at birth? What if she lived only a couple of years? What does it mean to get a DNR (a do-not-resuscitate order), for an infant? Hospitals are legally protected from trying to save a baby and not legally protected from letting a baby die. That was something we thought about, too.

We were in crisis, and in crisis, you don't talk very much. You say what you need to say, and the rest is just thoughts turning around in your head constantly. My husband was wonderful. I would cry until I didn't have any tears, and he would pick me up and carry me to our room. I knit and knit and knit. I knit in my worry and knit in my fear, and I finished the sweater. I wove in the ends, and then my husband and I got in the car and drove to the MRI.

It was a morning appointment, and at the end of that day we met with the neurologist, who told us that our baby had Dandy-Walker malformation, the most severe presentation of the syndrome. It basically meant there were holes in her brain. She also had agenesis of the corpus callosum, which meant the bridge between the two hemispheres of her brain didn't grow. So we had two malformations, each of which had a wide range of outcomes, but, combined, had a horrible prognosis. The doctor said, "We expect your baby to have moderate to severe mental retardation; she's going to have moderate to severe physical disability; she is probably never going to walk or talk; she will possibly never be able to lift her head; she is going to have seizures all of the time." At first, I was thinking, "This doesn't make sense, she's always moving," and then he mentioned seizures, and I understood.

In that moment, I had to shift my thinking. I was hoping for special ed, and had been focusing on questions like: How much should you save to know your special-needs daughter will be OK after you die? I was thinking about long-term care and mild to moderate disability. Instead, I had to think about a baby who was probably not going to live very long, and the longer she lived, the more pain she would be in. That realization—that I was more scared of her living than of her dying—is what made the choice for me.

When it comes to a decision like this, there is no good option. What you want is a happy, healthy baby. The doctor asked if we had any questions, and I said, "What does a baby like this do? Does she just sleep all day?" The doctor looked so uncomfortable. He said, "Babies like this one are not generally comfortable enough to sleep." That's when we thanked him and left.

On the way home, even though I knew what I wanted to do, I couldn't say the word. What kind of mother is eight months pregnant and wants an abortion? I turned to my husband and said, "Tell me what you think we should do." He said, "Kate, you do not have to do this, but I think we should ask about the abortion."

It was a gift. It felt like light and fresh air. I had been feeling so dark and so trapped, and when I realized we were together on this, I felt free. I knew what to do. It didn't matter anymore that people were going to call me a murderer, or that I'd never heard of anyone doing this. It didn't matter that we didn't even know if it was legal. If I had my husband, I could do this.

***

I called my doctor as soon as I got home. While we were waiting for her to call back, I didn't know if we had a safe and legal option. I remember thinking, "If we can't get the abortion, I'm going to run away somewhere rural and I'm going to have this baby by myself and let her die without intervention." That would have been so dangerous, and I could be dead right now. She was a high-risk birth, not a regular healthy birth. Her head could have swollen with fluid at any time. Even if it went smoothly, and I had my baby and she had died in a few hours, I could have been put under investigation. The risks that I was willing to take to let this baby go in peace, in the way I believed she deserved—it's terrifying. But I was desperate, and I was so untrusting. I was scared the police would get called on me for just having these thoughts.

My doctor called back at 6:30 that night. It was a Friday, and my husband and I were out for a walk when the phone rang. Immediately, the doctor said, "I am so sorry, but if you want the abortion you need to call before 7 pm, which is the end of the workweek Mountain Time, because the clinic closes for the week in a half an hour. And you have to be on a plane to Colorado on Monday." We were in Boston, where there are a million medical schools and hospitals, but the only doctor in the country who would perform this late an abortion was in Colorado. (Actually, there was one other, but that clinic was closed for the week.) My doctor barely had time to explain everything, she just said I'd have to be in the clinic on Tuesday. It was a four-day procedure, and I had to have it done by Friday, when I would be 36 weeks pregnant. There is no doctor in the country who performs abortions after 36 weeks.

Then she added, "You have to show up with $25,000." We didn't have $25,000 sitting around. We are a middle-class family. We don't have that kind of credit, either. But it didn't matter. I would figure it out.

So I called the Boulder Abortion Clinic in Colorado. We scheduled everything we needed to, but then I had to get money. I called my parents. I told my mom everything, and when I told her I wanted to get the abortion, she said, "That is what I would do, too."

It was such a relief to hear those words. It's one thing to get an abortion, it's another thing to get an abortion at eight months. I felt like such an outcast. It's so heavily tabooed that I was afraid to even tell my mother. But once I knew I had her support, I blurted out, "I need money." My parents took it out of their retirement fund, which is probably what we would have done if we'd had more time. But you can't do much with no business days.

On Monday, we flew to Colorado. I made up a story that I was six months pregnant with twins, in case someone tried to stop me from getting on the plane. I was so afraid that I was going to be found out, that someone was going to get in the way of me getting to the clinic.

The whole first day was counseling and testing to make sure it was safe to do the procedure. They want to make sure you completely understand what is going to happen and that no one is pressuring you into the deci-

sion. At the end of the day, I signed all the paperwork, and the doctor injected the baby with a drug that, over a few hours, slowed her heart to still. It was a very, very difficult day. Euthanizing the baby is, obviously, a very hard thing to do. After the injection, he asked how I was feeling, and I just said, "I feel so sad. I'm going to miss her."

My husband and I went back to the hotel and I lay down until she stopped moving. I could tell when she was gone. It feels very different. The second and third days were short appointments, so we took a nice drive through the Rockies to pass the time. Then on the fourth day, they induced my labor. I got Pitocin, and it was actually a very natural birth. It was quite healing for me. I couldn't do anything for this baby—I couldn't fix her brain or make her well, but I could deliver her from my body. I chose to view her, so they cleaned her up and brought her in and she looked a lot like my older daughter. She was beautiful and she was whole. I got her footprints and had her cremated and they sent us her ashes in the mail a few days later. We wanted to name her after a flower, so we called her Rose.

Ten days after we had that 35-week ultrasound, she was gone.

***

Late in my pregnancy, my older daughter would say, "Mama do you have a baby in your belly?" and I would say, "Yes honey! Want to give her a kiss?" After I got home, I knew she would ask, so I waited for that moment. When it came, my daughter put her hand on my stomach and said it: "Mama, do you have a baby in your belly?" And I said, "No, honey. Baby died. Baby's all gone."

She cried, but probably because I had spoiled the game. My daughter asked me every day for two weeks. Now, every six months or so, we talk about it again— her understanding of it evolves as she grows. At this point, she knows the baby died because she was sick in a way the doctors couldn't fix, because she had holes in her brain, and you need your whole brain to be healthy.

My 30th birthday party was scheduled for the Sunday after we got home—two days after I gave birth to Rose. It was only for close family and friends, so I decided not to cancel. I told people that the baby died and that we induced a stillbirth. I didn't tell them I went to Colorado. I didn't tell them the baby died because we gave her an injection. But eventually, I told my best friend, and she was wonderful. And that helped me tell other people and speak publicly. My husband is a private person, and he would rather I didn't tell anyone, but I have healed a lot from sharing and receiving support.

I've gone on to have another healthy little girl, who is 16 months. The MFM specialist I saw for my third pregnancy said that if it had been him, he would have caught Rose's condition sooner. I have explored the possibility of a medical malpractice suit, but in the end I decided against it. I decided that I can live in a world where people make honest mistakes.

My third pregnancy was hard, emotionally, but today I have a 5-year-old and a 1-year-old. I don't know about the future—I refuse to make a decision right now. I'm still healing. But I have two living children, and I had another baby, whom I still love every day.

"I Set Up #ShoutYourAbortion Because I Am Not Sorry, and I Will Not Whisper"

By Lindy West

Almost exactly five years ago, in September 2010, I took one pill, and then another, and lay in my bed for a night and a day, and then I wasn't pregnant any more. It was a fairly smooth experience, distressing only because my relationship was bad and I had no money. The procedure itself was a relief. Not being able to have it would have been the real trauma.

Suddenly, last week, in the thick of the rightwing, misogynist crusade to defund Planned Parenthood[1] (a vital American nonprofit that provides a broad range of healthcare services, including pelvic exams, STI screenings, contraception and abortion), a thought bowled me over: I never, ever talk about my abortion. I live in a progressive city, I have a fiercely pro-choice social circle and family, I write confessionally about myself for a living—so why is it that I never speak about abortion in anything beyond an abstract way, even with my closest friends? I know about who has a vagina infection, whose boyfriend's penis bends weird, who used to do drugs, who still does. And I know how all of them feel about abortion, policy-wise. But I don't know who has had one, and they don't know about mine. It's not a secret; it's just something we don't talk about.

Not talking about our personal experiences with abortion wasn't conscious—it felt like a habit, a flimsy ouroboros of obfuscation. We don't talk about it because we don't talk about it because we don't talk about it. So, on Saturday, when my friend Amelia Bonow posted this plainspoken, unapologetic announcement on her Facebook page,[2] it felt simultaneously so obvious, so simple and so revolutionary: "Like a year ago I had an abortion at the Planned Parenthood on Madison Ave, and I

remember this experience with a near inexpressible level of gratitude . . . I am telling you this today because the narrative of those working to defund Planned Parenthood relies on the assumption that abortion is still something to be whispered about. Plenty of people still believe that on some level—if you are a good woman—abortion is a choice which should be accompanied by some level of sadness, shame or regret. But you know what? I have a good heart and having an abortion made me happy in a totally unqualified way. Why wouldn't I be happy that I was not forced to become a mother?"

"The assumption that abortion is still something to be whispered about." That struck me hard. The fact that even progressive, outspoken, pro-choice feminists feel the pressure to keep our abortions under wraps—to speak about them only in corners, in murmurs, in private with our closest confidantes—means that opponents of abortion get to define it however suits them best. They can cast those of us who have had abortions as callous monstrosities, and seed fear in anyone who might need one by insisting that the procedure is always traumatic, always painful, always an impossible decision. Well, we're not, and it's not. The truth is that life is unfathomably complex, people with uteruses own their bodies unconditionally, and every abortion story is as unique as the person who lives it. Some are traumatic, some are even regretted, but plenty are like mine.

With her permission, I screengrabbed Amelia's post and put it on Twitter,[3] with a hashtag that seemingly wrote itself: Don't whisper, #ShoutYourAbortion.

The response was immediate and overwhelming—it felt, almost, as if many had been waiting for this moment to speak. People I've known for years told me stories

[1] http://www.theguardian.com/us-news/2015/sep/18/house-of-representatives-planned-parenthood-defunding-bills-shutdown
[2] https://www.facebook.com/amelia.bonow/posts/10152976598871666
[3] https://twitter.com/thelindywest/status/645368432666374144?ref_src=twsrc%5Etfw

I'd never heard before. Complete strangers shared a galaxy of personal experiences, from the harrowing to the mundane:

> **Letha** @lethacolleen
> if ever pregnant, i will have an abortion. i lay claim to my own life. that life will not include giving birth. #ShoutYourAbortion
> *11:32 PM—20 Sep 2015*

> **Anne Carlin** @sacarlin48
> I had to make the choice at 45 yrs after a number of miscarriages. V. Difficult #shoutyourabortion
> *11:26 PM—20 Sep 2015*

> **msmanet** @msmanet
> my abortion gave me my life back..started my healing from rape. no regrets ,not one.#ShoutYourAbortion
> *10:33 PM—20 Sep 2015*

> **—Asshole_Inkslut (@MeanNormaJean)**
> September 20, 2015
> Without my abortion, I'd be forever tied to the man who would go on to rape me 5 years into our relationship. #ShoutYourAbortion

> **Credible Phillips** @Jomegsallan
> No traumatic backstory: Didn't want kids. Couldn't afford kids. Contraceptive failure with casual bf. Not one regret.#ShoutYourAbortion
> *9:02 PM—20 Sep 2015*

All of those abortions are valid. None are shameful.

There are no "good" abortions and "bad" abortions, because an abortion is just a medical procedure, reproductive healthcare is healthcare, and it is a fact without caveat that a fetus is not a person. I own my body, and I decide what I allow to grow in it. Telling our stories at full volume chips away at stigma, at lies, at the climate of shame that destroys the lives (sometimes literally) of women and girls and anyone anywhere on the gender spectrum who can become pregnant, especially those living in poverty, in rural areas and in hyper-religious and conservative households. (It's vital to remember, too, that being able to tell my abortion story without feeling unsupported and unsafe—beyond the general unease of knowing my country is full of heavily armed, anti-intellectual GOP extremists—is a privilege. I speak out because I can.)

There's a reason why #ShoutYourAbortion has been getting mountains of positive, mainstream press attention, while the people terrorizing us (my feed is clogged with pictures of bloody fetuses and death threats—this is Twitter, after all) are ignored on the fringe. It's because we are right, and however glacially society evolves, it is evolving in the right direction. Abortion is common. Abortion is happening. Abortion needs to be legal, safe and accessible to everyone. Abortion[4] is a thing you can say out loud.

I am not sorry.

---

[4]http://www.theguardian.com/world/abortion

"Ask Bear: Is It Okay to Be So, So Sad About My Miscarriage?"

By S. Bear Bergman

Ask Bear[1] is an advice column written by S. Bear Bergman.[2] Bear is a busybody know-it-all with many opinions who is only too happy for a sanctioned opportunity to tell you what he thinks you ought to be doing (as well as a writer, storyteller, publisher, and activist who enjoys telling educational institutions, health care groups, and portions of government what he thinks they ought to be doing). To submit a question to Ask Bear, email asking.bear@gmail.com. Questions will remain 100 percent confidential, and may be edited for length.

Dear Bear,

I'm a good feminist. I know that at eight weeks of gestation a pregnancy does not yet mean a baby, and I absolutely would support a person's right to choose abortion at that point (or at any point, really). But I was personally just pregnant, and I miscarried at eight weeks and feel really sad. How can I recognize my grief and process that but also stand by my pro-choice values?

I keep thinking, "I lost a baby," even though I know eight weeks is actually about a sesame seed worth of barely differentiated cells. About which I am so, so sad. Help?

• • • •

Dear Brave Correspondent,

I'm so sorry. So sorry. In the least creepy way imaginable, I would like to give you a huge hug and make you a pot of soup so you can eat without having to think about it too much. My husband and I had two miscarriages on our way to our two children, who are currently making a lot of noise while I type, and I remember. I remember what that first week was like, especially.

As far as your feminism—which is probably very good indeed even though I am equally sure that there is no objective measure of such things—maybe we can leave it alone for the day. Feminism is about the idea that all people should have the same opportunities, regardless of sex or gender. Nothing in your letter suggests that you have abandoned that ideal. Your feminism is in whatever shape it was in before your miscarriage (though, since we're talking about it, I would like to vote for "intersectional" over "good" as the adjective to strive toward, feminism-wise). Let's talk about feminism again in a minute, after we tend to your feelings, okay?

As far as your heart, of course you're grieving. The loss of possibility with a wanted pregnancy is tremendous. Eight weeks means you've known you were pregnant for three or maybe even four weeks, and three or four weeks is plenty of time for thinking about names, for imagining how your friends will react to the news or how your Great Aunt Petunia will, for calling around to midwives, for eyeing cute pregnancy tops at Target. You created an entire room in your heart for this new human you had started gestating, and now it stays empty. There might well be more chances for you to build a similar room again anew—I really hope that, for your sake. But no amount of logical arguments or medically accurate fetal development timelines will change

[1] https://bitchmedia.org/topic/ask-bear
[2] http://sbearbergman.com/

the difficult emotional truth that this particular room will always be small and darkened.

I recognize that that's not an uplifting thought. However, it's a direct result of my family's experience with miscarriage, which sometimes felt like a musical with only one number: "You Can Always Try Again!" And we did, and the result of the "trying again" process was a great new human. But some people cannot try again; sometimes for reasons of health or money or circumstance there's no Trying Again available. It's not just the end of a chapter, but the end of a certain volume of the great story of hope.

Even though we were able to try again, and we made the decision to give it one more go, I struggled with not wanting to smack those very well-meaning people in the mouth. ("I understand how human reproduction works, thank you. I have studied for this quiz. Please stop talking now.") I wanted people to acknowledge what we'd lost, or at least to let me acknowledge it without trying to talk me out of my feelings. In my heart, that room became a quiet spot where my feelings could be protected in relative peace.

It may help you to know that many, many people have feelings and stories around miscarriage. It may not seem like it—it didn't to me—because people I knew hadn't disclosed that they had (unwanted, disappointing) miscarriages to us until we shared the news that we'd had one. It's like a giant secret club no one wants to belong to. The fact of which is further complicated by the reality that some people's miscarriages were not disappointing to them at all; they weren't occasions of grief but rather relief. However, I am willing to wager, Brave Correspondent, that if you quietly let it be known that you are having a hard time around this, some people will come and hold your hand and nod knowingly and listen to you talk (which is most of what we need when we feel really sad, I find).

It occurs to me as I write this that part of what the pro-choice movement is about is *choice*, the choice of a pregnant person to decide whether they can or should continue being pregnant. There are sometimes questions about when the incipient being in there could, possibly, manage on its own; at what developmental stage (grape? kiwi? orange? Why are they always fruits?) a fetus could reasonably said to be a separate being. Regardless of that, though, the salient point remains: In this case, your choice about your pregnancy got taken away from you. For you it was by circumstances rather than by law, but it still feels relevant. This is how I understand your grief as not being incongruous with feminist ideals in any way.

Another thing feminism is about is defining your body and your self on your own terms, and I would like to propose that this includes everything in it. If it is useful to you to define that which you lost as a baby, then I would consider that feminist. If—in another circumstance, or for another person—it's useful to think of it as a fetus, I believe that is also feminist. It's the self-determination that makes it feminist, by its very nature.

Anti-choice people are frequently concerned with the question of "when is it REALLY a baby?" When I did clinic defense for Planned Parenthood in the '90s, I was often surrounded by yelling people with big feelings about that topic and large posters to go with them. They did not tend to be especially concerned with the lives of the pregnant people or the children once they were born, however. Their actual anger about abortion services was about not being allowed to control the bodies of pregnant people or shame them for having engaged in sexual acts. If they *really* cared about limiting abortion, they'd be crazy-go-nuts for other family planning services like free contraception. But they're not. If they *really* cared about children, they'd be shoveling money at nutrition and wellness programs for babies and children. But they're not.

This "when is it really a baby" thing is a decoy. It's an anti-choice right-wing framing that tries to draw pro-choice people into an energy-sucking debate that has no clear answer, all the better to distract us from protecting the rights of people to become pregnant or not as they choose. For this reason, I don't really think you have to engage with it right now or ever. I think you can be sad without worrying that you are betraying the movement. I think your grief can be real and you owe nothing to the mean yelling people outside the clinics. I think the love and sweetness of possibility you began to feel can be banked like the coals of a fire and blaze brightly again when the time is right, whether by conception or adoption or blending of families.

In my life, the biggest places of sorrow have always been the loss of possibility. And the greatest joys have been the realization of it—the sweetness of being able to make real the wonders of my secret heart, which were long sought-for and long lavished with the many luminous glazings of hope and desire. I wish most sincerely for you, Brave Correspondent, that eventually you also feel this joy.

Love and courage,
Bear

Related Reading: What to Say—And What Not to Say—After Someone Has a Miscarriage[3]

---

[3]http://bitchmagazine.org/post/what-to-say%E2%80%94and-what-not-to-say%E2%80%94after-someone-has-a-miscarriage—This is a great piece in comic form. *Ed.*

"Expensive, Exhausting, And Deeply Unsexy: Babymaking While Queer"

By Lindsay King-Miller

Trying to conceive can be difficult and emotionally draining, no matter who's making the attempt. *For a queer couple like us, the process has been nothing short of excruciating.*

My partner Charlie and I had been married for a little over a year when we decided to start trying to have a baby in August 2013. Despite being the butch in our relationship and using male pronouns, Charlie knew from the start that he wanted be the gestational parent. He's always had a fascination with pregnancy and birth—a fascination that once led him to briefly pursue a midwifery apprenticeship—and he was excited to experience all the highs and lows of carrying a child. I, on the other hand, dread physical pain, and was overjoyed by the prospect of becoming a parent without going through pregnancy.

Charlie's cycle operates with clocklike precision, so we figured it would be easy enough to identify the opportune moment. We started by trying to conceive at home—all you need is a syringe and a clean jar. We painted our guest room in pastels, recruited a dude we know and love to donate sperm, and got underway.

Unfortunately, the magic I'd anticipated was pretty much gone the first time I went for a walk around the block so that our friend could jerk off in our bathroom. After that, we decided that it would be less awkward if he made his donation at his own home, then dropped by with the jar—sperm can live outside the body for several hours, especially if they're kept warm—but calling and saying, "Charlie's ovulating, can you come over?" wasn't very romantic either. We had to skip insemination one month because our donor couldn't escape his roommates, who didn't know about our conception attempts, for the requisite five minutes. Also unforeseen was the discomfort of making small talk every time he dropped off his jar, camouflaged in a paper bag—no one really wants to chat about how work is going at such a moment, but without a little conversation the whole thing felt too transactional. "Thank you for your genetic material, Unit B. Your service is no longer required."

And there was a squick factor that neither Charlie nor I anticipated. We were competent, sex-positive adults who wanted to have a baby—surely we could handle a jar with a little semen in it! Turns out that other people's bodily fluids are disconcerting, no matter how chill and mature you promise yourself you'll be about the whole thing. I'm sorry to contribute to the body-shaming and negativity that pervades our culture, but let's be real: A jar of sperm is super gross. Every month, Charlie would calmly draw up the sperm into the syringe while I shrieked and covered my eyes as though it was the gory scene in a horror movie (no, that's not true—movie gore bothers me way less).

The insemination wasn't much better. We had originally looked forward to this part—the two of us alone in our room, sharing the beautiful, intimate moment of creating our future child. Inseminating just before or even during sex is supposed to up your odds of success, which we figured was a bonus. We'd read about it online and it seemed easy, straightforward, and even fun. But it was almost impossible to get into the moment, since we were pressed for time (sperm were dying by the second!) and limited by the necessity that Charlie stay lying on his back with a pillow under his hips. I tried to help with the syringe, but couldn't find a comfortable angle, so Charlie had to take over.

Nothing kills a mood like a syringe.

Technically you're not considered infertile until you've tried to conceive for 12 months straight with no result, but five negative pregnancy tests in a row made us question the efficacy of our approach. First we investigated the possibility of Charlie taking Clomid, an ovulation-stimulating drug used to treat infertility—if we could up his egg production, we might increase our odds of a successful at-home insemination. But we couldn't get anyone to prescribe Clomid.

"It's not safe to take if your insemination isn't being overseen by a doctor," said the nurse Charlie talked to on the phone.

"But if we were a straight couple, we could just take Clomid and have sex, right?" Charlie argued.

"Well, yes, we would prescribe it for a normal couple," the nurse said.

Oh. Although in some subsets of our culture the phrases "artificial insemination" and "lesbians" go together like peanut butter and chocolate, the medical infrastructure surrounding assisted reproduction is still staunchly heteronormative. We tried to appeal the Clomid decision, but got nowhere; every doctor we talked to agreed that, for no reason they could pinpoint, taking fertility treatments and then trying to get knocked up at home was much more dangerous for lesbians than for straight people.

The next step was to try intrauterine insemination, or IUI. We had to set up a directed donation account with a local sperm bank, meaning that our donor's sperm could only be used by us, as opposed to anonymous donor sperm, which is available for purchase by any of the sperm bank's clients. Directed donation is expensive—they test the donor for all kinds of communicable or congenital diseases, and we had to pay for all those tests, whereas with an anonymous donor the cost is spread across multiple customers. We were spending hundreds of dollars and still acting as reluctant consultants for our donor's masturbation calendar, but at least there were no more jars of semen.

On our first visit to a reproductive endocrinologist (RE), Charlie was officially diagnosed with infertility, despite being well below the threshold for unsuccessful conception attempts. Being part of a reproductively incompatible couple is apparently, in itself, a medical condition. This reminded me of the time Charlie's doctor wrote down that his birth control method was "abstinence." Is there a rule somewhere that says doctors can't write or speak the word "gay"?

The IUI process, which was both invasive and impersonal, carried us even further from the romantic candlelit conception of our dreams. Charlie had to take pills, undergo transvaginal ultrasounds (which he termed "the snatch wand"),[1] have blood tests and X-rays, and get inseminated via a cervical catheter two days out of every month. Physical modesty and privacy went out the window. There were medications for everything. Charlie was briefly put on a diet—in fact, the doctor suggested that I should lose weight too, as though the size of my ass was somehow eclipsing Charlie's fallopian tubes. The underlying message was clear: There is something wrong with you, or you wouldn't be here. And of course, that "infertile" diagnosis lingered, growing more and more ominous as more months passed without a positive pregnancy test.

While Charlie's experience with IUI involved being constantly scrutinized and objectified, mine was alienating in a different way. Our doctors all but ignored me. I still remember the rush of excitement I felt when we came in on a Saturday and the weekend RE actually shook my hand. I exist! It's possible that as a male partner of a straight woman undergoing IUI, I would have been more included in the process, but maybe not. I only know that frequently, the doctor would come in, perform the procedure, and leave without so much as a word to me. I'm not sure any of our providers knew my name. Or Charlie's, for that matter—they continued calling him by his legal name, despite all the forms where he wrote CHARLIE in big letters under "name you prefer to be called." We could have made a drinking game out of it: Take a shot every time a doctor gets one of our names right on the first try! It would hardly have interfered with Charlie's medically endorsed sobriety.

Contrasted with the doctors and nurses in reproductive endocrinology were the lab techs in the basement, whom we saw several times a month—Charlie more often than me—for blood tests and to defrost our sperm samples. Knowing nothing about us except that we wanted to be parents, they were still warm and welcoming. Each month after the first time, they gave a sympathetic sigh as we walked through their door: "Back again, huh? Hopefully this time it will work!" They ushered us out with our thawed vial and a cheerful "Hope we don't see you again!" Upstairs, no one ever acknowledged that our repeat visits were a source of unhappiness and stress—they just pulled out the speculum and got down to business.

---

[1] Ultrasounds performed to assess and treat fertility, like ultrasounds in the first trimester of pregnancy, are generally *transvaginal*, meaning that a probe is inserted into the vagina for imaging. In states that mandate a pre-abortion ultrasound (including Wisconsin), the vast majority of people seeking abortions must also undergo a transvaginal ultrasound since the majority of abortions are performed in the first trimester (see Guttmacher Institute fact sheets elsewhere in this section). *Ed.*

One month, we happened to show up for Charlie's procedure on the office's unofficial Dyke Day. There were two other lesbian couples in the waiting room, clearly for the same reasons as us, and we all shared an informal little Queer Solidarity Salute.

"This has got to be a good omen," said one of the other women, who was a textbook Crunchy Granola Lesbian. "Awesome lady-power vibes." We smiled at each other, and I felt an irrational jolt of optimism. This was perfect! I was already imagining what I would say later: *We knew it was our lucky day when we walked in and saw that the waiting room was full of lesbians . . . .* Sadly, population density of queer women is not an accurate predictor of fertility. I don't know if either of those other couples came out of their visits expecting, but we did not.

After five months of IUI and five more negative pregnancy tests (necessitating five weekends spent at home, crying and watching *Juno*), we've moved on to in vitro fertilization, adding injections and hormone side effects to the list of things Charlie gets to guilt-trip our child for, assuming we ever have one. On top of that, we burned through our savings paying for IUI at a rate of about $1,000 a month, and had to take out a loan to cover the cost of IVF. With all the money we've spent trying to conceive a child, we joke that we can no longer afford to actually raise one. (It's a joke in that we laugh when we say it, but that's mostly just to mask our fear that it's true.)

We still have nothing to show for our efforts, and there's a part of me that feels like, for that reason, I should keep all this to myself. As a culture, we're very uncomfortable with the concept of trying and failing. We prefer to see the finished product, not the struggle and sacrifice it took to get there. Thus, many individuals and couples who are trying to conceive keep that fact to themselves until and unless they get pregnant, all the while fielding questions like "So when are you going to have kids?" from well-meaning family and friends.

I wish it were more acceptable to talk about this. Trying to get pregnant using assisted reproductive technology is *hard*, and people going through it deserve support and sympathy. We need to be able to talk about the sometimes obstacle-filled journey to parenthood openly, but without fielding tons of intrusive questions that further fracture our already tenuous privacy. And as queer people, we need culturally competent health care providers who understand and sympathize with what we're going through. Assisted reproductive technology isn't anyone's ideal way to start a family, but if it's needed it can be an enormous blessing. I think it's worthwhile to share our stories and realize that, while this issue is emotional and deeply isolating, those of us going through it are not alone. I'm tempted to end on some kind of platitude—like "I know it will all be worth it when I finally get to hold our child"—but the sad truth is that we might not succeed. Some couples don't. Some stories don't have happy endings, but that doesn't mean they don't deserve to be told.

Lindsay King-Miller is the author of Ask a Queer Chick: A Guide to Sex, Love, and Life for Girls Who Dig Girls *(2016).*[2]

---

[2]http://www.penguinrandomhouse.com/books/318341/ask-a-queer-chick-by-lindsay-king-miller/9780147516787/—Spoiler: One of the categories under which the book is listed is "Parenting." *Ed.*

CHILDBIRTH AND LACTATION

"Ideals vs. Reality in U.S. Births"

From Citizens for Midwifery
Developed by Carolyn M. Keefe

	WHO Recommendations	2004 U.S. Stats	CIMS Suggestions (4.1 million births)
Birth Attendants	Midwives for normal pregnancy and birth	Access to professional midwifery care	Midwives 7.9% (325,000)
Place of Birth	Out-of-Hospital preferred	Where mother prefers	Hospitals 99.% (4.07 million)
Electronic Fetal Monitoring	Not routine	Not routine	No longer reported Last reported 85.%
Pain Relief Drugs in Labor	Not routine	Only for complications	80%*
Induction of Labor	10% or less	10% or less	21.2% (870,000)
Episiotomies (Vaginal Births)	Systematic use not justified	Goal of 5%	23.7%** (667,000)
Cesarean Rate	10–15%	10–15%	29.1% (1.19 million)
Breastfeeding After Birth	Immediately	WHO-UNICEF BFHI Guidelines	67%***

- *WHO Recommendations*–taken from a report on the *Appropriate Technology for Birth*, published by the World Health Organization in April, 1985.
- *CIMS Suggestions*–taken from *The Mother-Friendly Childbirth Initiative* from the Coalition for Improving Maternity Services (CIMS), 1996, www.motherfriendly.org. BFHI = Baby-Friendly Hospital Initiative.
- *2004 US Stats*–most taken from *Births: Final Data for 2004*, National Vital Statistics Report Vol. 55, No. 1, September 29, 2006 http://www.cdc.gov/nchs/data/nvsr/nvsr55/nvsr55_01.pdf.

No longer reported—In revising birth certificate reporting, NCHS no longer collects this information. Last reported rate (2003) is included here

Listening to Mothers Report, October 2002, p. 18
**"National Hospital Discharge Survey 2004: Advance Data," *Vital Health Statistics*, No. 371, May 5, 2006.
***Mothering Magazine*, No. 112, May/June 2002

"Birth Trends in the United States: Understanding Outcomes and Maternal Agency/Autonomy in Pregnancy and Labor"

By Tanya N. Cook

Childbirth in the United States

Of the 3.93 million births in the United States in 2013, over 98% took place in hospitals and over one million were cesarean section births (MacDorman, Mathews, and Delcerq, 2014, Martin et al 2015). This represents a dramatic change from a century ago when most women[1] gave birth at home attended by midwives and family members. By the mid-twentieth century, women had been both pushed and pulled into the hospital. Women were pushed into the hospital by increasing urbanization and mobility and also the continuing trend of women calling on male physicians, who increasingly specialized in obstetrics, for home birth. At the same time, hospitals were explicitly marketed to women of means as safer places to birth and more pleasant settings for both labor (pain medications were becoming more available) and post-delivery care (providing a vacation from household duties) (Leavitt 1986).

The shift to hospital-based, obstetrician-attended birth did correlate with improved, lowered rates of both maternal and infant mortality, although these rates remain disproportionately high among minority and lower SES groups. Women giving birth, however, traded increased safety for loss of control over their labor and delivery experiences. As long as birth was an event that happened primarily in the private sphere of women's homes, Leavitt (1986) argues that the woman giving birth largely retained control over where she would give birth, who would attend her, and what technological interventions would be employed. This changed, however, with what Leavitt (1986: 195) labels the "most important transition in childbirth history": the move from birth in the home to birth in the hospital.

Women giving birth between the 1950s and 1980s were routinely subjected to standardized obstetrical practices including: generalized anesthesia, pubic area shaving, episiotomy, enema, having an IV lead inserted for fluids, labor-inducing drugs or emergency anesthesia, vaginal exams, fetal monitoring, moving from labor to delivery room, and delivery in the lithotomy (or flat on one's back with feet spread and raised in stirrups) position (Davis-Floyd 1992). Furthermore, women's significant others or family members were often excluded from the delivery room and women had to undergo separation from the newborn immediately after birth when the newborn was taken to a nursery for observation.

While hospital practices have changed to be more family and mother-centered in some ways, women still often birth in a context of limited agency and autonomy due to financial and policy constraints. Even if pre-existing, pregnancy-related health complications do not limit choices, obstetric practices may. For example, most providers will not allow women to carry a pregnancy more than a week "past term" even when the due date itself is more of an estimate than precise calculation. As Morris (2013: 93) explains, estimated due dates include a significant margin of error: "The 'normal' pregnancy length is defined as a four-week window

---

[1] Throughout this piece, the term "woman" is generally used to describe pregnant people and people giving birth due to the fact that existing scholarship overwhelmingly works from this assumption. It can also be argued that the cultural feminization of pregnant bodies and the birth process contributes significantly to the ways in which pregnant and birthing people's agency and autonomy are limited. However, we recognize that this is not the most accurate representation of who does and does not become pregnant or birth, and may have negative consequences both for women who do not birth and trans men, non-binary people, and other non-women who do. For more detailed discussion of this issue, see "Culturally Appropriate Doula Support for Queer and Transgender Parents" elsewhere in this section. *Ed.*

between thirty-eight and forty-two weeks since the start of the woman's last menstrual period." Interestingly, this limit may imply additional constraints on autonomy as induction of labor has been associated with an increased likelihood of cesarean section (Morris 2013). While the intention of both induction and cesarean is to save maternal and infant lives, cesarean in particular, as a major surgical procedure, is associated with an increased risk of complications and maternal mortality.

The United States recently ranked 33rd out of 179 countries on a Mother's Health Index which included measures of infant, child, and maternal health (Save the Children 2015). The relatively high rates of maternal and infant mortality in the U.S. are the main reason that it is ranked below most other highly industrialized nations including Spain, Portugal, Slovenia, Greece, and the Czech Republic (Save the Children 2015). Maternal mortality, defined as death during pregnancy or up to one year after birth or pregnancy termination, has more than doubled for U.S. mothers from 7.2 deaths per 100,000 in 1987 to 17.8 deaths in 2011 (CDC 2016). While some of this increase is due to a change how pregnancy and birth related deaths were noted on death certificates in 2003, the more recent number (17.8) is considered to be more accurate and demonstrates an unusually high maternal mortality rate compared with other nations (Maron 2015).

Rates of maternal mortality also differ dramatically by racial-ethnic group in the U.S. Alarmingly, non-Hispanic Black mothers have nearly three times the rate of maternal mortality as non-Hispanic White mothers at 42.8 versus 12.5 per 100,000, respectively. High and increasing rates of maternal mortality in the U.S. and among African American mothers in particular are associated with poverty and lack of health care access and coverage (CDC 2015). Untreated chronic health conditions such as hypertension, diabetes, and heart disease are listed as the primary causes of maternal death in most cases. Anesthesia complications (0.2%), hemorrhage (11.3%), infection and sepsis (12.7%), are other leading causes of maternal death while 6.2% of maternal deaths have no known cause (CDC 2015). Anesthesia complications, infection, and hemorrhage are also more likely to be associated with cesarean birth.

Disproportionate poverty rates, lack of access to health care or access to inappropriate care, stress, and untreated health conditions also contribute to disparities in infant mortality rates between racial-ethnic groups in the U.S. Internationally, the U.S. ranked 26th out of the 29 most developed Organization for Economic Cooperation and Development (OECD) countries with an infant mortality rate of 6.1 per 1,000 live births in 2010 (MacDorman et al 2014). Approximately 47% of these deaths were to infants born later than 37 weeks gestation

and 39% were due to the higher percentage of preterm births in the U.S. as compared to other countries (MacDorman et al 2014). African American infant mortality rates, however, were double the rates for non-Hispanic Whites at 11.11 versus 5.06 in 2013 (Mathews, MacDorman, and Thoma 2015). Part of this disparity could be explained by the higher rates of low birth weight and preterm births between non-Hispanic Black mothers and other groups. While this is partially associated with existing racial disparities in socioeconomic class and pre-pregnancy health, some researchers have found that that recent and lifetime experiences of racism specifically also account for some of this racial variation in low birth weight (Dominguez et al 2008) and that racial microaggressions may increase the risk of preterm birth for Black women who are not already categorized as "high risk" (Slaughter-Acey et al 2016). Low birth weight infants had 25% increased risk of mortality in 2013 (Mathews, MacDorman, and Thoma 2015). Maternal and infant mortality rates for some Americans, then, parallel rates in other OECD most-developed nations. For others, however, the experience of healthcare in America as measured by infant and maternal mortality rates is similar to that of a developing nation.

In 2009 the percentage of children born in the U.S. via cesarean section reached an all-time high of 32.9% (Martin et al 2012). Correspondingly, cesarean section was the most common operating room procedure in the U.S. by 2010, representing an increase of 41% from 1997 to 2010 (Pfuntnur, Wier, and Stocks, 2013). The overall rate of cesarean declined to 32.7% in 2013 but continues to be two to three times higher than the World Health Organization's recommendation of 10 to 15% (Martin et al 2015). (By comparison, in 1970, the overall U.S. cesarean rate was about 6%.) Additionally, cesarean has decreased for non-Hispanic White mothers but has remained higher for non-Hispanic Black mothers and Hispanic mothers at 35.8% and 32.3%, respectively (Martin et al 2015). While c-section certainly saves some lives and has become a much safer procedure over the past forty years, evidence indicates that overall cesarean rates above 15% are not associated with a significant decrease in maternal and neonatal mortality (WHO/RHR/15.2 2015).

Overall, there are more negative health consequences for mothers and infants from cesarean versus spontaneous vaginal birth. Mothers who deliver via planned cesarean versus planned vaginal birth are 2.3 times more likely to be re-hospitalized in the 30 days following the birth for infection and complications with the incision (Declercq et al 2007). Other studies suggest a link between cesarean delivery and an increased likelihood that a child will suffer allergies and asthma (Hampton 2008), and a decreased likelihood that a mother will breastfeed (Perez-Escamilla, Maulen-Radovan and Dewey 1996). Cesarean has also been associated with increased rates post-partum depression in some studies though not in others.[2] Cesarean deliveries are also more costly than vaginal births; cesarean delivery now averages $27,866 versus $18,329 for a vaginal birth.[3] There are high-risk birth situations in which cesareans save lives, but of particular concern for public health scholars is the growing rate of cesareans for low-risk mothers without a medical indication (MacDorman et al 2008b). One study found a 69% higher risk of neonatal mortality when comparing cesarean deliveries without labor complications to planned vaginal births (MacDorman et al 2008b).

Given the potential negative infant and maternal health outcomes and the higher costs, why then does the cesarean section rate remain over 30% in the United States? Cesarean delivery as a public health issue is intermixed with issues of gender, race/ethnicity, authority, and public understanding of risk. Some argue that fear of malpractice suits leads doctors to unintentionally fail to inform women of alternatives to cesarean. However, Morris (2013) found the relationship was less direct. Rather, it is an institutional focus on documentation as protection against liability lawsuits that is associated with practices that may increase the rate of cesarean. Nurses in particular are subject to this pressure to document labor events as their malpractice insurance is covered by the hospital.

Documentation of fetal heart rate during labor via electronic fetal monitoring (EFM) is prioritized as a defensive practice against a potential lawsuit should the newborn suffer an injury that could be argued was caused or not prevented by actions nurses and doctors did or did not take during labor. EFM records are constructed as the best indicator of fetal status during labor despite the well-documented evidence that EFM readings must be interpreted by providers, and in fact, as many as 99.8% of EFM readings that indicate fetal distress may actually be false positives (Morris 2013). Although EFM is emphasized for the prevention of cerebral palsy, evidence indicates that most cases of cerebral palsy are not caused by labor events (Morris 2013). The ubiquity of EFM and its association with false positive diagnoses of fetal distress, which in turn are associated with increased cesarean section, produces serious limitations on maternal agency and autonomy during labor (Cook 2012).

[2]For more information see Bland: http://clearinghouse.missouriwestern.edu/manuscrips/59.php

[3]For more information, see Eugene Declercq for CNN: http://www.cnn.com/2013/07/09/opinion/declercq-childbirth-costs/index.html

Possible Causal Explanations for Cesarean Rate Increase

Other studies have attempted to explain the increase in cesarean birth rates as the result of other associated variables including advanced maternal age, mother's overall health, a reduction in the rate of vaginal birth after cesarean (henceforth VBAC), and a larger percentage of women requesting cesarean birth. A closer examination of the data reveals, however, that these factors do not sufficiently explain the increase in the primary cesarean rate over the last decade. As maternal age at first birth has increased over the past few years in the U.S. to an average of 26 at first birth, and birth rates among women in the 30–44 cohort have increased, cesarean rates have actually declined slightly (Mart et al 2015). Based on a study of 512 women giving birth in 2006 in the UK, Naftalin and Paterson-Brown (2008) found a statistically significant relationship between obesity and cesarean section. Obese first-time mothers were found to be more than 5 times more likely to have a cesarean than non-obese first-time mothers (Naftalin and Paterson-Brown, 2008). The authors suggest obese patients may be more likely to experience a cesarean because their overall lack of conditioning results in the uterus being unable to contract sufficiently during labor. They also speculate that obese patients may suffer from "...the deposition of adipose tissue along the birth canal impeding the fetal passage" (Naftalin and Paterson-Brown 2008: 397).

As with many forms of healthcare delivered to obese patients and especially women, however, it seems that doctor's *beliefs* about obese patients' ability to labor may play a larger role here. While it is true that overall Americans are getting heavier, rates of cesarean are rising across demographic groups, not only in obese women (MacDorman et al 2008). The rate of obesity has climbed steadily, increasing approximately 1% per year from 1995 to 2006 from 15% to 26% (MacDorman et al 2008). Over the same time period, however, cesarean rates rose at a slower pace in the late 90s from approximately 18% in 1995 to 21% in 2000. From 2000, when the overall cesarean rate was 21%, the cesarean section rate rose 10% in six years, reflecting a more rapid increase in the rate of cesarean than in the rate of maternal obesity. If the rise in cesarean section rates were mostly due to advancing maternal age and obesity, one would see associated steady growth in cesarean section rates over time as we have seen in rates of obesity.[4]

[4]For more information about how health care providers' weight-related biases may negatively affect patient care, especially for women, see Lacey Alexander and Anna G. Mirer's work elsewhere in this volume. *Ed.*

Key to understanding the apparently dramatic increase in the rate of cesarean from 2000 onward is the American College of Obstetrician and Gynecologists' (ACOG) 1999 recommendation that women attempting a VBAC have the ability to deliver surgically, that is via cesarean, "immediately available (Roberts et al 2007)" if attempting a trial labor. As Roberts et al (2007) show in their study of hospitals in four states between 2003 and 2005, this policy had the consequence of significantly limiting access to VBAC delivery. Smaller hospitals were unable to have the recommended surgeons and anesthesiologists readily available for the duration of an attempted VBAC labor and delivery, leading many of them to require scheduled cesareans as a way to manage risk and scarce personnel resources. This policy shift has led to a return to the guideline "once a cesarean, always a cesarean" for more and more women.

In July 2010, responding to recommendations from a panel on VBAC convened by the NIH in March, ACOG revised its 1999 statement with the intention of increasing access to VBAC.[5] The new guidelines state that for women in low risk conditions with only one prior cesarean, VBAC may not involve more risk than cesarean. The language that surgical and anesthesia care be "immediately available" for emergency delivery remains, however, leading some childbirth advocates to speculate that the policy change will not produce an increase in VBAC.

The rate of VBACs peaked in 1996 at 28.3% but had declined dramatically to approximately 8–9% nationally by 2006 (NVSS 2009). Reductions in the rate of VBAC, however, are still not sufficient to explain the rise in overall cesarean section rates. Primary cesareans, that is, cesareans for women who have not had a previous cesarean, declined between 1989 and 1996 but rose after 1996 to a high of 23.5% in 2006. Zhang et al (2010) argue that reducing the overall cesarean rate is ultimately dependent on reducing the primary cesarean rate. It may also depend on reducing the rate of induction, as the authors found that cesarean rate was twice as high for women who experienced induced versus spontaneous labor (Zhang et al, 2010).

Some have argued that increases in the rate of primary cesarean are due to a trend toward maternally requested, but medically unnecessary, cesarean. I will refer to these as CDMRs (Cesarean Delivery based on Maternal Request). However, as few as 1 in 1600 women report a preference for cesarean delivery

without a medical indication (Declercq et al 2006). In a critical literature review of articles documenting CDMRs, Gamble et al (2007) argued that much of the inflation in the rate of women requesting cesareans was the result of decision-making in a context heavily influenced by provider suggestion, lack of complete information about the safety of cesarean birth, and a miscategorization of some cesareans that could have been listed as medically indicated.

Increasingly cesarean section is being used in a prophylactic sense to manage risk to the fetus. Medical professionals turn to cesarean, which is *presented* as an alternative with low risk to mother and even less risk to fetus, as a way to manage other risks. Cesarean is the go-to intervention for formerly vaginal births with higher risk such as breech, which may have previously been assisted with forceps or vacuum extraction, both of which have declined in use since 1996 (Martin et al 2012). Some studies have suggested that the increase in the use of cesarean perpetuates a cycle where cesarean becomes the dominant risk-management tool for difficult labors and provider competence in other methods is lost, which in turn leads to more cesarean (Block 2007, Morris 2013). In the case of a breech presentation, for instance, in the past medical professionals would attempt to turn the baby into a head down position prior to delivery (external cephalic version), or attempt a vaginal breech delivery with the use of forceps. With the increase in cesarean as a treatment for breech delivery, however, the likelihood that a new doctor will learn the external cephalic version technique is reduced. A pregnant person who is carrying a breech baby is faced with a choice between a somewhat painful procedure which may not work and carries a small amount of risk, or the option of scheduling a "safe" cesarean. Cesarean, however, is not without risk. Although the surgery has become much safer over the last 30 years, risks to the birthing person include: bladder injury, abdominal pain, intrauterine infection, uterine rupture, blood transfusion, risk of subsequent pregnancy ending in stillbirth, and death (Baxter 2007).

Whether or not women agree to cesarean delivery in the context of full disclosure or informed consent about these risks is another issue raised in the literature (Baxter 2007, Bergeron, 2007). For children born via cesarean, the risk of asthma and allergy increases, suggesting a link between the mode of delivery and immune system response (Hampton 2008). Cesarean delivery is also much more expensive than vaginal birth, as mentioned previously. A 2009 survey of 2800 hospitals nationwide by the International Cesarean Awareness Network (ICAN), however, indicated that up to 30% of hospitals nationwide have official prohibitions on VBAC deliveries, with an additional 20% of

---

[5]See Denise Grady's 2010 *New York Times* coverage of the revised ACOG statement here: http://www.nytimes.com/2010/07/22/health/22birth.html?_r=0

hospitals reporting they had no current doctors on staff who would accept a VBAC patient.[6]

Medicalized and Alternative Birth Movements

In *Birth as an American Rite of Passage*, Davis-Floyd (1992) argues that the medicalized model of childbirth common in the US is no less ritualized or symbolic because of its supposed rationality. Instead, Davis-Floyd (1992) analyzes birth as a rite of passage that re-creates society literally and culturally by transmitting key cultural values. New members are produced and women are re-produced as mothers through the socialization process of their birth experience. Although birth challenges the technocratic model's emphasis on the importance of technology's dominance over nature and its view of society, the ritualization and standardization of the childbirth experience through hospital birth serves to legitimate patriarchy (Davis-Floyd 1992). Under the medical/technocratic model, women's biology is seen as pathological and birth is an involuntary process that a woman's anatomy "does." Martin (1987) argues that this model views a woman as a worker producing a product (baby) with her machine (uterus) while being managed by a doctor (146). Women are thus alienated from both the product of their labor, their child, and from the process of producing the product, the birth. Casper's (1998) work on the developing field of fetal surgery also shows how medical professionals decontextualize the fetus by removing the mother from view in training materials. They do this in order to construct the fetus as an acceptable work object distinct from the mother (Casper 1998). As Casper (1998: 18) states: "Fetal subjectivities, like other social categories, are produced within social interactions rather than being endowed by nature-although materiality may be significant as we shall see."

Women who experience cesarean deliveries speak most strongly about this alienation/separation. They often mourn a loss of control over the process of birth and feel disconnected from the product—their child (Martin 1987, 79). Furthering the production/consumption metaphor, Taylor (2000) argues that prenatal technologies increase the commodification of fetuses. Women are the alienated unskilled workers whose production is increasingly subjected to the quality control of ultrasound and other prenatal diagnostic technologies. A qualitative study of 40 mothers' traumatic birth stories in English-speaking countries (US, UK, Australia and New Zealand) revealed that a lack of communication between mothers and providers during labor often leads women to identify as traumatic a birth that clinicians would see as routine (Beck 2004). Mothers specifically rejected the notion that "the ends justify the means" during labor. A healthy baby of course was prioritized, but not the only outcome important to mothers. Mothers also wanted to be cared for during birth and treated as active agents during labor (Beck 2004).

Mathews and Zadak (1991) show how alternative birth movements to the technocratic birth model emphasized consumer choice in order to motivate hospitals to change procedures. Organizations developed in the 1970s, like the International Childbirth Education Association and the American Society for Psychoprophylaxis in Obstetrics, advocated for changes in what had been seen as routine hospital procedures (Mathews and Zadak 1991, 44). When educated women began looking for alternatives, hospitals responded by allowing husbands/partners/labor support people to attend deliveries and by developing more home-like birthing centers within maternity wards. Stand-alone birthing centers opening around the country also put pressure on hospitals to respond to consumer demand. 80% of US hospitals with maternity care had single room care (labor and delivery in same room) available by 1987 (Mathews and Zadak 1991). The American College of Nurse Midwives and the American Public Health Association endorsed freestanding birth centers and established proposed guidelines for their use and screening out "at risk" cases. The American College of Obstetricians and Gynecologists and the American Academy of Pediatrics, however, both endorsed hospitals as the only safe place for labor and delivery in 1983 (Mathews and Zadak 1991). The established institutions had been threatened by changing consumer demands and the fact that stand-alone birth centers can often provide the same services for half of the cost of an OB-attended hospital birth.

As several authors (Martin 1987; Davis-Floyd 1992; Mathews and Zadak 1991) point out, however, alternative birth options are usually most available for well-educated middle class women. These women have the resources to educate themselves about their birth options and advocate for the choices they want (Mathews and Zadak 1991). As Davis-Floyd's (1992) research also suggests, most of these women find their birth philosophies somewhere in between the continuum of technocratic and holistic approaches to birth. They want control but also believe in the safety and security science and technology supposedly provide. Less well-educated women and women of color may not have these options. Economic factors including lack of insurance or limited insurance coverage may also restrict the choices available, and even when women

---

[6]For more information, see ICAN website: http://www.ican-online.org/

have a choice of provider types, women of color in particular may still struggle to find *culturally* competent care. There is significant under-representation of women of color among Certified Nurse Midwives (CNMs), the most educated type of midwife and the most likely to practice in a hospital or birth center and be covered by private insurance. 57% of White women versus 13% of African American women are cared for by a CNM and only 2% of midwives themselves identify as Black (Grace 2015). Additionally, women whose pregnancies have been identified as high risk will be more constrained with their birth choices.

As much as birth practices have changed over the last thirty or forty years, no or low-intervention vaginal birth (no epidural, no induction, etc) remains a small minority of all births in the US. A majority of women (68%) now opt for an epidural and birth without some form of anesthetic is virtually unheard of (Morris 2013). Stories of fetal and maternal loss due to home birth gone wrong undermine the efforts of advocates and contribute to legislative efforts to make home birth illegal. If, as advocates claim, home birth or low-to no intervention midwife-attended birth center experiences are safer than intervention-heavy hospital birth, more empowering for women, and less expensive, then why do so few American women seek out these options?

Estimating the risk of neonatal mortality for home birth is complicated. It is not always clear whether the home birth was intended or whether labor was brought on by an underlying condition that also affected the viability of the fetus. While most neonatal deaths are due to congenital abnormalities that exist prior to birth, other studies have demonstrated an association between type of provider, birth location, and neonatal mortality. In general, hospital births attended by Certified Nurse Midwives (CNMs) have lower rates of neonatal mortality than doctor-attended hospital births, CNM-attended home births, or other midwife (such as Certified Professional Midwife (CPM), also known as a lay midwife)-attended births either in the hospital or at home (Malloy 2010). After an analysis of vital birth statistics for the years 2000–2004, Malloy (2010) found the risk of neonatal mortality for a CNM-attended home birth was twice that of a CNM-attended hospital birth (3.45 vs 1.18 per 1000 live births, respectively).

Given data limitations and potential selection bias, however, it is difficult to know whether this increased risk was due to the type of provider and location of birth or to some other pre-existing or associated factor. Prenatal risks are often under-estimated and the population who tends to choose homebirth is disproportionately non-Hispanic White and over the age of 35 (Malloy 2010). Furthermore Malloy's (2010: 624) data show that those who birth at home with a CNM or other midwife were more likely to be at gestational ages 41–42 weeks (25.1% CNM and 26.8% other midwife versus 19.1% for hospital-attended CNM). Although Malloy (2010) does not address this issue, gestational age is associated with increased risk of neonatal mortality (Rosenstein et al 2013); therefore the percentage differences in populations here by provider type and location could explain some of the increased risk found in this data. Given how challenging estimating neonatal mortality risk is, if the goal is to understand how women understand risk and make decisions about childbirth options, we cannot take for granted the assumptions of either the medical-technical or alternative birth movements.

Martin's (1987) and Davis-Floyd's (1992) interview data point to the cultural dominance of the technocratic model of birth. According to these authors, women buy into the legitimacy of medicalized birth and the authority of obstetricians. They value science and technology and believe they provide the safest options for birth. Women want personal choice, but sometimes that means choosing pain medication and cesarean sections over more "natural" alternatives. Birth is painful and difficult, and some women view elective C-sections as the ultimate feminist control over nature and their biology, rather than as succumbing to the power of a patriarchal medical system. Indeed, much of the move to the physician-attended birth and hospital birth in the earlier part of the century was influenced by feminist women who believed in the ability of technology to liberate them from their biology. Bottle-feeding, anesthetized labor, and hospital stays were seen by some as freeing them from what had been defined as biological necessity of their sex (Davis-Floyd 1992). Retracing this history sheds light on how expecting mothers are enabled and constrained by their socialization within a larger social context dominated by the medical technical model of childbirth (Davis-Floyd 1992). Yet, as we have seen, women have successfully used frames from both the medical technical and alternative birth movements in order to achieve their own goals, and they need not be (and rarely really are) exclusively committed to a single frame.

But it is not only whether or not an individual woman believes more in the technocratic or holistic philosophy of birth that will determine her experience. As Leavitt (1986) pointed out, when birth moved to the hospital, women no longer had the social networks of home birth available to them. Although this is changing, many women do not know that home birth is a true option. Also, insurance and economic issues may rule out certain birth alternatives. Many insurance companies will only cover physician-attended hospital births.

Birth centers in Colorado, for example, have many restrictions on the types of birth services they offer, including a no VBAC policy. Although home birth may be a less costly option, depending on insurance coverage, if a company agrees to cover all of the costs of a hospital birth versus none of the costs of a home birth, this may influence a woman's decision. Given the rise of family-friendly birth centers in hospitals, laboring at home, especially if a woman has other children, may not sound as attractive as laboring in the hospital. Finally, the dominant medical community remains fairly successful in reinforcing our cultural understanding of birth as something inherently risky that requires medical intervention and supervision, even for women who may have reservations about granting health care providers unconditional trust.

Conclusion

Childbirth for American women has changed dramatically over the past century. Despite incredible improvements in reducing the rate of maternal and infant mortality, however, mothers and infants in the U.S. continue to die at much higher rates than those in similarly industrialized nations. Poverty, racism, lack of access to affordable and appropriate health care, stress, and other socioeconomic factors disproportionately affect the most vulnerable mothers. Differentiating between agency (choice) and autonomy (capacity) is vital for improving childbirth experiences for women. Birthing women arguably have more agency qua choices about childbirth preferences than ever. An examination of institutional and sociocultural constraints, however, reveals that American women do not always have the ability to act on these choices (autonomy). We can talk endlessly about improving childbirth with choices but that will not effect change for women. We need to understand how the meaning of EFM, cesarean, and VBAC, for example, are shaped through interaction between people and systems.

Studies that attempt to link population changes such as advancing maternal age and increased obesity cannot definitively establish a causal link between these changes and an increase in cesarean (Declercq et al 2008). What they have done, however, is show that maternally-requested cesarean is a mostly a myth (Listening to Mothers II, III). Whatever is driving the United States' high rate of cesarean birth with all its accompanying risks for birthing people and newborns, it is not the preferences of the people actually giving birth. Ensuring that people have access to quality prenatal care including education about pregnancy and birth, training providers in culturally-sensitive communication skills, and expanding anti-poverty programs would likely do more to reduce infant and maternal mortality rates than limiting access to VBAC or policing the low-risk woman's pregnancy weight gain.[7] We put a great deal of responsibility on pregnant people to make the "right" choices for their babies, but we do little to enable them to truly understand what those choices are for *them*, let alone to have the authority to reliably make them. In studying childbirth, we need to understand how mothers› decision-making is constrained and enabled lest we throw mothers as agents out with the proverbial bathwater.

REFERENCES

Association of Women's Health, Obstetric, and Neonatal Nurses (AWHONN). 2008. "Fetal Heart Monitoring." Position Statement: http://www.awhonn.org/awhonn/content.do?name=05_HealthPolicyLegislation/5H_PositionStatements.htm

Association of Women's Health, Obstetric, and Neonatal Nurses (AWHONN). 2011. "Introduction to Fetal Heart Monitoring." Online course.

Basset, K. 1996. "Anthropology, Clinical Pathology, and The Electronic Fetal Monitor: Lessons from the Heart." *Social Science and Medicine*, 42 (2): 281–292.

Basset, K., Iyer N., and Kazanjian A. 2000. "Defensive Medicine During Hospital Obstetrical Care: A By-Product of the Technological Age." *Social Science and Medicine*, 51: 523–537.

Baxter, J. 2007. "Do Women Understand the Reasons Given for their Caesarian Sections*?" British Journal of Midwifery*, 17 (9): 536–538.

Becker, Howard, Blanche Geer, Everett Hughes, and Anselm L. Strauss. 1961. *Boys in White: Student Culture in Medical School*. Chicago: University of Chicago Press.

Bergeron, V. 2007. "The Ethics of Cesarean Section on Maternal Request: A Feminist Critique of the American College of Obstetricians and Gynecologists' Position on Patient-Choice Surgery." *Bioethics*, 21 (9): 478–487.

Bessett, Danielle. 2010. "Negotiating Normalization: The Perils of Producing Pregnancy Symptoms in Prenatal Care." *Social Science and Medicine* 71: 370–377.

Bland, M. 1998. "The Effect of Birth Experience on Post Partum Depression." Missouri Western State University. http://clearinghouse.missouriwestern.edu/manuscripts/59.php

Block, J. 2007. *Pushed: The Painful Truth about Childbirth and Modern Maternity Care*. Cambridge, MA: Da Capo Press.

---

[7]Research suggests that perception of a patient as a *woman* leads providers to focus on weight at much lower absolute measurements than they would for men (see Lacey Alexander's work elsewhere in this volume). Also see Lindsay King-Miller's piece elsewhere in this volume for specific discussion of how providers' weight bias may influence even preconception fertility care. *Ed.*

Blumer, Herbert. 1969. *Symbolic Interactionism: Perspective and Method*. Englewood Cliffs, NJ: Prentice-Hall.

Borst, C. 1995. *Catching Babies: The Professionalization of Childbirth, 1870–1920*. Cambridge: Harvard University Press.

Boyd, Elizabeth and John Heritage. 2006. "Taking the History: Question Taking During Comprehensive History-Taking," pgs. 150–184 in *Communication in Medical Care: Interaction Between Primary Care Physicians and Patients*. John Heritage and Douglas Maynard, editors. New York, NY: Cambridge University Press.

Braunstein, Glenn. 2012. "The Realistic Skinny on Moms, Pregnancy, and Weight Gain." 11-5-12. Huffington Post Blog.

Brody, J. 2009. "Updating a Standard: Fetal Monitoring." *New York Times*: July 7, 2009.

Bryant, J., Porter, M., Tracy, S., .and Sullivan, E. 2007. "Caesarean birth: Consumption, safety, order, and good mothering." *Social Science and Medicine*, 34 (4): 1192–1201.

Buckley, S. 2005. "Epidurals: Risks and Concerns for Mother and Baby." http://www.sarahbuckley.com/epidurals-risks-and-concerns-for-mother-and-baby/

Canguilhem, George. 1989. *The Normal and The Pathological*. New York, NY: Zone Books.

Casper, M. 1998. *The Making of the Unborn Patient: A Social Anatomy of Fetal Surgery*. New Brunswick: Rutgers University Press.

CDC. 2015. "Pregnancy Mortality Surveillance System." Centers for Disease Control, http://www.cdc.gov/reproductivehealth/maternalinfanthealth/pmss.html, Accessed 4-10-16.

CDC. 2015. "Infant Mortality." Centers for Disease Control, http://www.cdc.gov/reproductivehealth/maternalinfanthealth/infantmortality.htm, Accessed 4-10-16.

CDC website accessed 4-10-16 http://www.cdc.gov/reproductivehealth/maternalinfanthealth/pmss.html

Charmaz, Kathy. 2006. *Constructing Grounded Theory: A Practical Guide Through Qualitative Analysis*. Thousand Oaks, CA: Sage.

Cherniak, D. and Fisher, J. 2008. "Explaining Obstetric Interventionism: Technical Skills, Common Conceptualisations, or Collective Countertransference." *Women's Studies International Forum* 31: 270–277.

Collins, James W., Richard J. David, Arden Handler, Stephen Wall and Steven Andes. 2004. "Very Low Birthweight in African American Infants: The Role of Maternal Exposure to Interpersonal Racial Discrimination. *American Journal of Public Health* 94 (12): 2132–2138.

Cook, Tanya. 2012 "Hooked Up: How Electronic Fetal Monitoring Affects Maternal Agency and Maternal Autonomy." *Techne*, 16(1): 45–61.

Cunningham, Gary F., Shrikant Bangdiwala, Sarah S. Brown, Thomas Michael Dean, Marilynn Frederisken, Carol J. Rowland Hogue, Tekoa King, Emily Spencer Lukacz, Laurence B. McCullough, Wanda Nicholson,

Nancy Frances Petit, Jeffrey Lynn Probstfield, Adele C. Viguera, Cynthia A. Wong, Sheila Cohen Zimmet—The NIH Consensus Development Panel. 2010. "National Institutes of Health Consensus Development Conference Statement. Vaginal Birth After Cesarean: New Insights March 8–10, 2010." *Obstetrics and Gynecology* 115 (6): 1279–95.

Davis-Floyd, R. 1992. *Birth as an American Rite of Passage*. Berkeley: University of California Press.

—. 1994. "The Technocratic Body: American Childbirth as Cultural Expression." *Social Science and Medicine* 38 (8): 1125–1140.

—. 1997. with Carolyn Sargent, co-editor. *Childbirth and Authoritative Knowledge: Cross-Cultural Perspectives*. Berkeley, CA: University of California Press.

Daviss, Betty Anne. 2001. "Reforming and (re))making midwifery in North America," in *Birth By Design*, eds. DeVries, R., Teijlingen, E., Wrede, S. and Benoit, C. New York: Routledge.

Declercq, E., Sakala, C., Corry, M. and Applebaum, S. 2006a. Listening to Mothers II: Report of the Second National U.S. Survey of Women's Childbearing Experiences. Childbirth Connections: http://www.childbirthconnection.org/article.asp?ck=10396

Declercq, E, Menaker, F, and MacDorman, M. 2006b. "Maternal Risk and the Primary Cesarean Rate in the United States, 1991–2002." *American Journal of Public Health* 96 (5): 867–872.

Declercq, E., Barger, M., Cabral, H., Evans S., Kotelchuck, M., Simon, C., Weiss, J., and Heffner, L. 2007. "Maternal Outcomes Associated with Planned Primary Cesarean Births Compared With Planned Vaginal Births." *Obstetrics & Gynecology*, 109 (3): 669–677.

Deline, James, Lisa Vernes-Epstein, Lee T. Dresang, Mark Gideonsen, Laura Lynch and John J. Frey III. 2012. "Low Primary Cesarean Rate and High VBAC Rate With Good Outcomes in an Amish Birthing Center." *Annals of Family Medicine* 10 (6): 530–537.

Dominguez, T.P., Dunkel-Schetter, C., Glynn, L.M., Hobel, C., and Sandman, C.A. 2008. "Racial Differences in Birth Outcomes: The Role of General, Pregnancy, and Racism Stress." *Health Psychology* 27(2): 194–203.

Duden, B. 1993. *Disembodying Women: Perspectives on Pregnancy and the Unborn*, Cambridge: Harvard University Press.

Fox, B. and Worts, D. 1999. "Revisiting the Critique of Medicalized Childbirth: A Contribution to the Sociology of Birth." *Gender & Society* 13: 326–46.

Fujimura, Joan. 1996. *Crafting Science: A Sociohistory of the Quest for the Genetics of Cancer*. Cambridge, Mass: Harvard University Press.

Gamble, J., Creedy, D. K., McCourt, C., Weaver, J. and Beake, S. 2007. "A Critique of the Literature on Women's Request for Cesarean Section." *Birth* 34 (4): 331–340.

Garfinkel, Harold. 1967. *Studies in Ethnomethodology*. Englewood Cliffs, NJ: Prentice-Hall.

Gill, Virginia Teas and Douglas W. Maynard. 2006 "Explaining Illness: Patients' Proposals and Physicians' Responses," pg. 115–150 in *Communication in Medical Care: Interaction Beteween primary Care Physicians and Patients*. John Heritage and Douglas W. Maynard, editors. New York: Cambridge University Press.

Gossman, Ginger, Jutta Joesch, and Koray Tanfer. 2006. "Trends in Maternal Request Cesarean Delivery 1991–2004.*" Obstetrics and Gynecology* 108 (6): 1506–1516.

Grace, Willie. 2015. "Black Org, Open Letter to US Midwifery Association." *Houston Style Magazine*, online edition, posted 6/9/2015.

Grivell, R. and Dodd, J. 2011. "Short- and Long-Term Outcomes after Cesarean Section." *Expert Review of Obstetrics and Gynecology* 6 (2): 205–215.

Guise J-M, Eden K, Emeis C, Denman MA, Marshall N, Fu R, Janik R, Nygren P, Walker M,McDonagh M. 2010. "Vaginal Birth After Cesarean: New Insights on Maternal and Neonatal Outcomes.*" Obstetrics and Gynecology* 116 (6): 1267–1278.

Hampton, T. 2008. "Researchers Probe Effects of Pregnancy, Birth on Childhood Asthma and Allergy." *Journal of the American Medical Association*, 300 (1): 29.

Heberlein, Thomas A. 1974. "The Three Fixes: Technological, Cognitive and Structural." Pp. 279–296 in *Water and Community Development: Social and Economic Perspectives*, edited by D. Field, J.C. Barren and B.F. Long. Ann Arbor, MI: Science Publishers, Inc.

Heritage, J. and Maynard, D. ed. 2006. *Communication in Medical Care: Interaction Between Primary Care Physicians and Patients*. New York: Cambridge University Press.

Jordan, Brigette. 1997. "Authoritative Knowledge and Its Construction," pg. 55–79 in *Childbirth and Authoritative Knowledge: Cross-Cultural Perspectives*. Robbie Davis-Floyd and Carolyn Sargent, editors. Berkeley, CA: The University of California Press.

Kotaska, A. 2011a. "Commentary: Routine Cesarean Section for Breech: The Unmeasured Cost." *Birth* 38 (2): 162–164.

Kotaska, A. 2011b. "Heads-Up: Defining Safe Breech Birth." Conference Presentation at the 8th Annual Women's Health Research Conference. University of Minnesota: 9-19-11.

Kotaska, Andrew. 2012. "Quantifying VBAC Risk: Muddying the Waters." *Birth* 39(4): 333–337.

Kozhimannil, Katy Backes, Michael Law, and Beth Virnig. 2013. "Cesarean Delivery Rates Vary Tenfold Among US Hospitals; Reducing Variation May Address Quality and Cost Issues. *Health Affairs* 32 (3): 527–535.

Kripke, C. 1999. "Why are We Using Electronic Fetal Monitoring?" *American Family Physician*, 59 (9): 2416–2420.

Kulka, R., Kuppermann, M., Little, M., Drapkin Lyerly, A., Mitchell, L., Armstrong, E., and Harris L. 2009. "Finding Autonomy in Birth." *Bioethics* 23 (1): 1–8.

Leeman, L., and Plante, L. 2006. "Patient-Choice Vaginal Delivery?" *Annals of Family Medicine* 4 (3): 265–268.

Lothian, J. 2008. "Choice, Autonomy, and Childbirth Education." *Journal of Perinatal Education* 17 (1): 35–38.

MacDorman, M., Menacker F., and Declercq, E. 2008. "Cesarean Birth in the United States: Epidemiology, Trends, and Outcomes." *Clinics in Perinatology* 35: 293–307.

MacDorman MF, Declercq E, Menacker F, Malloy MH. 2008b. "Neonatal mortality for primary cesarean and vaginal births to low-risk women: application of an "intention-to-treat" model." *Birth*.35(1): 3–8.

MacDorman, Marian F., Eugene Declercq, T.J. Matthews, and Naomi Stotland. 2012. "Trends and Characteristics of Home Vaginal Birth After Cesarean Delivery in the United States in Selected States." *Obstetrics and Gynecology* 119 (4): 737–744.

MacDorman, Marian F., T.J. Mathews, Ashna D. Mohangoo, and Jennifer Zeitlin. 2014. "International Comparisons of Infant Mortality and Related Factors: United States and Europe, 2014." *National Vital Statistics Report* 63 (5) Hyattsville, MD: National Center for Health Statistics.

MacDorman, Marian F., T.J. Mathews, and Eugene Declercq. 2014. "Trends in Out-of-Hospital Births in the United States, 1990–2012." NCHS data brief, no 144. Hyattsville, MD: National Center for Health Statistics.

Mackenzie, C. and N. Stoljar. 2000. "Introduction: Autonomy Refigured," *in Relational Autonomy: Feminist Perspectives on Autonomy, Agency, and the Social Self*. C. Mackenzie and N. Stoljar, eds. New York: Oxford University Press, 3–31.

Malloy, MH. 2010. "Infant Outcomes of Certified Nurse Midwife Attended Home Births: United States 2000 to 2004." *Journal of Perinatology* 30: 622–627.

Maron, Dina Fine. 2015. "Has Maternal Mortality Really Doubled in the U.S.?" *Scientific American*. 6-8-15.

Martin, Emily. 1987. *The Woman in the Body: A Cultural Analysis of Reproductio*n, Boston: Beacon Press.

Martin Joyce, Brady Hamilton, Stephanie Ventura, Michelle Osterman, Elizabeth Wilson, and T.J. Matthews. 2012. "Births: Final data for 2010." *National Vital Statistics Reports* 61 (1) Hyattsville, MD: National Center for Health Statistics.

Martin, Joyce, Brady Hamilton, Michelle Osterman, Sally Curtin, and T.J. Mathews. 2015. "Births: Final Data for 2013." *National Vital Statistics Reports* 64 (1) Hyattsville, MD: National Center for Health Statistics.

Martin, Karen. 2003. "Giving Birth Like a Girl." *Gender and Society* 17 (10): 54–72.

Mathews, Joan and Kathleen Zadak. 1991. "The Alternative Birth Movement in the United States: History and Current Status." *Women and Health* 17 (1): 39–56.

Mathews, T. J., Marian F. MacDorman, and Maria E. Thoma. 2015. "Infant Mortality Statistics From the 2013 Period Linked Birth/Infant Death Data Set." *National Vital Statistics Reports* Vol. 64 (9) Hyattsville, MD: National Center for Health Statistics.

Maynard, Douglas W. 2003. *Bad News, Good News: Conversational Order in Everyday Talk and Clinical Settings*. Chicago: University of Chicago Press.

McGrath, SK and JH Kennell. 2008. "A Randomized Controlled Trial of Continuous Labor support For Middle-Class Couples: Effect on Cesarean Delivery Rates." *Birth* 35 (2): 92–97.

McLeod, C. and S. Sherwin. 2000. "Relational Autonomy, Self-Trust, and Health Care for Patients Who are Oppressed," in *Feminist Perspectives on Autonomy, Agency, and the Social Self.* C. Mackenzie and N. Stoljar, eds. New York: Oxford University Press, 259–279.

Mead, George Herbert. 1967. *Mind, Self, and Society.* Chicago: University of Chicago Press.

Miller, Amy Chasteen and Thomas Shriver. 2012. "Women's Childbirth Preferences and Practices in the United States." *Social Science and Medicine* 75: 709–716.

Mishler, Elliot. 1984. *The Discourse of Medicine: Dialectics of Medical Interviews.* Norwood, NJ: Ablex.

Mol, Annemarie. 1998. "Lived Reality and the Multiplicity of Norms: A Critical Tribute to George Canguilhem." *Economy and Society* 27 (2–3): 274–284.

Morris, Theresa. 2013. *Cut It Out: The C-Section Epidemic in America.* New York University Press, New York, NY.

Naftalin, J. and Paterson-Brown, S. 2008. "A Pilot Study Exploring the Impact of Maternal Age and Raised Body Mass Index on Caesarean Section Rates." *Journal of Obstetrics and Gynaecology,* 28 (4): 394–397.

National Vital Statistics Reports (NVSR) 2010. "Births: Preliminary Data for 2009." 59 (3): http://www.cdc.gov/nchs/data/nvsr/nvsr59/nvsr59_03.pdf

National Institutes of Health: Office of Human Subjects Research. 2012. "Regulations and Ethical Guidelines: The Belmont Report, Ethical Principles and Guidelines for the Protection of Human Subjects of Research." OHSR http://hsr.od.nih.gov/guidelines/Belmont.html#goc1 accessed 1/2012.

Pateman, K., Khalil, A. and O'Brien, P. 2008. "Electronic fetal heart rate monitoring: help or hindrance?" *British Journal of Midwifery,* 16 (7): 454–457.

Pérez-Escamilla, R. I Maulén-Radovan, and K G Dewey. 1996. "The association between cesarean delivery and breastfeeding outcomes among Mexican women." *American Journal of Public Health.* 86 (6) 832–836.

Perez, Miriam. 2013. "New Study Shows Birth Centers are a Quality Option for Low Risk Births." Posted 2-20-13 at http://rhrealitycheck.org/article/2013/02/20/new-study-shows-birth-centers-are-a-quality-option-for-low-risk-births/

Pfuntner, A., Wier, LM, Stocks, C (AHRQ). Most Frequent Procedures Performed in U.S. Hospitals, 2010. HCUP Statistical Brief #149. February 2013. Agency for Healthcare Research and Quality, Rockville, MD. Available at http://www.hcup-us.ahrq.gov/reports/statbriefs/sb149.pdf

Placek, P.J. and S. M. Taffel. 1980. "Trends in cesarean section rates for the United States, 1970–78." *Public Health Reports* 95(6): 540–548.

Rapp, Rayna. 2000. Testing Women, Testing the Fetus: The Social Impact of Amniocentesis in America." New York, NY: Routlage.

Roberts, Richard G., Mark Deutchman, Valerie J. King, George E. Fryer, and Thomas J. Miyoshi. 2007. "Changing Policies on Vaginal Birth After Cesarean: Impact on Access." *Birth* 34 (4): 316–322.

Roberts, CL, S Tracy, and B. Peat. 2000. "Rates for Obstetric Intervention Among Private and Public Patients in Australia: Population Based Descriptive Study." *BMJ* 321: 137–141.

Rochman, Bonnie. June 25, 2012. "Midwife Mania? More US Babies than Ever Are Delivered by Midwives." For Time Healthland online http://healthland.time.com/2012/06/25/midwife-mania-more-u-s-babies-than-ever-are-delivered-by-midwives/.

Rosenstein, M. G., Cheng, Y. W., Snowden, J. M., Nicholson, J. M., & Caughey, A. B. (2012). "Risk of Stillbirth and Infant Death Stratified by Gestational Age." *Obstetrics and Gynecology, 120*(1), 76–82.

Sakala C, Yang YT, Corry MP. 2013. "Maternity care and liability: Pressing problems, substantive solutions." *Womens Health Issues* 23 (1): 7–13.

Sartwelle, Thomas. 2012a. "Electronic Fetal Monitoring: A Defense Lawyer's View." *Reviews in Obstetrics and Gynecology.* 5 (3–4) e121-e125.

Sartwelle, Thomas. 2012b. "Electronic Fetal Monitoring: A Bridge Too Far." *The Journal of Legal Medicine* 33: 313–379.

Save the Children, 2015. "The Urban Disadvantage: State of the World's Mothers 2015." Save the Children Foundation. Fairfield, CT.

Scott, James R. 2010. "Solving the Vaginal Birth After Cesarean Dilema." *Obstetrics and Gynecology* 115 (6): 1112–1113.

Sherwin, Susan. 1998. "The Politics of Women's Health: Exploring Agency and Autonomy." *The Feminist Health Care Research Network.* Philadelphia: Temple University Press.

Shibutani, Tamotsu. 1961. *Society and Personality.* Englewood Cliffs, NJ: Prentice-Hall.

Shibutani, Tamotsu. 1986. *Social Processes: An Introduction to Sociology.* Berkeley and Los Angeles, CA: University of California Press.

Simonds, W. "Watching the Clock: Keeping Time During Pregnancy, Birth, and Postpartum Experiences." *Social Science and Medicine,* 55: 559–570.

Slaughter-Acey, J.C., Sealy-Jefferson, S., Helmkamp, L., Caldwell, C.H., Osypuk, T.L., Platt, R.W., Straughen J.K., Dailey-Okezie, R.K., Abeysekara, P., and Misra, D.P. 2016. "Racism in the form of micro aggressions and the risk of preterm birth among black women." *Annals of Epidemiology* 26(1): 7–13.

Strauss, Anselm. 1978. *Negotiations: Varieties, Processes, Contexts, and Social Order.* San Francisco, CA: Jossey-Bass.

Strauss, Anselm. 1987. *Qualitative Analysis for Social Scientists.* New York, NY: Cambridge University Press.

Swedha, A., Hacker, T., and Nuovo, J. 1999. "Interpretation of the Electronic Fetal Heart Rate During Labor." *American Family Physician*, 59 (9): 2487–2506.

Tanassi, Lucia. 2004. "Compliance As Strategy: The Importance of Personalized Relations in Obstetric Practice." *Social Science and Medicine 59*: 2053–2069.

Tucker, S., Miller, L., and Miller, D. 2009. *Mosby's Pocket Guide to Fetal Monitoring: A Multidisciplinary Approach*, St. Louis: Mosby.

Wendland, C. 2007. "The Vanishing Mother: Cesarean Section and 'Evidence-Based Obstetrics.'" *Medical Anthropology Quarterly*, 21 (2): 218–233.

WHO/RHR/15.02. 2015. WHO Statement on Cesarean Section Rates. World Health Organization. http://apps.who.int/iris/bitstream/10665/161442/1/WHO_RHR_15.02_eng.pdf?ua=1, accessed 4-10-16.

Zhang,J., Troendle, J., Reddy, U., Laughon, S. K., Branch, D.W., Burkman, R., Landy, H., Hibbard, J., Haberman, S., Ramirez, M., Bailit, J., Hoffman, M., Gregory, K., Gonzalez-Quintero, V., Kominiarek, M., Learman, L., Hatjis, C., and van Veldhuisen, P. 2010. "Contemporary Cesarean Delivery Practice in the United States." *American Journal of Obstetrics and Gynecology*, 203 (4): 326. e1-326.e10

"Hard Labor: The Case for Testing Drugs on Pregnant Women"

By Emily Anthes

When the heart stops beating, minutes matter. With every minute that passes before a rhythm is restored, a patient's odds of survival plummet. Which is why Anne Lyerly was surprised when, one night 20 years ago, she got a phone call from a doctor who had paused in the middle of treating a patient in cardiac arrest. Lyerly was a newly minted obstetrician; the caller was an internal medicine resident who was desperately trying to resuscitate a dying patient. A pregnant dying patient. He had called because his supervisor wanted to know whether a critical cardiac drug would be safe for the woman's fetus.

Lyerly was stunned. Most medications are never tested in pregnant women and, although she knew that there was a chance the compound might harm the fetus, her response was unequivocal. "You need to tell him he needs to save her life," she told the resident. "It doesn't matter what drug he's using. She's dying."

In the years since, Lyerly, now an ob-gyn and bioethicist at the University of North Carolina,[1] has found herself fielding such questions again and again, from colleagues, patients and friends eager to know whether it is safe for a pregnant woman to stay on her antidepressants, take her migraine medication or use her asthma inhaler.

Sometimes the answer is obvious: a dying woman should get a drug that would save her life, regardless of the risk it might pose to the fetus. But often Lyerly didn't have such definitive answers. Because it has long been considered unethical to include expectant mothers in clinical trials, scientists simply don't know whether many common medicines are safe for pregnant women. Of the more than 600 prescription drugs that the US Food and Drug Administration approved between 1980

[1]https://www.med.unc.edu/socialmed/people/anne-lyerly

and 2010, 91 percent have been so meagerly researched that their safety during pregnancy remains uncertain.

Over the last few years, however, a small, tight-knit group of ethicists, including Lyerly, have become determined to reverse this longstanding scientific neglect of pregnant women. Science and society, they argue, have got it utterly wrong: our efforts to protect women and their fetuses have actually put them both in jeopardy. "Ethics doesn't preclude including pregnant women in research," says Lyerly. "Actually, ethics requires it."

§

On 16 December 1961, the *Lancet* published a short letter from an Australian obstetrician named William McBride. In the previous months, McBride wrote, he'd noticed a troubling pattern of birth defects: newborns with severely malformed arms and legs. Their mothers, he reported, had been taking a new drug called Distaval. Its active ingredient? Thalidomide.

Over the next few months, other doctors published similar observations. It soon became clear that thalidomide, a sedative that had been marketed as a safe treatment for morning sickness, was a major public health disaster, the cause of serious birth defects in as many as 12,000 children. A second crisis followed a decade later, when scientists realized that diethylstilbestrol, a drug widely prescribed to prevent miscarriages, increased the risk of cancer in girls who had been exposed to the drug while in the womb.

These tragedies left a lasting legacy. Expectant mothers became understandably nervous about taking medication. Scientists, drug companies and lawmakers grew reluctant to allow pregnant women—and even women who were merely of childbearing age—to participate in drug trials. Subsequent regulations designated pregnant women a 'vulnerable population' that could participate in clinical research only under limited circumstances.

On the face of it, this caution seems sensible. Many medicines cross the placenta, and a high dose of the wrong drug at the wrong time can disrupt fetal development, leading to miscarriages, stillbirths or birth defects. But many mums-to-be have a legitimate need for medication. "Pregnant women get sick, and sick women get pregnant," says Brian Cleary, Chief Pharmacist at the Rotunda Hospital in Dublin, Ireland.

This year, some 130 million women will give birth around the world. Expectant mothers grapple with all kinds of health conditions, from depression to diabetes, migraines to malaria, epilepsy, Crohn's disease and more. Many are offered medications for their maladies: precise figures are hard to pin down, but according to several reviews of prescription databases,[2] the share of pregnant women who receive at least one prescription during pregnancy is 56 per cent in Denmark and Canada, 57 per cent in Norway, 64 per cent in the USA, 85 per cent in Germany and 93 per cent in France.

But with so little data available about drug safety during pregnancy, many of these women will face a stark choice: use medications that have unknown effects on their developing children, or forgo treatments that are crucial to their own health.

§

In the autumn of 2013, Heidi Walker, a lab technician who lives in Nottingham, England, was hospitalized for severe depression. Over the course of her two-month stay, she slowly found her feet again, thanks, in part, to a drug regimen that included an antidepressant, an antipsychotic, an antianxiety medication and a sleeping pill. But just a few months after her release, Heidi unexpectedly found herself pregnant with her first child: a girl. "She was a surprise baby," Heidi recalls. "Whether the medications I was on at the time were safe during pregnancy wasn't something I'd considered at all."

Heidi soon learned that none of the four drugs she was taking had been well-studied in humans, though animal studies had raised some concerns. Like many women with chronic illnesses, she found herself facing an agonizing decision. On the one hand, Heidi feared what the pharmacopoeia might do to her developing daughter. "It was a lot of medication to be taking, and it's a risky thing to be doing," she says. "'Cause everyone's heard of thalidomide and things like that, haven't they?" At the same time, however, she worried about what might happen if she went off her meds and the

depression returned. "Am I going to be able to take care of her?" she wondered. "Are social services going to get involved if I'm unwell?"

In consultation with her doctor, Heidi decided to give up all four drugs, ultimately replacing them with a low dose of sertraline,[3] an antidepressant that has been relatively well-studied in pregnant women. But as she weaned herself from her old prescriptions, she experienced severe withdrawal. "It was physically quite rough," Heidi recalls. "I had brain zaps and shivers and was feeling very, very unwell." But she believes she made the right decision. "You just don't know," says Heidi, whose daughter was born last January. "Had something been wrong with her, and I'd carried on taking those medications, then you'd have a lot of guilt wouldn't you?"

Many other mothers-to-be come to the same conclusion. In the face of inadequate safety data, both women and doctors tend to err on the side of caution, discontinuing drugs with unknown risks.

After Rachel Tackitt conceived last autumn, her neurologist told her that there was little information available about the safety of a drug she was taking to control her chronic migraines. "My neurologist said she could not with good conscience recommend it or allow me to take it because we don't know the risks," says Rachel, an engineer who lives in Tucson, Arizona. Rachel ultimately stopped taking the drug, as well as two other migraine medications, only to see her headaches come roaring back. Until she gave birth to her son in July, she suffered from two or three debilitating migraines every week; she spent a lot of time, particularly in her first trimester, lying in a dark room and waiting for the headaches to pass.

In some cases discontinuing a drug can have tragic consequences. The Confidential Enquiry into Maternal Deaths, a periodic report on maternal fatalities in the UK and Ireland, has identified cases in which pregnant women have died after giving up their asthma or epilepsy medications. Poorly controlled maternal illness is dangerous for a fetus, too. Untreated depression, for example, increases the odds of fetal growth restriction, premature birth and low birth weight. So does untreated asthma. "Oftentimes we end up harming fetuses even more by not attending to the health needs of pregnant women," says Maggie Little, a bioethicist at Georgetown University in Washington, DC,[4] who specializes in reproductive and research ethics. "In general, what's good for a fetus is a healthy mom."

---

[2]http://www.ncbi.nlm.nih.gov/pmc/articles/PMC3423446/

[3]http://www.medicinesinpregnancy.org/Medicine—pregnancy/Sertraline/
[4]https://kennedyinstitute.georgetown.edu/people/maggie-little/

§

The guesswork involved in treating pregnant women has troubled Lyerly since her earliest days as a doctor. When she graduated from medical school in 1995, the field of medicine was just beginning to move toward an 'evidence-based' approach, in which doctors used rigorous clinical research, rather than intuition or anecdote, to determine the best way to care for a patient. But this new emphasis on evidence, Lyerly noticed, didn't seem to apply to the treatment of pregnant women. "It was well-known that we prescribed medications without a lot of good data about their safety or the right kind of dosing," she says.

This shortage of data frustrated Lyerly, who hated not being able to give her patients better guidance about their medications. And when, in the early 2000s, she began serving on institutional review boards—ethics committees that vet proposals for research involving human subjects—her frustration only grew. After spending hours with her pregnant patients, who peppered her with questions about their medications, Lyerly would then review proposals for studies that could potentially provide answers—and find that pregnant women were often excluded, as a reflex, even from research that posed minimal risk. "People were very quick to say, 'Well, it's unethical to include pregnant women in research,'" she recalls. "It struck me that people were hiding behind the veil of ethics."

Lyerly often found herself fighting back, arguing that the real danger to pregnant women was treating them without evidence, but for years, little changed. One day, in late 2007 or early 2008, a sympathetic-seeming scientist with a proposal before a committee she was serving on made a startling confession. As Lyerly recalls: "One of the researchers said, 'You know, I understand where you're coming from... but I gotta tell you, I just don't like including pregnant women in research. It's just my bias.'"

She had finally had enough. She reached out to two colleagues who had both done their own thinking on the issue: Maggie Little, the Georgetown bioethicist, and Ruth Faden, a bioethicist at Johns Hopkins University.[5] The women talked and eventually met in Washington, DC, where they sat on Faden's porch, drinking coffee and lamenting how little scientists still knew about drug safety during pregnancy.

They were not alone in their concerns. "There's still many, many drugs, including many relatively frequently used drugs, that we don't know very much about," says Jan Friedman, a medical geneticist at the University of British Columbia in Canada. "There's not a lot of funding for this kind of research and not a lot of work that's being done." At the same time, the scientists who are trying to gather this desperately needed data often struggle to get their studies approved.

Lyerly, Little, and Faden decided that the cause needed more proactive advocates. So in the spring of 2009, the 'troika', as they call themselves, formally launched the Second Wave Initiative:[6] a broad, multipronged campaign to promote ethically responsible research with pregnant women. Its name is a reference to the 'first wave' of clinical trial reform, in the 1990s, which spurred scientists to enroll more women in their studies. Since founding the Initiative, the troika have lobbied lawmakers, hosted and presented at conferences, and written a flurry of papers and editorials.

The Initiative flips the familiar script. For decades, ethics has been used to justify barring pregnant women from research. But now, Lyerly, Little, and Faden are making the opposite argument: that conducting research with pregnant women is an ethical obligation. Side-lining this entire population, they say, is fundamentally unjust, depriving pregnant women of equal access to medical advances. "We support biomedical research with all of our tax dollars, with the understanding that all of us will benefit," Faden explains. "And not that only people who are not pregnant will benefit."

In addition to being unjust, the knowledge gap is also downright dangerous, they argue. Although many untested drugs are likely to be safe if used during pregnancy, the failure to study medications specifically in pregnant women means that some are on the market for years before scientists discover that they pose a risk. In 2006, for example, a paper in the *New England Journal of Medicine* reported that women who took angiotensin-converting enzyme (ACE) inhibitors—an exceedingly common class of drugs for high blood pressure—during the first trimester were nearly three times more likely to have babies with major birth defects. By then, ACE inhibitors had been on the market for more than three decades, and they had traditionally been considered safe for use during the first trimester. If researchers had studied the drugs earlier, countless birth defects likely could have been prevented.

That's the irony of the thalidomide story. Traditionally, it is used to justify excluding pregnant women from research. **But thalidomide wasn't actually tested in pregnant women before it went on sale. The drug is so catastrophically disruptive to fetal development that even a small trial would likely have revealed its dangers, sparing thousands of children Ed.**

[5]https://kennedyinstitute.georgetown.edu/people/ruth-faden/

[6]http://secondwaveinitiative.org/

"If we did a better job of researching drugs in pregnancy before we approved them, we would have been able to avoid the thalidomide crisis," Little says. "The lessons we learn from the past aren't always the right lessons.

Denying pregnant women access to clinical trials also leaves doctors in the dark about how to treat expectant mothers who do fall ill. As Lyerly, Little, and Faden have written, "Pregnancy, it turns out, is an 'off label' condition."[7] In fact, in the months immediately after they founded the Second Wave Initiative, a wily new virus made this danger frighteningly clear. In April 2009, the US Centers for Disease Control and Prevention (CDC) announced that a previously unknown strain of H1N1, or swine flu, had sickened two American children. By June, the virus was in more than 70 countries, and the World Health Organization had declared a full-fledged pandemic. Pregnant women were at particular risk, being more likely to become seriously ill, require hospitalization and die than those in the general population; during the first two months the virus was in the USA, at least six pregnant women died from it.

CDC recommended oseltamivir—an antiviral medicine commonly known by its brand name, Tamiflu—for pregnant women. Although a few small observational studies had suggested that the drug was unlikely to cause birth defects, the data was limited. What's more, many of the body changes that accompany pregnancy, including increases in blood volume and changes in liver and kidney function, affect how the body processes drugs, often in unpredictable ways. Unless a compound has been tested in expectant mothers—and at the time, oseltamivir hadn't been—doctors can't be sure what dose to prescribe. "We were worried about the absence of good data about Tamiflu and the possibility that we might be dosing it wrong," Lyerly recalls.

They were right to be worried. Subsequent research, published in 2011, suggested that pregnant women clear the drug from their bodies more quickly than non-pregnant women, which means that expectant mothers who took the drug during the pandemic may have been significantly under-dosed. Indeed, some doctors speculated that one reason pregnant women appeared to be particularly vulnerable to the virus was because they were getting doses of antivirals that were too low. Pregnant women had been spared the risks of research, but they'd become guinea pigs all the same.

§

Over the past ten years, Shifneez Shakir, a former chemistry teacher who lives in the Maldives, has navigated three difficult—and very different—pregnancies.

---

[7]http://www.ncbi.nlm.nih.gov/pmc/articles/PMC2747530/

Shifneez has a severe form of sickle-cell disease, an inherited disorder that causes her red blood cells, which are normally plump and round, to transform into a crescent shape. These deformed blood cells can clog the circulation, starving the body's tissues of oxygen and causing periodic 'crises', or episodes of intense pain. Women with the disease are also at increased risk for having premature or abnormally small children, as well as miscarriages and stillbirths.

The only medication known to actually treat sickle-cell patients' underlying disease is an anticancer drug called hydroxyurea. Scientists have not systematically studied the drug's safety in pregnant women, but high doses can cause birth defects in lab animals, and women are typically advised to stop taking it before having children. And so during her first two pregnancies, in 2005 and 2008, Shifneez dutifully discontinued the only medication that could keep her blood flowing smoothly and her crushing bone pain at bay. Her health deteriorated rapidly, and 11 weeks into her first pregnancy, she miscarried. "I was devastated," Shifneez recalls. Although her second pregnancy gave her a beautiful, healthy son, she had a major crisis in her second trimester and had to be hospitalized.

In 2013, when Shifneez got pregnant for the third time, she was determined to avoid another crisis. This time, she decided, she would not give up the hydroxyurea. Although she remained healthy throughout her pregnancy, few of her doctors supported her decision. When they discovered she was taking the drug, they flat-out advised her to get an abortion. And at first, Shifneez and her husband were reluctant to tell their friends and family that they were expecting another child, in case a termination became necessary. Shifneez believed that she had made the best decision she could, given the limited data, but she remained worried about the consequences. Even regular ultrasounds failed to allay all her fears. What if the baby had a defect or abnormality that the scans could not detect? "I kept mentally preparing myself for the worst," she says.

On 1 July 2014, her daughter Eiliyah was born. "And the first thing I asked was, 'Is she OK? Is everything OK with her?' I was very nervous. And then I saw her." She was 2.9 kgs, and she was perfect. "It was the most incredible moment," Shifneez says. And yet, with her daughter more than a year old, Shifneez finds that the anxiety lingers. She worries that the medication may have caused abnormalities that are not yet apparent and keeps a close eye on her daughter's development. "It feels like such an achievement when she crosses every milestone," she says.

For the millions of women around the world who may need medication while pregnant, there are no easy choices, or right answers. Each patient, experts say, should think carefully about her own health needs and priorities and carefully weigh the benefits and risks of her specific drug regimen. Of course, that's difficult to do without data.

§

After the 2009 swine flu pandemic broke out, the US National Institutes of Health (NIH) launched a clinical trial of the new H1N1 vaccine specifically for pregnant women, who would be randomly assigned to receive one of two different dosages of the vaccine. The researchers filled their study quota quickly, and when Lyerly and Faden interviewed the volunteers, they learned that the women's motivations for participating were astute and varied. Some wanted early access to a potentially lifesaving vaccine, others wanted to help advance scientific knowledge, and others thought that it would be safest to get the vaccine within the context of a clinical trial, in which they'd be carefully monitored. "Women were beating down the doors to get into the flu vaccine study," Lyerly says. "The idea that pregnant women wouldn't participate in a study is not true."

But this willingness hardly matters if scientists don't launch such studies in the first place. Lyerly, Little, and Faden hope that their latest endeavor will help remedy this problem by encouraging more scientists to perform research with pregnant women and making it easier for them to do so. Their new, NIH-funded project focuses on HIV. Although preventing women from transmitting HIV to their children has long been a scientific priority, pregnant women are still largely excluded from trials of HIV-related drugs that could benefit their own health. In 2013, the troika set out to help close this research gap, joining with Anna Mastroianni, a legal scholar at the University of Washington, to launch a project they called PHASES (Pregnancy and HIV/AIDS: Seeking Equitable Study).

The four women are working to understand the reasons pregnant women are routinely excluded from these trials and to devise potential solutions. By the time the project wraps up in 2019, they plan to have produced a set of "practical, user-friendly" guidelines for studying pregnant women. Though their focus will be on HIV, the lessons they learn, and the guidelines they ultimately develop, should be relevant for scientists who want to study other illnesses. "Our goal is nothing less than coming up with an empirically grounded and consensus-based ethical and legal framework for how and when you can do research with pregnant women," Little says.

They will also highlight specific strategies for gathering data on pregnant women in an ethically defensible but scientifically rigorous manner. Although scientists can and should study expectant mothers who have already made the choice to take certain medications, tracking their pregnancy outcomes and drawing their blood to study how the drugs are being metabolized, these opportunistic studies have limitations. (Among them that it can take decades to find and enroll enough women to draw significant conclusions.)

Conducting a traditional clinical trial—the gold standard in medicine—is trickier, but not impossible, especially if scientists think creatively. The PHASES team has highlighted a series of trials of tenofovir gel, which can protect women from HIV when applied inside the vagina, as one particularly innovative model.

To learn about the drug's safety and dosing during pregnancy, a team of scientists based at the University of Pittsburgh gave a single dose of the gel to 16 pregnant women who had been previously scheduled to have Caesarean sections. The women received the drug just two hours before their deliveries, when the medication was unlikely to seriously harm a fetus. Once the researchers determined that pregnant women appeared to absorb the drug normally, and that very little of the compound reached the fetus, they pushed the exposure slightly earlier, giving the gel to women who were 37 to 39 weeks pregnant, and then to women who were 34 to 36 weeks along. Such studies will never be completely risk-free—nothing in clinical research or medicine is—but by being slow, deliberate and patient, researchers can minimize the chance of harm.

New laws could also help nudge drug companies in the right direction. The USA has spurred paediatric research by offering pharmaceutical companies extensions of their drug patents if they conduct studies with children;[8] a similar strategy might also stimulate research with pregnant women. (As it currently stands, pharmaceutical companies have powerful disincentives to conduct such studies. If a medication that's currently on the market turns out to cause birth defects, its manufacturer can argue that the compound was never approved for use in pregnant women. But if a company does conduct a small trial, labels a medication safe for use during pregnancy, and then the drug is later discovered to be dangerous? In that scenario, the pharmaceutical company has opened itself up to a barrage of lawsuits.)

There are small signs of progress. This autumn, the Council for International Organizations of Medical Sciences released a set of proposed revisions to its influential International Ethical Guidelines for Biomedical

---

[8]http://bpca.nichd.nih.gov/about/Pages/Index.aspx

Research Involving Human Subjects.[9] Among other changes, the new draft guidelines now emphasize the need for more research into the health needs of pregnant women[10] and more clearly detail the level of risk that is acceptable in such studies. "The hope is that with more guidance, people will be less reluctant to conduct research," says Annette Rid, a bioethicist at King's College London and a member of the working group that revised the guidelines.

Meanwhile, pregnancy registries are continuing to track women who take certain medications, and several organizations and institutions have launched programs to accelerate research. A handful of scientists are conducting full-fledged clinical trials with pregnant women, but the scale of the problem is huge, and experts say they need more funding for this work and more colleagues to join them in their efforts. In the meantime, pregnant women can seek advice on the risks and benefits of particular drugs from free teratology information services, and those who want to help advance scientific knowledge can volunteer for pregnancy registries. But until scientists do more controlled, rigorous studies, millions of women will be forced to muddle through, making medical decisions without the scientific evidence that many other patients take for granted.

§

For each of the last several years, a professor at the University of North Carolina's Gillings School of Global Public Health has invited Anne Lyerly to give a guest lecture to her class. And every year, after Lyerly finishes her lecture, the professor announces that during her own pregnancy, several decades ago, she took a drug called Bendectin. The drug, which was used to treat morning sickness, was later pulled from the market[11] after a barrage of lawsuits alleged that it caused birth defects. Reams of data now suggest that the medication is safe, and the Food and Drug Administration reapproved it, under a different name, in 2013. But this professor still couldn't quite shake the gut-wrenching fear that she had somehow hurt her child.

"This is no way to practice medicine," Lyerly says. "Women suffer. And they don't just suffer during pregnancy." Even when their stories have happy endings, the uncertainty can leave women with worries that ripple through their lives, an enduring unease that—simply by trying to alleviate their own nausea or headaches

or depression—they might have harmed the people they love most.

- Author: Emily Anthes
- Editor: Chrissie Giles
- Copyeditor: Rob Reddick
- Fact checker: Francine Almash
- Illustrator: Laura Breiling
- Art director: Peta Bell

ARTICLE EXTRA: "Knowledge is Power."

For questions about the use of specific medications during pregnancy and lactation, United States residents can use MotherToBaby. A service of the Organization of Teratology Information Specialists (OTIS), MotherToBaby provides counselling and advice to women and doctors throughout the USA and Canada. Callers may be routed to an affiliated service in their area.

Website: http://mothertobaby.org/
Call Toll-Free: 866-626-6847
Text (Standard messaging rates may apply): 855-999-3525

ARTICLE EXTRA: The End of Letter-Based Labels

For decades, the US Food and Drug Administration (FDA) has relied upon an alphabetic system for communicating the safety of drugs in pregnancy. Under this system, every medication is assigned to one of five categories: A, B, C, D or X. Drugs in category A are considered to be the safest for pregnant women; medications in this category have been well-studied and do not seem to pose a risk to a fetus. On the other hand, drugs that appear to present a serious danger to fetal health—with a risk that "clearly outweighs any potential benefit"[12]—are placed in category X. Drugs in categories B, C and D fall somewhere in between.

Experts, however, have complained that this simple-seeming system is, in fact, too simple. "For years we have had these ABCDX categories, which really I think have sort of lulled clinicians and patients into thinking that if something has a B designation we know that it's OK to use, and if something has a D designation you should never take it in pregnancy," says Christina Chambers, a perinatal epidemiologist at the University of California, San Diego. "These categories may provide, on the one hand, more confidence than the data support for some drugs that have a B category, and may

[9]http://www.cioms.ch/index.php/guidelines-test
[10]http://www.cioms.ch/index.php/guideline-19
[11]https://www.apgo.org/elearn/modules/nvpmodule/halenvp.pdf

[12]http://www.gpo.gov/fdsys/pkg/CFR-2006-title21-vol4/pdf/CFR-2006-title21-vol4-sec201-57.pdf

create more concern for a drug than the data show, even for drugs that have an X category."

The FDA has come to agree with these concerns. In December 2014, the agency announced that it would be officially dropping the familiar letter-based system. As the agency wrote: "FDA has decided to eliminate the pregnancy categories because they are often viewed as confusing and overly simplistic and don't effectively communicate the risk a drug may have during pregnancy and lactation and in females and males of reproductive potential."

Rather than a standardized letter grade, drugs will now carry more narrative: detailed summaries of whatever information exists on the safety of compounds when used in pregnancy, during lactation, and in men and women of reproductive age. Each label will summarize the overall likelihood that a drug poses risks to a developing fetus and lay out how the dosing and timing of the medication may affect those risks. (A drug that is perfectly safe in the second and third trimester, for instance, may cause birth defects if taken during the first trimester.) Labels will also be required to describe any risks—to the mother or fetus—from whatever underlying disease the drug is designed to treat.

The American College of Obstetricians and Gynecologists has praised the new labelling rule, as have other experts. "It's a huge improvement," says Janine Polifka, who manages the Teratogen Information System (TERIS)[13] at the University of Washington. "Eliminating those pregnancy categories is really going to be advantageous because they were so misleading." The new law also requires that labels prominently list any pregnancy registries that are currently tracking women who are taking a given medication—a move that researchers hope will spur more patients to volunteer for these studies. Some scientists also believe that the new labels could help raise awareness of how little is known about drug safety and dosing during pregnancy, ultimately driving a demand for more research.

"I think it will make it clear, when you look at that section of the label… where we really have gaps," Chambers says. "So I think it will prompt greater interest in the need for systematically collecting this data and making it available to clinicians and patients." All new drugs approved on or after 30 June 2015 will use the new system; manufacturers of older drugs will have several years to revise their labels.

- Author: Emily Anthes
- Editor: Chrissie Giles
- Copyeditor: Rob Reddick
- Fact checker: Francine Almash

---

[13]http://depts.washington.edu/terisdb/terisweb/index.html

"Culturally Appropriate Doula Support for Queer and Transgender Parents"

By Miranda Welch, MA, CD(DONA)

I'm an openly-queer, professional birth doula in what many would consider a progressive, hippie-dippie city. I frequently work with queer-friendly (and increasingly trans-friendly) medical care providers, birth workers, and healers. I also frequently work with queer and trans identified folks[1] who are seeking more than "friendly" as they grow their families because they know that "friendly" is never enough. Prenatal, intrapartum, and postpartum[2] standards of care developed within a medical establishment that is, at its core, heteronormative, often neglect the unique needs and experiences of queer and trans parents, perpetuating health disparities. As a doula, I cannot fully disrupt culturally inappropriate care that my clients may be receiving. However, I can and do provide fierce and unwavering culturally appropriate support to birthing families, helping them to clarify their needs and communicate them with professionals and make confident, informed decisions for themselves. All professional doulas should have the skills to provide culturally appropriate support; simply identifying our services as queer- or trans-friendly without the knowledge and skills to back it up is insufficient at best and harmful at worst.[3]

[1] I am using the term "queer" to refer to anyone who does not identify with societal norms in regards to sexuality. I use the term "trans" or "trans identified" to refer to anyone who does not identify with the gender binary.

[2] "Maternity care" can be an isolating term as it refers to women and more specifically, mothers, so I refer to this care as prenatal, intrapartum, and postpartum care or care in the childbearing year.

[3] Please note that I will not be discussing the experiences of two cisgender dads. As a birth doula, I have not had the opportunity to support surrogate women or dads in this capacity as it is uncommon to have families seeking doula support in these circumstances.

Birth Doulas 101

Professional birth doulas provide individualized and continuous labor support to birthing families; this support is informational, emotional, and physical. Doulas support all births and choices without judgment. Doulas do not provide any medical care or perform procedures, as they are not medical practitioners. Currently in the United States, somewhere between 5–8% of all births are doula supported.

Prenatally, doulas get to know the families they work with. This is a time for doulas and partners to discover how to best work together to support the birthing parent. It is also a time for the doula to support all parents and help them to feel as prepared as possible for the birth of their baby. Doulas meet with their clients to learn more about their preferences for birth, process fears and concerns, provide information and referrals, and help families to clarify support roles. However, doulas also want to know who their clients are as individuals and as a family. What are their values? How do the parents interact with each other? What does their birth and growing a family mean for them? What do they need from their birth? Generally, it is more important for a doula to understand and support their clients emotionally and relationally than it is for them to know every one of their clients' specific birth preferences.

During the labor and birth, doulas help families to navigate their birth and gather the necessary information to make confident and informed decisions for themselves. Doulas create a safe environment for families to move through their labor together, joining the family whenever they are ready, and remaining until everyone is settled after the birth. Wherever the birth ventures, whatever it asks of the parents, doulas are a continuous presence during labor, providing constant emotional support and tending to the family's needs. They assist birthing families in gathering information, including risks and benefits of options offered by care providers, and enhance communication between parents and providers by encouraging parents to ask questions and express their preferences and concerns. Regardless of other pain management chosen during labor, doulas provide physical support with a variety of comfort measures and relaxation techniques such as baths, birth balls, movement, music, breathing, touch, visualization, rebozo, counterpressure, muscle relaxation, hot and cold compresses, and dim lighting. Doulas also suggest positions and movements for helping birthing parents to feel strong and facilitate labor progression. Doulas inform families on the course of their labor, providing reassurance and encouragement along the way.

Whole family support, meaning all parents are adequately supported, is imperative. Partners know their birthing person better than anyone else; doulas are knowledgeable and experienced with birth. Together, they make the optimal support team. As an extra set of hands, an open heart, and a calm presence, doulas support parents who are not birthing, helping them to participate comfortably as they wish. Doulas enhance the relationship between parents by alleviating some of the pressure partners may feel and creating a safe space for parents to work together to welcome their new baby into the world.

Birth doulas also meet with the family at least once postpartum, generally in the first week following birth. During this visit, doulas help the family to process their birth, answer questions about the sequence and specifics of birth events, and provide information and referrals as necessary. As birth is a major transition, doulas try to get a sense for how the family is doing overall, mentally, emotionally, and physically, and triage and troubleshoot accordingly. If the family chooses to nurse, doulas also assess feeding and provide support, information, and referrals as necessary.

Benefits of Birth Doula Support

Mounting research finds that continuous support from a trained, professional doula[4] creates a more positive birth experience for families while improving labor and birth outcomes. The number one factor in having a positive birth experience is not the specific outcome but how families are treated during their birth. Specifically, receiving appropriate support, having a high-quality re-

lationship with care providers, and being involved in decision-making helps families to feel that they were treated with dignity and respect while birthing.[5] Doulas cannot force care providers to afford this dignity and respect; however, doulas can provide the strong, continuous support and facilitate the participation in decision-making that are also necessary to a positive birth experience.[6]

Professional doula support may:

- Help to create a positive birth experience for families
- Strengthen the family bond
- Reduce the risk of postpartum anxiety and mood disorders
- Enhance communication among members of the birth team
- Improve labor and birth outcomes
- Decrease the risk of surgical birth
- Decrease the risk of assisted delivery through vacuum or forceps
- Increase parental self-esteem
- Help parents who are not birthing to enjoy the birth more
- Increase success with nursing
- Allow partners to participate in the birth at their own comfort level[7]

Culturally Appropriate Doula Support

For queer and trans folks to receive the maximum benefits of doula support, that support must be culturally appropriate. Doulas must understand and anticipate the unique needs of queer and trans families in order to help them navigate a system of care that was not designed for them. This support begins with recognizing that our dominant model of prenatal, intrapartum, and prenatal care in the United States is heteronormative and cisnormative. Its one-size-fits-all approach can be alienating to queer and trans identified parents at best, and oppressive and harmful at worst.

---

[4]Research consistently indicates that this support must be from a professional doula, not a lay person.

[5]For more information regarding factors contributing to positive birth experiences, see Hodnett's 2002 study in the American Journal of Obstetrics and Gynecology.

[6]According to a 2013 study on the benefits of doulas, there is no risk to families and birth associated with professional doula support. For more information, see The Cochrane Collaboration study, as well as the follow-up joint statement from The American Congress of Obstetricians and Gynecologists and The Society for Maternal-Fetal Medicine recommending the use of professional doulas in births.

[7]For more information on the evidence for doulas and the benefits of support, see Rebecca Dekker.

Culturally appropriate care for queer and trans identified folks is, first, understanding the family's unique needs and second, adjusting standards to provide care that meets these needs. Culturally appropriate care involves the recognition of, and education about, specific issues affecting queer and trans families, such as:

Postpartum mood and anxiety disorders

Queer and trans friendly medical providers may ask the same questions and offer the same information or resources to their queer and trans patients as they do for their straight and cisgender patients, which is likely minimal. Medical practitioners providing culturally appropriate care may discuss the mental health histories of all parents and explain the heightened risk of experiencing postpartum mood and anxiety disorders for queer and trans folks. Care providers need to encourage families to prepare as much as possible for this reality, assess, and share culturally appropriate resources as necessary.

Language

Queer and trans friendly medical providers may refer to a two mommy family as "mom and her partner," "the birth mother and her partner," or some combination thereof. While many folks are okay with this terminology, many others are not, as it defines one parent (and often their relationship to the child) while excluding others. Medical practitioners providing culturally appropriate care may refer to this family as "a family." When having to distinguish parents, providers may refer to the parent giving birth as "the parent giving birth." And mom as "mom." My personal favorite is "the mom giving birth and mom."

Co-nursing

Queer and trans friendly medical providers may discourage co-nursing, or a nursing relationship in which more than one parent is regularly offering their nipple to baby.[8] Providers, including Internationally Board Certified Lactation Consultants (IBCLC's), may discourage co-nursing because co-lactating is very challenging and often leads to a rapid loss of milk supply in one or all of the lactating parents. Often queer and trans friendly medical providers will simply say, "don't do it." Medical practitioners and IBCLC's providing culturally appropriate care may open a conversation to determine the goals, wishes, and reasons for wanting to co-nurse.

They may also distinguish between co-nursing and co-lactating[9] and shape their discussion, care, information and resources accordingly. Rather than saying "don't do it," these practitioners may attempt to understand the desire to co-nurse, offer culturally sensitive information, accept whatever decision the family makes, and take care of them as best as possible.

Role of the Birth Doula in a Heteronormative System

The role of the birth doula in a heteronormative system of medical care is to provide professional, fierce, and unwavering culturally appropriate support to birthing families so that they may receive all of the benefits of doula support, particularly a positive birth and healthy postpartum experience. Doulas are agents of social change, and providing culturally appropriate support to queer and trans folks is a perfect example of how doulas can engage in reproductive justice.[10]

What culturally appropriate support actually looks like depends on the family and their needs. But let's begin with why "queer and trans friendly" isn't enough.

A prospective client asks a doula they consider working with: "Have you ever worked with a same-sex couple before, and what has been your experience at XYZ hospital?"

The doula responds: "I sure have. This is ABC City and everyone is super gay friendly, so I would say it really depends more on the care provider."

While ABC City might be queer friendly, that doesn't mean that this family will receive culturally appropriate care from their providers or support from their doula. One of the reasons they may be seeking a doula is anticipation of a lack of culturally appropriate care, or even discrimination. For families that are afraid of how they may be treated because of their queer or trans identities, the support of a doula is what may help them to feel safe. ABC City being "gay friendly" is not enough for this family. "Gay friendly" does not understand and anticipate this family's unique needs; rather, it ignores, refuses to notice, and/or excuses common behaviors and disparities that they may face as they grow their family.

---

[8]"Breastfeeding" and "breasts" are terms that can be alienating and harmful to some parents who don't identify with these terms. For the purposes of being all-inclusive, I use "nursing" and "nipple" instead.

[9]Co-nursing is more than one parent regularly offering their nipple to baby; co-nursing does not have to involve co-lactating as it can be done for comfort and bonding. Co-lactating is more than one parent producing milk and regularly offering their nipple to baby for nutrition.

[10]For more information, see Monica Reese Basile's "Reproductive justice and childbirth reform: doulas as agents of social change."

Key Disparities Facing Birthing Families

The disparities facing birthing queer and trans families are deeply institutionalized and systemic. The few I discuss here are brief and certainly not comprehensive. They are some things that I see regularly as a doula,[11] and while I categorize and distinguish them as best as possible, these experiences are complex, interrelated, and may be compounded by multiple marginalization of individuals.

Language

Language disparities include how we talk about birth, the body, families, and parents. How do we define parentage, and what is our obsession with doing so? Why are we so concerned with biology and genetics in growing families? Why are we, as a culture, attached to essentialist notions of femininity in pregnancy and birth? The heteronormative language that we commonly use when talking about birth, bodies, families, and parents can be isolating and oppressive to queer families and trigger dysphoria[12] in trans folks.

Common pregnancy and birth terminology is focused on "the female body," which can be a primary cause of gender dysphoria for trans folks. "Vagina" and "breasts" can be particular triggers for dysphoria. Replacing these words with alternatives or not using them at all can help trans folks feel safer, better supported, and present in their own bodies during their childbearing year. Instead of a "vaginal birth," for example, consider using the term "non-surgical birth." Instead of "breastfeeding," it may be helpful to say "nursing," or when talking about the breast itself (i.e. "offering the breast"), saying "nipple."

"Women were made to give birth."

As doulas, when we are encouraging laboring folks, reminding them that they can do it and that they are strong and working hard, sometimes a phrase like "women were made to give birth" slips in. Let's not do that. Not only is this harmful to folks who don't identify with this essentialist theory of womanhood, but it is harmful to birthing folks period. It negates the journey and work the birthing parent goes through to bring their baby into the world and in situations in which the birth does not go as desired or planned. Particularly when the birth is traumatic, this phrase can stick with birthing folks and make them feel like failures. Essentialist phrases like this always carry the potential for isolation and damage, even when we may not immediately recognize it.

When we attempt to define parentage and families, we often ask questions that, while they may come from a kind place, are actually destructive and regressive. Insensitive questions are particularly harmful during birth, as they can lead families to feel unsafe in their birthing environment and shut down. This is not fair to a family welcoming their newest addition. Typical questions asked of queer and trans families are not asked of heteronormative families, so why do we ask them? Why do we need to know so badly? We don't. It is always none of our business and never imperative to our work. All we need to know is that they are a loving, growing family.

Questions such as "have you decided what you are going to call yourselves yet"[13] can catch a family off guard, and it is probably one of the last things they are thinking about as they are taking their baby in for the first time.

"Are you going to do this next time" is frequently asked of parents who are not giving birth. When this happens, particularly during the birth, it is exceptionally harmful because there is a reason that one parent is pregnant and others are not. That reason is not important for us to know, but it is important for us to understand that it exists and it can be quite complex, personal, and raw. It is also important for us to understand that queer and trans parents who are not birthing experience their pregnancies and births differently than dads in heteronormative families do. As doulas, we should always be cognizant of these dynamics to provide adequate support to all parents.

Healthcare and Legal Systems

Systemic disparities include the legalities and other logistics associated with accessing health systems in the childbearing year, as well as creating and protecting families. Whose names go on the birth certificate? How many hospital bracelets are there, and will there be enough for all parents?[14] Will parents who are not birthing be "second parent adopting" their baby, and what does that process look like in their state? What are the options for growing families, what does access

---

[11]As I am discussing my experiences as a doula, these disparities are also somewhat specific to my geographic location.

[12]Gender dysphoria is a psychological term referring to the significant distress individuals may experience with their biological sex and/or the gender assigned to them at birth; dysphoria is common when folks feel that the sex and gender assigned to them at birth at are odds with one another.

[13]This is a question that has been asked by medical staff at every single birth I have supported in which there were queer or trans identified parents.

[14]Often, hospitals only give two bracelets, one to each parent to match them with their baby for security purposes. When there are more than two parents, this can be a serious concern.

to these options look like, and what is the best option for each family? What kind of support do families have through their conception process? What do legal protections for families look like, and how do families access those protections? How are families recognized (or not recognized) in various systems that they must access throughout the childbearing year, such as the hospital, judicial system, assisted conception clinics, insurance companies, etc.? Every system that queer and trans families encounter may require navigation, negotiation, and challenging decisions. Queer and trans families must be strong advocates for themselves at all times, and as doulas we are supporting them during a period of life when their engagement with these processes may be particularly painful or frustrating. As doulas, we must be sensitive to what families go through in order to be a family, and know that our emotional support is crucial.

A common question that families have prenatally is whether or not they need to pack their legal documentation (marriage certificates, power of attorney, living wills, wills, family attorney information, etc.) to bring to the hospital. While marriage is now legal in all fifty states, many family attorneys in my community are continuing to encourage families to participate in second parent adoptions and other legal protections for their families. Marriage is still new and there are still many discriminatory laws and practices on the books across the United States. Basically, we don't really know if families should bring them or not. So bring them. No doula wants to be the one who said "meh, you shouldn't need that; this is ABC City, super queermo friendly," only to end up in a situation in which the family truly needed it to protect themselves. No family wants to be without that protection, hence their question.

In pregnancy and birth, trans folks often experience additional challenges with health insurance. Insurance companies may require that patients be officially designated as female in order to receive coverage for their prenatal, intrapartum, and postpartum care. For some trans folks, this may mean contacting the insurance company and petitioning to have their sex changed in the records. Some insurance companies may not allow this if it is not an open enrollment period for coverage and policy changes. Even if folks are able to change their designated sex with their insurance provider, they may then have to change it back soon after the baby is born in order to receive proper health care coverage going forward. For example, a birthing individual identifying as male may need to be designated female during pregnancy to receive proper care and coverage during the childbearing year. However, after the birth, they will need to be designated as male again in order to receive coverage for their standard care, such as

testosterone. Insurance companies are challenging for everyone, but trans folks face additional complications and barriers even when they are not pregnant. Pregnancy and birth may add another layer to insurance navigation in their childbearing year.

Electronic medical records may also complicate care in the childbearing year for trans folks as many of these computer programs require female designation in order to even open pregnancy and birth modules. This means that, in computer programs that require female designation before proceeding (and for trans folks whom this applies to), providers must go into the medical records and change the identity of their patient. Female designation in medical records can distort care providers' understanding of how folks identify and what care they need. It can also confuse providers, particularly in the hospital during the birth, when they read that a patient is female but in reality, this is not the case. Female designation and accompanying provider reactions and treatment may trigger increased gender dysphoria for trans folks, which can also contribute to health disparities during their childbearing year.

Socialization and Constructions of Gender

Socialization and constructions of gender include our cultural ideas of what makes a mother, parent, and family and associated beliefs about connections between gender and biology. We often gender our bodily processes, especially pregnancy, birth, and nursing, and attach them to our identities. How is my menstrual cycle connected to my womanhood? How is the gestation process connected to my motherhood? How is nursing connected to my motherhood? How is a non-surgical birth connected to my womanhood and motherhood? Often, notions of "innate feminine wisdom" come to the surface here. When we want to highlight the incredible strength and power it takes to become a parent, we focus on the pregnancy and birth processes and we feminize them, but why? Who is it serving? Who is it isolating? What is at stake here? These ideas may create barriers to receiving culturally appropriate resources and doula support for queer and trans families in their childbearing year.

The needs of queer and trans parents who are not birthing can be quite different from the needs of dads in heteronormative relationships. Queer and trans partners often experience their pregnancy, birth, and postpartum uniquely as well. This is primarily because of how we define and gender motherhood, fatherhood, and parenthood in connection with heteronormative constructions of gender. For example, for a mom who is not birthing, how is she to define herself as a mother in a culture that refuse to recognize her as such because she did not birth her baby? For a mom who wants to birth but cannot, her partner's pregnancy and birth may be challenging for her. She may also struggle with how to define herself as a mother. As doulas, it is critical for us to be cognizant of and sensitive to the unique needs and experiences of queer and trans partners.

Body politics[15] may also affect the childbearing year, particularly for trans folks. How bodies look, how they are read by others, and how folks feel about them are vulnerable issues that may surface. Trans folks may have a heightened need for safety in order to feel comfortable in their own skin as they birth. This may also be an issue with nursing, whether lactating or not, and trans folks may need additional support to feel comfortable with nipple exposure and skin to skin bonding with their baby. Body politics may also increase gender dysphoria for trans identified folks. Sensitivity to a parent's relationship to their body, as opposed to beliefs that modesty always goes out the window when birthing (or should), may be of paramount importance to some families.

Nursing is frequently deeply associated with motherhood, and specifically touted as "good" motherhood. For some queer and trans mothers, lactation must be medically induced, or induced lactation simply will not work. Some parents who identify as mothers may wish to nurse so that they can establish and feel that "motherly bond" with their baby. They may nurse for comfort or they may induce lactation and nurse for nutrition. International Board Certified Lactation Consultant's (IBCLC) may encourage nutritive nursing because "breast is best," but when families wish to co-nurse it may be discouraged due to difficulty in balancing this relationship for baby. When we send the message that "breastfeeding" makes good mothers, how are queer and trans mothers supposed to navigate this message? For dads who choose to nurse, how safe will they be in public? How comfortable will they be providing milk for their babies? If nursing triggers dysphoria, how will that impact their postpartum period and what kind of support will they need? As doulas, we need to understand the complicated messages our culture sends to families about nursing and be sensitive to the needs of all parents.

Across books, videos, evidence-based research, childbirth education classes, nursing classes, etc. there is an incredible lack of resources for queer and trans families. In particular, there is a huge lack of culturally appropriate childbirth and postpartum preparation resources that adequately address the needs of queer and trans families. For these families, it can often feel that information doesn't apply to them. From two mommy families, I often hear "I didn't relate to this section about dads." No kidding! You're not a dad! The lack of culturally appropriate resources is reflective of our heteronormative constructions of birth and families. It can leave families feeling unprepared and abnormal in their experience.

Postpartum

Postpartum disparities include the heightened risk of developing postpartum mood and anxiety disorders for queer and trans folks, as well as the basic understanding that queer and trans folks will have a unique postpartum experience. As their postpartum period and establishment of themselves as a family is often eclipsed and influenced by heterosexism and transphobia, families face additional postpartum challenges to adjusting to having a new baby. Families may receive questions from people about their family and their parentage. When a new family is seen by others as different or strange, this impacts their ability to balance and find their "new normal" as a family.

Gender dysphoria, histories of mental health concerns, and heterosexism and transphobia substantially increase the risk of postpartum mood and anxiety disorders for queer and trans parents. How families are treated during their birth can also compound this risk. Generally, having support from family and friends during the postpartum period can help to alleviate some of the common challenges in baby's first weeks. For some queer and trans parents, however, relationships with their own parents and family members may not be the healthiest. What kind of help does the family have for when their baby arrives? What boundaries do they have with their parents? How is becoming a parent triggering past experiences with their own parents, and how is this impacting how they imagine themselves as parents? Navigating the postpartum period for queer and trans parents may take more fine-tuning to ensure that they are adequately supported, that old wounds are not re-opened, and that boundaries they have set in their lives remain intact.

How Doulas Can Support Birthing Families

- Use gender neutral language until you learn how parents refer to themselves and follow suit
- Refer to clients always as a family; there is no

---

[15]Briefly, body politics refers to institutional power over and regulation of bodies. Body politics asks who controls bodies and explores the struggle for bodily autonomy between society and individuals.

need to define them further

- Set a strong, consistent example for care providers during their birth and be consistently culturally appropriate for the family
- Provide fierce, unwavering emotional support during the birth; this can be as simple as saying "I heard that" when something offensive is said to them, or staying close when they are particularly vulnerable to discrimination
- Help the family to convey to medical staff their unique preferences and needs, particularly in written birth preferences
- Know what their values are as a family: what is important to them and why
- Help families to adequately prepare for specific culturally inappropriate care they may receive, discuss preferences and expectations for your role as a doula in these situations, and consider how you might navigate these interactions ahead of time
- Be knowledgeable and able to make referrals to providers, resources, information, education, therapy, etc. with an understanding of their level of cultural appropriateness
- Help families plan as much as possible for their postpartum experience with sensitivity to how it may be impacted by heterosexism and transphobia
- Discuss and understand the family's preferences regarding co-nursing

- Adequately support parents who are not birthing while understanding that their needs and their relationship to their birth may be unique
- Be mindful of intersectionality and how race and class may be impacting their experience as well[16]
- If you identify as queer or trans and are comfortable doing so, you can out yourself to medical staff during the birth to shift the power dynamic[17]

Works Cited

Basile, Monica Reese. "Reproductive justice and childbirth reform: doulas as agents of social change." *University of Iowa: Theses and Dissertations.* 2012 <http://ir.uiowa.edu/etd/2819/>.

Caughey, Aaron B., Alison G. Cahill, Jeanne-Marie Guise, Dwight J. Rouse. "Safe Prevention of the Primary Cesarean Delivery." *Obstetric Care Consensus Series.* 1 (2014). *American Congress of Obstetricians and Gynecologists.* Web. 4 Mar. 2016.

Dekker, Rebecca. "The Evidence for Doulas." *Evidence Based Birth.* Evidence Based Birth, n.d. Web. 4 Mar. 2016.

Hodnett, ED, S Gates, G Hofmeyr, C Sakala. "Continuous support for women during childbirth." *Cochrane Collaboration Library.* 15 July 2013 <http://www.cochrane.org/CD003766/PREG_continuous-support-for-women during-childbirth>.

Hodnett, ED. "Pain and women's satisfaction with the experience of childbirth: a systematic review." *American Journal of Obstetrics and Gynecology* 186.5 (2002): S160–172. Web. 4 Mar. 2016.

---

[16]For more information, please see the Wisconsin Doulas of Color Collective (https://www.facebook.com/WisDoulasOfColor/).
[17]Outing yourself as a professional is a personal choice that should be done wisely.

"State of Breastfeeding Coverage: Health Plan Violations of the Affordable Care Act"

From The *National Women's Law Center*

Introduction

The affordable care act's (ACA) coverage of breastfeeding equipment, support, and counseling is a groundbreaking new insurance benefit. In order to support women's efforts to breastfeed, and reduce cost barriers for women who want to breastfeed, the ACA requires insurance coverage of breastfeeding supplies, support, and counseling without co-payments, deductibles, or co-insurance.[1] This coverage is an important step to ensure women have the support and tools they need to breastfeed successfully.

However, some women do not fully benefit from this new coverage. In some cases, insurance policies fail to comply with the ACA's breastfeeding coverage requirements, or restrict coverage in ways that undermine the intent of the law.[2] In other instances, the federal guidance detailing coverage standards falls short of what women need to breastfeed successfully. Insurance plan noncompliance and the lack of clear federal standards and inadequate guidance means that women are not getting insurance coverage that meets their needs.

The National Women's Law Center (the Center) operates a nationwide hotline, CoverHer, which women can call when they face problems accessing the breastfeeding benefits to which they are entitled. Through this hotline, the Center has heard from women across the country. Women who contact the Center report spending hours on the phone with their insurance company trying to decipher what their insurance plan covers, and how they can get breastfeeding benefits as soon as possible. But, customer service representatives frequently give them conflicting information about their coverage, or wrongly tell them **their plan does** not provide coverage of breastfeeding support. Some women pay hundreds of dollars out-of pocket for services; other women who cannot afford to pay the full cost of services forgo getting breastfeeding help altogether.

In addition to reports received through CoverHer, the Center reviewed over 100 plan documents from issuers in the new marketplaces in 15 states.[3] This research, combined with stories from the hotline, points to three major trends that prevent women from getting breastfeeding benefits as required by law:

- Some insurance companies impose restrictions and limitations on breastfeeding support and supplies that explicitly violate the ACA or undermine the intent of the law;
- Some insurance companies do not have a network of lactation providers and are not following clear federal rules that allow women to obtain preventive services, including breastfeeding benefits, out-of-network, at no cost-sharing; and
- Some insurance companies impose major administrative barriers or offer insufficient coverage that prevents women from obtaining timely breastfeeding support and adequate equipment, as the ACA intended.

In addition to these three major trends, research and CoverHer contacts have reported other problems with the implementation of the ACA's breastfeeding benefit, such as plans limiting coverage to a manual pump, which is permitted by federal guidance but is a huge barrier to some women breastfeeding successfully.

This report highlights the obstacles women face when trying to get coverage for breastfeeding benefits and identifies strategies to remedy violations of the law and to revisit the insufficient federal guidance that leaves women without the coverage they need. To that end, the Center's recommendations call for insurance companies to come into compliance and correct any violations of the ACA. The recommendations also call for state and federal regulators to carefully review coverage policies and promptly respond to consumer complaints. And in order to ensure that federal guidance itself does not permit insurance company policies that leave w:Jmen with inadequate breastfeeding coverage, the recommendations call for the Departments of Health and Human Services, Treasury, and Labor (the Departments) to engage a range of stakeholders to reexamine coverage standards and develop new guidance that ensures women across the country get the tools they need to breastfeed successfully.

The Affordable Care Act's Coverage of Breastfeeding Support and Supplies

The ACA's breastfeeding benefits are part of the law's preventive health services coverage provision, which is designed to enable individuals to avoid preventable conditions and improve health overall by increasing access to preventive care and screenings. This provision requires health insurance plans to provide coverage for certain preventive services without out-of-pocket costs, including a set of preventive services for women.

To determine which women's preventive services would be covered without out-of-pocket costs, the Health Resources Services Administration (HRSA) of the Department of Health and Human Services commissioned the Institute of Medicine (IOM) to study gaps in coverage of women's preventive services and to recommend which additional women's preventive services should be included. After conducting its analysis, the IOM recommended eight additional preventive services for women, including breastfeeding support and supplies. HRSA adopted the recommenda tions set forth in the IOM's report[4]. According to the HRSA requirement, coverage is for comprehensive lactation support and counseling, including the costs of breastfeeding equipment, to ensure the successful initiation and continuation of breastfeeding.

The reason the IOM recommended adding coverage for breastfeeding support and supplies is because research has consistently shown that breastfeeding benefits the mother and the child. According to the Agency for Healthcare Research and Quality (AHRQ), breastfeeding reduces children's risk for a variety of common childhood illnesses and less frequent but serious conditions, including sudden infant death syn-

drome, ear infections, upper and lower respiratory disease, asthma, childhood leukemia, childhood obesity, and Type 2 diabetes.[5] It also reduces maternal risk for breast and ovarian cancer.[6] Based on this and other research, the American College of Obstetricians and Gynecologists and the American Academy of Pediatrics support exclusive breastfeeding for approximately six months, with continuation of breastfeeding, if possible, even longer.[7]

Despite the proven benefits of breastfeeding, there is a gap between women's decision to breastfeed their children and the support they need to successfully breastfeed for as long as intended. A majority of pregnant women plan to breastfeed and initiate breastfeeding at birth, but a much lower proportion of women continue to breastfeed. One study found that 76 percent of new mothers began breastfeeding, with 47 percent continuing to breastfeed at 6 months, and only 26 percent breastfeeding at 12 months.[8]

While breastfeeding rates have been growing steadily, there are significant gaps across racial, ethnic, and socioeconomic lines.[9]

The Surgeon General's Call to Action to Support Breastfeeding outlines several key barriers women face when breastfeeding. The report indicates that successful initiation of breastfeeding not only depends on experiences in the hospital but also depends on access to instruction on lactation from breastfeeding experts, particularly in the postpartum period.[10]

Affordable Care Act Requirements

The ACA requires health plans to cover breastfeeding support and supplies without co-payments, deductibles, or co-insurance, for the duration of breastfeeding.[11] The ACA requires this coverage for most employer health insurance plans, individual health coverage purchased on insurance Marketplaces operating in each state, and Medicaid enrollees who are newly eligible as part of a state's decision to adopt the ACA's Medicaid expansion.[12]

Insurance plans must cover breastfeeding support and supplies, for the duration of breastfeeding
According to the HRSA recommendations, insurance plans must cover comprehensive lactation support and counseling by a trained provider, and costs of breastfeeding equipment. This requirement applies in conjunction with each birth. Federal guidance specifies that coverage for breastfeeding support and supplies extends for the duration of breastfeeding.[13] This means that plans cannot impose time limits on when women can obtain lactation counseling and breastfeeding equipment.

Insurance plans must provide access to out-of-network providers at no cost-sharing
Federal guidance specifies that women must be able to obtain recommended preventive services with no cost-sharing, and, in some circumstances, obtain these services from out-of-network providers. Specifically, the guidance states, "if a plan or issuer does not have not have in its network a provider who can provide the particular service, then the plan or *issuer must cover the item or service when performed by an out-of-network provider and not impose cost-sharing* with respect to the item or service" (emphasis added).[14] This means that if an insurance company does not have a network of providers for women to receive lactation counseling, then the plan must allow them to obtain lactation counseling from an out-of-network provider, at no cost-sharing.

Insurance companies may use limited "reasonable medical management"
Under the regulations implementing the preventive health services, insurance companies are allowed to use "reasonable medical management techniques" to determine the "frequency, method, treatment, or setting for which a recommended preventive service will be available without cost-sharing requirements to the extent not specified in a recommendation or guideline."[15] But these medical management techniques are not unlimited. While plans may use reasonable medical management techniques, they cannot limit or restrict coverage in ways that conflict with federal guidance. For example, because coverage of breastfeeding benefits extends for the duration of breastfeeding, plans cannot impose an arbitrary time limit on when women can access these benefits.

Insurance companies can limit coverage to a manual pump
Unfortunately, the Department of Health and Human Services has clarified that the ACA does not require insurance plans to cover a certain type of pump.[16] However, a manual pump is insufficient for many women such as women returning to work, women who have preterm or ill infants, low milk supply, or women who have physical disabilities.[17]

Coverage Problems That Prevent Women From Getting Breastfeeding Benefits

Unfortunately, not every woman who should be geting coverage of breastfeeding support and supplies without cost-sharing has been able to access this important benefit. The Center has documented this through the review of coverage policies in 15 states' marketplaces. In addition, the Center receives calls and emails through a nationwide hotline from women who face significant barriers to getting coverage to which they are entitled under the ACA. The Center has identified three major trends that prevent women from getting breastfeeding benefits:

- Some insurance companies impose restrictions and limitations on breastfeeding support and supplies, which explicitly violate the ACA or undermine the intent of the law;
- Some insurance companies do not have a network of providers for women to get lactation counseling and are not following clear federal rules that allow women to obtain preventive services, including breastfeeding benefits, out-of-network, at no cost-sharing; and
- Some insurance companies impose major administrative barriers or offer insufficient coverage that prevents women from obtaining timely breastfeeding support and adequate equipment, as envisioned by the ACA.

Insurance companies impose unallowable limitations on breastfeeding support and supplies
Insurance companies have coverage policies for breastfeeding that are more limited than federal guidance allows. Women who have contacted the Center report that they had to obtain a breast pump within 6 months after their baby was born. In some cases, women report the insurance company only covers a breast pump 48 days after delivery.

In addition to reports from women trying to use this benefit, the Center's plan document research found similar restrictions. Three health issuers in two states only allow women to obtain a breast pump within 6 months of delivery.[18] Two issuers in one state limit

IN THEIR OWN WORDS: DENIED COVERAGE OF A BREAST PUMP

"I was going back to work and wanted to use a breast pump. My insurance company told me that I wasn't eligible for a breast pump because it had been over 180 days since I gave birth. I contacted the Center to see if this policy was correct. The Center helped me file a claim and later an appeal with my insurance company. Many months later they reimbursed me $200 for a breast pump. The whole ordeal was such a hassle."

-Nicole, California

IN THEIR OWN WORDS: DENIED COVERAGE OF LACTATION COUNSELING

"My daughter was only a few days old, and had been so dehydrated at the hospital (due to breastfeeding issues) that they almost put her in the NICU. I needed to see a lactation specialist immediately, but my insurance company didn't have any lactation providers in their directory. So I called my insurance company to find out if I could get coverage. They told me that their in-network provider was La Leche League and gave me the names and numbers of two women who run a local La Leche League meeting. But when I contacted these women, they explained that La Leche League is a breastfeeding support group, not a provider network! I ultimately saw a certified lactation consultant on my own, which solved my breastfeeding problems. Now I'm trying to get reimbursed. I've been fighting with my insurance company since July 2014 and I'm still trying to get reimbursed!"

—Aiysson, Washington DC

rental of a breast pump to 12 months.[19] Two issuers in two states indicate the plan determines the duration of rental.[20] One issuer limits coverage of a breast pump to one purchase every three years.[21] All of these restrictions are clear violations of the ACA's requirement to provide coverage for the duration of breastfeeding.[22]

Many women need access to breast pumps to maintain their milk supply, particularly when returning to work. In fact, one of the reasons the IOM recommended coverage of breastfeeding equipment was to ensure that women who return to work or have other obligations that separate them from their infant can continue to breastfeed, if they choose to, without cost barriers.[23]

Several hotline callers report similar limitations on breastfeeding support and lactation counseling. Women report that their insurance plan will only provide coverage for lactation counseling on an inpatient basis during the post-delivery hospital stay. If they are already home and having problems breastfeeding, their insurance plan says that lactation counseling is not covered.

In addition to reports from women facing barriers in accessing lactation counseling, the Center's plan document research found similar restrictions in lactation counseling. Six health insurance issuers in one state only allow women to get lactation services within two months of delivery.[24] Three issuers in one state limit coverage to a single lactation visit within two months of delivery.[25]

One company limits breastfeeding education to one visit per pregnancy.[26] Another company limits breastfeeding education to two services per calendar year (for pregnant women) and three counseling sessions in conjunction with each birth.[27] All of these examples conflict with federal guidance requiring insurance companies to cover breastfeeding equipment and support, in conjunction with each birth, for the duration of breastfeeding.[28]

Some women need intensive lactation support to manage initial breastfeeding challenges such as insufficient milk supply or a newborn's difficulty latching. Sometimes a woman will need lactation support after breastfeeding has been established, if she encounters medical issues associated with breastfeeding, such as thrush or mastitis that affect her ability to breastfeed. Even after breastfeeding is well-established, some women who return to work experience problems with their milk supply and may need additional lactation counseling to continue breastfeeding.

The HRSA guidelines recognize the various points at which women may need lactation support and breastfeeding equipment, and specifically recommend that benefits should encompass the initiation and duration of breastfeeding. In all of these examples, insurance companies are imposing benefit limits and restrictions that violate the law.

Insurance companies have not established a network of providers and are not following federal rules allowing women to obtain services out-of-network, at no cost-sharing

Despite the ACA's requirement to provide "comprehensive lactation support," insurance companies have not established networks of lactation providers.[29] In these instances, the plan typically refers women to their obstetrician or to the child's pediatrician-neither of whom usually offers lactation counseling. In some cases, women report that insurance companies have one in-network lactation provider (usually located in a hospital) to serve all of the plan's enrollees. And in the case of hospital-based lactation consultants, hospital policy often restricts these providers to inpatient clients, which means women cannot access these health professionals once they are discharged from the hospital.

The lack of a provider network for lactation counseling means that women must turn to out-of-network providers to get help with breastfeeding. Federal guidance clearly allows women to obtain required preventive services, including breastfeeding benefits, through out-of-network providers, at no cost-sharing, when the plan does not maintain a network of appropriate providers.[30] However, dozens of women have contacted the Center to report their insurance company is ignoring this rule and denying payment for services they obtained out-of-network. These denials violate the ACA.

When plans fail to establish a network of providers, women face significant barriers to accessing breastfeeding benefits that should be covered by law. Women have to pay at the point of service for lactation counseling, and seek reimbursement from their plan afterwards. Plans often deny these claims because the woman obtained benefits out-of-network. Upon appeal, some plans will partially reimburse the cost of lactation counseling—but they reimburse at the out-of-network rate which means women still pay significant money for services that should have been fully covered. Women report that some plans deny the claim altogether because they did not follow a lengthy and time-consuming administrative process to get approval from the plan to access out-of-network providers.[31] These practices effectively shift more costs to women. Some women—especially women with limited income or who may be taking unpaid family leave—will not be able to pay the full cost of lactation counseling at the point of service, and will not get the care they need. For these women, they effectively have no benefit at all.

Insurance companies impose major administrative barriers

Insurance companies impose administrative barriers that hamper women's ability to get timely breastfeeding benefits. These barriers include medical management techniques like prior authorization and restrictions on when women can get services. For example, women report that some insurance companies will not provide coverage of a breast pump until after the baby is born and only after going through some administrative barriers such as getting a prescription or prior authorization.

Women in these plans will not get their breast pumps until a few weeks after they give birth. This coverage policy is problematic because some women need a breast pump immediately. The newborn could be unable to latch properly, or need intensive medical services that require them to be admitted into the Neonatal Intensive Care Unit (NICU). Premature babies or newborns with other health challenges may have difficulty feeding and women will need to begin using a breast pump immediately to establish their milk supply.

In other instances, some women who previously faced breastfeeding challenges and are having subsequent children may already know they need to use a breast pump shortly after giving birth to help build their milk supply. Coverage policies that limit when a woman can get a breast pump can interfere with her attempts to initiate breastfeeding. Further, the IOM's recommendation is for comprehensive support "in conjunction with each birth." Nothing in the ACA or federal guidance indicates that the coverage only begins after delivery.

Federal guidance allowing coverage of only manual pumps is insufficient

Unfortunately, the Department of Health and Human Services indicates that, under the ACA, insurance plans are not required to cover a certain type of pump.[32]

For example, some plans only provide coverage of a manual pump and exclude all electronic or hospital grade pumps. Limiting coverage to a manual pump means that some women will not get access to the tools they need to successfully breastfeed.

Women need access to hospital grade pumps for various reasons. Women who have newborns in the NICU and are separated from their infant cannot initiate breastfeeding with a manual pump. Women in these circumstances will require an electric or hospital grade pump to establish their milk supply.[33] The American Academy of Pediatrics (AAP) strongly encourages feeding infants who are in the NICU human milk.[34]

Further, AAP recommends that breast pump coverage include all grades of breast pumps (manual, electric, hospital grade), indicating that "[m]anual breast pumps may not be appropriate in all situations and benefit plans should include coverage for electric and hospital grade breast pumps. Double electric or hospital grade pumps are often more efficient to maintain milk supply for mothers that return to work."[35] In addition, women returning to work may find a manual pump incompatible with their need to express milk quickly and efficiently during the work day.

> ### IN THEIR OWN WORDS:WOMEN NEED BETTER COVERAGE
>
> Debbie is a Clinical Nurse Specialist and International Board Certified Lactation Consultant. In her level 4 NICU, she works with new mothers who are separated from their infants and require a hospital grade breast pump to establish their milk supplies and feed their babies.
> "Providing a manual or consumer level pump to a mother who has a newborn in the NICU is totally insufficient. These mothers need a hospital grade pump, and lots of lactation support."
>
> —Debbie, Clinical Nurse 111/IBCLC

Recommendations

The ACA's breastfeeding benefits are a huge step forward that can remove the cost barriers associated with breastfeeding support and equipment and give women the tools they need to successfully breastfeed for as long as they want. However, because insurance companies are not following the law, women are not getting breastfeeding benefits as required by the ACA. To make certain that every woman gets the coverage guaranteed to her under the ACA, insurance companies and state and federal governments must take steps to ensure plans comply with the law.

Insurance companies: bring coverage into compliance

- Insurance companies **must carefully examine coverage documents to ensure the policy** complies with federal regulation and guidance. Plans should immediately remove restrictions or limitations that violate the ACA.
- Insurance companies **must-at a minimum establish a network of lactation providers** so women can obtain timely in-network lactation

services with no cost-sharing or up-front costs, within a reasonable distance. As plans build this network, however, they must allow women to obtain services from out-of-network providers, at no cost-sharing, as required by law.
- Insurance companies **must remove all administrative barriers to getting timely lactation support.** Women should not be required to pay the full costs of lactation counseling out-of-pocket and then seek reimbursement through a series of claims and appeals.
- Insurance companies **must remove all administrative barriers to getting a breast pump.** Insurance companies should permit women to obtain breast pumps prior to delivery. They should also have an expedited process so that women can acquire a breast pump quickly when they need it.

Federal and state regulators: enforce the law

- Federal regulators must **ensure plans comply with the ACA's breastfeeding benefits and enforce the law.** It is inexcusable to expect women to pay the full costs of lactation services, up-front, with no guarantee the costs will be fully reimbursed, as required by law. It is also inexcusable to allow insurance companies to circumvent reasonable network requirements.
- State regulators **must ensure health insurance complies with the ACA**, its implementing regulations, and related guidance. Most states are responsible for the initial certification of health plans on state and federal Marketplaces. State regulators must be diligent in their review of Qualified Health Plan documents and determined in their efforts to bring plans into compliance with the law during the certification process.
- State regulators **must be diligent about responding to complaints** about coverage violations. State regulators must respond to complaints from women about insurance practices that create administrative barriers to required coverage. Regulators should pay particular attention to complaints of an insufficient network for lactation counseling.
- State regulators should **inform women about the law** and its coverage requirements for women's health. For example, states should work with stakeholders to develop and distribute informational bulletins on the ACA's preventive services requirements and the scope of breastfeeding coverage. Women need this information to be informed consumers and to advocate for the coverage they need.

- State regulators should **broadly publicize the appeals process**. Women need to know the appropriate course of action when plans fail to provide the coverage the ACA requires, and plans need to be held accountable when they do not comply with the law.

Compliance with the existing law is not enough. To fulfill the promise of this benefit, policymakers need to reexamine what coverage should encompass, and should more closely align coverage requirements with the IOM's recommendations and input from a range of important stakeholders

The Departments of Health and Human Services, Treasury, and Labor: Revisit Guidance and Engage Stakeholders

- The Departments **should revisit current guidance** to ensure coverage of breastfeeding support and supplies aligns with the Institute of Medicine's recommendations and best practices.

- The Departments **should engage stakeholders**—breastfeeding experts, the medical community, advocates, and insurance companies—**to develop new federal standards for** breastfeeding coverage that takes into account the best evidence.

Conclusion

The ACA's investment in preventive services and breastfeeding benefits is a historic step forward. Access to breastfeeding equipment and the expertise of trained lactation providers is critical to removing barriers to breastfeeding. Millions of women across the country are already benefitting from the law, in terms of both their health and the impact it has on their families and lives. But, there is significant room for improvement—right now, women do not have access to coverage required by law and face inexcusable barriers to getting breastfeeding benefits. All stakeholders must work together to correct these problems and ensure that breastfeeding benefits fulfill the promise of the ACA.

"Everybody Calm Down About Breastfeeding"

By Emily Oster

In the run-up to my son's birth a couple of months ago, I spent a lot of time sitting in my midwife's office staring aimlessly at the posters on the wall. My favorite one depicted two scoops of ice cream with cherries on top, strategically set to look like breasts. The caption underneath suggested that exclusive breast-feeding for six months would lower a child's risk of obesity.[1] Presumably the implication was that if you chose to breastfeed, your child could later eat ice cream with impunity.

It was a great visual, and given the current rate of obesity in the United States, a compelling argument. The only trouble is that there is no good reason to think it is correct. The one high-quality randomized controlled trial of breast-feeding did not show[2] any impacts on childhood obesity.

Of course, it's not just childhood obesity. The purported benefits of nursing (here is one list[3] from the California Department of Public Health) extend to better mother-infant bonding, lower infant mortality, fewer infections in infancy, higher IQ, higher wages in adulthood, less cancer and on and on. If one takes the claims seriously, it is not difficult to conclude that breastfed babies are all thin, rich geniuses who love their mothers and are never sick a day in their lives while formula-fed babies become overweight, low-IQ adults who hate their parents and spend most of their lives in the hospital.

It shouldn't come as a surprise, then, that many women who struggle to breastfeed (or just find it annoying and want to quit) feel ashamed and sad that they are not giving their children the "best" start in life. It wouldn't be great to make women feel this way even if all the purported benefits of breastfeeding were real. It's even worse because the truth is that the vast majority of these claims are way overblown.

This is not to say that there aren't some benefits to breastfeeding. In poor countries where water quality is very poor, these benefits may be very large since the alternative is to use formula made with contaminated water. In developed countries—the main focus of the discussion here—this isn't an issue. Even in developed countries, there are a few health benefits of breastfeeding for children in the first year of life (more on this below).

In addition, many women enjoy nursing, so that's a benefit regardless of any long-term impacts. And if you are planning to be home with your baby for an extended period of time, breastfeeding can be convenient and inexpensive (if you are planning to return to work, this is largely not the case, given the time and costs of pumping[4]). But the vast majority of the claimed benefits of nursing simply do not hold up when we look at the best data.

---

[1] For critiques of the medicalization and pathologization of weight and larger bodies, see section 12 of this volume. You might also consider how breastfeeding is often promoted as a weight loss method for the person whose body is producing the milk, and how our negative cultural attitudes about fat affect pregnant people and those who have given birth, with narratives about "getting your body back," etc. *Ed.*

[2] http://www.ncbi.nlm.nih.gov/pubmed/18065591

[3] http://www.cdph.ca.gov/programs/breastfeeding/Documents/MO-BF-Benefits.pdf

[4] For more information about the **earnings loss** associated with breastfeeding by women in the paid labor force, especially those who breastfeed their infants past six months of age, see Rippeyoung & Noonan's 2012 *American Sociological Review* article, "Is Breastfeeding Truly Cost Free? Income Consequences of Breastfeeding for Women." *Ed.*

It is not that the claims about benefits are completely made up. They are mostly based on some data. The trouble is that the evidence they are based on is often seriously biased by the fact that women who breastfeed are typically different from those who do not. Breast-feeding rates differ dramatically across income, education and race.

In the U.S. (and most developed countries), white, wealthy women with a lot of education are much, much more likely to nurse their babies than the rest of the population. But these demographic characteristics are also linked to better outcomes for infants even independent of breastfeeding. This makes it very difficult to infer the actual *causal* effect of breastfeeding. Sure, there is a correlation between nursing and various good outcomes—but that doesn't mean that for an individual woman, nursing her baby would improve the child's life.

To give a concrete example, take this study[5] (conducted in the late 1980s) of 345 Scandinavian children that compared IQ scores at age 5 for children who were breastfed for less than three months versus more than six months. The authors find that the children who nursed for longer had higher IQ scores—about a 7 point difference. But the mothers who breastfed longer were also richer, had more education and had higher IQ scores themselves. Once the authors adjusted for these variables, the effects of nursing were much smaller.

The authors of this and other studies claim to find effects of breastfeeding because even once they adjust for the differences they see across women, the effects persist. But this assumes that the adjustments they do are able to remove *all* of the differences across women. This is extremely unlikely to be the case.

Think about it this way: Even holding constant maternal education levels, mothers with higher IQ scores are more likely[6] to nurse their babies. Maternal IQ is also linked directly with child IQ.[7] So even if researchers are able to adjust for a mother's education, they are still left with a situation in which breastfeeding behavior is associated with other characteristics (in this example, maternal IQ) that may drive infant and child outcomes.

I would argue that in the case of breastfeeding, this issue is impossible to ignore and therefore *any* study that simply compares breastfed to formula-fed infants is deeply flawed. That doesn't mean the results from such studies are necessarily wrong, just that we can't learn much from them.

You might wonder: If this is correct, why all the mania about breastfeeding? Why all the policy focus? Why put out a poster trumpeting the value of breast-feeding against obesity if it is wrong? The simplest reason is that people (including policymakers) may not stop to think about which research they should believe—and, as I've noted, there are plenty of (flawed) papers that would point to all kinds of breastfeeding benefits. It often takes time for good research to trump bad—many people still think a low-fat diet is a good idea even though randomized trial data[8] has not supported that belief.

It's also the case that when it comes to our kids, we all want to believe that what we are doing is the best thing for them. Ensuring that your child gets exclusively breast milk for six months or a year can be very challenging, and it may be that we want to believe the sacrifice has some benefits. And it does. Just not nearly as many as we might think.

To actually learn about the impacts of breastfeeding, we need to rely on studies in which breastfeeding is assigned randomly (the best option) or, in the absence of that experiment design, studies that somehow fully adjust for differences across women.

This leaves us with a small but informative set of studies. In the first camp—the randomized trial camp—we have one very large-scale study from Belarus. Known as the PROBIT trial,[9] it was run in the 1990s and continued to follow up as the children aged.[10] The study randomized women into two groups, one in which breastfeeding was encouraged and another in which it wasn't, and found that the encouragement treatment increased breastfeeding rates. The trial has studied all sorts of outcomes, including infant and child health and cognitive development.

Given how much interest there is in this topic, it is perhaps surprising that we have only this one large randomized trial of breastfeeding. It's not clear to me why this is the case. People may be so convinced of the benefits of breastfeeding that they see no need for further testing. Or it may be that a large enough study is too daunting and expensive to run. Whatever the reason, the randomized evidence is limited to this single case.

The other group of helpful studies are those of siblings—that is, studies that compare a sibling who has

---

[5]http://www.ncbi.nlm.nih.gov/pmc/articles/PMC1718901/
[6]http://www.bmj.com/content/333/7575/945.full.pdf+html
[7]http://www.bmj.com/content/333/7575/945.full.pdf+html

[8]http://www.ncbi.nlm.nih.gov/pubmed/16467234
[9]http://jama.jamanetwork.com/article.aspx?articleid=193490
[10]One concern in drawing conclusions using this study is that Belarus is not similar to the U.S., and it is certainly true that Belarus is on average poorer. The most significant concern is that the water and formula quality may be worse in the study population than in the U.S. currently. This will bias us in favor of finding larger benefits of breastfeeding than there actually are. *(Footnote in original)*

been breastfed with one who has not. These aren't as good as randomized trials, since there must be some reason why one child was nursed and one was not, but they do get around the issue of mothers who breastfeed being different from those who don't.

When people cite the benefits of breastfeeding, those benefits typically fall in one of three groups: early life health, later life health and IQ. So, what does the data say?

Breastfeeding and Infant Health

Among the most straightforward benefits claimed for breastfeeding are improvements in infant health. The randomized trial in Belarus evaluated a very large number of infant health outcomes. The results[11] are decidedly mixed.

Infants in the treatment group—who, remember, were more likely to be breastfed—had fewer gastrointestinal infections (read: less diarrhea) and were less likely to experience eczema and other rashes. However, there were no significant differences in any of the other outcomes considered. These include: respiratory infections, ear infections, croup, wheezing and infant mortality.

In other words, the evidence suggests that breastfeeding may slightly decrease your infant's chance of diarrhea and eczema but will not change the rate at which he gets colds or ear infections and will not prevent death.

Breastfeeding and Child Health and Behavior

Many sources (for example, that poster in my midwife's office) go further and claim that breastfeeding has health benefits for the child in the long term—lower obesity risk, better blood pressure and so on. And on top of this, there are the claimed benefits on behaviors—less hyperactivity, fewer behavior problems, more maternal attachment, etc.

Here, the evidence is not mixed. It rejects these claims across the board.

The PROBIT randomized trial is again the best source. The researchers analyzed the impacts of breastfeeding on allergies and asthma;[12] on cavities;[13] and on height, blood pressure, weight and various measures of obesity.[14] They found no evidence of nursing's impacts on any of these outcomes. They also found no

evidence of impacts on child behavior issues, emotional problems, peer issues, hyperactivity or maternal-child connection.[15]

These non-results are also present when we look at sibling data. This study,[16] published last year in the journal Social Science & Medicine, compares siblings who were and were not breastfed on various health and behavior outcomes—obesity, asthma, hyperactivity, parental attachment, compliant behavior. They find no impact of breastfeeding on any outcome.

These sibling results also provide a sense of why less effective research methods would have shown impacts. The researchers demonstrate that if you simply compare breastfed to formula-fed infants, there are significant differences on virtually all outcomes. However, once you compare siblings—where differences among mothers are fully adjusted for—you no longer see any positive impacts of breastfeeding.

Breastfeeding and IQ

The final area in which the benefits of breastfeeding are often proclaimed is children's cognitive development. All those fatty acids in breast milk are supposed to raise your child's IQ. Perhaps more than any other benefit, this possible IQ effect is what drives the shaming of women who choose to bottle feed (at least in certain social circles).

The randomized trial in Belarus did evaluate IQ.[17] Its results are mixed and a little confusing.

First, researchers looked at all the kids in the study. For this sample, the evaluation of IQ was done by evaluators who knew whether or not a child was in the breastfeeding-encouraged treatment group. There were no significant effects of breastfeeding on overall IQ. In addition, breastfeeding had no effect on teachers' evaluation of the children's school performance. But the researchers observed large effects of breastfeeding on verbal IQ.

Because the researchers were concerned about evaluator bias, they also had a subset of children evaluated by independent evaluators who did not know which children were breastfed. The differences in verbal IQ disappeared. This, in combination with the teacher evaluations, makes it seem likely that the overall effect was driven by the evaluators, not by true differences among children because of breastfeeding.

[11]http://www.ncbi.nlm.nih.gov/pubmed/11242425
[12]http://www.ncbi.nlm.nih.gov/pubmed/17855282
[13]http://www.ncbi.nlm.nih.gov/pubmed/17878730
[14]http://www.ncbi.nlm.nih.gov/pubmed/18065591
[15]http://www.ncbi.nlm.nih.gov/pubmed/18310164
[16]http://www.sciencedirect.com/science/article/pii/S0277953614000549
[17]http://www.ncbi.nlm.nih.gov/pubmed/18458209

This explanation seems especially likely since the effects observed in the full sample are too large to be plausible. Taking into account the impact of the program on breastfeeding rates, the results suggest that nursing increases child IQ by about 24 IQ points, which is far outside of what any other study—even one seriously biased by differences across mothers—would suggest. Overall, as others have noted,[18] this study doesn't provide especially strong support for the claim that breastfeeding increases IQ.

Comparisons among siblings (i.e., this[19] and this[20]) also show no IQ impacts. Again, these studies make clear that if you ignore differences across mothers, you can find large impacts of breastfeeding on IQ. It is only when you compare within the same family that you reveal the fact that it really doesn't seem to matter.

---

[18]http://archpsyc.jamanetwork.com/article.aspx?articleid=482895

[19]http://www.ncbi.nlm.nih.gov/pubmed/17020911

[20]http://www.sciencedirect.com/science/article/pii/S0277953614000549

The Bottom Line

Many women find breastfeeding to be an enjoyable way to bond with their babies. There is certainly no evidence that breastfeeding is any worse for a baby than formula. And maybe there are some early-life benefits in terms of digestion and rashes, which you may or may not think are important. But what the evidence says is that the popular perception that breast milk is some kind of magical substance that will lead your child to be healthy and brilliant is simply not correct.

That ice cream poster is wrong. If you want to help your child avoid becoming obese, breastfeed or not as you please. The key is to hold off on the ice cream.[21]

---

[21]For critique the efficacy of weight loss dieting specifically, see Anna G. Mirer and Lacey Alexander's work in this volume. For a more general critique of negative attitudes towards larger bodies in our culture, see Michaela Null's piece elsewhere in this volume. *Ed.*

"Black Teen Mom Manifesto: For Your Child"

by Jasmia Hamilton (writing as Jas)

Parenting is highly based on cultural and community dynamics. No one set of characteristics defines black parenting, white parenting, Asian parenting, poor or rich etcetera. However, we do have in our minds as children, adults, and parents stereotypes about the way 'our' group or some other group parenting styles and which style is superior. I think that with all the other challenges you faced or will face you should not be concerned with parenting 'like them'. Being a 'good' parent is dependent upon the ways in which you see fit raising your child and your resources and the accommodations/help you will receive. I will not touch on the disciplining of your child here because I think that is beyond the scope of my call to you to raise your child as you see fit. But I would like tell you that you are never a bad parent for the following reasons: 1—because you do not breastfeed your child, 2—because your child is not like "normal" children, 3—because you cannot give your child everything you *think* she/he needs, or 4—because you feel it is too hard.

On breastfeeding: There are a lot of campaigns to increase rates of breastfeeding among poor and minority women. The logic to breastfeed it simple, it is cheaper (not free) and it help you bond with your child. People say breastfeeding is free; it is not first of all because you should eat 'healthier' foods and eat more to make sure you are maintaining your own body's health for milk production as you try to maintain that of your baby. What is known without a doubt is that women who are able to breastfeed is that they are usually stay at home moms, women who are lucky enough to receive maternity leave (pray even harder if it is paid). Chances are that if you have yet to graduate high school, unless your child is born in the summer or during winter recess, you are right back to working with books on your bosom. Breastfeeding is a privilege and as are all relationships of privilege-penalty this fact is invisible. The teen mother peers of mine who were able to breastfeed were the ones who did not receive the support needed to stay in school and were effectively pushed out. While bonding through "the breast" is one way to attach with your child physically, psychologically, and emotionally, there will be opportunities for deep bonding (like reading, many daily hugs, museum trips, and a lot of movie time).

On a "normal" child: Every person that suppose that your child is not "normal" wish to them to be bitten by bees. Normal is the notion that your child should walk at a certain time, weigh a certain amount at a certain age and not an ounce more or less, speak at a certain time, and so forth is a half-truth. Human diversity means that sometimes we do not conform to the "normal standard" and people who seek to make everyone the same is deeply scared by difference. Now, this discussion of "normalness" does not mean that you should not communicate with healthcare providers if you are concerned with the growth or verbal/physical development of your child. You must also know that the environment that you allow your child to be in contributes to the increase or decrease of growth, sometimes you just have to take great time to talk *with* your child and not *at* your child. My mother tells me stories of how some people were concerned that I talked late yet I am excelling very fine in my life. I suppose now that maybe I was simply saving my words for people that mattered.

Do not assume that you are doing something wrong because the doctor or people who have children older than yours assume that something is wrong with your child and your style of parenting. There are a few things that should be true; your child should eventually crawl, gain weight regularly, walk and talk eventually. For example, in general kids learn to be use the toilet on their own between three and four years old, but it would *not* be abnormal if a child learns right at five or a little earlier than three. If someone tries to forcefully convince you that your need to sit your one year old on the toilet for six hours a day that is indeed not the proper way to teach a child to learn when to empty the tank. It even sounds to me like abuse, six hours is a lot of time that could be used for early language development, singing songs, and physical play. Anyhow, if you are to be concerned with something normal about your child, it should be if he or she is happy. Happy is not a very descriptive thing but when I say happy it could be smiling, hugs, excitement when you enter the door, etcetera. Happiness to me is one of the most important things to encourage all other forms of your child's development.

On giving them "everything": Every black mom and for sure every teen mom (and dads of the spectrum) that I know in my life say some variation of the following. 'All I want for my child is for them to have everything I did not have'. I am twenty-one and have never been to Disney World, maybe it is the case that I would someday like to take my children there but I am not with sadness that my mom could not afford to take me and my siblings there. That place is expensive as hell and there is a high chance I would imagine for contracting horrible colds, flus, and stomach bugs. In college my peers talked about being out of the country and having been to Disney World so many times that they became bored with it—that tells me that well maybe it is not so good after all. In these moments, I must remind them that on the first day of class and during anecdotal discussion that when I say, "I am from Chicago", "in Chicago", "Chicago is different than my college town because", I really mean Chicago and not Naperville, Elgin, or Skokie. Money and spending it in capitalistic commercial places is one part of giving your child everything or better than what you had but it is not everything.

One indisputable way to give your child everything is to give him/her what is needed to survive. The basics: food, clothes, a clean bottom, shelter, and human contact. One of my high school teachers, who I assumed to be middle class, as he and his wife were both employed, said that he did not purchase his children shoes until they were one year old. My classmates and I casually called him a cheapskate but in actuality it made sense. Babies usually do not walk a lot on their own until they

are one year old and up until that point you would have to otherwise buy shoes every 2–5 weeks if you were committed to keeping their feet fly. I am sure that all of the money my partner, family, and I spent on Baby Jordan's and Nike's would have been better invested in these same companies to help contribute to a college fund. If you will not budge on fly feet, that is fine, however, I think that there is a clear line between silly spending and giving your child the things in life that they will remember such that you feel that you are giving them everything you never had. If Mike's every few weeks means that you need to borrow money for essentials (diapers, sanitary napkins, formula) then maybe this is not actually giving your child everything they need. Again, even as I try to only engage you and not be 'like them' I want you to be critical in your goals for yourself and your child.

On being too hard: Feeling (or believing) that being a parent is too hard is not a feeling of only black young teen moms or 'weak' mothers. Life is hard, damn sure being a parent is hard. I do not know any mom, dad, or parental figure who ever said parenting is easy regardless of race, class, educational status, ability, or political status. Now I must not sugarcoat the fact that some people have less stress doing so because they have a lot of support (to sleep, eat, educate themselves, etc.) usually we may think that money is the most important thing for ease of parenting. Money is important, but human support is also very, very essential to not experiencing post-birth depression, incidents with your child, missed feedings, and maintaining a functioning mental status.

When things are "too hard" this simply means that you are learning to master or become more efficient at something that you have never experienced before and this is completely expected. Like I said before and probably will say again over the course of this text, there is no one way to be a 'good' parent. My experience as a parent was not as hard as I know it could have been because my sons were co-raised in their early years by their dad, my mother, my brothers, my sister, their paternal grandmother, and many aunts and uncles. As I mentioned earlier there are certainly push and pull factors to not asking for help (i.e. help does not exist, your pride is in the way, you do not know who to ask, the people who would otherwise help will not in this instance) you should do so anyway. Black women as parents and certainly black teen moms (it would be unfair for me not to note that poor mothers too and all teen moms more broadly) are socially plagued by the bad parent stereotype. The illogical and often racist and classist arguments you may hear are that: we are welfare queens, we are so unbearable that we are driving men away, blah blah, and because of all this many of our sons aspire to be drug dealers. It is not unreasonable of me to generalize the statement that black women have it harder because of our race, gender, and in general lower economic status. So with this on being too hard, I feel that you have the right to say and feel it is too hard. The biggest challenge is recognizing that the hardness is not strictly because of your position as a teen mom. Parenting and guardianship is hard for everyone. Rest assured that things will get better and less hard (even if they may feel as though they become worse before the sun shines again).

GENDER-BASED VIOLENCE

"Breaking the Silence"

By Megan Steffer

Rape and sexual assault are public health issues that most of us would prefer to ignore. In 1987, it was first reported that approximately 27 percent of college-aged women had been rape victims since age 14.[1] Further studies have gone on to specify that anywhere from 15–20 percent of women are raped during their time as an undergraduate student.[2] These numbers rise significantly when statistics also include attempted rape and sexual assault: studies report that as many as 57 percent of college women have been victims of some kind of sexual assault during their college careers.[3] Despite having rape prevention programs in place at almost every major university in the country, current figures still estimate that one in four college women are survivors of rape or attempted rape.[4]

When many people think of rape, they imagine a sinister-looking man sexually assaulting a woman in a dark alley. While these situations do occur, the vast majority of rapes (80%) occur between people who know each other, and take place in environments that are generally considered to be safe.[5] Rapists also do not match most stereotypes: men who commit rape are our friends, co-workers, neighbors, and relatives. In some groups (such as sports teams and fraternities) sexual aggressiveness is seen as a positive trait for men to have. From conversations I've had, it seems that many rapists don't even know what they have committed is rape, assuming that it was okay because a girl was drunk, provocatively dressed, or displaying "suggestive" behavior.

Something clearly needs to be changed in our society when this kind of violence towards women is accepted or ignored by the majority of the population. Even women at the highest risk of becoming victims of rape seem ultimately unconvinced that it could happen to them. Even me.

My story is all too typical. I am the one college woman in four. My experience began on an average Saturday night, partying with my roommates at a co-worker's house outside campus. Not in the mood to drink, I shared a beer with a roommate so people would stop pestering us about the fact that we weren't holding red cups of beer.

As the night wore on, my roommates grew bored and wanted to go home, but I was having fun with my co-worker and his friends. He assured me that he would get me home safely. I bid my roommates adieu, refilled my red cup with water, and returned to the party. Less than 15 minutes later, I had my last memory of the evening.

I opened my eyes the next morning, naked, in a room I had never seen before. Next to me was my co-worker, naked and sound asleep. Large purple bruises covered both of my arms and legs, two parallel lines were burned into my right forearm, and dried blood covered my thighs and the sheets all around me. I saw my clothes nearby. My only thought: "Get out now." As I climbed out of the bed, he opened his eyes and gazed at my bloody, bruised, and burned body. "Good morning, beautiful."

When I asked him what had happened he just laughed. "You had a good time," he told me, after grumbling about how he'd have to wash my blood out of his formerly clean sheets. "Take me home now," I demanded. After assuring him that I did not, in fact, want to stay for breakfast, he got his keys.

The following days were extremely difficult, as I tried to determine what actually happened. To me, it is pretty clear that "date-rape drugs" were involved. These sedatives, which include GHB, Rophynol, and Ketamine, usually are colorless and odorless when added to a drink. The sedatives often make the person who drinks them appear to drunk and makes them lose their memory; for this reason, they have become widely known for their use in conjunction with rape and sexual assault. Although I will never be completely sure that someone gave me such a sedative, the blood and pain clearly tell me I was raped.

Thankfully, although I knew him from work, our interactions there were few and far between. I saw him in the building two or three times after that night, and did my best to avoid him. When I saw him at work, he acted as if nothing had happened, asking: "Why haven't you called?" Some days he would show up in the parking lot or outside my apartment complex, but I refused to talk to him. The last time I saw him was when he showed up at a restaurant where I worked, told me he missed me, and kissed me on the cheek. I almost slapped him. He sat in another server's section, and I avoided that part of the restaurant until he was gone.

It has been a year and a half since that night. At first, I couldn't even think about what had happened, not wanting to face the reality of what I had been through. I did not report the crime. I knew that my lack of memory about the evening would weaken my case. I was also confused because I had once seen this man as a friend and wanted to believe that he had not betrayed my trust.

Eventually, I began talking about my experience. Some friends seemed hesitant to believe my story, suggesting that I could have been drunk and blacked out, or that I had led him on. Others did believe me, but continued to interact with him like nothing had happened.

Similar reactions have been documented across the country. We simply don't want to believe that rape happens. We especially don't want to accept that our friends or family members could be perpetrators or victims of rape. Before this experience, I didn't either.

As difficult as it was, I found that talking about what had happened was the most helpful thing in allowing me to move on with my life. Even after I had shared my story, it seemed as though I was talking about something I had seen in a movie or heard from a friend, not an experience that I had lived through. It wasn't until about three months later, when I was beginning a romantic relationship with another man, that the reality of it all finally hit me.

When he touched me in certain ways, or even cast certain looks at me, it could cause bouts of uncontrolled panic and grief. Fortunately, he was very understanding, talked with me about my experience, and helped me to work through the pain. I was very lucky to have someone who was so patient and supportive of me as I tried to make sense of my feelings and reactions. After accepting the fact that this experience was not something that I could simply block out of my life, I decided to seek counseling at the campus health center. Through the support of some close friends and the counseling sessions, I am finally able to speak openly about my experience, and recognize the value of being able to share it with others.

If one benefit can come from this, it is that I can tell you that rape does happen, it is a problem, and we can make a difference. Please, if you are a victim of sexual violence, start talking about it. Ask your daughters and friends about their experiences. Most importantly, be ready to listen and support these women as their stories unfold.

REFERENCES

1. Koss MP, Gidycz CA, Wisniewski N. "The scope of rape: incidence and prevalence of sexual aggression and victimization in a national sample of higher education students." *Journal of Consulting and Clinical Psychology* 1987; 55(2): 162–170.

2. Koss MP, Dinero TE, Siebel CA et al. "Stranger and acquaintance rape: are there differences in women's experiences." *Psychlogy of Women Quarterly* 1988; 12: 1–24.

3. Gary JM. "An overview of sexual assault on campus." In: Gary JM (ed). *The Campus Community Confronts Sexual Assault: Institutional Issues and Campus Awareness*, Holmes Beach, FL: Learning Publications, 1994, 1–9, Brener ND, McMahon PM, Warren CW et al. "Forced sexual intercourse and associated health-risk behaviors among female college students in the United States. *Journal of Consulting and Clinical Psychology* 1999; 67(2): 252–9; Fisher B, Cullen F, Turner M. *The Sexual Victimization of College Women*. Washington, DC: U.S. Dept. of Justice, 2000.

4. Fisher, Cullen, and Turner, see above.

5. Tjaden P, Thoennes N. *Full Report of the Prevalence, Incidence, and Consequences of Violence Against Women: Findings from the National Violence Against Women Survey* (Report NCJ 183781). Washington, DC: National Institute of Justice, 2000.

"The Ashley Treatment and Who Tells the Story"

By s.e. smith

Growth attenuation—also known as the Ashley Treatment—is one of the most bizarre, deeply troubling, and horrific 'treatments' inflicted on disabled children, with their parents performing surgical mutilation and aggressive hormone treatments on nonconsenting children because, they claim, it's better for them. While it is thankfully unusual, it has been used in a number of places around the world with little criticism, except from disabled people,[1] who have been largely ignored—and while nondisabled bioethicists may express some discomfort with the idea, they still seem to think it's more or less okay.[2]

The Ashley Treatment entered the public sphere in 2007, when the parents of "Ashley X" spoke out about a series of medical procedures they'd subjected their developmentally disabled daughter to, ostensibly with the purpose of improving her quality of life and making it easier for them to care for her. The procedures involved removing her breast buds and uterus to keep her in a state of permanent infantilism, paired with the use of growth attenuation hormones to keep her artificially small—her parents referred to her as a "pillow angel." This horrific treatment attracted worldwide discussion and triggered an ethics review and widespread condemnation from disability rights activists concerned about the procedures in light of the long history of medical experimentation with disabled bodies. Despite vocal opposition to the treatment, however, numerous other parents have imitated it, largely to widespread praise from other parents and the media, including in a March 2016 *New York Times* piece discussed below.

Periodically, it pops up in the news again, the obnoxious pimple of disability news, and every time, the people who get to talk about it are 'experts' who aren't disabled, and parents. Stories are inevitably framed from a parental perspective, talking about how *difficult* it is to care for disabled people, and how we should have sympathy for parents who were expecting beautiful perfect children and instead ended up with broken duds, people who would need extensive support and care throughout their lives. But lo, there's a 'treatment' that facilitates care, turning children into 'pillow angels' who are lightweight, less messy and inconvenient. Perpetual innocents.

I remarked in 2012 that this is incredibly dehumanizing,[3] as such aggressive 'treatment' would never be considered acceptable if nondisabled children were involved, but it's reasoned to be a 'moral compromise' when children are 'confined to a wheelchair' or 'nonverbal' or 'profoundly disabled.' Yet, people still do it, and they keep being the subjects of uncritical stories — or stories that talk about their 'difficult choice' to mutilate their children, but don't really explain *why* this choice is difficult, how harmful it is to children and the disability community, why disabled people are so upset by it.

---

[1] While "person-first" language is still generally promoted in the United States, "disabled people" and "disabled person" have been the preferred language for disabled people in the United Kingdom for some time. Many disability activists in the United States are now adopting similar language to make the point that they do not think that the person can, or should, be separated from their disability, especially in a social environment that creates or intensifies many of the negative effects of disability through a general lack of accommodations. *Ed.*

[2] http://meloukhia.net/2011/01/on_growth_attenuation_and_moral_compromise/

[3] http://www.theguardian.com/commentisfree/2012/mar/16/ashley-treatment-disabled-people

The *New York Times* has been the latest to join the fray, with a March feature by Genevieve Field[4] in which she managed to go on at length about how disability is inconvenient for parents, interviewing parents and 'experts' in a piece she claimed was supposed to be a neutral, evenhanded representation of 'both sides' of a hotly-contested issue. The fact that the basic humanity of disabled people is still considered to be a contested issue is a disturbing testimony to the disablism that runs rampantly through society. It's hard to believe that a feature on forced sterilization and surgical torture along with nonconsensual use of hormones and other drugs would be considered 'balanced' only if it included the other side unless it was a story about people who aren't considered humans.

But in this case, 'the other side' is the side directly affected by such surgeries and the continued tolerance for them. The article didn't include a single quote from a person who identified as disabled, let alone quotes from disabled parents, disabled bioethicists, or other disabled people who are also experts in this field. Only a handful of references were made, one including a snide comment about being 'bitter,' and the article centered squarely on the parental experience, which is a common trend—as is assuming that disabled people can't be parents, as the article lingered over how *hard* parenting is when your children aren't born perfect.

Features on practices like these are critically necessary. Many nondisabled people don't know that the Ashley Treatment exists, or they aren't familiar with the specifics involved. They should be aware that disabled children with some developmental impairments are being subjected to horrific medical procedures without consent or respect for autonomy by nondisabled people, surrounded by an approving audience of nondisabled people including physicians, surgeons, bioethics committees, and the like. But these stories shouldn't be narrated by nondisabled people: They should be narrated by disabled people, speaking for themselves.

Numerous disabled journalists would be great candidates for writing an excellent, strong, powerfully-researched feature on the Ashley Treatment, one that would involve interviewing lots of people about their lived experience as well as having conversations with disabled experts in the medical and bioethics field. Such a feature would focus on the real stakeholders in this conversation, the people with bodies and lives on the line in a culture where they are hated, feared, and presented as incalculable burdens that ruin their parents' lives. Features like this are disablist, and also

incredibly harmful. They're a reminder to disabled readers — yes, disabled people read things — that they don't belong in society, and will always be considered lesser, not quite human. Only through infantalization will their humanity be recognized. Only through procedures that keep them 'innocent' will they be considered acceptable.

Criticism of growth attenuation is complicated and extensive, but one important facet is the denial of autonomy, giving disabled people no control over their bodies. By keeping developmentally disabled people in a permanently childlike state, the treatment makes them entirely dependent on parents and caregivers — defenders argue that the procedure is only used on those with "severe" disabilities who would already be reliant on assistance with tasks of daily living, and that by keeping disabled people smaller, it facilitates ease of care and makes it easier for parents to keep their children at home, rather than in institutions.

However, this permanent infantilism is also extremely dehumanizing, and as the treatment tends to be deployed specifically for keeping female-assigned disabled people small, it carries heavy implications in a society that already exerts tremendous control over women's bodies — this is a procedure that literally strips women and girls of agency, desexualizing them and turning them into passive objects. One thing it doesn't do, however, despite claims from some defenders, is remove the risk that women and girls will be sexually assaulted and abused. Disabled people, especially disabled women, particularly those with developmental disabilities, are at a very high risk of sexual and physical assault[5] — and keeping them in a state of eternal childhood could exacerbate that problem.

The *New York Times* feature didn't talk about sexual and physical assault and disability, let alone how forcible sterilization can facilitate these acts. It didn't talk about the thoughtful, thorough dissections of the Ashley Treatment from the disability community. It didn't talk about objectification, infantalization, or dehumanization. It made a passing reference to the 'social model' of disability that looked like it was pulled straight from Wikipedia, occupying not even an entire sentence — that was it.

Of course, when things like this are published and the disability community comments on them, most people don't listen. Those who do are swift to defend the prac-

---

[4]http://www.nytimes.com/2016/03/27/magazine/should-parents-of-severely-disabled-children-be-allowed-to-stop-their-growth.html

[5]Some sources estimate the rate of sexual assault for women with intellectual disabilities at about 80%, with half of those who have been assaulted experiencing more than ten separate assaults. Research in the mid-1990s found that only 3% of abuse cases involving developmentally disabled people were ever reported. For sources and more information on this issue, see: http://www.wcsap.org/disability-community *Ed.*

tices discussed, as Field certainly did when people challenged her. Parents come pouring out of the woodwork to talk about how difficult their children are and how they wish they could have this series of procedures done on their own children. Nondisabled people lecture about disabled lives and the value of disabled bodies. At the end of the day, the disabled critics are labeled 'bitter' and their voices discarded, because, really, who needs to pay attention to a bunch of whiny cripples?

When talking about disability issues, the media has a duty of care to center disabled voices in those conversations, and *Times* editors did a tremendous disservice to this piece by not demanding that Fields educate herself. Given the low representation of disabled people in editorial, that's not a big surprise — because it's very rare to see a nondisabled editor carefully considering the potential repercussions of a disability-related piece, let alone learning from critiques of things like this.

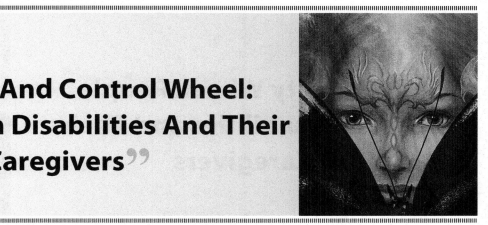

"Power And Control Wheel: People With Disabilities And Their Caregivers"

Physical VIOLENCE Sexual

POWER & CONTROL

COERCION AND THREATS:
Threatening to hurt the person; withold basic support and rights; terminate relationship and leave the person unattended; report noncompliance with the program; use more intrusive equipment. Using consequences and punishments to gain compliant behavior. Pressuring the person to engage in fraud or other crimes.

INTIMIDATION:
Raising a hand or using looks, actions, or gestures to create fear. Destroying property and abusing pets. Mistreating service animals. Displaying weapons.

EMOTIONAL ABUSE:
Punishing or ridiculing. Refusing to speak and ignoring requests. Ridiculing the person's culture, traditions, religion, and personal tastes. Enforcing a negative reinforcement program or any behavior program the person doesn't consent to.

CAREGIVER PRIVILEGE:
Treating person as a child, servant. Making unilateral decisions. Defining narrow, limiting roles and responsibilities. Providing care in a way that accentuates the person's dependence and vulnerability. Giving an opinion as if it were the person's opinion. Denying the right to privacy. Ignoring, discouraging, or prohibiting the exercise of full capabilities.

ISOLATION:
Controlling access to friends, family, and neighbors. Controlling access to phone, TV, news. Limiting employment possibilities because of caregiver schedule. Discouraging contact with the case manager or advocate.

ECONOMIC ABUSE:
Using person's property and money for staff's benefit. Stealing. Using property and/or money as a reward pr punishment in a behavior program. Making financial decisions based on agency or family needs. Limiting access to financial information and resources resulting in unnecessary impoverishment.

WITHHOLD, MISUSE, OR DELAY NEEDED SUPPORTS:
Using medication to sedate the person for agency convenience. Ignoring equipment safety requirements. Breaking or not fixing adaptive equipment. Refusing to use or destroying communication devices. Withdrawing care or equipment to immobilize the person. Using equipment to torture people.

MINIMIZE, JUSTIFY, AND BLAME:
Denying or making light of abuse. Denying the physical and emotional pain of people with disabilities. Justifying rules that limit autonomy, dignity, and relationships for program's operational efficiency. Excusing abuse as behavior management or as due to caregiver stress. Blaming the disability for abuse. Saying the person is not a "good reporter" of abuse.

Physical VIOLENCE Sexual

Reprinted by permission of the National Center on Domestic and Sexual Violence.

"Equality Wheel: People with Disabilities and Their Caregivers"

NONVIOLENCE

NEGOTIATION AND FAIRNESS:
Discussing the impact of the caregiver's actions with the person. Accepting change. Compromising. Seeking mutually satisfying resolutions to conflict. Using positive reinforcement to affect change.

NON-THREATENING BEHAVIOR:
Creating a safe environment through words and actions. Treating property, pets, and service animals with care. Having no weapons on the premises.

CHOICE AND PARTNERSHIP:
Listening to the person. Acting as agent of person rather than agency. Sharing caregiving responsibilities with other caregivers and family. Being a positive, non-violent role model. Encouraging the person to speak freely and to communicate with others. Focusing on the person's abilities and maximizing their independence.

DIGNITY AND RESPECT:
Encouraging positive communication. Honoring culture, tradition, religion, and personal tastes. Allowing for differences. Developing service and behavior program collaboratively.

ECONOMIC EQUALITY:
Acting responsibly as fiscal agent. Developing a plan where access to money or property is not contingent on appropriate behavior. Having purchasing decisions represent preferences/needs of the person. Advocating and brokering all possible resources of the person. Sharing and explaining financial information.

EQUALITY with inter-dependence

INVOLVEMENT:
Encouraging personal relationships. Assisting in gaining access to information and employment. Facilitating involvement within residence and job site. Encouraging contact with the case manager or advocate.

RESPONSIBLE PROVISION OF SERVICES:
Using medications properly. Maintaining and using equipment in timely and appropriate manner. Encouraging access to and use of adaptive equipment. Showing sensitivity to the person's vulnerability when providing care.

HONESTY AND ACCOUNTABILITY:
Admitting being wrong. Understanding that everyone has feelings. Being flexible in policies and practices. Using positive behavioral practice. Communicating openly and truthfully. Acknowledging that abuse is never an acceptable practice.

NONVIOLENCE

Reprinted by permission of the National Center on Domestic and Sexual Violence.

"Violence Against Native Women: Battering"

From *Sacred Circle – National Resource Center to End Violence Against Native Women & the Domestic Abuse Intervention Project*

PHYSICAL VIOLENCE ~ pushing ~ slapping ~ pulling hair ~ punching ~ kicking ~ choking

physically attacking the sexual parts of her body ~ **SEXUAL VIOLENCE** ~ treating her like a sex object

MALE PRIVILEGE
Treats her like a servant. Makes all the big decisions. Acts like the "king of the castle." Defines men's and women's roles.

ISOLATION
Controls what she does, who she sees and talks to, what she reads. Limits her outside involvement. Uses jealousy to justify actions.

INTIMIDATION
Makes her afraid by using looks, actions, gestures. Smashes things. Destroys her property. Abuses pets. Displays weapons.

EMOTIONAL ABUSE
Puts her down. Makes her feel bad about herself. Calls her names. Makes her think she's crazy. Plays mind games. Humiliates her. Makes her feel guilty.

MINIMIZE, LIE, AND BLAME
Makes light of the abuse and doesn't take her concerns seriously. Says the abuse didn't happen. Shifts responsibility for abusive behavior. Says she caused it.

USING CHILDREN
Makes her feel guilty about the children. Uses the children to relay messages. Uses visitation to harass her. Threatens to take away the children.

ECONOMIC ABUSE
Prevents her from working. Makes her ask for money. Gives her an allowance. Takes her money. Doesn't let her know about or access family income.

COERCION AND THREATS
Makes and/or carries out threats to do something to hurt her. Threatens to leave her, to commit suicide, to report her to welfare. Makes her drop charges. Makes her do illegal things.

CULTURAL ABUSE
Competes over "Indian-ness." Misinterprets culture to prove male superiority/female submission. Uses relatives to beat her up. Buys into "blood quantum" competitions.

RITUAL ABUSE
Prays against her. Defines spirituality as masculine. Stops her from practicing her ways. Uses religion as a threat: "God doesn't allow divorce." Says her period makes her "dirty."

UNNATURAL POWER AND CONTROL

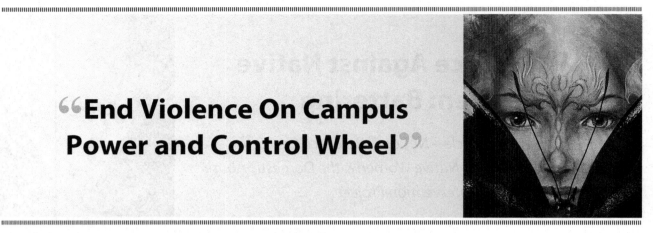

"End Violence On Campus Power and Control Wheel"

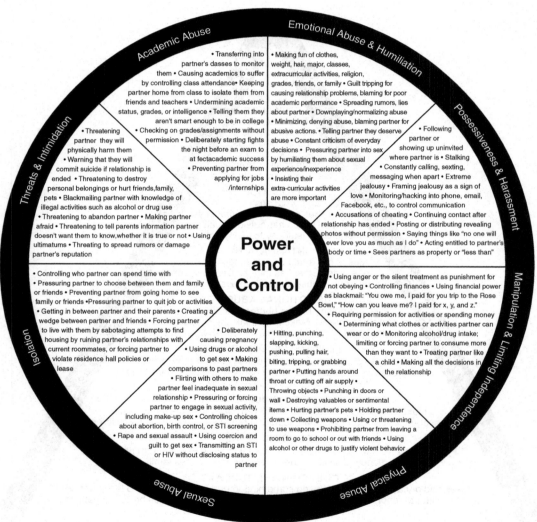

Power and Control (center)

Academic Abuse
• Transferring into partner's classes to monitor them • Causing academics to suffer by controlling class attendance• Keeping partner home from class to isolate them from friends and teachers • Undermining academic status, grades, or intelligence • Telling them they aren't smart enough to be in college • Checking on grades/assignments without permission • Deliberately starting fights the night before an exam to at fectacademic success • Preventing partner from applying for jobs /internships

Emotional Abuse & Humiliation
• Making fun of clothes, weight, hair, major, classes, extracurricular activities, religion, grades, friends, or family • Guilt tripping for causing relationship problems, blaming for poor academic performance • Spreading rumors, lies about partner • Downplaying/normalizing abuse • Minimizing, denying abuse, blaming partner for abusive actions. • Telling partner they deserve abuse • Constant criticism of everyday decisions • Pressuring partner into sex by humiliating them about sexual experience/inexperience • Insisting their extra-curricular activities are more important

Threats & Intimidation
• Threatening partner they will physically harm them • Warning that they will commit suicide if relationship is ended • Threatening to destroy personal belongings or hurt friends,family, pets • Blackmailing partner with knowledge of illegal activities such as alcohol or drug use • Threatening to abandon partner • Making partner afraid • Threatening to tell parents information partner doesn't want them to know,whether it is true or not • Using ultimatums • Threating to spread rumors or damage partner's reputation

Possessiveness & Harassment
• Following partner or showing up uninvited where partner is • Stalking • Constantly calling, sexting, messaging when apart • Extreme jealousy • Framing jealousy as a sign of love • Monitoring/hacking into phone, email, Facebook, etc., to control communication • Accusations of cheating • Continuing contact after relationship has ended • Posting or distributing revealing photos without permission • Saying things like "no one will ever love you as much as I do" • Acting entitled to partner's body or time • Sees partners as property or "less than"

Isolation
• Controlling who partner can spend time with • Pressuring partner to choose between them and family or friends • Preventing partner from going home to see family or friends •Pressuring partner to quit job or activities • Getting in between partner and their parents • Creating a wedge between partner and friends • Forcing partner to live with them by sabotaging attempts to find housing by ruining partner's relationships with current roommates, or forcing partner to violate residence hall policies or lease

Manipulation & Limiting Independence
• Using anger or the silent treatment as punishment for not obeying • Controlling finances • Using financial power as blackmail: "You owe me, I paid for you trip to the Rose Bowl," "How can you leave me? I paid for x, y, and z." • Requiring permission for activities or spending money • Determining what clothes or activities partner can wear or do • Monitoring alcohol/drug intake; limiting or forcing partner to consume more than they want to • Treating partner like a child • Making all the decisions in the relationship

Sexual Abuse
• Deliberately causing pregnancy • Using drugs or alcohol to get sex • Making comparisons to past partners • Flirting with others to make partner feel inadequate in sexual relationship • Pressuring or forcing partner to engage in sexual activity, including make-up sex • Controlling choices about abortion, birth control, or STI screening • Rape and sexual assault • Using coercion and guilt to get sex • Transmitting an STI or HIV without disclosing status to partner

Physical Abuse
• Hitting, punching, slapping, kicking, pushing, pulling hair, biting, tripping, or grabbing partner • Putting hands around throat or cutting off air supply • Throwing objects • Punching in doors or wall • Destroying valuables or sentimental items • Hurting partner's pets • Holding partner down • Collecting weapons • Using or threatening to use weapons • Prohibiting partner from leaving a room to go to school or out with friends • Using alcohol or other drugs to justify violent behavior

Help is available.

University Health Services
End Violence on Campus (UHS EVOC)
608-265-5600 (option 3)
evoc@uhs.wisc.edu
evoc.wisc.edu

Domestic Abuse Intervention Services (DAIS)
24-hour helpline: 608-251-4445
abuseintervention.org
24-hour texting helpline:
Text "HOPE" to 20121

Reprinted by permission of UW-Madison University Health Services.

"2014 Report on Intimate Partner Violence in Lesbian, Gay, Bisexual, Transgender, Queer and HIV-Affected Communities in the U.S. Released Today"

From the *National Coalition of Anti-Violence Programs* (October 27, 2015)

- For a fourth year in a row cisgender men killed by their male partners were most impacted by IPV homicide
- LGBTQ and HIV-affected communities of color, bisexual survivors, transgender communities, and cisgender male survivors were uniquely and disproportionately impacted by IPV
- LGBTQ and HIV-affected survivors on public assistance were more likely to face physical violence and injury as a result of IPV
- A higher percentage of LGBTQ and HIV-affected survivors of intimate partner violence attempted to access the police, courts, and domestic violence shelters for support compared to previous years

NATIONAL—Today the National Coalition of Anti-Violence Programs (NCAVP)[1] released its report *Lesbian, Gay, Bisexual, Transgender, Queer and HIV-Affected Intimate Partner Violence in 2014*. For this report - the most comprehensive of its kind—NCAVP collected data concerning intimate partner violence (IPV) within LGBTQ and HIV-affected relationships from 16 anti-violence programs in 13 states across the country, including Arizona, California, Colorado, Illinois, Massachusetts, Michigan, Minnesota, Missouri, New York, Ohio, Rhode Island, Texas and Vermont.

General Findings

In 2014, NCAVP programs received **2,166 reports of IPV, a decrease of nearly 20%** from the 2,697 reports received in 2013. This decrease between 2013 and 2014 follows an increase between 2012 and 2013, and variation in the total number of reports received each year are a normal occurrence from year to year. Several contributing NCAVP member programs which saw a decrease attributed the decrease in their area to less visibility for their organization due to staffing changes, including

OutFront Minnesota, the New York City Anti-Violence Project, and Community United Against Violence in San Francisco. "While NCAVP saw a decrease in reports in 2014, this data remains some of the most comprehensive data available and includes reports of LGBTQ and HIV-affected IPV which may not have been reported to the police," said Beverly Tillery from the New York City Anti-Violence Project. "The need to bring visibility and resources to the experiences and needs of LGBTQ survivors of IPV remains a critical issue facing our country."

Homicide Rates

NCAVP documented **15 IPV homicides in 2014**. This is down 29% from 21 IPV homicides in 2013. For a fourth year in a row, cisgender men were disproportionately affected by IPV homicide. **Of the 15 homicides documented in 2014, 8 (53%) of the victims were cisgender men, 7 of whom were killed by current or former male partners. In 2014, 47% of all reported IPV homicide victims were cisgender men killed by their male partners.** "We know from the National Intimate Partner Violence Survey (NISVS) by the Centers for Disease Control that lesbians, gay men, and bisexual people experience IPV at the same

[1]http://www.ncavp.org

or higher rates as non-LGB people, and actual homicide numbers are likely much higher," said Vanessa Volz from Sojourner House in Providence, Rhode Island. "The lack of awareness and visibility in the media—and in society generally—around fatal intimate partner violence as it affects LGBTQ and HIV-affected people needs to change[2]."

Disproportionate Experiences of Violence

People of Color Survivors

For the fourth year in a row, LGBTQ and HIV—affected people of color made up the majority (51%) of IPV survivors. Specifically, LGBTQ Black/African American survivors were 1.89 times more likely to experience physical violence within IPV when compared to all non-black survivors. Latin@[3] survivors were 1.59 times more likely to experience threats by their partners when compared to all non-Latin@ survivors. "LGBTQ and HIV-affected survivors of color often face racism along with homophobia, biphobia and transphobia when interacting with first responders or attempting to access supportive services," said Lynne Sprague from Survivors Organizing for Liberation in Colorado. "It is imperative that responses to LGBTQ and HIV-affected intimate partner violence survivors of color address not just institutional anti-LGBTQ and HIV bias - but also racism."

Transgender Survivors

The 2014 report found that transgender survivors were 1.98 times more likely to experience IPV in public areas, and 3.39 times more likely to experience discrimination than people who did not identify as transgender. "Transgender people face increased risk of violence for many reasons, including transphobia and discrimination on the basis of gender identity," said Mieko Failey, from the Los Angeles LGBT Center. "It is critical that we address the barriers transgender survivors experience in accessing resources and provide supportive programs that explicitly include the

transgender community," added Susan Holt, also from the Los Angeles LGBT Center.

Bisexual Survivors

The 2014 report found that for a second year in a row, bisexual survivors were more likely to experience sexual violence within IPV. People who identified as bisexual were 2.02 times more likely to experience sexual violence than people who did not identify as bisexual. NCAVP's 2014 data reinforces the findings of the NISVS. The NISVS report revealed that 61% of bisexual women and 37% of bisexual men experienced rape, physical violence, and/or stalking in their lifetimes within IPV. "Research indicates that bisexual survivors are impacted by intimate partner violence in a way that is both distinct and concerning," said Eva Wood from OutFront Minnesota. "Comprehensive and inclusive information on sexual orientation is necessary in data collection, research studies and elsewhere so that we can better understand the unique ways that bisexual survivors are impacted by IPV and their experiences in accessing care."

Undocumented Transgender Survivors

The 2014 report showed that **undocumented transgender survivors were more likely to experience discrimination and harassment.** Undocumented transgender survivors were 3.83 times more likely to experience discrimination, and 1.78 times more likely to experience harassment than people who do not identify as transgender and undocumented. "Undocumented transgender survivors are at a unique risk for IPV because abusive partners can threaten them with their immigration status, and survivors may be reluctant to seek support for fear of revealing their immigration status to law enforcement and immigration authorities," said Lidia Salazar from Community United Against Violence in San Francisco. "Now is the time to enact compassionate, comprehensive immigration reform to reduce barriers for LGBTQ and HIV-affected immigrant survivors of IPV."

LGBTQ Survivors and Public Assistance

For the first time, NCAVP collected data on experiences of LGBTQ and HIV-affected survivors who are on public assistance in an effort to expand current research to analyze the economic impacts of violence and relationship between socio-economic status and violence. The 2014 report found that **LGBTQ survi-**

---

[2]Note that while cisgender men are the largest group of IPV homicide victims in this study, overall violence against the "LGBTQ+ community" still tends to disproportionately affect transgender women, especially transgender women of color. Additionally, many homicides of transgender women might be considered IPV but for various reasons are not officially categorized that way. *Ed.*

[3]Latin@' is a term often used to avoid the default gendering inherent to nouns and adjectives in Spanish. You may also see people use 'Latinx.' Both terms avoid treating masculinity as the unmarked state, and are inclusive of non-binary people as well. *Ed.*

vors of color were **3.34 times more likely to be on public assistance** than people who do not identify as LGBTQ people of color, and **transgender women of color were 8.43 times more likely to be on public assistance** than people who did not identify as transgender women of color. Additionally, **survivors on public assistance in 2014 were 3.13 times more likely to experience physical violence and 5.71 times more likely to be injured** than survivors who were not on public assistance. "Economic violence is often a central form of abuse within IPV, and survivors who face societal economic vulnerabilities may be more vulnerable to economic abuse and exploitation from their abusive partners," said Chai Jindasurat from the New York City Anti-Violence Project. "Policymakers and funders should fund economic empowerment programs targeted at LGBTQ and HIV-affected communities, particularly LGBTQ and HIV-affected communities of color, transgender communities, immigrant communities, and low-income communities."

Service Provision

NCAVP's 2014 report found that a higher percentage of survivors attempted to access formal systems and services, and when they did, example, **in 2014 a higher percentage of LGBTQ and HIV-affected survivors (24%) sought orders of protection compared to 2013 (17%). Of those orders of protection, 85% were granted in 2014 compared to 58% in 2013.** With regard to shelter services, **15% of survivors sought shelter access in 2014**, compared to 6% in 2013. Finally, the report revealed that **55% of survivors provided information about police engagement reported their experience of IPV to the police in 2014**, a substantial increase from 2013, when 37% of survivors reported to police. "The fact that LGBTQ and HIV-affected people were more likely to access systems and services in 2014 is encouraging, and speaks to the work of LGBTQ organizations, and others, to reform violence response systems and expand the national discourse on intimate partner violence," said Aaron Eckhardt from BRAVO in Ohio, "As we begin to reach a collective understanding that anyone can experience IPV in their relationships, systems and

services will have to continue to evolve to support these survivors."

Recommendations

The report includes specific policy recommendations, including the following key recommendations related to the findings highlighted above. There are further recommendations published in the full report.

- Policymakers should ensure that the federal government collects comprehensive and inclusive information on sexual orientation and gender identity, whenever demographic data is requested in studies, surveys, and research, including IPV.
- Policymakers, researchers and advocates should ensure that LGBTQ survivors are included in all prevention assessments, including homicide and lethality assessments, and that coordinated community responses include specific and targeted programming for LGBTQ survivors.
- Policymakers and funders should fund LGBTQ and HIV-affected specific IPV prevention initiatives.
- Policymakers and funders should fund economic empowerment programs targeted at LGBTQ and HIV-affected communities, particularly LGBTQ and HIV-affected communities of color, transgender communities, immigrant communities, and low-income communities.
- Policymakers should enact compassionate, comprehensive immigration reform to reduce barriers for LGBTQ and HIV-affected immigrant survivors of IPV.

NCAVP works to prevent, respond to, and end all forms of violence against and within lesbian, gay, bisexual, transgender, queer (LGBTQ), and HIV-affected communities. NCAVP is a national coalition of 53 local member programs and affiliate organizations in 25 states, Canada, and Washington DC, who create systemic and social change. We strive to increase power, safety, and resources through data analysis, policy advocacy, education, and technical assistance.

NCAVP is coordinated by the New York City Anti-Violence Project.

"Black Teen Mom Manifesto: Secession Pressures: Situating Experience, Madness, and Activist Viewpoint (excerpt)"

By Jasmia Hamilton (writing as Jas)

My story of understanding would have virtually been non-existence without the emancipation of my mind through GWS and early childhood rebellion and taking hold of my sexuality and my physical body. I was expected to be normal in my body and my mind when I had to process things alone and without answers or the solemn "it will never happen again" as I lay in the arms of someone's warm body. I had processed an army vet grasping my arms, my frail seven or eight year old arms. The room was dimly lit by the rays that poured into the living room of the windows in the housing project apartment. I didn't move, my lungs began to collapse, I thought my voice box simply disappeared. I was forced to look into his yellow pedophile eyes. If they were clear they would have looked exactly like those of his daughter, my grandmother. My vulva irked as he grasped and I didn't gasp for a breath. Granddad. He made me feel as close as I can ever remember of being close to death. I remember my aunt saving me, screaming as she peeked across the narrow hallway "come here." "What did he do to you," she asked. Did I really have to answer I know she saw? My stone body stood still in front of a man for who I can now sense I was not his first victim. There may have been plenty of young Vietnamese eight year olds who were damaged by his yellow eyes. I told her. My mom arrived home and my aunt said "tell her." Must I tell her again, must I explain the actions without an understanding of why I had become a victim. My mom questioned, I said, "No, it was just on the outside of them."

Had I just given this dirty man a break? I wish I had the skills to lie to make him be in more trouble I wish he had died while he abused me not in the safety of one of his other daughter's homes, I would have had so much power and not have become a victim to his crusade. I had wished I could have been bigger and not in particular regards to age but to my ability to think, to act, and to scream. At his funeral I felt his dominating presence in the restroom, as many doors peaked open, I felt his spirit hovering over me. I returned to my seat and held my urge to urinate probably for half a day. I did not want to be in the bathroom and see his spirit. I wish I had pushed his coffin and pissed on it. Or learned to set a fire and had burned his body in front of the army men who had come to honor him. What I got from my mom is "maybe he abused mom (her mother) and that's why she is crazy" she had said this not to me of course but to my aunt in my eight year old presence. If he had abused my grandmother, I really wanted him to go to hell. Not just down there, but to hell and be whipped by the Devil. But I have seen his body closed in a coffin, and placed in a pit in the ground so my vengeance would not be fulfilled or potentially that of my grandmother. It only takes in most instances five pounds or less to shoot a firearm, I wish there had been one in our dwelling so I could have blown his brains out.

How could he hurt her? Her dark brown skin, and short stocky body she was the only God to me she was all that mattered and to think she could have experienced the same turmoil that I did but for an extended period. I was glad he died. My abuse did not have a name, I still can't name it, was it sexual assault or molestation or some other thing. Laws and statutes characterize these actions very peculiarly. I am sure it occurred before because I refrained from coming near him on that day my aunt saved me, maybe I suppressed the prior memories and remember the one vividly and excruciatingly because his terror ended. I do not even know for sure if he is an army veteran. Nor do I know if to see him as a veteran helped me stay sane through strategic coping or if constructing this narrative actively assisted in recognizing there were many more bad men that the US government endorsed. It is not my duty to confirm this. Nor is it yours. That did not end the crusade of fear that was sparked by potential assaults on my body.

"I need my dick sucked" a young man said in the smelly hall of our concrete building. "Do you want to do it." I went away, he probably was four years older than me but he never touched me, he played games with my brothers and ate dinner at our dwelling when his mother struggled with caring for her six children in a two-bedroom unit that often was the dwelling place of extended family members. Besides, he was so malnourished and self-medicating his own wounds with weed that even at my age I could have successfully put him on his back. I had always lived in fear running through the halls of the projects because I knew worse things could happen to my body. I had dreamt of being raped before I had a definition for it. That was less horrific than being fondled by someone whose funeral I would have to attend several months later and a month or so apart from that of my maternal grandmother. He is I guess technically my great grandpa (second maternal grand male) but nothing was great about him and I will leave the story at that.

I had many years later in a conversation with my mother about nothing and somehow we entered a conversation about how she desperately made sure to protect my little sister from bad men I received the statement 'he was sick'. That was an excuse; she had not had an explanation for why it happened or no logical explanation for not protecting me. She was not trying to excuse him and I do not blame her for that phraseology. No one has the right words to console someone after these situations. Not even God. Some sick people deserve medical attention and therapy. Some others the real 'sick' people deserve for their brains to be shattered, and or their hands to be cut off. The thing about Gender and Women's studies as my academic choice not being an accident is applicable here. Scholars who have come to terms with their own abuse or have generated discourses about sexual abuse as a structural form of domination are not far off from the truth. My body had to be ten times smaller and I was a child in order for this domination to work. And of course, it was not standard practice for parents to say don't go around you grandpa, or if he offers you gum from his mouth, it's because he want to make your vulva his own.

I had come to terms. Not only with my own abuse but the fact that it was commonplace. In 1997, Girl X had been raped and poisoned in the hall of a nearby building in the Cabrini Greens, I would have never known her pain as I was only three. She was left mute, physically disabled, and confined to a state care institution. In the fourth grade, a dear friend of mine, out of nowhere while the girls lined up to use the restroom said, "I was raped". She just needed to be heard and hugged and loved and acknowledged. But another girl in our class who I despised so much said "you are not supposed to tell anyone that." How did she know? Maybe she had been raped too, and was told not to tell? Whatever the case was, abuse sexual and the like was clearly under-addressed. That was the story, I was not the only one without answers or an understanding that perpetrators use their dominance to make us hate our body and set us up for an unhealthy relationship with our sexuality. If no one ever tells these stories then there will many thousands of girls (and boys) who will continue to be traumatized by the fear of not telling. I am not ashamed of my abuse. I am not ashamed of my blackness. I am not ashamed of my sexuality. I am not ashamed of my sex. I am not ashamed of my teen parent identity. I am not ashamed of any aspect of my identity. I will continue to be in anyone's face about the hard, bleak truth if it means that I can "save" someone from their fear closet.

While I was fortunate and lucky to have never been raped, for much of my conscious life I carried various forms of defense tools because I could never assume my body to be safe. And I was very sure that if I needed to that I would fight for my life and would was adamant if killing someone was the vehicle for my survival then so be it. I took ownership of my body by giving an affirmative and un-fearful "Yes" to my partner. Girl X and my friend from elementary school did not have that choice. I was using my body and my words to say *fuck you granddad I hope you rot in hell you dirty motherfucker*. It did not matter to me that I ran the chance of contracting a STI (as my high school physical education teacher was taught to make us fear as a reason for not having sex) or getting pregnant and ending up like a young lady in my high school who gave birth in the middle of high school freshman year. I wished there were more people like this young lady. I had once said in conversation "what a shame" to one of our peers, but I really meant that she was brave. She still managed to come to school and smiled practically every time she was in someone's company. She was brave because she didn't give a shit about what people thought. One day in homeroom I daydreamed about the many nights she might have cried at home though. I had got the chance to know her personally, but I never asked to confirm whether my daydream was accurate. I cannot attribute not choosing to abort my children to her but she always remained in my mind.

MENTAL HEALTH

Mad Women or Mad Society
"Towards a Feminist Practice with Women Survivors of Child Sexual Assault"

By Fiona Rummery

This chapter examines an aspect of structural violence as embodied in traditional psychiatric labels of mental ill health. Although this discussion revolves around the issues of child sexual assault (which is constituted by physical violation) it does not focus on the interpersonal aspects of such abuse. Rather, it explores the subtler abuse which often informs the framework of societal institutions, such as medicine. When considering violence against women, it is usually overt and direct experiences of violence which are highlighted. It is arguable that women's experiences of systemic violence when seeking assistance are as worthy of detailed assessment. As Irwin and Thorpe argue in the opening chapter in this collection, systemic violence plays a crucial role in allowing interpersonal violence to continue, partly through the processes of silencing and discrediting, as this chapter details.

This chapter considers the question of what it is about a feminist counselling practice that differentiates it from other, more traditional modes of working. It will thus utilise an illustrative discussion of an issue which arose for me whilst working as a sexual assault counsellor. This involved working with an incest survivor who had an extensive history with the psychiatric profession, and my subsequent investigation into this area. As such, this chapter encompasses discussions of the issues involved in child sexual assault generally; women and notions of madness and the way these intersect with constructions of femininity; as well as ideas about working as a feminist practitioner. This is not an exhaustive discussion but rather exists as an exploration of some of the more subtle ways in which we, as workers, must always consider and reconsider the theoretical underpinnings of any practice, as well as constantly

analyzing the practical implications of any theoretical formulation.

Child Sexual Assault

Misconceptions, fear and denial surround the issue of child sexual assault, as its existence problematises popular ideas about the fundamental institution of the family. In most cases of child sexual assault the perpetrator is known to the child, and the abuse continues over some time (Waldby 1985). The dominant cultural discourses which attempt to deal with child sexual assault form a powerful and ubiquitous part of the social fabric. More importantly (and confusingly) they are bizarrely contradictory in their nature:

> It doesn't happen; it only happens to poor families; it doesn't happen to THIS family; men do it when their wives are frigid or otherwise unavailable; children are naturally seductive; it doesn't do any harm; it damages for life. (Linnell & Cora 1993, 24)

The sexual assault of children usually involves progressive intrusion over a long period of time, with gradual coercion or co-option of the child, and with disclosure not occurring until some time after the abuse has ended (Cashmore & Bussey 1988). Child sexual assault is a particularly silenced experience; still commonly eliciting responses of disbelief and stigmatisation. It is also a particularly silencing experience in that the intensity and intimacy of violation often leads women to such a state of depression, self-hatred and/or distrust that they are unable or reluctant to talk about it (Stanko 1985; Ward 1984). Much of the early literature on child sexual assault documented the ravages of abuse, focussing on the tragedy of supposedly ruined lives. More recently the focus has shifted towards the process of recovery, with the aid of appropriate intervention. Incest survivors need to be provided with appropriate supportive services that allow them to actively and consciously confront the legacy of their abusive history.

One of the issues that I experienced when I began working with incest survivors, was that a high number had some psychiatric history or diagnosis. Approximately seventy percent of the clients I had seen had been categorised with Borderline Personality Disorder, or as Manic Depressive or as having psychotic episodes and as a result had been hospitalised or prescribed medication. When I questioned these women as to the details of the exact nature of the causes of their depression—or psychotic episodes—I was again surprised by the manner in which the symptoms manifested by these women seemed to me to be normal reactions to abusive situations. This led me to do some reading into women and psychiatry so that I could better understand theoretically the unease I felt intuitively to such psychiatric labelling of women's distress. Moreover, I wanted to incorporate this unease more effectively into my practice.

Women and Madness

The history of the connections between women and madness has been examined by a number of feminist writers in the last twenty years. These have ranged from historians (such as Matthews 1984) through to psychiatrists and social workers (such as Penfold & Walker 1983) and to philosophers (Russell, 1986, 1995). They have examined the manner in which what is defined as "madness" has changed over time according to context. In addition, they have exposed the manner in which the mental health profession has been used as a mechanism of social control, inextricably intertwined with notions of what constitutes "femininity".

The "science" of mental health will be treated in this discussion as an elastic and value-driven social science. Whilst I acknowledge that some women may be genuinely suffering from psychiatric illnesses, there are also many whose emotions, responses and "symptoms" are unnecessarily deemed "sick" within a psychiatric framework. It is this process of pathologising women's behaviour with which this paper is most concerned.

Phyllis Chesler says of her interviews with sixty women aged 17–70 with regard to their experiences in both private therapy and mental asylums: "Most were simply unhappy and self-destructive in typically (and approved) female ways. Their experiences made it very clear to me that help-seeking or help-needing behaviour is not particularly valued or understood in our culture" (Chesler 1973, XXII).

Central to the definition of what constitutes madness then, is the manner in which femininity is socially constructed. Caplan like Chesler, asserts that: "A misogynist society has created a myriad of situations that make women unhappy. And then that same society uses the myth of women's masochism to blame the women themselves for their misery" (Caplan 1985, 9).

The traditional "psychology of women" correlates closely with the "characteristics of oppression" (Penfold & Walker 1983). Women's sane, average, even self-preserving responses to situations of abuse or oppression are often used as evidence of their own lack of mental health.

Debra

I want at this point to introduce a case example in order to highlight some of the issues referred to throughout. Whilst I am loathe to do this in some senses—as it easily becomes voyeuristic and simplistically condenses a woman's struggle and life—it elucidates my point at different stages of this discussion more effectively than any abstract discussion of "women" can.

Debra was a woman whom I saw for counselling after she referred herself to the sexual assault service. It was largely through my contact with her that I undertook this research into women and psychiatry. She was thirty-four at the time and had a nine-year-old daughter. She was chronically and sadistically sexually abused by a male family member from the age of approximately eight until sixteen. She has had extensive contact with the psychiatric profession, has had a variety of diagnoses and been prescribed nearly every type of medication. Her first contact with psychiatrists was at age eight when she attempted suicide. After hospitalisation she was labelled "depressed" and given Valium and sleeping tablets for a number of years.

Her first psychotic episode occurred after the birth of her daughter, at which time she was placed in a psychiatric institution for some months. Since then, intrusive flashbacks of the sexual abuse she had experienced as a child have increased and intensified. She regularly had bouts of depression, suicidal feelings and tendencies as well as repeated psychotic episodes during which time she was hospitalised. She had been prescribed a plethora of drugs, none of which alleviate either the psychotic episodes or her flashbacks. Debra sought counselling at the sexual assault service as her flashbacks had further intensified since the time her daughter turned eight, and she felt strongly that there were things about the sexual assault which she needed to resolve.

Although Debra had a history of extensive contact with health professionals, at no time was she asked about her childhood. Even at age eight, and during her adolescence when Debra was medicated and hospitalised a number of times, the safety and stability of her family life was not questioned. The psychiatrists she saw did not ask her whether she had any ideas about what might be causing her distress. Rather, the manifestations of her emotional distress in response to abuse were treated as symptoms of an illness which could be cured by psychiatric intervention, such as medication.

It became clear to me quite early on that the messages which I was giving Debra directly contradicted those of her psychiatrist, whom she was still seeing. The things that he said to her are best encapsulated in the following examples:

> You have no control over this.
> You don't know what you need, I know what's *best for you.*
> Just do as I say and take the medication.
> The sexual assault is not *particularly relevant.* You must not indulge in self-pity and dwell on it. Put it out of your mind, it is in the past now.
> You are psychotic and manic depressive. There is nothing you can do about it. You must learn to live with your mental illness.

The work that I undertook with Debra, some of which will be described here, focussed upon validating both her feelings and memories, believing her, and giving her control over the counselling relationship. This approach stems from the belief that the core experiences of child sexual assault are disempowerment and disconnection from self and others. Recovery, therefore, is based primarily upon the empowerment of the incest survivor and the creation of new relationships which are non-abusive. "No intervention that takes power away from the Survivor can possibly foster her recovery, regardless of how much it appears to be in her best interest" (Herman 1992, 133).

The way in which Debra's psychotic episodes were dealt with by psychiatrists provides an illuminating illustration of the manner in which women's distress is pathologised rather than validated. When I questioned Debra as to the exact nature of her psychotic episodes, these were revealed (over some time) to be a series of extremely distressing memory flashbacks. To label these "psychotic" effectively removes them from her reality, thereby denying her the opportunity of integration. Whilst these memories were extremely distressing and often bizarre in nature, it was only through exploring them fully that Debra was able to become less afraid of them. As one survivor of childhood sexual abuse

wrote: "I've looked memories in the face and smelled their breath. They can't hurt me any more" (Bass & Davis 1988, 70).

The validation that her terror of flashbacks was an expression of the terror she had felt at the time of the abuse enabled Debra to remove these from the realm of paranoia. By extension, she was then able to turn fear into (justifiable) rage toward a perpetrator who could do such cruel things to a child. This change was in direct contrast to her previous self-blame and confusion about feeling crazy due to her mood hallucinations. The process of remembering and mourning has been well-documented by feminist practitioners as a crucial stage in recovery from childhood trauma of any kind, as it is only through knowing what happened that women can begin to heal and recover from the damage done to them (Herman 1992, 155).

The Problems with Categorisation

A major part of the construction of femininity is the emphasis which is placed upon serving others. This is ex-emplified in the importance which is accorded to mother-hood and women's roles in providing for children. This role, however, has gradually become devalued in western society, so women are ensnared within the paradox of being both glorified and trapped within an oppressive definition of what they should be. At its extreme, some feminist commentators have argued that concepts of femininity and madness are actually interchangeable.

Numerous psychological studies have pointed out that what in the west is generally regarded as the woman's role happens to coincide with what is regarded as mentally unhealthy (Russell 1986, 86; Russell 1995). *The Diagnostic and Statistical Manual of Mental Disorders* (DSM-IIIR), created by the American Psychiatric Association, lists symptoms of all psychiatric disorders and is considered to be the essential reference for those working in Mental Health in the western world. Whilst the length of this chapter prevents greater exposition, it is useful to compare the set of criteria for certain diagnoses, particularly those which are most often assigned to women.

Kaplan (cited in Russell 1986, 82–90) undertook a comparison of the DSM-III description of Histrionic Personality Disorder (which is far more frequently diagnosed in women than in men) with the findings of Broverman's (1972, in Russell) research into what constitutes a mentally healthy woman. The criteria for a diagnosis of Histrionic Personality Disorder are "self-dramatization, for example exaggerated expression of emotions, overreaction to minor events" (Spitzer & Williams 1987). Remarkably similar is the woman deemed mentally healthy in Broverman's research "being more emotional and more excitable in minor crises" (as cited in Russell 1986, 82–90).

This comparison illustrates the paradox in which women are placed, in that what are described as healthy feminine attributes can equally be seen as symptoms of psychiatric disorders. Thus, through assumptions about appropriate sex roles on the part of practitioners, a woman who is "successfully" fulfilling the feminine role by "revealing emotional responsibility, naivete, dependency and childishness" (Lerner & Wolowitz as cited in Russell 1986, 88) can be very easily diagnosed and labelled. The example used here is by no means the only one. A woman conforming to the female role can also be deemed to have a "dependent personality disorder", or "avoidant personality disorder". These definitions also include a high level of ambiguity, allowing for much interpretation on the part of the practitioner.

Whether women comply with or rebel against traditional precepts of femininity, we risk being labelled "dysfunctional". As the above examples reveal, compliance with femininity is not necessarily the safer option, as it can imply any variety of mental disorders; but rebellion against it can be seen as signifying aggressiveness, lack of gender identity, and social maladjustment. The "catch-22" inherent in this paradox is treacherous for women.

Constructing Reality

The dominant group in any society controls the meaning of what is valid information. For women and other subordinate groups, the version of the world which has been sanctioned as reality does not address their lived experience . . . (Penfold & Walker 1983, 56)

When there is a disjunction between the world as women experience it and the terms given them to understand the experience, women often have little alternative but to feel "crazy". Labels of mental ill-health thus create and authorise ways in which women can conceptualise their unhappiness and despair, in a societally acceptable manner. In struggling against this, rather than treating Debra's symptoms as hers alone, a feminist approach seeks to normalise these by placing them within a context. Whilst this does not necessarily alter the feelings she experiences, it does alleviate accompanying feelings of isolation and fault. For example, when I pointed out to Debra that many women experience an increase in intensity and number of memory flashbacks after the birth of a child, or when a daughter reaches

the age that they were when the abuse began, she was relieved, and we were able to explore what a daughter's vulnerability might mean to her. I would stress again that this does not necessarily relieve the distress experienced during these flashback episodes, but rather that the panic of feeling "crazy" and out of control during and afterwards is alleviated. Thus, Debra was able to view her symptoms as having a cause, rather than being something intrinsic to her as an individual which she needed to "learn to live with". It is important to remember that women's symptoms are real. Although this chapter criticises the fact that these symptoms are seen to constitute an identifiable (or classifiable) mental illness, this does not negate the fact that the symptoms as experienced by individual women can be intense and overpowering. Thus, the theoretical underpinnings of one's practice are revealed in the manner in which one defines women's distress. The psychiatrists who saw Debra acknowledged her distress, as did I. It is the framework in which we interpreted this that differed dramatically.

Mental Illness as Social Control

The institution of psychiatry presents itself as healing, benign and compassionate while obscuring its function as part of the apparatus through which society is ordered. (Penfold & Walker 1983, 244)

Depressed or subservient women serve a social function in that they are unlikely to question their subordinate gender roles nor challenge broader social structures. This is exemplified by Miles (1988) in her discussion of the role of housewife:

The stresses inherent in domestic work and the role of the housewife can lead to neurosis which in its turn is likely to make her even more home-centered and thus vulnerable to further stress . . . [T]he home can become . . . a setting which, by its peculiar strains, "drives her mad" yet which provides asylum from the impossible demands of the world outside with which she feels that she can no longer cope. (Miles 1988, 7)

If one accepts the premise that the construction of mental health reflects a social ordering of gender, one must then ask what purpose the pathologising of women's behaviour serves. To medicate Debra meant that she remained socially compliant. To label her as crazy enabled both professionals and her family to dismiss those disclosures she did make about the child sexual assault as imagined or exaggerated. This silenced her more effectively than any terror she may have felt.

Jordanova (1981, 106) expands upon this idea, by examining depression within the paradigm of an "illness". She compares those illnesses from which men most commonly suffer, with those of women, highlighting how rarely women are allowed to take on the "sick role": a role which provides relief from day-to-day burdens of work. This is not to negate the underlying framework which operates to posit the female condition as continuously or innately "sick". Rather, my point is that men are given societal access to a "legitimate" sick role. Jordanova effectively contrasts a woman who is depressed and on medication but still expected to perform familial duties, with the more "serious" illnesses which lead to time spent in bed, relaxation, holidays, and time off work for men. Again, Debra had been medicated and encouraged to "cope". For ten years her ability to care for her child and elderly relatives (including her and her partner's grandparents) domestically was actively rewarded, and the time that she spent in hospital frowned upon as indulgent. At no point was she offered the space, time or care to understand and deal with the cause of her distress.

Strategies for a Feminist Practice

Practicing from a feminist perspective will involve a variety of methodological approaches depending upon the context in which one is working. Thus, I do not intend to discuss method, but rather the underlying ideals informing a feminist approach. The ideal is to empower clients to challenge both external power structures and their own internalised oppression. This is necessary because both external and internal oppression can be equally debilitating and disempowering in the manner in which they are personally experienced (Fook 1990, 30).

A feminist approach cannot be a set of "how-to's" which can be easily adopted. A feminist framework is flexible and evolving, and involves as much an analysis of one's self, as that of the women with whom one is working. This is not to simplify feminism, nor to unify all feminist counsellors into the one category. I acknowledge the diversities within the existing definitions of feminism (and women) and the way in which these manifest in work practices. In order to establish and maintain a feminist practice, the worker must firstly be a feminist. This is in some senses stating the obvious, but I would reiterate that undertaking counselling in a feminist manner is not simply a job or framework which can be utilised and then discarded. Feminist practice is also not merely client-focused. Rather, it extends into all areas of work, examining and analysing the structures in which one is working and in the dynamics between staff members. An example which is

pertinent is that of working within a psychiatric institution. In such an environment, one's feminist perspective would be of crucial motivation when interacting with other staff members in the organisation, particularly doctors, and others in positions of power in the hierarchy—in challenging the established frameworks in which they think and label people and which influence their practice.

A feminist approach values collective rather than hierarchical structures and seeks to deconstruct the "expert worker"—"client in need of help" dynamic, favoring instead empowerment of clients. This is particularly pertinent to a discussion on working with incest survivors. Working from a feminist perspective in essence allows women to be the expert of their own lives. This structuring of one's practices, so that the client is more than merely a recipient, allows the space for them to control the relationship. This is crucial as Herman points out, "The first principle of recovery is the empowerment of the Survivor. Others may offer advice, support, assistance, affection and care, but not cure" (Herman 1992, 133).

A feminist focus upon validating women's experiences is paramount—indicating to them that they have been listened to, heard, and believed, as this so rarely occurs elsewhere. This again is particularly pertinent to working with victims of sexual assault whose experiences of abuse may have been denied, trivialised or ignored—as in Debra's situation. The silence surrounding sexual assault makes it incredibly difficult for women to speak of their experiences; thus it is not possible to underestimate the impact on a personal level of a worker hearing and believing a woman's disclosure. Working with Debra involved providing constant reassurance that I did believe her memories and that I did not think that she was lying. At times, her fear of having spoken the abuse was palpable. This again reinforces the transformative power of merely disclosing the abusive experiences. It has been stressed that as workers we should never lose sight of the terror of disclosure, adding that on many occasions it is actually as if the perpetrator were in the room: "The terror is as though the patient and therapist convene in the presence of yet another person. The third image is of the victimiser, who . . . demanded silence and whose command is now being broken" (Herman 1992, 137).

This also highlights the importance of the manner in which the counsellor perceives of change. The worker should not view change simply as a change in behaviour, but rather expand this to create an environment in which it is recognised that change does not have to be structural or large to be of importance. The emphasis is therefore shifted so that an apparently slight change in awareness is valued and its ability to facilitate considerable difference in a woman's life is acknowledged. For Debra this type of change in awareness allowed her to begin to redefine her self and formulate a differing self-image from that previously provided to her. The creation of a new manner in which to perceive her self and her life allowed her to reinterpret her own life experience (Linnell & Cora 1993, 36). This new-found ability to resist the dominant discourse of her experience facilitates the potential for both social and personal empowerment. Goldstein comments that the personal narrative has been the way in which women have attempted (often privately and without recognition) to link up their lived experiences and feelings in the face of social definitions: "The use of this method is most instructive for social work because it reveals how personal and social change may be spurred by the kind of consciousness raising that occurs when people explore their own stories" (Goldstein 1990, 40).

Another essential feature of a feminist practice is that the worker's values are stated, and there is no pretence at objectivity or impartiality: "The consciousness of oppression has implications for alternative approaches such as those developed in self-help groups, women's studies, political action and consciousness raising" (Penfold & Walker 1983, XI).

In my practice, in order to challenge dominant constructions of power and knowledge, I take an overtly non-neutral position. This is achieved through providing the woman with the space, opportunity and information which is necessary for her to begin to consider her own experiences in the light of the broader cultural and social context. An example of this involves providing women with knowledge of the incidence of child sexual assault (as well as common reactions and experiences as detailed previously). This broader context allows the woman's perspective to encompass her own experience as well as the knowledge of a complex social dynamic. It is then possible to provide questions and possibilities which facilitate the reframing of personal experience within the context of this new knowledge (Linnell & Cora 1993, 34). Whilst this mode of working could be accused of not being "impartial" enough by traditional practitioners, it is important to differentiate here between making one's political and social ideologies clear without rupturing the boundaries of the counselling relationship, and importing the worker's own emotional personal agenda into the working relationship. Herman provides a poignant explanation of the difference between the technical neutrality of the practitioner as opposed to what she calls moral neutrality: "Working with victimised people requires a committed moral stand. The therapist is called upon to bear witness to a crime. She must affirm a position of solidarity with the victim" (Herman 1992, 135).

She further extends this notion to explain that it does not necessitate a simplicity which assumes that the victim can do no wrong and asserts that rather it involves an understanding of the fundamental injustice of the child sexual assault and the victim's subsequent need for "a resolution that restores some sense of social justice" (Herman 1992, 135).

If we see that the depression of women speaks their lived experiences and represents a feminised manner of calling for some kind of understanding, then "a detailed examination is called for which concerns itself not just with which women in the population get depressed, but how and why" (Jordanova 1981, 106–07).

Social analysis does not necessarily help those women who feel unable to cope with their day-to-day existence. Knowledge that their "illness" is part of broader structural problems, and attributable to their social situation does not automatically endow them with feelings of joy and liberation. Whilst this is an important long-term aim, it does little to alleviate the suffering women individually experience. It "highlights the immediacy of the problem for women, and the need to think in terms of immediate action, not just the distant solutions implied in abstract analysis" (Jordanova 1981, 105).

If counselling is about negotiating an adjustment between client and environment (Fook 1990), then the treatment undertaken for women deemed "mentally unhealthy" has largely sought to adapt them to their environment. A feminist approach, however, would necessitate an examination of the societal factors which have led to the level of emotional distress present. Essentially then, public and private struggles are as inextricably linked as are theory and practice. Most importantly, neither partner in either equation should be treated as superior as each is crucial to the other.

Conclusion

It is necessary for a feminist practice to examine the oppression of women in both private and public, individual and institutional, structural contexts. Although this chapter has utilised the example of parts of one woman's story, as stated earlier this is representative of the experiences of many of the women with whom I have worked. The process of labelling these women when they exhibit intense emotional distress as "disordered" or "sick", effectively silences their disclosures of abuse. To accept that there are extremely cruel and sadistic acts perpetrated against children within our society is confronting and difficult. The manner in which social institutions and scientific discourse interact with the ideologies of patriarchy, needs to be exposed, and such interactions condemned for the manner in which they subjugate women.

Labels of mental illness do not exist in a social vacuum. To deny the importance of an individual's abusive childhood is to abdicate the responsibility that we all have for the impact of our actions on others. Such denial contributes to the continuation of such abuse. Links between madness as a social construction, and madness as a subjective experience (or as a "sane" response to abusive or oppressive experiences) need to be explored. Further, the label of "madness" when applied to women needs to be viewed with utter skepticism before being accepted as an appropriate diagnosis.

REFERENCES

A list of references is available in original source.

"Frequency, Causes, and Risk Factors for Depression"

From *Report of the Task Force on Women and Depression in Wisconsin*

Prevalence and Consequences of Depression

Depression is a common, under-diagnosed, yet highly treatable disorder. This section examines national data, and the next section reviews available data specific to Wisconsin. In any given 1-year period, 9.5% of the adult population in the United States, or almost 20 million adults, suffers from a depressive illness. There are similarly high rates of subclinical symptoms, which, although less debilitating, also interfere with psychological and interpersonal well being and can lead to the development of a depressive disorder. While the economic costs to society are enormous, the cost in human suffering is incalculable. Depressive illnesses and symptoms interfere with normal functioning. They cause pain and suffering not only to those with the problems, but also to partners, children, other family members, friends, and co-workers. Serious depression left untreated can irreparably damage family life as well as the life of the ill person.

Depression leads to workplace absenteeism twice as often as in non-depressed persons and interferes with work productivity. Compared with community samples, depressed persons are 7 times more likely to be unemployed, employed part-time, or in jobs below their education levels (Druss, et al., 2001). In addition to these occupational costs, the medical costs of depressed persons average twice those of non-depressed persons. Depression is one of the most common conditions found in the primary care setting. It can increase the risk of cardiac problems, cerebrovascular events, overall mortality, and other physical health-related problems (Van Rhoads & Gelenberg, 2005). Depressive disorders also raise the risk for suicide attempts and suicide completions.

THE EXPERIENCE OF DEPRESSION

I felt like I would never stop crying. Everything around me felt like a blur. Everyday decisions were so difficult and when I finally did make a choice I would get so upset because it was always the wrong one. Once in a blue moon, though, I would have good days; I would be laughing and having fun and the next thing I knew things would seem even worse than before. Then I started having anxiety attacks. Sometimes it would be twice a week or none for two weeks. There was never a pattern.

Gender Differences in Depression

Women are at least twice as likely as men to experience depressive disorders and symptoms, and some studies report even higher ratios (Kessler, et al., 1993; Piccinelli & Wilkinson, 2000; Weissman, et al., 1988). Thus women and those close to them are much more likely than men to suffer the economic, psychological, and social consequences. Women consistently have higher rates of depression than men across all cultures (Kleinman & Cohen, 1997), though the ratios vary. For example, women in China have rates of depression nine times that of men and also higher rates of completed suicides.

Because depression is so much more common in women than men, the search for causes has begun to focus on reasons for their greater susceptibility. Before adolescence, rates of depression are low and similar for boys and girls. Depression becomes more prevalent in females than males beginning around ages 13–15, according to studies based both on diagnostic interviews and standardized self- reports (Hankin, et al., 1998; Zahn-Waxler, et al., 2004). By 15–18 years the gender disparity reaches the 2:1 ratio that persists throughout most of adulthood. Adolescence is a developmental period of high risk for many girls. Anxiety becomes more prevalent as do eating disorders. Depression is also linked with drug use, heavy alcohol use, and cigarette smoking, which may serve as ways to self-medicate for depression. Since girls are likely to become physiologically dependent on substances more quickly than boys (Andrews, 2005) and have greater difficulty stopping, there may be greater adverse consequences for their physical health as well as their mental health. Because depression co-exists with these and other problems in females more than males starting in adolescence (Loeber & Keenan, 1994), females are likely to become more functionally impaired with these symptoms earlier in their lives (Zahn-Waxler, et al., 2006).

Depression that begins in childhood and adolescence often continues into adulthood and is especially likely to be associated with risk for suicide. A large proportion of apparent new cases of depression in adulthood, in fact have origins in childhood or adolescence (Kessler, et al., 2005). At the same time, many new cases are diagnosed in women at different points in adult development. Depression has been called the most significant mental health risk for women, especially younger women of childbearing and child-rearing age, and the rate appears to be increasing in recent decades (Cross National Collaborative Group, 1992). Postpartum depression is particularly serious, both for the mother and for the offspring. Due to the dramatic increase in rates of depression in girls in adolescence, most explanations for the causes have focused on this period of development and beyond (as new cases of depression emerge in adulthood). Even in childhood, though, some risk factors are more common among girls than boys and may contribute to their later, greater vulnerability (Zahn-Waxler, et al., 2004).

There are gender differences in how adolescents and adults show their depression (Zahn-Waxler, et al., 2004). In addition to their greater anxiety, depressed females also show more physical symptoms, including excessive sleep, weight gain, increased appetite, fatigue, slowed motor activity, and body image disturbance. Higher rates of crying, sadness, self-control, and negative self-concept are also seen in depressed girls than boys, as well as less irritability and self-aggrandizement. Although many of the symptom differences are physiological in nature and could suggest biological differences, others are likely to reflect environmental processes.

Although some causes and risk factors for depression are similar for males and females, others are likely to differ. The explanations for higher rates of depression in females than males include a number of biological, psychological, and social factors.

Genetic and Other Biological Causes and Risk Factors

Genetic Factors   Major depression clusters in families and depression in a first-degree relative is a risk factor for depression. Although some investigators find similar levels of heritability of depression in women than men, several others have found higher genetic loadings for females. Moreover, some genetic linkage studies suggest that the impact of some genes on risk for major depression differ in women and men (Kendler, et al., 2001). Genes are also involved in the causes of depression through their effect on sensitivity to environmental events. Persons who are at greater genetic risk for depression are twice as likely to develop depression in response to severe stress as those at lower genetic risk.

Puberty and Sex Hormones   Because the unique biology of women may explain, in part, their greater prevalence of depression beginning in adolescence, early puberty and sex hormones are likely to play a role (Ge, et al., 1996, 2003; Zahn-Waxler, et al., 2004). Early puberty is a risk factor for depression for girls, but not boys. Genes, as well as environmental factors like nutrition, exercise, and weight, play a role in the onset of puberty. Depression in mothers may induce early puberty in daughters; the presence of unrelated male father figures in the home may also induce early puberty for girls. Animal studies suggest that chemicals known as pheromones produced by unrelated adult males accelerate female pubertal development. In addition to the hormonal and other biological changes that come with early menarche, young adolescent girls also may not have acquired sufficient skills for coping with the social pressures and stresses of early physical maturation. There is no biological counterpart for boys that creates a similar level of risk for depression.

The sex hormones testosterone and estrogen, which are associated with pubertal development and reproduction, are related to depression in adolescent girls (Angold, et al., 1999). Estrogen has been shown to predict depression in adolescent girls, even as long as a year later (Paikoff, et al., 1991). There is some support for the hypothesis that women may be vulnerable to disturbances in the interaction between the sex hormone system and brain chemistry (neurotransmitters such as serotonin). This dysregulation may also make women more sensitive to psychosocial, environmental, and other physiological factors (Mazure, et al., 2002).

Premenstrual Depressive Symptoms As many as 75% of women experience some premenstrual behavioral and emotional symptoms (Mazure, et al., 2002). These depressive menstrual symptoms are disabling in small but sufficient numbers of women to warrant a diagnosis of premenstrual dysphoric disorder (PMDD). The positive response of these women to treatment with antidepressants (specifically, selective serotonin re-uptake inhibitors or SSRIs) suggests that their serotonin may be altered via hormone-neurotransmitter interactions. Other treatment studies have shown that the female hormone progesterone may promote the cyclic symptoms of PMDD, while a metabolite of this hormone (allopregnanalone) may have a calming effect.

Postpartum and Menopausal Phases Depression associated with the postpartum and menopausal times of life is now being studied in relation to hormonal factors and interactions between hormones, neurotransmitters, and other biological systems (Mazure, et al., 2002). The shifts in sex hormones and major changes in the stress-response physiological system (the hypothalamic-pituitary-adrenal [HPA] axis) during these periods are well known. Pregnancy and delivery produce marked changes in estrogen and progesterone levels as well as major shifts along the HPA axis. Depression in pregnancy is associated with biological disturbances that may affect the developing fetus. Postpartum depression may interfere with the development of a secure mother-child attachment and hence with the quality of the relationship that is established. Failures to reproduce, such as infertility, miscarriage, and surgical menopause, are also associated with depression. Natural menopause results in substantial fluctuations in estrogen and changes in other hormones as well. The effects of these changes have not yet been clearly linked to the onset of depression but the questions merit further inquiry.

While maternal depression is a consistent risk factor for childhood anxiety, depression and disruptive disorders, the positive news is that recent research shows that vigorous treatment of a mother's depression can reduce symptoms of anxiety and depression in her child. A 2006 study of 151 mother-child pairs, with children ranging from 7 to 17 years old, found 33% remission among children with a base-line diagnosis for depression whose mothers' depression remitted, compared to 12%

remission among children whose mothers' depression did not remit (Weissman, et al., 2006).

Psychological and Social Factors

Socialization Experiences Parental depression (most often studied in mothers) creates substantial risk for depression in offspring and more so if both parents are depressed (Rohde, et al., 2005; Williamson, et al., 2004; Zahn-Waxler, et al., 2004). The lifetime risk for depression in children with a depressed parent has been estimated at 45%. It is often assumed that these children are at risk due to genetic risk factors; however, these children's experiences often differ markedly as well. Depressed mothers are less reciprocal, attuned, and engaged in interactions with their children beginning in infancy. Depressed mothers often model helpless, passive styles of coping and negative emotions that their children also then experience and may imitate. A number of problematic child-rearing and discipline practices have also been identified. In childhood and adolescence, girls of depressed mothers are more susceptible to the influences of maternal depression than boys, showing greater depression and anxiety.

The effects of maternal depression on adolescent girls' depression become stronger as girls mature (Zahn-Waxler, et al., 2004). Adolescent daughters provide more support to their depressed mothers than do the sons. They also express more sadness, worry and responsibility for the mother's depression. Parental conflict and divorce (which often accompany parental depression) are more likely to lead to depression and related problems in girls than boys. In adulthood, too, women's higher levels of caring for others more often become burdensome and create risk for depression. Maternal depression often occurs in the context of other environmental factors that create additional risk.

Socialization practices directed more often to girls than boys can reflect the beginnings of the adverse environments that create risk for depression (Zahn-Waxler, et al., 2006). Parents are less likely to encourage independence and more likely to foster interpersonal closeness in their daughters than their sons. Girls are more often socialized in ways that interfere with self-actualization, that is, to be dependent, compliant, and unassertive. Parents are more restrictive and demanding of mature interpersonal behavior in girls than boys and are less tolerant of girls' anger, aggression, and mistakes. Such practices may contribute to the development of maladaptive cognitive styles and coping patterns that can contribute to depression. In early adolescence, pubertal changes combine with intensified pressure for gender-role conformity increase the likelihood of depression in girls.

Life Stress, Trauma, and Violence[1] Life stress and trauma throughout the life cycle play a major role in the onset and continuation of depression (Mazure, et al., 2002). More than 80% of cases of depression are preceded by a serious adverse life event. Women are more likely than men to experience depression in response to stressful life events. Traumatic stressors such as childhood sexual abuse, adult sexual assault, and male partner violence are consistently linked to higher rates of depression, other psychiatric disorders, and physical illness in women. National statistics indicate that the lifetime chance of a woman being raped is between 15 and 25 percent (Koss, 1993). The psychological impact of rape can be severe. It includes not only major depression and long-term depressive symptoms, but also smoking, alcohol use, reduced activity, and physical injury. Each year an estimated 588,000 women in the United States are beaten by their intimate partners (U. S. Department of Justice, 2003). Thus depression among women who experience male partner violence is very high and male partner violence is the greatest single cause of injury to women who require emergency medical treatment. Women more often experience other stressors associated with depression, including caring for elderly parents (often with severe physical and cognitive impairments), while simultaneously caring for their own children.

Higher rates of depression in women have also been linked to other forms of chronic stress, including poverty, little education, inequality, immigration, and discrimination. Depression is more common among low-income persons, particularly mothers with young children (Belle, 1982; Brown & Moran, 1997). The more children a woman has, the more likely she is to experience depression. Depression is more common in single mothers and women of color; women are also more likely than men to have incomes below the poverty line. Seventy-five percent of people living in poverty in the U.S. are women and children, reflecting a trend termed the feminization of poverty. Because adults in poverty are over twice as likely to experience major depression as adults who are not poor (Bruce, et al., 1991), poor women are disproportionately at risk. Poor women have more frequent and uncontrol-

lable adverse life events than the general population, which are known to contribute to depression. In addition to dire poverty, economic inequality contributes to negative health outcomes and is linked to depression in women. Similarly, sex discrimination in the work place and elsewhere is associated with depression, anxiety, and an overall diminished sense of well being (Klonoff, et al., 2000). Refugee women, particularly those who escaped from traumatic situations such as war, are at heightened risk for depression or post-traumatic stress disorder (Fazel, et al., 2005).

The stress associated with discrimination can be particularly severe for women of color since they experience both racial/ethnic and sex discrimination (Reskin, 2000). The higher rates of depression for these women primarily reflect their poorer life circumstances rather than their ethnicity. That is, women from ethnic and racial minorities in the U.S. are more likely than White women to experience social and economic inequities that include greater exposure to racism, discrimination, violence, and poverty (U.S. Department of Health and Human Services, 2001). They also are more likely to experience lower educational and income levels, segregation into low-status and high-stress jobs, unemployment, poor health, larger family sizes, marital dissolution, and single parenthood.

Personality Characteristics Some psychological characteristics make people more likely to become depressed in the face of life stress (Abramson, et al., 1989; Mazure, et al., 2002; Nolen-Hoeksema, 2001). These include maladaptive beliefs (for example, that they are at fault for most of their own and others' problems), accompanied by feeling helpless and hopeless. One predisposing style seen more often in women than men is ruminative thinking. Rumination involves a repetitive and passive mental focus on one's symptoms of distress and their causes and consequences. It leads to impaired problem solving and difficulty engaging in actions that would allow one to take greater control over one's life. Excessive rumination predicts longer and more severe episodes of depression and an increased likelihood of being diagnosed with major depressive disorder (Nolen-Hoeksema, 2000).

In childhood girls are more likely than boys to experience anxiety that includes dwelling on problems even before depressive symptoms are identified. This may help to set the stage of later depression. Early socialization practices that emphasize gender-stereotyped roles for girls and discourage independence and active problem solving may contribute to dysfunctional beliefs and rumination, which help to create risk for later depression (Zahn-Waxler, et al., 2004).

---

[1]See previous section in this volume for pieces discussing various aspects of gender-based violence. Also note that "the lifetime prevalence of PTSD for women who have been sexually assaulted" is at least 50% (http://www.ncbi.nlm.nih.gov/pmc/articles/PMC2323517/) and that in the United States, women are about twice as likely to develop PTSD as are men (http://www.ptsd.ne.gov/what-is-ptsd.html). *Ed.*

By adulthood, women who build their identity narrowly, e.g. mainly around family (a possible consequence of assuming gender-stereotyped roles as children) are more prone to rumination and depression in part due to their narrow base for self-esteem and social support (Law, 2005). More generally, depression is associated with perfectionism and an excessive relational focus (Law, 2005). Excessive relational focus, more common to women than men, is the valuing of relationships to the point of maintaining them regardless of personal costs. Women are more sensitive than men to relationship-based stressors, which can lead to depression.

Other Factors Family history and context also influence the expression of depression in women. Many depressed women were raised in dysfunctional families with parents who had mental health problems (Hammen,

1991). These conditions contribute to antisocial behavior in girls and antisocial girls are prone to depression (Gunter, 2004). Compared with nondepressed women, depressed women are more likely to experience conflict in their marriage and divorce, in part because depressed women are more likely to marry men with psychiatric disorders, which include antisocial behaviors that can be directed toward the woman (Hammen, et al., 1999). Depressed women also have fewer social networks and supports (Belle, 1982) and their friendships tend to be with other depressed women. Thus when their young children do get to play with other children, the mothers of their playmates are more often depressed. Although some of these factors are reflections rather than causes of depression, they tend to perpetuate problems by creating adverse experiences for children that contribute to intergenerational transmission of depression.

SECTION HIGHLIGHTS

- Depression is a very common, but under-diagnosed, disorder. Both nationally and in Wisconsin, twice as many women as men are depressed.
- One of the key factors contributing to depression is poverty. Policies that reduce poverty and that give greater access to treatment for those in poverty will reduce the number of cases of depression.
- The gender difference in depression is not present in childhood, but emerges by 15 years of age. Policies should address the risk factors for depression among adolescent girls.
- Women are especially at risk for depression during the postpartum period. Postpartum depression can be debilitating for the woman and can have negative effects on her child and other family members. Policies must focus on postpartum depression.
- Both biological factors (genetics, hormones) and stressors contribute to depression. Rape and battering are two extreme stressors that disproportionately affect women and increase their risk for depression. Policies that reduce the incidence of rape and battering will help to reduce women's depression.
- Chronic stressors, such as poverty and discrimination, also contribute to depression, putting poor women and women of color at greater risk.

"Depression in Wisconsin Women"

From *Report of the Task Force on Women and Depression in Wisconsin*

The research reviewed in the previous section is based on national data. What is known specifically about women and depression in Wisconsin? According to a 2001 national study, the gender difference found nationally is evident specifically in Wisconsin (National Center for Chronic Disease Prevention, 2005). Thirteen percent of Wisconsin women, compared with six percent of men, reported that they had been diagnosed with depression at least once in their lifetime. In raw numbers, this equates to 259,000 women and 124,000 men who have been diagnosed. This is an underestimate, of course, because many people with depression never seek treatment and therefore are never diagnosed. A longitudinal study conducted with all graduates of Wisconsin high schools from the class of 1957 also found a 2:1 ratio of depressed women to men when assessed at 54 years of age (Wisconsin Longitudinal Study, 2005).

In 2002, Wisconsin Lieutenant Governor Barbara Lawton launched the *Wisconsin Women=Prosperity Initiative* to improve the well-being of women in the state. The Initiative has its roots in a national report, *Status of Women in the States*, a biennial state-by-state comparison compiled by the Institute for Women's Policy Research (IWPR). Among other troubling findings, the IWPR gave Wisconsin a poor evaluation on women's mental health (Institute for Women's Policy Research, 2002).

As part of their overall health index, the Institute for Women's Policy Research used two measures to assess states on women's mental health: poor mental health days and mortality from suicide. On poor mental health days, Wisconsin ranked a low 48 of 51 states. Wisconsin women self-reported an average of 4.4 poor mental health days (depressed and anxious) per month compared with 3.8 for women nationally. On death from suicide, Wisconsin ranked more favorably at 16 of 51 states.

Caution should be used when interpreting the meaning of the IWPR rankings because they are based on few measures and a broad definition of mental health. These data cannot be viewed as a substitute for a more comprehensive, uniform assessment of depression in Wisconsin women, which is needed to assess the true extent of the problem. The findings, however, suggest that women in Wisconsin experience high levels of subclinical depression, which when ignored, often escalates to more severe clinical depression. At the end of this section we highlight a number of factors that may put Wisconsin women at greater risk for depression.

The other measure of mental health status in the IWPR report was suicide, which is most likely a result of depression. While the rates of suicide are relatively low in Wisconsin women, there is still cause for concern. Although men more often complete suicide attempts, women are much more likely to make them. In the past these attempts have been viewed as cries for help and not taken seriously; however, the reason women often do not "succeed" may have more to do with their inability to access methods that more likely guarantee completion of the attempt. As more women gain access to firearms and other more certain methods, these ratios may change. The most promising way to prevent suicide is through early recognition and treatment of depression (Wisconsin Department of Health and Family Services, 2002).

Suicide is the second leading cause of death for individuals between the ages of 15 and 34 years. Young people in Wisconsin may be particularly vulnerable. Suicidal thoughts among Wisconsin teenagers are high, with 1 in 5 high school students having considered suicide. While the rate of youth suicide has declined by 24% nationally over a 9 year period, the rate in Wisconsin declined by only 8% (Eisenberg, et al., 2005). As with older adults, young females are less likely than males to commit suicide; however, they are over twice as likely to be hospitalized for self-inflicted injuries and the medical costs are high. American Indian youth have the highest rates of suicide and hospitalization of all ethnic groups (Eisenberg, et al., 2005).

Other causal factors that increase risk for depression have special relevance to Wisconsin women, e.g. economics, location, education, employment status, reproductive control, and health risk behaviors. Although Wisconsin has a high proportion of high school graduates (ranking 21st in the nation), it ranks low (40th in the nation) relative to other states in terms of levels of higher education (graduate and post-graduate) (U.S. Census Bureau, 2004). Although this education deficit will affect incomes for both women and men, it may have a greater negative impact on women. Women in Wisconsin also rank low on self-owned businesses (33rd in the nation), and, compared with women in the nation as a whole, they work less frequently at higher level jobs such as managers or professionals.

Low income and poverty are associated with higher rates of depression and Wisconsin women have a lower income than women in most other states. Moreover, the wage gap—the *differential* between the income of men and women—is also greater in Wisconsin than the national average. Women's earnings as a percent of men's in 2004 was 80.3% in the United States as a whole and 75.2% in Wisconsin, with Wisconsin ranking 40th in the country on this measure (U.S. Department of Labor and U.S. Bureau of Labor, 2005). The wage gap would be expected to increase women's rates of depression and cause greater economic disadvantage and deprivation, as well as contributing to their lower status as members of society.

Because a relatively large proportion of Wisconsin women live in rural areas they may experience greater isolation, which also contributes to depression. Northern climates, with their shorter days and longer nights during part of the year, are associated with a seasonal form of depression. Another major risk factor for Wisconsin women involves substance abuse, particularly their rates of binge drinking that are almost twice as high as the national average. Alcohol use is commonly linked to depression. It may be a form of self-medication for existing depression, but it may also lead to the development of depression. There are physical health consequences as well, both for the woman and for her children, if she drinks during pregnancy. A risk factor particularly germane to Wisconsin women concerns their lack of control (a factor that contributes to depression) of their own bodies (Institute for Women's Policy Research, 2002). Wisconsin ranked near the bottom of all states (48th) on reproductive rights.

The vast majority of women in Wisconsin (90%) are White. In absolute numbers they represent most of the depressed women in need of treatment; however, as noted, women of color are disproportionately more likely to experience depression and are less likely to be in a position to access treatment. Therefore, it is important to be sensitive to their special needs as can be seen in several examples. Although African American women make up only 6% of the Wisconsin population, they account for 20% of all sexual assault victims (Wisconsin Women's Health Foundation, 2001). They are also incarcerated at disproportionate rates (Gunter, 2004). Both violence against women and women's antisocial behavior are linked to higher rates of depression. These conditions occur most commonly in circumstances of poverty. The city of Milwaukee, with a large African American population, has the seventh highest poverty rate of all cities in the nation, with 26% of all individuals and 41% of children living below the poverty line (U.S. Census Bureau, 2004).

Poverty is also characteristic of large numbers of other ethnic minority women in Wisconsin. Hmong have an unemployment rate of 27% (Hmong Population Research Project, 2000). In a study conducted in western Wisconsin, among Hmong postpartum women, 43% met the criteria for depression (Schaper, 2000). Depression is also common among American Indians in Wisconsin. American Indian women have the highest rates of hospitalization for depression in Wisconsin—1.8 times greater than the rate for White women (Wisconsin Department of Health and Family Services, 2005b).[1]

As ethnic minority populations in Wisconsin increase, more attention will need to be paid to depression in these groups. To the extent that women in Wisconsin, regardless of race/ethnicity, disproportionately experience risk factors for depression, their mental health will remain a significant problem unless these needs are further addressed. There is little reason to think that Wisconsin women differ from women in other states in terms of biologically based vulnerability factors; however, the environmental factors discussed here may contribute to even higher levels of depressive symptoms in Wisconsin women than women in most other states. Cumulatively these risk factors function to interfere with the self-actualization, independence, and positive contributions to society that help to prevent depressive experiences.

READING HIGHLIGHT

Several factors in Wisconsin specifically may increase women's risk for depression. These include a larger gender gap in wages compared with the nation, leaving women more economically distressed, and high rates of poverty in Milwaukee.[1]

---

[1]For more information about the impact of the gender wage gap on women's mental health, see the following piece by Suzannah Weiss. *Ed.*

"The Wage Gap Correlates With Anxiety and Depression in Women, and It's Just One of Many Ways Societal Gender Roles Are Hurting Us"

By Suzannah Weiss

It has long been known that women suffer from higher levels of depression and anxiety than men, and like many gender differences, this discrepancy has frequently been attributed to biology. But a recent study suggests another culprit—or at least another significant factor: The wage gap contributes to women's anxiety and depression.[1] After all, let's face it: Women getting paid less than men is pretty depressing and anxiety-provoking.

The study, conducted at Columbia University's Mailman School of Public Health and published in *Social Science & Medicine*, found that women's depression and anxiety levels correlate with the difference between their earnings and those of men with similar work experience and education levels. While it's true that correlation is not causation, the effect was still drastic and therefore notable: Women with lower earnings than comparable men were 2.5 times more likely than men to be depressed. Women whose incomes equaled or exceeded those of their male counterparts had the same levels of depression as men did. That's right—**the wage gap accounted entirely for gender differences in depression.**

For generalized anxiety disorder, the results were similar: **Women were four times as likely as men to have suffered from anxiety over the past year when they were victims of the wage gap.**

"If women internalize these negative experiences as reflective of inferior merit, rather than the result of discrimination, they may be at increased risk for depression and anxiety disorders," said the study's lead author Jonathan Platt in a press release.

Additionally, senior author Katherine Keyes said that "while it is commonly believed that gender differences in depression and anxiety are biologically rooted, these results suggest that such differences are much more socially constructed that previously thought, indicating that gender disparities in psychiatric disorders are malleable and arise from unfair treatment."

Other studies have indicated that depression and anxiety are, at least to an extent, influenced by societal gender roles. According to research published in the *Journal of the American Academy of Child and Adolescent Psychiatry*, girls and boys are equally anxious[2] until around age 11, yet girls are six times as anxious by age 15. Why? "There's quite a lot of evidence that little girls who exhibit shyness or anxiety are reinforced for it, whereas little boys who exhibit that behavior might even be punished for it," anxiety expert Michelle Craske told *Slate*. In other words, we make a big deal out of girls' troubles while we teach boys to toughen up.

Taylor Clarke pointed out in the same *Slate* article that people consider women (and women consider themselves) more emotional than men, leading to more diagnoses, even when women complain of physical symptoms like chest pain.[3] On top of that, our culture of toxic masculinity discourages men from discussing

---

[1]http://www.eurekalert.org/pub_releases/2016-01/cums-wgc010416.php

[2]http://www.slate.com/articles/life/family/2011/04/nervous_nellies.html
[3]Unfortunately, some of these women with chest pain are actually experiencing heart attacks. Women's heart attack symptoms often differ from the "classic" symptoms based on medical research conducted entirely on men, but even when they present with such classic symptoms, women are still more likely to have their health problem misdiagnosed as psychological. This is despite the fact that more women than men have died from cardiac disease every year in the United States since 1984 (see: http://www.theheartfoundation.org/heart-disease-facts/heart-disease-statistics/). *Ed.*

mental health or seeing a therapist, which could lead men who are anxious or depressed to go undiagnosed.

Lastly, the pressures of being a woman in our society can be anxiety-inducing in of themselves. Ally Boguhn wrote of her anxiety in *Everyday Feminism*: "a lot of the stressors that impact me the most are actually stressors put upon women by society[4] to look and act in certain ways. Some of my biggest stressors have always been about what others think of me: my appearance, my weight, my accomplishments." Women are more likely to dislike their bodies,[5] for example, and that's a stressor right there.

"Considering that on the whole, women are paid less, find it harder to advance in a career, have to juggle multiple roles and are bombarded with images of apparent female 'perfection,' it would be amazing if there wasn't some emotional cost," Daniel and Jason Freeman, authors of *The Stressed Sex: Uncovering the Truth about Men, Women and Mental Health*,[6] wrote in *Time*.

The depression and anxiety gap is one of many examples of gender differences we need to stop dismissing so quickly as "natural." When we attribute these discrepancies to biology, we overlook the structural oppression that contributes to them, which masks how harmful these injustices are.

It shouldn't be surprising to us that women and LGBT people[7] are more anxious and depressed. Sexism, homophobia, and other forms of discrimination are not abstract concepts but phenomena that affect us every day. It's no wonder women have higher levels of anxiety and depression when being a woman in our society is just plain anxiety-provoking and depressing.

[4]http://everydayfeminism.com/2014/05/feminism-and-anxiety/
[5]http://www.bustle.com/articles/133579-men-are-twice-as-likely-as-women-to-love-their-bodies-plus-4-more-stats-proving

[6]http://ideas.time.com/2013/07/18/its-not-just-sexism-women-do-suffer-more-from-mental-illness/#ixzz2ZolPjjPJ
[7]http://www.apa.org/monitor/feb02/newdata.aspx

"Selfies and Health: Self-Care and Self-Representation"

By Elise Nagy

"We don't know how to exist any more without imagining ourselves as a picture."
— Amelia Jones

"You get displaced, and then taking self-portraits becomes a way of hanging on to yourself."
— Nan Goldin

1. Objectification, Gender, and Health

Sometimes it seems like every day comes with a new mountain of essays and articles and studies and casual conversations and offhand comments about selfies. Selfies have been seen as a harbinger of the "end of civilization," a predilection of shallow women and girls who aren't contributing anything to the world—living lives of frivolity and vapid uselessness—or worse, are narcissists and sociopaths. A small portion of these have acknowledged the autonomy and agency that selfies afford the people who take and share them. They may examine the way that selfies exist within, and are often used to resist, a culture wherein girls and women are constantly encouraged to think of their physical appearance as the ultimate determination of their worth.

Whether you're pro- or anti-selfie (or hopefully hold a more nuanced place somewhere in the middle) it's obvious that an overwhelming number of people like to take and share selfies, and that selfies therefore must serve some function in many people's lives. If selfies allow us to relate to our embodiment in new and compelling ways, it's important to understand the old ways we might be trying to outrun or successfully navigate.

Living immersed in a culture where women and girls (and anyone whose gender expression is generally

read as feminine)[1] are constantly objectified—that is, commonly viewed not as individuals but as objects that exist primarily for the pleasure, entertainment, or aesthetic enjoyment of others—creates a phenomenon where many women, girls, and femme people are unable to resist relating to themselves at least partially as objects as well. We are often hyperaware of how we assume other people perceive us, and many of us put an extraordinary amount of time and money into creating and maintaining carefully cultivated appearances. Sometimes this means striving to meet a culturally imposed (and deeply heteronormative and White supremacist) standard of "professionalism" in order to survive under capitalism. Sometimes this means trying

---

[1] I'd like to be very clear that when I use the term "women" I am referring to all people who identify as women, regardless of their sex/gender assignment at birth. I think it's important to also explicitly include "femme people" and "people whose gender expression is usually read as feminine" under the umbrella of people I'm discussing in this essay because they often share the experiences I'm talking about, though not all femme-identified people or people who are read as feminine identify as women. The experiences of cisgender and transgender women, non-binary femme people, femme-identified women, and butch-identified women are necessarily different because of their social locations and the different axes of marginalization they experience, and this article is unfortunately too short to give those differences all of the nuance they deserve, but I hope to leave space for those disparate experiences. I want to specifically acknowledge that everything I discuss here is not only a burden placed on cisgender traditionally feminine-presenting women and girls.

to attain or maintain a compulsorily thin embodiment to avoid body shaming and harassment. Sometimes this involves a time consuming daily hygiene and cosmetic routine. And it often means carrying out a number of short-term body modifications in order to be seen as a desirable romantic or sexual partner.

This time, money, and effort goes towards things like makeup for decoration or camouflage; tanning; waxing and shaving; various "fitness" routines that are more about appearance than health; waist trainers and shape-wear; hair cuts, color, and styling; and even surgery. We can talk about how these expectations are a problem without condemning individual women, girls, and femme people who take steps to meet them for survival, personal enjoyment, or (most often) both. Many people find a meaningful joy, affirmation, and satisfaction in using makeup and other ornamentation to change how they look, and that's important! The problem is not that women and femme-identified people do these things; the problem is that they are *expected and required* to do these things, and that they are vulnerable to financial, social, and physical punishment for not conforming (or trying to conform) to these "feminine ideals." If they fail to meet these expectations they aren't hired, are hired but paid less, aren't promoted, aren't seen as potential romantic or sexual partners, and are subtly or overtly socially excluded or seen as "others." People who are read as women but also read as "masculine" (whether as butch women, transgender women, or both) are particularly vulnerable to physical harm and abuse. In many cases women, girls, and femme people are also punished for partaking in these "rituals" in the "wrong" way, such as by modifying their bodies "too much" or wearing makeup that is seen as transgressive or "unflattering." When the trappings and processes of maintaining or attaining femininity are hyper-visible rather than mystified and passed off as "just how women are," the "naturalness" of femininity is threatened.

Living under this pressure not only has incalculable negative effects on mental and physical wellbeing. It also actively prevents women from taking up personal and collective political and social power. As Susan Bordo wrote in her foundational book *Unbearable Weight: Feminism, Western Culture, and the Body* (1993):

> Through the pursuit of an ever-changing, homogenizing, elusive ideal of femininity—the pursuit without terminus, requiring that women constantly attend to minute and often whimsical changes in fashion—female bodies become docile bodies—bodies whose forces and energies are habituated to external regulation, subtrac-
> tion, transformation, "improvement." Through the exacting and normalizing disciplines of diet, makeup, and dress—central organizing principles of time and space in the day of many women—we are rendered less socially oriented and more centripetally focused on self-modification. Through these disciplines, we continue to memorize on our bodies the feel and conviction of lack, of insufficiency, of never being good enough. At the furthest extremes, the practices of femininity may lead us to utter demoralization, debilitation, and death. (166)

Not only are we extremely stressed and convinced that we're somehow simultaneously inadequate and excessive (often developing mental and physical illnesses as a result) but we also have very little leftover energy to effectively participate as social and political agents in the world. When so much energy goes towards worrying about and maintaining this "elusive ideal of femininity" we don't have as much time to devote to political organizing, or our work, or our art, or our friends and family, or all of the other things we'd rather be doing with our lives than feeling corporeally inadequate or unacceptable.

So this is the context we currently exist in, as women and girls and femme and feminine-read people. Many of us often have a hard time fully inhabiting our bodies without feeling a little like we're floating outside of ourselves looking back at the object we've carefully cultivated, making sure everything is in place. Taking and sharing selfies can of course just be another brick in that wall of self-monitoring and insecurity, but it can also be a subversive and innovative way to resist and survive within this context. Often this resistance and survival goes hand in hand with self-care practices. Throughout 2014 and 2015 I conducted a study consisting of discourse analysis, visual analysis, and ethnographic interviews to better understand how people use selfies to navigate identity, community, and self-care in ways that are often overlooked or underestimated.

2. Selfies as Self-Care

Selfies are devalued in society. Many people assume that they're a waste of time and energy and that they serve no meaningful function. This devaluation happens in a number of ways, particularly through sexist and ableist mechanisms. Because everything coded as "feminine" is socially devalued under patriarchy, selfies are seen as useless and ridiculous specifically through their association with girls and women—especially teenage girls. We've all encountered condescending representations of the stereotypical selfie-taker as a frivolous teenage girl whom we're supposed to regard with derision and dismissal. As one of my interviewees, Sierra, noted:

> "High school aged girls get judged most, I think, for taking photos of themselves because everyone tries to condition them to be the most insecure about their appearance. They're the ones that get bombarded with advertisements [that say] 'have better skin, have eyes like this, do this with your makeup, wear these clothes, this is the kind of body you should have' so as soon as they turn that camera on themselves and are just taking photos for themselves then suddenly it's like 'what are you doing, how dare you be this confident, girls aren't supposed to have that confidence.' Now they're 'arrogant' and now they're 'bitches' and now they're 'sluts' and I hate those words. Like, why would you assign those to 14-year-old girls who are having a good time with their friends? Calm down." (Interview, 2/13/15)

The devaluation of selfies as worthless or actively harmful relies on a society that sees teenage girls as silly and inconsequential.

It also relies on a society that sees disability and mental illness as either terrifying or pitiful, and the rhetoric surrounding selfies taps into these constructs as well. Many people have made offhand associations between selfies and narcissism or selfies and sociopathy/psychopathy, with very little understanding of—or empathy for—people with narcissistic personality disorder or anti-social personality disorder. Certain researchers have in fact conducted studies trying to show observable and significant ties between people's selfie practice and mental illness.[2] In addition to the harm done by othering/dehumanizing real people with personality disorder diagnoses, such work ignores how people with mental illness actually use and conceptualize selfies. While most research and writing exploring the relationship between selfies and mental health reinforces negative perceptions of people with disabilities, including mental illness, and is centered around selfies as a sign of pathology, the way selfies are used to cope with or protect against mental illness has been largely ignored. For people with disabilities, including mental illness, selfies can be a form of self-care.

"Self-care" has various gradations of meaning; it's sometimes understood as necessarily involving community (as a way to take care of each other outside of formal healthcare institutions) and sometimes understood as something more individualistic or personal. Sometimes self-care is thought of as specifically focused on a health issue—in this case, healthcare professionals will sometimes refer to at-home health monitoring and adjustments as "self care" to cope with a specific illness (for example: people with diabetes check their blood sugar and adjust what they eat or how much they exercise to bring their blood sugar within more desirable levels, independently at home without the supervision of a doctor or nurse). Self-care can also be seen as more general and holistic, and not necessarily in response to a specific illness or health concern. As one of my interviewees, Taylor, explains:

> "Self-care is an ongoing process. [. . .] It's something that has to be not like a one-time individual moment but it has to be several small moments rolled into one. I think that it is the act of slowing down, putting yourself first, and trying to understand what your needs are in that moment and meeting them in the best way possible." (Interview, 2/1/15)

My study participants use selfies as a self-care practice to cope with or combat issues including dissociation, depersonalization, body dysmorphia, depression, and anxiety.

In order to understand these strategies, we need to understand what all of those terms really refer to and why their use isn't necessarily straightforward or always beneficial. These are all diagnostic terms that are found in the *Diagnostic and Statistical Manual of Mental Disorders*, used by psychiatrists and psychologists to categorize mental and emotional variations. Diagnostic terms are medicalized terms, and are essentially a way to categorize people who fall outside of the neutral/ideal socially constructed body. In 1963 Erving Goffman described the "mythical norm"—or the human subject seen as both neutral/default and ideal in American society—as a "young, married, white, urban, northern, heterosexual, Protestant" man who is a father, college educated, and is "fully employed, of good complexion, weight and height, and a recent record in sports" (Garland-Thomson 8). As Rosemarie Garland-Thomson, co-director of the Emory University Disabilities Studies Initiative, notes, "Corporeal departures from dominant expectations never go uninterpreted or unpunished, and conformities are almost always rewarded" (ibid. 7). To put it simply: the further you fall from the mythical norm, the more marginalization and structural oppression you experience.

Diagnoses are one way in which we mark or make note of those so-called "deviations" from the mythical

---

[2]Both narcissistic personality disorder and anti-social personality disorder are medicalized and pathologizing terms set forth by the Diagnostic Statistical Manual V (DSM-V).

norm, and they can have violent and harmful effects. Diagnoses have historically been used as a mechanism to deprive people of political and personal autonomy: to justify institutionalization, imprisonment, bodily violation, and forced sterilization, among other forms of exclusion, abuse, and harassment. While diagnostic terms are often helpful as shorthand for describing common bodily and mental experiences, and many people also find personal comfort or utility in the diagnoses they are given (as validation, a first step to a plan for necessary healthcare, etc.), we should be wary of accepting diagnostic terms as carrying some inherent deterministic meaning. Diagnostic terms and individual diagnoses are made by people and are therefore deeply influenced by cultural assumptions and norms. Bearing that in mind, I'm not using these diagnostic terms as if they carry some inherent essential truth about the people or experiences they're applied to, but I do think they're useful in discussing common—sometimes distressing—experiences that people who take selfies talk about going through.

"Dissociation" refers to a sense of disconnection between things that ostensibly should be connected. This might mean emotional numbness in the face of something that would reasonably provoke strong emotions, a sense of disconnection from the physical world or your body, an inability to remember previous experiences, or a sense of disconnection from aspects of your own identity/sense of self. Most of us will experience some degree of dissociation at some point. However, more severe dissociation can lead to significant distress. The International Society for the Study of Trauma and Dissociation (ISSTD) describes "depersonalization" as "the sense of being detached from, or 'not in' one's body. This is what is often referred to as an 'out-of-body' experience. However, some people report rather profound alienation from their bodies, a sense that they do not recognize themselves in the mirror, recognize their face, or simply feel not 'connected' to their bodies in ways which are challenging to articulate" (ISSTD).

While people who experience depersonalization may feel uneasy about their embodiment because of this perceived detachment from their bodies (without necessarily feeling like there's anything flawed about that body) people who experience "body dysmorphia" feel discomfort about their embodiment because they feel that something is inherently wrong with their physical body. According to the Anxiety and Depression Association of America (ADAA), body dysmorphia is characterized by "persistent and intrusive preoccupations with an imagined or slight defect in one's appearance."

Depression and anxiety are becoming more colloquially known, but their symptoms and realities are still widely misunderstood and minimized. Depressive disorders are mood disorders in which people can experience extremely low moods, emotional numbness or disconnection, irritability, hopelessness, lack of interest or pleasure, exhaustion and fatigue, sleep problems, suicidal ideation, difficulty performing basic life tasks, and physical pain such as headaches, muscles aches, gastrointestinal discomfort (NIMH). Symptoms of anxiety disorders can include restlessness, fatigue, difficulty concentrating, irritability, muscle tension and soreness, excessive worrying, sleep problems, debilitating fear, intense avoidance, blushing, sweating, shaking, and nausea (NIMH). These are just some of the things that my interview participants talked about experiencing, and for which they used selfies as a self-care coping technique.

As Emily McCombs writes in a personal essay defending selfies against accusations of "vanity" and "narcissism,"

"For someone like me, behaviors that can be read as vanity are often actually markers of insecurity. In particularly dysmorphic times, I'm checking myself out in every reflective surface to make sure that I am OK, to remind myself that I have not, in the last few minutes, become hideous to look upon, that the proportions of my body are still of the general size and shape favored by humans."

This sense that our bodies might—if not under constant surveillance—become monstrous, embarrassing, or "hideous" is a common experience for many people struggling with depersonalization and dysmorphia. (Of course, this quote and this concern are also undergirded by pervasive social devaluation of people with physical disabilities whose bodies might *not* be "the general size and shape favored by humans.")[3] This sense that we need to monitor ourselves is an effect of the omnipresent cultural pressure for girls, women, femme-identified, and feminine-read people to aspire to a very narrow and prescriptive embodiment of femininity, and to put significant effort into achieving and maintaining that embodiment.

Selfies can also be used as self-care in situations where dissociation and depersonalization go hand in hand with depression. Taylor specifically talked about how she used selfies to cope with this:

"I have depression, so there have been quite a few times when I've been crying because I'm in a depressive episode and I feel sort of alone and I

---

[3]This is one of *many* reasons we need additional future research that specifically considers how people with visible physical disabilities use selfies, particularly to navigate the complexities of embodiment and self-representation.

need to remind myself that my emotions are real and that the things that I'm feeling and going through are real, so I've taken quite a few selfies of me [. . .] in the process of crying for that purpose. Sometimes I've saved them just for me and other times I've posted them in order to facilitate a conversation about mental health or depression specifically, and my struggles with mental health. To give a visual to that is really powerful." (Interview, 2/1/15)

In this way Taylor's self-care is not just an individual practice, but one that involves and even creates community. These selfies help her remind herself that her feelings are "real" (combating dissociation/depersonalization) but then the images and her accompanying captions also go out into the world to create more self-determined and positive representations of mental illness, and to open up opportunities to talk about mental illness despite pervasive stigma and silence. Another interviewee, Kenzie, talked about how selfies let her get comfortable with new aspects of identity and presentation before facing the stress of situations where her body might be read in a way she doesn't want:

"I have a chronic depressive disorder and I also have a generalized anxiety disorder, and so going into situations where I'm not sure how people are going to receive me is almost enough to make me completely avoid that situation forever. And it depends on whether I'm medicated or not, or what kind of day I've had, but there are absolutely times in the course of my life where if I feel like anything about my visual representation of myself is going to draw attention to me, I'm not going to put myself in that situation. So having a space where I feel like I know how I'm going to be received is very important for me coming to terms with that, and beginning to feel so natural that I just don't give a shit. Selfies do and have in the past occupied a space for me to get to that level of comfort with other [. . .] new ways of portraying and negotiating [my identity] to a point where I feel comfortable enough with it to venture out." (Interview, 1/21/15)

Even if we aren't extremely distressed about a sense of disconnection from our bodies, selfies can help navigate that nagging slight discomfort and reaffirm our physical existence in the world. One of my interviewees, Katie, explained:

"Sometimes selfies are 'look at how I exist' but sometimes they are just 'look: I exist' and that is also really important. Sometimes they are a way for me to remind myself that I have a body and for me

to see what that body looks like at that particular moment in time, because often I have no idea. I spend a lot of time in my own head and selfies can be a way to take me out of that a little, a way for me to see myself existing in the world." (Interview, 2/8/15)

Seeing yourself existing in the world is important. It can be disconcerting to not have a reliable and holistic sense of what you look like, to not have a sense of yourself as a real and embodied person. When we're implicitly and explicitly encouraged to think of ourselves as objects to modify for the pleasure or placation of others, it can be difficult to inhabit our bodies as subjects.

In addition, for many of us creating a sense of distance from our bodies can feel protective, especially when we have bodies that are marginalized and vulnerable to fat hatred, racism, sexism, heterosexism, cissexism, and ableism. Taylor explained:

"I ignore my body, I specifically tried to disassociate myself from my body for a really long time, so when I found fat positive spaces it was really important to me to play with my body through the act of taking pictures of it. [. . .] I found that while my thoughts and my opinions of my body would

FIG 1. Katie's Selfie

constantly fluctuate pictures always stayed the same. So it was really helpful for me if I was feeling really down on myself to look back at a picture that I enjoyed and to be able to see that I liked the way I looked; that was really important to me. [. . .] I definitely try to explore different angles or different poses, things like that, just to see what my body looks like in different situations, and it helps me really learn about myself. [. . .] I think as a fat person growing up you are taught to sort of separate yourself from your body if you're not actively trying to change it, so being able to see myself from all different kinds of angles and poses and all of that was really important to me." (Interview, 2/1/15)

Kenzie also noted:

"I've spent a lot of my life living in very conservative very judgmental atmospheres, and having selfies and having the online communities in which I currently share selfies and which I did at the time was certainly an avenue for [playing with personal presentation]. I was very up front about being bisexual and playing with these ideas of queering your visual presentation, and those were not things that would have been safely received had I ventured into the gas station at the corner where everybody's hanging out, you know?" (Interview, 1/21/15)

It's important to be able to (even if only sometimes) see yourself existing in the world as the whole and varied person that you experience yourself to be. While mass media representations are becoming more varied, there is still a dearth of positive and complex representations of women, people of color, LGBTQ+ people, and people with disabilities in mainstream movies, TV shows, ad campaigns, etc. Selfies are used to explore identity and to experiment with bodily expression in a relatively safe environment. Many people use selfies to try to get comfortable with or exert some sense of agency and autonomy over how they are perceived and how they see themselves. Endless aspects of identity and self-expression can fall under this umbrella, but looking at how people navigate gender, sexuality, and (dis)ability is particularly interesting.

3. Selfies as Representation: Disability and Fat Embodiment

Mainstream representations of fat people and people with disabilities are usually in some sense dehumanizing. Mainstream media present pitiful figures played solely to provide comedy, or a tragic storyline, or a narrative of a "miraculous" cure or transformation. Because our society equates thin and abled bodies with health, and health with moral superiority,[4] the bodies of fat people and people with disabilities are often supposed to represent ill health and moral inferiority. Selfies allow people to create more complex conversations around health and to complicate the idea that health is always possible or a worthy aspiration. There is still pervasive shame and silencing around chronic illness, disability, and fat embodiment, and selfies are one way some people can talk about their complicated health status and the way that understanding health as compulsory and morally good can be very alienating and hurtful.

People use selfies to talk about health and disrupt dominant discourses of health in several ways. Many people post selfies that are meant to show that they are closer to or further from normative ideals of "health" than they are assumed to be by people who assess their health status visually—e.g. fat people laying claim to health, or people with invisible illnesses revealing their experience with chronic illness. This shifts the discourse on fatness, making room for the understanding that fat is not inherently linked to illness or poor health; it also shifts the discourse around disability, pushing back against the idea that disability is always visible or legible. It also allows people who are both fat and ill or disabled to talk about their experiences with their embodiment, and to create self-determined representations of an experience that is most often shamed, ridiculed, or ignored.

FIG 2. Paige's Selfie

---

[4]The harmful and unscientific character of these associations is discussed at length elsewhere in this volume. *Ed.*

Within mainstream media and shared cultural narratives, fat women and women with disabilities are rarely allowed or encouraged to be seen as complex, variable, autonomous subjects. The alternate representation of selfies provides a strategy to push back against pervasive, reductive dehumanization. It can be immensely satisfying and important to create counter-representations that more fully show us as we are. People can also use selfies to make "invisible" identities more legible in ways that aren't so limited or determined by (often dehumanizing) medical and social institutions, or to reclaim a sense of bodily autonomy from those institutions. As one of my interviewees, Paige, said:

"I feel like I have more decisions over how my body is presented [in selfies]. And I like that especially because [. . .] everyone wants to control my body. [. . .] I just feel like in a world where everyone is trying to regulate my body selfies give me the chance to do that myself and present it how I want to and own it in a way that I'm not able to as both disabled and a woman, and that's fucking awesome to be able to have that sort of bodily integrity and empowerment that I don't get 90% of the time. Especially when you're poked and prodded by doctors all the time. There's a sense that your body isn't yours when you have imaging done and when you get so many infusions, and you take chemo, [. . .] my hair is not the same. My body isn't mine, it's my disease's at this point. Selfies give me a way where I can be like 'fuck you, this is how I want to present my body, this is how I posed it, this is how I'm filtering it, and that's how I'm presenting it,' in a way I can't do 24/7." (Interview, 1/24/15)

Considering the historical and ongoing phenomenon of people with disabilities being represented in medical literature and popular news stories in non-consensual and dehumanizing ways, being able to create counter-representation that feels more self-determined creates a real sense of empowerment and reclamation.

When selfies are shared—on various social networking and blogging platforms—the effect representation can have goes far beyond the individual posting the image. They can provoke awe, anger, inspiration, hope, disgust, desire, reassurance, unease, and the list goes on. Describing a selfie where she is wearing red lipstick and a blue bra and looking right into the camera (fig. 3) Taylor said:

"I know that people who aren't used to seeing fat bodies or aren't really used to really looking at a fat person would be really shocked by this, probably maybe disgusted, confused at how my body looks the way it does, things like that. [. . .] I remember taking it [. . .] and thinking 'holy shit, I love this.' I remember being afraid to post it a little bit because I didn't know what people would say, which is exactly why I went ahead and posted it, because I knew that if I was hesitant that there would be people who would hate it and there would be people who would have really horrible things to say about it. When I have these moments I encourage myself and force myself to power through because it means that I'm in this moment where I have internalized these really toxic thoughts. If I can overcome them and I can say 'fuck it, I don't care, this is who I am,' then hopefully it can help other people do the same. [. . .] I'm a larger fat person

FIG 3: Taylor's Selfie

and so I think that's inspiring for a lot of people, because if they see a larger fat person especially is embracing their body and is appreciating their body, that makes people want to strive [to appreciate and embrace their own bodies] even more. [...] It's also just sort of fun to piss off people who hate fat people." (Interview, 2/1/15)

We can never be sure what the impact of our selfies will be, but one of the best things they can be is an act of solidarity, a call to action or understanding, and a stubborn insistence that we should be allowed to exist in the world as we are. When we discourage others from taking and sharing selfies, we are not only being invasive and unnecessarily paternalistic; we might also be directly limiting the potential for contagious self-acceptance and self-love. If selfies can encourage us to have compassion for ourselves and for others, and to push for further social justice for people with all kinds of embodiment, it might just be impossible to take or post "too many" selfies.

4. Conclusion

The relationship between selfies and health is anything but straightforward, and further research into the way selfies and health are intertwined is clearly needed. Selfies are often used in ways that are beneficial to health; they are sometimes used to represent people's complicated health status in self-determined ways; they are also used to disrupt ableist and anti-fat discourse surrounding the concept of health. Discussions about selfies are limited and unrealistic when they assume that all selfie-takers are thin, non-disabled, and solely interested in representing hegemonic femininity or accentuating the ways in which they most closely align with normative/idealized embodiments and identities. If Kim Kardashian is the only point of reference for what selfies can be, our conversations on the subject will be severely and unrealistically limited.[5] Ultimately, anti-selfie discourse relies mainly on sexism and ableism (especially scapegoating teenage girls and people with personality disorders) and it unnecessarily pathologizes a behavior that can actually have protective health effects.

WORKS CITED

"Body Dysmorphic Disorder (BDD)." *Understand the Facts: Related Illnesses*. Anxiety and Depression Association of America, Sept. 2014. Web. 16 Mar. 2016. <http://www.adaa.org/understanding-anxiety/related-illnesses/other-related-conditions/body-dysmorphic-disorder-bdd>.

Bordo, Susan. Unbearable Weight: Feminism, Western Culture, and the Body. Berkeley: U of California, 1993. Print.

Diagnostic and Statistical Manual of Mental Disorders: DSM-5. Washington, D.C.: American Psychiatric Association, 2013. Print.

"Dissociation FAQs." *Dissociation FAQs*. International Society for the Study of Trauma and Dissociation, n.d. Web. 16 Mar. 2016.

Garland-Thomson, Rosemarie. *Extraordinary Bodies: Figuring Physical Disability in American Culture and Literature*. New York: Columbia UP, 1997. Print.

McCombs, Emily. "In Defense Of Selfies: Why I'll Never Stop Taking Photos Of Myself." xoJane, 5 Mar. 2013. Web.

"NAMI: National Alliance on Mental Illness." *NAMI: National Alliance on Mental Illness*. NAMI, n.d. Web. 17 Mar. 2016. <https://www.nami.org/>.

---

[5]An avid selfie-taker who has publicly defended her prolific selfie practice both on her TV show, *Keeping Up With The Kardashians* and on Twitter, Kardashian West published a book titled *Selfish* in 2015 that mostly consists of selfies. Kardashian West is often publicly criticized for her selfie practice and the fact that this collection was **not** categorized as an "art book" or similar is necessarily informed by pervasive cultural misogyny and the specific devaluation of women's selfies as visual objects. I don't mean to pile onto that criticism, only to suggest that selfies can exist as a great many things beyond displays of hegemonic and normative femininity.

SECTION 11

SOCIAL STRUCTURE AND ENVIRONMENTAL FACTORS

"Sick Woman Theory"

By Johanna Hedva

All photos by Pamila Payne;[1] Styling, hair and makeup: Myrrhia Rodriguez; Art Direction: Johanna Hedva

Johanna Hedva lives with chronic illness and her sick woman theory is for those who were never meant to survive but did.

1.

In late 2014, I was sick with a chronic condition that, about every 12 to 18 months, gets bad enough to render me, for about five months each time, unable to walk, drive, do my job, sometimes speak or understand language, take a bath without assistance, and leave the bed. This particular flare coincided with the Black Lives Matter protests, which I would have attended unremittingly, had I been able to. I live one block away from MacArthur Park in Los Angeles, a predominantly Latino neighborhood and one colloquially understood to be the place where many immigrants begin their American lives. The park, then, is not surprisingly one of the most active places of protest in the city.

I listened to the sounds of the marches as they drifted up to my window. Attached to the bed, I rose up my sick woman fist, in solidarity.

I started to think about what modes of protest are afforded to sick people—it seemed to me that many for whom Black Lives Matter is especially in service, might not be able to be present for the marches because they were imprisoned by a job, the threat of being fired from their job if they marched, or literal incarceration, and of course the threat of violence and police brutality—but also because of illness or disability, or because they were caring for someone with an illness or disability.

[1]http://www.pamilapayne.com/

Originally published in Mask Magazine, January 2016. Edited by Hanna Hurr and Isabelle Nastasia. Reprinted by permission. www.maskmagazine.com

I thought of all the other invisible bodies, with their fists up, tucked away and out of sight.

If we take Hannah Arendt's definition of the political—which is still one of the most dominant in mainstream discourse—as being any action that is performed in public, we must contend with the implications of what that excludes. If being present in public is what is required to be political, then whole swathes of the population can be deemed *a*-political—simply because they are not physically able to get their bodies into the street.

In my graduate program, Arendt was a kind of god, and so I was trained to think that her definition of the political was radically liberating. Of course, I can see that it was, in its own way, in its time (the late 1950s): in one fell swoop she got rid of the need for infrastructures of law, the democratic process of voting, the reliance on individuals who've accumulated the power to affect policy—she got rid of the need for policy at all. All of these had been required for an action to be considered political and visible as such. No, Arendt said, just get your body into the street, and *bam*: political.

There are two failures here, though. The first is her reliance on a "public"—which requires a private, a binary between visible and invisible space. This meant that whatever takes place in private is *not* political. So, you can beat your wife in private and it doesn't matter, for instance. You can send private emails containing racial slurs, but since they weren't "meant for the public," you are somehow not racist. Arendt was worried that if everything can be considered political, then nothing will be, which is why she divided the space into one that is political and one that is not. But for the sake of this anxiety, she chose to sacrifice whole groups of people, to continue to banish them to invisibility and political irrelevance. She chose to keep them out of the public sphere. I'm not the first to take Arendt to task for this. The failure of Arendt's political was immediately exposed in the civil rights activism and feminism of the 1960s and 70s. "The personal is political" can also be read as saying "the private is political." Because of course, *everything* you do in private is political: who you have sex with, how long your showers are, if you have access to clean water for a shower at all, and so on.

There is another problem too. As Judith Butler put it in her 2015 lecture, "Vulnerability and Resistance,"[2] Arendt failed to account for who is allowed in to the public space, of *who's in charge* of the public. Or, more specifically, *who's in charge of who gets in*. Butler says that there is always one thing true about a public demonstration: the police are already there, or they are coming. This resonates with frightening force when considering the context of Black Lives Matter. The inevitability of violence at a demonstration—especially a demonstration that emerged to insist upon the importance of bodies who've been violently un-cared for—ensures that a certain amount of people won't, because they can't, show up. Couple this with physical and mental illnesses and disabilities that keep people in bed and at home, and we must contend with the fact that many whom these protests are for, are not able to participate in them—which means they are not able to be visible as political activists.

There was a Tumblr post that came across my dash during these weeks of protest, that said something to the effect of: "shout out to all the disabled people, sick people, people with PTSD, anxiety, etc., who can't protest in the streets with us tonight. Your voices are heard and valued, and with us." Heart. Reblog.

So, as I lay there, unable to march, hold up a sign, shout a slogan that would be heard, or be visible in any traditional capacity as a political being, the central question of Sick Woman Theory formed: How do you throw a brick through the window of a bank if you can't get out of bed?

---

[2]View the lecture here: https://www.youtube.com/atch?v=fbYOzbfGPmo

2.

I have chronic illness. For those who don't know what chronic illness means, let me help: the word "chronic" comes from the Latin *chronos*, which means "of time" (think of "chronology"), and it specifically means "a lifetime." So, a chronic illness is an illness that lasts a lifetime. In other words, it does not get better. There is no cure.[3]

And think about the weight of time: yes, that means you feel it every day. On very rare occasions, I get caught in a moment, as if something's plucked me out of the world, where I realize that I haven't thought about my illnesses for a few minutes, maybe a few precious hours. These blissful moments of oblivion are the closest thing to a miracle that I know. When you have chronic illness, life is reduced to a relentless rationing of energy. It costs you to do anything: to get out of bed, to cook for yourself, to get dressed, to answer an email. For those without chronic illness, you can spend and spend without consequence: the cost is not a problem. For those of us with limited funds, we have to ration, we have a limited supply: we often run out before lunch.

I've come to think about chronic illness in other ways.

Ann Cvetkovich[4] writes: "What if depression, in the Americas, at least, could be traced to histories of colonialism, genocide, slavery, legal exclusion, and everyday segregation and isolation that haunt all of our lives, rather than to be biochemical imbalances?" I'd like to change the word "depression" here to be all mental illnesses. Cvetkovich continues: "Most medical literature tends to presume a white and middle-class subject for whom feeling bad is frequently a mystery because it doesn't fit a life in which privilege and comfort make things seem fine on the surface." In other words, wellness as it is talked about in America today, is a white and wealthy idea.

Let me quote Starhawk, in the preface to the new edition of her 1982 book *Dreaming the Dark*: "Psychologists have constructed a myth—that somewhere there exists some state of health which is the norm, meaning that most people presumably are in that state, and those who are anxious, depressed, neurotic, distressed, or generally unhappy are deviant." I'd here supplant the word "psychologists" with "white supremacy,"

"doctors," "your boss," "neoliberalism," "heteronormativity," and "America."

There has been a slew of writing in recent years about how "female" pain is treated—or rather, not treated as seriously as men's in emergency rooms and clinics, by doctors, specialists, insurance companies, families, husbands, friends, the culture at large. In a recent article in *The Atlantic*, called "How Doctors Take Women's Pain Less Seriously,"[5] a husband writes about the experience of his wife Rachel's long wait in the ER before receiving the medical attention her condition warranted (which was an ovarian torsion, where an ovarian cyst grows so large it falls, twisting the fallopian tube). "Nationwide, men wait an average of 49 minutes before receiving an analgesic for acute abdominal pain. Women wait an average of 65 minutes for the same thing. Rachel waited somewhere between 90 minutes and two hours," he writes. At the end of the ordeal, Rachel had waited nearly fifteen hours before going into the surgery she should have received upon arrival. The article concludes with her physical scars healing, but that "she's still grappling with the psychic toll—what she calls 'the trauma of not being seen.'"

What the article does not mention is race—which leads me to believe that the writer and his wife are white. Whiteness is what allows for such oblivious neutrality: it is the premise of blankness, the presumption of the universal. (Studies have shown that white people will listen to other white people when talking about race, far more openly than they will to a person of color. As someone who is white-passing, let me address white people directly: look at my white face and listen up.)

The *trauma of not being seen*. Again – *who is allowed in* to the public sphere? Who is allowed to be visible? I don't mean to diminish Rachel's horrible experience—I myself once had to wait ten hours in an ER to be diagnosed with a burst ovarian cyst—I only wish to point out the presumptions upon which her horror relies: that our vulnerability should be seen and honored, and that we should all receive care, quickly and in a way that "respects the autonomy of the patient," as the Four Principles of Biomedical Ethics puts it. Of course, these presumptions are what we all should have. But we must ask the question of who is allowed to have them. In whom does society substantiate such beliefs? And in whom does society enforce the opposite?

Compare Rachel's experience at the hands of the medical establishment with that of Kam Brock.[6] In

---

[3]For more information on how women are disproportionately affected by chronic illness and how our current healthcare systems often fail to provide appropriate care, see the National Women's Law Center report "State of Women's Coverage: Health Plan Violations of the Affordable Care Act Key Findings" elsewhere in this volume. *Ed.*
[4]http://www.anncvetkovich.com/

---

[5]http://www.theatlantic.com/health/archive/2015/10/emergency-room-wait-times-sexism/410515/
[6]http://www.nydailynews.com/new-york/exclusive-woman-held-psych-ward-obama-twitter-claim-article-1.2159049

September 2014, Brock, a 32-year-old black woman, born in Jamaica and living in New York City, was driving a BMW when she was pulled over by the police. They accused her of driving under the influence of marijuana, and though her behavior and their search of her car yielded nothing to support this, they nevertheless impounded her car. According to a lawsuit brought against the City of New York and Harlem Hospital by Brock, when Brock appeared the next day to retrieve her car she was arrested by the police for behaving in a way that she calls "emotional," and involuntarily hospitalized in the Harlem Hospital psych ward. (As someone who has also been involuntarily hospitalized for behaving "too" emotionally, this story feels like a rip of recognition through my brain.) The doctors thought she was "delusional" and suffering from bipolar disorder, because she claimed that Obama followed her on twitter – *which was true*, but which the medical staff failed to confirm. She was then held for eight days, forcibly injected with sedatives, made to ingest psychiatric medication, attend group therapy, and stripped. The medical records of the hospital—obtained by her lawyers—bear this out: the "master treatment plan" for Brock's stay reads, "Objective: Patient will verbalize the importance of education for employment and will state that Obama is not following her on Twitter." It notes her "inability to test reality." Upon her release, she was given a bill for $13,637.10.

The question of why the hospital's doctors thought Brock "delusional" because of her Obama-follow claim is easily answered: Because, according to this society, a young black woman can't possibly be that important—and for her to insist that she is must mean she's "sick."

3.

Before I can speak of the "sick woman" in all of her many guises, I must first speak as an individual, and address you from my particular location.

I am antagonistic to the notion that the Western medical-insurance industrial complex understands me in my entirety, though they seem to think they do. They have attached many words to me over the years, and though some of these have provided articulation that was useful—after all, no matter how much we are working to change the world, we must still find ways of coping with the reality at hand—first I want to suggest some other ways of understanding my "illness."

Perhaps it can all be explained by the fact that my Moon's in Cancer in the 8th House, the House of Death, or that my Mars is in the 12th House, the House of Illness, Secrets, Sorrow, and Self-Undoing. Or, that my father's mother escaped from North Korea in her childhood and hid this fact from the family until a few years ago, when she accidentally let it slip out, and then swiftly, revealingly, denied it. Or, that my mother suffers from undiagnosed mental illness that was actively denied by her family, and was then exasperated by a 40-year-long drug addiction, sexual trauma, and hepatitis from a dirty needle, and to this day remains untreated, as she makes her way in and out of jails, squats, and homelessness. Or, that I was physically and emotionally abused as a child, raised in an environment of poverty, addiction, and violence, and have been estranged from my parents for 13 years. Perhaps it's because I'm poor—according to the IRS, in 2014, my adjusted gross income was $5,730 (a result of not being well enough to work full-time)—which means that my health insurance is provided by the state of California (Medi-Cal), that my "primary care doctor" is a group of physician's assistants and nurses in a clinic on the second floor of a strip mall, and that I rely on food stamps to eat. Perhaps it can be encapsulated in the word "trauma." Perhaps I've just got thin skin, and have had some bad luck.

It's important that I also share the Western medical terminology that's been attached to me—whether I like it or not, it can provide a common vocabulary: "This is the oppressor's language," Adrienne Rich wrote in 1971, "yet I need it to talk to you."[7] But let me offer another language, too. In the Native American Cree language, the possessive noun and verb of a sentence are structured differently than in English. In Cree, one does not say, "I am sick." Instead, one says, "The sickness has come to me." I love that and want to honor it.

So, here is what has come to me:

Endometriosis, which is a disease of the uterus where the uterine lining grows where it shouldn't—in the pelvic area mostly, but also anywhere, the legs, abdomen, even the head. It causes chronic pain; gastrointestinal chaos; epic, monstrous bleeding; in some cases, cancer; and means that I have miscarried, can't have children, and have several surgeries to look forward to. When I explained the disease to a friend who didn't know about it, she exclaimed: "So your whole body is a uterus!" That's one way of looking at it, yes. (Imagine what the Ancient Greek doctors—the fathers of the theory of the "wandering womb"—would say about that.) It means that every month, those rogue uterine cells that have implanted themselves throughout my body, "obey their nature and

---

[7]While Rich remains an extremely important figure in contemporary gender studies and activism, we should also recognize her active support of some of her second-wave feminist contemporaries who worked to deliberately exclude transgender women from feminist movements and even block their access to necessary resources, including healthcare. *Ed.*

bleed," to quote fellow endo warrior Hilary Mantel. This causes cysts, which eventually burst, leaving behind bundles of dead tissue like the debris of little bombs.

Bipolar disorder, panic disorder, and depersonalization disorder have also come to me. This means that I live between this world and another one, one created by my own brain that has ceased to be contained by a discrete concept of "self." Because of these "disorders," I have access to incredibly vivid emotions, flights of thought, and dreamscapes, to the feeling that my mind has been obliterated into stars, to the sensation that I have become nothingness, as well as to intense ecstasies, raptures, sorrows, and nightmarish hallucinations. I have been hospitalized, voluntarily and involuntarily, because of it, and one of the medications I was prescribed once nearly killed me—it produces a rare side effect where one's skin falls off. Another cost $800 a month—I only took it because my doctor slipped me free samples. If I want to be able to hold a job—which this world has decided I ought to be able to do—I must take an anti-psychotic medication daily that causes short-term memory loss and drooling, among other sexy side effects. These visitors have also brought their friends: nervous breakdowns, mental collapses, or whatever you want to call them, three times in my life. I'm certain they will be guests in my house again. They have motivated attempts at suicide (most of them while dissociated) more than a dozen times, the first one when I was nine years old. That first attempt didn't work, only because after taking a mouthful of sleeping pills, I somehow woke up the next day and went to school, like nothing had happened. I told no one about it, until my first psychiatric evaluation in my mid-20s.

Finally, an autoimmune disease that continues to baffle all the doctors I've seen, has come to me and refuses still to be named. As Carolyn Lazard has written about her experiences with autoimmune diseases: "Autoimmune disorders are difficult to diagnose. For ankylosing spondylitis, the average time between the onset of symptoms and diagnosis is eight to twelve years. I was lucky; I only had to wait one year." Names like "MS," "fibromyalgia," and others that I can't remember have fallen from the mouths of my doctors—but my insurance won't cover the tests, nor is there a specialist in my insurance plan within one hundred miles of my home. I don't have enough space here—will I ever?—to describe what living with an autoimmune disease is like. I can say it brings unimaginable fatigue, pain all over all the time, susceptibility to illnesses, a body that performs its "normal" functions monstrously abnormally. The worst symptom that mine brings is chronic shingles. For ten years I've gotten shingles in the same place on my back, so that I now have nerve damage there, which results in a ceaseless, searing pain on the skin and a dull, burning ache in the bones. Despite taking daily medication that is supposed to "suppress" the shingles virus, I still get them—they are my canaries in the coalmine, the harbingers of at least three weeks to be spent in bed.

My acupuncturist described it as a little demon steaming black smoke, frothing around, nestling into my bones.

4.

With all of these visitors, I started writing Sick Woman Theory as a way to survive in a reality that I find unbearable, and as a way to bear witness to a self that does not feel like it can possibly be "mine."

The early instigation for the project of "Sick Woman Theory," and how it inherited its name, came from a few sources. One was in response to Audrey Wollen's "Sad Girl Theory,"[8] which proposes a way of redefining historically feminized pathologies into modes of political protest for girls: I was mainly concerned with the question of what happens to the sad girl when, if, she grows up. Another was incited by reading Kate Zambreno's fantastic *Heroines*,[9] and feeling an itch to fuck with the concept of "heroism" at all, and so I wanted to propose a figure with traditionally anti-heroic qualities—namely illness, idleness, and inaction—as capable of being the symbol of a grand Theory. Another was from the 1973 feminist book *Complaints and Disorders*, which differentiates between the "sick woman" of the white upper class, and the "sickening women" of the non-white working class.

Sick Woman Theory is for those who are faced with their vulnerability and unbearable fragility, every day, and so have to fight for their experience to be not only honored, but first made visible. For those who, in Audre Lorde's words, were never meant to survive: because this world was built against their survival. It's for my fellow spoonies.[10] You know who you are, even if you've not been attached to a diagnosis: one of the aims of Sick Woman Theory is to resist the notion that one needs to be legitimated by an institution, so that they can try to fix you. You don't need to be fixed, my queens—it's the world that needs the fixing.

---

[8]http://www.cultistzine.com/2014/06/19/cult-talk-audrey-wollen-on-sad-girl-theory/
[9]http://www.amazon.com/Heroines-Semiotext-Active-Agents-Zambreno/dp/1584351144
[10]For more discussion of the terms "spoonies" and "spoons," see Christine Miserandino's "Spoon Theory": http://www.butyoudontlooksick.com/articles/written-by-christine/the-spoon-theory/ *Ed.*

I offer this as a call to arms and a testimony of recognition. I hope that my thoughts can provide articulation and resonance, as well as tools of survival and resilience.

And for those of you who are not chronically ill or disabled, Sick Woman Theory asks you to stretch your empathy this way. To face us, to listen, to see.

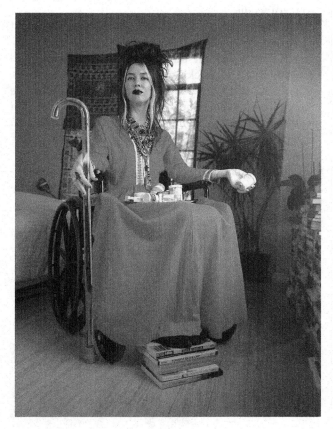

5.

Sick Woman Theory is an insistence that most modes of political protest are internalized, lived, embodied, suffering, and no doubt invisible. Sick Woman Theory redefines existence in a body as something that is primarily and always vulnerable, following from Judith Butler's work on precarity and resistance. Because the premise insists that a body is defined by its vulnerability, not temporarily affected by it, the implication is that it is continuously reliant on infrastructures of support in order to endure, and so we need to re-shape the world around this fact. Sick Woman Theory maintains that the body and mind are sensitive and reactive to regimes of oppression—particularly our current regime of neoliberal, white-supremacist, imperial-capitalist, cis-hetero-patriarchy. It is that all of our bodies and minds carry the historical trauma of this, that it is *the world itself* that is making and keeping us sick.

To take the term "woman" as the subject-position of this work is a strategic, all-encompassing embrace and dedication to the particular, rather than the universal. Though the identity of "woman" has erased and excluded many (especially women of color and trans and genderfluid people), I choose to use it because it still represents the un-cared for, the secondary, the oppressed, the non-, the un-, the less-than. The problematics of this term will always require critique, and I hope that Sick Woman Theory can help undo those in its own way. But more than anything, I'm inspired to use the word "woman" because I saw this year how it can still be radical to be a woman in the 21st century. I use it to honor a dear friend of mine who came out as genderfluid last year. For her, what mattered the most was to be able to call herself a "woman," to use the pronouns "she/her." She didn't want surgery or hormones; she loved her body and her big dick and didn't want to change it—she only wanted the word. That the word itself can be an empowerment is the spirit in which Sick Woman Theory is named.

The Sick Woman is an identity and body that can belong to anyone denied the privileged existence—or the cruelly optimistic *promise* of such an existence—of the white, straight, healthy, neurotypical, upper and middle-class, cis- and able-bodied man who makes his home in a wealthy country, has never not had health insurance, and whose importance to society is everywhere recognized and made explicit by that society; whose importance and care *dominates* that society, at the expense of everyone else.

The Sick Woman is anyone who does not have this guarantee of care.

The Sick Woman is told that, to this society, her care, even her survival, does not matter.

The Sick Woman is all of the "dysfunctional," "dangerous" and "in danger," "badly behaved," "crazy," "incurable," "traumatized," "disordered," "diseased," "chronic," "uninsurable," "wretched," "undesirable" and altogether "dysfunctional" bodies belonging to women, people of color, poor, ill, neuro-atypical, differently abled, queer, trans, and genderfluid people, who have been historically pathologized, hospitalized, institutionalized, brutalized, rendered "unmanageable," and therefore made culturally illegitimate and politically invisible.

The Sick Woman is a black trans woman having panic attacks while using a public restroom, in fear of the violence awaiting her.

The Sick Woman is the child of parents whose indigenous histories have been erased, who suffers from the trauma of generations of colonization and violence.

The Sick Woman is a homeless person, especially one with any kind of disease and no access to treatment, and whose only access to mental-health care is a 72-hour hold in the county hospital.

The Sick Woman is a mentally ill black woman whose family called the police for help because she was suffering an episode, and who was murdered in police custody, and whose story was denied by everyone operating under white supremacy. Her name is Tanesha Anderson.[11]

The Sick Woman is a 50-year-old gay man who was raped as a teenager and has remained silent and shamed, believing that men can't be raped.

The Sick Woman is a disabled person who couldn't go to the lecture on disability rights because it was held in a venue without accessibility.

The Sick Woman is a white woman with chronic illness rooted in sexual trauma who must take painkillers in order to get out of bed.

The Sick Woman is a straight man with depression who's been medicated (managed) since early adolescence and now struggles to work the 60 hours per week that his job demands.

The Sick Woman is someone diagnosed with a chronic illness, whose family and friends continually tell them they should exercise more.

The Sick Woman is a queer woman of color whose activism, intellect, rage, and depression are seen by white society as unlikeable attributes of her personality.

The Sick Woman is a black man killed in police custody, and officially said to have severed his own spine. His name is Freddie Gray.[12]

The Sick Woman is a veteran suffering from PTSD on the months-long waiting list to see a doctor at the VA.

The Sick Woman is a single mother, illegally emigrated to the "land of the free," shuffling between three jobs in order to feed her family, and finding it harder and harder to breathe.

The Sick Woman is the refugee.

The Sick Woman is the abused child.

The Sick Woman is the person with autism whom the world is trying to "cure."[13]

The Sick Woman is the starving.

The Sick Woman is the dying.

And, crucially: The Sick Woman is who capitalism needs to perpetuate itself.

Why?

Because to stay alive, capitalism cannot be responsible for our care—its logic of exploitation requires that some of us die.

"Sickness" as we speak of it today is a capitalist construct, as is its perceived binary opposite, "wellness." The "well" person is the person well enough to go to work. The "sick" person is the one who can't. What is so destructive about conceiving of wellness as the default, as the standard mode of existence, is that it *invents illness as temporary*. When being sick is an abhorrence to the norm, it *allows us to conceive of care and support in the same way*.

Care, in this configuration, is only required sometimes. When sickness is temporary, care is not normal.

Here's an exercise: go to the mirror, look yourself in the face, and say out loud: "To take care of you is not normal. I can only do it temporarily."

Saying this to yourself will merely be an echo of what the world repeats all the time.

---

[11]http://www.cleveland.com/metro/index.ssf/2014/11/cleveland_woman_with_mental_il_1.html

[12]http://data.baltimoresun.com/news/freddie-gray/

[13]Many *allistic* (not autistic) people have been taught to see a "cure" for autism as a laudable goal. Many autistic people (an identity label often preferred over "people with autism"), however, point out that to "cure" autism would be to completely redesign their brains. That is, it would mean replacing autistic people with completely different beings who just happened to look exactly like the people who had been destroyed. For allistic people, this would not be a "medical advance"; it is essentially the plot to *Invasion of the Body Snatchers. Ed.*

6.

I used to think that the most anti-capitalist gestures left had to do with love, particularly love poetry: to write a love poem and give it to the one you desired, seemed to me a radical resistance. But now I see I was wrong.

The most anti-capitalist protest is to care for another and to care for yourself. To take on the historically feminized and therefore invisible practice of nursing, nurturing, caring. To take seriously each other's vulnerability and fragility and precarity, and to support it, honor it, empower it. To protect each other, to enact and practice community. A radical kinship, an interdependent sociality, a politics of care.

Because, once we are all ill and confined to the bed, sharing our stories of therapies and comforts, forming support groups, bearing witness to each other's tales of trauma, prioritizing the care and love of our sick, pained, expensive, sensitive, fantastic bodies, and there is no one left to go to work, perhaps then, finally, capitalism will screech to its much-needed, long-overdue, and motherfucking glorious halt.

***

This text is adapted from the lecture, "My Body Is a Prison of Pain so I Want to Leave It Like a Mystic But I Also Love It & Want It to Matter Politically," delivered at Human Resources, sponsored by the Women's Center for Creative Work, in Los Angeles, on October 7, 2015. The video is here.[14]

***

RECOMMENDED TEXTS[15]

Arendt, Hannah. The Human Condition. Chicago: University of Chicago Press, 1958.

Berkowitz, Amy. Tender Points. Oakland: Timeless, Infinite Light, 2015.

Berlant, Lauren Gail. Cruel Optimism. Durham: Duke University Press, 2011.

Brown, Stephen Rex. "Woman Held in Psych Ward over Obama Twitter Claim." *NY Daily News*. March 23, 2015.

Butler, Judith. "Vulnerability and Resistance." REDCAT. December 19, 2014.

Cvetkovich, Ann. *Depression: A Public Feeling*. Durham, N.C.: Duke University Press, 2012.

Ehrenreich, Barbara, and Deirdre English. *Complaints and Disorders; the Sexual Politics of Sickness*. Old Westbury, N.Y.: Feminist Press, 1973.

Fassler, Joe. "How Doctors Take Women's Pain Less Seriously."*The Atlantic*, October 15, 2015.

Federici, Silvia. *Caliban and the Witch: Women, the Body and Primitive Accumulation*. New York: Autonomedia, 2003.

Halberstam, Jack. "Zombie Humanism at the End of the World." Lecture, *Weak Resistance: Everyday Struggles and the Politics of Failure*, ICI Berlin, May 27, 2015.

Harney, Stefano, and Fred Moten. *The Undercommons: Fugitive Planning & Black Study*. New York: Minor Compositions, 2013.

Hedva, Johanna. "My Body Is a Prison of Pain so I Want to Leave It Like a Mystic But I Also Love It & Want It to Matter Politically." Lecture, Human Resources, Los Angeles, October 7, 2015.

Lazard, Carolyn. "How to Be a Person in the Age of Autoimmunity." The Cluster Mag. January 16, 2013.

Lorde, Audre. A Burst of Light: Essays. Ithaca, N.Y.: Firebrand Books, 1988.

Lorde, Audre. The Cancer Journals. Special ed. San Francisco: Aunt Lute Books, 1997.

Mantel, Hilary. "Every Part of My Body Hurt." *The Guardian*, June 7, 2004.

Miserandino, Christine. "The Spoon Theory Written by Christine Miserandino." But You Dont Look Sick: Support for Those with Invisible Illness or Chronic Illness. April 25, 2013.

Rich, Adrienne. "The Burning of Paper Instead of Children." In *Adrienne Rich's Poetry and Prose: Poems, Prose, Reviews, and Criticism*, edited by Barbara Charlesworth Gelpi. New York: W.W. Norton, 1993.

Salek, Yasi. "Audrey Wollen on Sad Girl Theory." CULTIST ZINE. June 19, 2014.

Starhawk. Dreaming the Dark: Magic, Sex, & Politics. 2nd ed. Boston: Beacon Press, 1988.

Thurman, Judith. "A Loss for Words: Can a Dying Language Be Saved?" The New Yorker, March 30, 2015.

Vankin, Jonathan. "Kam Brock: The Reason They Threw Her In A Mental Ward Was Crazy—What Happened Next Was Even Crazier." The Inquisitr News. March 24, 2015.

Zambreno, Kate. Heroines. Semiotext(e) / Active Agents, 2012.

---

[14]https://vimeo.com/144782433

[15]Original color photographs and active links to recommended texts may be found in the original online version of this article here: http://www.maskmagazine.com/not-again/struggle/sick-woman-theory

"Four Critical Questions to Ask Before You Buy Pink"

From *Breast Cancer Action*

Pinkwashing

Breast Cancer Action coined the term *pinkwashing* as part of our **Think Before You Pink®** campaign.

Pinkwasher: (pink'-wah-sher) noun.

A company or organization that claims to care about breast cancer by promoting a pink ribbon product, but at the same time produces, manufactures and/or sells products that are linked to the disease.

1. Does any money from this purchase go to support breast cancer programs? How much?

Any company can put a pink ribbon on its products. The widely recognized pink ribbon symbol is not regulated by any agency and does not necessarily mean it effectively combats the breast cancer epidemic. Some products sport pink ribbons to try to communicate that they are "healthy" and don't contribute to breast cancer, such as a number of natural health and beauty products. Other products have a pink ribbon in order to indicate that the company supports breast cancer programs even if the company's contributions are not tied to the purchases of the specific product bearing the ribbon. Still other companies give a portion of an item's cost to a breast cancer organization but may require further action on the part of the consumer for the donation to be realized. Can you tell how much money from your purchases will go to support breast cancer programs? If not, consider giving directly to the charity of your choice instead.

EXAMPLE: In 2010, Dansko shoe company sold pink ribbon clogs. Consumers likely thought that a portion of their purchase of pink ribbon clogs went to a breast cancer program. However, purchase of the pink ribbon clogs was not connected to Dansko's donation—none of the portion of the sales went toward their already set donation of $25,000 to Susan G. Komen for the Cure. No matter whether or not you bought the clogs, their donation was the same.

2. What organization will get the money? What will they do with the funds, and how do these programs turn the tide of the breast cancer epidemic?

Many companies that sell pink ribbon products and donate a percentage of each sale to breast cancer programs fail to indicate which of the many different breast cancer organizations will get the money. Furthermore, the consumer is left to trust that these organizations are engaged in work that is meaningful and makes the greatest difference. If money goes to "services," are they reaching the people who need them most? How do screening programs ensure that women can get treatment? And how do breast cancer awareness programs address the fact that we already know that breast cancer is a problem and that action is needed in order to end the epidemic? Does the money go to truly addressing the root causes of the epidemic, like social inequities that lead to women of color and poor women dying more often of breast cancer, or environmental toxins that are contributing to high rates of breast cancer? Before donating, check the recipient organization's website to make sure that its mission and activities are in line with your personal values. If you can't tell, or you don't know what the organization does, reconsider your purchase.

EXAMPLE: The KISSES for a Cure music box is advertised by its maker, The Bradford Exchange, online with the following: "A portion of the proceeds from this music box will be donated to help fight breast cancer." It is not clear what breast cancer organizations would benefit, how much money they would receive, and what programs or work would be funded by the donation.

3. Is there a "cap" on the amount the company will donate? Has this maximum donation already been met? Can you tell?

Some companies that indicate that a portion of the proceeds from the sale of a particular pink ribbon product will go to support breast cancer programs put an arbitrary "cap" on their maximum donation. Once the maximum amount has been met, the company may continue to sell the product with the pink ribbon without alerting customers that no additional funds will be donated to breast cancer organizations. This means you may be buying a product for which none of your purchase price will go to a breast cancer cause but only to the bottom line of the company.

EXAMPLE: In 2010, Reebok marketed a line of pink ribbon emblazoned footwear and apparel at prices ranging from $50 to $100. Though it heavily promoted the fact that some of their pink ribbon product sales would be donated to the Avon Breast Cancer Crusade, they set a limit of $750,000, regardless of how many items were sold, and there was no mechanism in place to alert consumers once the maximum donation had been met.

4. Does this purchase put you or someone you love at risk for exposure to toxins linked to breast cancer? What is the company doing to ensure that its products are not contributing to the breast cancer epidemic?

Many companies have sold pink ribbon products that are linked to increased risk of breast cancer. We believe that companies that are profiting from building a reputation based on their concern about breast cancer have a responsibility to protect the public from possible harms when scientific research indicates that there is a risk or plausible reason for concern. Some of the earliest cause-marketing companies were well-known cosmetics companies that continue to sell cosmetics containing chemicals that have been linked to breast cancer. Even car companies have gotten in on the action and sell cars that emit toxic air pollutants in the name of breast cancer. In considering a pink ribbon purchase, does the product contain toxins or otherwise increase our risk of breast cancer?

EXAMPLE: In 2011, Susan G. Komen for the Cure commissioned a perfume called Promise Me[1] that contains unlisted chemicals that are regulated as toxic and hazardous, have not been adequately evaluated for human safety, and have demonstrated negative health effects. Although Komen said they would reformulate future versions of the perfume, without official adoption of the precautionary principle, there is no guarantee that future versions would be better.

If you have doubts about your pink ribbon purchase after reviewing these critical questions:

Think before you spend your money on pink items. Download a handy PDF of critical questions,[2] find out the real story behind where the pink ribbon came from,[3] learn more about cause marketing[4] and make a direct donation to Breast Cancer Action.[5]

Write a letter asking the company to be transparent about its donations.

Consider giving directly to a breast cancer organization whose work you believe is most essential to addressing the breast cancer epidemic.

---

[1] http://thinkbeforeyoupink.org/?page_id=1627
[2] http://thinkbeforeyoupink.org/wp-content/uploads/2012/03/Share-Critical-Questions.pdf
[3] http://thinkbeforeyoupink.org/resources/before-you-buy/?page_id=26
[4] http://thinkbeforeyoupink.org/resources/before-you-buy/?page_id=36
[5] https://bcaction.secure.nonprofitsoapbox.com/thinkbeforeyoupink

"Toxins in Nail Salons: When Environmental and Reproductive Justice Meet"

By Turner Willman
For the *National Women's Health Network*

Article taken from September/October 2012 Newsletter

In 1978, tanker trucks loaded with oil, on a mission from the Ward Transformer Company, drove along the roads of rural North Carolina, illegally dumping toxic Polychlorinated Biphenyls (PCBs) everywhere they went. PCBs have been linked to endocrine disruption, neurotoxicity, and cancer, and the Environmental Protection Agency (EPA) has rules governing their safe disposal.[1] So, all of this PCB-contaminated soil had to be dug up and securely stored somewhere safer. In 1982, Governor Hunt's administration, with the EPA's approval, chose Warren County as the PCB landfill site. The residents of this poor, rural, mostly African-American community banded together to fight the dump, but eventually it went through. Despite their failure, today the Warren County battle is seen as a pivotal moment that merged the civil rights and environmental movements—and gave rise to the Environmental Justice movement.[2]

It is no surprise that low-income individuals, immigrants, and people of color get the short end of the stick when it comes to big issues like wages, access to health care, incarceration, and education. But, inequality can work in more subtle ways, as well. Disempowered communities with limited resources and representation have little recourse against polluters and ineffective regulators. To address this problem, the Environmental Justice movement addresses the presence of environmental hazards where we work, live, and play—a danger that often goes undetected and unreported.

Decades after the Warren County protests, the National Asian Pacific American Women's Forum (NAPAWF) is combating environmental injustice in an unexpected place—the beauty shop. Every day, thousands of women stream in and out of nail salons and spas with little thought to the chemical fumes swirling in the air. These fumes come from nail polish and remover, disinfectants, and hair straightening treatments.

Of particular concern are products containing the aptly titled "Toxic Trio" of chemicals: formaldehyde, dibutyl phthalate, and toluene. Formaldehyde (familiar to many from the preserved frogs in high school biology class) easily vaporizes as a toxic gas, in which form it can cause asthma-like respiratory irritation and cancer.[3] Formaldehyde is most often used as a nail-hardening agent. Dibutyl phthalate has been linked to menstrual disorders, miscarriages, and spasms in the extremities.[4] It provides flexibility and a moisturizing sheen to nail polishes. Toluene is a reproductive toxin that also affects the central nervous system, causes kidney and liver damage, and irritates the respiratory system.[5] Toluene is added to polishes to ensure a smooth finish on the nail. Under current laws, it is perfectly legal for products containing the Toxic Trio to be sold in the United States.

Now, thanks to pressure from health advocates, some top brands are beginning to phase the Trio out and labeling their products as "Three-Free." These brands include Acquarella, Zoya, and Revlon nail polishes. A recent study has revealed, however, that some nail products have been falsely labeled as Three-Free and still contain the Toxic Trio.[6] Without comprehensive laboratory testing of all cosmetics, claims that a product is Three-Free will be unsubstantiated.

Advocating for Change

Ventilation systems pull some of the chemical fumes out of the environment, and customers probably don't think about them at all as they walk out into the fresh air after their appointments. For salon workers, however, chemical exposure is not such a fleeting concern. Most beauty and nail salons are small, enclosed spaces where it is easy to come into contact with toxic chemical products, even when safety precautions are taken. These chemicals can enter a worker's body in a variety of ways: they can be inhaled, absorbed through the skin, or accidentally ingested during handling. Logging in months or years at a beauty or nail salon carries serious health risks, including damage to the reproductive system.

Salon workers are often classified (or *misclassified*) as "independent contractors" instead of "employees" under U.S. labor laws. This classification renders them ineligible for many workers' rights, including minimum wage, workers' compensation, and health and safety protections.[7] Moreover, because of low socioeconomic status, language barriers, and lack of health insurance, salon workers often cannot access health care services after their bodies react to the Toxic Trio.

Most salon workers already know the health risks associated with cosmetic products. NAPAWF began to focus on this issue after receiving phone calls from distraught workers who experienced spontaneous miscarriages and had trouble conceiving. These women knew their health problems were caused by the toxins they were exposed to on a daily basis. Over 40 percent of salon workers are Asian Americans, and many are immigrant women of reproductive age. In nail salons, their bodies are ground zero.[1]

In partnership with Women's Voices for the Earth and the California Healthy Nail Salon Collaborative, NAPAWF co-leads the National Healthy Nail and Beauty Salon Alliance. Through strategic movement-building, policy advocacy, and nationwide media efforts, the Alliance works to increase salon workers' health, safety, and rights.

One of the Alliance's major concerns is the lack of adequate regulation of the cosmetics industry. Currently, the Food and Drug Administration (FDA) does not test cosmetics before they are released on the market, and cannot order a recall of hazardous cosmetics. Additionally, for products that are marketed only to salon professionals, manufacturers are not required to provide ingredient lists. This limits workers' ability to determine the content, and the safety, of the products they use every day.

Federal agencies must be empowered to provide effective oversight and ensure salon products are safe. The Alliance is advocating for the *Safe Cosmetics Act* (HR 2359). This bill would require manufacturers to remove toxic chemicals from cosmetics, require accurate ingredient labeling, provide translated safety-handling information, and give the FDA the power to recall toxic products.

The Alliance has also established the first Interagency Working Group on Salon Safety to ensure that the FDA, EPA, Occupational Safety and Health Administration (OSHA), and the National Institute for Occupational Safety and Health (NIOSH) collaborate and share resources to regulate salon products. The Alliance has submitted recommendations to these agencies, which have begun to make progress on meeting our goals of worker health and safety.

And, from July 24-26, 2012, the Alliance hosted a *Salon Week of Action* in Washington, DC. During the event, salon workers from across the nation met with policymakers and legislators to demand safer work environments so they do not have to choose between having work and being healthy.

Through collaborative efforts with health advocates, salon workers, and government agencies, the Alliance is working to ensure Warren County does not happen to a new generation. To learn more about NAPAWF's work to improve the health of nail salon workers, visit www.nailsalonalliance.org.

Turner Willman is a reproductive justice intern at the National Asian Pacific American Women's Forum through support from the Civil Liberties and Public Policy Program of Hampshire College.

REFERENCES

1. US Environmental Protection Agency (EPA), *Basic Information: Polychlorinated Biphenyl (PCB)*, Washington, DC: EPA, 2012. Retrieved July 6, 2012 from http://www.epa.gov/epawaste/hazard/tsd/pcbs/pubs/about.htm.

2. McGurty E, Transforming Environmentalism: Warren County, PCBs, and the Origins of Environmental Justice, Piscataway, NJ: Rutgers University Press, 2009.

3. Occupational Safety and Health Administration, *OSHA Factsheet: Formaldehyde*, Washington, DC: OSHA, 2011. Retrieved July 6, 2012 from http://www.osha.gov/OshDoc/data_General_Facts/formaldehyde-factsheet.pdf.

4. Occupational Safety and Health Administration, *Occupational Health and Safety Guideline for Dibutyl Phthalate*, Washington, DC: OSHA, no date. Retrieved July 6, 2012 from http://www.osha.gov/SLTC/healthguidelines/dibutylphthalate/recognition.html.

5. Occupational Safety and Health Administration (OSHA), *Safety and Health Topics: Toluene*, Washington, DC: OSHA, 2004. Retrieved July 6, 2012 from http://

---

[1]For more recent news coverage of the experiences of these marginalized women who make up the majority of salon workers, see Sarah Maslin Nir's 2015 investigative piece for the *New York Times*, "Perfect Nails, Poisoned Workers": http://www.nytimes.com/2015/05/11/nyregion/nail-salon-workers-in-nyc-face-hazardous-chemicals.html?_r=0 *Ed.*

www.osha.gov/dts/chemicalsampling/data/CH_272200. html.

6. California Department of Toxic Substances Control, *Summary of Data and Findings from Testing of a Limited Number of Nail Products*, Sacramento: California: California Department of Toxic Substances Control, 2012. Retrieved on July 6, 2012 from http://dtsc.ca.gov/ PollutionPrevention/upload/NailSalon_Final.pdf.

7. Occupational Safety and Health Administration, *Stay Healthy and Safe While Giving Manicures and Pedicures: A Guide for Nail Salon Workers*, Washington, DC: OSHA, 2012. Retrieved on July 6, 2012 from http://www. osha.gov/Publications/3542nail-salon-workers-guide.pdf.

"Cervical Cancer Vaccines in Context"

By Adriane Fugh-Berman

In Washington D.C., in the 1970s, I volunteered at a Latino health fair that offered various health screenings, including Pap smears to look for pre-cancerous cells. When the results came back, about one of four of the Paps was abnormal. An abnormal Pap doesn't equal a diagnosis of cervical cancer, but follow-up colposcopy (examination of the cervix with a lighted microscope) is necessary, and some women should have further procedures as well. Colposcopy is a specialized procedure, usually done by gynecologists, and we couldn't identify qualified physicians who were willing to perform this procedure without charge, so we couldn't provide this follow-up. I don't know what happened to the women whose abnormal Paps were identified during the health fair; without adequate follow-up, some may have developed cervical cancer by now.

Paps are crucial to preventing deaths . . . but only if women can get them, and if they're followed up by appropriate diagnostics and treatment. Worldwide, cervical cancer rates are much higher in other countries than in the U.S.; more than 80% of cases occur in underserved, resource-poor communities. In parts of Africa, Central and South America, and Micronesia, there are more than 50 cases of cervical cancer per 100,000 women.

In the U.S., there are 6.6 cases of cervical cancer for every 100,000 White women, and 10.5 cases for every 100,000 African American women. Since the Pap smear was introduced in 1949. U.S. cervical cancer incidence and mortality have dropped by three-quarters, although rates are higher in the rural South and some cities, including D.C. (The combined Pap/human papilloma virus test that's now common was invented in the 1990s.) Today, about half of the U.S. women diagnosed with cervical cancer had never been screened by a Pap test prior to their diagnosis.

There are hundreds of types of human papilloma virus (HPV), some of which cause genital warts (especially HPV types 6 and 11), and others of which cause cervical cancer (especially HPV types 16 and 18). Infection with HPV, including with the cancer-associated types, is *extremely* common: about 15% of the population's infected with some form of HPV. Yet, most women with HPV, including those with types 16 and 18, never develop either cervical cancer or abnormal cells. In fact, in most people, HPV cures itself. About 70% of women test negative for the virus a year after their diagnosis and about 90% test negative after two years.

Only about 10% of women who are infected with HPV stay infected; it is these women with persistent infections who are at the highest risk for HPV to progress to cervical cancer. In the U.S., even presistent HPV rarely causes cervical cancer, as regular screening catches precancerous changes and available treatment of precancerous changes prevents cancer. In the U.S., in 2006, an estimated 9,710 cases of invasive cervical cancer occurred, and about 3,700 women died from it. Worldwide, however, cervical cancer is the 2nd most common cancer death among women, causing about 288,000 deaths annually. In June 2006, the Food and Drug Administration (FDA) approved Gardasil, a vaccine against HPV types 6, 11, 16 and 18 Gardasil is the first vaccine against cervical cancer to be approved, although a second vaccine will reach the market soon. The development of a cervical cancer vaccine is a public health breakthrough with the potential to save many lives worldwide. It won't end cervical cancer, however, although it will reduce the need for Pap smears over time. This is because some cervical cancers are caused by viral strains not covered by the vaccine, and we don't know yet how long protection lasts for the covered strains (we do know that it's still going strong at five years), so booster shots may be required.

The vaccine only works well if it is administered before a woman is exposed to HPV. Merck (Gardasil's manufacturer) just curtailed its efforts to lobby state legislatures to require vaccination of schoolgirls, as part of which it donated an undisclosed sum to Women in Government, an advocacy group of women state lawmakers. Bills have been introduced, or are being drafted, in about 20 states to require HPV vaccination for schoolgirls.

There's been a public backlash against the idea of this mandatory vaccination. I support the backlash, but I also support the use of HPV vaccines. HPV vaccines are expected to reduce deaths from cervical cancer, and to reduce the risk of precancerous changes, which are not trivial. Treatment of precancerous conditions involves cutting, burning, or freezing part of the cervix, and can cause complications that affect childbearing. Reducing the number of these procedures will benefit women's health.

There should be a public outcry against mandatory HPV vaccine laws not because the vaccines are experimental (they are well-tested) or because they are dangerous (they aren't). The currently proposed laws should be opposed because public health policy should never be orchestrated by corporations. The debate over mandatory HPV vaccination is an important one, but the debaters should be restricted to those who will not turn a profit from the decisions.

Although the HPV vaccine's touted as the first vaccine against cancer, the hepatitis B virus (which can be transmitted sexually) increases the risk of liver cancer, and hepatitis vaccines are available. And in terms of sexually transmitted infections, hepatitis and HIV together cause many more deaths than HPV, Condoms, of course, are still the best protection against all sexually transmitted infections, including HPV. But these are not mutually exclusive strategies. We need public health education about condoms, cervical cancer screening—and cervical cancer vaccines.

See: The Centers for Disease Control and Prevention (CDC). "Human papillomavirus; HPV information for clinicians." Atlanta: CDC. Nov. 2006. Online: http://cdc.gov; and Saslow D, Castle PE, Cox JT et al. "American Cancer Society Guidelines for human papillomavirus (HPV) vaccine use to prevent cervical cancer and its precursors." *Cancer J Clin* 2007; 57:7–28. Online. http://caonline.amcancersoc.org/cgi./content/full/57/1/7.

"The New HPV Vaccine Better Protects Black Women—But Does It Go Too Far?"

By JR Thorpe

The new and improved HPV vaccine that's just gotten approval for mass production on the U.S. market[1] is getting a lot of attention. Mostly, people are celebrating the fact that it finally covers a larger number of HPV strains[2] — nine, to be exact, up from the last vaccine's two. Which is, any way you slice it, amazing news.

HPV, or the human papillomavirus, is a sexually transmitted disease that's estimated, according to a landmark study in 2008, to be linked to a huge swath of cancers:[3] up to 40 percent of vulvar, 60 percent of vaginal, and 80 percent of anal cancers can be traced back to it, plus most of the incidences of genital warts. So a nine-strain vaccine must be very, very good for everybody. Right?

Unfortunately, not so much for black American women, who've already been let down massively by the vaccines currently on the local market.[4] So what's really going on—and will the new vaccine provide genuine change for those who were left behind before?

Let's break one thing down first: the human papillomavirus isn't actually a single virus at all. It has up to 100 different strains or types. They're all handily numbered, for our convenience, and are sorted into "high grade" and "low grade." High grade HPV means that HPV cells carry a high risk of developing into cancer,[5] while low grade cells may just go back to normal on

their own. If you've ever had a Pap smear with abnormal results, somebody has (hopefully) explained this to you.[6]

But there's another aspect to HPV subtypes, as the strains are called: who gets what seems partially determined by racial background. Research in the past few years has shown that, in the American population, women most often get HPV subtypes 16, 18, 56, 39, and 66, while black women most often contract HPV subtypes 33, 35, 58, and 68.[7] See a lot of crossover there? Neither do we.

As of yet, we don't know why black American women (and other women of color) develop different HPV strains than white women.[8] But it seriously affects treatment—particularly because the vaccines currently on the US market only vaccinate girls against two subtypes.

Duke University did a now-famous study laying this disparity out back in 2013,[9] and pointed out a pretty

---

[6]In our experience, many young people who receive abnormal pap smears unfortunately get very little patient education about their results. In most cases if you are told to come back for a follow-up in six months or some other timeframe, it is because providers expect the abnormal cells to gradually disappear on its own, without medical intervention. For a provider who sees abnormal pap smears on a regular basis, this is routine, but they don't always seem to remember that for an individual patient, it probably isn't! We hope that you will find providers who remember to explicitly provide this kind of information, or at least answer questions professionally and completely when asked. *Ed.*

[7]http://www.bustle.com/articles/29300-what-its-like-to-have-hpv-how-the-vaccine-failed-to-protect-me-as-a-black

[8]Much of the variation is likely explained by the fact that people tend to select romantic and sexual partners from within their own racial groups. *Ed.*

[9]http://corporate.dukemedicine.org/news_and_publications/news_office/news/hpv-strains-affecting-african-american-women-differ-from-vaccines

---

[1]https://www.sciencenews.org/article/new-hpv-shot-fends-more-types-virus

[2]http://www.bustle.com/articles/29300-what-its-like-to-have-hpv-how-the-vaccine-failed-to-protect-me-as-a-black

[3]http://onlinelibrary.wiley.com/doi/10.1002/ijc.24116/abstract;jsessionid=C3DB8ED56D3B2BAF04B26F8BBFF5BD11.f01t02

[4]http://www.bustle.com/articles/29300-what-its-like-to-have-hpv-how-the-vaccine-failed-to-protect-me-as-a-black

[5]http://www.cdc.gov/std/hpv/pap/

enormous problem: the then-current HPV vaccines, Gardasil and Cervarix, only targeted subtypes 16 and 18.[10] Yep: the vaccines weren't targeting any of the subtypes common in black American women. They were being left incredibly vulnerable.

"I endured the three painful shots—and thought it was a form of punishment for not using condoms— never knowing that Gardasil may not have been the correct option for me," Evette Dione wrote for Bustle[11] when she discovered her own HPV-positive status. "Had there been funding for a vaccine specifically designed for my black, female body, a shot that protects my body as well as it does white women, I might very well be HPV-free today."

This is a hideous situation — but it's one which the new HPV vaccine is trying to (partially) improve. The new shot is designed to target HPV types 31, 33, 45, 52, 58, 6, 11, 16 and 18. Two of these are on the list of types most commonly found in black American women: 33 and 58. Both are "high grade" HPV subtypes, likely to lead to cancer (58 has been found in a high proportion of Chinese sufferers of cervical cancer,[12] too). So: dancing in the streets. Right? Not so fast.

Hopefully, with this first nine-strain vaccine approved by the Centers for Disease Control this month,[13] black American women will begin to be (at least partially protected) by their HPV vaccinations. But there continues to be resistance to tailoring vaccine study to particular races, and a blame game has started that goes something like this: that not enough scientists are including different races in their HPV studies, that not enough black women are volunteering for experiments, that studies ignoring "low grade" subtypes as less important, the list goes on.

And, despite both the FDA and CDC's approval, the timeline for when the nine-strain vaccine will become available remains hazy.

But this is urgent. Four of the HPV subtypes[14] that Duke identifies as common in black women are classified as «high grade,» and two of them still have no vaccine. Gardasil and Cervarix, which have been on the market since 2008, have failed thousands of black American women; research into vaccines that target high grade subtypes across the entire racial spectrum would go at least some way towards fixing that.

Perhaps understandably, Duke's findings didn't go down well. The developers of Gardasil argued that 16 and 18 are the ones responsible for 70 percent of all HPV-related cancers—which was the conventional wisdom—but Duke's scientists maintained that more subtypes were involved. And while the scientists bickered, more and more black American women were getting a vaccine that, it turned out, wasn't targeted at their most common foes at all. (There have, as of yet, been no studies published[15] of the HPV subtypes typically contracted by women in other parts of the world, and Gardasil and Cervarix remain the global go-tos for HPV vaccines[16] — including in developing countries, where 85 percent of worldwide deaths from cervical cancer occur.[17])

Targeting vaccines to particular races is a sticky issue. A *TIME* magazine article in 2013 pointed out that scientists are often reluctant to factor race into medical discussions,[18] mostly because it's extremely complicated: race-based medicine, as it's called, is based on genetic factors far more complicated than just skin color.[19] And it's a seriously touchy subject, politically; claiming that different races require different medical care is seen as a "slippery slope"[20] that might lead to deepened racial divides as medical treatment becomes more segregated, and to people excusing the health effects of social inequality as "just the way that race is."

As of right now, nobody's announced any studies into why American black and non-Caucasian women sustain different HPV subtypes, and it's likely because of this worry; scientists who tried to delve into the area might be unlikely to get funding from squeamish authorities. But without understanding the real roots of the divide, it may be tricky for scientists to develop more targeted vaccines.

Fortunately, there's hope in other areas of medicine even for those whose common strains aren't covered

[10]http://www.bustle.com/articles/7771-hpv-vaccine-might-not-protect-african-american-women-says-duke-university-study

[11]http://www.bustle.com/articles/29300-what-its-like-to-have-hpv-how-the-vaccine-failed-to-protect-me-as-a-black

[12]http://jnci.oxfordjournals.org/content/94/16/1249.long

[13]https://www.sciencenews.org/blog/science-ticker/cdc-panel-gives-thumbs-vaccine-against-nine-hpv-types

[14]http://www.cdc.gov/vaccines/pubs/pinkbook/hpv.html

[15]https://scholar.google.co.uk/scholar?q=hpv+subtypes+study&hl=en&as_sdt=0&as_vis=1&oi=scholart&sa=X&ei=fXz4VN36MJCV7AaUoYGABg&ved=0CB4QgQMwAA

[16]http://www.who.int/bulletin/volumes/85/2/07-020207/en/

[17]http://www.gavi.org/library/news/press-releases/2013/hpv-price-announcement/

[18]http://healthland.time.com/2013/11/01/the-hpv-vaccine-and-the-case-for-race-based-medicine/

[19]Note that human racial groups are socially defined (which doesn't mean race isn't "real," but that it is a social category) and that geneticists have clearly demonstrated that there is greater variation **within** these individual racial groups than **between** different racial groups. For a simple discussion of human racial categories and genetics, try this ~10-minute TEDx talk on the subject: https://www.youtube.com/watch?v=G3BIIIPlahw *Ed.*

[20]http://papers.ssrn.com/sol3/papers.cfm?abstract_id=2187359

by the latest vaccine. In Mexico, a treatment has been authorized by the government that treats women who already have HPV with a therapeutic vaccine,[21] and it's been a big success in clinical trials: every subject either had their HPV cells massively diminish, or saw them vanish entirely.

If the racial disparities prove too difficult for science to manage, this may be the way the game goes: just let people get HPV, and treat them for it afterwards. But surely an ounce of prevention is still better than a pound of cure—and every woman deserves to be protected.

---

[21]http://online.liebertpub.com/doi/abs/10.1089/10430340460745757

"Screening Mammograms When Fighting for Coverage and Quality Isn't Enough"

By Cynthia Pearson
For the *National Women's Health Network*

Article taken from January/February 2007 Newsletter

Sometimes the work of women's health activists is easy. We find out that a new procedure or service can help improve women's health, we advocate for all women to have access to it, we do everything we can to ensure that it is provided in a high quality way, and then we celebrate the gains made. Sometimes it's more complicated, though, and the case of mammography screening for breast cancer is a painful example of a complicated women's health issue.

Mammography was originally studied as a screening tool in the 1960s. The first trial seemed to show screening saved lives: asymptomatic women were screened every year or two; smaller cancers were found than in similar, but unscreened women; these cancers were treated promptly; and fewer women died of breast cancer. This trial was followed by a large demonstration study that showed the average radiologists outside a highly structured clinical trial could identify small breast cancers. Based on these promising results, it appeared that mammography screening should be made available to all women at-risk of developing breast cancer.

In the aftermath of this early research, NWHN advocated strongly for mammography access. In the late 1980s, we lobbied Congress for Medicare coverage of screening mammograms. At that time, Medicare didn't cover any screening tests, and its managers were reluctant to expand the program's scope. In fact, I still remember testifying before Congress in favor of Medicare coverage of screening mammograms—and being opposed by a government accountant who said that it would be "too expensive" to pay the health care costs for all the women who would live many years longer if their breast cancer was cured after being found on a screening mammogram! Thankfully, Congress expanded Medicare's coverage even after the accountant's dire warning.

After Medicare began to cover screening mammograms, private insurance companies followed suit, and programs aimed at reaching women without insurance began. With access expanding, NWHN next turned its advocacy efforts to quality—and found we had work to do. Provision of screening mammography wasn't regulated back then, and the quality of machines used varied greatly, as did the training and experience of technicians and radiologists. Many women received very high-quality services, but not everyone did. And, as we pointed out, a bad mammogram is worse than no mammogram at all. The Network created a guide to the important elements of high-quality mammography, and many NWHN members volunteered to check out facilities in their hometowns. When members found inconsistent quality, we took this information to Congress and sought federal regulations. Other women's and cancer advocacy groups joined in this effort and, in the early 1990s, the Mammography Quality Standards Act was passed. We were especially proud that the Act gave women the right to get their own copy of their mammograms.

But, just when we thought we'd accomplished our work, the original premise of mammography (that screening saves women's lives) came into question. In 1992, NWHN began analyzing the benefit women really got from mammography screening. And, it turned out, the benefit wasn't as big as originally thought, nor did it apply equally to women of all ages. NWHN dove into this work, not because we thought we were exposing a sham—we'd promoted screening mammography, after all—but because our members want to know if researchers had doubts about the effectiveness of any treatment. NWHN members have told us that they don't want overly optimistic information or simplistic messages that are better at motivating than educating.

What we discovered in the 1990s was disheartening. In the aftermath of mammography screening's first trial, several other trials were undertaken, without impressive results. Screening's life-saving benefit was not found in all trials. It certainly wasn't found in the one trial designed to show the benefit of beginning mammography at age 40. NWHN went public with this information, and in 1993, issued a position paper recommending against screening mammography for premenopausal women—a very controversial position. The breast cancer advocacy movement was just getting started back then, and many organizations had a hard time accepting the idea that screening mammography might not really be very effective.

We also found that many people were shocked at the very idea that screening could, in fact, be harmful. Here's why: screening leads diagnosis, which leads to treatment. There is no treatment without risks. Treatment is often worth the risk when a condition is causing symptoms or is dangerous. But early cancer found through screening, when no symptoms are present, doesn't always progress to life-threatening, advanced cancer. We wanted to be sure that treating everyone found to have early cancer would actually help save women's lives. It was these considerations that led NWHN to tell women we believe that breast cancer screening should not be recommended for pre-menopausal women until it's been well-proven to do more good than harm.

Times have changed but, unfortunately, the complicated nature of mammography screening hasn't. The same seven screening mammography trials still generate controversy, just as they did in the early '90s. But the emergence of several wonderful breast cancer advocacy organizations that do their own independent analysis of science and clinical trials now makes it much easier for women to find excellent information on this complicated subject. The Network stopped doing our own analysis of the issue a few years ago, when we realized that other organizations can follow and analyze breast cancer screening reports as well as, and often more quickly than, NWHN.

The Myth of the Baseline Mammogram

While many things about screening mammograms are uncertain, there's at least one thing that is certain: baseline mammograms shouldn't be recommended as a routine part of health care for women. There is complete agreement about this, even among organizations that disagree on almost every other aspect of mammography.

But, despite this agreement that baseline mammograms aren't necessary and shouldn't be recommended, many women tell us that their practitioners start recommending baseline mammograms at age 35. Why is this? In part, it's because the American Cancer Society (ACS) spent over a decade promoting baseline mammograms as an essential part of screening for breast cancer. The ACS recommendation had no scientific evidence to support it—there are absolutely no studies showing any benefit of a baseline mammogram in women under 40—but the ACS recommendations reached and influenced the majority of U.S. physicians, nurse practitioners, and physician assistants.

The ACS received steady criticism of its recommendation in favor of baseline mammograms and finally withdrew it in 1992. The ACS did not, however, promote this change and the message still hasn't gotten out to well-meaning practitioners who continue to tell women in their 30s that its time for their baseline mammogram.

For more information about the history of the mammography debate, see: Sharon Batt, *Patient No More: The Politics of Breast Cancer*, Charlottetown, PE: Gynergy Books, 1994. Barron Lerner, MD., *The Breast Cancer Wars: Hope, Fear and the Pursuit of a Cure in Twentieth-Century America*, New York: Oxford University Press, 2001.

REFERENCE

"Chronological History of ACS Recommendations on Early Detection of Cancer." On-line at: http://www.cancer.org/docroot/PED/content/PED_2_3X_Chronological_History_of_ACS_Recommendations_on_Early_Detection_of_Cancer.asp?sitearea=PED.

BODY IMAGE IN THE INDIVIDUAL AND SOCIETY

"Weight Bias in Healthcare"

By Lacey Alexander, MS, RN

Seeking Care while Fat

In response to the American Medical Association's 2013 decision to classify obesity as a disease, the academic journal *Narrative Inquiry in Bioethics* put out a call for lay people to submit stories about discussions they had had with physicians concerning their weight, weight management, and overall health. Lauren Moore (2014) was one of the people who responded, writing about her experiences as a fat woman navigating the healthcare system. Biometrically speaking, other than weight, health professionals consider all of Lauren's[1] lab values and vital signs within normal limits for a person without disease. Lauren wrote,

> "I can visit for a rash, or a stomach bug, or contraception, or just be registering with a new doctor, but every appointment will become about my weight. No one will explain how my rash is symptomatic of my weight, but somehow it is. As a fat woman, any health problem, however temporary or seemingly unrelated to body size, is put down to my weight" (p. 110).

Based on elevated weight alone, healthcare clinicians have often insinuated that Lauren must be lying about dieting and exercising, and that refusing bariatric surgery means she is in denial. Lauren wrote that she believes her doctors think she is deserving of any disease that comes her way—because, of course, her body size will inevitably cause subsequent diseases.

Similar to Lauren's story, Catherine Seo (2014) submitted a narrative about what it was like to be a person of size who sought healthcare for potentially serious symptoms (e.g. pain, fatigue, etc.), but was dismissed by clinicians who automatically attributed her ailments to her BMI measures and the poor health behaviors that clinicians assumed were behind them. More specifically, Catherine wrote about having undiagnosed lipedema, an inherited genetic chronic disorder that caused localized and painful fat deposits in her arms and legs (Seo, 2014). Prior to receiving her lipedema diagnosis, Catherine suffered from a surgical complication that left her with uncontrollable and painful swelling of fat in her arms and legs. Her surgeon insisted that the fat accumulation was Catherine's fault, and told her that she must lose 75 pounds to "reverse the damage she had done" before they would treat her with additional surgery.

Essentially, the surgeon placed blame on Catherine for her health complication, and provided her with a blanket recommendation to lose weight without providing any clinical resources or evidence-based methods or interventions for weight management. The surgeon did not seem concerned that it might be difficult for Catherine to lose weight while in pain and immobile. Most importantly, the surgeon did not investigate her pain and weight gain as symptoms of an underlying health problem, instead seeing the weight itself as the only problem worth identifying. After a year of suffering, Catherine was finally diagnosed with lipedema by a different doctor, allowing her to get proper treatment. The diagnosis also carried the relief of recognizing that her suffering was not her own fault. It turned out that

---

[1]Because these are personal narratives that highlight the humanity of individuals experiencing weight bias in healthcare, the author refers to them by first name. In general, bear in mind that you should use surnames to refer to people whom you do not know in academic writing; as gender scholars, we often notice that students extend this courtesy to people they read as men, but not to those they read as women. Just be aware when you write of the specific context and implications of different modes of address. *Ed.*

the initial surgery had actually aggravated Catherine's lipedema, but because her care team held strong weight biases, they did not treat her promptly or properly. Subsequently, the condition left her with even more complications, including immobility.

Unfortunately, these experiences are not isolated incidents in healthcare. People of size who enter the healthcare system often have different experiences than thin people. One reason for this is that medical professionals have categorized obesity as a disease. Treating obesity as a disease encourages medical professionals to assume a person is unhealthy based simply on their physical appearance or their body mass index (BMI). Lauren elaborated on the far-reaching consequences of medicalizing obesity in the conclusion of her article. As she explained,

> "The...decision to further medicalize my body and refer to it as diseased—a body that I love, a body that is carrying me around with no health problems, is just another reason for me to fear the medical establishment that wants to hurt me and have me thank them for it" (p. 112).

Lauren emphasizes the harm done by the strong weight bias that exists among healthcare clinicians, who are often quick to accept the medicalization of obesity due to widespread social stigma associated with fat. Just because a clinician has a medical or healthcare degree does not mean that they are immune to the harsh weight bias prevalent in American society.

Unfortunately, the cultural weight biases that clinicians bring into their practice is another major reason why people of size are less likely to receive appropriate care for their health problems. The term "weight bias" refers to harmful prejudicial assumptions regarding personality characteristics based on a person's size, such as assuming fat people are unintelligent, unsuccessful, inactive, weak-willed, ugly, overindulgent, awkward, not hygienic, etc. (Puhl & Heuer, 2009). In this article, I will discuss the mounting evidence that weight bias is prominent in many aspects of healthcare. I will argue that health professionals often base their weight loss recommendations on false assumptions about BMI and health as well as the efficacy of diet and exercise for long-term weight changes.

Please note that "fat" and "people of size" are terms that I consciously use in place of language that may be inaccurate and stigmatizing, such as "overweight" and "obese." Some fat studies scholars and activists, denouncing the use of terms such as "overweight" and "obese" as neither neutral nor benign, have reclaimed the word "fat" as a neutral adjective (Wann, 2009). However, I acknowledge that some people might not want others, perhaps especially healthcare clinicians, to refer to them as "fat." Thus I often use the term "people of size" to avoid assigning unwanted labels or medicalized descriptors, both of which may contribute to stigma. I only use the words "overweight" and "obese" when drawing from specific studies that (like most medical research) have adopted this system of categorization from the Centers for Disease Control and Prevention (CDC).

Evidence of Weight Bias in Healthcare

The CDC categorizes people by their weight status using a measure called Body Mass Index (BMI). The CDC (2015) considers people underweight with a BMI of less than 18.5, normal or healthy weight with a BMI of 18.5 to 24.9, overweight with a BMI of 25.0–29.9, and obese with a BMI of 30 or greater. Some scholars have criticized this measure because researchers, policymakers, and clinicians use BMI as a measure of individual health, when researchers did not design it for use on an individual basis. As a result, health insurance companies, the pharmaceutical industry, clinicians, researchers, and patients are all guilty of conflating individual BMI with individual health (Bacon & Aphramor, 2014), assuming health to deteriorate as BMI increases.

Not only is this inaccurate, but people with "overweight" BMIs actually have the longest overall lifespans (Flegal, Graubard, Williamson, & Gail, 2005; Janssen, 2007; Lantz, Golberstein, House & Morenoff, 2010; McGee, 2005). Researchers conducted a meta-analysis and found a statistically significant relationship between BMI and mortality only when BMI reaches 40 and above (Troiano, Frongillo, Sobal, & Levitsky, 1996), raising questions about why the "obese" BMI category starts at 30. Some scholars argue that the cutoffs for the categories of overweight and obesity were set low because those who created the obesity standards were stakeholders in the weight loss industry (Bacon, 2013; Bacon & Aphramor, 2014). The CDC's categorization of "overweight" and "obese" is an example of weight bias in research that has influenced policy and practice in such profound ways that it is impossible to entirely excise even from critical works like this one. This certainly contributes to the weight bias that patients experience in individual healthcare settings.

Many studies have confirmed that weight-based discrimination is a problem in healthcare. Foster and colleagues (2003) found that one-third of primary care physicians (N=620) described their obese patients as weak-willed and lazy, more than half described obese patients as noncompliant, and most viewed obesity as a behavioral problem due to inactivity and overeating.

A recent study on implicit and explicit weight biases in a large national sample of medical students (N = 4,732) found high levels of implicit (74%) and explicit (67%) weight bias. Explicit attitudes were more negative toward obese people than toward racial minorities, gay men, lesbians, or poor people (Phelan et al., 2014).[2] Puhl and Brownell (2006) assessed overweight and obese adults' experience of weight stigmatization and found that 69% of participants reported experiencing weight-related stigma from doctors, and 46% reported it from nurses. Patients' perceived stigma is likely an accurate reflection of the weight prejudice some clinicians hold, as many studies have found that physicians find counseling patients about weight loss "professionally unrewarding" (Campbell, Engall, Timperio, Cooper & Crawford, 2000, p. 464; Bocquier et al., 2005; Thuan & Avignon, 2005). Clinicians may find counseling patients about weight loss unrewarding because they often have low expectations of the effectiveness of weight loss interventions (Campbell et al., 2009).[3]

This well-demonstrated weight bias impedes clinicians' ability to give accurate, unprejudiced diagnoses, interventions, and treatment options. One study found that 84% of obese adults believed that clinicians blame weight for most medical problems, and obese women were more likely than men to report that clinicians do not consider any possible medical reason for why they might be overweight (Thompson & Thomas, 2000). In another study, mental health clinicians were more likely to give fat patients psychiatric diagnoses that are more serious, and physicians were more likely to spend less time and order more tests for their overweight and obese patients compared with thin patients (Hebl & Xu, 2001). Ordering more tests despite spending less time with a patient might mean that clinicians are forgoing thorough mental and physical assessments, assuming patients have pathologies based on their body size, and ordering diagnostic tests for confirmation.

Ordering more tests for obese people could also be a reflection of clinical guidelines to screen all patients who are overweight or obese for certain metabolic disorders. However, if a clinician thinks a patient might be at risk for a metabolic disorder, it is puzzling that they would actually spend less time with the patient, as people at risk for metabolic disorders may benefit

from patient education. However, researchers have also found that physicians are less likely to provide health education to obese patients (Bertakis & Azari, 2005). This might be due to clinicians assuming that obese patients are noncompliant, or, in a for-profit healthcare system, clinicians feeling that health insurance systems do not appropriately reimburse them for providing weight management education (Foster, 2003).

These obvious patterns of weight bias in healthcare lead people of size to delay seeking treatment or even avoid the healthcare system all together (Ferrante et al., 2006; Mitchell, Padwal, Chuck & Klarenbach, 2008; Rosen & Schneider, 2004). Weight bias in healthcare, which mirrors larger gendered social attitudes toward weight, especially affects women's care-seeking behaviors. Women experience noticeable weight bias in society when their BMI reaches 27.5, while men do not experience noticeable weight bias until they reach a BMI of 35 (Puhl, Andreyeva, & Brownell, 2008). As a result, women tend to view themselves more critically than men do at the same level of BMI (Bookwala & Boyar, 2008). This might explain why women who are categorized as overweight or obese based on their BMIs are less likely to partake in (or be offered) preventative health screenings than are men with higher BMIs (McGuigan & Wilkinson, 2015). Women who have higher BMIs receive fewer preventive health screenings, such as for breast and cervical cancer (Coughlin et al., 2004; Ferrante, Chen, Crabtree & Wartenberg, 2007; Østbye et al., 2005).

People of size sometimes fear going to clinics and hospitals due to poor previous experiences, such as clinicians telling them to lose weight at appointments that have nothing to do with weight, feeling embarrassed by clinicians weighing them, and receiving care without appropriate equipment, such as larger exam tables or scales with higher weight limits (Amy, Aalborg, Lyons & Keranen, 2006). Despite poor experiences in the healthcare system, people of size rely on health services across their lifespan. Researchers who examine weight bias continue to discuss the importance of developing and testing effective stigma reduction strategies for health clinicians, as they are in a unique position to improve the holistic well-being of people of size (Puhl & Heuer, 2009). However, to combat weight bias in healthcare, we cannot simply look at individual-level bias. We also have to address the biases in research that inform and reinforce individual clinician bias.

Why do Clinicians Recommend Diet and Exercise for Weight Loss?

There is limited long-term evidence about the efficacy of diet and exercise for sustained weight loss. Weight

---

[2]We should also consider how providers' beliefs about the noncompliance of obese patients may intersect with similar beliefs about patients of color as noncompliant or less intelligent, or LGBTQ+ patients as untrustworthy, to give just a couple of examples of how outcomes may be even worse for multiply marginalized people of size. *Ed.*

[3]Ironically, such low expectations are justified (see below in this piece and Anna Mirer's work elsewhere in this section); however, like most people (including many of the dieters themselves), providers are sadly likely to blame the patient rather than the intervention! *Ed.*

is a complex variable that sometimes reflects eating excess calories and a living a sedentary lifestyle, but it also reflects genetics, ability, underlying pathologies, and access to nutritious foods, such as fresh fruits and vegetables. A health clinician should consider how biological (e.g. genetic, nutrition), psychological (e.g. behavior, coping), social (e.g. socioeconomic, medical) and environmental (e.g. neighborhood, rurality) factors influence wellness and disease. When clinicians critically and consciously apply these considerations to weight, most have the knowledge that many complex variables influence patient weight. However, this does not mean that clinicians are immune to weight bias, as clinicians often believe that people of size could easily modify their behaviors and become, and stay, thin.

A review on weight bias in society demonstrated that health clinicians often assume that all people of size eat too much and are not physically active (Puhl & Heuer, 2009). It is important to note that despite discussing weight at about 50% of primary care visits (Befort et al., 2006), many health clinicians do not feel equipped to provide guidance regarding weight loss or to recommend weight loss programs (Befort et al., 2006; Bocquier et al., 2005; Thuon & Avignon, 2005). This might explain why clinicians routinely provide blanket recommendations to lose weight without patient education on how to execute weight management strategies, or refer them to weight loss programs without proven efficacy.

Researchers have reviewed outcomes from private sector weight loss programs (Dansinger et al., 2005; Tsai & Wadden, 2005), but most programs have only been examined in industry-sponsored trials, and rarely include long-term follow-up (Fogel, 2014). Long-term follow-up is imperative because people who lose weight and keep it off for two to five years are more likely to maintain the weight loss long-term (Wing & Phelan, 2005). Even if these diet programs had robust evidence, consumers of commercial diet programs often report that these diets encouraged unhealthy eating behaviors, such as extreme caloric restriction or consuming low-calorie foods with significantly reduced nutritive value (Gailey, 2014). To date, most commercial weight loss programs, such as Nutrisystem, Jenny Craig, and Medifast, have limited research of their short-and long-term effectiveness. Weight Watchers is one of the only programs available that offers peer-reviewed evidence of weight loss efficacy, but actual average weight loss is usually modest and does not persist in the long term (Djuric et al., 2002; Heshka et al., 2003).

Many clinicians would argue that there are many examples of evidence-based, peer-reviewed studies that demonstrated empirical support for weight-loss dieting. On one level, this is true, because calorie restriction reliably leads to short-term weight loss for most people. However, reviews of the scientific literature have shown that weight loss dieting interventions have not been effective in changing weight *long-term* (Bombak, 2014). The idea that weight loss dieting is only effective short-term is not novel.[4] In fact, the National Institutes of Health published reviews confirming that weight loss dieting is not a long-term solution more than twenty years ago (Goodrick, Poston & Foreyt, 1996). More recently, one group of researchers (Mann et al., 2007) conducted a comprehensive review of seven randomized control trials with long-term follow-up assessments and concluded that across all studies, there was no strong evidence that weight loss dieting can lead to long-term weight loss. The group also found strong biases within the reviewed studies to mislead clinicians into interpreting the interventions under study as having demonstrated long-term efficacy. Biases included confounding diet and exercise, low follow-up rates, reliance on self-reports of weight, and participants engaging in different subsequent diets during study follow-up.

Similar to weight loss dieting, health clinicians often assume there is abundant evidence that exercise leads to weight loss. People of size are often shamed in healthcare for not exercising enough, which heavily implies that thin people exercise more fat people do. Clinicians commonly encourage patients to use pedometers to track their activity or engage in exercise programs to facilitate weight loss. However, there is very little evidence that pedometer-based programs or exercise programs in the absence of weight loss dieting can lead to significant weight loss (Swift, Johannsen, Lavie, Earnest, & Church, 2014). Although there are many physical and mental health benefits of physical activity, when people do lose weight while engaging in exercise and dieting simultaneously, the vast majority of weight loss is due to weight loss dieting (Swift et al., 2014). Yet, clinicians still routinely prescribe exercise for weight loss, and when it fails to produce that result, patients may be discouraged from engaging in physical activity.

The lack of effectiveness of exercise alone is because the clinically recommended amount of moderate intensity exercise does not produce clinically significant weight loss (Donnelly et al., 2009). Clinical guidelines actually indicate that people of size need to be more physically active than people with "normal" BMIs are in order to be "healthy." In fact, The American College of Sports Medicine (ACSM) has created

[4]For more detail on the lack of efficacy for weight-focused interventions in general, including diets as well as medications and surgeries, see Anna Mirer's piece elsewhere in this section. *Ed.*

distinctions between minimum physical activity levels to maintain health, lose weight, and maintain weight loss. The ACSM recommends that all people in good health should get 150 minutes of physical activity per week to maintain or improve their health. However, to prevent weight gain a person must exercise 150–250 minutes a week, to promote clinically significant weight loss a person must exercise 225–420 minutes a week, and to prevent weight regain after weight loss a person must exercise 200–300 minutes a week (Donnelly et al., 2009). The takeaway message here is that there is a large body of evidence showing that exercise will only lead to weight loss if the dose of exercise is extremely high (Swift et al., 2014). It also means that the amount of recommended exercise for a person who has been thin their entire life will be lower. Most importantly, clinicians need to be sensitive to the fact that when they recommend that a patient should lose weight via physical activity, they are asking them to exercise more than double the standard recommendation of 150 minutes per week.

It is important to understand that people of size cannot simply adopt the same behaviors as thin people and get the same results. It is true that diet and exercise plays an important role in maintaining health and may support weight maintenance in some individuals, but this is distinctly different from using weight loss dieting and exercise to lose weight and then maintain that weight loss (Swift et al., 2014). Clinicians and patients must acknowledge that routine recommendations that are thrown at people of size to "lose weight" and to seek a "healthy BMI" may be setting many people up to fail—but this failure to reach a certain BMI does not mean that these people are not healthy.

What is Healthy?

A growing amount of evidence suggests that being physically fit and eating a calorically balanced and nutritious diet may improve health status completely independent from BMI. There is a concept in health literature called "metabolically healthy obese," which refers to people who are categorically "obese" yet have normal metabolic parameters (e.g. blood pressure, cholesterol, blood sugar, etc.). Some researchers have demonstrated that eating well and exercising partially explain why many people with higher BMIs are metabolically healthy (Ortega et al., 2013; Phillips, 2013). For example, people who are categorized as obese and engage in 150 minutes of physical activity a week have half the death rate and a lower incidence of cardiovascular disease compared to people who are categorized as normal weight and do not engage in significant physical activity (Blair & Church, 2004). However, "metabolically healthy obese" is still not a concept that the medical community entirely accepts, as it contradicts the standard belief that fat is itself unhealthy and can and should be changed.

There is also a concept in the literature called "metabolically unhealthy normal weight," which refers to people who are categorically "normal weight" yet still have metabolic abnormalities (e.g. high blood pressure, high cholesterol, high blood sugar, etc.). This concept is relevant to the many thin people who may be at risk for a metabolic disease, such as diabetes or cardiovascular disease (Aung, Lorenzo, Hinojosa & Haffner, 2013). I have outlined many ways in which fat bias in healthcare is harmful to people of size, but we must also consider how weight bias in healthcare is actually harmful for thin people, too. Just as clinicians assume that people with higher BMIs overeat and live sedentary lifestyles, clinicians often assume that people with lower BMIs are healthy and do not need to make any behavioral changes. It is likely that clinicians are assuming that all thin people eat nutritious and calorically balanced diets and engage in regular physical activity. If clinicians are over-emphasizing risk for metabolic diseases in people of size, then it is likely that they are also insufficiently screening thin people who have these same diseases (Aung et al., 2013), because a high BMI is often what signals clinicians to screen patients for chronic diseases in the first place.

Despite what credentialed health clinicians might tell you, fatness and fitness are not mutually exclusive. The clinical obsession with weight as an indicator of health is problematic because we are creating more reasons for people of size to forgo seeking healthcare. Because there is ample evidence that weight loss dieting and exercise are not leading to long-term weight loss, then we must question why the majority of health professionals are advocating for weight loss as the only approach to health.

Health at Every Size (HAES) is a weight-neutral approach to health that includes balanced and healthy eating and promoting physical activity without weight loss as the goal (Bacon, 2013). Rather than relying on weight as an indicator of health, HAES supporters believe that these health behaviors determine our true state of health and well-being. Rather than teaching patients to count calories, the dietary component of HAES promotes intuitive eating, which means that people should rely on internal cues of hunger rather than external cues from dieting programs or being coaxed to eat to excess in social settings (Bombak, 2014).

Because both HAES and the traditional weight-focused public health approach emphasize the need for healthy eating and exercise, this means the main difference between HAES and the traditional public health approach is that HAES does not involve a scale. Without a scale, clinicians could talk to their patients to assess their health and well-being. The larger institutionalized problem at hand is that the social stigma attached to fat has led to clinical weight biases, which has led to many clinicians treating patients as measurements rather than whole individuals. By limiting or eliminating the importance of the scale in healthcare, clinicians could begin to consider the many complex factors that influence their health, rather than focusing on a single measurement.

REFERENCES

Amy, N. K., Aalborg, A., Lyons, P., & Keranen, L. (2006). Barriers to routine gynecological cancer screening for White and African-American obese women. *International Journal of Obesity*, 30(1), 147–155.

Aung, K., Lorenzo, C., Hinojosa, M. A., & Haffner, S. M. (2013). Risk of developing diabetes and cardiovascular disease in metabolically unhealthy normal-weight and metabolically healthy obese individuals. *The Journal of Clinical Endocrinology & Metabolism*, 99(2), 462–468.

Centers for Disease Control and Prevention. (2015). *About adult BMI*. Retrieved from http://www.cdc.gov/healthy-weight/assessing/bmi/adult_bmi/index.html

Bacon, L. (2013). *Health at every size*. Dallas, TX: BenBella Books

Bacon, L., & Aphramor, L. (2011). Weight science: Evaluating the evidence for a paradigm shift. *Nutrition Journal*, 10(9), 2–13.

Befort, C. A., Allen Greiner, K., Hall, S., Pulvers, K. M., Nollen, N. L., Charbonneau, A., . . . & Ahluwalia, J. S. (2006). Weight-related perceptions among patients and physicians: How well do physicians judge patients' motivation to lose weight?. *Journal of General Internal Medicine*, 21(10), 1086–1090.

Blair, S. N., & Church, T. S. (2004). The fitness, obesity, and health equation: Is physical activity the common denominator?. *Journal of the American Medical Association*, 292(10), 1232–1234.

Bertakis, K. D., & Azari, R. (2005). Obesity and the use of health care services. *Obesity Research*, 13(2), 372–379.

Bookwala, J., & Boyar, J. (2008). Gender, excessive body weight, and psychological well-being in adulthood. *Psychology of Women Quarterly*, 32(2), 188–195.

Bombak, A. (2014). Obesity, health at every size, and public health policy. *American Journal of Public Health*, 104(2), e60–e67.

Bocquier, A., Verger, P., Basdevant, A., Andreotti, G., Baretge, J., Villani, P., & Paraponaris, A. (2005). Overweight and obesity: Knowledge, attitudes, and practices of general practitioners in France. *Obesity Research*, 13(4), 787–795.

Campbell, K., Engel, H., Timperio, A., Cooper, C., & Crawford, D. (2000). Obesity management: Australian general practitioners' attitudes and practices. *Obesity Research*, 8(6), 459–466.

Coughlin, S. S., Uhler, R. J., Bobo, J. K., & Caplan, L. (2004). Breast cancer screening practices among women in the United States, 2000. *Cancer Causes & Control*, 15(2), 159–170.

Dansinger, M. L., Gleason, J. A., Griffith, J. L., Selker, H. P., & Schaefer, E. J. (2005). Comparison of the Atkins, Ornish, Weight Watchers, and Zone diets for weight loss and heart disease risk reduction: A randomized trial. *Journal of the American Medical Association*, 293(1), 43–53.

Djuric, Z., DiLaura, N. M., Jenkins, I., Darga, L., Jen, C. K. L., Mood, D., . . . & Hryniuk, W. M. (2002). Combining weight-loss counseling with the weight watchers plan for obese breast cancer survivors. *Obesity Research*, 10(7), 657–665.

Donnelly, J. E., Blair, S. N., Jakicic, J. M., Manore, M. M., Rankin, J. W., & Smith, B. K. (2009). American College of Sports Medicine Position Stand. Appropriate physical activity intervention strategies for weight loss and prevention of weight regain for adults. *Medicine and Science in Sports and Exercise*, 41(2), 459–471.

Ferrante, J. M., Chen, P. H., Crabtree, B. F., & Wartenberg, D. (2007). Cancer screening in women: Body mass index and adherence to physician recommendations. *American Journal of Preventive Medicine*, 32(6), 525–531.

Flegal, K. M., Graubard, B. I., Williamson, D. F., & Gail, M. H. (2005). Excess deaths associated with underweight, overweight, and obesity. *Journal of the American Medical Association*, 293(15), 1861–1867.Fogel, S. C. (2014). But I have big bones! Obesity in the lesbian community. In S. L. Dibble & P. A. Robertson (Eds.). *Lesbian Health 101: A clinician's guide* (pp.165–181). UCSF Nursing Press: San Francisco, CA. Foster, G. D., Wadden, T. A., Makris, A. P., Davidson, D., Sanderson, R. S., Allison, D. B., & Kessler, A. (2003). Primary care physicians' attitudes about obesity and its treatment. *Obesity research*, 11(10), 1168–1177.

Gailey, J. A. (2014). *The hyper (in) visible fat woman: Weight and gender discourse in contemporary society*. New York, NY: Palgrave Macmillan.

Goodrick, G. K., Poston, W. S., & Foreyt, J. P. (1996). Methods for voluntary weight loss and control: Update 1996. *Nutrition*, 12(10), 672–676.

Hebl, M. R., & Xu, J. (2001). Weighing the care: Physicians' reactions to the size of a patient. *International Journal of Obesity*, 25, 1246–1252.

Heshka, S., Anderson, J. W., Atkinson, R. L., Greenway, F. L., Hill, J. O., Phinney, S. D., . . . & Pi-Sunyer, F. X. (2003). Weight loss with self-help compared with a structured commercial program: A randomized trial. *Journal of the American Medical Association*, 289(14), 1792–1798.

Janssen, I. (2007). Morbidity and mortality risk associated with an overweight BMI in older men and women. *Obesity*, 15(7), 1827–1840.

Lantz, P. M., Golberstein, E., House, J. S., & Morenoff, J. (2010). Socioeconomic and behavioral risk factors for mortality in a national 19-year prospective study of US adults. *Social Science & Medicine, 70*(10), 1558–1566.

Mann, T., Tomiyama, A. J., Westling, E., Lew, A. M., Samuels, B., & Chatman, J. (2007). Medicare's search for effective obesity treatments: Diets are not the answer. *American Psychologist, 62*(3), 220.

McGee, D. L., & Diverse Populations Collaboration. (2005). Body mass index and mortality: A meta-analysis based on person-level data from twenty-six observational studies. *Annals of Epidemiology, 15*(2), 87–97.

McGuigan, R. D., & Wilkinson, J. M. (2015). Obesity and healthcare avoidance: A systematic review. *AIMS Public Health, 2*(1), 56–63.

Mitchell, R. S., Padwal, R. S., Chuck, A. W., & Klarenbach, S. W. (2008). Cancer screening among the overweight and obese in Canada. *American Journal of Preventive Medicine, 35*(2), 127–132.

Moore, L. (2014). I'm your patient, not a problem. *Narrative Inquiry in Bioethics, 4*(2), 110–112.

Ortega, F. B., Lee, D. C., Katzmarzyk, P. T., Ruiz, J. R., Sui, X., Church, T. S., & Blair, S. N. (2013). The intriguing metabolically healthy but obese phenotype: Cardiovascular prognosis and role of fitness. *European Heart Journal, 34*(5), 389–397.

Østbye, T., Yarnall, K. S., Krause, K. M., Pollak, K. I., Gradison, M., & Michener, J. L. (2005). Is there time for management of patients with chronic diseases in primary care?. *The Annals of Family Medicine, 3*(3), 209–214.

Phelan, S. M., Dovidio, J. F., Puhl, R. M., Burgess, D. J., Nelson, D. B., Yeazel, M. W., . . . & Ryn, M. (2014). Implicit and explicit weight bias in a national sample of 4,732 medical students: The medical student CHANGES study. *Obesity, 22*(4), 1201–1208.

Phillips, C. M. (2013). Metabolically healthy obesity: Definitions, determinants and clinical implications. *Reviews in Endocrine and Metabolic Disorders, 14*(3), 219–227.

Puhl, R. M., Andreyeva, T., & Brownell, K. D. (2008). Perceptions of weight discrimination: Prevalence and comparison to race and gender discrimination in America. *International Journal of Obesity, 32*(6), 992–1000.

Puhl, R. M., & Brownell, K. D. (2006). Confronting and coping with weight stigma: An investigation of overweight and obese adults. *Obesity, 14*(10), 1802–1815.

Puhl, R. M., & Heuer, C. A. (2009). The stigma of obesity: A review and update. *Obesity, 17*(5), 941–964.

Rosen, A. B., & Schneider, E. C. (2004). Colorectal cancer screening disparities related to obesity and gender. *Journal of General Internal Medicine, 19*(4), 332–338.

Swift, D. L., Johannsen, N. M., Lavie, C. J., Earnest, C. P., & Church, T. S. (2014). The role of exercise and physical activity in weight loss and maintenance. *Progress in Cardiovascular Diseases, 56*(4), 441–447.

Thompson, R. L., & Thomas, D. E. (2000). A cross-sectional survey of the opinions on weight loss treatments of adult obese patients attending a dietetic clinic. *International Journal of Obesity & Related Metabolic Disorders, 24*(2).

Seo, C. A. (2014). You mean it's not my fault: Learning about lipedema, a fat disorder. *Narrative Inquiry in Bioethics, 4*(2), E6-E9.

Thuan, J. F., & Avignon, A. (2005). Obesity management: Attitudes and practices of French general practitioners in a region of France. *International Journal of Obesity, 29*(9).

Troiano, R. P., Frongillo Jr, E. A., Sobal, J., & Levitsky, D. A. (1996). The relationship between body weight and mortality: A quantitative analysis of combined information from existing studies. *International Journal of Obesity and Related Metabolic Disorders: Journal of the International Association for the Study of Obesity, 20*(1), 63–75.

Tsai, A. G., & Wadden, T. A. (2005). Systematic review: An evaluation of major commercial weight loss programs in the United States. *Annals of Internal Medicine, 142*(1), 56–66.

Wann, M. (2009). Forward. In E. D. Rothblum, & S. Solovay (Eds.). *The fat studies reader.* New York Unviersity Press: New York, NY.

Wing, R. R., & Phelan, S. (2005). Long-term weight loss maintenance. *The American Journal of Clinical Nutrition, 82*(1), 222S-225S.

"Let's Talk About Intentional Weight Loss and Evidence-Based Medicine"

By Anna G. Mirer, Ph.D., M.P.H.

You are a doctor. You are trying to get through a busy clinic day when there is a knock at your office door. It is a pharmaceutical rep. Before you can say anything, he lets himself in, saying, "I'll only take up a minute of your time, but I just have to tell you about this exciting new weight loss drug. It's 95% effective at treating obesity in adults." Sounds good right? Oo, he's giving away a free pocket knife with the drug's logo on it. Maybe you do have a minute to spare. You know you have some questions about the study that got this new drug approved.

You start by asking how much weight the study participants lost on average. Turns out it's about 10% of their body weight in the first year. So women weighing 250 pounds at the start of the study weighed, on average, 225 pounds after a year.

Well ok, so it's not a cure for obesity, but it still sounds useful. Everyone's always telling you how small weight loss can have a dramatic effect on health. And besides if you took the drug for five years you could lose 50% of your body weight, right?

Well… the rep tugs at his collar… not exactly. By the end of the second year, people in the study had started to regain the weight.[1] At the end of the study subjects taking the drug weighed, on average, about six pounds[2] less than the control group. In fact, by the end of year five, less than half[3] the subjects had sustained their modest weight loss. Somewhere between 20–80% of subjects[4] (depending on who you counted and how

long they stayed in the study) had gained even more weight than they lost.

Ouch. So in the long run this drug could actually hurt more people than it helps? That can't be right, can it? Still, that's still a lot of people who are able to sustain weight loss in the long term. Given the terrible consequences of obesity, maybe a small chance at weight loss is worth the risk. Well, actually, now that you think of it, what are the other risks? That is, what are the side effects?

The rep clears his throat and begins to mumble a list.[5] Depression, worsened self-esteem, difficulty concentrating, constant hunger, obsession with food, increased risk of eating disorders. Also bone loss.

But the side effects were rare, right? Was the drug well tolerated? The rep scratches the back of his neck. Actually not so rare. Actually about half of people assigned to take the drug dropped out of the study[6] and no one's sure[7] what happened to them.

Whoa. That doesn't sound harmless at all. Still, if it's a choice between depression and obesity, you know most of your patients will choose depression. So which of your patients might be good candidates for this new drug? It's a new treatment, so maybe all of your patients should try it, just in case it works.

But then the rep starts shuffling his feet. He mutters something and you realize that this supposedly new drug is just a reformulation of a drug that has been around for a long, long time. In fact, it's been around so long that people accept it as dogma that it works, despite its lack of evidence base. It's extremely popular.

[1] http://www.ncbi.nlm.nih.gov/pmc/articles/PMC3135022/figure/F2/
[2] http://onlinelibrary.wiley.com/doi/10.1002/14651858.CD005270/abstract
[3] http://ajcn.nutrition.org/content/74/5/579.long
[4] http://motivatedandfit.com/wp-content/uploads/2010/03/Diets_dont_work.pdf
[5] http://www.nutritionj.com/content/10/1/9
[6] http://www.ncbi.nlm.nih.gov/pubmed/16755283
[7] http://motivatedandfit.com/wp-content/uploads/2010/03/Diets_dont_work.pdf

In fact, now that you think about it, you don't have very many obese patients who *haven't* tried this drug in one form or another, on and off for most of their lives. Does it really makes sense to make them try the same drug that has failed them so many times?

But you're not ready to give up yet. What about the control group in this drug study? What about the poor souls who did not even get to try the drug, who were just abandoned to their disease? I mean, whatever the drug's effects, it can't be worse than just continuing to live with obesity, can it?

The rep is ready for this. There was a control group in this trial, he is excited to tell you. He is excited, because it turns out the numerous prior studies of this drug rarely have a well-chosen control group; they just compare different formulations of the same drug if they even have a comparison group. But this control group was given no weight loss intervention at all! Instead of being encouraged to lose weight, they were just counseled on their "health" (the rep uses air quotes for this word, as though people like that could even have health[8]). They were given mental health interventions, including learning how to read their body's cues for hunger and satiety, and support for body image issues. They were encouraged and supported in physical activity, and taught to find ways to move their body that felt good and were sustainable. The rep is giggling now.

So it sounds like the control group must have gained a lot more weight? He stops giggling. Actually no.[9] And how did the two groups compare in terms of other metabolic outcomes like blood pressure and cholesterol? The control group did better. And mental health outcomes? The control group did way better (though the rep whispers *But who cares, it's not like mental health is really health.*) And did half of this group drop out too? No, they mostly stayed.

You politely escort the pharmaceutical rep out, thanking him for the pocket knife and accepting his card. He has given you a lot to think about.

Will you recommend the new drug? To anyone? Only to the few people that have never tried it before? How many times should you require your patients to try and fail with this drug before you recommend they stop?

Well, friends, by now you see where I'm going with this: the drug in this story is not really a drug invented by some sleazy big pharma boogeyman. It is every weight loss intervention there is.[10] It is Weight Watchers, Jenny Craig, Nutrisystem, the Atkins Diet, the Paleo Diet, the Blood Type Diet, the French Woman's Diet, the Aerobic Housecleaning Lifestyle, the Grapefruit Diet, the Sugar-Free Diet, the Ice Cream Diet, a sensible low fat diet, and MyPyramid. It is Orlistat[11] (slower regain but more fecal incontinence) and all the other weight loss drugs.[12] It is gastric bypass surgery and lap bands (those probably produce slower regain,[13] but no one really knows because the quality of the evidence is so poor,[14] though it clearly involves greater risk of being hospitalized for things that happen when someone surgically remodels your stomach). The diets, the pills, the surgeries, they all work the same[15]—for the vast majority there will be temporary weight loss followed by weight regain,[16] often at serious cost to mental and physical health.

Please remember this when some recommendation[17] comes out suggesting "treat the weight first" and that all other health problems will have to take a back seat. Remember this when academics are slap-fighting[18] about whether BMI is linked to mortality. None of it actually matters at all to the patients you have today, because existing weight loss interventions don't work. Even with outcomes for which weight loss could be beneficial, the benefit will be temporary if and when the weight comes back. Quickly or slowly it will come back for all but a very few. The best most people can expect for their pain and suffering is to be about five to ten pounds lighter, and those are the minority for whom the treatment succeeds. It doesn't matter how big a problem you think obesity is, and it doesn't matter whether or not you're right about it, because we do not have any tool that will make obesity go away.

Like the villain in this story, there are a lot of people and a lot of companies who make money off of the

---

[8]http://www.fatnutritionist.com/index.php/when-health-is-not-on-your-side/

[9]http://www.ncbi.nlm.nih.gov/pubmed/15942543

[10]http://www.ncbi.nlm.nih.gov/pubmed/21261939

[11]http://www.sciencedirect.com/science?_ob=MiamiCaptionURL&_method=retrieve&_eid=1-s2.0-S1521691814000936&_image=1-s2.0-S1521691814000936-gr1.jpg&_cid=272484&_explode=defaultEXP_LIST&_idxType=defaultREF_WORK_INDEX_TYPE&_alpha=defaultALPHA&_ba=&_rdoc=1&_fmt=FULL&_issn=15216918&_pii=S1521691814000936&md5=71f53ef678650267f7ee190a8b6a795f

[12]http://circ.ahajournals.org/content/125/13/1695/T1.expansion.html

[13]http://link.springer.com/article/10.1007/s11695-007-9265-1/fulltext.html

[14]http://onlinelibrary.wiley.com/doi/10.1002/14651858.CD003641.pub4/full

[15]http://annals.org/article.aspx?articleid=477646

[16]http://ac.els-cdn.com/S0002822307014836/1-s2.0-S0002822307014836-main.pdf?_tid=506f9872-a333-11e4-8c78-00000aab0f6b&acdnat=1422040339_41a41b729d09949aeeb3782cc6139550

[17]https://danceswithfat.wordpress.com/2015/01/21/horrible-new-medical-guidelines-for-fat-patients/

[18]http://www.ncbi.nlm.nih.gov/pubmed/23280227

promise of weight loss. It's a great business model; the more the intervention fails, the more money people pour into it. These people and companies have a vested interest in perpetuating the lie that anyone can and should become thin. But medicine doesn't have to be a part of it.

To any reader who would like an overview of these issues in scientific language rather than in the form of a short story, I highly recommend Bacon & Aphramor's 2011 Nutrition Journal review article, "Weight science: evaluating the evidence for a paradigm shift": http://www.ncbi.nlm.nih.gov/pubmed/21261939

"Making 'A Way Outa No Way'"

By Becky W. Thompson

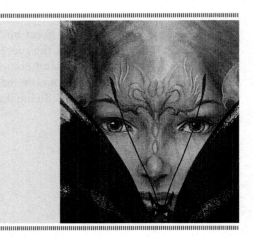

. . . Rethinking biased assumptions in the literature on eating problems begins with scrutinizing ideas about femininity and gender socialization. For example, the belief that women's bodily insecurities are fueled by lessons about femininity that teach women to be passive and complaint may accurately describe socialization patterns among middle- and upper-class Protestant white women, but this does not apply to many African-American and Jewish women, who are often encouraged to be assertive, self-directed, and active both within their families and publicly. Nor do passivity and dependence accurately describe lesbians and single, divorced, and widowed women who do not rely upon men for economic support and who tend to work in the paid labor market all of their lives. The notion that an institutional imperative toward thinness is a backlash against women's economic gains does speak to the advances of white middle-and upper-class women. But, as these women have been struggling to move up the occupational ladder, working-class women of all races have been striving simply to stay on the ladder—a ladder that, for them, has been horizontally rather than vertically positioned. While women of all classes and races are affected by a backlash Susan Faludi rightfully termed "the undeclared war against American women," the link some theorists draw between this backlash and augmented economic power is a race- and class-specific supposition that reinforces the association of eating problems with "achievement-oriented" business and professional women. Once again, anorexia and bulimia are rendered invisible among working-class women.

Similarly, the connection drawn between an increase in eating problems and "superwoman" expectations—as more women juggle careers and family responsibilities—accurately identifies changes in the participation of white middle-class women in the paid labor market. More middle-class white women are balancing two full-time jobs, but this double duty is not new for working- and middle-class women of color, lesbians, and single mothers. As white middle-class women have been fighting for the right to work outside the home, many black and Latina women have been fighting for the opposite: a chance to stay home with their children.

Race and class stratification breaks apart a singular reliance upon sexism as the underlying cause of eating problems. The women I interviewed linked the origins of their eating problems to many different types of trauma, many of which have received scant attention from researchers or the media. More than half of them—across race and class—were survivors of sexual abuse, which was often peppered with racism or anti-Semitism. Some women tied eating problems to a range of class factors, including poverty and stress caused by upward class mobility. Among the lesbians, some developed eating problems to cope with homophobia. Other traumas women linked to eating problems were emotional and physical abuse, often laced with racism, and witnessing abuse of siblings or parents.

The multiple traumas women link to their eating problems do not discount the important feminist analyses of the impact of sexist assaults against women's bodies and appetites. A multiracial focus, however, complicates the picture considerably. While feminists have shown how emotional, physical, and sexual abuse may lead women to binge or purge, little attention has been given to how inequalities besides sexist ones change women's eating patterns. Such a focus requires an expanded understanding of trauma that includes not only physical but also psychic injuries. In this way, trauma may include what Harriette McAdoo has

"Making 'A Way Outa No Way,'" from *A Hunger So Wide and So Deep* by Becky Thompson, University of Minnesota Press, 1994, pp. 7–20. Reprinted by permission.

termed the "mundane extreme environmental stress" of racism,[1] injuries from poverty, incest and other sexual abuse, physical and emotional abuse, immigration, battery, heterosexism, and a variety of other socially induced injuries.

It is frightening to consider that the many extraordinary and harrowing accounts of trauma the women I interviewed identified may not, in fact, be uncommon. One African-American woman began bingeing when she was four years old because it gave her reliable comfort from the pain of sexual abuse, racism, and witnessing the battering of her mother. A white upper middle class Jewish woman attributed fasting for days on end to sexual and emotional abuse by her boyfriend. Pressed into isolation with the threat of further abuse, this woman began to think she deserved no pleasures—eating, seeing people, or even going out in the sunlight. She locked herself up in her dormitory room, sometimes even in her closet, and starved herself. A Latina woman described her body as a "shock absorber" that attracted the "world's pain," going back as far as she could remember. She ate to buffer herself from this pain. She remembered wondering at the age of five if an entire picnic table of hot dogs, hamburgers, chips, potato salad, and buns would be enough to fill her. Beset by emotional abuse and her relatives' constant criticism of her weight, she had little chance to understand either her body or her appetite as trustworthy or safe.

Identifying the traumatic bases of many eating problems reveals the dangers of labeling a common way women cope with pain as an appearance-based disorder. One blatant example of sexism is the notion that women's foremost worries are about their appearance—a belittling stereotype that masks women's worries about paying the bills, keeping their children off the streets and in school, and building loving and egalitarian relationships. By highlighting the emphasis on slenderness, the dominant imagery about eating problems falls into the same trap of assuming that difficulties with eating reflect women's "obsession" with appearance. This misnaming fails to account for the often creative and ingenious ways that girls and women cope with mul-

---

[1] In recent years, there has been a fair amount of discussion among psychiatrists, psychologists, and other professionals on how the experience of racism might produce mental health problems similar to post-traumatic stress disorder (PTSD). While this discussion generally focuses on ongoing "low level" experiences of racism, some professionals have also pointed out that viral media content featuring the deaths of people of color, especially Black people, may also function as a kind of vicarious trauma and lead to the development of more classically understood PTSD. This may happen even when such content is shared with the goal of raising awareness about and promoting action to change disproportionate violence against POC in our culture. *Ed.*

tiple hardships, quite frequently with no one's help but their own.

The culture-of-thinness model has also been used, erroneously, to dismiss eating problems among women of color based on the notion that they are not interested in or affected by a culture that demands thinness. This ideology lumps into one category a stunning array of racial and ethnic groups—Japanese-Americans, Chicanas, Hopi, Puerto Ricans, Amerasians, and African-Americans, to name just a few. The tremendous cultural, religious, and historical diversity among these groups of people makes the notion that they are—as a whole—invulnerable to eating problems dubious at best.

Emphasis on thinness is certainly not universal or equally tenacious across race and ethnicity. There are aspects of African-American culture, for example, that historically have protected against a demand for very thin bodies. In addition, festivities that take place when food is being prepared and eaten are key aspects of maintaining racial identity. Many black women writers, for example, include positive images of physically large women who enjoy food, and celebrate women of varying shapes and sizes. In fact, Alice Walker's definition of "womanist" includes a woman who "loves love and food and roundness." In her poem "Song for a Thin Sister," Audre Lorde also celebrates size and rejects the notion of thinness as an ideal:

> *Either heard or taught*
> *as girls   we thought*
> *that skinny was funny*
> *or a little bit   silly*
> *and feeling a pull*
> *toward the large and the colorful*
> *I would joke you   when*
> *you grew too thin.*
> *But your new kind of hunger*
> *makes me chilly   like danger*
> *I see you forever retreating*
> *shrinking   into a stranger*
> *in flight*
> *and growing up*
> *Black   and fat*
> *I was so sure that   skinny*
> *was funny   or silly*
> *but always*
> *white.*

In her poetic voice, Lorde associates "skinny" with whiteness and a culture outside her own. One African-American woman I interviewed was raised in a rural community in Arkansas that valued women of ample proportions. One Puerto Rican woman was given appetite stimulants as a child because her mother thought that skinny children looked sickly.

This ethic did not, however, stop either of them from developing eating problems. In her chronicle about eating problems, Georgiana Arnold, an African-American health educator, identifies dual and conflicting patterns about food. While eating was a joyful part of family life, fat was a topic that the family avoided:

> In our home, food was a source of nourishment, a sign of love, a reward and the heart of family celebrations. It was also a source of ambivalence, guilt, shame, and conflict. Our "family fat" issues descended into the same cavern of silence that housed my father's alcoholism, gambling and willful disappearance from our lives. There was no talking about it and there were no tears.

Ironically, an ethic that celebrates food and protects against internalizing a value of thinness can work against identifying and getting help for eating problems. Furthermore, since there is no such thing as a monolithic "black community," any attempt to identify a single idea about weight, size, and food quickly breaks down.

A multiracial focus does not make the culture of thinness insignificant, but shows that its power needs to be understood in the context of other factors. For some girls, an imperative toward thinness initially has little or nothing to do with their eating problems. They link other social injustices to their eating difficulties. Furthermore, those who do internalize an emphasis on thinness also attribute other injustices to anorexia or bulimia.

By questioning the prominence of the culture-of-thinness model, I do not want to suggest that women avoid talking about their desires to be thin. Issues of appearance are essential currency for women's access to power in this country, and thinness is a critical component. While fat men are vulnerable to ridicule and discrimination, the standards are clearly gendered: being a fat woman is a far graver "mistake" than being a fat man. For white young women, thinness may, in fact, be the most powerful marker used to judge their physical attractiveness. But for women of color, body size is only one of many factors used to judge attractiveness. For older women of any race, the approval of thinness is countered by disdain for wrinkles and an aging body. For lesbians, cashing in on the power of thinness depends upon taking care not to look too "butch." Stereotypes aimed at lesbians of color who are not thin

are a stark example of what Barbara Smith termed the "simultaneity of oppression." Nedhera Landers, a black lesbian who is fat, explains:

> My mere existence shows up society's lies in great relief. Being Black (and a chick) would eliminate my being fat. But since I am fat, young and childless, that must mean I'm a whore out of desperation for a man. But, since I am a lesbian and men aren't central to my life, that would eliminate my whore status. So, according to the current myths, I don't exist. When I assert my presence and insist that I am indeed fully present, I become an object of ridicule.

Ultimately, more troubling than what the reliance on the ideal of thinness reveals about health research is what it may signal about U.S. society in general: it speaks to a social inability to openly confront and deal with the results of injustice. In a country brimming with glorified images of youth, whiteness, thinness, and wealth, it makes painful sense that dissatisfaction with appearance often serves as a stand-in for topics that are still invisible.

In fact, it is hard to imagine what the world might be like if people were able to talk about trauma and the ways they cope with it with the same ease as they talk about dissatisfaction with their weight and appearance. The fact that Anita Hill was herself put on trial for testifying about sexual and racial harassment is a glaring indicator that much that we need to know about injustice and people's responses to it is still "unspeakable." The fact that more energy has been spent taking the hateful images of Public Enemy off the music racks—on the premise that the lyrics incite violence—than regulating the guns responsible for the death of thousands of young people is a glaring example of the politics of distraction. The Bush and Reagan administrations' use of the military term "vertical insertion"—a euphemism for the bombing and death of human beings—is a searing example of how language is used to hide violence and violation. In the words of Judith Herman, the "ordinary response to atrocities is to banish them from consciousness. Certain violations of the social contract are too terrible to utter aloud: this is the meaning of the word unspeakable." For a staggering number of women, atrocities done to them have been rendered unspeakable. In the place of this unuttered language are symbolic representations of their traumas—often manifested in unwanted eating patterns and supreme dissatisfaction with appetites and bodies.

Of course, not all women with eating problems have developed them to cope with trauma. The fact that 80 percent of fourth grade girls in one large study said they were on diets and that dissatisfaction with weight and size is in fact normative for women in the United States indicates the danger of such a sweeping generalization. A key distinction between periodic dieting and body disapproval and potentially life-threatening and long-term eating problems may be the history of abuse underlying them. Different exposure to trauma may distinguish a young girl who constantly worries about her weight from a woman for whom bulimia is the centerpiece of her day, a woman who occasionally uses liquid diets from a woman who, at eighty pounds, remains afraid to eat. Explicating possible distinctions like these would require examining trauma in different categories of women. This is a study yet to be done. But the experiences of the women whose lives form the basis of this book reveal that discomfort with weight, bodies, and appetite are often the metaphors girls and women use to speak about atrocities. To hear only concerns about appearance or gender inequality is to miss the complex origins of eating problems

The Politics of Invisibility

How were women of color and lesbians left out of media attention and research on eating problems in the first place, given that the stereotype of eating problems as a golden girl's disease is probably more indicative of which women have been studied than of actual prevalence? Certainly, the common reliance on studies conducted in hospitals, clinical settings, private high schools, and colleges skewed public perceptions of those most vulnerable to developing anorexia or bulimia. Basing theory on studies restricted to these locations has limited knowledge of women who are not in college, of women of color, of older women and poor women.

This skewed focus has long-term and potentially debilitating consequences. The stereotype that eating problems are "white girl" phenomena has led many highly trained professionals to either misdiagnose or ignore women of color. Maria Root explains that "social stereotypes of plump or obese Black, Latina or American Indian women may avert the therapist from examining any issues around food and body image. Similarly a thin, Japanese American woman may not be assessed for an eating disorder." When women of color are treated, their eating problems tend to be more severe as a result of delays in diagnosis. Among the women I interviewed, only two had been diagnosed bulimic or anorexic by physicians, yet all who said

they were anorexic or bulimic fit the diagnostic criteria (DSM-111) for these diagnoses.

Given these realities, a more important question than *how* these groups of women have been made invisible may be *why* theorists and the media have been dedicated to stereotyped images of eating problems. The answer to this question lies in the way that ideology about black women's bodies has been invisibly inscribed onto what is professed about white women's bodies. In her work on biases in higher education curricula, Patricia Hill Collins explains, "While it may appear that the curriculum is 'Black womanless' and that African-American women have been 'excluded,' in actuality subordinated groups have been included in traditional disciplines through the groups' invisibility." Toni Morrison also offers essential tools for uncovering ideology about race and racism in literature, tools that apply well to developing race-conscious health research. In her groundbreaking essay "Unspeakable Things Unspoken: The Afro-American Presence in American Literature"—which she later expanded into the book *Playing in the Dark*—Morrison unravels the illusion that traditional literature in the United States has been "race free" or "universal," recognizing the presence of Afro-Americans, whether spoken or not, in the work of such well-known white writers as Melville, Poe, Hawthorne, Twain, Faulkner, Cather, and Hemingway, to name a few. Using Melville as a case in point, Morrison recognizes the presence of Afro-Americans and slavery in *Moby Dick*, pointing out that traditional American literature is both informed and determined by this presence. For Morrison, this analysis doubles the fascination and power of the great American writers. She warns us that "defending the Eurocentric Western posture in literature as not only 'universal' but also 'race-free' may have resulted in lobotomizing that literature, and in diminishing both the art and the artist." Avoiding future lobotomies, she writes, depends on excavating the "ghost in the machine"—the ways in which the "presence of Afro-Americans has shaped the choices, the language, the structure and the meaning of so much American literature."

Morrison's method of searching for the ghost in the machine of American literature can reveal substantial biases in research on women's mental health. This tool for theoretical excavation dredges up stereotypes of women of color, lesbians, and working-class women that not only are debilitating for these women but also ultimately backfire on white heterosexual women as well.

The portrayal of bulimia and anorexia as appearance-based disorders is rooted in a notion of femininity in which white middle- and upper-class women are presented as frivolous, obsessed with their bodies, and accepting of narrow gender roles. This representation, like the reputation of AIDS and some cancers, fuels people's tremendous shame and guilt about them. The depiction of middle-class women as vain and obsessive is intimately linked to the assumption that working-class women are the opposite: one step away from being hungry, ugly, and therefore not susceptible to eating problems. The dichotomy drawn between working-class and middle-class women reflects the biased notion that middle-class people create symbolic, abstract relations through their actions and thought while working-class people relate to the world in literal, concrete ways. Within this framework, middle- and upper-class women's eating patterns are imbued with all kinds of symbolic significance—as a way of rebelling against parents, striving for perfection, and responding to conflicting gender expectations. The logic that working-class women are exempt from eating problems, by contrast, strips away any possible symbolic significance or emotional sustenance that food may have or give in their lives. Recognizing that women may develop eating problems to cope with poverty challenges the notion that eating problems are class bound and confirms that both middle- and working-class women are quite capable of creating sophisticated and symbolic relations with food that go far beyond a biological need for calories.

Like biased notions about class, the belief that African-American women are somehow untouched by the cult of thinness is built on long-standing dichotomies—good/bad, pretty/ugly, sexually uptight/ sexually loose—about white and black women. These divisions feed into an erroneous notion of black women as somehow separate from a society in which beauty standards are an integral part of the socialization of all women. The portrayal of white women as frivolous and obsessed with their appearance is linked to the presentation of black women as the opposite: as unattractive "mammies' who are incapable of being thin or who are not affected by pressures to be thin. With these multiple distortions, the fact that the dress and "look" of black youth have frequently set the standard for what constitutes style in the fashion industry is entirely unaccounted for.

In an autobiographical account, Retha Powers, an African-American woman, describes being told not to worry about her eating problems because "fat is more acceptable in the Black community." Stereotypical perceptions held by her peers and teachers of the "maternal Black woman" and the "persistent

mammy-brickhouse Black Woman image" added to Powers's difficulty in finding people willing to take her problems with food seriously. The association of eating problems with "whiteness" has made some women of color unwilling to seek help. Getting help may feel like "selling out" or being treated as an oddity by friends or medical professionals. The racist underpinnings of some health care policies historically have also led some women of color to avoid seeking help out of fear of being treated in a prejudicial way. Furthermore, the historical view of black women as bodies without minds underlies their invisibility in the frame of reference; they are dismissed as incapable of developing problems that are both psychological and physical. With the dichotomy drawn between black and white women, Latinas drop out of the frame of reference altogether.

Failing to consider eating problems among lesbians reflects the unwritten but powerful belief that lesbians are not interested in or capable of being "attractive" in the dominant sense of the word. This reflects stereotypical notions of "butches" who are too ugly to care about their weight; women who have "become" lesbians because of fear of men and who have subsequently lost touch with "mainstream" society; and women who settle for women after being rejected by men. As biased notions about race reflect racial fears, so distorted ideas about sexuality reflect fears about sexuality in general, and these fears historically have been projected onto lesbians' bodies. These distortions have not only pushed attention to lesbians with eating problems out of the frame of reference, they have also rendered invisible the many ways lesbian communities have refashioned what constitutes beauty in ways that nurture multiple versions of style, glamour, and grace. It is no coincidence that much of the activism and scholarship opposing "fat oppression" has been spearheaded by lesbian feminists who astutely analyze how discrimination against fat women reflects a society hostile to women who take up space and refuse to put boundaries around their hunger for food, resources, and love.

The notion that eating problems are limited to heterosexual women has also contributed to some lesbians' secrecy. The historical association of lesbian sexuality with mental illness and deviance undercuts many lesbians' willingness to identify themselves with any stigmatizing illness. This institutional bias has been coupled with secrecy among lesbians based on the fear of being misunderstood or rejected by other lesbians. The connotation of anorexia and bulimia as problems developed by those who accept male models of beauty means that a lesbian with an eating problem is admitting to being malecentered and therefore not appropriately lesbian. In this way, linking eating problems with appearance rather than trauma has impeded lesbians' self-diagnosis.

Pioneering research on lesbians has confronted the problematic assumptions underlying their invisibility. Like the emerging research on race, this scholarship links unwanted eating patterns and internalized oppression—the process by which people from subordinated communities accept negative attitudes about themselves that are created by the dominant culture. In addition, although lesbian communities may offer women more generous versions of what constitutes health and beauty, this ethic may not be able to compete with dominant cultural beliefs about body size and weight. The scholarship on lesbians, like that on African-American women, reveals cultural methods of protection against harmful social standards previously missing in research that treated white heterosexual women as the standard.[2]

The intricacies of race, class, and sexuality encourage us to rethink demeaning assumptions about white middle-class femininity and racist assumptions about women of color and to consider bulimia and anorexia serious responses to injustices. At their core, bulimia and anorexia are not signs of self-centered vanity and obsession with appearance but rather, at least in their initial stages, are sensible ways women cope with the difficulties in their lives. Reexamining split and oppositional images about race, class, and sexuality with a wide-angle lens reveals a single complicated frame. A multiracial focus shows that distorted notions about black, Latina, and lesbian women are embedded—both explicitly and implicitly—in notions about white heterosexual women, and that it is impossible to understand any of them without the others.

Body Consciousness

The traumatic basis of many women's eating problems can teach us much about bodies and embodiment, for trauma often disrupts an intact sense of one's body. Women's ways of using food are emblematic of a rupturing of women's embodiment, of their ability to see themselves as grounded in and connected to their bodies.

---

[2]Recent research shows that among adolescent girls, lesbian girls have higher rates of disordered eating than heterosexual ones, and bisexual girls have the highest rates of all identity categories included. Despite this, one of the federal government's first public health initiatives targeting adult lesbian and bisexual women after the passage of the Affordable Care Act was a program meant to promote weight loss among members of this groups. *Ed.*

When I first began to ask women about their relationships to their bodies, I asked them to tell me about their body images, but I soon realized a basic conceptual problem in my question. By inquiring about their body "image" I was taking for granted that they imagined themselves as having bodies, an assumption that many women quickly dispelled. The notion that someone can imagine her body assumes that she considers herself to have a body. Some women do not see themselves as having bodies at all.

This painful reality is partly a consequence of oppression that has both historical and contemporary manifestations. The more than three hundred years of slavery in this country robbed African-American men and women of the right to own their own bodies. African-American women were forced into this country as pieces of property "whose purpose was to provide free labor. . . . Their roles in U.S. society were synonymous with work, labor outside of the home, and legitimized sexual victimization from the very outset." In the existential nightmare of slavery, no self was legally recognized, and therefore the body could not exist for the self either. Once slavery was abolished, all that black people had were their bodies. The legal right to own one's body, however, does not in itself ensure that one can claim this right. The legacy of slavery still informs black women's experiences of their bodies in profound ways. The portrayal of black women as mammies (women incapable of being sexual), as Sapphires (women who dominate in the family and in the bedroom), and as Jezebels (sexually promiscuous women who willingly participate in sexual exploitation) reflects the projection of white fantasies and sexuality onto black women's bodies. The idea that white women needed protection was build on seeing black women as their opposite—neither worthy of protection nor wanting to be free of sexual violation.

Debilitating and contradictory stereotypes of Latina women are among the complex and limiting messages against which Latinas have struggled. They have been viewed both as highly sexual, irrationally flamboyant temptresses and as obedient, subservient, fat, and passive—good Catholic mothers. In both their historic and contemporary versions, these stereotypes have long-lasting effects on embodiment and physical presence for Latinas. The existence of these stereotypes does not mean they are inevitably internalized. But what embodiment means for black and Latina women cannot be understood without awareness of the struggle and impact of these stereotypes on self-consciousness.

For many women, responding to social injustices directed at their bodies includes trying to escape what seems like the very location of that pain—their bodies. Pecola, a character in Toni Morrison's *The Bluest Eye,* tries to make her body disappear in response to incest, racism, and poverty:

> Letting herself breathe easy now, Pecola covered her head with the quilt. The sick feeling, which she had tried to prevent by holding in her stomach, came quickly in spite of her precaution. There surged in her the desire to heave, but as always, she knew she would not.
>
> "Please, God," she whispered into the palm of her hand. "Please make me disappear." She squeezed her eyes shut. Little parts of her body faded away. Now slowly, now with a rush. Slowly again. Her fingers went, one by one; then her arms disappeared all the way to the elbow. Her feet now. Yes, that was good. The legs all at once. It was hardest above the thighs. She had to be real still and pull. Her stomach would not go. But finally it, too, went away. Then her chest, her neck. The face was hard, too. Almost done, almost. Only her tight, tight eyes were left. They were always left.

Pecola's wish to make her body disappear dramatizes the destructive intersection of sexual abuse, racism, and poverty as no statistic can. Trying to disappear is an immediate and logical strategy to escape what Pecola came to believe caused her pain—her brown eyes and brown body. Her attempt to slip out and away from the reality of a world bent on destroying her is a vivid example of how women's embodiment is compromised. People facing these injustices cannot take for granted such a basic and elemental capacity as being able to reside comfortably in their bodies. And yet the costs of leaving one's body are monumental.

Ultimately, I put aside the concept of body image and instead thought about women's relationship to their bodies as forms of consciousness. Body consciousness is shaped by biological changes common to all women—growth spurts during childhood, puberty, menstruation, menopause, and the aging process—and by the changes of pregnancy and birthing. People are born with a self-consciousness of mind and body, with an internal body image, and a "sixth sense"—a body self-awareness and a sense of mind-body integration. It is through body consciousness that people can often sense danger, intuitively know what to do, and identify how they feel. These elemental and substantial capacities depend on residing within one's body. Embodiment that allows a person to know where his or her body stops and another's physical body begins may be at the root of a person's capacity to know him/herself as simultaneously unique and connected to the world.

Although everyone is born with a sense of embodiment, experience of it is not universal. The meanings people ascribe to their bodies and the social injustices that violate embodiment vary across gender, race, sexuality, class, religion, and nationality. Unlike the term "image," which has a psychological, individual connotation, the etymology of "consciousness" links an awareness of one's social standing directly to social conditions. Consciousness, as Karl Marx used the term, links individual people's social realities, opportunities, and perspectives to class. In a similar way, one's body consciousness is linked to one's race, gender, and sexuality. This connection more accurately captures women's complicated relationship to their bodies than is conveyed in the term "image." Representations of black and Latina women's bodies and their body consciousness are profoundly different from those of white women. Class stratification also shapes body consciousness. Poverty, for example, can significantly alter a woman's relationship to her body. Being denied the chance to own a car, a house, or even furniture can make a poor woman feel as if her body is all she has left.

Women with eating problems certainly do not have a corner on the market in terms of having difficulty residing comfortably within their bodies. As Emily Martin chronicles in her research on women's reproduction, medical and social processes of birthing, menopause, and puberty in the United States fragment women's embodiment. Feminist theorists on disability offer rich analyses of how disability changes women's embodiment. Discriminatory practices against people with disabilities—including limited access to education, employment, independent living, and sexual freedoms—are typically more restricting than actual physical conditions.[3]

The essential issue may not be if women struggle to claim their bodies as their own, but rather the differing ways that embodiment is disrupted. Adrienne Rich writes:

> I know no woman—virgin, mother, lesbian, married, celibate—whether she earns her keep as a housewife, a cocktail waitress, or a scanner of brain waves—for whom her body is not a fundamental problem: its clouded meaning, its fertility, its desire, its so-called frigidity, its bloody speech, its silences, its changes and mutilations, its rapes and ripenings.

In her poetic way, Rich captures the contradictions and complexities of living in one's body.

---

[3] Discriminatory practices and cultural transphobia also drive high rates of disordered eating among trans people of all genders, but especially trans women. *Ed.*

To complicate this further, women employ a variety of survival strategies in response to violations of their bodies. The poet Wanda Coleman writes:

> The price Black girls pay for not conforming to white standards of beauty is extracted in monumental amounts, breath to death. We bend our personalities, and sometimes mutilate our bodies in defense. Sometimes that bent is "bad attitude," perhaps accompanied by a hair-trigger temper, ready to go off at the mildest slight: neck-wobbling, hands to hips, boisterous, hostile, niggerish behavior.

Women may also respond to psychic and physical assaults with silent refusals to engage or show rage. They may run away from home or never leave their apartments. They may flunk out of school or hide behind books. The reasons for these coping strategies are complicated and not easily predicted—just as it is not easy to explain why some women develop eating problems and others do not.

Women with eating problems, however, offer special insights about body consciousness because they respond to trauma in particularly bodily ways. Their stories reveal how bingeing, purging, and dieting can change a woman's embodiment, and they provide vivid examples of what it means for a woman to "leave her body."

Leaving the body is a survival strategy many women use when they see no other alternatives. The sophisticated ways in which the women I talked with describe their experiences of their bodies originate in part in their having had to grapple—seriously and over the long term—with the discomfort of being in their bodies. Their stories reveal the social inequalities that whittle away at a woman's ability to identify her body as her own. They explain what it means to be in exile from one's own body, and why this is common. Their testimonies reveal why sexual abuse and racism can lead a teenager who weighs 110 pounds to see herself as fat and to consider her body the cause of her pain. Their stories also highlight the consequences of drastic weight loss and gain on a woman's sense of her body's shape and size. The average weight fluctuation among the women I talked to was seventy-four pounds. Many of the women's weight changed several times in their lives. Substantial and recurrent weight fluctuation raises complicated and painful questions about what it means to be "embodied" since a woman's possession of a significant portion of her body may be in constant flux.

The women's stories reveal that body consciousness is a highly imaginative and simultaneously concrete ability to see one's self as part of one's body and to draw upon the power generated from this embodiment. It is a concrete reality in that, regardless of one's relation to one's body, breathing, eating, sleeping, and simply being require some consciousness of one's body. But body consciousness occurs at the imaginative and symbolic level as well. In the face of debilitating stereotypes and injustices, women do struggle to claim their bodies as their own. The struggle requires being able to see one's own image of one's body rather than the images projected onto it. Consciousness both takes into account oppressive perceptions of the body and rejects what is debilitating about them.

The women's stories also reveal the often ingenious and creative strategies they develop to counter various assaults, strategies that are at the core of their journey toward self-love and empowerment. Self-love and empowerment are profoundly related to the body. Cornel West writes:

> The issue of self-regard, self-esteem, and self-respect is reflected in bodily form. . . . Toni Morrison would say, "Look you've got to love yourself not only in the abstract; you've got to love your big lips; you've got to love your flat nose; you've got to love your skin, hands, all the way down."

The women whose experiences form the basis of this book identify their injuries and their resistance with honesty and insight. In so doing, they chronicle their despair and resilience, their depression and fortitude, their ingenuity in taking care of themselves.

"Fat People Deserve Dignity and Societal Change"

By Michaela A. Null,
University of Wisconsin-Fond du Lac

Body size and health are contentious issues, especially in recent years. Recently, "obesity" has been designated a disease (Pollack, 2013). There have been many public health campaigns in the United States targeting "obesity" and "childhood obesity" as health problems in and of themselves, including a campaign led by First Lady Michelle Obama. "Anti-obesity" campaigns tend to shame people for their bodies and the choices that are presumed to produce those bodies.

These campaigns aim to "eliminate obesity." This means the goal of the campaign is to eliminate fat people. When I see these campaigns, they tell me that my country's leaders, my government, and my fellow citizens are placing great importance on the creation of a world where no one looks like me. My body is representative of a scourge on America that must be eradicated. National officials, like former U.S. Surgeon General Richard Carmona, have likened "obesity" to terrorism (Los Angeles Times, 2006). "Childhood obesity" campaigns intentionally shame children and adolescents. For example, many schools now send home BMI report cards (Vogel, 2011; Hoffman, 2015) and a 2011 Strong4Life ad campaign stigmatized kids so directly that it sparked a counter-campaign (Nader, 2012). Shaming people has a negative effect on our health rather than a positive one. When we address health, we may do better to focus on structural and systematic issues rather than individuals.

My area of scholarly interest within sociology and gender, sexuality, and women's studies is fat studies. Fat studies is an interdisciplinary area of study that uses a critical lens when looking at body weight and constructions of fat, fat bodies, and fat individuals. As women' studies is the scholarly wing of the women's movement, fat studies is the scholarly wing of the fat activist movement. While the contemporary fat activist movement started in the 1960s, fat studies is a more recent endeavor. Fat studies scholars are not necessarily fat activists, but fat activism certainly paved the way for scholarly work in a similar vein.

Our critical lens allows us to reject the terms "overweight" and "obesity" and embrace the word "fat." While many people see fat as a negative word and an insult, we see in "fat" the potential for use as a simple physical descriptor like "thin" or "tall" or "brunette." Our use of the word fat is a political strategy aimed at reclaiming the word in order to destigmatize it. While "fat" may be a relative term, it makes no specific claims to authority. In contrast, medicalized terms claim authority over bodily norms. "Obesity" identifies bodies as inherently diseased, linking body size to pathology. "Overweight" denotes that there is a "normal" weight to be over (or under). Many in the fat acceptance movement ask, "Over whose weight am I?"

It's widely known that the Body Mass Index (BMI) is flawed as an indicator of health (Burkhauser and Cawley, 2008; Finer, 2012), especially when applied to individuals rather than the entire populations for which it was designed (Flegal, 2010). "Normal" weight and "overweight" are arbitrary. In fact, in 1998 the BMI thresholds for "overweight" and "obesity" were lowered, causing over 25 million Americans to become overweight overnight (Cohen and McDermott, 1998). Regardless of where the lines are drawn, our understanding of the relationship between BMI and health is skewed. Two common measures of health are morbidity (the presence of disease) and mortality rate (incidence of death). However, if we are using those measures as proxies for health, "overweight" is the healthiest category. Katherine M. Flegal of the CDC found that people in the "overweight" category actually have the best statistical outcomes for morbidity and mortality—better than the "normal" weight category (Flegal et al, 2013; Flegal and Kalantar-Zadeh, 2013).

Further, "obesity" literally pathologizes an individual based on their body size alone. According to this logic, a fat person's very existence is what makes them diseased. Labeling a person "obese" asserts that they are diseased based only on their height and weight ratio, disregarding other health indicators such as blood sugar, cholesterol, and self-reported quality of life, such as satisfaction with life, quality of relationships, and resiliency. For these reasons, fat studies scholars avoid using the terms "overweight" or "obesity" except when referring to medical literature or categories, and typically use quotations around them to denote our critical perspective.

Most popular representations of fat people are dehumanizing and encourage a decoupling of the person and the body. For example, a popular notion in weight loss rhetoric is to refer to the "thin person inside" "waiting to get out." This encourages us to imagine that thin people are *people* and fat people are simply… thin people smothered by their fat exterior. Fatness and personhood are situated in opposition. This reflects common notions that fat people must lose weight before they can live their lives or be "good" at life activities. For example, many *Biggest Loser* contestants say they entered the competition so that they could lose weight in order to be better parents.[1] It is also incredibly common for individuals to embark on weight loss to present their "best bodies" for particular life events—getting married, beach season, etc. This means that fat people often put off engaging in social, physical, and even intellectual activities until they lose weight. Fat people often dissociate from their bodies, which have become symbols of their failure as people.

Not only do we see this dehumanization in our language, but also in our visual representations. The use of fat suits in TV and movies furthers the notion that the individual and fat are separate, and that fat is sheddable excess (Mendoza, 2009). Even more widespread is the phenomena of the "headless fatty"—a term coined by

---

[1]For recent coverage of the long-term outcomes of *Biggest Loser* contestants, see Gina Kolata's work for the *New York Times*: http://www.nytimes.com/2016/05/02/health/biggest-loser-weight-loss.html Notice that even coverage like this, which describes how participants soon regained weight and in fact found that their metabolisms had been permanently altered to burn fewer calories, does not reject the underlying assumption that dieting should—and can, if we can just figure out how to "do it right"—be pursued for weight loss! Compare this articles and others like it to the evidence showing the overall inefficacy of dieting discussed by Anna Mirer elsewhere in this section. *Ed.*

activist and scholar Charlotte Cooper (2007). News media, and stock photos used in media, regularly represent fat people without a head; that is, they show them only from the shoulders down. This form of objectification, while perhaps intended to remove the identity of the person in the image, results in removing the personhood from images of fat people and reinforces the notion that fat people should be ashamed. As Jean Kilbourne has said, "Reducing a group of people to an object is the first step in justifying violence against them" (Kilbourne, 2010). While some might see these patterns as attempts to protect fat people from stigma, the headless representation of fat people creates a larger pattern of intensified stigma around fatness and fat people. If people see fat people as objects or "bodies" they see them as less than people—instead, they are things without humanity, personhood, or dignity.

How does this relate to fat people's health? For one, fat people internalize this stigma and often dissociate from their bodies in an attempt to separate themselves from the shame of fatness. In her short film "Fat," Margaret Donahoe says, "My whole life growing up I had been taught to dislike my body, and specifically my fat. I had been dissociating [sic] from my body. You really cement this separation between your self and your body" (Donahoe, 2011). Fat stigma and shame have a negative effect on health behaviors. (Muennig, 2008; Latner et al, 2013). While a common tactic is to try to shame fat people so that they become thin (and, we presume, thereby healthy), shame triggers negative health behaviors, not positive ones. For example, people who feel ashamed may avoid physical activity, isolate themselves socially, engage in disordered eating (binge eating, not eating, etc.), or lapse in their self-care. Feeling ashamed does not inspire people to treat themselves well.

On a larger, systemic level, fat stigma effectively promotes the exclusion of fat people from areas of society that are supposed to encourage and enhance individual health. For example, physical fitness is typically represented and understood in complete opposition to fatness. Spaces for physical activity are thus not made to be fat friendly—in fact, the opposite is typically true. When I go to a gym, spaces in between cardio machines are often so small that I have to squeeze between them, possibly disrupting someone else's exercise in order to access the equipment. Further, the harassment of fat people in public discourages physical activity. Many gym goers are there specifically because they don't want their bodies to look like mine, and they may not welcome my presence. In 2009, a woman wrote about her experience passing an anti-fat PETA billboard advertisement in Jacksonville, FL (Valenti, 2009). The ad featured a headless fat person in a swimsuit with the tag line "Save the Whales." Upon seeing the ad, the woman felt so ashamed she went home while her family stayed to enjoy the beach. While mainstream rhetoric around "obesity" would claim to encourage physical activity, spaces understood as being for physical fitness or physical activity almost always exclude fat people.

Fat stigma and discrimination is estimated to be as prevalent as gender and racial discrimination (Puhl, Andreyeva, and Brownell 2008). Unlike gender and racial discrimination, there are practically no legal protections against fat discrimination. In the United States, laws that protect people from fat discrimination are only in place in the state of Michigan and the cities of Madison, WI, Santa Cruz, CA, San Francisco, CA, Urbana, IL, Washington, DC, and Binghamton, NY (NAAFA, 2016).

A literature review conducted by weight bias scholars Puhl and Brownell (2001: 797) revealed that:

> "28% of teachers in one study said that becoming obese is the worst thing that can happen to a person; 24% of nurses said that they are 'repulsed' by obese persons; and, controlling for income and grades, parents provide less college support for their overweight than for their thin children. There are also suggestions but not yet documentation of discrimination occurring in adoption proceedings, jury selection, housing, and other areas."

While all of these figures might shock and upset anyone who values fat people as people, we might be especially concerned about the ways in which fat stigma is endorsed, reproduced, and enforced by health care providers. This is particularly significant because all individuals need health care and yet health care is one of the main areas where fat people experience fat stigma and discrimination (Puhl and Brownell, 2001).

Researchers continue to examine the effects of racial stigma and discrimination on the health of people of color, independent of income, wealth, and education (Williams, Neighbors, and Jackson, 2003; Williams et al, 2010). For example, African Americans are more likely to experience post-traumatic stress disorder (PTSD), with increased experiences of racial discrimination correlating with even higher risk. There is also evidence that structural, cultural, and interpersonal racism have psychological and even physiological effects (Williams and Mohammed, 2013). Given the relative prevalence of fat stigma, and especially given its medicalization, we are beginning to see widespread evidence that fat stigma and racial discrimination have some similar effects on health and health care. It is clear that fat stigma impacts whether people seek medical care, how

easy that care is to access, and the quality of the care that they receive.

Ostbye et al. (2005) found that middle-aged White women and elderly White men and women were less likely to receive preventative services as their BMI increased. Fat people often avoid medical care, but they may also be less likely to get recommendations for preventative care because medical professionals focus on weight and ignore other problems or make treatment contingent on weight loss. For example, I once sought a referral for physical therapy for foot and ankle pain that affected my ability to be active. Before even examining me, the doctor lectured me on my weight and recommended I see a nutritionist specifically for a weight loss plan and that I exercise more. Once the doctor finally examined me, he found that the pain in my feet and ankles was not weight related, and he no longer recommended anything but physical therapy. For any given medical issue, fat people may face these stigmatizing barriers.

Medical care is intimate and often involves physical contact. What courage must it take for fat patients to access medical services when (as noted above) many medical professionals are repulsed by them?[2] And further, what sort of quality of care can you expect when fat stigma is woven into the only system available for you to access? A 2008 study found that fat women in medical settings suffered stigma because the equipment did not fit them, they received inadequate support, they were "demeaned or embarrassed" by interactions with medical professionals, and they felt dehumanized (Merrill and Grassley).

Further, fat stigma and discrimination intersect with class, gender, and racial discrimination and other axes of oppression. Women experience more stigma and discrimination at lower weights than do men (Maranto and Stenoien, 2000; Morris, 2005; Puhl and Heuer, 2009). That is, fat stigma is gendered. Similarly, S. Bear Bergman (2009) has written about how he is not treated as fat when he is perceived as a man, but is considered fat when perceived as a woman. Being fat is associated with being of a lower socioeconomic class; although many have posited that being poor causes you to be fat, others have suggested that being fat causes you to be poor because of the discriminatory society fat people live in. In particular, research shows that "overweight" women face a wage penalty (Shinall, 2015). Weight bias is also often used as a proxy for racial bias and fatness in our culture is often associated with Black

---

[2]For resources on how to navigate the medical establishment as a fat person, see Marianne Kirby's piece immediately following this one. The fact that a guide like hers is necessary—that body size is such a barrier to health care—is devastating. *Ed.*

and Latin@ people. This means that fat stigma and discrimination disproportionally impact groups of people who are already oppressed—and who are more likely to be stigmatized in medical settings.

One might still ask, "Isn't it legitimate to be concerned about fat people's health?"

First, neither shame, stigma, nor discrimination improve health. Framing fat as inherently bad and insisting that fat people must become thin in order to be healthy actually discourages healthy behaviors, such as physical activity, accessing regular medical care, etc.

Second, the way we think and talk about fat people's health is skewed. We tend to over-focus on the individual in the United States and frame health issues in terms of "healthy behaviors" rather than social structures. "Concern for fat people's health" is typically expressed by imploring fat people to be different or do different things: Fat people should eat less. Fat people should exercise more. Fat people need to learn about portion control. Fat people who lose weight and become thinner will be healthier.

We place the blame for poor health on fat people themselves and ignore other causal factors of health. What we rarely see, if ever, is concern for the structural conditions that negatively impact fat people's health on a massive scale. If we, as a society, are really interested in the health and well-being of fat people, we would address the structural issues and stigma and discrimination that have a wide array of negative effects on fat people's health.

Finally, it should be clear that people deserve human rights, dignity, and respect regardless of their body size *or* their health. We should not condone or encourage any stigma or discrimination on either basis. Using weight or health to justify personal behavior or institutional policies that dehumanize a group of people is harmful and makes little sense.

Those who care about the health of fat people will advocate for inclusion, respect for all bodies, and interpersonal and structural changes that improve fat people's material and psychic access to physical activity, nutritious food, and quality, weight-neutral medical care.

References

Burkhauser, Richard V. and John Cawley. 2008. "Beyond BMI: The value of more accurate measures of fatness and obesity in social science." *Journal of Health Economics* 27(2): 519–529.

Cohen, Elizabeth and Anne McDermott. 1998. "Who's fat? New definition adopted." *CNN*. June 17. http://www.cnn.com/HEALTH/9806/17/weight.guidelines/

Cooper, C. 2007. *'Headless Fatties' [Online]*. London. *Available:* http://charlottecooper.net/publishing/digital/headless-fatties-01-07

Donahoe, Margaret. 2011. "Fat." https://vimeo.com/27254425

Finer, Nick. 2012. "Better Measures of Fat Mass—Beyond BMI." *Clinical Obesity* 2(3–4): 65.

Flegal, Katherine M. 2010. "Katherine M. Flegal, Weight and Mortality: The Population Perspective." *UCLA Center for the Study of Women.* https://www.youtube.com/watch?v=cUqhR9cYMaA

Flegal, KM, Kit BK, Orpana H, Graubard BI. 2013. "Association of all-cause mortality with overweight and obesity using standard body mass index categories: a systematic review and meta-analysis." Journal of the American Medical Association 309(1):71–82.

Flegal, Katherine M. and Kamyar Kalantar-Zadeh. 2013. "Overweight, Mortality, and Survival." *Obesity* 21(9): 1744–1745.

Hoffman, Jan. 2015. "Body Report Cards Aren't Influencing Arkansas Teenagers." New York Times. August 10. http://well.blogs.nytimes.com/2015/08/10/body-report-cards-arent-influencing-arkansas-teenagers/

Kilbourne, Jean. 2010. *Killing Us Softly IV*. Media Education Foundation.

Latner, Janet D., Laura E. Durso, and Jonathan M. Mond. 2013. "Health and health-related quality of life among treatment-seeking overweight and obese adults: associations with internalized weight bias." *Journal of Eating Disorders* 1: 3.

Los Angeles Times. 2006. "Fat is 'Terror Within,' Surgeon General Warns." March 2. http://articles.latimes.com/2006/mar/02/nation/na-briefs2.1

Maranto, Cheryl L. and Ann Fraedrich Stenoien. 2000. "Weight Discrimation: A Multidisciplinary Analysis." *Employee Responsibilities and Rights Journal* 12(1): 9–24.

Mendoza, Katharina R. 2009. "Seeing Through the Layers: Fat Suits and Thin Bodies in *The Nutty Professor* and *Shallow Hal.*" *The Fat Studies Reader* edited by Esther Rothblum and Sondra Solovay. New York: New York University Press.

Merrill, Emily and Jane Grassley. 2008. "Women's stories of their experiences as overweight patients." *Journal of Advanced Nursing.* 64(2): 139–146.

Meunnig, Peter. 2008. "The body politic: the relationship between stigma and obesity-associated disease." *BMC Public Health* 8: 128.

Morris, Stephen. 2006. "Body Weight and Occupational Attainment." *Journal of Health Economics* 25(2): 347–364.

NAAFA. 2016. "Weight Discrimination Laws." *National Association to Advance Fat Acceptance.* http://www.naafa-online.com/dev2/education/laws.html

Nader, Alexia. 2012. "Activists For the Overweight Stand Up to Obesity Campaign in Georgia." *Village Voice.* February 13. http://www.villagevoice.com/restaurants/activists-for-the-overweight-stand-up-to-obesity-campaign-in-georgia-6537214

Ostbye, Truls, Donald H. Taylor Jr, William S. Yancy Jr, and Katrina M. Krause. 2005. *American Journal of Public Health* 95(9): 1623–1630.

Pollack, Andrew. 2013. "A.M.A. Recognizes Obesity as a Disease." *New York Times.* June 18. http://www.nytimes.com/2013/06/19/business/ama-recognizes-obesity-as-a-disease.html?_r=2

Puhl, Rebecca and Kelly Brownell. 2001. "Bias, Discrimination, and Obesity." *Obesity Research* 9(12):788–805.

Puhl, R. M., T. Andreyeva, and K. D. Brownell. 2008. "Perceptions of weight discrimination: prevalence and comparison to race and gender discrimination in America." *International Journal of Obesity* 32: 992–1000.

Rebecca M. Puhl and Chelsea A. Heuer. 2010. Obesity Stigma: Important Considerations for Public Health. *American Journal of Public Health* 100(6): 1019–1028.

Shinall, Jennifer Bennett. 2015. "Occupational Characteristics and the Obesity Wage Penalty." *Working Paper.*

Valenti, Jessica. 2009. "PETA Fat Shames in "Save the Whales" Campaign." *Feministing.* August 17. http://feministing.com/2009/08/17/peta-fat-shames-in-save-the-whales-campaign/

Vogel, Lauren. 2011. "The skinny on BMI report cards." *Canadian Medical Association Journal* 183(12): E787–E78.

Williams, DR, HW Neighbors, and JS Jackson. 2003. "Racial/ethnic discrimination and health: findings from community studies." American Journal of Public Health 93(2):200–208.

Williams, David R., Selina A. Mohammed, Jacinta Leavell, and Chiquita Collins. 2010. "Race, socioeconomic status, and health: Complexities, ongoing challenges, and research opportunities." *Annals of the New York Academy of Sciences* 1186: 69–101.

Williams, David R. and Selina A. Mohammed. 2013. "Racism and Health I: Pathways and Scientific Evidence." *American Behavioral Scientist* 57(8): 1152–1173.

"A Doctor Walks Into A Bar; Finding A New Doctor When You Don't Like The Doctor In The First Place"

By Marianne Kirby

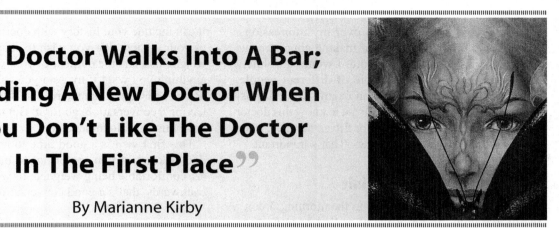

Alas, this is not a post about Doctor Who. Going to the gynecologist. Ah, that imperative ritual of having a uterus.

It's just about that time of year for me again—but because my doctor moved out of state, I have to find a new person I can trust to examine my area, inside and out, for general healthfulness. Finding someone to poke at my parts in a medical sense is actually way more aggravating to me than the exam itself. So I have some techniques for making the whole process a lot less painful. Metaphorically. If there's physical pain, there's something else going on. I thought it would be a good idea to share these tactics—I know going to the doctor is almost always fraught. It can be even more so when you're going to wind up wide-legged on a table.

Prep Work

Before I take my pants off with anyone, I need to know a little bit about them.

This counts for dates and it counts for doctors, too. In fact, it counts EXTRA for doctors—they're working for me and I'm paying them!

Before I go to any doctor, much less one who expects me to get naked on a table and submit to invasive exams, I call and do a quick phone interview. These are the questions I ask:

- What is your office policy when it comes to the treatment of fat patients?
- Is the practice familiar with and do you support Health At Every Size (HAES)?
- What's the largest size gown you have readily available?
- How likely are you to market weight loss surgery to me?

- Do you have large-size blood pressure cuffs in your exam rooms?
- How do you respond if patients refuse to be weighed? Do you allow people to be weighed standing backwards?

These are some pretty straightforward questions. Not knowing what HAES is doesn't have to be a deal-breaker—but the reaction of whoever is on the phone with me can be very revealing about the culture of that particular doctor's office.

Remember—if you have any other concerns, this phone screening is a good time to mention them. Are you a trans man? This is a vital chance to make sure no one is going to give you any grief. Are you disabled? This is a vital chance to make sure they'll accommodate you as needed without making you feel like shit. And so on.[1]

Note that, at this point, you're probably talking to whoever is on the phone. That is totally cool. Nurses and nurse practitioners are a huge part of creating and maintaining the environment and atmosphere of a practice. Even if the doctor is friendly, if the nurses aren't, it might not be an office you want to visit.

Make sure to have a couple of offices you can call—don't put all your eggs in one, um, ovary. So to speak. It's also best to make these calls when you don't have a particularly urgent issue. Remember, this person is going to be working for you. You want to come at this from a place of comfort and power, not a place of fever and emergency.

---

[1] Although this piece primarily addresses people who have concerns about mistreatment by healthcare providers due to weight bias, this is a really important point—this advice is useful for **anyone** with previous negative experiences with or concerns about receiving compassionate and appropriate care. *Ed.*

Once I have my list, I'll go over my impressions. I don't have the fiscal luxury of making appointments with multiple doctors, but if I did, I would absolutely schedule consults with a couple of different people. Schedule a consultation—not an exam—if at all possible. That'll give you a chance to get to know this doctor in person, even if it's just for ten or fifteen minutes, when you aren't under the gun of illness. That's important.

Setting Up the First Visit

I like to schedule appointments in the morning. I don't really like going to an office after I've been running around all day—it always makes me worry that I'm sweaty and gross. Rather than worry, I schedule for my preferred time as often as possible.

Remember, you want to arrange this appointment in a way that minimizing your own anxiety. Doctors are busy, absolutely. But you have to ask for what you need—if you need to arrange a time when you won't be waiting in the lounge out front for very long, tell the person scheduling the appointment that and explain it's due to anxiety. They'll often be very willing to work with you.

And if they aren't, it might be a good idea to move to the next doctor on your list.

The First Visit Itself

Remember all that advice people give to teenagers about how to take tests like the SAT and the ACT? That's pretty good advice for your first visit to a new doctor, too.

If you're able, get a good night's sleep beforehand. If you're able, eat something small and easy on the stomach to help settle you.

Have your important paperwork (insurance cards, any necessary medical documents, etc.) ready beforehand so you aren't scrambling to find it once you get to the office.

Remember, you can take a letter to be included in your file (I think I got this from Stef at cat-and-dragon).

It can include your history with doctors, any discussion of your anxiety that you wish to share, your stance on weight loss, and the purpose of your visit. It can include anything you want it to. And you can hand that to the doctor and expect them to read it. If you're comfortable having a conversation, go for it. But it's always good to have this stuff documented.[2]

This first visit is a good time to let the nurse and/or doctor know if you prefer not to be weighed. If you are comfortable being weighed, or with being weighed backwards, that's a good conversation to have, too.

After The First Visit

Evaluate—how'd it go? Did the doctor treat you with respect? Did the doctor make eye contact? Would you feel comfortable going to this person with an actual medical issue? If yes, schedule an appointment for an exam! If no, if at all possible, repeat the process with a different doctor from your list.

This applies no matter what kind of doctor you're seeing. You are putting yourself in a vulnerable position when you go to the doctor, particularly the gynecologist. That means it needs to be someone you can at least trust not to abuse you.

An actual gynecological exam isn't running through a field with rainbows and kittens. But it also tends to be fairly quick, and most doctors seem to be at least cognizant that it isn't a happy fun position to be in. Doctors conduct exams differently, of course. But most will do the initial intake exam before you have to take off your clothes. A good doctor will talk to you and let you know what's going on throughout the exam—which, again, shouldn't take all that long once they get going. If you are ever uncomfortable or feeling panicky, tell the doctor to stop. Even when they're in the middle of an intrusive exam, they work for you.

---

[2]The editor of this volume has personally found this suggestion invaluable in coordinating her own often complex medical care. *Ed.*

"Where Are The Fat Activists Of Color?"

By Shannon Barber

For a few years I spent a lot of time in the Fatosphere and engaging with a lot of online fat activism (FA). In my time writing about fatness, I've seen many POC give up and focus on other things. Every now and then, someone involved in FA looks up and realizes that as it is today, it is a very White centric landscape. Why?

I believe my own experiences can shed some light.

The first and biggest problem, as a Black fat person, is that I personally wasn't doing fat fashion in a serious way. I love fat fashion and believe it is an important part of the discourse about being a fat person; however, I found that frequently POC have been relegated to only being taken seriously in the context of fat fashion. Everyone loves a fashionable Black fatty in a kickass outfit, but things get too real when we step out of that realm and talk about other things.

That brings us to intersectionality. The problem I ran into time and again was that my approach to writing about fatness was purposefully and forcefully intersectional. Fatness is not only physical, it is cultural and contextual and that makes things difficult for people who are new to the basic ideas of fat acceptance or any other movement such as feminism, etc.

I need to stop here. I had a very grand fancy plan to explain in depth in very fancy language why a lot of POC myself included have stepped back from fat activism in a very public way. What it boils down is the unrelenting pressure and intimidation of Whiteness. As with any type of activism where the most visible people are White and in the case of Fat Acceptance tended towards being within shouting distance of normative Western beauty ideals and with a very particular way of speaking/writing—people like me had (have) to struggle past it and then constantly engage in the backlash of not adhering to Whiteness.

In the realm of Fat Acceptance here is what that looked like for me. Post something about being fat and Black. Screen out comments about how divisive that is, how racist I am, how race and fatness have nothing to do with each other. Have to deal with being reminded that, however I say something, I am only ever angry and since I am angry (rightfully or not), I am not to be listened to.

After that, often days or weeks later, I would find another fat-related blog where what I said was watered down and my Blackness was stripped in order to make it more palatable to White people, White women in particular. My identity as it influenced what I had to say was removed.

For me, this continual intellectual theft is what finally silenced me and drove me out of the community. White women, the same women who frequently and ferociously talked about feminism, the same women who liked to claim ally status and talk about not being racist, were the ones who stole from me and made money from work I did. Not only did they take money out of my pocket and thus food out of my mouth, they stole my ability to trust my community. When they stole from me, it was nothing to them. Rearrange a few words and voila, they had instant intersectional work. What they got for free I paid for in time, pain, and emotional/intellectual labor. All performed for free, for the good of my community, often for no thanks and at great emotional cost to myself.

Add in to that happening with regularity, there were also random racist responses to my original work from other people in the FA community. I was accused on a personal level of trying to start "race wars" because I deleted a comment that used racial slurs. I was subject to drunken racist comments because I had the audacity to question a White woman's project. I saw my thoughts dragged in passive-aggressive ways, I was instructed by well-meaning White women to tone it down and maybe not talk about race so much.

Fast forward to 2016. I am no longer heavily involved in fat activism. After one too many instances of nonsense I had to withdraw. I needed to not engage with that dynamic because it was just too much stress. I actually retired from fat blogging in 2014 and took some time to recover.

Here in 2016, there is a well-established pattern of POC, especially Black women, bowing out of public discourse in certain activist movements. Feminism, judicial activism, environmentalism, LGBTQ activism, literary activism—almost any level of activism that exists, these patterns of Whiteness being enforced as the center and norm exist. Dealing with this stuff is exhausting.

I had to make a very conscious decision to decenter Whiteness in my activism. I had to decide between staying the foul-mouthed Shannon some folks got to know and love, or to shut down a large part of my voice and experience so I could cut down on the crap that got flung my way whenever I opened my mouth. In speaking to other POC about how we deal with this many of the people I know reach a point where the only choice that allows for self-preservation is to disengage. Not ideal, but needed.

In the intervening couple of years I've learned something very important. There is no separating my Blackness from any opinion I have. If that makes people uncomfortable that is not my problem. I don't have to cave to the strong arm coercion of racism. My voice, what reach I have matters.

I want to end with some solutions. I don't want my experience of fat activism to discourage others from engaging.

For those who benefit from Whiteness or are otherwise in a position of privilege in any given activist conversation learn to decenter yourself. Learn to acknowledge when your voice doesn't need to be the loudest or only voice in the conversation. Do your research on 101 level <insert identity thing you aren't here>. Before you enter a conversation with people who are not you, get to a basic level of understanding.

After you've done that, do a whole lot of listening. Sometimes you may want to stand up for Whiteness, heterosexuals, etc.—step back and check yourself. Wait out the initial impulse and think about it again, figure out why you're feeling how you're feeling before you comment or talk to whomever has triggered that feeling.

For marginalized people. A few tips. You do not always have to do racism/whatever-ism 101 with everyone. You are allowed to get deep and intersectional in your politics. I encourage it. Your voice matters. Speak up, don't forget to self-care, and most importantly keep yourselves safe.

Everyone—

Whether or not an issue impacts you directly, we live in the most amazing time where you can learn about it. We can work from our small circles outward to create change and awareness. This is how we expand and improve our world. Good luck.

INDEX

CPSIA information can be obtained
at www.ICGtesting.com
Printed in the USA
LVOW03s2131230816

501403LV00004B/4/P